The
Complete
Bev·er·age
Dictionary

Second Edition

Bob and Kathie Lipinski

VNR

VAN NOSTRAND REINHOLD

I(T)P® A Division of International Thomson Publishing Inc.

New York • Albany • Bonn • Boston • Detroit • London • Madrid • Melbourne
Mexico City • Paris • San Francisco • Singapore • Tokyo • Toronto

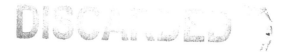

Copyright © 1996 by Van Nostrand Reinhold

I(T)P® A division of International Thomson Publishing, Inc.
The ITP logo is a registered trademark under license

Printed in the United States of America

For more information, contact:

Van Nostrand Reinhold
115 Fifth Avenue
New York, NY 10003

Chapman & Hall GmbH
Pappelallee 3
69469 Weinheim
Germany

Chapman & Hall
2-6 Boundary Row
London
SE1 8HN
United Kingdom

International Thomson Publishing Asia
221 Henderson Road #05-10
Henderson Building
Singapore 0315

Thomas Nelson Australia
102 Dodds Street
South Melbourne, 3205
Victoria, Australia

International Thomson Publishing Japan
Hirakawacho Kyowa Building, 3F
2-2-1 Hirakawacho
Chiyoda-ku, 102 Tokyo
Japan

Nelson Canada
1120 Birchmount Road
Scarborough, Ontario
Canada M1K 5G4

International Thomson Editores
Seneca 53
Col. Polanco
11560 Mexico D.F. Mexico

2 3 4 5 6 7 8 9 10   QEB-FF   01 00 99 98 97

Library of Congress Cataloging-in-Publication Data

Lipinski, Robert A.
   The Complete beverage dictionary / Bob and Kathie Lipinski. —2nd ed.
      p.   cm.
   ISBN 0-442-02208-5
   1. Beverage—Dictionaries.   2. Alcoholic beverages—Dictionaries.
I. Lipinski, Kathleen A.   II. Title
TP503.L56 1996   95-49070
663' .03—dc20   CIP

This book is dedicated to my family: my two sons, Johnnie and Matt,
and especially my loving and special wife Kathie,
for without her support, love, dedication, loyalty, and understanding
...you wouldn't be reading this book.

PREFACE TO THE SECOND EDITION

When the Complete Beverage Dictionary was titled back in 1992, we naïvely believed that we had covered virtually all the terminology as it related to beverages on a global perspective. After all, the first edition contained more than 6,100 terms (and about 150,000 words), many of them international in scope, and it was the first beverage dictionary ever written. So how many more terms could there really be that we did not cover? Well, since then, we have added about 1,500 new terms, in addition to more than 24,000 words, and we are now convinced that the quest to make this book all-encompassing will never end.

This dictionary is written for the hospitality industry, which is made up of importers, wholesalers, retailers, managers of on- and off-premise facilities, foodservice operators, restaurateurs, hoteliers, educators, bartenders, and food and beverage directors, as well as interested consumers. It is needed to fill a vacuum that exists in the beverage industry relative to correct terminology usage and accurate definitions.

ABAFADO *(PORTUGAL)* *See* Vinho Abafado.

ABBADIA *(ITALY)* Abbey.

ABBEY ALE Ales made for centuries by Cistercian monks in Belgium, who brewed them for personal consumption and enjoyment with guests. Typically, they are deep golden to coffee in color, with a heavy, pronounced, malty bouquet.

ABBOCCATO *(ITALY)* Also known as *amabile*. *See* Semidry Wine.

ABBONDOSA *(ITALY)* *See* Nuragus.

ABC LAWS Alcoholic beverage control laws.

ABFÜLLER *(GERMANY)* Bottling or bottler—must be listed on all quality wines.

ABFÜLLREIF *(GERMANY)* Describes a wine that is ready for bottling.

ABGANG *(GERMANY)* *See* Aftertaste.

ABGEFÜLLT DURCH *(GERMANY)* Bottled by.

ABGEFÜLLT FÜR *(GERMANY)* Bottled for (the firm that bottled the wine).

ABOCADO *(SPAIN)* *See* Semidry Wine.

A BOIRE *(FRANCE)* Ready to drink.

ABONDANCE Wine diluted with water; often served in European restaurants to children.

ABONNEMENTS *(FRANCE)* Fixed contracts between proprietors and groups of *négociants* wherein the merchants guarantee to purchase the next five or ten years' grape crop for a fixed price.

ABOURIOU A red grape variety. Also known as *Early Burgundy* and *Gamay St-Laurent*.

ABRUZZI *(ITALY)* *See* Abruzzo.

ABRUZZO (ITALY)   One of twenty wine-producing regions, located in a mountainous region just south of Latium in the south-central part of Italy, off the Adriatic Sea. Known as *Abruzzi* in Italy.

ABSCISSION   The normal separation or dropping-off of leaves or fruits from plants as a result of a breakdown of a thin layer of pithy cells at the base of their stems.

ABSINTHE   An aromatic, yellow-green distilled spirit flavored with oil of wormwood. This anise-based distilled spirit was officially banned throughout most of the world on March 16, 1915 (Spain in 1937). The technical name of the main ingredient is *Artemisia absinthium* (wormwood), an Old World plant or herb that grows about three feet high and is botanically related to the sagebrush of the southerwestern United States. The oil from the leaves, called *absinthol*, contains a rather strong narcotic, *thujone*; it is poisonous in large doses. Thujone is colorless and has a pleasant smell; however the taste is astringently bitter, as bitter as digitalis, cinchona, quinine, or hops. At one time, thujone was prescribed by alchemists for everything from increasing sexual prowess and virility to the elimination of such thoughts, which required larger doses.

Absinthe was first created by Dr. Pierre Ordinaire (he was a general practitioner; his actual name is not known), a French country physician. Fleeing from France and Napoléon in 1790, when all royalists were revolutionary targets for the guillotine, he settled in Neuchâtel, Switzerland, whose population and countryside reminded him of his home in the Jura Mountains. Like most country doctors in those days he prepared his own remedies and, on his little horse La Rouquette, crisscrossed the Val-de-Travers to gather the many wild and medicinal herbs and plants that grew on the mountain slopes. Among them was wormwood (*Artemisia absinthium*), which was then widely used in various herbal compounds for its medicinal properties. In his ten- to twenty-liter still, the doctor discovered that the value of absinthium heightened when it was steeped in a high-proof alcohol, anywhere from 130 to 161 proof. In 1792, the doctor concocted an elixir nicknamed "The Green Fairy," which was an infusion of fifteen herbs including the dried wormwood, aniseed, parsley, chamomile, hyssop, melissa (a type of mint), badiane (Turkish or star anise), coriander, veronica (a plant or shrub of the figwort family), persil, and, of all things, spinach! Absinthe, which was sold as a digestive, gained its light yellow-green color by the addition of chlorophyll from nettle juice or spinach.

The doctor died in 1793 and his secret formula or recipe for the making of absinthe was given to La Mère Henriot, his housekeeper and occasional lover, who continued to make the potion. Major Henri Dubied, a Frenchman, while on vacation in Switzerland, used absinthe for its curative effects on his stomach as well as a treatment for chills, fever, bronchial inflammation, and low appetite. He believed that, if taken in moderation after dinner, absinthe was a marvelous and safe aphrodisiac. Ernest Hemingway was one of the many writers who praised the erotic powers of absinthe, claiming that it worked by changing the ideas rather than by irritating the sexual glands, as do most aphrodisiacs.

Whether or not it was for the aphrodisiac qualities of absinthe that Major Dubied wanted the recipe is not known. In 1797, the same year his daughter married, Dubied bought the recipe and, with his new son-in-law, Henri-Louis Pernod, opened the world's first absinthe distillery in Couvet, Switzerland. As sales of absinthe increased, the distillery had to be enlarged. Eight years later, in 1805, Pernod opened a larger factory in Pontarlier, about twenty-five miles from Couvet.

Absinthe's popularity still hadn't caught on and it wasn't until the 1840s that the French government ordered rations of absinthe be given to their troops who had contracted malaria and other maladies while fighting in Algeria. The formula was simply to add several drops to wine at mealtime. The side effect was that hundreds of thousands of soldiers developed a taste and yearning for the tasty licorice and anise-flavored beverage. This taste spread throughout France like a plague and by the 1890s absinthe, or the "Green Goddess" or "Green Muse," was synonymous with Paris café and bistro life. The Bohemians sat and talked for hours over marble-topped tables about their absinthe, as if it had a magical ability to stimulate the mind and assist the flow of ideas. Indeed, absinthe was so popular that the hour of the apéritif was known as *l'heure verte* (the green hour). Degas, Picasso, Modigliani, and Toulouse-Lautrec all painted under its influence. "The Absinthe Drinker," a painting by Degas, which is in the Louvre, immortalizes its sweet melancholy. The dissipations of French absinthe drinkers have been dramatized in the film story of Toulouse-Lautrec, the artist of the Moulin Rouge, who drank himself to madness and death at the age of thirty-seven. Poets Rimbaud and Verlaine were addicted to absinthe and wrote from a more-or-less permanent state of intoxication of the exaltation, freedom from inhibitions, wildness of ideas, and the sensations, sexual excitement, and terrible hangovers and physical ravages it inflicted.

Garçons in every bistro knew the correct way to pour absinthe. A little absinthe was poured into the bottom of a tall glass. A long-handled spoon whose bowl was filled with small holes was placed over the drinker's glass. A lump of sugar was put in the spoon and ice-cold water was slowly added, drop by drop, through the sugar (which sweetened the absinthe). This process blended the water into a liquor so gradually that it did not separate but turned an opalescent green—actually a result of the water consolidating the flavor-generating oils and resins, but perhaps the true source of aphrodisiacal power.

Some of the problems associated with absinthe ingestion were convulsions, mania, gastrointestinal irritation, extreme nervousness, drugged stupor, hallucination, and loss of hearing and sight. In large doses, absinthe induced a coma or even death. Epileptic reactions could be created by the interaction of absinthe, hyssop, and fennel, while stupor sometimes resulted from the combination of anise, badiane, angelica, oregano, melissa, and mint.

In 1905, a drunken and crazed man killed his wife and two daughters but failed to kill himself. His daily alcoholic consumption was six quarts of wine, six brandies, and a couple of absinthes; he was said to be in an absinthe-induced delirium. Stories of the outrage spread throughout the world, fired by temperance groups, and caused the courts to ban the production of absinthe first in Switzerland, then in France. The French government, waiting until 1915 to finally prohibit the manufacture and sale of absinthe, used the pretext that alcohol was needed for the manufacture of gunpowder for the war, thus putting an end to a century of popularity.

Absinthe, with its dry, bitter, licorice-like flavor and herbal aroma, was resurrected in 1922 under the name Pernod, minus the toxic wormwood. In its place, anise was substituted; the alcohol content was lowered to 86 proof and the drink's popularity was once again on the rise. Paul Ricard, aged twenty-three, while working in his father's wine wholesale business, decided to produce his own aniseed drink, design his own label and posters, and begin marketing "Pastis."

In 1940, the French Vichy government once again banned the making of aniseed-based alcoholic liquor at more than 16 proof, allowing for the return of bootlegging, as during World War I. After the Second World War, legislation dragged on and it was not until 1951 that a 45-proof Pastis, at which strength the anise essence is properly stabilized, became once again legal. Paul Ricard filled the market with a campaign based around the slogan "The True Pastis from Marseilles." Pernod invented their Pastis 51, which not only marked the year it was first introduced but also the proportions, five parts water to one part Pernod.

The French drink their anise-based distilled spirits in a tall glass with ice-cold water, one part anise distilled spirit to five parts water. If these spirits are consumed either chilled directly from the refrigerator or over ice, a cloudiness or opalescence appears, which adds to the beauty of the drink.

ABSOLUTE ALCOHOL   Clinically pure or 200-proof (100 percent) ethyl alcohol. Pure ethyl alcohol does not really exist because alcohol and water form an azeotropic mixture—one with a boiling point lower than either pure alcohol or water, which does not separate during simple distilling. The final portion of water can be removed by distilling in a system under vacuum by adding a solvent such as benzene that "breaks" the azeotrope, or by passing the liquid through an absorbent column.

Measurements in absolute alcohol provide a meaningful way of describing alcohol consumption in a population or of relating the alcohol content of different beverages. Also known as *anhydrous alcohol*.

ABSOLUTE THRESHOLD   The sensory threshold of a given compound or substance. It is the minimum concentration in an aqueous (water-containing) solution that a person is able to correctly identify.

ABSORPTION   The taking in of nutrients and other minerals by a plant's feeder roots or through the cuticle of its foliage.

ABSORPTION   The process by which alcohol enters the bloodstream or body tissues.

ABSTICH (GERMANY)   *See* Racking.

ABSTICHREIF (GERMANY)   Describes a wine that is ready for racking.

ACACIA   A chemical used to clarify and stabilize wine.

ACADÉMIE DU VIN DE BORDEAUX (FRANCE)   Bordeaux Wine Academy, created in 1948 to spread the word about Bordeaux wines. It has forty members, including shippers, brokers, and producers.

ACCIAIO INOSSIDABILE (ITALY)   *See* Stainless Steel.

ACCLIMATIZATION   Involves the greenhouse transfer of plants cultivated *in vitro* to a horticultural substrate and the gradual readjustment of these plants to open air and to the usual level of humidity.

ACCOUNTS PAYABLE   Debts to suppliers of goods or services.

ACCOUNTS RECEIVABLE   Amounts due from customers.

ACERBE (FRANCE)   *See* Acerbic.

ACERBIC   Describes an unpleasant, bitter, tart, astringent, coarse, or disagreeable taste that comes from unripe grapes. Also known as *acerbe* and *acerbo*.

ACERBO (ITALY)   *See* Acerbic.

ACESCENCE   A name given to the vinegar smell and taste of a wine that has undergone aerobic bacterial spoilage; it is equivalent to *volatile acidity* (VA). In some wines, notably port and well-wood-aged red table wines, a small amount of acescence is considered a desirable part of the wine's nose. However, when excessive, acescence will completely destroy the acceptability of any wine. When a wine contains an excessive amount of acetic acid and ethyl acetate, a translucent gray film often forms on the surface and acescency occurs; the wine acquires a stinging, sharp, vinegary taste. Also known as *goût de piqué*. See Acetic Acid, Acetobacter, and Volatile Acidity.

ACETALDEHYDE   A colorless, soluble, volatile liquid formed when the enzyme carboxylase forms acetaldehyde and carbon dioxide from pyruvic acid. It is at this next and final stage of a complete fermentation that acetaldehyde is reduced to ethyl alcohol, but a minute quantity remains and adds to the flavor of the wine. In large amounts, acetaldehyde has a sharp, vinegary odor. See Volatile Acidity.

ACETAMIDE   *See* Mousy.

ACETATE   An ester of acetic acid.

ACETIC   Describes a wine that has gone irredeemably bad through prolonged exposure to oxygen. Acetic acid combines with ethyl acetate to give the vinegary smell and taste that a spoiled wine emits. Also known as *acide acétique, agrio, aigre*, and *vappa*. See Acetic Acid and Volatile Acidity.

ACETIC ACID   A colorless, volatile acid found in all wines. It is usually present in tiny quantities; if there is excessive development of it, the wine turns to vinegar. A pungent substance that is the chief ingredient of vinegar. Also known as *acetic*. See Acetobacter and Volatile Acidity.

ACETIC ACID   Used to correct natural deficiencies in grape wine.

ACETIFICATION   The formation of vinegar.

ACETO (ITALY)   *See* Vinegar.

ACETOBACTER   Airborne aerobic microorganisms (bacteria) that cause the oxidation of alcohol (wine) primarily to acetaldehyde by prolonged exposure of oxygen. Oxygen is essential for its formation; therefore, barrels should be kept *topped* and air spaces in bottles kept to a minimum. See Acetic Acid, *Mycoderma* aceti, and Volatile Acidity.

ÄCHERICH (GERMANY)   *See* Powdery Mildew.

ACID   A substance having a sharp and biting taste; it is present in all grapes. See Acetic, Ascorbic, Citric, Lactic, Malic, and Tartaric Acids.

ACID BLEND   A mixture of organic acids—citric, malic, and tartaric—generally added to the *must* prior to fermentation to correct acid deficiencies.

ACIDE ACÉTIQUE (FRANCE)   *See* Acetic.

ACIDE TARTRIQUE (FRANCE)   *See* Tartaric Acid.

ACIDEZ (PORTUGAL AND SPAIN)   *See* Acidity.

ACIDIC   Describes wines (often very young or very old) that are improperly balanced because of an abnormally high acid content. The total acid in this case is so high that it tastes sour and has a sharp feel in the mouth.

ACIDITÀ (ITALY)   *See* Acidity.

ACIDITÀ FISSE (ITALY)   *See* Fixed Acidity.

ACIDITÄT (GERMANY)   *See* Acidity.

ACIDITÀ TOTALE (ITALY)   *See* Total Acidity.

ACIDITÀ VOLATILE (ITALY)   *See* Volatile Acidity.

ACIDITÉ (FRANCE)   *See* Acidity.

ACIDITY   The quality of tartness or sharpness in the taste of wine due to the presence of agreeable fruit acids. An important constituent that contributes flavor and freshness to wine when it is in proper balance and contributes to its aging. Not to be confused with sourness, dryness, or astringency. The principle acids found in wine are tartaric, citric, malic, and lactic. Also known as *acidità, acidität, acidez, acidité, acido*, and *säure*.

ACIDO (ITALY)   *See* Acidity.

ACIDO CARBONICO (ITALY)   *See* Carbonic Acid.

ACIDOPHILUS MILK   Lowfat milk that has a bacteria culture, known as "*lactobacillus* added." It is made for individuals who are lactose sensitive or intolerant.

ACID SOIL   Soil with a pH measurement of 6.9 or less.

ACIDULÉ (FRANCE)   *See* Acidulous.

ACIDULO (ITALY)   *See* Acidulous.

ACIDULOUS   Describes a wine that displays an unpleasantly sour taste due to high acidity, often more than one percent of total acid. Also known as *acidulé, acidulo, agrillo*, and *säuerlich*.

ACKER (GERMANY)   *See* Feld.

ACQUA (ITALY)   *See* Water.

ACQUA MINERALE (ITALY)   *See* Mineral Water.

ACQUAVITE (ITALY)   *See* Aqua Vitae.

ACQUIT (FRANCE)   A key document controlling all transportation of wines or distilled spirits on which government taxes have not been paid. Its color depends upon the category of wine designated: green for AOC, yellow-gold for Cognac and Armagnac, orange for *appellation contrôlée* dessert wines, and manila for ordinary wines.

ACRE   American and English surface measurement equivalent to 4,047 square meters (0.4047 hectares) or 43,569 square feet. Also known as *morgen*.

ACRE (ITALY)   *See* Astringency.

ÂCRE (FRANCE)   *See* Astringency.

ACRE FOOT OF WATER   The amount of water covering an acre one foot deep; equals 325,851 gallons.

ACRID   Describes a sharp, bitter, stinging, or irritating taste or smell. Also known as *mordant*. *See* Astringency.

ACTIFERM (ROVIFERM)   A fermentation adjunct.

ACTIVATED CARBON A highly absorbent black powdery substance of vegetable origin used for removing undesirable colors and odors in certain beverages and occasionally as a fining agent. Also known as *carbon, carbonio*, and *carbono*. *See* Fining and Fining Agents.

ACTIVATED CHARCOAL A highly absorbent granular carbon used in filtering some whiskies as well as for removing undesirable colors and odors in certain beverages; it is occasionally used as a fining agent. Also known as *carbón, carbonella*, and *charcoal*. *See* Charcoal Mellowed, Fining, Fining Agents, and Leaching.

ACTUAL BEVERAGE COST The cost of beverages sold, as determined by a factual weekly or monthly record.

ACTUAL BEVERAGE COST PERCENTAGE The actual cost divided by sales and multiplied by one hundred.

ACTUAL COST PRICING Pricing based on what the actual costs for the item are, including purchase, labor, and operating costs.

ACUTE Strong or sharply defined.

ADAMADO (PORTUGAL) *See* Sweet.

ADDED BRANDY Brandy or wine spirits for use in fortification of wine as permitted by internal revenue law.

ADDITIVES A group of materials, such as preservatives, that are added to beverages to improve or strengthen them. Some additives are colors, flavors, acids, vitamins, minerals, yeast, and bacterial inhibitors. While these might not be essential to the product, they could be added to improve or ease production.

ADEGA (PORTUGAL) *See* Wine Cellar.

ADJUNCT Unmalted grains used mostly in American-made beer, including corn, corn grits, and brewer's rice. Refined corn grits tend to produce the milder, lighter-bodied beer preferred by the American consumer. Like malt, corn is a source of starch that is converted to sugar in the brewing process.

ADONIS COCKTAIL Named after the first Broadway musical to run for more than five hundred performances. The musical first opened at the Bijou Opera House on September 9, 1884. The cocktail consists of dry sherry, sweet vermouth, and a dash of bitters (preferably orange).

AD REPRINT Copy of an ad published in an identified print medium; it is often used as a selling tool.

AD SLICK Sheet of paper with various illustrations of brands of alcoholic beverages. Illustrations can be cut out and used by retailers in their own ads.

ADSTRINGENTE (PORTUGAL) *See* Astringency.

ADSTRINGEREND (GERMANY) *See* Astringency.

ADULTERATED WINE A wine that has been treated with, exposed to, or had unauthorized or prohibited ingredients or materials added to it, or that possesses excessive levels of a permitted substance. Also known as *adulterato*. *See* Bacterial Spoilage and Spoiled.

ADULTERATO (ITALY)   See Adulterated Wine.

AD VALOREM   A phrase applied to certain duties levied on imported alcoholic beverages according to their invoiced value.

ADVECTION FROST   A frost that occurs when freezing air blowing into an area displaces warmer air that was present before the frost occurrence. Moderate to strong winds, no inversion, cloudy or clear skies, and freezing temperatures even during daylight typically characterize advection frosts. In some cases, the temperature can remain below freezing for several successive days.

ADVOCAAT   See Advokatt.

ADVOKATT   A 30-proof, creamy yellow eggnog liqueur made in Holland and Germany from egg yolks, brandy, cream, and sugar. Also spelled *advocaat*. See Eggnog.

ADZ   An ancient long-handled, ax-like tool used to cut and shape the staves or sides of wooden barrels.

AERATE   See Aeration.

AÉRATION (FRANCE)   See Aeration.

AERATION   The process of letting a wine "breathe" in the open air or swirling it in a glass. Also known as *aerate* and *aération*. See Breathing and Decanting.

AERATION   A process by which oxygen in the soil is replaced by oxygen in the atmosphere.

AEROBIC FERMENTATION   A fermentation conducted in the presence of oxygen.

AFERRIN   A substance used to reduce trace metals from wine.

AFFINÉ (FRANCE)   See Fining.

AFRUTADO (SPAIN)   See Fruity.

AFSTIRÓS (GREECE)   See Austere.

AFTER-DINNER WINES   Sweet fortified and nonfortified wines.

AFTERTASTE   What lingers or remains in the throat or on the tongue after a beverage is swallowed. Some beverages have a long, crisp, clean, and fruity aftertaste, while others are short or nonexistent. Also known as *abgang, arrière goût, length, lingering, long, nachgeschmack, ressaibo, retrogusto, schwanz*, and *schweif*. See Finish and Length.

AGAR   A gelatinous polysaccharide material extracted from certain saltwater algae and used in bacterial cultures to grow yeast and to thicken foods. See Alginate and Yeast.

AGAVE   A huge plant, indigenous to Mexico, with large leaves and prickly, needlelike thorns, resembling cactus. The agave, which belongs to the botanical family *Amaryllidaceae*, is used in the making of tequila and mezcal. It is occasionally called *maguey*. See Tequila.

AGAWAM   A red grape variety developed in 1861 from a cross of Mammoth Sage and Black Hamburg by Edward S. Rogers of Salem, Massachusetts. Formerly known as *Rogers 15*.

AGE   Period of storage of spirits in oak containers, after distillation and before bottling, to develop character and palatability.

For most American whiskies, it means storage in charred, new oak barrels. The exceptions are corn and light whiskies, which may be aged in uncharred, new or charred, reused oak barrels. Rum, brandy, and Scotch are generally aged in used oak containers. Age may not be designated for gin. According to the United States government standards of identity, the time a whiskey spends outside of an oak container does not add to its age.

AGE INCONNU (FRANCE) A label designation used on calvados bottles that indicates that the youngest brandy used in the blend is at least six years old, although they contain a very high percentage of brandy that has been aged for twenty, thirty, or forty years or more.

AGGLOMERATED CORK This unusual cork, developed in 1925, consists of scraps of cork glued together and then reformed into the shape of a cork. Also known as *aggloméré, composition cork*, or *particle cork*.

AGGLOMERATION *See* Flocculation.

AGGLOMÉRÉ (FRANCE) *See* Agglomerated Cork.

AGGRESSIVE Describes a young wine or brandy whose fiery taste has not yet mellowed or become harmonious. Also known as *aggressivo* and *agressif*.

AGGRESSIVO (ITALY) *See* Aggressive.

AGING The process whereby wine, beer, whiskey, or brandy is stored in oak barrels, stainless steel tanks, or glass so that complex changes that only time can implement take place. Aging smoothes a rough, new wine, beer, whiskey, or brandy and adds bouquet and character. Also known as *invecchiamento*. *See* Barrel Aging, Bottle Aging, Maturity, Ripe, and Ripe For Bottling.

AGIORGITIKO (GREECE) A red grape variety.

AGITADOR (SPAIN) *See* Rousing.

AGLIANICO (ITALY) A very dark red grape variety producing full-bodied wines. According to legend, the Aglianico grape was brought to Italy by ancient Greek settlers around 800 B.C. Its name is a corruption of the ancient Greek grapevine *Ellenico* or *Hellenica*. Today the Aglianico grape is widely grown throughout much of southern Italy, especially in Basilicata and Campania.

AGOSTADO (SPAIN) A deep plowing of the soil for vineyards carried out during the month of August as a first step for planting the new grapevines. Due to this plowing, the soil is completely free from the deepest weeds and roots.

AGOSTINELLA (ITALY) A white grape variety.

AGRAFE The metal clip that holds a champagne cork in place during the secondary fermentation. Incorrectly spelled *agraffe*. Also known as *grapa*.

AGRAFFE *See* Agrafe.

AGRÉABLE (FRANCE) *See* Pleasant.

AGREEABLE Also known as *agréable*. *See* Pleasant.

AGRESSIF (FRANCE) *See* Aggressive.

AGRICULTURAL WINE Wine made from agricultural products other than the juice of grapes, berries, or other fruits.

AGRILLO (SPAIN) *See* Acidulous.

AGRIO (SPAIN) *See* Acetic.

AGUA (SPAIN) *See* Water.

ÁGUA (PORTUGAL) *See* Water.

AGUAMIEL (SPAIN) The sticky sap (or *honey water*) released from the agave plant, used in making tequila or mezcal.

AGUARDENTE (PORTUGAL) Brandy used to fortify port wines. *See* Eau-de-Vie.

AGUARDENTE DE BAGACEIRA (PORTUGAL) *See* Grappa.

AGUARDIENTE (SPAIN) *See* Eau-de-Vie.

AGUARDIENTE DE ORUJO (SPAIN) *See* Grappa.

AH-SO A very popular and easy-to-use two-prong corkpuller. It is short for *ah-so-easy*.

AHR (GERMANY) One of thirteen Qualitätswein (quality) grape-growing regions, located in the north, noted for its excellent red wines produced from the Spätburgunder and Portugieser grape varieties.

AIGNE (FRANCE) A *marc* of grapes. *See* Marc of Grapes.

AIGRE (FRANCE) *See* Acetic.

AIMABLE (FRANCE) *See* Amiable.

AÎNÉ (FRANCE) Elder.

AIRELLE A fruit brandy made from the red mountain cranberry. *See* Myrtle.

AIRÉN (SPAIN) A white grape variety used in Brandy de Jerez and wines for málaga. Also known as *Lairén*.

AIRLINE BOTTLES *See* Miniature Bottles.

AIRLOCK *See* Fermentation Lock.

AJEÑJO (SPAIN) Wormwood. *See* Vermouth.

AKTIEN GESELLSCHAFT (AUSTRIA) The "A.G." after the name of a firm on a wine label, equivalent to *incorporated*.

AKVAVIT A high-proof distilled spirit made from a distillate of grain or potatoes and redistilled in the presence of caraway seeds, fruits, herbs, and spices. Because of its potency, it was nicknamed "Black Death." Akvavit is quite popular in the Scandinavian countries, where it is spelled *aquavit* and also known as *brännvin*.

ALAAI (CHINA) An ancient spirit distilled from rice in about 800 B.C. Also known as *Santchoo*.

ALAMBIC (FRANCE) *See* Alembic.

ALAMBIQUE (SPAIN) *See* Alembic.

ALAMBRADO (SPAIN) The wire net often found on wine bottles; it was introduced to prevent the fraudulent replacement of the bottle's contents. Also known as *arame*.

ALAMEDA   A grape-growing county in northern California, east of San Francisco Bay. The principal growing area is Livermore.

ALAR   The trade name for daminozide, a pesticide. Its use is now prohibited by the United States Food and Drug Administration.

ALBA (ITALY)   An important red-wine-producing province in the northwest region of Piedmont. Alba is also the location of one of Italy's important viticultural and enological schools, founded in 1881.

ALBALONGA (GERMANY)   A white grape variety developed from a cross of Sylvaner and Rieslaner in Würzburg. Its name was taken from Alba Longa, the oldest town in Latium and the mother city of Rome.

ALBAN (SPAIN)   *See* Palomino.

ALBAN   An ancient Roman wine.

ALBANA (ITALY)   A white grape variety grown primarily in the Emilia-Romagna region, where it produces Albana di Romagna. Also known as *Greco, Greco di Ancona*, and *Biancame*.

ALBANA DI ROMAGNA (ITALY)   A dry white wine produced from the Albana grape variety in the eastern region of Emilia-Romagna. On April 13, 1987, it became the first white wine to receive the DOCG designation.

ALBANELLO (ITALY)   A white grape variety grown in Sicily.

ALBANO (ITALY)   *See* Trebbiano.

ALBARIÑO (SPAIN)   A white grape variety grown primarily in Galicia, Spain, and Portugal, where it is used to produce Vinho Verde wine.

ALBARIZA   A chalky type of soil, considered by many to produce the very best sherry. Its texture is a spongy clay that soaks up and traps the winter rains and stores them, a plus because irrigation is not permitted. This texture also provides a perfect aeration of the soil and allows deep penetration by the grapevine roots. The soil contains approximately 40 percent white chalk, so the grapevines are nourished by its lime content. Approximately 85 percent of the soil in Jerez, Spain, is made up of albariza. However, the yield per acre from albariza is the lowest of any soil type. *See* Barro and Arena.

ALBAROLA (ITALY)   A white grape variety grown in Sicily.

ALBEISA (ITALY)   A classic, robust-shouldered bottle inspired by a local design of the eighteenth century, which was adopted by the wineries of Alba, Piedmont. Some of the wines stored in this unique bottle are Barbera, Barbaresco, Barolo, Dolcetto, and Freisa.

ALBERELLO (ITALY)   A system of head-pruning "little trees," created by training the taller grapevine shoots back on themselves and tying them in looped supports for the fruit. While this can be accomplished by individual grapevine dressers working on one plant at a time, it limits the exposure of the leaves and the graftable limbs on which additional grape clusters can be encouraged to grow. A major drawback of this method is that the grapevines are grown close to the ground so that they derive reflected heat from the ground onto the leaves. This method of training is seldom employed in Italy nowadays.

ALBESE *(ITALY)*   *See* Negro Amaro.

ALBILLO CASTELLANA *(SPAIN)*   *See* Pardina.

ALBUME *(ITALY)*   *See* Albumen.

ALBUMEN   Egg whites, in either a fresh or a dried state, that are used as a fining agent, mostly in winemaking. Albumen carries a positive charge and can cause a protein haze if excessive amounts are used. Also known as *albume, albumin*, and *egg whites. See* Fining and Fining Agents.

ALBUMIN *(GERMANY)*   *See* Albumen.

ALCOHOL   The unqualified term for a colorless, volatile, flammable liquid contained in all beverages that are fermented and/or distilled. Alcohol is an important by-product of the fermentation process. Yeasts working upon the sugar contained in a liquid transforms it into carbon dioxide and alcohol. The substance known as alcohol is technically *ethyl alcohol* (ethanol) (C_2H_5OH)—the preservative and intoxicating constituent of wine, beer, and distilled spirits. *See* Aqua Ardents, Ardent Spirits, and Ethyl Alcohol.

ALCOHOL BY VOLUME   The alcoholic content of a liquid expressed as a percentage of the volume. Also known as *alcool. See* Alcohol Content.

ALCOHOL CONTENT   A statement of alcohol content in percentage by volume appears on the labels of most alcoholic beverages. As an alternative, some bottlers prefer to label wine with an alcohol content between 7 and 14 percent as "table wine." For table wines, the law allows a 1.5 percent variation in either direction from the stated percentage as long as the alcohol does not exceed 14 percent.

In order to provide the consumer with clearer and more useful information on labels for distilled spirits, the United States Bureau of Alcohol, Tobacco, and Firearms (BATF) also issued regulations (November 10, 1986) for labeling: alcohol content must be indicated by percentage—not just in proof. This is a more readily understood way to convey alcohol content to the purchaser.

Since the repeal of Prohibition, the requirement that labels state alcohol content (formerly expressed in degrees of proof) has remained unchanged. Proof is a traditional term for alcohol content (equal to twice the percentage by volume). Thus, 80 proof means 40 percent alcohol by volume, 100 proof means 50 percent alcohol by volume, and so on.

According to the regulations, labels must show percentage by volume of alcohol, but both forms (proof and percentage) may be used. If a proof statement is used, it must be shown in direct conjunction with the percent by volume, emphasizing the fact that both expressions mean the same thing. Also known as *alkoholgehalt. See* Alcohol By Volume.

ALCOHOLERIA *(SPAIN)*   A distillery where the stems, skins, and seeds are sent to be made into *aguardiente*.

ALCOHOL FERMENTATION   *See* Primary Fermentation.

ALCOHOL-FREE WINES   Wines whose alcohol is removed after fermentation; they are 99.5 percent alcohol free.

ALCOHOLIC   A person who suffers from alcoholism. *See* Alcoholism.

ALCOHOLIC   Describes a wine or distilled spirit that has an excess of alcohol for its body and weight, making it unbalanced. This can be discerned either in the nose or mouth. Also known as *alkoholreich* and *burning. See* Hot.

ALCOHOLIC BEVERAGE As defined by United States law, the term refers to any beverage in liquid form that contains not less than one-half of one percent (0.5 percent) of ethyl alcohol (ethanol) by volume and is intended for human consumption.

These beverages are classified by their method of production:

Fermented beverages: Produced through fermentation alone, these beverages are of two kinds: malted beverages, brewed principally from cereal grains and malted barley, flavored with hops; and wine, the result of fermentation of grape or other fruit juices.

Distilled spirits: Produced by distillation of any alcohol-containing mixture—wine or the distiller's beer from a fermentation process. Whiskey, vodka, rum, brandy, gin, and tequila comprise the principal classes of distilled spirits. Another class, liqueurs, is not directly distilled but consists of beverage spirits treated with flavoring materials.

These versatile beverages play a continuing role in human history as sacred symbol, medicine, social lubricant, adjunct to gracious living, and thirst quencher.

ALCOHOLISM The chronic or habitual use of alcohol to the extent that its use contributes to sickness, accidents, or dependency on it to avoid withdrawal symptoms. *See* Alcoholic.

ALCOHOLIZED A slang term for an individual significantly under the influence of beer, wine, or distilled spirits.

ALCOHOLOMETER An instrument utilized for determining the quantity of pure alcohol in a liquid. *See* Ebulliometer.

ALCOL COMPLESSIVO (ITALY) The actual alcohol in finished wine plus the potential alcohol in the residual sugar.

ALCOL DA SVOLGERE (ITALY) *See* Potential Alcohol.

ALCOLISADO (PORTUGAL) *See* Vinho Alcolisado.

ALCOOL (ITALY) *See* Alcohol By Volume.

ALCOOL ÉTHYLIQUE (FRANCE) *See* Ethyl Alcohol.

ALCOOLS BLANCS (FRANCE) White or clear distilled spirits. Generally refers to brandies distilled from fruits other than grapes: cherries, pears, raspberries, and others. They are clear because they are not aged in wooden barrels. Also known as *virgin brandy*. *See* Grappa and Eau-de-Vie.

ALDEHYDE A colorless, volatile fluid with a distinct odor; it is a natural by-product of fermentation and increases in concentration as a wine or distilled spirit ages. One of the organic chemical ingredients of wine and distilled spirits formed by the partial oxidation of alcohol. It adds to the beverage's aroma, but may be unpleasant if present in large quantities.

ALDEN A red grape variety developed in 1952 from a cross of Ontario and Gros Guillaume at the State Experimental Station in Geneva, New York.

ALE A top-fermented beer with a slightly darker color than lager beer. It usually has more hops in its aroma and taste and is often lower in carbonation than lager-type beers. Ale is usually bitter to the taste, with a slight tanginess, although some ales can be sweet. Ales are usually fermented at warmer temperatures than are lager-type beers (60 to 70 degrees Fahrenheit) for three to five days, and generally mature faster. Ale is originally from England, where it is often referred to as *bitters*.

ALEATICO   A dark red grape variety of the Muscat family, grown primarily in Italy. Aleatico generally produces sweet dessert wines, although some table wines can be found. Some is also grown in California, but its acreage is dwindling.

ALEBERRY   An alcoholic beverage made from boiled ale with various spices and sugar.

ALECONNERS   An old title for an English town official or officer in London whose business was to inspect public houses or ale houses for fraud. He was also in charge of the testing and tasting of ale to determine its authenticity.

ALEHOUSE   A store where ale is retailed.

ALEMBIC   A large, onion-shaped copper pot still used for the double distillation of cognac and other brandies. It was originally used by the Moors, who used it to distill the nectar of flowers for perfume. (Later, it was used by medieval alchemists in attempts to turn nonprecious metals into gold.) Also spelled *alambic*. Also known as *alambique* and *chaudière*. *See* Pot Still.

ALEMBIC BRANDY   Grape brandy made in accordance with the methods utilized in France's Cognac and Armagnac regions, which rely solely on the *alembic pot still*.

ALE POSSET   A mildly intoxicating English drink made from a mixture of heated ale and curdled milk, with spices added. Also the name of an English beer, lightly hopped and slightly bitter.

ALERAMO *(ITALY)*   A large glass bottle with a capacity of 3.8 liters, used to store wine.

ALEXANDER   A cocktail made with brandy or gin, white crème de cacao, and heavy cream.

ALEXANDER   A red grape variety first discovered between 1732 and 1741. It was miscalled Black Cape, Black Madeira, Cape, Cape Constantia, Clifton's Constantia, Constantia, Rothrock of Prince, Schuylkill Muscadelle, Spring-Mill Constantia, Tasker's Grape, Vevay, Winnie, and York Lisbon. James Alexander, a gardener to Thomas Penn (son of Governor William Penn), found it growing near the Schuylkill River in Philadelphia, Pennsylvania.

ALEXANDER VALLEY   A grape-growing area located in northern Sonoma County, California.

ALFROCHEIRO PRETO *(PORTUGAL)*   A red grape variety grown in the Dão and Alentejo regions.

ALGINATE   A gelatinous compound extracted from certain seaweeds and used in the food and beverage industry as a thickener, stabilizer, and gellifier. *See* Agar, Encapsulated Yeast, and Yeast.

ALICANTE BOUSCHET   A red-juice grape variety, developed in France in 1865 by Henri Bouschet, a viticulturist. It is a cross of Petit Bouschet and Grenache. Alicante Bouschet is used for blending because of its deep, dark color and abundance of juice;

however, it is rarely bottled as a separate variety. It is grown in California, southern France, and Algeria.

ALICANTE GANZIN   A red grape variety.

ALIGOTÉ   A white grape variety grown primarily in France and California. It produces a highly acidic white wine, which has been used for years in Burgundy, France, as a base for the popular drink kir. Also known as *Plant Gris*.

ALIOTIQUE (FRANCE)   A type of sandstone indigenous to the southwest.

ALISIER (FRANCE)   A fruit brandy made from rowanberries in Alsace.

ALKALINE SOIL   Soil with a pH in excess of 7.0.

ALKOHOLGEHALT (AUSTRIA)   *See* Alcohol Content.

ALKOHOLREICH (GERMANY)   *See* Alcoholic.

ALKY   *See* Intoxicated.

ALLAPPANTE (ITALY)   *See* Astringency.

ALLEGAGIONE (ITALY)   *See* Berry Set.

ALLEGRO (ITALY)   *See* Bright.

ALLIED PRODUCTS   Commercial fruit products and by-products (including volatile fruit-flavor concentrate) not taxable as wine.

ALLIER OAK (FRANCE)   A small forest centered around the city of Moulins, noted for its production of wooden barrels, which are between Tronçais and Nevers in terms of hardness. Allier oak has a medium-tight grain, with moderate oak flavor and tannin extraction; it displays an intense, earthy component and a floral perfumed character.

ALL-IN-BOND   *See* In Bond.

ALL-MALT   A beer made exclusively with barley malt and without adjunct grains.

ALLUVIAL FAN   Soil deposited by a stream onto an open plain or valley. *See* Alluvial Soil.

ALLUVIAL SOIL   A type of soil predominantly made of sand and gravel. It is formed by gradual deposits left by moving water in the bottomlands along rivers, as along a riverbed or lakeshore. Also known as *alluvions*. *See* Alluvial Fan.

ALLUVIONS (FRANCE)   *See* Alluvial Soil.

ALMACENISTA (SPAIN)   Shopkeepers who purchase sherry wine, then carefully mature it in their cellars.

ALMA DEL VINO (SPAIN)   Soul of wine.

ALMERIA   A white grape variety grown primarily in California. Also known as *Ohanez*.

ALMIBAR (SPAIN)   A solution of invert sugar that is occasionally used to sweeten pale sherries.

ALMIJAR (SPAIN)   An outside location or open house where grapes are left to dry prior to being pressed.

ALMISSION A red grape variety developed from a cross of Mission and Carignan.

ALMOND Describes an odor or taste found in some wines or even beers that recalls almonds. The chemical responsible for this odor or taste is *benzaldehyde*.

ALMUDE (PORTUGAL) A seldom-used measure of volume equal to twenty-five liters of liquid.

ALOXE-CORTON (FRANCE) A red-wine-producing village in Côte de Beaune in the region of Burgundy. Aloxe-Corton was the favorite wine of French satirist, philosopher, and historian Voltaire (1694–1778). In 1862, the village of Aloxe added its name to that of its most illustrious vineyard, Corton.

ALPHA A red grape variety.

ALSACE One of France's six major wine-producing regions, located in the northeast. This region, dotted with picturesque villages, occupies a narrow strip of land between Strasbourg and Mulhouse. It is less than two miles wide and about sixty miles long, with an area of approximately thirty thousand acres. It is nestled between the Vosges Mountains and the Rhine River, just east of Champagne and Burgundy.

Alsace produces one-fifth of all of France's white wines entitled to the AOC designation. Because it is located so far north, there is generally insufficient sunshine to fully ripen the red grapes. Therefore, more than 90 percent of all wines of Alsace are white.

ALSTERWASSER (GERMANY) *See* Shandy.

ALT (GERMANY) Old—meaning beer brewed in the old style. A top-fermented beer popular in Germany prior to the 1800s, when *lager* was first produced. It is often reddish-brown in color with an abundant hop flavor.

ALTAR WINE *See* Sacramental Wines.

ALTBIER (GERMANY) A top-fermented beer (ale) with a high barley and hops content; it is quite bitter.

ALTERATO (ITALY) *See* Spoiled.

ALTESSE (FRANCE) A white grape variety grown in the south. Also known as *Roussette*.

ALUS Lithuanian and Latvian term for beer.

ALVARELHÃO (PORTUGAL) A red grape variety grown in the Douro region. Also known as *Pilongo*.

ALVARINHO (PORTUGAL) A white grape variety used mostly in the production of Vinho Verde.

ALWOOD A red grape variety developed in 1967 from a cross of Fredonia and Athens at the State Experimental Station in Geneva, New York.

AMA SPECIAL GELATIN A chemical substance approved for the clarification of wine.

AMABILE (ITALY) *See* Semidry Wine.

AMADURECIDO (PORTUGAL) *See* Mellow.

AMANGO *(PORTUGAL)* *See* Bitter.

AMARETTO A generic almond-apricot liqueur, russet in color; flavored with bitter-sweet almond oils obtained from the coasts of the Mediterranean. It is produced in Italy and the United States.

AMARGO *(SPAIN)* *See* Bitter.

AMARO *(ITALY)* *See* Bitter.

AMAROGNOLO *(ITALY)* Slightly bitter.

AMARONE *(ITALY)* *See* Amarone della Valpolicella.

AMARONE DELLA VALPOLICELLA *(ITALY)* A wine produced on hilly portions of the Valpolicella Classico Zone in the northeastern part of Veneto, bordered on the west by the Adige River.

The word *amarone* comes from the Veronese dialect; it means bone-dry almost to the point of bitterness. The grapes used are the same as those in Valpolicella: Corvina Veronese, Rondinella, Molinara, Rossignola, Negrara, Sangiovese, and Barbera. Amarone, however, unlike Valpolicella, is made exclusively from the best grapes, which are located at the top and outside perimeter of the clusters. The grapes used for Amarone are grown on three-foot-high trellises in the hills of Valpolicella that rise one to two thousand feet above sea level. The best grapes, those that receive the most direct sunshine, are called *recie* or *orecchie* (ears), hence the formerly used name Recioto della Valpolicella Amarone (*recioto* is a word from the old Veronese dialect of the area).

In the picking process, more than 50 percent of the grapes are immediately rejected because they are not ripe enough. In addition, the bunches that are selected are those whose grapes are sufficiently spaced to allow air to circulate between them in the eventual drying process (this limits the formation of *gray mold*). These grapes, whose sugar levels are the highest because of the amount of sunlight they receive, are picked and then arranged on flat drawers that easily fit into racks that allow a good circulation of air. It is very important that they be kept in a dry, cool, well-ventilated room. In years past, bamboo, straw mats, or trellises were used to dry the grapes. Each mat is clearly marked with the day the grapes were picked and the part of the vineyard from which they originate. The grapes are cleaned and turned about every twenty days and are constantly inspected during the three- to four-month drying period. This drying period causes a 30 percent loss of juice, resulting in grapes low in juice but extremely high in sugar and varietal character. The best Amarones depend on the formation of *Botrytis cinerea*, which releases gluconic acid during the drying process. Enzymatic action also changes the properties of the acids and sugar balance. The dried grapes, which resemble shriveled raisins, are pressed just after Christmas and fermented slowly for approximately forty-five days with the skins and stems intact. The wine is aged for a minimum of two years in wood (DOC regulation), but it is not uncommon for Amarone to be aged for five years or more in barrels prior to bottling and further bottle aging.

The resultant wine is, not surprisingly, highly alcoholic: a minimum of 14 percent under DOC law. However, most Amarones are even higher in alcohol, sometimes as high as 17 percent. When produced in the heart of the DOC production zone, the wine may be labeled *classico*. Amarone received its DOC status on August 21, 1968. Formerly known as Recioto Della Valpolicella "Amarone." *See* Recioto della Valpolicella.

AMBER As a white wine ages, it takes on golden tints reminiscent of the color *amber*. This color change results from oxidation of the anthocyanins (coloring matter). The term can also be used to describe the color of some sherries. Also known as *ambra, ambrato*, and *ambre*.

AMBER   A white grape variety.

AMBER ALE   An ale with a light amber color.

AMBER FLUID *(AUSTRALIA)*   *See* Beer.

AMBRA *(ITALY)*   *See* Amber.

AMBRATO *(ITALY)*   *See* Amber.

AMBRE *(FRANCE)*   *See* Amber.

AMBROS   A white grape variety developed by Albert Seibel. Formerly known as *Seibel 10713.*

AMELIORATION   The addition to juice or natural wine before, during, or after fermentation, of either water or pure dry sugar, or a combination of water and pure dry sugar, or liquid sugar, or invert sugar syrup, to adjust the acid level. Also known as *amélioré. See* Calcium Carbonate and Gallization.

AMÉLIORÉ *(FRANCE)*   *See* Amelioration.

AMER *(FRANCE)*   *See* Bitter.

AMERICA   A red grape variety developed by Thomas Volney Munson (1843–1913) of Denison, Texas.

AMÉRICAIN GOÛT *(FRANCE)*   A term meaning fairly sweet (in relation to champagne). More vulgarly, it implies a sugared-up blend of wine for the American market.

AMERICAN-MADE WHISKEY   Whiskey defined by the United States Federal Alcohol Administration Regulations, formulated in 1935. The maximum proof at which American-made whiskey can leave the still is 160, although most whiskey is actually distilled at 120 to 140 proof. American whiskey can only be made from grains specified for each category; potatoes and beets, used in vodka-making, cannot be used to make whiskey. *See* Whiskey.

AMERICAN OAK   Commonly considered higher than European oak in odorous components, including vanillin and related compounds and especially "oak lactone." European oak, on the other hand, has about one and one-half times the total extractables, double the extractable phenols including tannins, and considerable colored components compared to American oak.

AMERICAN WINE   Any wine (table, sparkling, fortified) produced in the United States that meets the requirements of the BATF as well as conforms to the requirements of a particular state in which the wine is made.

AMERTUME *(FRANCE)*   *See* Bitterness.

AMETHYST   A grape variety developed by Thomas Volney Munson (1843–1913) of Denison, Texas.

AMIABLE   Also known as *aimable* and *garbato. See* Pleasant.

AMIGNE *(SWITZERLAND)*   A white grape variety.

AMINO ACIDS   Essential components of protein, present in grape juice, that play an important role in the production of aroma in wine. Due to their nitrogenous organic compounds, they are indispensable to yeasts for the fermentation process.

AMMONIUM CARBONATE   A yeast nutrient used to facilitate fermentation in wine. It was removed from the authorized wine-treating materials list in 1993.

AMMONIUM PHOSPHATE   An available nitrogen and nutrient source, sometimes added to fermentations where there is doubt about the level of available nitrogen. Nitrogen is needed for healthy yeast growth and fermentation. *Ammonium sulfate* can be substituted, but ammonium phosphate is preferable. *See* Energizer.

AMMONIUM SULFATE   *See* Ammonium Phosphate.

AMMOSTARE (ITALY)   *See* Crushing.

AMMOSTATE (ITALY)   Grapes that are partially pressed.

AMMOSTATURA (ITALY)   *See* Crushing.

AMMUFFITO (ITALY)   *See* Musty.

AMONTILLADO (SPAIN)   A style of sherry that has more color and body than *fino*, with a medium dry taste and nutty flavor. True *amontillado* sherries are the best to use for cooking, for they impart a nutty-tangy flavor to food. *Fino* sherry is too dry for cooking and seems to lack the *amontillado* sherries' charm and depth, while *oloroso* and cream sherries are simply too sweet. Also known as *cocktail sherry* or *dry sherry*.

AMOROSO (SPAIN)   A seldom-used term that refers to a sweet oloroso sherry.

AMPELIDACEAE   The botanical family to which all grapevine species belong.

AMPELOGRAPHY   The descriptive study and identification of grapevines or grapevine botany. The science, the study, and the knowledge of *Ampelidacedes*—in Greek, *ampelos* means vine—teaches us that there exist almost unlimited varieties of grapevines resulting from different modes of cultivation or from the innumerable mutations and crossings that have taken place over the centuries. Also known as *ampélographie*.

AMPÉLOGRAPHIE (FRANCE)   *See* Ampelography.

AMPELOS (GREECE)   *See* Grapevine.

AMPHORA   An ancient vessel, often made of ceramic or earthenware, usually with two handles, which was used as a container for wine.

AMPIO (ITALY)   *See* Round.

AMPLE   Also known as *ampio*. *See* Round.

AMPLEUR (FRANCE)   *See* Well-Balanced.

AMPUL   A small glass container that can be sealed and its contents sterilized, intended for hypodermic injections. Also spelled *ampule*.

AMPULE   *See* Ampul.

AMTLICHE PRÜFSTELLE (GERMANY)   State Institute for Quality Control.

A

AMTLICHE PRÜFUNGSNUMMER (GERMANY) The "A.P." number that appears on the bottom of some wine labels. It certifies that the wine met all legal requirements and passed a rigid battery of laboratory and sensory tests. Also known simply as *prüfungsnummer*.

AMUADO (PORTUGAL) *See* Cooked Wine.

AMYLASE Any of various enzymes that convert starch to sugar. *See* Dextrin and Diastase.

AÑADA (SPAIN) Year of the harvest. Also known interchangeably as *año, cosecha*, and *vendimia*. *See* Harvest.

ANAEROBIC FERMENTATION A fermentation during which the atmosphere is oxygen-free.

ANCELLOTTA (ITALY) A red grape variety grown primarily in Emilia-Romagna.

ANCIENNE (FRANCE) Ancient.

AÑEJO OR AÑEJADO POR (SPAIN) Aged by.

AÑEJO (SPAIN) Aged, in reference to rum and tequila.

ANESONE (ITALY) A high-proof, dry, generic anise-and-licorice-flavored liqueur, clear in color. *See* Anise-Based Spirits.

ANGEGOREN (GERMANY) *See* Fermentation.

ANGELICA A sweet fortified wine, generally produced in California, which is seldom made today.

ANGEL'S SHARE *See* Evaporation.

ANGLAIS GOÛT (FRANCE) A term whose meaning depends on the district and context: in Champagne, dry; in Burgundy, big and smooth.

ANGOSTURA BITTERS A concentrated, aromatic bitter flavoring from the island of Trinidad, used in certain cocktails.

ANGULAR Describes wines without charm or grace, often referred to as being stiff or hard, often with bitter or tart flavors. Angular is the opposite of soft, yielding, and supple.

ANHYDROUS ALCOHOL *See* Absolute Alcohol.

ANIDRIDE SOLFORSO (ITALY) *See* Sulfur Dioxide.

ANIMAL BLOOD A fining agent used in ancient times. Also known simply as *blood*. *See* Fining and Fining Agents.

ANÍS (SPAIN) *See* Anisette.

ANISE The dried ripe fruit (incorrectly called seeds) of an annual umbelliferous plant (*Pimpinella anisum*) that is native to Egypt and the Mediterranean region. It has a definitive licorice-like taste and is used globally as a flavoring base of many liqueurs, candies, breads, and pastries.

ANISE-BASED SPIRITS Distilled spirits produced by either infusion or by the addition of flavoring (usually licorice and aniseed); they have a high alcoholic content and contain a minimum of 2.5 percent sugar. These beverages, which are produced globally, include Anesone, Chinchon, Masticha, Ojen, Ouzo, Pernod, and Ricard.

ANISETTE   A generic anise-and-licorice-flavored liqueur, clear in color, which is mostly produced in Italy, although it is also produced globally. Also known as *anís*.

ANJOU (FRANCE)   A grape-growing district in the central Loire Valley famous for its Rosé d'Anjou wine (made from mostly Cabernet Franc and Groslot grapes).

ANNATA (ITALY)   Year of the harvest. Also known interchangeably as *vendemmia*. *See* Harvest.

ANNÉE (FRANCE)   Year of the harvest. Also known as *millésime, récolte*, and *vendange*. *See* Harvest.

AÑO (SPAIN)   *See* Añada.

ANO (PORTUGAL)   *See* Ano de Colheita.

ANO DE COLHEITA (PORTUGAL)   Year of the harvest. Also known interchangeably as *ano*. *See* Harvest.

ANON BRAICH   A Gaelic term meaning *single malt* that appears on certain Scotch whisky labels.

ANREICHERN (GERMANY)   *See* Chaptalization and Verbessern.

ANSONICA (ITALY)   *See* Inzolia.

ANSPRECHEND (GERMANY)   *See* Pleasant.

ANSTELLEN (GERMANY)   The addition of yeast to *wort* in order to start a fermentation in the making of beer.

ANTHOCYANIN   A phenol that gives wine its red color. The red color of a wine is almost exclusively caused by fairly unstable anthocyanin molecules (which are basically a colored form of tannin). Also known as *pigment, pigmentazione*, and *pigmento*. *See* Phenol and Tannin.

ANTHOSIMÍA (GREECE)   *See* Bouquet.

ANTICRITTOGAMICO (ITALY)   *See* Fungicide.

ANTIOXIDANT   Tablets or crystals (often *ascorbic acid*) added to wine or beer at the time of bottling to prevent excess oxidation, browning, and deterioration of flavor. *See* Campden Tablet.

ANTITRUST LAWS   Laws designed to control monopoly power and practices.

AOC (FRANCE)   *See* Appellation d'Origine Contrôlée.

AOUTEMENT (FRANCE)   The moment when the soft, green tendrils on a grapevine become hard and woody.

AP   *See* Amtliche Prüfungsnummer.

AP   *See* As Purchased.

APAGADO (SPAIN)   *See* Feeble.

APALEADOR (SPAIN)   *See* Rousing Stick.

APÉRITIF (FRANCE) An alcoholic beverage taken before meals to stimulate the appetite. Also known as *aperitivo*.

APÉRITIF WINE A wine having an alcoholic content of not less than 15 percent by volume, compounded from grape wine containing added brandy or other distilled spirits. It is flavored with herbs and other natural aromatic flavoring materials, with or without the addition of caramel for coloring purposes, and possesses the aroma and characteristics generally attributed to an apéritif wine. It is so designated unless designated as "vermouth."

There are many factors that must be considered when determining which wines are apéritifs. The beverage should be dry, light, chillable, and refreshing; it should be relatively acidic, to cleanse the palate; it should perhaps also be slightly bitter. Also referred to as *flavored wines* and *vinho aperitive*. See Aperire and Low-Alcohol Refreshers.

APERIRE Latin for *to open*, which is the origin of the word *apéritif*, a wine that usually opens lunch or dinner as a stimulant to the appetite. Most apéritifs have an initial sweet taste with a somewhat bitter aftertaste due to the use of quinine as one of the ingredients. This slight bitterness tends to whet the appetite and cleanse the palate. The French government mandates that apéritifs be produced from at least 80 percent wine with a minimum alcoholic strength of 10 percent, prior to alcohol being added to raise the strength to between 16 and 19 percent. See Apéritif.

APERITIVO (ITALY) See Apéritif.

APEX The lower or tip end of a grape.

APIANO (ITALY) The name of an ancient Roman wine made from the Muscat grape and named after the Latin word *apis* for bee, because the bees would be alerted to the sweet taste.

APFELSCHNAPPS (GERMANY) See Applejack.

APPARENT CONSUMPTION Estimate of the gallons of distilled spirits sold at retail; based on state excise tax receipts, sales by state stores, shipments by producers to wholesalers, or shipments by wholesalers to retailers.

APPASSIMENTO (ITALY) The drying (or *resting*) of the best clusters of grapes for the making of Amarone wine. See Amarone and Ripasso.

APPEARANCE Refers to clarity, not color. Wines should be free of cloud and suspended particles when evaluated in a glass.

APPELLATION OF ORIGIN Refers to the name of the place where the dominant grapes used in the wine are grown. It can be the name of a country, state, county, or geographical region, also known as a viticultural area. Also known as *denomination of origin*.

APPELLATION D'ORIGINE CONTRÔLÉE (AOC) (FRANCE) The *appellation d'origines contrôlées* were created by the French authorities in 1935 to establish areas of production, grape varieties, minimum levels of sugar in the *must* and of alcohol in the wine, maximum yield per hectare, and pruning, grape-growing, and vinification methods.

APPETIZER WINES An incorrect term to denote wines taken before dinner; the correct term is apéritif. Appetizers are foods. Beverages, especially wine-based, are *apéritifs*.

APPLE   A fruit smell (*hexyl acetate*) and sometimes taste in some wines (Chardonnay and Johannisberg Riesling), associated with the presence of *malic acid*. Also an odor characteristic of *manzanilla* sherries.

APPLE BRANDY   *See* Applejack.

APPLEJACK   American brandy distilled from apples. Also known as *apple brandy, apfelschnapps*, and *batzi*. *See* Blended Applejack and Calvados.

APPLE JUICE   The natural, unsweetened juice from apples; it is pasteurized and may be partially or completely filtered. *See* Cider, Hard Cider, and Sweet Cider.

APPLE WINE   Sweet cider is *chaptalized* and allowed to ferment, as would white grapes. The final product, also like wine, has a fairly long shelf life. *See* Cider, Hard Cider, and Sweet Cider.

APPLIED CARBON DIOXIDE PRESSURE   Carbon dioxide gives beverages their carbonization and is used as a liquid gas under pressure. During service, gas leaves the cylinder and its pressure is reduced to a desired level by a regulator. This type of system is often used for soft drinks or beer dispensing.

APPROVED VITICULTURAL AREA (AVA)   In the United States, a delimited, geographical grape-growing area that has officially been given appellation status by the BATF. Two examples are Napa Valley and Sonoma Valley.

ÂPRE (FRANCE)   *See* Rough.

ÂPRETÉ (FRANCE)   *See* Hard.

APRICOTS   An odor present in wines affected by *Botrytis cinerea* (the noble rot) that totally masks the varietal character and substitutes an odor reminiscent of apricots. Some of the grapes affected are Sauvignon Blanc, Sémillon, Muscat, and Johannisberg Riesling.

APRICOT-FLAVORED BRANDY   A mixture of brandy, minimum of 2.5 percent sugar, flavored and colored with apricots. By United States federal law it cannot be bottled at less than 60 proof (30 percent alcohol by volume).

APRICOT LIQUEUR   A sweetened alcoholic beverage consisting of a base of alcohol, minimum 2.5 percent sugar, flavored and colored with apricots. It is sweeter and lower in proof than apricot-flavored brandy.

ÁPSITOS (GREECE)   *See* Young.

APULIA (ITALY)   One of twenty wine-producing regions, it stretches from the "spur" to the "heel" of the boot-shaped Italian peninsula. Apulia is bordered by Molise to the north and Campania and Basilicata to the west. The region's climate is temperate and the country is mainly flat.

For years this region was considered by many to be incapable of producing high-quality table wines because of its intense heat and arid climate. The wines that were produced (mostly reds) were heavy, dark in color, highly alcoholic, and flat-tasting (lacking acidity). Therefore, a good percentage of the wines were shipped north to Piedmont where they were blended with other varieties and used in making vermouth.

Within the last few years, however, modern technology has overtaken the region's vineyards, drastically lowering its total wine production. In place of the heavy alcoholic wines, Apulia's vineyards today produce lighter, fresher wines with surprisingly good acidity levels. Known as *Puglia* in Italy.

AQUAVIT   *See* Akvavit.

AQUA ARDENTS   The Latin term for alcohol, frequently used by writers of early treatises. *See* Alcohol.

AQUA VITAE   From Latin, literally meaning *water of life*, used by the French to refer to clear distillates or brandies. Also known as *acquavite, okowita, usquebaugh*, and *uisge-beatha*.

AQUEOUS   Containing water, or watery.

AQUIFER   Moderately to highly permeable rocks through which water readily moves. An important consideration when growing grapes or grains intended for use in making beverages.

AQUILEIA (ITALY)   A wine-producing area within the region of Friuli-Venezia Giulia. *See* Friuli-Venezia Giulia.

AQUITAINE (FRANCE)   The ancient name given to the region of Bordeaux.

ARABINOSE   A crystalline sugar of the pentose class, obtained from plant polysaccharides such as arabic or cherry-tree gum.

ARAGONEZ (SPAIN)   *See* Tempranillo.

ARAME (PORTUGAL)   *See* Alambrado.

ARAMON   A red grape variety grown in California and southern France. Also known as *Ugni Noir*.

ARANCIATO (ITALY)   Orangish.

ARANZADA (SPAIN)   A land measurement equal to 0.475 hectares or 1.1737 acres.

ARATURA (ITALY)   Plowing.

ARCHES   *See* Legs.

ARDENTE (ITALY)   *See* Hot.

ARDENT SPIRITS   An ancient name used to describe distilled spirits. *See* Alcohol.

ARE (FRANCE)   One-hundreth of a *hectare*.

ARENA   A type of soil found in approximately 17 percent of the Sherry region of Spain. It is about 80 percent sand, red-yellow in color, and contains alumina, silica, and clay. The soil is very tillable but produces coarser wines than either *albariza* or *barro* soils. *See* Albariza and Barro.

AREOMETER   *See* Hydrometer.

ARGILE (FRANCE)   *See* Clay.

ARGOLS   *See* Potassium Bitartrate.

ARINTO (PORTUGAL)   A white grape variety grown in the regions of Bucelas and Bairrada. Also known as *Pedernão*.

ARINTO DO DÃO (PORTUGAL)   See Assario Branco.

ARIS (GERMANY)   A white grape variety developed from a cross of *Vitis riparia* and Gamay (and Johannisberg Riesling) in Siebeldingen.

ARISTOCRATIC   Also known as *aristocratico*. See Breed.

ARISTOCRATICO (ITALY)   See Breed.

ARJAN   See Kumiss or Koumiss.

ARJOADO (PORTUGAL)   See Training.

ARM (GERMANY)   See Thin.

ARMAGNAC (FRANCE)   A brandy made in the demarcated region of Armagnac, which comprises approximately 52,000 acres of quite sandy soil mixed with some limestone, clay, and chalk. It is bounded roughly by the Garonne Valley to the north, Toulouse to the east, Bayonne and Bordeaux to the west, and the Pyrenees to the south. Its average annual production of wine is under seventy-nine million gallons. About one-quarter of this wine is distilled into brandy; the remainder is consumed as table wine.

The Armagnac region is divided into three zones: Upper Armagnac (Haut-Armagnac), the smallest area (3 percent of the total brandy production comes from this zone), which is often called "White Armagnac" because of its chalky, limestone-containing calcareous soil; Lower Armagnac (Bas Armagnac), which is by far the largest zone (57 percent of production) and is often called "Black Armagnac" because of its forests; and Ténarèze (40 percent of production). The quality, style, and taste of armagnac varies from zone to zone; it is generally agreed that the finest armagnacs come from Bas-Armagnac.

ARMAZÉM (PORTUGAL)   Warehouse.

ARMONICO (ITALY)   See Balance.

ARMS   The major branches of the trunk of a grapevine on which canes and renewal spurs are borne. These are the branches of older wood extending from the trunk. In a well-pruned vineyard they should not be more than one to two feet in length. Several ages of wood may make up an arm, all more than one year of age. The best arms, however, are of wood that is two or three years old.

ARNAISON (FRANCE)   The local name in Touraine for the Chardonnay grape variety.

ARNEIS (ITALY)   A local white grape variety grown exclusively in the Piedmont region. The origins of Arneis are not known but it has been traditionally grown in the area around Alba—always in a secondary role. Also known as *Bianchetta, Bianchetto*, and *Nebbiolo Bianco*.

ARNSBURGER (GERMANY)   A white grape variety developed from a cross of Müller-Thurgau and (Madeleine Angevine and Calabrese).

ÁROMA (GREECE)   See Aroma.

AROMA   The particular smell, odor, or fragrance of a specific grape used to produce the wine. White wines usually produced by a single grape variety are associated with aroma and are said to have *varietal character*. Also known as *ároma* and *arôme*. See Bouquet and Nose.

AROMATIC   A term for wines that have intense aromas—fruits, herbs, or other odors either directly from the grape or developed by the winemaking process. Also known as *aromatico*.

AROMATICO (ITALY)   *See* Aromatic.

AROMATIC RUM   The combination of the special quality of the river water on the island of Java in Indonesia and the addition of the dried red Javanese rice cakes that are added to the mash during fermentation results in the highly aromatic nature and dry taste of this rum. Aromatic rums are generally aged for three to four years in Java, then shipped to the Netherlands, where additional aging takes place prior to blending and bottling. One brand available in the United States is Batavia Arak. (It was so named by ancient Arabian seafarers voyaging to the Caribbean islands.)

AROMATIC WINE   *See* Aromatized Wine.

AROMATIZED WINE   A fortified wine that has any number of related aromatic plants (*Artemisia absinthium*) or bitter herbs, roots, bark, or other plant parts infused into its bouquet. An example of an aromatic wine is vermouth. Also known as *aromatic wine* and *aromatizzato*.

AROMATIZZATO (ITALY)   *See* Aromatized Wine.

ARÔME (FRANCE)   *See* Aroma.

ARPENT (FRANCE)   During the eighteenth century, one *arpent* varied in size between thirty-five and fifty acres of vineyard land.

ARRACK   An alcoholic beverage distilled from the juice or sap of palm trees, as well as other ingredients in different parts of the world. Arrack is produced mainly in the Middle East and Egypt and is referred to by many names: Arack, Arak, Arrac, Arrak, Arraki, or Raki. *See* Batavia Arrack.

ARRIÈRE-GOÛT (FRANCE)   *See* Aftertaste.

ARROBA (SPAIN)   A measurement of approximately 16 to 16.5 liters, or slightly more than four gallons.

ARROBO (PORTUGAL)   *See* Cooked Wine.

ARROPE (SPAIN)   Concentrated, unfermented grape juice used to color and sweeten some sherries. Also known as *sancocho*. *See* Cooked Wine.

ARRUMBADOR (SPAIN)   A vineyard or bodega worker.

ARSAC (FRANCE)   One of the five communes in the Bordeaux region entitled to the appellation *Margaux*.

ART (GERMANY)   A wine that is characteristic of its origin.

ARTIFICIAL CARBONATION   Probably the quickest and cheapest method of making wines sparkle is similar to the way sodas are made to fizz—that is, by pumping them full of carbon dioxide. With this method the bubbles are not an integral part of the wine and do not last long after it is poured. Sparkling wines made via this method are easy to spot; their bubbles are very large and the wine froths up very quickly for a few moments and then appears to go flat. *See* Artificially Carbonated Wine, Carbonated Beverages, and Carbonated Water.

ARTIFICIALLY CARBONATED WINE   Grape wine made effervescent with carbon dioxide other than that resulting solely from the secondary fermentation of the wine within a closed container, tank, or bottle. Effervescent wine is artificially charged with carbon dioxide and contains more than 0.392 grams of carbon dioxide per 100 milliliters. Also known as *gaseoso, gazèifiè,* and *perlwein. See* Artificial Carbonation.

ARTISAN DISTILLERS OF CALIFORNIA   An organization formed in September 1990 to develop marketing strategies and promotion of what members consider traditional European distilling methods. Their method requires more time to make smaller, higher-quality batches, and uses equipment originally developed in Europe.

ARVINE (SWITZERLAND)   A white grape variety.

ARVINO (ITALY)   *See* Magliocco Canino.

ASALI   The name of a fermented beverage made from honey in East Africa.

ASCIUTTO (ITALY)   A wine that is extremely dry.

ASCORBIC ACID (VITAMIN C)   *See* Antioxidant and Campden Tablet.

ASEPTIC   Describes substances such as sorbic acid or sulfur dioxide that can kill bacteria or microorganisms.

ASKOS (GREECE)   A wine skin or a small vase or jug shaped like a leather bottle. *See* Wine Skin.

ASPARTAME   An artificial low-calorie sweetener made from a compound of phenylalanine and aspartic acid. It is about two hundred times sweeter than sucrose and is used in the manufacture of soft drinks. Its trade name is Nutra-Sweet.

ASPERGILLUS ORYZAE   A mold that is responsible for converting the starch in rice into sugar when making *saké.*

ASPILLA (SPAIN)   A wooden dipstick used for gauging the capacity of the butts containing sherry wine.

ASPRIGNO (ITALY)   *See* Sour.

ASPRINIO (ITALY)   A white grape variety grown in the south. Also known as *Asprino, Asprinio d'Aversa,* and *Uva Asprina.*

ASPRINIO D'AVERSA (ITALY)   *See* Asprinio.

ASPRINO (ITALY)   *See* Asprinio.

ASPRO (ITALY)   *See* Rough.

AS PURCHASED (AP)   As the item is purchased or received from the supplier.

ASSAGGIO (ITALY)   *See* Degustazione.

ASSAM TEA   A very strong, full-bodied, and malty-tasting tea made from leaves grown in India's northeastern Brahmaputra Valley. In 1823, Robert Bruce discovered the plant growing wild in India.

ASSARIO BRANCO (PORTUGAL)   A white grape variety. Also known as *Arinto do Dão.*

ASSEMBLAGE (FRANCE)   The *assembling* or putting together of the base wines, known as the *cuvée*. *See* Blending.

ASSET   Something that is owned.

ASSOCIADO (PORTUGAL)   An associate or partner in a cooperative winery.

ASSYRTIKO (GREECE)   A white grape variety.

ASTE (FRANCE)   A fruit-bearing branch on a grapevine, roughly twenty-inches long, from which the end buds are cut off to leave only four live buds.

ASTESANA (ITALY)   An ancient wine bottle of Piedmont.

ASTI (ITALY)   A town in southern Piedmont famous for production of its sparkling wine, Asti, a DOCG spumante. It also produces some DOC red wines (Barbera, Dolcetto, Grignolino, and Freisa) and another DOCG white wine, Moscato d'Asti.

ASTI (ITALY)   A white, sweet sparkling wine produced in the southern area of Langhe (province of Cuneo) and Monferrato (province of Asti and Alessandria), in the region of Piedmont. The production area was delimited on March 7, 1924, when Asti Spumante was classified as a "typical wine." In 1994 Asti Spumante was granted its DOCG and with it came a name change to *Asti* with the suffix *Spumante* deleted.

Asti is made from 100 percent Moscato Bianco grapes and must contain a minimum of 7 to 9.5 percent residual sugar as well as alcohol.

ASTRINGENCY   A taste sensation that is unpleasant, harsh, rough, sharp, bitter, or with a biting quality. It is often caused by excess levels of acidity or tannin in wine or beer. Also known as *acre, âcre, adstringente, adstringerend, allappante, astringent, astringente, harsh, puckery, rude,* and *stryfnós. See* Acrid, Phenol, and Tannin.
Astringente (*Italy* and *Spain*) *See* Astringency.

ASTRINGENTE (ITALY AND SPAIN)   *See* Astringency.

ASTRINGENT   *See* Astringency.

ASZTALI BOR (HUNGARY)   Table wine.

ASZÚ (HUNGARY)   Overripe, dried-out grapes used in the making of Tokay wine.

ATESINO (ITALY)   A term occasionally encountered on wine labels that describes wines produced along the Adige River in the region of Trentino-Alto Adige.

ATF   *See* Bureau of Alcohol, Tobacco, and Firearms.

ATHIRI (GREECE)   A white grape variety.

ATHOL BROSE   A Scottish drink made with Scotch whisky, honey, and oatmeal.

ATM   *See* Atmosphere.

ATMOSPHERE (ATM)   In physics, a unit of pressure equal to 14.69 pounds of force per square inch, or the pressure exerted upon the human body at thirty feet under water. In bottles of sparkling wines, there are usually five to seven atmospheres of pressure, or about 110 pounds per square inch of CO_2 are formed.

ATTITUDE ADJUSTMENT HOUR   *See* Happy Hour.

AUBAINE (FRANCE)   The local name for the Chardonnay grape in the Chablis district of Burgundy.

AUBE *(FRANCE)* The southern province of the Champagne appellation vineyards, mostly planted with Pinot Noir grapes.

AUBUN *(FRANCE)* A red grape variety grown primarily in the southeast. Also known as *Counoise*.

AUFZIEHEN *(GERMANY)* The agitation or aeration of yeast during the fermentation process of beer.

AU LAIT *(FRANCE)* Served with added milk.

AUM *(GERMANY)* A barrel with a capacity of thirty gallons. *See* Barrel.

AUME *(FRANCE)* A large barrel for storage purposes used in Alsace, usually containing as much as a thousand liters (260 gallons). *See* Barrel.

AURORA *See* Aurore.

AURORA BLANC *See* Aurore.

AURORE A white grape variety developed by Louis Seibel in the late 1880s near the Burgundy region of France. Aurore was introduced into the Finger Lakes region of New York in the early 1940s and is used for white table wines and sparkling wines. Formerly known as *Seibel 5279*. Aurore is also incorrectly known as *Aurora* or *Aurora Blanc*.

AUSBRUCH AUSTRIA Very overripe sweet grapes, often infected with *Botrytis cinerea*.

AUSDRUCK *(GERMANY)* *See* Character.

AUSDÜNNEN *(GERMANY)* *See* Crop Thinning and Leaf Thinning.

AUSEIGENEM LESEGUT *(GERMANY)* Estate bottled.

AUSGEBAUT *(GERMANY)* *See* Maturity.

AUSGEGLICHEN *(GERMANY)* *See* Balance.

AUSLESE *(GERMANY)* A *prädikat* wine made from particularly ripe, selected, late-harvested bunches of grapes. Auslese wines are especially full, rich, and somewhat sweet; however, they may not be *chaptalized*. Auslese wines are generally sweeter and more expensive than *spätlese* wines. Also known as *szemelt*.

AUSTERE Describes wines that are generally dry, high in acidity, and bitter from excessive tannin. It implies a tactile sensation of relative hardness and an uncomplex, possibly undeveloped character in a wine that may be caused by grapes grown in cool climates or harvested earlier than usual. Also known as *afstirós, austère, austero*, and *severe*.

AUSTÈRE *(FRANCE)* *See* Austere.

AUSTERO *(ITALY)* *See* Austere.

AUSTRALIA A wine-producing country that is slightly smaller than the United States and has more than five hundred wineries, although most of them are quite small. Basically, the same grape varieties flourish in Australia that grow in Europe and California: Cabernet Sauvignon, Merlot, Pinot Noir, Chardonnay, Sauvignon Blanc, and Sémillon. However, Australia's most interesting grape variety (by far) is Syrah, generally referred to as *Shiraz*.

Australia is divided into three major grape-growing states: New South Wales, South Australia, and Victoria. Wine is also produced (to a lesser degree) in Queensland,

Tasmania, and Western Australia.

AUTOCLAVE (ITALY)   *See* Charmat Method.

AUTOLYSIS   Self-destruction of yeast cells, which release their different aromatic and flavor compounds into the surrounding medium. These compounds are amides, amino acids, and esters. In sparkling-winemaking, it is the breakdown of yeast cells inside the sparkling wine bottle after the secondary fermentation is completed that contributes to the complexity and elegance of the wine. *See* Sur Lie.

AUTOMATIC BAR   A type of self-service bar that, at the push of a finger, dispenses a predetermined, portion-controlled quantity of distilled spirit.

AUTONOMIC NERVOUS SYSTEM   The subsystem of the motor branch of the nervous system that regulates the glands and cardiac muscles.

AUTUMN FREEZE RISK   The percentage of chance that frost will hit the vineyards before the entire harvest can take place.

AUXERROIS (FRANCE)   *See* Malbec.

AUXERROIS BLANC (FRANCE)   A white grape variety grown in the Alsace region. The grape was named in honor of the Earldom of Auxerrois in Northern Burgundy. Also known as *Pinot Auxerrois*.

AUXERROIS GRIS (FRANCE)   *See* Pinot Gris.

AUXEY-DURESSES (FRANCE)   A small red-wine-producing village in Côte de Beaune in the Burgundy region. In the ninth century, Auxey was known as *Aulessiacum*. In July 1924, the village of Auxey added its name to that of its most illustrious vineyard, Duresses.

AVA   *See* Approved Viticultural Area.

AVAILABLE WATER STORAGE CAPACITY   The amount of water soil can store that can be readily absorbed by grapevines.

AV ALARM   A system that broadcasts irritating sounds to harass birds; commonly used during harvest.

AVELUDADO (PORTUGAL)   *See* Luscious.

AVESSO (PORTUGAL)   A white grape variety grown in the Minho area.

AVIGNON (FRANCE)   A small but historic city, located in the Rhône region. From 1309 to 1377 it was the papacy stronghold. *See* Châteauneuf-du-Pape.

AVILLO (SPAIN)   *See* Folle Blanche.

AWAMORI (JAPAN)   A high-proof spirit distilled from rice, made in Okinawa.

AWARE   American Wine Alliance for Research and Evaluation.

AWKWARD   Describes a wine or beer that is crude, has poor structure, or is out of balance. Also known as *plump*.

AXIL   The acute angle formed between the *petiole* and the shoot from which the leaf extends on a grapevine.

AXINA DE MARGIAI (ITALY)   *See* Nuragus.

AXINA DE POPORUS (ITALY)   *See* Nuragus.

AŸ (FRANCE)   A village in the Champagne region that grows primarily Pinot Noir grapes for champagne.

AZAL (PORTUGAL)   A red grape variety used in the production of Vinho Verde wine.

AZIENDA AGRARIA (ITALY)   *See* Azienda Agricola.

AZIENDA AGRICOLA (ITALY)   Only companies that can prove that their wines have been made solely from grapes gathered in their own vineyards and vinified in their own cellars have the right to describe themselves as an *azienda agricola* or winery. Also known as *Azienda Agraria*.

AZIENDA VINICOLA (ITALY)   Winery; agricultural concern.

AZIENDA VITIVINICOLA (ITALY)   Vintner; a grape-growing and winemaking company. Generally means the same as *azienda vinicola*.

b \ bē \ *n, often cap, often attrib*

BABEASCA NEAGRA (RUSSIA) A red grape variety, originally from Romania, which displays an unusual spicy odor for a red wine, like that of a Muscat or perhaps a Gewürztraminer.

BAC *See* Blood Alcohol Count.

BAC À GLÂCE (FRANCE) A shallow brine bath used to freeze the neck of champagne bottles prior to *dégorgement*.

BACARDI A cocktail containing Bacardi rum, grenadine syrup, sugar, and lime juice. Also the brand name of a rum originally produced in Cuba but now made in Puerto Rico.

BACH (GERMANY) Stream.

BACCHAE (FRANCE) The female companions of Bacchus.

BACCHUS The Roman god of wine; related to *Dionysus*, the Greek god of wine. Also known as *Bacco*.

BACCHUS A red grape variety developed in the 1870s by James H. Ricketts in Newburgh, New York.

BACCHUS (GERMANY) A white grape variety developed from a cross of (Sylvaner and Johannisberg Riesling) and Müller-Thurgau at the Geilweilerhof Research Station in the Pfalz.

BACCO (ITALY) *See* Bacchus.

BACK BAR The cabinet or display area behind the bar usually used for merchandise, the cash register, supplies, and storage.

BACK BLENDING Prior to fermentation, some of the unfermented juice, which is high in natural sugar, is filtered and held under refrigeration until after the fermentation is complete. At this point, a small amount of this sugar-rich juice is then added back to the wine to create a sweet flavor. Also known as *muté* and *süssreserve*. *See* Filtrato and Mistelle.

BACKBONE   A term used in describing those wines that are full-bodied, well structured, and balanced by a desirable level of acidity. Also known as *rückgrat*.

BACKINGS   *See* Tails.

BACK OF THE HOUSE   Those areas of a hotel, restaurant, tavern, or any facility that are not in the public eye; the work areas where guests and customers are not permitted. The kitchen, storeroom, and food preparation area are examples.

BACKWARD   Describes a young wine that is less developed than others of its type and class from the same vintage. When referring to red wines, it means they are still somewhat harsh from youthful tannin, and closed in.

BACO 1   *See* Baco Noir.

BACO 22A   *See* Baco Blanc.

BACO 2-16   *See* Totmur.

BACO BLANC   A white grape variety developed in 1898 by Maurice Baco from a cross of Folle Blanche and Noah. It is the only French-American hybrid grape variety used for blending permitted in France in an AOC region (Armagnac). Formerly known as *Baco 22A*.

BACO NOIR   A red grape variety named after François Baco (1865–1947), the French hybridizer (often confused with his son Maurice, for whom Baco Blanc is named), who developed this grape variety in 1902 near the Burgundy region. Baco is a cross of Folle Blanche and a wild *Vitis riparia* variety from the United States. It is believed to be the first commercially grown French hybrid in the United States (Finger Lakes Region, 1949). Baco Noir is mostly grown in the northeast of the United States. Formerly known as *Baco 1*.

BACTERIAL SPOILAGE   A general name for most types of spoilage bacteria that attacks *must*, wine, or beer during and after fermentation. Often due to formation of mold from improperly cleaned equipment, sloppy winemaking or brewing practices, lack of sterile conditions, or faulty sanitation procedures. In those instances where bacterial infestation is present, the wine or beer often turns to vinegar or becomes spoiled, and is unfit for consumption. *See* Adulterated Wine and Spoiled.

BADEN *(GERMANY)*   One of thirteen qualitätswein (quality) grape-growing regions, located in the southwest along the Rhine River, known for its full-flavored wines. Baden is marked by the Kaiserstuhl, an extinct volcano whose soil helps produce wines that are powerful and aromatic. The predominant grape varieties are Müller-Thurgau, Pinot Gris, Weissburgunder, and Gewürztraminer.

BADISCH ROTGOLD *(GERMANY)*   The designation for a rosé wine from the Baden region.

BAGA *(PORTUGAL)*   A red grape variety grown in the Bairrada, Dão, and Ribatejo regions.

BAGA *(PORTUGAL)*   Elderberry juice, used in ancient times to add color to some port wines.

BAGACEIRA *(PORTUGAL)*   *See* Grappa.

BAGAÇO *(PORTUGAL)*   *See* Pomace.

BAGASSE   The sugar-laden center of the sugar cane.

BAG-IN-A-BOX   A food-grade plastic bag containing wine (generally three, four, or five liters), that is enclosed in a cardboard box with an attached spigot.

BAGUE CARRÉ *(FRANCE)*   The rounded lip or edge on a sparkling wine bottle, similar to that on a bottle of still wine.

BAGUE COURONNE *(FRANCE)*   The rounded lip or edge on a sparkling wine bottle, similar to that on a beer bottle.

BAILEY   A red grape variety developed by Thomas Volney Munson (1843–1913) of Denison, Texas.

BAILHOT *(FRANCE)*   *See* Grape-Picking Basket.

BAIRRADA *(PORTUGAL)*   A red- and white-wine-producing region located south of Oporto. The principal grape varieties for the reds include Baga, Periquita, and Tinta Pinheira. For white wines they include Bical and Rabo de Ovelha.

BAKED   A caramel-like odor or flavor of being cooked or baked found in certain wines. Generally these wines have been heated at too high a temperature for too long. Often descriptive of wines from Madeira, Portugal, and Marsala, Italy. Also known as *brandig* and *burnt*. *See* Caramelization, Cooked, Hydroxymethylfurfural, and Maderized.

BAKING   *See* Estufa.

BALANCE   Pleasant harmony of the elements and components of a beverage, especially of wine. A balanced wine is one whose components—sugar, fruit, tannin, acid, alcohol, wood, extract, and so forth—are evident, but do not mask or dominate one another. Acid is balanced by sweetness, fruit by oak and tannin, alcohol by acidity and flavor. The olfactory and tactile elements are cohesive, proportioned, and seem to blend or meld together. Also known as *armonico, ausgeglichen, equilibrado, equilibrato, équilibré, harmonica, harmonious, harmonisch*, and *proportioned*. *See* Round and Well-Balanced.

BALANCED PRUNING   The pruner adjusts the crop at pruning time so that it is in balance in relation to the grapevine's potential to produce a crop in the subsequent growing season. Balanced pruning also regulates cane and shoot growth. *See* Brush Weight and Pruning.

BALADÍ *(SPAIN)*   A white grape variety used to produce sherry.

BALBINO *(ITALY)*   A white grape variety.

BALLING   Name of a system developed in 1868 by Karl J.N. Balling, a German scientist. It is used by American and other English-speaking countries' winemakers to measure the sugar content of grapes, *must*, and occasionally wine. *See* Brix.

BALLONGES *(FRANCE)*   *See* Gondola.

BALLOON GLASS   An oversized wineglass with a balloon-shaped bowl, having a capacity of between ten and twenty-six ounces.

BALSAM   A banana-flavored liqueur produced in the West Indies.

BALSEIRO *(PORTUGAL)*   A large wooden barrel on legs, often used to transport or hold wine. *See* Barrel.

BALTHAZAR   An oversized bottle equal in capacity to sixteen 750 milliliter bottles or twelve liters (405.6 ounces). Balthazar was the name given to one of the three Wise Men, known as the "Lord of the Treasury." He was a sixth-century B.C. king of Babylon and a grandson of Nebuchadnezzar, the first king of Babylon.

BAMBOO JUICE   The name given to alcoholic beverages by members of the United States Air Force who were stationed in the South Pacific during the Korean War.

BANANA LIQUEUR   *See* Crème de Banana.

BANANAS   With some very young white wines (tank samples as well as freshly bottled), there is either a faint smell or noticeable odor of bananas, a by-product of fermentation. The chemical responsible for this is *amyl* or *isoamyl acetate*, which diminishes with age.

BANAT RIESLING (*ROMANIA* AND *YUGOSLAVIA*)   A white grape variety. Also known as *Creata*.

BAN DE VENDANGE (*FRANCE*)   The official ceremony announcing the beginning of the harvest.

BANDOL (*FRANCE*)   A province located just to the west of Toulon, Provence, along the Mediterranean coast. In the vineyards of Bandol, the grapevines are planted in terraces made of chalky, silicate soil, which is also very arid. To be entitled to the appellation for its red and rosé wines, a high percentage of Mourvèdre and Grenache must be used; for its whites, Clairette and Ugni Blanc are utilized.

BANG   A wine made in India from hemp leaves and twigs infused in water. Also spelled *bhang*.

BANYULS (*FRANCE*)   A sweet, fortified wine made predominantly from the black Grenache grape variety. Banyuls is produced in the Languedoc Roussillon region on the Mediterranean coast, near Spain.

BAPTISM (*FRANCE*)   A process formerly used to collect bad wine and improve it by the use of chemicals.

BAR   A place of business that sells and serves alcoholic beverages by the drink. There are three parts of a bar: the front bar or countertop where alcoholic beverages are served to customers; the underbar or work station where bartenders assemble drinks; and the back bar, usually a cabinet or display area agaist a wall, used for merchandise, the cash register, supplies, and storage. Also known as *bar and grill*. *See* Barroom, Cocktail Lounge, Inn, Pub, Saloon, Tavern, and Watering Hole.

BARACK PÁLINKA (*AUSTRIA* AND *HUNGARY*)   A fruit brandy made from apricots.

BARADA DA MOSCA (*PORTUGAL*)   *See* Bical.

BAR AND GRILL   *See* Bar.

BAR BACK   A bartender's helper or an apprentice bartender. A bar back replenishes ice, nonalcoholic beverages, and mixes; cuts up garnishes; cleans the bar area; and generally assists in all but the final presentation of drinks and collection of money.

BARBADOS BRANDY   *See* Rum.

BARBADOS WATER   *See* Rum.

BARBARESCO *(ITALY)* A dry red wine produced from 100 percent Nebbiolo grapes (or the subvarieties Lampia and Michet) grown in vineyards located in the towns of Barbaresco, Neive, Treiso, and Alba, all in the southern province of Cuneo in the northwest region of Piedmont. The Barbaresco vineyards consist of twelve hundred acres with an annual yield of approximately two hundred thousand cases.

Barbaresco is often referred to as "Barolo's younger brother" or the "queen of Piedmont's wines." While not quite as powerful, Barbaresco does share Barolo's robust and austere qualities. Although it only received its DOCG in 1981, Barbaresco's production has actually been subject to local government regulations since 1908. A quality control group was set up at that time which, among other things, established the precise boundaries of the Barbaresco production zone. These boundaries were officially recognized by the DOC law of 1963.

Barbaresco must have an alcoholic content of no less than 12.5 percent and be aged for a minimum of two years, one in wood; when aged four years (three in wood), it may be labeled *riserva*. The Barbaresco *consorzio* features on its neck label the ancient tower of Barbaresco in gold on a blue background.

BARBAROSSA *(ITALY)* A red grape variety.

BARBERA A red grape variety grown primarily in Piedmont, Italy, and in small quantities in the United States. It produces wines that are generally full-bodied and slightly tannic, with a high natural amount of acidity and a tart berry, fruity taste.

Although its exact origins are uncertain, it is believed to have originated from a spontaneous crossing of seeds from ancient grapevines growing in the hilly area known as Monferrato in southern Piedmont; in fact, its ampelographical name is *Vitis vinifera Montisferratensis*.

BARBERONE A made-up California name for inexpensive, heavy, full-bodied red wines that are likely to be slightly sweet. Popular during the 1950s and 1960s, these wines are of little consequence today.

BAR BRANDS *See* Well Brands.

BARCELO *(PORTUGAL)* A white grape variety grown in the Dão region.

BARDO *(SPAIN)* *See* Training.

BARDOLINO *(ITALY)* A dry, light-bodied red wine produced in the northeastern region of Veneto. From the Brenner-Verona highway, the classico zone of Bardolino can be seen in the rolling hills between the Adige and Lake Garda. Bardolino is produced in the area southeast of Lake Garda, including all or parts of the communal territories of Bardolino, Garda, and others, in the province of Verona. The name Bardolino is relatively recent; at the beginning of this century, it was called *Garda wine*, although the wine itself is very old indeed.

Bardolino, a DOC wine since 1968, contains a minimum of 10.5 percent alcohol. If 11.5 percent and aged one year, it may be labeled *superiore*. Bardolino Classico must come from a strictly delimited area of production. Under DOC, there is also a Bardolino Spumante. Bardolino is a blend of Corvina Veronese, Rondinella, Molinara, Negrara, and other grape varieties.

There is also a very light Bardolino, resembling a rosé, called Bardolino Chiaretto. Bardolino bottled by December 31 of the year of the harvest can be identified on the label as *novello* (nouveau). The *consorzio* of Bardolino features a Roman arena at Verona on its neck label.

BÄRENTRANK *(GERMANY)*   The name of a spirit distilled from potatoes and flavored with honey.

BAR FLY   A term from the 1940s to 1970s used to describe someone (usually female) who spends time hanging out and drinking alcoholic beverages at bars.

BARISTI *(ITALY)*   *Bartenders* specially trained in the use of Italian espresso machines.

BARK   The outermost layer of a woody stem or plant, especially a grapevine.

BARKEEPER   A bartender or owner who is charge of the establishment and responsible for serving and selling alcoholic beverages. Also known as *bartender*.

BARLETTANA *(ITALY)*   *See* Uva di Troia.

BARLEY   A widely cultivated cereal plant. Its seed or grain is extracted, then converted into malt for making beer or whiskey.

BARLEY BEER   A drink of the ancient Greeks.

BARLEY MALT   *See* Malt.

BARLEY WATER   A nonalcoholic grain beverage made by boiling the grain in water and cooling it to room temperature. Popular in Victorian England, the drink is commonly served with meals in present-day Korea.

BARLEY WINE   Not actually a wine, but an English term for an extra strong dark ale.

BARLINKA   A red grape variety grown in the United States and South Africa.

BARMAID   A cocktail waitress or female worker who works behind the bar mixing, serving, and selling alcoholic beverages.

BAR MANAGER   *See* Beverage Manager.

BARNYARD   An unpleasant odor occasionally found in some wines due to unsanitary winemaking techniques or facilities. *See* Brettanomyces.

BAROLISTA *(ITALY)*   Someone who makes Barolo wine.

BAROLO *(ITALY)*   A renowned, full-bodied, dry red wine produced all over the DOCG area of Barolo, particularly in Serralunga d'Alba, Castiglione Falletto, and La Morra (traditionally the best communes within the DOCG area of production for Barolo), the area centering around the town of Barolo in the Langhe Hills just southeast of Alba in the northwest region of Piedmont.

The Barolo vineyards of Piedmont consist of three thousand acres with an annual yield of approximately four to six hundred thousand cases. Barolo must be produced from 100 percent Nebbiolo grapes or the subvarieties Lampia and Michet.

Barolo must be aged at least three years, (two in wood) and have a minimum alcohol content of 13 percent. When aged five years (four in wood) it may be labeled *riserva*.

Barolo received its DOCG status on January 22, 1981. The Barolo *consorzio* features on its neck label a golden lion or a helmeted head on a blue background, according to the particular district it comes from.

BAROLO CHINATO *(ITALY)*   A special wine produced by flavoring Barolo with various botanicals including cinchona bark, gentian root, rhubarb, cardamom, and others, which are extracted by maceration.

BARREL   A container of any size in which wine, beer, or distilled spirits is stored, aged, and sometimes shipped. The barrel can be made of any material, such as wood or stainless steel. A finished fifty-gallon wooden barrel typically weighs 110 pounds empty and about 525 pounds full. The head diameter is twenty to twenty-one inches, stave length thirty-three to thirty-five inches. The individual staves vary in width from two to four inches. Barrels, depending on capacity, country of origin, and what type of alcoholic beverage they contain, are referred to by many names. Among them are Aum, Aume, Balseiro, Barrica, Barril, Barrique, Barriquot, Bocoy, Bode, Bordelesas, Bota, Bota Chica, Bota Bodeguera, Bota De Embarque, Bota De Recibo, Bota Gorda, Botte, Butt, Caratello, Casco, Cask, Corredor, Cuva, Demi-Muid, Déposito, Doppleohm, Dopplestück, Double Aum, Fass, Fatte, Feuillette, Firkin, Foudre, Fuder, Fusto, Fût, Gönc, Halbfuder, Halbstück, Hogshead, Keg, Kilderkin, Media, Octave, Pièce, Pin, Pipe, Puncheon, Quartaut, Queue, Rood, Rundlet, Scantling Pipe, Stück, Tank, Tercero, Terzo, Tierce, Tina, Tonel, Tonne, Tonneau, Tun, Viertelstück, and Vat.

BARREL AGING   The process of mellowing an alcoholic product through extraction, as the alcohol dissolves flavor-affecting chemicals present in the wood of the barrels. Flavor components, aromatic substances, and wood tannin all contribute to the body, character, and complexity of the wine. The pine-type trees (Douglas fir, pine, and spruce) have resinous flavors that are undesirable to wine, while acacia imparts a yellow pigment.

During aging, the liquid nearest the barrel wall becomes more dense from taking on the added weight of the extractables; this heavier liquid then falls away, causing circulation, which brings the lighter liquid from the center of the barrel to the walls to pick up added extractable elements. The smaller the barrel, the more rapid the circulation and the extraction, and hence the more rapid the aging process. Also known as *wood aging*. *See* Aging, Bottle Aging, Maturity, Ripe, and Ripe For Bottling.

BARREL DOGGING   A seldom-used moonshining operation where wooden barrels (formerly utilized by legal distilleries) are disassembled and steamed or sweated in order to capture any residual alcohol that soaked into the wood during aging.

BARREL FERMENTATION   A technique utilized in Burgundy, France, for centuries, and now in wine regions around the world, for the production of certain white wines (primarily Sauvignon Blanc and Chardonnay). The *must*, after being separated from its stems, skins, and seeds, is fermented in wooden barrels (usually fifty-five gallons) rather than temperature-controlled stainless steel containers. During this process, extractables, such as tannin, color, odors, and flavors are leached into the wine, creating more complexity and depth. Certain flavor extractables are available to a wine only at certain levels of alcohol. In other words, some flavor compounds found in oak might be available to a wine only at an alcohol level of 2 percent, while other flavors might be available only at 10 percent, and so forth. Therefore, if the wine is not in wood at these times, the extractives will not be in the wine.

Some winemakers believe that certain white wines benefit from barrel fermentation for harmony of taste and increasing body. The cost and risk of spoilage often outweigh the benefits obtained. Also referred to as *barrel-fermented* on certain wine labels.

BARREL HOUSE (ENGLAND)   An establishment that primarily serves lager and ale.

BARREL LEAK   *See* Leakage.

BARREL OF BEER   A stainless steel barrel containing thirty-one gallons (13.8 cases of twelve-ounce cans or bottles of beer).

BARREL PROOF   Whiskey as it comes out of the barrel, without reducing the proof.

BARREL-STORE   Large storeroom where the young wine, beer, or distilled spirits are kept in oak barrels prior to bottling.

BARREL THIEF   *See* Wine Thief.

BARRICA (SPAIN)   *See* Barrel and Barrique.

BARRIL (PORTUGAL)   *See* Barrel.

BARRIQUE (FRANCE)   A small barrel. A law that appeared in the "Moniteur" on June 13, 1866, ratified a meeting of the Bordeaux Chamber of Commerce, held on May 12, 1858, which established that barrels' dimensions should be uniformly expressed in metric terms. It stipulated that the volume of the Bordeaux barrique should be precisely 225 liters (59.4 gallons); length ninety-one centimeters (35.8 inches); external circumference at the bilge 218 centimeters (7 feet 1.8 inches); an extrusion of seven centimeters (2.8 inches) from the closed head of the barrel to the end of the staves; thickness of head sixteen to eighteen millimeters (6/10 to 7/10 of an inch); thickness of the staves at the bilge twelve to fourteen millimeters (8/16 to 9/16 of an inch); and so forth. Also known as *barrica*. *See* Barrel.

BARRIQUOT (FRANCE)   An old term for a small barrel. *See* Barrel.

BARRO   A heavy, dark soil (due to the high iron oxide content) with some chalk, but mostly made of clay and sand. Barro is often found in valleys between hills of *albariza* soil. It is more fertile and yields about 20 percent more grapes per ton than albariza. Barro soil is important in the sherry-producing vineyards of Jerez de la Frontera, Spain. *See* Albariza and Arena.

BARROOM   A room with a bar or counter at which alcoholic beverages are sold. Also known as *taproom*. *See* Bar, Cocktail Lounge, Inn, Pub, Saloon, and Tavern.

BARSAC (FRANCE)   A sweet white wine made from a blend of Sauvignon Blanc, Sémillon, and Muscadelle grape varieties. It is also one of the five communes within Bordeaux's Sauternes district entitled to be called "Sauternes." Only wines from the commune of Barsac are entitled to the Barsac *appellation contrôlée*; however, a decree in 1936 gave this commune the right to the illustrious Sauternes appellation as well. On September 11, 1936, Barsac was officially given its *appellation contrôlée* designation.

BAR SPOON   An elongated stainless-steel spoon used behind the bar for stirring cocktails, especially those containing carbonated beverages.

BAR STRAINER   *See* Cocktail Strainer.

BAR SUGAR   *See* Superfine Sugar.

BARTENDER   An employee responsible for the operation of a bar, including the mixing, serving, and selling of alcoholic beverages. Also referred to as "tapman" when the operation sells a large volume of beer. Also known as *barkeeper* and *mixologist*.

BARTZCH   A local Asian distilled beverage made from fermented hogweed, a general name for any coarse plant, such as ragweed or sow thistle.

BAR WHISKEY   *See* Well Brands.

BAR WORKBOARD   Area below the top of a bar containing sinks, drainboards, glass washers, glass chillers, beverage coolers, ice storage compartments, cocktail mix stations, beer system, and so on. Also known as *sink workboard*.

BASAL   A shoot originating on the trunk area of a grapevine.

BAS ARMAGNAC (FRANCE)   A zone in the Armagnac region that produces the finest armagnacs.

BASE   The flat bottom of a tumbler or stem glass. Also known as *foot*.

BASI (PHILIPPINES)   The name of a spirit distilled from sugar cane.

BASIC PERMIT   Formal document issued under the United States Federal Alcohol Administration Act authorizing the person named (individual or firm) to engage in specified activities at the stated location. Such permits are required for importers, domestic producers, blenders, and wholesalers.

BASILICATA (ITALY)   One of twenty wine-producing regions located in the south, best known for its steep, rugged mountains, hot weather, and full-bodied red wines. Its most famous wine is Aglianico del Vulture, a dry and full-flavored red wine.

BASKET   *See* Wine Cradle.

BASKET PRESS   A type of press wherein grapes are put in a wooden tub with slotted sides. Pressure is applied by means of a large screw, which presses the grapes and allows the juice to run out through the slots. *See* Wine Press.

BASQUAISE (FRANCE)   An oval bottle traditionally used for armagnac.

BASTARDO (PORTUGAL)   A red grape variety grown in the Dão and Bairrada regions as well as in the Douro, where it is used in making port wine. Also known as *Trousseau*.

BASTER   *See* Wine Thief.

BASTO (SPAIN)   *See* Rough.

BAT AND A BALL   Slang term for a shot of whiskey accompanied by a glass of beer. Also known as a *beer and a ball* and *puddler and his helper*.

BATAVIA ARRACK   A highly aromatic rum distilled in Java from dried red Javanese rice cakes. *See* Arrack.

BATF   *See* Bureau of Alcohol, Tobacco, and Firearms.

BATH   A red grape variety developed in 1952 from a cross of Fredonia and N.Y. 10805 at the State Experimental Station in Geneva, New York.

BATHTUB GIN   An illicit alcoholic beverage made in the United States during Prohibition by mixing together neutral spirits, glycerin, and extracts or oils of juniper berries inside a bathtub. After being stirred with an oar, it was bottled and either sold or consumed.

BÂTONNAGE (FRANCE)   Describes the process of stirring up the *lees* regularly so as to keep the solids in suspension.

BATZI (SWITZERLAND)   Apple brandy. *See* Applejack.

BAUM (GERMANY)   Tree.

BAUMÉ (FRANCE)   Name of a system (after Antoine Baumé, 1728–1804, a French chemist) used to measure the level of unfermented sugar present in the *must*. If degrees Baumé are multiplied by 1.8, the result is degrees Brix. To determine Baumé, take degrees Brix and divide by 1.8. *See* Brix.

BAVARIAN PURITY ORDER   *See* Reinheitsgebot.

BAYLETON   The trade name of a systemic fungicide called Triadimefon (common name) that is effective against powdery mildew and black rot.

BEACON   A red grape variety developed by Thomas Volney Munson (1843–1913) of Denison, Texas.

BEAD   *See* Rim.

BEADS   Term often used to describe the chains of pinpoint bubbles found in sparkling wines, beers, and carbonated soft drinks, formed by the presence of carbon dioxide. Also, the bubbles that form on the surface of a distilled spirit when shaken. *See* Pinpoint Bubbles.

BEAUCAILLOU (FRANCE)   Beautiful pebbles.

BEAUJOLAIS (FRANCE)   Extremely fruity, fresh, and light-bodied red, white, and rosé wines produced in the southern part of Burgundy. White Beaujolais is made from a blend of Chardonnay and Aligoté grapes. Most Beaujolais wines are made by carbonic maceration and are meant to be consumed young.

BEAUJOLAIS DE L'ANNÉE (FRANCE)   *See* Beaujolais Nouveau.

BEAUJOLAIS NOUVEAU (FRANCE)   The new Beaujolais that is rushed through fermentation, then sold only a matter of weeks after harvest. Nouveau is at its best when it first appears on the market. After one year it is tired and with few exceptions should be forgotten.

Beginning in 1967, the official date of first release or sale of the nouveaus was November 15. However, since 1985, the official date is the third Thursday in November, regardless of the specific date. Also known as *Beaujolais de l'année* and *Beaujolais primeur*. *See* Carbonic Maceration and Nouveau.

BEAUJOLAIS PRIMEUR (FRANCE)   *See* Beaujolais Nouveau.

BEAUJOLAIS-SUPÉRIEUR (FRANCE)   A designation of wine containing 1 percent more alcohol than simple Beaujolais and probably from one of the fifty-nine communes in the Bas-Beaujolais area. It rarely is exported to the United States.

BEAUJOLAIS-VILLAGES (FRANCE)   Wines produced in the thirty-nine communes located in the northernmost section of the Haut-Beaujolais area. These wines contain more body and flavor than ordinary Beaujolais wines.

BEAUMES-DE-VENISE (FRANCE)   A white-wine producing vineyard located in the southern part of the Rhône Valley, noted for a sweet, fortified white made exclusively from Muscat grapes.

BEAUNE (FRANCE) A principal town in the southern half of Burgundy's Côte d'Or, noted for its exceptional white and red wines.

BEAUNOIS (FRANCE) The local name for the Chardonnay grape in the Chablis district of Burgundy.

BEAUTY SEEDLESS A red grape variety developed in 1946 by Dr. Harold P. Olmo at the University of California, Davis.

BÉCLAN A red grape variety grown in California and in Jura, France.

BEECHWOOD AGING As practiced by Anheuser-Busch, beechwood aging is quite different from aging wine in barrels at a winery. In beechwood aging, either beechwood chips or a number of short slats of beechwood are tied together and then immersed in a tank where the beer is undergoing a process known as *kräusening*. The beechwood does not impart any particular flavor to the beer but rather attracts impurities and promotes clarification of the yeast. It accomplishes this by increasing the surface area for encouraged fermentation. After use, these slats are washed off and used over and over again.

BEER Generic term for all alcoholic beverages that are fermented and brewed from malted barley, hops, water, and yeast. Other starchy cereals, such as corn and rice, may also be used where legal. Also known as *amber fluid, bere, bier, bière, bira, birra, biru, biyar, cerveja, cerveza, kiu, mai chiu, öl, oluteza, pivo, piwo, serbesa, sor, ubhiya*, and *zythos*.

BEER *See* Wash.

BEER AND A BALL *See* Bat and a Ball.

BEER AND SKITTLES (ENGLAND) Slang term for drinks and enjoyment or pleasure.

BEER BALL A nonreturnable, plastic, oversized ball containing one or more gallons (128 ounces) of beer. It is generally fitted with a type of spigot for dispensing.

BEER BASH Campus, college fraternity, or teen term for a party at which the primary beverage is beer, often served from a keg. Also known as *keg party*.

BEER BOTTLE A glass container for the storage and service of beer. In 1940, Owen-Illinois Glass introduced *duraglass*, which enabled beer bottlers to reuse bottles and consumers to return them for deposit. In 1953, the nonreturnable beer bottle made its debut.

BEER BOX A specially constructed refrigerated compartment or cooler used for the storage of draft beer and its corresponding system. Also known as *tap box*. *See* Beer Cooler.

BEER CAN A metal container for the storage and service of beer. First introduced on January 24, 1935, in Richmond, Virginia, by the Kreuger Brewery of Newark, New Jersey. In 1960, the soft top aluminum end was introduced to the beer can.

BEER CLEAN GLASS A glass that is free of grease (petroleum and its products), lint, soap, and odor; this is necessary for the proper service of beer.

BEER COOLER An enclosed refrigerated cooler (includes walk-in) used for the storage of kegs, cans, and bottles of beer. *See* Beer Box.

BEER DISPENSER *See* Beer Standard.

BEERENAUSLESE (GERMANY) (Sometimes abbreviated BA.) Berry selection wines made from individually picked, extremely overripe grapes, produced in very small quantities in the best vintages only. Out of each bunch of grapes, the pickers might only select one or two berries to use. Obviously the result is an extremely high production cost. In addition, the grapes generally have been attacked by the mold *Botrytis cinerea* (known in Germany as *edelfäule*). The resultant wine is intensely sweet and can generally age for several decades.

BEERENTON (GERMANY)   The taste of fully ripened or mature grapes.

BEER FLIP   *See* Flip.

BEER GARDEN   Slang term for a pub.

BEER HALLS   Seldom-used term for social gathering centers (usually for the lower and middle classes, and senior citizens) that serve primarily beer. Also known as *beer houses*.

BEER HOUSES   *See* Beer Halls.

BEER PACKS   Containers such as bottles, cans, or barrels with various capacities used for the storage and service of brewed beverages.

BEER STANDARD   That portion of a draft beer system that is above the counter and visible to the eye. It includes the tap, faucet, drain, and stainless steel housing. Also known as *beer dispenser* or *tapping cabinet*.

BEER SYSTEM   A draft beer system consisting of a keg of beer, CO_2 tank, regulator, beer box, beer lines, and beer standard.

BEERY   Describes an odor or taste that is typical of beer or other malt beverages with a pronounced odor of hops.

BEESWAX   Soft, pliable wax generally used to fill in or seal minute leaks in a barrel.

BEESWINE   *See* Mead.

BEESWING   The light, thin crust that resembles the transparent wing of a bee and often forms in bottles of port. *See* Sediment.

BEET SUGAR   A sugar used in Europe for *chaptalization*.

BELDI   A white grape variety grown in Tunisia.

BELEMNITA QUADRATA (FRANCE)   The chalky soil that composes the hills of the Champagne region; it evolved during subterranean earthquakes millions of years ago.

BELL   A white grape variety developed by Thomas Volney Munson (1843–1913) of Denison, Texas.

BELLANDAIS   A red grape variety developed from a cross of Seibel 6468 and Plantet. Formerly known as *Seibel 14596*.

BELLINI   A cocktail consisting of peaches, lemon juice, dry Italian spumante, and grenadine syrup. This drink was created in 1948 by Giuseppe Cipriani at Harry's Bar in Venice, Italy, to commemorate the Renaissance artist Giovanni Bellini.

BELLONE (ITALY)   A white grape variety native to Latium.

BELLO VELLETRANO (ITALY)   A white grape variety.

BELL PEPPER   An odor characteristic of bell peppers, occasionally detected in Cabernets (Franc and Sauvignon), Sauvignon Blanc, and certain other grape varieties.

The source of this odor has been identified as a pyrazine compound, *2-methoxy-3-isobutyl pyrazine* (MIP).

BELLY SPOT   A surface depression on a cork caused by inner density of the cork.

BELOE (RUSSIA)   *See* White.

BELVERDINO (ITALY)   A white grape variety.

BENCH GRAFTS   A common propagation method of producing grafted grapevines of a desired fruiting species on rootstocks resistant to *phylloxera* or nematodes. Also referred to indoor grafting because the grafting usually takes place during the winter in appropriate warm environments like greenhouses.

BENCH GRAFTING   Indoor grafts done during late winter or early spring during the dormant season, calloused-in, in a warm environment, rooted and grown for one year in the nursery, then vineyard planted in the second spring. Normal take for bench grafts is well above 90 percent, making for uniform stands (vineyards with grapevines of similar maturity). The term came about since these grafts were accomplished during the winter while sitting comfortably at a warm bench rather than stooping in a cold field. Also referred to as *field budding* and *chip budding*.

BENCH TESTING   Also referred to as *laboratory testing*.

BENDING AN ELBOW   A slang term for drinking beer or whiskey at a bar.

BENEAU (FRANCE)   *See* Grape-Picking Basket.

BENIN WINE   A distilled spirit made from fermented palm sap, which is produced in Nigeria.

BENTONITE   An excellent fining agent, first used in 1931 by Lothrop and Paine for fining honey. It is basically a granular clay (resembles gray crystalline powder) originating from the states of Wyoming and South Dakota and consisting of montmorillonite, produced from decomposition under water of volcanic glass. Chemically, bentonite is hydrated aluminum silicate and carries a negative charge. *See* Fining and Fining Agents.

BENZALDEHYDE   *See* Almond.

BEOR (ENGLAND)   An old term for beer.

BERE (ROMANIA)   *See* Beer.

BEREICH (GERMANY)   A subregion within a Gebiet (region).

BEREITUNG (GERMANY)   The preparation, manufacture, or making of alcoholic beverages.

BERENDA RED   A red grape variety grown in California.

BERG (GERMANY)   Mountain or hill.

BERLINER WEISSE (GERMANY)   Berlin's classic wheat beer. *See* Wheat Beer.

BERM   A ledge or ridge of soil in between grapevine rows, generally 1-1/2 to 3 feet wide.

BERNKASTEL (GERMANY)   The principle vineyard town of the Mittelmosel.

BERRIES   This berry-like quality is a nebulous, fruity characteristic often associated with young red wines such as Zinfandel, Gamay-Beaujolais, and others.

BERRY   An individual grape. Berries vary in color, size, and the number of seeds they contain.

BERRY DESSERT WINE   *See* Fruit Dessert Wine.

BERRY-LIKE   Term equated with the fruity olfactory qualities associated with such berries as blackberry, cherry, cranberry, raspberry, strawberry, and others. Berry-like can be used to describe young red wines such as Zinfandel, Gamay-Beaujolais, Beaujolais, and so on.

BERRY SET   The successful pollination of grape flowers. The pollinated grape blossoms start to develop, with each flower in the floral cluster transformed into a miniature grape berry about the size of a small BB. Also known as *allegagione* and *set*. *See* Shatter and Shot Berries.

BERRY TABLE WINE   *See* Fruit Table Wine.

BERRY WINE   Fruit wine produced from berries.

BERTILLE-SEYVE, JR. (1895–1959)   A French hybridizer who married the daughter of hybridizer Victor Villard. He distinguished his hybrids from those of his father (Seyve) and father-in-law (Villard) by naming them Seyve-Villard.

BERZAMINO *(ITALY)*   A red grape variety.

BESTE *(GERMANY)*   Best.

BESTES FASS *(GERMANY)*   The best barrel or the producer's best wine.

BETA   A red grape variety of the Concord family developed in the late nineteenth century by Louis Suelter of Minnesota.

BEVA *(ITALY)*   A wine term denoting a pleasurable dry taste and drinkability.

BEVANDA *(ITALY)*   *See* Beverage.

BEVERAGE   Any liquid for drinking, whether alcoholic or nonalcoholic. Also known as *bevanda*.

BEVERAGE COST   The total costs for all ingredients necessary to make the drink served in a beverage facility. It includes alcoholic as well as nonalcoholic beverages. Factors such as pilferage, waste, overproduction, and so on must also be included because they tend to raise the cost. Also known as *standard beverage cost* or *standard cost*.

BEVERAGE COST PERCENTAGE   The costs incurred for each one dollar of sales. Beverage cost is expressed as a percent of sales. Costs divided by sales equals cost percentage (C/S= C%). Also known as *cost percentage* and *standard cost percentage*.

BEVERAGE INVENTORY TURNOVER   The number of times the dollar value of the beverage inventory turned over.

BEVERAGE MANAGER   A person who forecasts, directs, organizes, and controls every phase of a beverage operation or bar. Also known as *bar manager*.

BEVERAGE MULTIPLIER   Beverage costs divided into one hundred will yield a number called a multiplier. Multiply this and beverage costs to determine selling price.

BEVERAGE SALES   Total revenue for a given or projected period of time that can include all beverages (alcoholic and nonalcoholic). Can also be segmented by specific type: wine, beer, distilled spirits, and nonalcoholic beverages.

BEVERAGE TRANSFERS   The wholesale cost of beverages, both alcoholic and nonalcoholic, that are used in departments other than bar operations.

BEYAZ (TURKEY)   See White.

BEYLERCE (TURKEY)   A white grape variety.

BHANG   See Bang.

BIANCA (ITALY)   See Biancolella.

BIANCAME (ITALY)   See Albana.

BIANCHELLO (ITALY)   A white grape variety.

BIANCHETTA (ITALY)   See Arneis.

BIANCHETTO (ITALY)   See Arneis.

BIANCO (ITALY)   See White.

BIANCO ACQUA (ITALY)   Water white.

BIANCO CARTA (ITALY)   A white wine so light in color that it is said to be paper-white.

BIANCO D'ALESSANO (ITALY)   A white grape variety grown in the region of Apulia.

BIANCOLELLA (ITALY)   A white grape variety grown in the south. Also known as *Bianca* and *Teneddu*.

BIANCONE   A white grape variety from Corsica.

BIBIERE   The ancient Latin term for beer.

BIBLINO (ITALY)   An ancient white wine from Sicily.

BICA ABERTA (PORTUGAL)   See Blanc de Noirs.

BICAL (PORTUGAL)   A white grape variety grown in the Bairrada region. Also known as *Barada da Mosca*.

BICANE (ITALY)   A white grape variety.

BICCHIÈRE (ITALY)   A drinking glass.

BIDULE   A small, circular polyethylene cap or plug that fits securely inside the neck of a sparkling wine bottle to form a tight seal. During secondary fermentation and during *remuage*, the bidule will capture some of the decomposed yeast before it is expelled prior to the final *dosage*.

BIEN EQUILIBRÉ (FRANCE)   See Well-Balanced.

BIENTEVEO (SPAIN)   A kind of rustic observatory built of wooden trunks, covered with straw or straw mats, above the level of the grapevines, from which the vineyard keeper dominates the widest view of the property unobserved and protected from the hot sun,

BIER *(GERMANY AND NETHERLANDS)* *See* Beer.

BIÈRE *(BELGIUM AND FRANCE)* *See* Beer.

BIERHALLE *(GERMANY)* Beer hall. Also known as *bierstube.*

BIERSTUBE *(GERMANY)* *See* Bierhalle.

BIG Also known as *robust. See* Full-Bodied.

BIGOLONA *(ITALY)* A white grape variety grown primarily in the northern regions.

BIGOT *(FRANCE)* A special hoe occasionally used in parts of northern Rhône Valley vineyards.

BIJELO *(YUGOSLAVIA)* *See* White.

BILBERRY A species of North American blueberry occasionally used in the production of fruit-flavored liqueurs or brandies.

BILGE The greatest diameter or widest part at the center of the staves on a wooden barrel.

BILLBOARD *See* Horizontal Set.

BILL OF LADING A contract between the shipper and carrier to transport the shipment from origin to destination. It includes delivery instructions, consignee, party to notify, freight payment, shipment description, and so on.

Port/Port: From port of loading to port of unloading.

Point/Port: From inland place of receipt to discharge port.

Port/Point: From loading port to named place of delivery.

Point/Point: Normally used for door to door service.

BILLY *(AUSTRALIA)* A tin container used for boiling water to make tea.

BINA *(SPAIN)* A yearly labor consisting of lightly digging earth and then flattening it to make the surface more compact, thus avoiding evaporation of moisture during the dry season.

BIN CARD A small storeroom card, usually attached to shelves, showing the bin number and stock on hand for each beverage item. It is a form of a perpetual inventory.

BINNING Putting away or storing bottles of wine in the cellar for further aging.

BIR Indonesian term for beer.

BIRA *(BULGARIA AND TURKEY)* *See* Beer.

BIRAH Hebrew term for beer.

BIRCH BEER A sweetened, carbonated soft drink flavored with sap from the black birch tree.

BIRD-BATH GLASS *See* Saucer-Shaped Glass.

BIRRA *(ITALY)* *See* Beer.

B

BIRRE   Albanian term for beer.

BIRU (JAPAN)   *See* Beer.

BISCHOF (GERMANY)   Bishop.

BISER (YUGOSLAVIA)   *See* Sparkling Wine.

BISHOP   One of the many versions of a mulled wine. It is made from port wine, sugar, spices, and an orange stuck with cloves. The drink is then heated and served warm. *See* Mulled Wine.

BISON VODKA   *See* Zubrówka.

BISTRO (FRANCE)   A small, generally outdoor café or restaurant where beverages are served.

BITARTRATE   A salt of tartaric acid. *See* Tartaric Acid.

BITE   Infers a substantial degree of acidity and/or tannin and alcohol in wine, generally from excessive levels of any of these.

BITTEN BY THE BREWER'S HORSE (ENGLAND)   *See* Intoxicated.

BITTER (GERMANY)   *See* Bitter.

BITTER   Describes amber-colored, well-hopped beers that display a rather strong alcohol content. A strong ale with certain levels of hops or barley will also exhibit levels of bitterness. Also an English term for amber to dark-colored, bitter beers. If measured by utilizing International Bittering Units, it refers to the degree of bitterness in the hops. *See* Ale.

BITTER   A sharp, often unpleasant taste sensation found in wine due to excessive levels of tannin. Also known as *amango, amargo, amaro, amer*, and *pikrós*.

BITTER   One of the four basic sensations recognized by the taste buds, the others being salt, acid, and sweetness. Bitterness is detected on the palate on the rear, flat part of the tongue.

BITTERNESS   A taste in wine that usually indicates it was kept too long on the skins or in the barrel. Also known as *amertume*.

BITTER ROT   Recognized as a disease of grapes since 1887. The name was derived from the bitter taste that develops in infected berries. Bitter rot is caused by the fungus *Melanconium fuligineaum*.

BITTERS   Distilled spirits containing an infusion of bittering compounds such as herbs, roots, or barks. The basic elements are aromatic herbs such as gentian, rhubarb, quinine, saffron, calamus or sweet rush, and centaury, among others. Bitters usually contain alcohol and were originally produced to soothe and relax the stomach after meals and therefore are often referred to as "digestives." They are also used as a medicine or tonic and as an ingredient in some cocktails. Also served as apéritifs or digestives. *See* Digestive.

BITTER STOUT   *See* Stout.

BITTERSWEET   Describes bitters or some beers that display an underlying bitterness while at the same time are also sweet.

BIYAR (INDIA)   *See* Beer.

BJALO (BULGARIA)   *See* White.

BLACK   Opaque; sometimes used to describe stout or porter-type beers.

BLACK   Coffee served without milk, cream, or other products used to lighten its color.

BLACK AND TAN   A drink consisting of equal parts of stout and British ale.

BLACKBERRY-FLAVORED BRANDY   A mixture of brandy, a minimum of 2.5 percent sugar, flavored and colored with blackberries. By United States federal law it cannot be bottled at less than 60 proof (30 percent alcohol by volume).

BLACKBERRY LIQUEUR   A sweetened alcoholic beverage consisting of a base of alcohol, minimum 2.5 percent sugar, flavored and colored with blackberries. It is sweeter and lower in proof than blackberry-flavored brandy.

BLACK CAPE   *See* Alexander.

BLACK COFFEE   A term often used when referring to or ordering espresso coffee.

BLACK CORINTH   A red grape variety grown in California. Also known as *Zante Currant*.

BLACK CURRANT   A smell characteristic of some red wines, especially Cabernet Sauvignon.

BLACK CURRANT LIQUEUR   *See* Cassis.

BLACK DEATH   *See* Akvavit.

BLACK HAMBURG   *See* Schiava Grossa.

BLACKISH   Describes an extremely young red wine, usually very tannic, which often takes a long time to mature.

BLACK MADEIRA   *See* Alexander.

BLACK MALT   Partially malted barley roasted at high temperatures. Black malt lends a beer both dark color and roasted flavor.

BLACK MALVOISIE   A red grape variety, part of the Malvasia grape family.

BLACK MONUKKA   A red seedless grape variety.

BLACK MOROCCO   A red grape variety grown primarily in the Central Valley of California.

BLACK MUSCAT   *See* Muscat Hamburg.

BLACK OLIVES   An odor often found in wines made from Cabernet Sauvignon or Cabernet Franc grapes.

BLACK PATENT   Malted barley that has been roasted for a prolonged period of time at a high temperature until it is black in color and displays a bitter sweet taste.

BLACK PEARL   A red grape variety.

BLACK PRINCE   A red grape variety grown in California.

BLACK ROSE   A red grape variety.

BLACK ROT   A fungus rot of the grapevine caused by the fungus *Guignardia bidwellii*, usually occurring in moist areas with relatively high humidity. This disease appears as black spots on the leaves of the grapevine and shrivels the fruit.

BLACK SPANISH   *See* Lenoir.

BLACKSTRAP MOLASSES   *See* Molasses.

BLACK ST. PETERS   *See* Zinfandel.

BLACK TAYLOR   *See* Taylor.

BLACK TEA   A rolled, dried leaf of the tea plant, fully fermented and dried with hot air over charcoal or in drying ovens to stop further oxidation and fermentation. Black tea accounts for more than 90 percent of the tea consumed in the United States. Black teas are from India, Sri Lanka, China, Java, and Sumatra.

BLACK VELVET   A mixture of stout and champagne popular in England during the Edwardian days (nineteenth century). It was created when Prince Albert died, an event which sent Queen Victoria (mother of Edward VII, King of England 1901-1910), along with the entire country, into shock. Everything was shrouded in black, including champagne, which was mixed with stout.
   The Black Velvet has had a resurgence in popularity; today, ginger ale is usually substituted because of the high cost of champagne.

BLACK ZINFANDEL   *See* Zinfandel.

BLADE   The flat, expanded portion of a leaf on a grapevine.

BLANC (FRANCE)   *See* White.

BLANC D'ANJOU (FRANCE)   *See* Chenin Blanc.

BLANC DE BLANCS (FRANCE)   White wine made entirely from white grapes. Champagnes or sparkling wines so labeled are usually lighter in body.

BLANC DE MORGEX (ITALY)   A white grape variety grown in the Valle d'Aosta region.

BLANC DE NOIRS (FRANCE)   White wine made entirely from black grapes without skin contact, which prevents extraction of tannin and color. Champagnes or sparkling wines so labeled are usually fuller in body. Also known as *bica aberta, en blanc,* and *vinificato in bianco.*

BLANC DOUX (FRANCE)   *See* Sémillon.

BLANC DU BOIS   A white grape variety developed in 1968 in Florida. The grape was named for Emile Dubois, a Frenchman who made wines in the Tallahassee area in the 1880s.

BLANC FUMÉ (FRANCE)   The local name for the Sauvignon Blanc grape variety around the town of Pouilly-sur-Loire in the Loire Valley. *See* Sauvignon Blanc.

BLANCO (SPAIN)   *See* White.

BLAND   A term describing a mild, neutral wine or beer with modest discernible odor or taste.

BLAND   A white grape variety named after Colonel Theodore Bland, soldier of the Revolutionary War and a candidate for governor of Virginia. Also known as *Bland's Madeira*.

BLAND'S MADEIRA   *See* Bland.

BLANDO (SPAIN)   *See* Mellow.

BLANK *(GERMANY)*   *See* Bright.

BLANQUETTE   *See* Clairette Blanc.

BLASS *(GERMANY)*   *See* Pale.

BLATINA *(YUGOSLAVIA)*   A red grape variety.

BLATTFALLKRANKHEIT *(GERMANY)*   *See* Downy Mildew.

BLAU *(GERMANY)*   Blue; a term used to describe the red or black color grapes.

BLAUBURGER *(AUSTRIA)*   A red grape variety developed from a cross of Portugieser and Blaufränkisch at the Klosterneuburg Institute.

BLAUBURGUNDER *(GERMANY)*   *See* Pinot Noir.

BLAUER KLEVNER *(GERMANY)*   *See* Pinot Noir.

BLAUER PORTUGIESER *(GERMANY)*   A red grape variety that produces mild wines with a delicate spicy flavor, and characterized by a deep red color. The grape variety was brought to the Pfalz in the middle of the nineteenth century. Its area of origin was Hungary and Austria, where it has been grown for many centuries. Also known as *Portugieser*.

BLAUER SPÄTBURGUNDER *(AUSTRIA)*   *See* Pinot Noir.

BLAUER WILDBACHER *(AUSTRIA)*   A red grape variety grown primarily in Weststeiermark.

BLAUFRÄNKISCH (TRANSLATES AS "RED FRANCONIAN")   A red grape variety. Also known as *Kékfrankos* and *Limberger*.

BLEICHERT *(GERMANY)*   *See* Rosé Wine.

BLEEDING   Reducing the amount of juice in the barrel prior to fermentation. Also known as *saignée*.

BLENDED AMERICAN WHISKEY   A mixture that contains at least 20 percent of straight whiskey on a proof basis and, separately or in combination, whiskey or neutral distilled spirits. A blended whiskey containing not less than 51 percent, on a proof gallon basis, of one of the types of straight whiskey is further designated by that specific type of straight whiskey; for example, "blended rye whiskey." The blending usually takes place after the whiskies reach full maturity; they are then allowed to rest for further aging. Caramel coloring is usually added prior to bottling.

Blended whiskies made with distilled neutral spirits carry a label on the back of the bottle showing the percentages of distilled neutral spirits and straight whiskies contained.

BLENDED AND BOTTLED BY   Means that the named winery mixed the wine with other wines of the same class and type at the stated address.

BLENDED APPLEJACK   A mixture that contains at least 20 percent apple brandy (applejack) on a proof gallon basis, stored in oak containers for not less than two years, and is not more than 80 percent distilled neutral spirits, on a proof gallon basis, if such mixture at the time of bottling is not less than 80 proof. *See* Applejack.

BLENDED SCOTCH WHISKY   A blend of pot-stilled malt whiskies with whiskies produced in Scotland by the column still method from a cereal mix that may contain unmalted as well as malted barley and other grains.

Blended Scotch whisky, as we know it today, was first produced in 1853 by Andrew Usher in Edinburgh. Prior to that, Scotches were distilled in old-fashioned pot stills at lower proof levels, which produced Scotches with a full body and heavy taste. In 1832, the continuous still was perfected by Aeneas Coffey for use in the distillation of Scotch whisky. This enabled distillers to produce a lighter-bodied and -flavored Scotch whisky, which was then blended with the heavier malted Scotches.

BLENDING   One of three methods of incorporating ingredients into a cocktail, in this case, by use of an electric blender.

BLENDING   A process used in the production of still and sparkling wines as well as beer and distilled spirits.

Blending in the making of wine is utilized in many circumstances. In a given grow-ing season, for instance, two red grapes might ripen completely, but one of the grapes may be deficient in natural acidity and the second grape have an excess of it. By blend-ing together these two wines, the acid level will even out somewhat, producing a rela-tively smooth wine. Other factors, among which are the amount of sugar, the pH, flavonoids, anthocyanins (red pigmentation), and tannin, must be considered prior to the blending. Blending two or more wines together, either from the same or different years, creates a synergistic effect; the total is greater than the sum of its parts. In addi-tion, with blending, a consistent product can be produced year after year that some winemakers call the "house style." This is quite important in the production of sparkling wines, where the base cuvée is first assembled prior to secondary fermentation. Also known as *coupage, cutting wine, marrying wines, taglio, verschnitt, verschneiden*, and *vino da taglio*. *See* Assemblage, Nonvintage, and Reserve Wine.

BLEND OF STRAIGHT WHISKIES   A mixture of straight whiskies. A blend of straight whiskies consisting entirely of one of the types of straight whiskey and not con-forming to the standard for "straight whiskey" is further designated by that specific type of straight whiskey; for example, "a blend of straight rye whiskies" (blended straight rye whiskies).

BLIND   *See* Intoxicated.

BLIND (GERMANY)   *See* Cloudy.

BLINDPROBE (GERMANY)   *See* Blind Tasting.

BLIND RECEIVING   Receiving goods either without an accompanying invoice or with an invoice that contains no more than the names of the items delivered. Information relative to quantity, quality, weight, and price are omitted from the invoice. The receiver is then forced to count, weigh, and record each item individually.

BLIND TASTING   An evaluative tasting of alcoholic beverages without knowledge of the name of the product, the brand name, the country of origin, the vintage year, and so on. It forces the taster to concentrate on quality and other sensory perceptions rather than predisposed decisions based on bias. Also known as *blindprobe*.

BLIND TIGER   A place of concealment where illicitly made distilled spirits can be purchased.

BLISTERS   Blemishes that occur inside glass during the glassmaking process. These blemishes resemble air bubbles.

BLOCKADER   Slang term for one engaged in the transportation or possible sale of non-tax-paid distilled spirits.

BLOND   Describes beer that is deep yellow-golden in color.

BLONDE & RED HEAD   A cocktail consisting of equal parts of white (dry or sweet) and red vermouth.

BLOOD   *See* Animal Blood.

BLOOD ALCOHOL COUNT (BAC)   Blood alcohol concentration is a measurable level of the amount of alcohol found in the human body at a given time. It reflects the amount of alcohol a person has consumed and is expressed in a percentage.

BLOODY MARY   A cocktail created by Ferdinand Petiot, a bartender at Harry's Bar in Paris in the 1920s. It was named after Queen Mary I of England who, because of her persecution of Protestants, attained the nickname Bloody Mary. It was later called a *Bucket of Blood*, then *Red Snapper*, and *Morning Glory*. It was introduced into the United States in the 1930s. It consists of vodka, Tabasco sauce, Worcestershire sauce, tomato juice, lemon juice, salt, and pepper.

BLOOM   In the vineyard, the time when the young flowers open and caps (calyptras) fall from the flowers.

BLOOM   The visible white, powdery coating of the grape berry, known as *micro-flora*. It is more noticeable on dark-colored grapes. Also known as *pruina* and *pruinose*. *See* Cutin and Micro-Flora.

BLUE ANCHOR   The first American tavern, said to have been opened as a safe haven for seafaring men. It opened its doors in Philadelphia early in the 1600s.

BLUE EYE   A red grape variety named after a small town in southern Missouri.

BLUE FINING   *See* Ferrocyanide Compounds.

BLUE IMPERIAL *(AUSTRALIA)*   *See* Cinsaut.

BLUE JAY   A red grape variety.

BLUE LAKE   A red grape variety developed in 1950 (named in 1960), from a cross of Florida 43–47 and Caco, by Professor Loren Stover of the Florida Agricultural Experimental Station; it is grown primarily in the southeast United States.

BLUE LAWS   State and local laws that regulate or prohibit certain business operations on Sunday.

BLUME *(GERMANY)*   *See* Bouquet.

BLUMIG *(GERMANY)*   *See* Flowery.

BLUSH WINE   *See* Rosé Wine.

BNIA *(FRANCE)*   *See* Bureau National Interprofessionel de l'Armagnac.

BNIC *(FRANCE)* *See* Bureau National Interprofessionel du Cognac.

BOAL *(PORTUGAL)* *See* Bual.

BOBAL *(SPAIN)* A red grape variety.

BOCK BEER A beer produced from grain that is considerably higher in extracts than the usual grains destined for use in lager beers. Bock, in German, means a male goat. Bock beer was originally produced around 1200 A.D. in the town of Einbeck, Germany. Today it is produced in virtually every country, in one form or another, on a seasonal basis, mostly during the winter so that it can be consumed in the early spring. Bock beers are usually quite dark in color, with an intense, sharp, sweet aroma. They have a full-bodied flavor followed by a slightly sweet, malty taste. A stronger version produced in very limited quantities in Germany is called double bock (*doppelbock*). Also spelled *bockbier*. *See* Maibock and Ur-Bock.

BOCKBIER (GERMANY) *See* Bock Beer.

BOCKSBEUTEL An unusual short, flat-sided, flask-shaped bottle introduced in 1728 in Franken, Germany. It is also used in parts of Chile and Portugal. Incorrectly spelled *boxbeutel*.

BÖCKSER *(GERMANY)* The smell of rotten eggs. *See* Hydrogen Sulfide.

BOCOY *(SPAIN)* A large barrel with a capacity of approximately 160 gallons. *See* Barrel.

BODE *See* Barrel.

BODEGA *(SPAIN)* Literally, a wine storage and aging cellar, but the term is also used to designate the producer and shipper. *See* Wine Cellar.

BODENGESCHMACK *(GERMANY)* *See* Earthy.

BODEGUERO *(SPAIN)* *See* Winemaker.

BODY The tactile sensation of weight or fullness (roundness) on the palate, usually from a combination of alcohol, extracts, glycerin, possibly residual sugar, tannin, and other physical components. Light-bodied wines tend to be low in alcohol, tannin, and extract. Full-bodied wines tend to be alcoholic, tannic, and, if white, occasionally sweet. Also known as *corpo, corps, cuerpo, koerper*, and *körper*.

BOGAZKERE *(TURKEY)* A red grape variety.

BOILER Any container, such as a still, evaporator, kettle, or cooker, where clarified wort or cooked mash are added for boiling, in either brewing or distillation. Also known as a *brew kettle*.

BOILERMAKER A shot of whiskey drunk straight and immediately followed by a glass of beer.

BOIRE *(FRANCE)* To drink.

BOIS À COMMUNS *(FRANCE)* *See* Bois à Terroir.

BOIS À TERROIR *(FRANCE)* A district in the region of Cognac. Also known as *Bois à Communs*.

BOISÉ *(FRANCE)* *See* Oaky.

BOIS ORDINAIRES *(FRANCE)* A district in the region of Cognac.

BOLGNINO *(ITALY)* A red grape variety.

BOLL An ancient measurement equivalent to roughly six bushels (one bushel equaling 25.4 kilograms) of malt, utilized in the production of Scotch whisky.

BOLO *(ITALY)* The blob of molten glass that is gathered on the end of a metal tube prior to being blown and shaped by a glassblower.

BOMBA *(SPAIN)* A pump or siphon necessary for moving wine from tank to tank.

BOMBED *See* Intoxicated.

BOMBINO BIANCO *(ITALY)* *See* Bonvino.

BOMBINO NERO *(ITALY)* A red grape variety grown primarily in the south.

BOMBONA *(SPAIN)* *See* Demijohn.

BOMMES *(FRANCE)* A sweet white wine made from a blend of Sauvignon Blanc, Sémillon, and Muscadelle grape varieties. It is also one of the five communes within Bordeaux's Sauternes district entitled to be called "Sauternes."

BONARDA *(ITALY)* A red grape variety known locally in Lombardy as *Croatina*.

BON BOIS *(FRANCE)* A district in the region of Cognac.

BONDE *(FRANCE)* *See* Bung.

BONDED WINE CELLAR A wine premises designated a bonded winery is also a bonded wine cellar. *See* Bonded Wine Premises and Bottled-In-Bond.

BONDED WINE PREMISES Authorized operations in untax-paid wine. *See* Bonded Wine Cellar, Bonded Wine Warehouse, Bonded Winery, Bottled-In-Bond, and In Bond.

BONDED WINE WAREHOUSE Bonded warehouse facilities on wine premises by a warehouse company or other person for the storage of wine and allied products for credit purposes. *See* Bonded Wine Premises and Bottled-In-Bond.

BONDED WINERY A winery where wine production operations are conducted and other authorized operations may be conducted. *See* Bonded Wine Premises and Bottled-In-Bond.

BONDING A government-controlled maturing of whiskey, regulated by a United States federal law that dates back to 1887.

BONE CHARCOAL Ground charcoal used to clarify wine.

BONE DRY A meaningless term that usually denotes wines or beers with no residual sugar; they often display a certain austerity and high acidity. Also known as *knochig*.

BONNE-CHAUFFE *(FRANCE)* The second distillation in the cognac process.

BON GOÛT *(FRANCE)* A good or pleasing taste.

BONITO *(SPAIN)* *See* Elegant.

BONTEMPS *(FRANCE)* A small, shallow wooden or ceramic bowl traditionally used in the Bordeaux region for mixing of egg whites for fining purposes. Also known as *desquet*.

BONUS CASE   Any case where the number of bottles included in the case varies from the standard configuration (e.g., fifteen 750-milliliter bottles instead of twelve). These cases are usually used in introducing a product or in special promotions.

BONVINO *(ITALY)*   A white grape variety native to Latium. Also known as *Bombino Bianco*.

BOOTLEGGER   In the United States, it was a practice of stagecoach travelers to conceal a pint-sized, flat bottle of thick glass in their boot, to have refilled at taverns along their way. It was also a way to secrete bottles of distilled spirits for later illegal sale to the Indians.

BOOZE   From E. G. Booz, a grocer in Philadelphia around 1840. He used to bottle and sell bourbon whiskey, which he bought in barrels.

BOR *(HUNGARY)*   *See* Wine.

BORACHO *(PORTUGAL)*   *See* Wine Skin.

BORDEAUX *(FRANCE)*   One of France's six major wine-producing regions, located approximately three hundred miles southwest of Paris, known the world over for its incomparable red, equally fine dry white, and superb sweet white wines. Major districts include Médoc, Saint-Émilion, Pomerol, Graves, and Sauternes.

The Bordeaux appellation vineyard area covers approximately 260,000 acres, accounting for 2 percent of the world's wine production. There are fifty-four appellations within Bordeaux, encompassing dry white, sweet white, rosé, sparkling, and world-renowned red wines. Bordeaux is the largest AOC wine-producing region, producing approximately 25 percent of all of France's AOC wines. Bordeaux's production of AOC wines is approximately 80 percent reds and 20 percent whites.

On May 18, 1152, Eleanor of Aquitaine, aged 30, heiress to William X, Duke of Aquitaine, divorced Louis VII, King of France (1137–1180), and married Henri Plantagenet (Henry II), aged 19, King of England. As her dowry, she gave him all of the land that was then called Aquitaine, now known as Bordeaux.

BORDEAUX BOTTLE   A bottle shape originating in Bordeaux, France, easily recognizable by its regular cylindrical form, characterized by a short neck and high shoulders. Also the standard 750-milliliter bottle traditionally used in the Bordeaux region. Also known as *bordelaise bottle*.

BORDEAUX BLANC *(FRANCE)*   White table wine, dry or sweet, from the Bordeaux region.

BORDEAUX MIXTURE   A blend of copper sulfate and slaked lime, used as a fungicide spray in the vineyards against oïdium, mildew, and other disorders. First introduced into Europe from the United States in 1878 and in 1885, French viticulturist Professor Millardet continued its use. Also known as *bouillie Bordelaise*. *See* Fixed Copper and Lime.

BORDEAUX ROUGE *(FRANCE)*   Dry, red table wine.

BORDEAUX WINE ACADEMY   Modeled after the French Academy and resembling it in its statues, constitution, and aims, the Bordeaux Wine Academy was created in February 1948. It is intended to defend, protect, and maintain the purity and quality of Bordeaux wines. There are forty academicians who comprise a forum of connoisseurs and counselors of unequaled competence.

BORDELAISE (FRANCE)   The inhabitants of Bordeaux.

BORDELAISE BOTTLE (FRANCE)   *See* Bordeaux Bottle.

BORDELESAS (SPAIN)   A barrel with a capacity of 225 liters (fifty-nine gallons). *See* Barrel.

BORDERIES (FRANCE)   A district in the region of Cognac.

BORE   *See* Worm.

BORGOGNA BIANCO (ITALY)   *See* Pinot Blanc.

BORGOGNO NERO (ITALY)   *See* Pinot Noir.

BORGOÑA (SPAIN)   *See* Burgundy.

BORRAÇAL (PORTUGAL)   A red grape variety used in the production of Vinho Verde wine.

BORRACHO (SPAIN)   *See* Intoxicated.

BOSADOR (SPAIN)   *See* Fermentation Lock.

BOSCO (ITALY)   A white grape variety grown in Liguria.

BOTA (SPAIN)   A bag, usually made of goatskin, from which some Spaniards and Portuguese squirt wine into their mouth. Also a sherry butt or barrel with a capacity of approximately 130 gallons. *See* Barrel and Porrón.

BOTA CHICA (SPAIN)   *See* Barrel.

BOTA BODEGUERA (SPAIN)   *See* Barrel.

BOTA DE EMBARQUE (SPAIN)   *See* Barrel.

BOTA DE RECIBO (SPAIN)   *See* Barrel.

BOTA GORDA (SPAIN)   *See* Barrel.

BOTANICALS   Those parts of a plant suitably used for the production of various alcoholic beverages. They include roots, stems, barks, leaves, flowers, berries, fruit, beans, seeds, pits, stems, skins, and so on.

BOTELLA (SPAIN)   *See* Bottle.

BOTRYTICIN   An antibiotic substance produced during fermentation that inhibits total fermentation of sugars in the *must*.

BOTRYTIS CINEREA   From the Greek *botrus*, grape, and the Latin *cineris*, ashes or cinders. *Botrytis cinerea* is a hairy mold, gray or even pinkish-brown in color. This mold is present as spores at all times in most vineyards. Depending on the grape variety, the time of year, and climatic conditions, it can greatly enhance or severely damage the grapes in a vineyard. Thinner-skinned grape varieties such as Johannisberg Riesling, Sauvignon Blanc, and Sémillon are the most susceptible to *Botrytis cinerea* attack and most benefited by the resultant sweetness.

Affected berries may resemble dark, purplish-brown, desiccated, cracked raisins, but retain much more natural fruit acid than raisins and do not have their caramelized taste. Long vegetative filaments (*mycelia*), threads resembling spikes, penetrate the outer layer of the berry's skin (*cuticula*), allowing the spores to grow safely inside, protected by the biological barrier.

There is no exposure of the pulp or juice to air. The action of the *micellae* of the mold causes dehydration. Water is evaporated as sugar concentration increases some 30 to 40 percent. Flavor, grape acids, grape essence, and aromatic compounds in the remaining juice are greatly magnified. Glycerin is produced in high levels, giving the wine a soft, almost oily tinge on the tongue and palate.

The vineyard conditions that encourage *Botrytis cinerea* start with high humidity (ideally near 100 percent) from an early rainfall or fog just before harvest time, this allows moisture to form on the surface of the fruit. If this is followed by dry, warm (65 to 75 degrees Fahrenheit) air, the desired *Botrytis cinerea* growth can form in as little as eighteen hours. If, on the other hand, the high humidity is followed by cold weather and the skins crack, a deleterious infection occurs. The fungus that forms on the moist grape skins is quite uneven in any given grape cluster and often requires multiple pickings, berry-by-berry, to obtain the maximum amount of affected berries.

The grapes that have been attacked by the noble rot are extremely overripe and may be handpicked individually after the ripeness has been determined. From each bunch of grapes the pickers might select one or two berries for use. The same vineyard might have to be picked over several times in order to obtain all the affected grapes. It is said that it takes one picker one full day to pick enough grapes to produce one bottle of this sweet wine. Obviously, the result is an extremely high cost of production.

Fermentation can last as long as the harvest (two months), due to the fact that the high sugar content retards yeast activity. In addition, the extremely sweet and syrupy juice can jam standard wine filters, taxing pumps that can easily transport dry wines.

Wines made from these grapes are yellow to gold-amber in color with a distinctive honeylike, raisiny character. They are extremely sweet and have an unusually long bottle life, lasting easily five to ten years and, if from an excellent vintage, as long as fifty years or more.

Botrytis is also known as *Botrytis bunch rot* (or simply *bunch rot*), edelfäule, *muffa nobile, noble rot, podridão dos cachos*, and *pourriture noble*. *See* Desiccated Grapes.

BOTRYTIZED   Wines made from grapes affected by the noble rot (*Botrytis cinerea*).

BOTTE (*ITALY*)   *See* Barrel.

BOTTE MADRE (*SPAIN*)   "Mother-Barrel," in the *solera* system used in the production of sherry wines.

BOTTIGLIA (*ITALY*)   *See* Bottle.

BOTTLE   A container four liters or less in capacity, regardless of the material from which it is made, used to store wine or to remove wine from the wine premises.

BOTTLE   A glass container that typically holds 750 milliliters (25.4 ounces). Derived from the French *bouteille*, which in turn was probably from *bautille*, the familiar wine flask. While early bottles had many names, such as flask, flagon, and carafe, only a vessel containing wine could correctly be called a bouteille. Also known as *botella, bottiglia, flasche*, and *garrafa*.

BOTTLE AGING   The aging process that takes place in the bottle at the winery and/or in private cellars.

As used in sparkling wines, it allows the wine to acquire complexity, depth, and fine texture in the bottle. Also known as aging *on-the-yeast, sur lies*, or *en tirage. See* Aging, Barrel Aging, Mature, Ripe, and Ripe for Bottling.

BOTTLE-BREAKER   A motor-driven machine utilized for the destruction of empty bottles by means of steel bars. Also known as *bottle crusher* or *bottle disposer*.

BOTTLE CAP   The beer bottle *cap* was introduced in the 1880s; previously, beer in bottles had been corked.

BOTTLE CHUTE   A flexible cylindrical tube where empty bottles are conveyed to the bottle-breaker for eventual destruction.

BOTTLE CLUB   Slang for a bar.

BOTTLE CODING   A special code put onto each bottle as it leaves the storeroom to the bar as a means of controlling inventory.

BOTTLE CRUSHER   *See* Bottle-Breaker.

BOTTLED-IN-BOND   Whiskey that is bottled in bond is mandated by United States federal regulations to be produced by one distillery in one distilling season, aged a minimum of four years in new charred oak barrels, and bottled at 100 proof. Whiskey that is bottled in bond has also been stored and bottled in a Treasury Department bonded warehouse; no excise tax is paid on the whiskey until the beverage is withdrawn or shipped from the warehouse. The term bonded on the label, therefore, does not refer to quality; it means nothing more than that the treasury agent was present to collect the taxes. *See* Bonded Wine Premises and In Bond.

BOTTLE DISPOSER   *See* Bottle-Breaker.

BOTTLED SUNSHINE   Slang term used by the British during World War II for a bottle or can of beer.

BOTTLED WATER   Water that is sealed in bottles or other containers and intended for human consumption.

BOTTLE FERMENTED   On a sparkling wine label, the term means that the secondary fermentation took place in the bottle or that the transfer method was used. It could also apply to all méthode-champenoise-produced sparkling wines.

BOTTLE-FOR-BOTTLE   The practice of turning in an empty bottle for a full one as a means of inventory checks and balances. Also known as *empty bottle return*.

BOTTLE LABEL   A paper label suitably glued onto the front and sometimes rear flat part of a glass bottle that depicts certain mandatory information.

BOTTLE MAKING MACHINES   In 1903, the routine use of paper labels closely followed the invention of the fully automatic bottle-making machine by Michael J. Owen, plant manager of Libbey Glass Company of Toledo, Ohio.

BOTTLE MARKING   The practice of marking bottles of alcoholic beverages by means of stickers, adhesive labels, magic markers, and so on in order to identify them as house property. The marked bottles are then recorded in a ledger and placed into use.

BOTTLE NECKER   Coupon, rebate, or other attention-getting promotion vehicle that fits around the neck of a bottle.

BOTTLER   A proprietor of wine premises who fills wine bottles.

BOTTLE SALES INCOME SYSTEM   A method of estimating the sales potential and income expected to be generated by the sale of each bottle of alcoholic beverage.

BOTTLESCREW   The original name for a corkscrew used around 1720. *See* Corkscrew.

BOTTLE SHOCK   *See* Bottle Sickness.

BOTTLE SICKNESS   A stage that may affect a wine or beer just after bottling. After bottling, the aroma, flavor, and/or balance of a wine or beer may be temporarily diminished. It affects some wines and beers and is characterized by a flat, lifeless taste. Also known as *bottle shock*.

BOTTLE SIZES   The BATF has authorized only certain metric sizes for wines and distilled spirits sold in the United States.

WINE (ALL TYPES)

Liters	750 milliliters	Ounces	Other Names
15 liters	20	507	Nebuchadnezzar
12 liters	16	405.6	Balthazar
9 liters	12	304.2	Salmanazar
6 liters	8	202.8	Imperial
4.5 liters	6	152.1	Rehoboam (not used in USA)
4 liters	5.32	135.2	
3 liters	4	101.4	Double Magnum or Jeroboam
1.5 liters	2	50.8	Magnum
1 liters	33.8		
750 milliliters	25.4		Standard-size bottle
500 milliliters	16.9		
375 milliliters	12.7		Half-bottle
187 milliliters	6.3		Split
100 milliliters	3.4		

DISTILLED SPIRITS (ALL TYPES)

Bottle size	Capacity in ounces
1.75 liters	59.2
1 liter	33.8
750 milliliters	25.4
500 milliliters	16.9
200 milliliters	6.8
50 milliliters	1.7

BOTTLES SUR LATTE *(FRANCE)*   Bottles laid horizontally during the *prise de mousse* (secondary fermentation of sparkling wine) and aging processes. They formerly used wooden slats in order to make the piles of bottles more stable.

BOTTLES SUR POINTE *(FRANCE)*   Bottles placed neck downwards, awaiting *dégorgement* (expulsion of the sediment) in sparkling winemaking.

B

BOTTLES SUR POINTE (FRANCE)

BOTTLE STINK   An odor occasionally found in some wines or beers that may be an indication of bacterial spoilage or wine- or beermaking flaw. The odor may dissipate with aeration. *See* Moldy, Mousy, and Musty.

BOTTLE TROUGH   *See* Speed Rack.

BOTTLING   The procedure of packaging all types of alcoholic beverages, usually in glass containers.

BOTTOM-FERMENTED   Describes beers produced by the use of a type of yeast (lager yeast) that generally converts sugars to alcohol and CO_2 at lower temperatures, at the tank's bottom. The most common type of bottom-fermented beer is lager, which ferments at cooler temperatures for a longer period of time than ales (which are top-fermented beers).

BOTTOMS   *See* Lees.

BOUCHÉ (FRANCE)   *See* Corked.

BOUCHET (FRANCE)   The local name in Saint-Émilion and Pomerol for the Cabernet Franc grape variety. *See* Cabernet Franc.

BOUCHON (FRANCE)   *See* Cork.

BOUCHON DE TIRAGE (FRANCE)   The temporary cork sometimes used to close the bottle during secondary fermentation of sparkling wines.

BOUCHON D'EXPÉDITION (FRANCE)   The final cork used in a finished bottle of sparkling wine.

BOUCHONNÉ (FRANCE)   *See* Corked.

BOUILLAGE (FRANCE)   In the making of champagne, the initial tumultuous fermentation.

BOUILLEURS DE PROFESSION (FRANCE)   Professional distillers.

BOUILLIE BORDELAISE (FRANCE)   *See* Bordeaux Mixture.

BOUNTIFUL   A red grape variety.

BOUQUET   The various fragrances noted by smell, created by the development of a beverage (wine, beer, and distilled spirits) and imparted to it from the fermentation and aging process, whether in barrel or bottle. The many acids present and the combination of organic acids with alcohol are vital contributions to the bouquet. Also known as *anthosimía, blume, bukett*, and *fumet*. *See* Aroma and Nose.

BOURBON AND BRANCH   *See* Branch Water.

BOURBON LIQUEUR   A liqueur bottled at not less than 60 proof, in which not less than 51 percent, on a proof gallon basis, of the distilled spirits used is bourbon whiskey, and which possesses a predominant characteristic bourbon flavor derived from such whiskey.

BOURBON WHISKEY   Bourbon whiskey is a distinctive whiskey of Kentucky, made predominantly from corn. Federal regulations require that bourbon whiskey be made from a minimum of 51 percent corn; generally, 65 to 75 percent is used. When the corn in the mash reaches 80 percent, the product, by government definition, becomes corn whiskey—not bourbon. The higher the corn content and the lower the percentage of other grains, the lighter the whiskey. The blend of the other grains is dictated by the distiller's own private formula; rye, wheat, or barley malt can be used in the grain mix.

The bourbon must be barreled at not less than 80 proof and not more than 125 proof. The raw bourbon is then put into new, large charred white oak barrels ranging in capacity from 50 to 66 gallons.

Bourbon whiskey, by law, must be aged for a minimum of two years. Most distillers age their bourbon anywhere from four to ten years.

BOURBOULENC (FRANCE)   A white grape variety grown primarily in Provence and the Rhône Valley.

BOURGEOIS GROWTHS (FRANCE)   *See* Cru Bourgeois.

BOURGOGNE (FRANCE)   *See* Burgundy.

BOURGOGNE OAK (FRANCE)   A forest in the hills behind and on the plains in front of the Côte d'Or, in Burgundy, noted for its production of wooden barrels, similar to Allier in terms of hardness. Bourgogne oak has a medium-open grain, with moderate flavor and tannin extraction. It displays some of the buttery flavors of Nevers, with a bitter, slightly weedy component. Bourgogne oak helps soften wine's acidity and gives a slightly richer feel to the wine. Bourgogne is traditionally used for Pinot Noir, Gamay, Sauvignon Blanc, Sémillon, and barrel-fermenting of Chardonnay. It gives a very rich vanilla character that mingles beautifully with the fruit in the wine.

BOURGUEIL (FRANCE)   A red wine produced almost exclusively from the Cabernet Franc grape in the Loire Valley.

BOURGUIGNON NOIR (FRANCE)   *See* Gamay.

BOURRET (FRANCE)   The new wine in Gascony, Armagnac, destined for distillation.

BOURRU (FRANCE)   Meaning surly or rude; used for a wine, still resting on the *lees*, that has not yet deposited its yeasts and impurities. With white wines, it applies to the fresh, still-fermenting grape *must* of characteristically cloudy appearance.

BOUTEILLAN (FRANCE)   A red grape variety grown primarily in the south.

BOUTIQUE WINERY   The name applied to small wineries of modest size and production, usually in reference to California wineries.

BOUTIQUE WINES   Wines made in very limited quantity by boutique wineries.

BOUTEILLE (FRANCE)   *See* Bottle.

BOUTON (FRANCE)   *See* Bud.

BOUTS (FRANCE)   Hand-shaping of the soil at the ends of the rows of grapevines to facilitate drainage of the water.

BOUVIER (AUSTRIA AND YUGOSLAVIA)   A white grape variety grown primarily in Burgenland. Also known as *Ranina*.

BOUZY (FRANCE)   A still red wine produced in the village of Bouzy in the Champagne region.

BOVALE DI SPAGNA (ITALY)   A red grape variety grown in the regions of Sardinia and Sicily.

BOVALE SARDO (ITALY)   A red grape variety grown in the regions of Sardinia and Sicily.

BOWL   That part of a goblet or glass that holds the liquid.

BOWLE (GERMANY)   A goblet that is filled with wine, fresh fruit, herbs, and occasionally liqueurs.

BOXBEUTEL   *See* Bocksbeutel.

BOXES   *See* Case.

BRACHETTO (ITALY)   A red grape variety grown in the Piedmont region, where it produces a dry or slightly sweet spumante wine.

BRACKISH   A term sometimes applied to beers that display a salty taste.

BRAGGET (ENGLAND)   An alcoholic beverage brewed from honey and ale.

BRAMBLE   Describes the zesty, fruity, berry-like characteristic of wines made from the Zinfandel grape. Also known as *briary*.

BRANCELLAO (SPAIN)   A red grape variety.

BRANCH WATER   Cold water, specifically from small spring-fed streams, creeks, or brooks, known in the southern United States as *branches*, often added to distilled spirits. One such drink is known as *Bourbon and Branch*.

BRANCO (PORTUGAL)   *See* White.

BRANDA (ITALY)   A term for grappa formerly used in Piedmont. *See* Grappa.

BRANDIG (GERMANY)   *See* Baked.

BRAND LABEL   The label carrying, in the usual distinctive design, the brand name of the wine.

BRAND NAME   Usually, the bottling or producing winery, brewery, or distillery owns the name so that competitors are barred from its use. Also known as *proprietary brand name, proprietary name*, or *proprietary wine. See* Logo and Trademark.

BRANDY   A spirit made by distilling (less than 190 proof) wines or the fermented mash of fruit, which then may or may not be aged in oak barrels. The varying characteristics of different brandies are the result of differences in fruit and grape varieties, climate, soil, and production methods, which vary from district to district and country to country. If a brandy is produced from fruits other than grapes, then the name of the fruit must be stated on the label.

The name brandy originates with the Dutch, who are believed to have been the first great connoisseurs of this drink; they called it *brandewijn*, meaning burnt wine. This referred to the process by which brandy was made: wine was heated and the resulting vapor distilled. This term was carried over into Germany as branntwein (weinbrand) and into France as brandevin. The English adopted the word as brandywine, which was later shortened to brandy. Also known as *gnôle*.

BRANDY GLASS   *See* Snifter.

BRANDY HEATER   A popular item, often sold in specialty stores or catalogues, which features a brandy snifter perched at a 45-degree angle on a metal holder above a short candle. According to the directions, pour some brandy into the glass, light the candle below the bowl of the glass, and allow the candle to gently warm the liquid. In reality, if one follows these directions, one will burn one's hands on the glass. And, subjected to an intensified heat, the brandy's vapors, which are an intrinsic part of its enjoyment, will burn off. Also known as a *heater*.

BRANDY SNIFTER   *See* Snifter.

BRÄNNVIN   *See* Akvavit.

BRASSERIE (FRANCE)   A brewery or small restaurant.

BRAUER (GERMANY)   *See* Brewmaster.

BRAUEREI (GERMANY)   *See* Brewery.

BRAUEREIWESEN (GERMANY)   Brewing trade or industry.

BRAUNER (AUSTRIA)   Coffee with a little milk.

BRAWNY   A term loosely used to describe a muscular red wine with high levels of tannin and alcohol. It usually refers to young red wines that are low in elegance, breed, and suppleness. *See* Powerful and Muscular.

BREAKAGE   Losses in shipment.

BREAK-EVEN POINT   The output at which costs just equal revenues, making the profits equal zero.

BREATHING   The practice of allowing air to reach wine by uncorking and pouring it. Wine breathes to shed any unpleasant odors and bring out its aroma or bouquet. *See* Aeration and Decanting.

BREED   A loosely used term for a wine or beer that is prominent, of distinguished character, and distinctive quality. A balance of qualities in good wine due to a combination of grapes, soil, and skill of the producer. Also known as *aristocratic, aristocratico, chratteristico, markant,* and *razza*.

BREF (FRANCE)   *See* Short.

BREIDECKER (GERMANY)   A white grape variety developed from a cross of Müller-Thurgau and Chancellor at the Geisenheim Institute in the Rheingau.

BREIT (GERMANY)   *See* Dull.

BRENTA (ITALY)   *See* Grape-Picking Basket.

BREPON (ITALY)   *See* Molinara.

BRETON (FRANCE)   The local name in the Loire Valley for the Cabernet Franc grape variety, named after Abbé Breton. *See* Cabernet Franc.

BRETTANOMYCES   A sulfur-resistant yeast spoilage organism occasionally found in wine or beer; it has an odor of manure, a barnyard, or a sweaty saddle. *See* Barnyard.

BREW   A slang term or name for a beer, especially draught.

BREW   To make coffee or tea by steeping or boiling in a liquid.

BREWAGE   Anything brewed, especially beer.

BREWER   *See* Brewmaster.

BREWER'S GRAINS   The residue of the mash run after *sparging*; usually sold as cattle feed.

BREWER'S YEAST   *Saccharomyces cerevisiae*, a yeast that is specifically cultured and used in brewing beer.

BREWERY   An establishment where beer is brewed. Also known as *brauerei, brewhouse, cervecería,* and *fabbrica di birra*.

BREWHOUSE   An archaic term for a brewery. *See* Brewery.

BREWING   The process of making malt beverages (as beer) by grinding the various grains, then mixing separately with hot water to produce *wort*, flavoring the wort with hops, fermenting the hopped wort with yeast, and drawing off the fermented wort for storage and bottling.

BREWING SALT   Mixture of Epsom salt, gypsum, noniodized salt, or other minerals, occasionally added to water that is considered too soft for the fermentation of beer.

BREW KETTLE   *See* Boiler.

BREWMASTER   The master blender who oversees the entire brewing process. Also known as *brauer, brewer, brugh-fer,* and *cervecero*. *See* Lehre Bube.

BREWPUB   A tavern that brews its own beer for on-premise consumption as well as off-premise sales. *See* Microbrewery.

BREWSTERS   A name given during the Middle Ages to the female member of the family who was in charge of brewing in the home.

BRIARY   *See* Bramble.

BRICCO *(ITALY)*   A prime hilltop vineyard site.

BRICK   A shade of red-brown often found in well-aged, mature red wines or slightly old red wines.

BRIGHT   Describes a wine or beer that is clear, shining with light, or brilliant in appearance and color. A better term to use, however, would be *brilliant*. Also known as *allegro, blank,* and *lumineux*. *See* Brilliant and Falling Bright.

BRIGHTON   A red grape variety developed from a cross of Diana Hamburg and Concord by Jacob Moore in Brighton, New York.

BRILHANTE *(PORTUGAL)*   *See* Brilliant.

BRILLANTE *(ITALY* AND *SPAIN)*   *See* Brilliant.

BRILLIANT   The appearance of a wine or beer that is free of visible, suspended material or haziness and has a sparkling clarity. Also known as *brilhante, brillante,* and *glänzend*. *See* Clear.

BRILLIANT   A grape variety developed by Thomas Volney Munson (1843–1913) of Denison, Texas.

BRIOSO *(ITALY)*   *See* Vivacious.

BRISK   A wine that displays a high level of acidity, making it crisp and refreshing.

BRITISH GALLON   *See* Imperial Gallon and Gallon.

BRITISH PROOF GALLON   An imperial gallon of 277.4 cubic inches containing 57.1 percent by volume of ethyl alcohol (50 percent of alcohol by weight). Same as *Canadian Proof Gallon*.

BRIX   Name of a system (developed in 1870 by Adolf F. Brix, a German scientist) used by American and Australian winemakers to measure the sugar content of grapes, *must*, and occasionally wine. A measure of total soluble solids in grape juice, more than 90 percent of which are fermentable sugars. Hence, degrees Brix essentially indicates sugar content. Brix is expressed as grams of sucrose in one hundred grams of solution at 68 degrees Fahrenheit (20 degrees Celsius). For every gram per hundred grams of solution, the hydrometer reads "one degree Brix." For most table wines, the usual range at the harvest is 20 to 25 degrees Brix. By multiplying the stated Brix at harvest by roughly 0.55, the potential alcohol-by-volume (if the wine were fermented to dryness) may be obtained. Also known as *Balling* in the United States; *Baumé* in France; *Essenz* in Hungary; *Klosterneuburg* in Austria; and *Öechsle* in Germany and Switzerland. Also known as *degrees balling* or *degrees Brix. See* Plato.

BROACH   A seldom used term that refers to the opening of a barrel of wine or beer.

BROCTON   A white grape variety developed in 1919 from a cross of Brighton and (Winchell and Diamond), at the State Experimental Station in Geneva, New York.

BROKEN CASE   A case of bottles made up of several brands or types of wine or distilled spirits when purchased from a wholesale distributor. Also known as *split case.*

BROKEN CASE ROOM   A locked storage room where opened cases of alcoholic beverages are stored.

BROKEN ORANGE PEKOE   *See* Orange Pekoe Tea.

BROKEN PEKOE   *See* Orange Pekoe Tea.

BROKER   A middleman, whether an individual or a firm, that buys from the grower and sells to the shipper or is the shipper. An important player in distribution channels, the broker brings good, marketable wine to the trade. Also known as *commerciante, commissionaire, courtier, dealer, éleveur, négociant, négociant-eleveur, partidista, trader*, and *wine broker.*

BROKERAGE   Services performed by a Customs Broker for preparing documentation to obtain release of merchandise from Customs custody.

BROKER COMMISSIONS   Payments made to brokers for handling alcoholic beverages.

BRONZE   The amber hue apparent around the rim of a glass of aged red or white wine.

BROU (FRANCE)   A sweet liqueur made from walnut shells.

BROUILLIS (FRANCE)   The heart of the first distillate in the making of cognac. Also known as *flema.*

BROUILLY (FRANCE)   The largest producer of the ten *cru* communes in Beaujolais producing wines with a distinct flavor of black and red currants.

BROWN ALE A dark brown or cocoa-colored ale that has a malty bouquet and bittersweet taste. It is light to medium in body, usually rather low in alcohol, and traditionally produced in Great Britain, Belgium, and occasionally Canada. Sometimes called *nut brown ale*.

BROWN-BAGGING A practice of allowing customers in an on-premise unlicensed or occasionally licensed facility to bring in their own bottles of alcoholic beverages for consumption on the premises. Many facilities often charge a corkage fee.

BROWN BRANDY During the second half of the last century, this was a beverage made in France that consisted of brandy mixed with molasses.

BROWN GOODS A term often used for those distilled spirits (generally whiskey) that posses a brown color and are generally aged in wood. Examples are blended, Bourbon, Canadian, Irish, light, rye, Scotch, and Tennessee. *See* White Goods.

BROWNIAN MOVEMENT Irregular, random, and continuous erratic zigzag movement of minute microscopic solid particle (colloidal) dispersions in a liquid medium, caused by collision with other molecules in the liquid. The small particles remain in suspension because they are kept agitated and vibrate by the normal movement of molecules in the liquid. This movement is unrelated to outside disturbances; however, variation in external temperature could influence this. This phenomena was first studied in 1827 by the Scottish botanist Robert Brown.

BROWNING The oxidative effect on the color, odor, or taste of a wine or beer that is past its prime or has been carelessly exposed to a prolonged period of aeration.

BROWN SHERRY An old British term for a particular type of dark sweet sherry wine from Spain.

BRUGH-FER An ancient Gaelic term for a brewer. *See* Brewmaster.

BRUGNOLA (ITALY) A red grape variety grown in Lombardy.

BRUISED BEER Beer that has been cooled, allowed to return to room temperature, and then cooled again. A loss of carbonation and quality results.

BRÛLANT (FRANCE) *See* Burning.

BRUNELLO (ITALY) *See* Brunello di Montalcino and Sangiovese Grosso.

BRUNELLO DI MONTALCINO (ITALY) An extremely full-bodied, dry red wine made of 100 percent Sangiovese Grosso (also known as *Brunello*) grapes in the Tuscany region. It is one of Italy's finest and longest-lived wines and received its DOCG status on July 1, 1980.

The first documented use of the name Brunello was in 1842, when Canon Vincenzo Chiarini of Montalcino praised the wine produced from the Brunello grape. In 1862, Clemente Santi (of the Biondi-Santi family) first made a wine called "Brunello di Montalcino," which won several citations for its excellence at expositions in London and Paris. However, it wasn't until 1880 that Ferruccio Biondi-Santi, grandson of Clemente Santi and son of Caterina (Clemente's daughter) and Jacopo Biondi, first discovered the clonal selection (subvariety) of the Sangiovese grape in his family vineyards (called "Il Greppo").

In 1967, the producers of Brunello voluntarily formed a *consorzio* to establish a uniform price structure and quality control system. The seal of the consorzio is a south European evergreen oak with holly-like leaves on a green background. *See* Montalcino, Rosso di Montalcino, and Sangiovese Grosso.

BRUSH WEIGHT   A viticultural term for the ratio of vegetative growth of a grapevine to fruit production; this computation determines if the two are in balance. *See* Balanced Pruning and Pruning.

BRUT (VERY DRY)   Among the driest French champagnes. According to the European Common Market, brut champagnes contain less than fifteen grams of sugar per liter (most brut champagnes have eight to ten grams per liter). When the term is used elsewhere, there is an absence of a legal definition as to the relative dryness or sweetness of the sparkling wine.

Until the 1840s, champagne was a sweet to very sweet wine. In 1848, Mr. Burne, a London wine merchant, persuaded the champagne house of Perrier-Jouët to ship him some *un-dosaged* 1846 vintage champagne. Unfortunately, Mr. Burne's customers found the champagne to be undrinkable. In 1850, Mr. Burne approached the champagne house of Roederer to produce a brut champagne, but they flatly refused. After a few more years of trying, several champagne houses agreed and sent him cases of 1865 brut champagne, which the French referred to as *English cuvée*. Also known as *bruto, English cuvée, reserved for England*, and *strencherb*.

BRUT ABSOLUT   *See* Extra Brut.

BRUT DE BRUT   *See* Extra Brut.

BRUT INTÉGRAL   *See* Extra Brut.

BRUT NON-DOSAGE   *See* Extra Brut.

BRUTO (*PORTUGAL* AND *SPAIN*)   *See* Brut.

BRUT SAUVAGE   *See* Extra Brut.

BRUT ZÉRO   *See* Extra Brut.

BUAL   A red grape variety, which is descended from the Pinot Noir of Burgundy, France. It is used to make a semisweet style of madeira, a fortified wine. The Portuguese spelling is *Boal*.

BUAL MADEIRA   A white grape variety used for madeira wines.

BUBBLY   A slang term for any wine that sparkles.

BUCELAS (*PORTUGAL*)   A predominantly white-wine-producing region northeast of Lisbon that was demarcated in 1911. Its wines are made predominantly from the Arinto grape variety.

BUCK   A type of cocktail.

BUCKET   Slang term for an oversized (double) "rocks" glass.

BUCKET OF BLOOD   *See* Bloody Mary.

BUCKET OF SUDS   A slang term for beer. *See* Suds.

BUCKMAN'S TAVERN   When Paul Revere made his historic ride on April 19, 1775, announcing that the British were marching on Lexington, Massachusetts, he stopped at this tavern and relayed the message.

BUD   A compressed shoot located at the node of a cane. The bud of the grape is a compound bud, usually made up of three buds. The center bud at a node is the one that usually starts growth in the spring and produces the fruit. Often, one of the smaller buds will make a short growth but not produce any fruit. If a late frost kills the main shoot, another shoot will grow that will usually produce a half crop. Also known as *bouton* and *gemma*.

BUD BREAK   As sap rises in a grapevine, its pressure increases, forcing the buds to swell until their protective cover, called *corolla* or *calyptra*, splits, and the first tiny leaf, new shoots, and floral cluster emerges. This usually occurs about forty-five days after the buds form. Also known as *bud burst*.

BUD BURST   *See* Bud Break.

BUDDING   Asexual form of reproduction occurring in yeasts.

BUDDING   *See* Field Grafting.

BUBBLE CAP   *See* Fermentation Lock.

BUDGET   An operational plan for the income and expenditure of money for a given period.

BUFFALO   A red grape variety developed in 1938 from a cross of Herbert and Watkins at the State Experimental Station in Geneva, New York.

BUFFALO VODKA   *See* Zubrówka.

BUKETT (GERMANY)   *See* Bouquet.

BUKETTRAUBE (SOUTH AFRICA)   A white grape variety that makes wines with a light Muscat scent.

BUKETTREICH (GERMANY)   A wine with a rich bouquet.

BULK   Any container that has a capacity in excess of one wine gallon. In practice, shipments in bulk involve much larger containers.

BULK BUYING   Purchasing beverages in quantity, usually at a lower "as purchased" price per unit cost. Also known as *discount purchasing* or *quantity purchasing*.

BULK CONTAINER   Any container larger than sixty liters (15.8 gallons). *See* Container.

BULK-FERMENTED   *See* Charmat Method.

BULK GALLON   *See* Gallon.

BULK PROCESS   According to BATF, sparkling wines made through the bulk process may be labeled as "fermented outside the bottle," "secondary fermentation outside the bottle," "secondary fermentation before bottling," "not fermented in the bottle," or "not bottle fermented," as alternatives to the term bulk process. The term charmat method is allowed as additional (but not as a substitute for) information to describe this process, provided it appears immediately before or after one of the above-mentioned phrases. Also known as *charmat method* or *charmat process*. *See* Charmat Method.

BULK WINE   *See* Jug Wine.

BULLITT   *See* Taylor.

BUMPER   A cup or glass filled to the brim with an alcoholic drink. An old English toast, "to drink a bumper."

BUNCH   *See* Cluster.

BUNCH ROT   Same as *Botrytis* Bunch Rot. *See Botrytis Cinerea.*

BUNDESSORTENAMT *(GERMANY)*   Federal Bureau for Grape Cultivars.

BUNDESWEINPRÄMIERUNG *(GERMANY)*   National Wine Judging.

BUNG   A plug or stopper (usually cork, wood, or silicon) that fits into the opening at the top of a barrel for a tight seal. Bungs should be made of a fairly soft wood and definitely softer than the type of wood used for the barrel. It will swell faster and, what's more, a hard wood bung could crack the wooden barrel's opening. Also known as *bonde, spile*, and *spund.*

BUNG HOLE   The opening at the top of the barrel where liquids are added and removed.

BUNGING   The process of hammering a bung into the bunghole of a barrel.

BUNGSTARTER   A rubber mallet used to tap open or closed a bung on a barrel. *See* Zwickle.

BUONAMICO *(ITALY)*   A red grape variety from the northwest.

BURDIGALA *(FRANCE)*   The name that the region of Bordeaux was known as when the Romans took it in 55 B.C. from the Celtic Gauls.

BURDIN 4672   A white grape variety.

BURDIN 5201   A white grape variety.

BURDIN 7705   *See* Florental.

BURDIN 8753   A red grape variety

BUREAU OF ALCOHOL, TOBACCO, AND FIREARMS (BATF)   This bureau of the United States Department of the Treasury regulates the production, transportation, and sale of alcoholic beverages, enforces legal sale, and ensures the collection of federal excise taxes that are sent to the Internal Revenue Service. Also known as *ATF.*

BUREAU NATIONAL INTERPROFESSIONEL DE L'ARMAGNAC (BNIA)   The professional body in Armagnac controlling and safeguarding the production and quality of armagnac.

BUREAU NATIONAL INTERPROFESSIONEL DU COGNAC (BNIC)   A governing agency that oversees production, quality, labeling designations, and exportation for the cognac industry of France.

BURG *(GERMANY)*   *See* Schloss.

BURGAW   A red grape variety.

BURGER   A white grape variety grown in many parts of the world, producing mostly neutral-tasting wines with a pronounced aroma, suitable for sparkling-winemaking. Also known as *Elbling, Kleinberger*, and *Monbadon.*

BURGUNDY (FRANCE)   One of France's six major wine-producing regions. It produces both red and white dry wines. Approximately 80 percent of the Burgundy wine produced is red; most of it is from the Côte de Nuits. The other 20 percent is white, mostly from the Côte de Beaune. Burgundy's four wine-producing districts (Sâone-et-Loire, Côte d'Or, Rhône, and Yonne), are known around the world. Burgundy is the northernmost great red-wine-producing region in the world. Also known as *Borgoña* and *Bourgogne*.

BURGUNDY   Term used in the United States and Australia for generic red wines. They have little or no resemblance to the French product.

BURGUNDY-BOTTLE   A bottle of conical shape, although not regular in form and rather fat-bellied, used to house both red and white wines of Burgundy, France.

BURNED DRINKS   Standard drinks served in a small glass so that there is only a minor amount of mixer. *See* Overpouring and Short Drink.

BURNING   Also known as *brûlant* and *spritig*. *See* Alcoholic and Hot.

BURNT   Also known as *brandig*. *See* Baked.

BURNT ALE   *See* Pot Ale.

BUSCHENSCHANK (AUSTRIA)   Seasonal wine taverns.

BUTT   A barrel used to store or ship ale, sherry wine, or other wines. It varies in proportion to the area in which it is used. *See* Barrel.

BUTTAGE (FRANCE)   A plowing method similar to the *chaussage*, but deeper.

BUTTER BEER   A beer flavored with butter, cinnamon, and sugar.

BUTTERMILK   A cultured milk, minus the butterfat, that has been treated with certain bacteria.

BUTTERY   *See* Diacetyl.

BUTTONS UP   An old Scandinavian custom at formal gatherings to drink as many toasts, often with Aquavit (or Akvavit), as there were buttons on a man's dress coat.

BUTYRIC ACID   A spoiling acid caused by micro-infection (bacteria) that gives a rancid odor (reminiscent of perspiration or rancid butter) and a bitter, disagreeably acid taste to wine or beer. Fortunately, its occurrence is now rare. Also known as *goût de rance*.

BUVETTE (FRANCE)   Slang for beer.

BUY BACKS   A manager's customary method of showing customer appreciation with a free drink offered for every three or four purchased. Not a legal term, nor widely practiced.

BUZA   The name of an alcoholic beverage distilled from dates in Egypt.

BUZZING   The now defunct custom of buzzing a bottle of port (wine) consisted of placing a wager on your ability to determine if the remaining port in a specified decanter could fit into your glass without spilling a drop of the precious liquid. If you were correct and all fit, you were then "buzzed" (bought) a bottle by all of those who lost the wager. However, if you lost the wager, you would then have to "buzz" (buy) the winner a bottle. The bottles won would then have to be consumed during the setting! This is the origin of the expression "I feel quite a buzz on," or "I have a little bit of a buzz on," when referring to the inebriating effect that alcohol has on the body.

BYBLINE (GREECE)   An ancient wine.

CABACEO *(SPAIN)* A wine blend or the blending of wine.

CABARET A restaurant or nightclub providing live entertainment.

CABARNELLE *(FRANCE)* *See* Carmenère.

CABERNET FRANC A red grape variety grown extensively in Bordeaux, France, where it is used in small amounts as a blending grape in the Médoc as well as Pomerol and Saint-Émilion. Cabernet Franc also grows in other parts of France, including the Loire Valley. Some Cabernet Franc is also grown in California, Australia, Chile, throughout eastern Europe, and some northern regions of Italy. Cabernet Franc produces wines with a distinct aroma and taste of blackberry, cherry, elderberry, green olive, mint, raspberry, strawberry, and sometimes herbs. Also known as *Bouchet, Breton*, and *Carmenet*.

CABERNET PFEFFER A red grape variety, native to California, popular back in the 1880s and 1890s. The grape takes its name from William Pfeffer, a grapevine breeder, who developed it in his Santa Clara Valley vineyard. Although the grape is named Cabernet, it is uncertain if either of its parents was actually the Cabernet Sauvignon grape variety.

CABERNET SAUVIGNON A major red grape variety grown primarily in the Médoc district of France, sometimes accounting for as much as 90 percent of blend; known locally in Graves as *Vidure*. The grape also flourishes in many countries of the world, including California, Chile, Italy, and Australia. Cabernet Sauvignon produces wines with a distinct aroma and taste of black or green olives, black tea, blackberry, black currants, chocolate, cedar, coffee, bell pepper, eucalyptus, mint, and various herbs. It is often referred to as the noblest of all red grape varieties.

Around 1860, Almadén Vineyards produced California's first commercial Cabernet Sauvignon.

CABINET *(GERMANY)* Term used until July 1971 to denote a quality wine.

CACCIONE *(ITALY)* *See* Canaiolo Nero.

CACO SEEDLESS   A red grape variety.

CAECUBAN   An ancient Roman wine.

CAFE   A coffeehouse or small restaurant serving alcoholic beverages.

CAFÉ *(FRANCE, PORTUGAL, AND SPAIN)*   *See* Coffee.

CAFÉ AU LAIT *(FRANCE)*   *See* Caffè Latte.

CAFÉ FILTRE *(FRANCE)*   Coffee made by pouring hot water through ground coffee beans in a filtering device that fits over a cup or pot.

CAFÉ NOIR *(FRANCE)*   Black coffee.

CAFFÈ *(ITALY)*   *See* Coffee.

CAFFÈ AMERICANO *(ITALY)*   Espresso coffee diluted with hot water to make it the strength of American coffee. Occasionally called *caffè lungo*.

CAFFÈ CON PANNA *(ITALY)*   An espresso served with a dollop of whipped cream on top.

CAFFÈ CORRETTO *(ITALY)*   An espresso coffee that has been "corrected" by the addition of grappa or other types of distilled spirits or bitters.

CAFFÈ FREDDO *(ITALY)*   Simply a chilled espresso, occasionally served with ice. *See* Espresso Con Ghiaccio.

CAFFEINA *(ITALY)*   Caffeine.

CAFFEINE   A crystalline, bitter, but odorless alkaloid present in coffee, tea, and certain soft drinks. It acts as a stimulant to the heart and central nervous system.

CAFFÈ LATTE *(ITALY)*   Strong coffee mixed with equal parts of scalded or steamed milk. Also known as *café au lait*.

CAFFÈ LUNGO *(ITALY)*   A "long" espresso that has been made weaker by the addition of water. *See* Caffè Americano.

CAFFÈ MOCHA *(ITALY)*   Espresso mixed with mocha and steamed milk, then topped with whipped cream.

CAFFEOL   The natural oil responsible for the characteristic odor and taste of coffee.

CAFFÈ RISTRETTO *(ITALY)*   A thicker, more concentrated version of espresso, usually one ounce or less. It is made by turning off the water pump a few seconds sooner than normal.

CAGE   *See* Wire Hood.

CAGNULARI *(ITALY)*   A red grape variety.

CAILLOU *(FRANCE)*   Pebbles.

CAIÑO BLANCO *(SPAIN)*   A white grape variety.

CAJUADA   A West African beverage made from fermented cashew nuts.

CAKE   *See* Pomace.

CALABRESE *(ITALY)*   *See* Nero d'Avola.

CALABRIA (ITALY)   One of twenty wine-producing regions. Calabria traces its history back more than 2,500 years to when it was called *Magna Grecia* by the ancient Greeks who occupied this barren, dry region located at the "toe" of boot-shaped southern Italy.

CALAMICH (ITALY)   *See* Cooked Wine.

CALCAIRE (FRANCE)   Limestone soil.

CALCAREOUS   A soil containing high levels of calcium carbonate (usually lime) and often magnesium carbonate.

CALCIUM ALGINATE BEADS   *See* Encapsulated Yeast.

CALCIUM CARBONATE   A compound used to reduce the excess natural acidity in high acid wines. Precipitated *chalk* is sometimes used for amelioration of the acidity. *See* Amelioration.

CALCIUM SULFATE (GYPSUM)   A pH-lowering compound often used in making Spanish-type or *flor* sherry wine. *See* Plastering.

CALDO (ITALY)   *See* Warmth.

CALEGRAÑO (SPAIN)   A white grape variety.

CALER (FRANCE)   The attaching of each grapevine stem to a stake by means of tying.

CALIENTE (SPAIN)   *See* Fiery.

CALIFORNIA BRANDY   All California brandy must be made, by state law, from grapes grown and distilled in California. It must be aged a minimum of two years in oak barrels and, if aged for less time, it must be labeled an "immature brandy." For brandies that are aged more than two years, the age may be stated on the label.

There is no required grape variety for use in brandymaking in California; many different varieties are used. Most distillers use the Thompson Seedless or Flame Tokay grapes as they are inexpensive, nondescript, and produce a fairly good product.

CALISAY (SPAIN)   A very bitter quinine-based liqueur that derives its taste from cinchona bark and other parts of the tree.

CALL BRAND   *See* Call Liquor.

CALL LIQUOR   Those brands of alcoholic beverages that have brand recognition for which the customer will call by name. Also known as *call brand* or *name brand*.

CALMERIA   A white grape variety developed in 1939 from Almeria grapes. It is grown in California.

CALORIC VALUE   This number varies with the percent alcohol by volume and the weight of sugar present in the finished product. To determine the calories of a dry wine, beer, or distilled spirit. 0.8 times proof times ounces = calories per drink size—but only the alcohol, not any added mixers, water, and so on.

CALORIES   A measure of the energy produced by a given amount of food or beverage when it is ingested and burned in the body.

CALVADOS   An apple brandy made from different varieties of apples that grow in the Normandy, Brittany, and Maine regions of northwest France. Calvados is actually an *eau-de-vie* of cider or a brandy distilled from either cider or the juice of fresh apples. Also known as *sargadoz*. *See* Applejack.

CALYPTRA The fused petals of the grape that fall off the flower at *anthesis*. *See* Bud Break.

CALZIN A red grape variety introduced in 1958 from a cross of Zinfandel and Refosco (Mondeuse) by the University of California at Davis.

CAMBIUM LAYER A thin, green layer just under the outer bark of grapevines that gives rise to new cells and promotes secondary growth. It is the artery of life for the grapevine.

CAMERA (SPAIN) *See* Candling.

CAMINA (GERMANY) A red grape variety developed from a cross of Pinot Noir and Portugieser.

CAMOMILE *See* Chamomile.

CAMPANIA (ITALY) One of twenty wine-producing regions, it is on the coast of the country south of Rome. Campania is famous for its Lacryma Christi, Fiano di Avellino, and Taurasi wines.

CAMPBELL EARLY A red grape variety developed in the mid-1930s by George W. Campbell on Stretch Island in Washington State. Formerly known as *Island Belle*.

CAMPBELTOWN MALTS Campbeltown is a barley-growing, Scotch-producing area noted for whiskies (Campletown Malts) that are very full-bodied and quite smoky.

CAMPDEN TABLET A seven-grain tablet of potassium metabisulfite that dissolves in the *must* or wine and releases sulfur dioxide, which acts as a sterilant and antioxidant. *See* Antioxidant, Potassium Metabisulfite, and Sulfur Dioxide.

CAN A form of packaging for beer and some wines.

CANADA (PORTUGAL) An old measure equal to 1.7 liters or approximately 59 ounces.

CANADA MUSCAT A white grape variety released in 1961 from a cross of Muscat Hamburg and Hubbard.

CANADIAN PROOF GALLON *See* British Proof Gallon.

CANADIAN WHISKY (In Canada, it is spelled *whisky*.) Although Canadian whisky is a distinctive product of Canada, the Canadian government doesn't set regulations relative to the mixture of the grain blend (providing no one grain exceeds 49 percent), the proof level at which it is distilled, or the type of barrel used. Distillers are allowed to make their own whisky as they see fit. Canadian whisky is matured most frequently in white oak barrels and, for the American market, is bottled at a minimum of 80 proof. Canadian whisky is made only from grains (corn, rye, and barley malt) and may be bottled after three years of age. Canadian whisky sold in the United States is generally four to six years old. Canadian whisky cannot be designated as a "straight" whisky. In 1891, a United States law required the country of origin to appear predominantly on a product's label.

CANADICE SEEDLESS A red grape variety developed in 1977 from a cross of Bath and Himrod at the State Experimental Station in Geneva, New York.

CANAIOLO BIANCO *(ITALY)* *See* Drupeggio.

CANAIOLO NERO *(ITALY)* A red grape variety used in small proportions in the making of Chianti, Torgiano, and Vino Nobile di Montepulciano wines. The Canaiolo grape variety was already growing in Tuscany during the thirteenth century. Also known as *Caccione*.

CANARY SACK *See* Sack.

CANARY WINES *(SPAIN)* Red and white wines from the Canary Islands, where only small quantities of wine are produced.

CAÑAS *(SPAIN)* A small, stumpy, cylindrical glass in which Manzanilla sherry is traditionally drunk.

CANCELLATION SYSTEM A system whereby the bartender or other service personnel tears, punches a hole through, or draws a red mark across a stub, indicating that drinks that have been recorded on a guest's check have in fact been served.

CANDIDA MYCODERMA *See* Flowers of Wine.

CANDLES Used as a substitute for paraffin on leaking wooden barrels. Candles are a necessary piece of equipment for decanting wines and are used for *candling* (testing the clarity of) wine. *See* Candling.

CANDLING A process that determines the clarity and amount of sediment, if any, which has formed in the bottle. To candle the bottle, carefully hold it, horizontally, in front of an exposed light bulb (60 to 100 watts) so that light penetrates the glass, displaying any sediment on the bottom side of the bottle. Knowing which wines have started to "throw" sediment aids in the serving process. Also known as *camera* or *obscura*.

CANDYLIKE Attributes often associated with very young, fruity red wines vinified for early consumption. These wines display extremely fruity, berry-like aromas, likened to candy.

CANE *See* Straw Mats.

CANE The stem or woody structure of a grapevine on which leaves, flowers, and fruit grow. In autumn, after the leaves fall off, canes darken and harden. *See* Shoot.

CANE PRUNING A yearly pruning method in which all of the extraneous growth is pruned from the grapevine, retaining only the strongest canes to bear fruit the following fall. These canes, usually four, are tied to a two-tiered trellis for support. With cane pruning, the grapevine is vertical in its growth (except for the fruit-bearing canes), whereas with cordon pruning the grapevine is rather T-shaped. The obvious advantage with the cane system over the head-trained system, where the grapevine is shaped rather like a bush, is that the grapevine is stretched out on a lateral plane and is considerably more open to sunlight and air. The one disadvantage of the cane system is that sometimes crop levels are hard to control. *See* Pruning and Spur Pruning.

CANE SUGAR Sucrose, obtained from sugar cane, sometimes used in fermentation.

CANE WEIGHT This is multiplied by a factor in order to determine the number of buds (potential crop) that the grapevine could bear. Also known as *vine size*. *See* Vine Capacity.

CANNA *(ITALY)* *See* Straw Mats.

CANNAMELU *(ITALY)*   *See* Guarnaccia.

CANNER SEEDLESS   A red grape variety developed in 1946.

CANNICI *(ITALY)*   Straw mats utilized for the drying of grapes to be used in the *governo Toscano* method of producing very young Chianti wine. *See* Governo and Straw Mats.

CANNONADU *(ITALY)*   *See* Grenache.

CANNONATU *(ITALY)*   *See* Grenache.

CANNONAU *(ITALY)*   Also known as *Canonau, Cannonadu,* and *Cannonatu. See* Grenache.

CANOA *(SPAIN)*   A wedge-shaped metal or wooden funnel used to fill a wooden barrel with wine.

CANONAU *(ITALY)*   *See* Grenache.

CANOPY   The entire foliage of a grapevine as it is positioned on the trellis.

CANTENAC *(FRANCE)*   One of the five communes entitled to the appellation *Margaux* in the Bordeaux region.

CANTINA   An establishment, generally found in Europe, which serves primarily wine and beer.

CANTINA *(ITALY)*   *See* Wine Cellar.

CANTINA SOCIALE *(ITALY)*   A cooperative winery.

CANTINIERE *(ITALY)*   *See* Cellarmaster.

CANUTO *(SPAIN)*   *See* Wine Thief.

CAP   During fermentation of red wine, the grape skins, stems, seeds, and so forth, rise to the surface of the tank or barrel due to the fact that pigments, flavonoids, tannins, and other compounds are being extracted, making the skins lighter than the *must.* When the skins reach the surface they harden, forming what is known as the cap or hat. Several times a day this cap must be broken up to allow the carbon dioxide gas to escape. It is also important for the skins to stay in contact with the fermenting juice, to aid extraction. To accomplish this, the wine is pumped from the bottom of the tank over the cap of floating skins and seeds at the top of the tank three times a day. Some wineries, with the aid of long paddles or oars, break up the cap and stir the skins back into the juice. Also known as *cappo, chapeau, hat,* and *manta.*

CAPATAZ *(SPAIN)*   A cellarmaster, as used in Jerez de la Frontera. *See* Cellarmaster.

CAP CLASSIQUE *(SOUTH AFRICA)*   The official designation for sparkling wines made by the *méthode champenoise* technique. *See* Sparkling Wine.

CAPE   *See* Alexander.

CAPE CONSTANTIA   *See* Alexander.

CAPITEUX *(FRANCE)*   *See* Heady.

CAPITOLARE WINES *(ITALY)*   The term means "title of relevance or merit," which indicates a particular typology and can only be exploited by estates that belong to the Authority for Protection of the Wines of the Hills of Central Tuscany.

Capitolare is a classification of high-quality wines that utilize nontraditional Tuscan grapes. The wines were first introduced into Italy in 1982 and into the United States market in 1986. Capitolare was formerly known as *Predicato*.

Capitolare regulates vineyard location, techniques of viticulture, and altitude. It forbids the inclusion of wines produced from grapes other than those grown in the zones singled out as having ideal soil and altitude for each of the four grape varieties. Capitolare unites these Tuscan wines and is basically their family name. The four categories are:

Capitolare del Muschio—A white wine from 100 percent Chardonnay grapes.

Capitolare di Bitùrica—A red wine, basically Sangiovese with a minimum of 30 percent Cabernet Sauvignon grapes.

Capitolare di Cardisco—A red wine from 100 percent Sangiovese grapes.

Capitolare del Selvànte—A white wine from 100 percent Sauvignon Blanc grapes.

CAPPELLO GALLEGIANTE *(ITALY)* *See* Extended Skin Contact.

CAPPING MACHINE A hand-operated device (it is seldom employed today) utilized for putting crown caps on soft drink and beer bottles.

CAPPO *(ITALY)* *See* Cap.

CAPPUCCINO *(ITALY)* An espresso coffee served with a creamy head made from steamed or scalded milk or cream. It is often dusted with a bit of chocolate, cocoa, or nutmeg.

Cappuccino is named after the Capuchin monks (Cappuccio), a Roman Catholic order, reformed in 1524, who had a special way of making their coffee, adding in a little cream and heating the mixture. The monks wore long pointed hoods, beige in color, known as *capuche*, from which they derived their own name. *See* Chocolaccino and Kapuziner.

CAPPUCCINO CHIARO *(ITALY)* A light cappuccino prepared with less espresso.

CAPPUCCINO SCURO *(ITALY)* A dark cappuccino prepared with more espresso.

CAP STEM The stem of individual flowers or grape berries.

CAPSULA *(ITALY)* *See* Capsule.

CAPSULE A plastic, lead, aluminum, or wax cover placed over the cork of a wine bottle to give a more secure closure and to improve the appearance of the package. Originally, lead capsules were utilized in England to deter rats living in the old underground cellars from eating through the old standard paraffin and corks. Also known as *capsula*.

CAPTIVATOR A red grape variety developed by Thomas Volney Munson (1843–1913) of Denison, Texas.

CAQUE *(FRANCE)* *See* Grape-Picking Basket.

CARACTÈRE *(FRANCE)* *See* Character.

CARAFE *(FRANCE)* A decanter or glass bottle used in restaurants for serving house wines. *See* Decanter.

CARAMEL Burnt sugar or roasted barley, slightly bitter but otherwise tasteless, used for coloring whiskey, rum, brandy, beer, and so forth.

CARAMEL COLORING   Caramel added to brown whiskey or brandy prior to bottling for color adjustment.

CARAMELIZATION   A condition often associated with wines that have been exposed to artificially high temperatures for prolonged periods of time, causing an odor and taste of caramel. It is a characteristic of some fortified wines. *See* Baked, Estufa, Hydroxymethylfurfural, and Maderization.

CARAMELIZE   To heat sugar to the point of browning.

CARAMEL MALT   Made from "green malt," malted barley that has had its sugars crystallized while still in the form of grain. It has not yet been kiln dried and is produced by drying the wet germinated barley at controlled temperatures. It enriches the color, giving a reddish-golden color and a caramel, almost sweet taste to the beer. Caramel malt also increases the body and aids in the head retention. Also known as *crystal malt* or *specialty malt*.

CARASSON (FRANCE)   Acacia (ornamental tree) stake used to support each grapevine stem.

CARATELLO (ITALY)   A fifty-liter (thirteen-gallon) barrel used for making Vin Santo.

CARATTERE (ITALY)   *See* Character.

CARATTERISTICO (ITALY)   Characteristic. *See* Breed.

CARBOHYDRATES   Chemicals produced by living organisms from carbon, oxygen, and hydrogen; used as the main currency for the distribution of chemically stored energy among living organisms, or within the body. Common carbohydrates include cellulose, starch, glycogen, and the simpler sugars.

CARBON   *See* Activated Carbon.

CARBÓN (SPAIN)   *See* Activated Charcoal.

CARBONATED BEVERAGES   Those beverages, both alcoholic and nonalcoholic, that obtain their carbonation from CO_2 that has been added or obtained naturally from fermentation. *See* Artificial Carbonation, Carbonated Water, and Artificially Carbonated Wine.

CARBONATED BEVERAGE SYSTEM   *See* Postmix Soda System and Premix Soda System.

CARBONATED SODA WATER   *See* Carbonated Water.

CARBONATED WATER   Ordinary water to which carbon dioxide gas has been injected under pressure. Also known as *carbonated soda water* and *soda water*. *See* Artificial Carbonation, Carbonated Beverages, and Artificially Carbonated Wine.

CARBONATION   The amount of carbon dioxide in a given amount of water or other liquid. The ideal conditions for carbonating water are relatively low water temperature (35 degrees Fahrenheit) and a high level of carbon dioxide pressure.

CARBONATION BURN-OFF   The escape of carbon dioxide from a beverage (alcoholic or nonalcoholic) that was not previously chilled when poured over ice, resulting in a diminished level of carbonation.

CARBONATOR   A mechanical device that mixes (at point of delivery) water, carbon dioxide, and syrup to produce soft drinks.

CARBONATOR TANK   A tank where the water and carbon dioxide are exposed to each other, preferably at a low temperature, above freezing. The carbonator includes a pump that injects water into the tank at a fixed ratio of water pressure to carbon dioxide.

CARBON DIOXIDE   A naturally occurring, odorless, colorless, inert gas, a by-product of fermentation. During fermentation, roughly half the weight of sugar is converted into CO_2, the other into ethyl alcohol. Carbon dioxide is allowed to dissipate into the atmosphere when making still wines. However, during the production of sparkling wines and beers, the carbon dioxide gasses are trapped to retain the effervescence in the product. Carbon dioxide will increase the perceived impression of acidity on the palate when converted to carbonic acid in a wine.

CARBONELLA *(ITALY)*   *See* Activated Charcoal.

CARBONIC ACID   A weak, colorless acid formed by the solution of carbon dioxide in water and existing only in solution. It is produced during fermentation and remains in the wine for varying periods of time. Also known as *acido carbonico*.

CARBONIC MACERATION   A very technical and complex procedure in which whole, uncrushed clusters of grapes are placed into a stainless steel fermenter. Care is taken to maintain the anatomical integrity of the berries without cuts, scrapes, or bruises. The tank is then pumped full with carbon dioxide and sealed. The sheer weight of the grapes is sufficient to break the skins, beginning an intracellular fermentation. The grapes are held under carbon dioxide pressure, causing the malic acid to break down while a complex fermentation takes place within the berries themselves. Because of the lack of oxygen, the skin cells asphyxiate and die, permitting color pigments to diffuse into the pulp. As a result of this, both tannin and the development of volatile acidity is kept to a minimum.

The juice is pressed and conventionally fermented, producing light-bodied, less alcoholic, young, and fruity wines meant for consumption several weeks after fermentation. In the United States, this process is often referred to as "whole berry fermentation." Carbonic maceration is used to make the Beaujolais *nouveau* wines of France. Also known as *macération carbonique, macerazione carbonica*, and *méthode carbonique*. *See* Beaujolais Nouveau, Flanzy, Morel, and Nouveau.

CARBONIO *(ITALY)*   *See* Activated Carbon.

CARBONO *(SPAIN)*   *See* Activated Carbon.

CARBOY   *See* Demijohn.

CARDBOARD   An odor or taste found in some beers or wines that is reminiscent of wet cardboard or newspaper. Usually the result of the formation of mold or other types of bacterial growth.

CARDINAL   A red grape variety released in 1946 from a cross of Flame Tokay and Ribier by E. Snyder and Harmon.

CARDINALE *(ITALY)*   A white grape variety grown in Sicily.

CAREGNANO *(ITALY)*   A red grape variety.

CARICO *(ITALY)*   Deeply colored.

CARIGNAN   A red grape variety used for blending, grown primarily in the south of France's Midi region and in Africa. It produces wines that are cherry-colored, with a delicate, aromatic bouquet and a fruity, light-bodied taste. Some Carignan is also grown in Spain and California (where it is spelled Carignane). Also known as *Carignano, Carineña,* and *Mazuelo.*

CARIGNANE ROUSSE *(FRANCE)*   *See* Grenache.

CARIGNANO *(ITALY)*   *See* Carignan.

CARINEÑA *(SPAIN)*   *See* Carignan.

CARLOS   A white grape variety introduced in 1970 by the North Carolina Agricultural Experimental Station.

CARMAN   A red grape variety developed by Thomas Volney Munson (1843–1913) of Denison, Texas in 1940.

CARMENÈRE *(FRANCE)*   A red grape variety grown in Bordeaux. Also known as *Cabarnelle.*

CARMENET *(FRANCE)*   The local name in the Médoc for the Cabernet Franc grape variety. *See* Cabernet Franc.

CARMIGNANO *(ITALY)*   A red DOCG wine produced in the region of Tuscany from a grape blend—essentially the same grape blend as for Chianti (Sangiovese and Canaiolo Nero), except that white grapes may be left out. Also, the maximum percentage of other red grapes (Cabernet Sauvignon and Cabernet Franc) has increased to a maximum of 15 percent.

CARMINE   A red grape variety developed in 1975 from a cross of (Cabernet Sauvignon and Carignan) and Merlot by Dr. Harold P. Olmo of University of California, Davis.

CARNELIAN   A red grape variety developed in 1973 from a cross of (Cabernet Sauvignon and Carignan) and Grenache by Dr. Harold P. Olmo of University of California, Davis.

CARNERO *(SPAIN)*   Ram.

CAROLINA BLACKROSE   A red grape variety grown in Texas.

CARRICANTE *(ITALY)*   A white grape variety native to Sicily, used in the blend for Etna Bianco wines.

CARRIER   A railroad car, motor truck, ship, airplane, or other vehicle used for transporting beverages and supplies. Sometimes used to denote an entire rail, trucking, shipping, or air transport system. Also known as *common carrier.*

CARTA BLANCA *(SPAIN)*   White label.

CARTA ORO *(SPAIN)*   Gold label.

CARTON   *See* Case.

CARTONS   Short for gift cartons.

CASA ESTABLECIDA *(SPAIN)*   Estate bottled.

CASA FONDATA *(ITALY)*   Winery founded... followed by a date.

CASA VINICOLA *(ITALY)*   *See* Winery.

CASCADE   A red grape variety developed from a cross of Seibel 7042 and Seibel 5409. Formerly known as *Seibel 13053*. Incorrectly referred to as *Cascade Noir*.

CASCADE NOIR   *See* Cascade.

CASCINA *(ITALY)*   An estate or farm.

CASCO *(SPAIN)*   Oak barrels of varying capacities utilized for aging and/or shipping wines. *See* Barrel.

CASCULHO *(PORTUGAL)*   A red grape variety grown in the Douro region.

CASE   Two or more bottles or one or more containers larger than four liters, enclosed in a box or fastened together by some other method.

CASE   A container that houses bottles or cans of wine, beer, or distilled spirits. A case of three or four liters contains four individual units; a case of 1.5 or 1.75 liters contains six individual units; a case of 750 milliliters or one liter contains twelve individual units; a case of 375 milliliters contains twenty-four individual units; a case of beer contains twenty-four individual units. Also known as *cartons* or *boxes*.

CASEIN   A positively charged protein fining agent derived from milk. Also known as *caseina, caseína,* and *caséine. See* Fining and Fining Agents.

CASEINA *(ITALY)*   *See* Casein.

CASEÍNA *(SPAIN)*   *See* Casein.

CASÉINE *(FRANCE)*   *See* Casein.

CASE CARD   *See* Cut Case Card.

CASE PRICE   The wholesale price per case, rather than price per individual unit that makes up the case. The case price is generally lower per unit than purchasing the same units individually.

CASH BAR   The bar at a private function where guests pay for their individual drinks. Also known as a *no-host* bar.

CASHIER'S BANK   The opening cash available at the start of a shift, necessary to make appropriate change for customers.

CASK   *See* Barrel.

CASKINESS   A flavor imparted to wine by barrels that have not been properly cleaned or maintained.

CASSADY   A red grape variety.

CASSE   A cloudiness present in some wines due to the formation of colloidal complexes of metals, most notably iron and copper. In some European countries, these excess metals may be removed by the addition of potassium ferrocyanide. However, this practice is not accepted in the United States. Instead, *Cufex*, a proprietary product, is the acceptable treatment. Also known as *iron haze. See* Citric Acid.

CASSIS *(FRANCE)*   Black currant flavored liqueur.

CASTA (PORTUGAL) *See* Grape Variety.

CASTEL 19637 A red grape variety.

CASTELA (PORTUGAL) A red grape variety grown in the Douro region.

CASTELÃO FRANCES (PORTUGAL) *See* Periquita.

CASTELLI (ITALY) *See* Straw Mats.

CASTELLO (ITALY) Castle.

CASTILLO (SPAIN) Castle.

CATADOR (SPAIN) A wine taster.

CATARRATTO (ITALY) A white grape variety grown primarily in Sicily, where it is used as a blending grape. Two of its subvarieties are known as *Catarratto Bianco Comune* and *Catarratto Bianco Lucido*.

CATARRATTO BIANCO COMUNE (ITALY) A subvariety of Catarratto.

CATARRATTO BIANCO LUCIDO (ITALY) A subvariety of Catarratto.

CATAVINO (SPAIN) A fine crystal glass for tasting and drinking sherry wine. It resembles a small glass chalice with a circular pedestal, thin cylindrical stem, and elongated, tulip-like receptacle.

CATAWBA A red grape variety that takes its name from the Catawba River in western North Carolina, where it was first recorded growing in 1802 by a man named Murray. In 1847, Nicholas Longworth made the first American sparkling wine from Catawba grapes in Cincinnati, Ohio.

CATCH WIRE Any horizontal wire used for catching and training grapevine tendrils or canes. Also known as *foliage wire*.

CATECHINS Phenolic compounds that are extracted from the skins and seeds in the *must* during the primary alcohol fermentation. They assist in the browning of damaged fruit and are sometimes the cause of bitterness.

CATION EXCHANGE CAPACITY The measured ability of a soil to hold nutrients to soil particles or colloids.

CATION EXCHANGE PROCESS A process where sodium chloride is used as a regenerator to help eliminate sediment from wine.

CATRAME (ITALY) Also known as *catramoso*. *See* Tarry.

CATRAMOSO (ITALY) *See* Tarry.

CAUDLE *See* Hot Caudle.

CAVA (SPAIN) The official designation for sparkling wines made by the *méthode champenoise* technique. The sparkling wine must have at least nine months of second fermentation and aging in the bottle and carry a four-cornered star on the bottom of its cork. Cava can be produced from approved grape varieties only, including Macabeo (called Viura in Rioja), Xarel-lo, Parellada, Subirat (called Malvasía in Rioja), and Chardonnay. For rosé Cavas, the red grape varieties Garnacha Tinta and Monastrell are permitted. Cava can be produced only in the delimited Cava region in northern Spain comprising parts of the provinces of Barcelona, Tarragona, Lérida, Gerona, Alava, Rioja, Navarra, and Zaragoza. *See* Sparkling Wine.

CAVALLA *(ITALY)* A red grape variety. Also known as *Soricella*.

CAVATAPPI *(ITALY)* *See* Corkscrew.

CAVE *(FRANCE)* *See* Wine Cellar.

CAVEAU *(FRANCE)* A tasting cellar open to the public.

CAVE COOPÉRATIVE *(FRANCE)* The source of many of the well-made, regional, non-estate wines.

CAVES Underground cellars.

CAVISTE *(FRANCE)* *See* Cellarmaster.

ÇAY *(TURKEY)* *See* Tea.

CAYETANA BLANCA *(SPAIN)* A white grape variety.

CAYUGA WHITE A white grape variety developed in 1945 (released in 1972) from a cross of Seyval and Schuyler (Zinfandel and Ontario).

CEDAR A characteristic smell often associated with oak-aged red wines of Bordeaux, France, and Rioja, Spain.

CELERY SODA A carbonated soft drink, first made in 1868 by the American Beverage Company of Brooklyn, New York. This celery-flavored beverage is made of oils extracted from celery seeds and other natural flavors. The most popular brand found on the East Coast is Dr. Brown's (fictitiously named) Cel-Ray Tonic.

CELL The basic unit of all living things; it is surrounded by a membrane and contains gel-like cytoplasm and various membrane-encased structures.

CELLAR Also known as *cantina* and *keller*. *See* Wine Cellar.

CELLARED AND BOTTLED BY A statement that means the named winery, at the stated address, subjected the wine to cellar treatment. The term is synonymous with *vinted and bottled by* and *prepared and bottled by*.

CELLARMAN A winery worker who is responsible for the movement or transferring of wines, sanitary conditions of the facility, and general maintenance.

CELLARMASTER An individual of considerable importance to both the vineyard and winery, who is responsible for the vinification and aging of all wines. The cellarmaster plays a most significant role in the cellar, for the success of a wine depends on his technical skills, experience, and judgment.

One characteristic of a European cellarmaster is the clothing (the same for centuries), consisting of a black jacket and a leather apron. Also known as *cantiniere, capataz, chef de cave, kellermeister,* and *maître de chais*.

CELLAR RAT A self-description of a winery worker. During the harvest, crush, and subsequent fermentation, the cellar rat stays in the cellar, busily working, never seeing the sun.

CELLAR TEMPERATURE The proper cellar temperature is 52 to 55 degrees Fahrenheit, but a few degrees higher or lower is satisfactory, providing that the temperature is constant. Wide and frequent fluctuations in temperature should be avoided. Wines can be safely stored for years in a fairly stable temperature, ranging from 55 to 70 degrees Fahrenheit. The cooler the bottle's aging conditions, the more a young wine's character is retained over a longer period of time. Temperatures are cooler at floor level and on interior walls or closets; exterior walls are affected by sunlight and daily temperature changes. Uninsulated rooms should not be used, as their wide temperature changes damage the wine and shorten its life. *See* Wine Cellar.

CELLIER *(FRANCE)* An above-ground storeroom for food and beverages.

CELL WALL The outer layer of a cell of a microorganism directly in contact with the surrounding external medium.

CENCIBEL *(SPAIN)* The local name in LaMancha for the Tempranillo grape variety. *See* Tempranillo.

CENIZA *(SPAIN)* *See* Powdery Mildew.

CENTIGRAM A metric unit of weight equal to one one-hundredth of a gram.

CENTILITER A metric unit equal to one one-hundredth part of a liter.

CENTIMETER A metric unit of length equal to one one-hundredth of a meter.

CENTRIFUGE A machine whose inner cylinders spin and utilize centrifugal force to separate particles of varying density, as yeast from wine. It is also used to remove solids (pulp, skin, etc.) from wine.

CENTURION A red grape variety developed in 1975 from a cross of Cabernet Sauvignon and Carignan (and Grenache) by Dr. Harold P. Olmo at the University of California, Davis.

CENTURY I A white grape variety.

CENTURY PLANT A name given incorrectly to the agave plant by early pioneers in the southwestern United States, because it was mistakenly believed to bloom only once every one hundred years.

CEP *(FRANCE)* Grapevine stock.

CEPA *(PORTUGAL* AND *SPAIN)* Grape or grapevine.

CÉPAGE *(FRANCE)* *See* Grape Variety.

CEPPO *(ITALY)* The trunk of a grapevine.

CERASUOLO *(ITALY)* Deep pink or cherry-red-colored.

CERCIAL DO DOURO *(PORTUGAL)* A white grape variety grown in the Douro region.

CEREALS A broad base of grains, including barley (malted and unmalted), wheat, oats, rye, corn, dried corn maize, rice, and many others. All of these grains contain starch that must be converted into a readily fermentable sugar before fermentation can take place. Cereals are necessary for the production of beer, whiskey, and some other alcoholic products.

CERTIFIED ORGANIC Private certification organizations registered with the state certify farmers' compliance with the California Organic Foods Act of 1990. Some groups have supplementary requirements that are more stringent. *See* Organically Grown Wine.

CERTIFIED STOCK   A grapevine stock that is certified free from known virus diseases and has been heat treated under a government certification program.

CERVECERÍA (SPAIN)   *See* Brewery.

CERVECERO (SPAIN)   *See* Brewmaster.

CERVEJA (PORTUGAL)   *See* Beer.

CERVEZA (SPAIN)   *See* Beer.

CESANESE COMMUNE (ITALY)   A red grape variety.

CESANESE DE AFFILE (ITALY)   A red grape variety of Latium.

CÉSAR (FRANCE)   A red grape variety grown primarily in the Chablis district.

CESTO VINDIMO (PORTUGAL)   *See* Grape-Picking Basket.

CEYLON TEA   A rich and pungent tea from the island of Sri Lanka. It has an intense flavor, pleasant aroma, and bright golden or orange color.

CHÁ (PORTUGAL)   *See* Tea.

CHABLIS (FRANCE)   A grape-growing area that takes its name from the village of Chablis, which is nestled by the side of the Serein River in the northern part of Burgundy. The chalky soil gives the wines of Chablis their clean taste, while fruitiness and a bouquet are contributed by the Chardonnay grape. Chablis is an extremely dry, crisp white wine with a refreshing acidity. By law there are four Chablis: *grand cru, premier cru,* chablis, and *petit chablis.* Chablis is also a generic name for mostly nondescript white wines produced in California and some other parts of the world.

CHAH (INDIA)   *See* Tea.

CHAI (FRANCE)   An above-ground facility for the storage and aging of wines.

CHALK   *See* Calcium Carbonate.

CHALYBON (GREECE)   An ancient wine.

CHAMBERTIN (FRANCE)   A famous *grand cru* vineyard located in the Côte de Nuits area of Burgundy, noted for its exceptional red wines.

CHAMBOLLE-MUSIGNY (FRANCE)   A red wine commune in the Côte de Nuits area of Burgundy, noted for its exceptional red wines. Chambolle was known as *Cambolla* in 1010. In 1875, the village of Chambolle added its name to that of its most illustrious vineyard, Musigny.

CHAMBOURCIN   A red grape variety that was developed in the Rhône Valley of France. Formerly known as *Joannes-Seyve 26205.*

CHAMBRÉ (FRANCE)   Room temperature. Cellars are always cool and red wines, when they are taken out of the cellar, have to be brought to the temperature of the room in which they are to be drunk for proper enjoyment.

CHAMOMILE   A plant (*Anthemis nobilis*) whose dried, daisy-like white flower heads are brewed and used in a medicinal tea. Chamomile has a very powerful, fragrant scent and a calming, antispasmodic effect on the stomach. Also spelled camomile.

CHAMPAGNE   A red grape variety.

CHAMPAGNE (FRANCE)   A sparkling wine produced in the Champagne region and by the *méthode champenoise*, from which it derives its characteristic sparkle from a secondary fermentation in a stoppered bottle. The word "champagne" must be stamped on every cork that is used for a bottle of French champagne. French champagne corks must also contain three layers, usually two solid and one particle-type.

The Champagne region is ninety miles northeast of Paris. A law passed on July 22, 1927, demarcated a zone of that region that, by virtue of its natural characteristics, is capable of supporting the vineyards whose product has the exclusive right to be called champagne. In the United States, the name "champagne" is often used as a generic name for a sparkling wine.

CHAMPAGNE (RUSSIA)   *See* Sparkling Wine.

CHAMPAGNE BOTTLE   The typical bottle of the Champagne region, used for sparkling wines. In shape, it greatly resembles the Burgundy bottle, but it is slightly puffed out in the middle and has an inverted bottom called a *punt* or *kick*. The specifications for the classic champagne bottle were first laid down by order of King Louis XV on March 9, 1735.

CHAMPAGNE GLASSES   *See* Flute-Shaped Glass, Saucer-Shaped Glass, and Tulip-Shaped Glass.

CHAMPAGNE METHOD   *See* Méthode Champenoise.

CHAMPAÑA (SPAIN)   A term, no longer legal, in the making of sparkling wines.

CHAMPANEL   A red grape variety developed by Thomas Volney Munson (1843–1913) of Denison, Texas.

CHAMPANSKI (BULGARIA)   *See* Sparkling Wine.

CHAMPION   A red grape variety.

CHANCELLOR   A red grape variety developed by Louis Seibel near the Burgundy region of France. The grape, although originally developed in the Rhône Valley of France, flourishes in the eastern United States. Formerly known as *Seibel 7053*.

CHANCELLOR SEEDLESS   A red grape variety developed by Dr. Kenneth Hanson at the Mountain Grove Missouri Fruit Substation.

CHANNEL   A lengthwise groove on corks caused by cutting them too close to each other.

CHANNELS OF DISTRIBUTION   Vehicles through which products or services may be marketed by suppliers and/or purchased by consumers.

CHANNEL STRIP   The metal strip on the front edge of a package store shelf; it accommodates inventory and stock numbers, promotional information, and retail price tags.

CHANTEPLEURE (FRANCE)   *See* Wine Thief.

CHAPEAU (FRANCE)   *See* Cap.

CHAPTALIZATION (FRANCE)   In certain wine-producing countries there is sometimes an insufficient amount of sugar present in the grapes at harvest to produce a stable wine. The finished wine would have a very low alcohol level and would thus be unstable for travel and subject to bacterial infestation.

A limited amount of sugar, set by law, can be added to the *must* (unfermented grape juice) prior to or during fermentation when a lack of natural sugar exists. The term *chaptalization* is derived from Dr. Jean-Antoine Chaptal, Comte de Chanteloup (1756–1832), Minister of the Interior and Agriculture and President of the Academy of Science under Napoleon I from 1800 to 1805.

This sugar addition increases the sugar content of the must, producing a higher degree of alcohol. When the fermentation is complete, the wine is dry. The purpose of sugaring the must is only to raise the alcoholic content of the finished wine and has nothing at all to do with producing a wine with noticeable residual sugar. No sugar can ever be added after fermentation. The sugar that has been added for chaptalization must always be completely converted into alcohol during fermentation.

Sugar to be used for chaptalization must be technically clean, noncolored sucrose and must contain at least 99.5 percent fermentable sugar. Sugar containing starch is no longer permitted and the use of syrup is also not permitted. According to European Economic Community regulations, sufficient sugar can be added to increase the alcohol content of a wine by up to 2.5 percent.

Adding sugar to the must is permitted in most grape-growing countries north of the Alps (Austria, Germany, Luxembourg, and Switzerland) and in many northern regions of France, including Alsace, Bordeaux, Burgundy, Champagne, and the Loire Valley. It is also practiced in New York and Oregon, but not in California, Italy, Spain, Portugal, or Greece. Also known as *anreichern, lesegutautbesserung, sucrage, sugaring of wine, sun in sacks*, and *zuccheraggio*. *See* Martin Method and Verbessern.

CHARACTER   Attributes of a wine typical to vintage, soil, climate, and treatment (aging in wood, steel, etc.). Also known as *ausdruck, caractère, carattere, charakter* and *kharaktir*.

That combination of a whiskey's sensory qualities that distinguishes it from another whiskey.

CHARAKTER (GERMANY)   *See* Character.

CHARBONO   A red-skinned grape variety of uncertain origin, but believed to have originated in the Iseré Valley near the foothills of the Alps, between the Italian, French, and Swiss borders. Some ampelographers believe Charbono is possibly Italian or French, related to the Corbeau, Charbonneau, or Douce Noir grape variety. Charbono displays sensory characteristics similar to that of the Barbera grape variety.

CHARCOAL   *See* Activated Charcoal.

CHARCOAL MELLOWED   A term used on whiskey labels to indicate that the distilled spirit has been filtered through charcoal for a smoother taste. *See* Activated Charcoal and Leaching.

CHARDONEL   A white grape variety developed in 1953 from a cross of Seyval and Chardonnay at the State Experimental Station in Geneva, New York.

CHARDONNAY   A major white grape variety acknowledged worldwide as producing some of the finest dry white wines. It is grown extensively in Burgundy and Champagne, France, as well as in most other wine producing countries. In 1934, Wente Brothers Winery of California was the first winery to bottle Chardonnay as a separate varietal.

Chardonnay ranges from pale yellow to medium gold in color, depending on the length of time the wine was aged in both the barrel and bottle. Chardonnay exhibits some of the following odor and taste characteristics: apples (sometimes green apple), butter, clove, coconut, figs, melon, peaches, pears, and pineapples. If barrel-fermented or aged in wood, overtones of caramel, fresh wood, smoke, spice, toasted bread, vanilla, butter, and even butterscotch are often prevalent.

The small village of Chardonnay is nestled among the vineyards, just three miles from the celebrated Romanesque church of Tournus in Burgundy; this, supposedly, is where the grape got its name. Formerly known as *Pinot Chardonnay*.

Chardonnay is known as *Beaunois* in the Chablis district of Burgundy, *Arnaison* in the Touraine district, and *Melon d'Arbois* in the Jura region of France.

CHARENTE *(FRANCE)*　A valley in the southwest, lying in the Cognac region.

CHARGE　Distiller's term meaning a single filling of a pot still prior to heating and distilling.

CHARGE *(FRANCE)*　The number of buds left on grapevine shoots after pruning (generally from four to twelve).

CHARM　*See* Pleasant.

CHARMAT METHOD　Named after its inventor, Eugène Charmat, a French wine scientist who developed the process in 1910 to save both the time and money involved in the classic method of producing sparkling wines. The original Charmat process (which is still, with some modifications, used today) requires three tanks. Still wine is run into the first tank and heated for twelve to sixteen hours, then immediately cooled. This wine is then pumped into a second tank, where yeast and sugar are added. It then ferments for fifteen to twenty days. The wine is then pumped into the third tank, where it is clarified by cooling the tank to about 30 degrees Fahrenheit; this also aids in tartrate stabilization. Finally, the wine is filtered and then bottled under pressure. This method usually produces sparkling wines within one month and is the least expensive of the higher quality methods. Because all of the fermentation takes place in temperature-controlled stainless steel pressurized tanks, bottle breakage is virtually nonexistent. Cooler fermentation allows for greater retention of fresh grapy flavors and the fermentation can be halted at any point by simply chilling the wine. This method is also known as *autoclave, bulk-fermented, bulk process, charmat process, chaussepied, cuve close, gasificado, granvas, metodo charmat, schaumwein, tank method*, and *vino gasificado*.

CHARMAT PROCESS　*See* Charmat Method.

CHARNU *(FRANCE)*　*See* Full-Bodied.

CHARPENTÉ *(FRANCE)*　*See* Full-Bodied.

CHARRING　The burning of the inside of a wooden barrel to be used for wine, whiskey, brandy, or other distilled spirits. The char helps to mellow or age the wine or distilled spirit while at the same time adding coloring matter. The use of charred oak barrels for the aging of whiskey first began in the United States in 1850. Also known as *toasted barrels* and *tostatura*.

CHARTRONS *(FRANCE)*　The name of the quayside in Bordeaux, derived from *Chartreuse* (a French term for the Carthusian monks who at one time occupied the location), where many *négociants* used to have their wine warehouses and offices.

CHASER A slang term for water, seltzer, or even a glass of beer that is drunk immediately after consuming a shot of neat or unmixed distilled spirits.

CHASSAGNE-MONTRACHET (FRANCE) A white wine commune in the Côte de Beaune area of Burgundy. Chassagne was once known as *Cassaneas* in 886 A.D. and as *Chaissaigne* in 1321 A.D. In 1879, the commune of Chassagne added its name to that of its most illustrious vineyard, Montrachet.

CHASSELAS (FRANCE) *See* Chasselas Doré.

CHASSELAS DORÉ (SWITZERLAND) A white grape variety. Also known as *Chasselas, Dorin, Fendant*, and *Gutedel*.

CHÂTEAU (FRANCE) A wine estate, particularly in the Bordeaux region.

CHÂTEAU BOTTLED (FRANCE) Literally, "estate bottled." Wine bottled at an estate, château, or domaine, made from its own grapes. Also known as *Mise en Bouteilles au Château* and *Mise en Bouteilles au Domaine*. *See* Estate Bottled and Domaine Bottled.

CHÂTEAUNEUF-DU-PAPE (FRANCE) This most popular of all Rhône Valley wines is produced out of some 7,500 acres of vineyards. By law Châteauneuf-du-Pape wine must attain a minimum alcoholic content of 12.5 percent and although it can be made from a blend of up to thirteen grape varieties, it is usually a blend of 65 percent Grenache and 35 percent Syrah grapes. The thirteen grapes that are allowed to be used by law are: Bourboulenc, Cinsaut, Clairette, Counoise, Grenache, Mourvèdre, Muscardin, Picardin, Picpoul, Roussanne, Syrah, Terret Noir, and Vaccarèse. A small percentage of white Châteauneuf-du-Pape is produced from a blend of Grenache Blanc, Clairette, Roussanne, and Bourboulenc grape varieties.

The village of Châteauneuf-du-Pape was the summer residence of the papacy from 1309 to 1377, beginning with Archbishop Bertrand de Goth, who had succeeded to the papacy as Pope Clement V. On June 28, 1929, Châteauneuf-du-Pape became the first wine in France to be granted its AOC.

CHAUCHÉ GRIS A white grape variety that is known by different names depending where it is propagated: *Grey Riesling* in California and *Trousseau Gris* (its proper name) in the Jura region of France.

CHAUD (FRANCE) *See* Warmth.

CHAUDIÈRE (FRANCE) The alembic boiler pot. *See* Alembic.

CHAUFFE (FRANCE) The first distillation in the making of cognac.

CHAUSSAGE (FRANCE) A plowing method that heaps the soil onto the row of grapevines. *See* Buttage.

CHAUSSEPIED (FRANCE) *See* Charmat Method.

CHEESE BOARD A board that fits around the screw of an old-fashioned basket winepress and rests directly on top of the grapes. It is shaped like boards used to press cheese.

CHEF DE CAVE (FRANCE) *See* Cellarmaster.

CHEF DE CULTURE (FRANCE) A vineyard manager.

CHEF DE TROUPE (FRANCE)   An experienced grape picker or foreman, generally put in charge of other less experienced pickers. Also known as *mayoral*. *See* Cuadrilla Forestera and Porteur.

CHELOIS   A red grape variety developed in the late 1880s from a cross of Seibel 5163 and Seibel 5593 by Louis Seibel in France, and brought to the United States sometime after World War II. Formerly known as *Seibel 10878*.

CHEMISE   *See* Sediment.

CHEMISE (FRANCE)   Jacketed or wrapped. It refers to the cloth towel servers use to gently wipe the bottle's neck after each and every pouring of wine. It also refers to the cloth placed around a bottle removed from an ice bucket, to pat dry.

CHÉNAS (FRANCE)   A *cru* commune of Beaujolais named after the oak trees (*chêne*) that at one time covered all of the Beaujolais area. They are among the sturdiest of the crus.

CHÊNE (FRANCE)   Oak (as in tree).

CHENEL (SOUTH AFRICA)   A white grape variety developed from a cross of Chenin Blanc and Trebbiano by Professor Chris Orffer. A subvariety of this crossing is known as *Weldra*.

CHENIN BLANC   A white grape variety grown primarily in California and the Loire Valley of France, where it is known as *Blanc d'Anjou* or *Pineau de la Loire*. In 1954, the Charles Krug Winery of Napa Valley, California, was the first winery to offer Chenin Blanc as a separate variety.

　　The taste of wines made from Chenin Blanc grapes can range from bone-dry to semidry and even sweet. Chenin Blanc produces wines that are pleasantly fruity and melonlike, resembling a fresh fruit salad. Also known locally in South Africa as *Steen*.

CHEROKEE   A red grape variety developed by Dr. J. Stayman of Leavenworth, Kansas.

CHERRY   Describes the aroma or taste of cherries found in some light-bodied red wines such as Zinfandel, Gamay Beaujolais, and Pinot Noir.

CHERRY-FLAVORED BRANDY   A mixture of brandy, minimum of 2.5 percent sugar, flavored and colored with small, wild black cherries. By United States federal law it cannot be bottled at less than 60 proof (30 percent alcohol by volume).

CHERRY LIQUEUR   A sweetened alcoholic beverage consisting of a base of alcohol, minimum 2.5 percent sugar, and flavored and colored with small, wild black cherries. It is sweeter and lower in proof than cherry-flavored brandy.

CHERRY SODA   A soft drink usually made with carbonated water, sugar or sweetener, caramel coloring, acids, and a syrup made from small, wild black cherries.

CHERVENO (BULGARIA)   *See* Red.

CHEVRIER (FRANCE)   *See* Sémillon.

CHEWY   Describes wines having a rich texture on the palate, often described as full-bodied, and slightly alcoholic, with greater than average tannin. It is usually accompanied by a strong flavor intensity, creating the impression that flavor particles can actually be sensed or "chewed." Also known as *dusty, mâche*, or *meaty*.

to be extremely sweet.

CHIANTI *(ITALY)*   Geographically and historically, Chianti is an area lying in the hills between Florence and Siena, encompassing the towns of Arezzo, Pistoia, and Pisa in the region of Tuscany. In the heart of this area lies Chianti Classico, the largest of the seven Chianti zones. The historic center of this area belonged to an ancient military league, formed in 1270, called the *lega del Chianti*. Although its primary purpose was to defend both its land and people, it was probably the first organization in the world to establish a wine quality law.

Chianti Classico is the oldest classified wine region in the world. Grapevines were already growing in Tuscany and central Italy when the Etruscans settled there in about the tenth century B.C. and as early as the ninth century B.C. produced wine. Since then, the history of the area has been tumultuous, complex, and illustrious.

Chianti was known as Vermiglio in the latter part of the fourteenth century. While today's Chianti is red, documents of the fourteenth century A.D. (tracing its origin to 1260) call a local white wine Chianti. Baron Ricasoli, descendant of Baron Bettino Ricasoli, has in his possession a document dated June 18, 1696, that is believed to be the certificate of origin for Chianti wine. In 1835, Baron Bettino Ricasoli (1809–1880) developed and defined the grape variety formula for Chianti, consisting of a blend of Sangiovese, Canaiolo Nero, and Malvasia del Chianti grapes. Chianti DOCG virtually eliminates the addition of white grapes and allows the addition of nontraditional grapes such as Cabernet Sauvignon, Merlot, and Cabernet Franc.

A technique known as *governo Toscano* used in making Chianti during Ricasoli's time was to induce a secondary fermentation by the addition of 5 to 10 percent *must*, pressed from selected grapes partly dried on straw mats known as *cannici*. This secondary fermentation took place immediately after the first racking of the wine before December 31. This process produced wines meant for early consumption. Most of the wines made by the *governo* technique were, and still are, bottled in squat bottles covered with straw, called *fiaschi*.

Since 1932 Chianti has been produced in an area encompassing five provinces—Arezzo, Florence, Pisa, Pistoia, and Siena—that is further subdivided into seven areas. These are listed below, with descriptions of their *consorzios'* neck labels:

Chianti Classico: the label shows a black rooster or cock (*consorzio del Marchio Storico*); this was the crest of the thirteenth century Chianti Defense League; first used on May 14, 1924.

Chianti Montalbano: the label shows the Tower of Montalbano.

Chianti Rufina: the label of this *consorzio* (founded in 1927) shows a *putto* (chubby baby cherub).

Chianti Colli Fiorentini: also known as Putto. The label of this *consorzio* (founded in 1927) shows the infant Bacchus, naked and entwined in a grapevine with clusters of purple grapes, a detail from Della Robbia's painting *Hospital of the Innocents*.

Chianti Colli Senesi: the label depicts Romulus and Remus with the she-wolf.

Chianti Colli Aretini: the neck label shows a *chimera*.

Chianti Colline Pisane: the label shows a centaur, or more commonly, the Leaning Tower of Pisa.

CHIANTIGIANA (ITALY)   In Chianti, a one-and-a-half-liter bottle.

CHIARA (ITALY)   *See* Albumen.

CHIARETTO (ITALY)   A lightly colored red wine.

CHIARIFICARE (ITALY)   *See* Fining.

CHIARIFICANTE (ITALY)   *See* Fining Agent.

CHIARO (ITALY)   *See* Clear.

CHIAVENNASCA (ITALY)   The local name used for the Nebbiolo grape variety in the province of Sondrio in the region of Lombardy. *See* Nebbiolo.

CHICHA   A corn-based beer brewed by the ancient Incas.

CHIEF   A red grape variety.

CHIEW   *See* Chiu.

CHILL HAZE   Formed by the bonding of malt protein particles to phenols (also called tannins) in beer. The unsightly haze will settle out during cold storage.

CHILLING A GLASS   Placing a glass in the refrigerator or glass chiller, with or without first wetting it, for the service of beer and cocktails usually served straight up. *See* Glass Chiller and Frosting.

CHILOGRAMMO (ITALY)   *See* Kilogram.

CHIME   The rim or beveled extensions formed by the staves that overlap the heads on a wooden barrel.

CHINCHÓN (SPAIN)   An anise-flavored distilled spirit, often diluted with water and drunk in a tall glass. *See* Anise-Based Spirits.

CHINON (FRANCE)   A red-wine-producing commune in the Loire Valley; however, it also makes a small amount of white and rosé wine. The red is made from the Cabernet Franc, while the white is made from the Chenin Blanc grape.

   Chinon is located on the southern bank of the Loire and both banks of its tributary, the Vienne.

CHIP   An irregular missing piece on a cork.

CHIP BUDDING   *See* Bench Grafting.

CHIROUBLES (FRANCE)   A *cru* commune in Beaujolais producing robust wines of distinctive flavor; however, they mature quickly and should be drunk within a year or two after harvest.

CHIU (CHINA)   Wine. Terms used prior to *chiu* were *Li* or *Chang*. Also known as *chiew*. *See* Wine.

CHLORINE DETERGENT   A powerful bleaching and sterilizing agent utilized for cleaning bottles and equipment.

CHLOROPHYLL   The green pigment found in the chloroplasts of plant cells that absorbs light energy; it is involved in the photosynthesis process. Chlorophyll is also used as a coloring agent. *See* Chloroplasts and Photosynthesis.

CHLOROPLASTS   Microscopic bodies, located within the cells of every green leaf, that store the green pigmentation. *See* Chlorophyll and Photosynthesis.

CHLOROSIS   The fading or yellowing of leaves or other green parts of a grapevine.

CHOCOLACCINO *(ITALY)*   A *cappuccino* served in a tall glass, topped with whipped cream and chocolate shavings.

CHOCOLATE MILK   A dairy beverage made with whole, pasteurized, homogenized milk containing up to 1.5 to 2 percent liquid chocolate plus a sweetener and stabilizer.

CHOCOLATY   A term that conveys the odor and taste components of chocolate, noted in some late-harvested Zinfandels and certain other red wines.

CHRISTINE   *See* Telegraph.

CHUG   A slang term that means to drink the contents of a glass, can, or bottle of beer or wine in large gulps. Also known as *chug-a-lug*. *See* Quaff.

CHURCH KEY   A slang term for a beer bottle opener.

CHURCH WINDOWS *(GERMANY)*   *See* Legs.

CIDER   A beverage made from freshly pressed apples or apple juice that may or may not be fermented, without added sugar. It can be nonalcoholic or alcoholic and it may contain carbon dioxide. Cider may be still or sparkling, sweet or dry. *See* Apple Juice, Apple Wine, Hard Cider, and Sweet Cider.

Most countries that produce cider utilize their own spelling versions:

Australia	*Cyder*	England	*Cyder*
France	*Sidre*	Greece	*Sikera*
Hebrew	*Shekar*	Latin	*Sicera*
Spain	*Sidra*		

CIDER PRESS   A machine that presses the juice out of apples for making cider.

CIDERY   An undesirable aroma or flavor caused by bacterial infestation, occasionally found in spoiled beer. It resembles apple cider, a trait of Prohibition-style home brew.

CILIEGIOLO *(ITALY)*   A red grape variety.

CINSAULT   *See* Cinsaut.

CINSAUT   A red grape variety grown in many parts of the world, producing deeply colored, full-bodied wines with good acidity and a distinctive, fruity taste. Also known as *Blue Imperial, Espagne, Hermitage, Oeillade, Ottavianello, Picardan Noir,* and *Plant d'Arles.* Also spelled *Cinsault.*

CISTERN   A large receptacle used for storing newly distilled spirits.

CITRIC ACID   Acid found most notably in citrus fruits in varying quantities and also present, although in lesser quantity, in grapes. As an additive in the production of alcoholic beverages, it is controlled by regulations and may only be used in certain circumstances and in certain quantities. It has the beneficial property of combining with iron in the wine. An excess of iron causes a type of clouding called *iron haze*; however, citric acid forms a soluble compound with the iron, preventing the formation of this clouding. It should only be added to the finished wine. *See* Casse and Cufex.

CITRUS   A family of fruits characterized by a high level of citric acid: black currants, boysenberries, elderberries, figs, grapefruit, lemons, limes, oranges, red currants, strawberries, and white currants.

CITRUS DESSERT WINE   *See* Citrus Fruit Dessert Wine.

CITRUS FRUIT DESSERT WINE   A citrus wine having an alcoholic content of more than 14 percent but not in excess of 24 percent by volume. Also known as *citrus dessert wine.*

CITRUS FRUIT TABLE WINE   A citrus wine having an alcoholic content not in excess of 14 percent by volume. Such wine may also be designated "light citrus wine," "light citrus fruit wine," and so forth. Also known as *citrus table wine.*

CITRUS FRUIT WINE   A wine produced by the normal alcoholic fermentation of the juice of sound, ripe citrus fruit with or without the addition, after fermentation, of pure condensed citrus *must,* and with or without added citrus brandy or alcohol, but without any other addition or abstraction. Also known as *citrus wine.*

CITRUSY   A characteristic of certain white wines that is similar to citrus fruits, such as high acidity and some tartness.

CITRUS TABLE WINE   *See* Citrus Fruit Table Wine.

CITRUS WINE   *See* Citrus Fruit Wine.

CIVB   *See* Conseil Interprofessionnel du Vin de Bordeaux.

CIVC   *See* Comité Interprofessionnel du Vin de Champagne.

CLADOSPORIUM CELLARE   *See* Torula.

CLAIR (FRANCE)   *See* Clear.

CLAIRET (FRANCE)   A red wine fermented for a relatively short period of time and having a somewhat deeper color than rosé.

CLAIRETTE BLANC (FRANCE)   A white grape variety grown primarily in the southeast. Also known as *Blanquette.*

CLARET   The British name for Bordeaux red wines, derived from an old French adjective meaning a wine that was clear, light, and bright enough to be distinguished from other red wines. Claret supposedly derives from the Earl of Clare, who served under Henry II of England (1154–1189), although there is some evidence to suggest that claret was first used about 1565, thus dispelling the Earl of Clare story.

CLARETE (PORTUGAL AND SPAIN)   A term that applies to wines made from a mixture of either red and white grapes that experiences part of its fermentation in the presence of the skins of red grapes. The fermentation in contact with red grape skins generally gives the clarete a deeper color and more robust flavor than the *rosado.* Although these two wines may often have similar hue, normally rosados are pink to very light red, while claretes vary from light red to red. Also known as *vinho clarete* and *vino clarete. See* Rosé Wine.

CLARIFY   *See* Clarifying.

CLARIFYING   The process of making a wine, beer, or distilled spirit clear or free of haze by means of a fining or filtering agent. Also to clean up a wine by causing a settlement of the minute particles that had made it cloudy or unclear. Other clarification methods may include cold-stabilization and racking. Also known as *clarify*. *See* Filtering, Fining, and Sterile Filtration.

CLARITY   The relative brilliance or absence of haze in beer or wine. In general, persistent hazes are due to very small particles ranging in diameter from 0.005 to 0.00005 millimeters. Larger-sized particles also cause haze, but they usually settle out rapidly.

CLARO (SPAIN)   *See* Clear.

CLASS   Generic classification of alcoholic beverages used in the Universal Numeric Code (UNIMERC), the primary statistical code identifying brands and vendors in the alcoholic beverage industry. A class may be further divided into types. Whiskey, gin, vodka, rum, brandy, liqueurs, cocktails, and tequila are the separate classes for *distilled spirits*. *See* Type.

CLASSÉ (FRANCE)   A classified wine; a wine purported to be a high quality wine.

CLASSEMENT (FRANCE)   Classification.

CLASSIC   A term often used to describe alcoholic beverages; it has no legal meaning.

CLASSIC METHODS/CLASSIC VARIETIES (CMCV)   A group of California sparkling wine producers that formed an alliance that maintains high standards in the making of sparkling wines.

CLASSICO (ITALY)   A geographic term applied to DOC or DOCG wines and referring to the central or original area of a production zone.

CLASSIFICATION OF 1855   The classification of 1855 applies to the wines of the Médoc (with the exception of Château Haut-Brion, in Graves) and the wines of Sauternes and Barsac in France.

   In the Médoc, the classification divides the sixty-two great vineyards into five categories, known as *crus* or "growths," according to their recognized quality in 1855, based on the prices obtainable for their wine at that time (a first-growth or *premier cru* vineyard, for instance, is of the highest quality, and a fifth-growth one or *cinquième cru*, the lowest). The Bordeaux Wine Classification of April 18, 1855, was established under the sponsorship of Emperor Napoleon III, who wanted to showcase the classification at the 1855 Paris Exposition (World's Fair).

CLASSIFIED GROWTHS (FRANCE)   The sixty-two red wines and twenty-five white sweet wines (from Bordeaux) that were classified in 1855 according to quality and price. A similar classification was done in 1953 in Graves and in 1954 in Saint-Émilion.

CLAVELIN (FRANCE)   A special bottle, squat in shape, used for wines of the Jura district.

CLAY   A type of soil that, due to its density, compactness, and resultant poor drainage, retains too much moisture, especially during the early spring and just prior to harvest. There is also a problem of excessive bulk density that hampers good root penetration. Because of the problem of bulk density, roots are unable to obtain sufficient oxygen and often lie in the waterlogged soil for days on end. Also known as *argile*.

CLEAN   Describes a beverage that is free from bacterial and processing defects. Also indicates the absence of any unpleasant odor or taste. Also known as *net, nett, netto, pulito, reintönig,* and *sauber*.

CLEAN TASTE   A taste that is palatable, agreeable, and refreshing; free from off aroma or taste.

CLEAR   A term applied to wines or beers that are perfectly clear and brilliant, with no suspended solids or cloudiness. Often referred to as *crystal-clear*. Also known as *chiaro, clair, claro, klar, limpid*, and *vin clair*. *See* Brilliant.

CLEFT GRAFTING   A method of grapevine propagation that gives more strength to the grapevine and hastens the maturing of grapes. The propagation is accomplished by joining branches of a grapevine called a scion (a short section of the stem) with a diameter of one-half inch to two inches to an understock in such a manner that the two grow together and continue development as a single plant without change in stock or scion.

CLEVNER *(FRANCE)*   *See* Pinot Blanc.

CLIENTELE   Patrons who are served inside a beverage facility.

CLIFTON'S CONSTANTIA   *See* Alexander.

CLIMAT *(FRANCE)*   A vineyard; as used in Burgundy, it defines a single field or plot in a vineyard or even a single vineyard, as in a "single-vineyard" designation.

CLINTON   A red grape variety, whose origin is unknown, although it can be traced back to 1815 to Hamilton College, New York.

CLOETA   A red grape variety developed by Thomas Volney Munson (1843–1913) of Denison, Texas.

CLONAL SELECTION (CERTIFIED PLANTS)   This entails *genetic clonal selection* (e.g., the search for intravarietal genetic variability in a given grapevine population) and *sanitary clonal selection*, with reference to dangerous viral infections. Clonal selection is far more rigorous than selection in the mass and it entails quantitative control over the principal parameters of quality.

CLONE   A particular strain of grape variety that developed either slowly, through natural adaptation, to a set of growing conditions, or asexually, propagated vegetatively from an original mother grapevine at a viticultural research institute. A plant genetically identical to all its siblings. One mother grapevine, through careful propagation, can produce thousands of perfect replicas. A clone is selected for its special viticultural and wine merits (productivity, adaptability to particular growing conditions, and wine quality).

CLONING   The process by which clones are propagated.

CLOROSE *(PORTUGAL)*   *See* Floral Abortion.

CLOS *(FRANCE)*   An enclosure or field; similar to the word *château* and used throughout France.

CLOS DE VOUGEOT *(FRANCE)*   *See* Vougeot.

CLOSED IN   Describes a condition present in some young wines, especially reds, which have not yet come together and are still displaying youthful characteristics. Also known as *closed up, tight*, and *verschlossen*. *See* Dumb and Numb.

CLOSED UP   *See* Closed In.

CLOSURE   Corks, crown caps, screw caps, and any other devices that seal bottles of wine, beer, or distilled spirits.

CLOUDINESS A state, often characteristic of wines of low alcoholic content, in which some albuminous substances refuse to settle.

CLOUDY Describes wines and beers containing excess colloidal material, protein instability, yeast spoilage, refermentation in the bottle, or sediment in suspension, which impairs the clarity. The wine or beer appears hazy and dull. Also known as *blind, hazy, louche*, and *nube*.

CLOUDY A temporary condition of beer exposed to temperatures below 34 degrees Fahrenheit for prolonged periods of time.

CLOYING A term applied to a sweet, often tiresome wine, which lacks acidity and is unbalanced and flabby. Also known as *dick, doucereux*, and *stucchevole*.

CLUB SODA Ordinary water that has been filtered, artificially carbonated, and has had mineral salts added for flavoring. *See* Seltzer.

CLUMPING *See* Flocculation.

CLUSTER A bunch of grapes, during maturation and prior to harvesting. Also known interchangeably as *bunch*. Also known as *grappe, racimo*, and *weintraube*.

CLUSTER THINNING *See* Crop Thinning.

CM (FRANCE) *See* Cooperative de Manipulant.

CMCV *See* Classic Methods/Classic Varieties.

COA (MEXICO) The long pole utilized for harvesting the matured agave heart used in making tequila.

COAN (GREECE) An ancient wine.

COARSE *See* Rough.

COARSE SALT Salt used for drinks that call for their glass rims to be salted. Also known as *kosher salt*. *See* Salt.

COASTER A small disk or napkin placed under a glass or bottle to protect a table or other surface.

COBBLER A tall iced drink containing fruit juices, wines, or distilled spirits, and decorated with pieces of fruit and laden generously with ice.

COBWEBS Often found in old wine cellars, cobwebs are really fungi that have been nurtured by alcohol fumes.

COCEDERO (SPAIN) *See* Wine Cellar.

COCHINEAL A red dye sometimes used in the nineteenth century by the French to darken the wines of Bordeaux.

COCHYLIS A disease of grapevines.

COCKTAIL A class of alcoholic beverages that is derived by mixing one or more of the other classes (whiskey, gin, vodka, rum, brandy, liqueurs, wine, or beer) with or without flavorings, eggs, nonalcoholic beverages, juices, or water. Also known as a *mixed drink*.

In 1776, Betsy Flanagan invented the American cocktail. It was in her bar, Halls Corners, in Elmsford, New York, which was decorated with brightly-colored tail feathers of cocks, that she had the notion to add a cock's tail feather as a stirrer to each drink. Hence the name cocktail. During that time, cocktails were often referred to as "roosters."

COCKTAIL GLASS   A squat-shaped bar glass, usually holding four to seven ounces.

COCKTAIL LOUNGE   A facility that offers customers the opportunity to have an alcoholic beverage. *See* Bar, Inn, Pub, Saloon, and Tavern.

COCKTAIL MIX STATION   A side bar equipped with ice compartments, condiment trays, and speed racks containing both distilled spirits and mixers, used for the preparation of cocktails. Also known as *stationary bar*.

COCKTAIL NAPKIN   A small square paper napkin usually served along with a cocktail. Used as an underliner or coaster.

COCKTAIL STRAINER   A perforated stainless steel spoon or a round, metal-handled strainer often surrounded by a flexible metal coil or wire spring, with ears that fit over the rim of a shaking glass, used for straining certain cocktails that contain seeds, fruit, pulp, or ice. Also known as *bar strainer* or *strainer*.

COCKTAIL SHERRY   An American term for a dry sherry wine from Spain or the United States, presumably an Amontillado rather than the bone dry Fino sherry. Also known as *dry sherry*.

COCKTAIL TRAY   A circular or oval tray, generally ten or twelve inches in diameter, used to serve drinks. It is usually cork-lined to prevent the glasses from slipping.

COCOA   Powder made from cocoa seeds that has been roasted and ground, with some of the fat removed; pulverized chocolate. The process was developed in 1828 by Conrad J. van Houten, who pressed vegetable fat from the liquor paste prepared from cocoa beans.

COCOA   A drink made by adding sugar and hot water or milk to cocoa powder.

COCONUT LIQUEUR   A sweetened alcoholic beverage consisting of a base of alcohol, minimum 2.5 percent sugar, and flavored and colored with the juice or milk of fresh coconuts.

COCQUARD (FRANCE)   The traditional champagne wine press; it is quite shallow, which allows the grapes to be spread out in a thin layer, reducing skin contact and limiting color extraction. *See* Marc of Grapes and Wine Press.

CODA DI VOLPE (ITALY)   *See* Pallagrello.

CÓDEGA (PORTUGAL)   A white grape variety grown in the Douro region.

COFFEE   A dark brown, aromatic drink made by brewing in water the roasted and ground bean-like seeds of a tall tropical evergreen shrub (genus *Coffea*) of the Madder family. Each small tree yields about two thousand berries a year, enough for a pound of roasted coffee beans.

In its two most widely cultivated species—the Arabica (high grown, high quality) and the Robusta (hardier, lower grown, mostly in Africa)—coffee comes in about one hundred different varieties. The individual characteristics are determined by many factors, such as the original strain, soil conditions, climate, growing altitudes, and preparation. Also known as *café*, *caffè*, *kaffee*, and *Kahve*.

COFFEE BREAK   A brief work stoppage or break where workers usually drink coffee or other refreshments.

COFFEE-FLAVORED BRANDY   A mixture of brandy with a minimum of 2.5 percent sugar, flavored and colored with coffee beans. By federal law it cannot be bottled at less than 60 proof (30 percent alcohol by volume).

COFFEE GRINDER   A machine that grinds the roasted coffee beans prior to brewing. Also called a *coffee mill*.

COFFEE HOUSE   A place where coffee and other refreshments are served and people gather to socialize.

COFFEE LIQUEUR   A sweetened alcoholic beverage consisting of a base of alcohol, minimum 2.5 percent sugar, flavored and colored with coffee beans. It is sweeter and lower in proof than coffee-flavored brandy.

COFFEE MILL   *See* Coffee Grinder.

COFFEE POT   A container (glass, ceramic, metal, etc.) with a lid and spout used to brew and serve coffee.

COFFEE URN   A large pot with a capacity of up to 150 gallons, in which coffee is brewed by pumping hot water over ground coffee beans.

COFFEY STILL   A type of still named after Aeneas Coffey, Inspector-General of Irish Excise, who invented the *continuous* still and was granted a patent for it in 1832. Prior to that, all distillations took place in *pot stills*. *See* Column Still, Continuous Still, Patent Still, and Still.

COGNAC (FRANCE)   A brandy-producing region located in the departments of Charente and Charente Maritime (which were established in 1791 by combining the provinces of Aunis, Saintonge, and Angoumois), approximately 315 miles southwest of Paris. The Cognac region's stony, chalk-rich soil (due to ancient oyster beds), its climate, and the specific grape varieties grown there, as well as the methods used in distilling, blending, and aging, give cognac its unique flavor. The grape varieties utilized are St-Emilion (known as *Ugni Blanc* in California and France and *Trebbiano* in Italy), Folle Blanche, and Colombard, which make for an exceedingly acidic white wine.

In 1936, the French government officially divided the delimited Cognac region into seven sections (the Bois Ordinaires and Bois à Terroir are usually grouped together; there is thus sometimes confusion over whether there are six or seven districts). The seven sections, which very roughly describe concentric circles around the town of Cognac, are Grande Champagne; Petite Champagne; Borderies; Fin Bois; Bon Bois; and Bois Ordinaire and Bois à Terroir (also called Bois à Communs). The highest quality cognacs are produced in Grande Champagne and Petite Champagne.

From 1946 until 1986, French law prohibited a vintage date on a bottle of cognac. In 1987 this prohibition was lifted. Also known as *Coñac*.

COGNITELLA (ITALY)   An ancient, big-bellied terra-cotta jug used until 1589 for the service of wine. *See* Fojetta.

COING (FRANCE)   A fruit brandy made from quince in Alsace.

COLA   An African tree (*Cola nitida*) of a family whose seeds or nuts contain caffeine and yield an extract used in soft drinks. Also known as *kola*.

COLA   A soft drink usually made with carbonated water, sugar or sweetener, caffeine, caramel coloring, acids, and a cola flavoring derived from the extract of cola seeds or nuts.

COLA DE PESCADO (SPAIN)   *See* Isinglass.

COLARES (PORTUGAL)   A white-wine-producing region located in the south. This region is probably one of the most difficult places in the world to grow grapes. The principal grapevine, Ramisco, must be planted in clay, fifteen feet below the surface of the sandy soil of the wind-blasted shores of the Atlantic Ocean. Cone-shaped holes, several yards across, are dug down through the sand by workers who wear baskets over their heads to allow them to breathe in the event of a cave-in. After planting, the grapevines are covered with sand. When the grapevine breaks the sand's surface, bamboo palisades and stone walls have to be built around to protect it against constant ocean gales. This is why so precious little wine is produced in this region and why it is so expensive.

COLD BOX   A large room where champagne and sparkling wines are placed to prepare for disgorging; it is pre-chilled to 35 degrees Fahrenheit.

COLD BOX   A large, walk-in cooler room kept at temperatures between 34 to 40 degrees Fahrenheit where beer, wine, and other beverages are often stored. Also known as *keg refrigerator* and *walk-in refrigerator*.

COLD DUCK   *Kalte Ende* means "cold ending" and is the name that identified this blend of red and white wines rumored to have been concocted by an eighteenth century German Baron. When it was introduced into the United States, the name was slightly changed to Kalte Ente, meaning cold duck.

COLD FERMENTATION   A method usually employed for making white wines. The grape juice is fermented at temperatures colder than traditional (below 55 degrees Fahrenheit), which retains much of the fruit, aroma, and varietal character of the grape.

COLD FILTERED   *See* Cold Stabilization.

COLD HARDINESS   The ability of the grapevine to resist injury during exposure to low temperature. The survival capability of a specified tissue of a grapevine following a specified exposure to a low temperature.

COLD INJURY   The killing by low temperature of some portion of the grapevine. Seriousness of cold injury is the amount of decrease in fruit production or fruit quality resulting from cold injury.

COLD METHOD   *See* Maceration.

COLD ONE   A slang term for a beer.

COLD PAN   After champagne or sparkling wines are pre-chilled to 35 degrees Fahrenheit, the bottle is placed, neck down, in the *bac à glâce*, which contains a brine bath at −20 degrees Fahrenheit. This freezes the neck of the bottle to a depth of about one inch, trapping the sediment in ice.

COLD STABILIZATION   A clarification technique that involves lowering the temperature to 25 to 30 degrees Fahrenheit from one to three weeks. The cold encourages the potassium bitartrate and other insoluble solids to crystallize and precipitate, rendering the wine or beer clear. These tartrates are actually tasteless and harmless and are

COLD TENDERNESS   The opposite of cold hardiness.

COLHEITA *(PORTUGAL)*   Basically an aged tawny port, Colheita is another term often used to denote a "port of (year)." Colheita ports must be a minimum of seven years of age prior to bottling.

COLLA DI PESCE *(ITALY)*   *See* Isinglass.

COLLAGE *(FRANCE)*   *See* Fining.

COLLAR OF FOAM   A brewer's term for the froth or creamy head that sits on top of a glass of beer. *See* Foam and Coney Island Head.

COLLE *(ITALY)*   Slope or hillside where grapes grow. Also known as *collina*.

COLLER *(FRANCE)*   *See* Fining.

COLLI *(ITALY)*   Hills.

COLLINA *(ITALY)*   *See* Colle.

COLLINE *(ITALY)*   Lower hills (than *colli*).

COLLINS   Tall, cool drinks (part of the punch family) that contain gin or vodka, lemon juice, sugar, and carbonated water. Called Tom (with gin) and John (with vodka).

COLLINS GLASS   A tall, narrow glass with a capacity of twelve to fourteen ounces.

COLLIO *(ITALY)*   A wine-producing area within the region of Friuli-Venezia Giulia. *See* Friuli-Venezia Giulia.

COLLI ORIENTALI DEL FRIULI *(ITALY)*   A wine-producing area within the region of Friuli-Venezia Giulia. *See* Friuli-Venezia Giulia.

COLLOIDAL SUSPENSION   A state that exists in liquids when certain semisolid and albuminous particles remain suspended. *See* Particle Matter.

COLLOIDS   A solid, gelatinous substance, made up of very small, insoluble, nondiffusible particles (as single large molecules or masses of smaller molecules) that are noncrystalline and semisolid, which remains suspended or dispersed in a surrounding liquid medium of different matter. Examples are gums, pectic substances, and proteins that, as hydrocolloids, cause hazing. They carry minute electrical charges.

COLMATURA *(ITALY)*   *See* Topping.

COLOBEL   A red grape variety that contains red-colored juice. Formerly known as *Seibel 8357*.

COLOGNE SPIRITS   *See* Neutral Spirits.

COLOMBARD   A white grape variety grown primarily in California as a blending grape and in France for making both cognac and armagnac. Colombard grape was brought to California some time in the 1870s. Colombard produces a fairly thin wine with high fixed acidity and a lively applelike flavor, which makes it ideal for distillation. It is also known as *French Colombard* and *Pied Tendre*.

COLOMBIA   A major coffee bean-growing region located in South America.

COLOMBIER (FRANCE)   See Sémillon.

COLOR   Each wine has its own "right" color that is correct for each wine type. Golden or amber is right for many dessert wines, but not for dry, white table wines. Whites can be yellow, gold, or straw color, but are flawed if they're too dark or too "water white." Rosés or blush wines should be distinctly pink with only a suggestion of orange or red. Reds can have violet hints if young and amber tints if aged. Brown is a flaw, as is too little red color. Also known as *colore* and *couleur*.

COLORE (ITALY)   See Color.

COLORINO (ITALY)   A red grape variety grown primarily in Tuscany.

COLTIVAZIONE BIOLOGICA (ITALY)   See Organically-Grown Wine.

COLUMN STILL   Two cylindrical columns (about forty to fifty feet high) fitted with a system of interconnecting steam-heated tubes. The alcoholic liquid is fed into the tubes, where it is distilled, redistilled, and taken off as highly concentrated and purified alcohol. *See* Coffey Still, Continuous Still, and Still.

COME-IN   Full-year forecast made for the current uncompleted fiscal year.

COMITÉ INTERPROFESSIONNEL DU VIN DE CHAMPAGNE (CIVC) (FRANCE) The interprofessional organization, founded in 1941, which consolidates relations between growers and producers and does considerable work for the champagne community.

COMMANDARIA (GREECE)   A fortified dessert wine from Cyprus, originally known as *Nama*. According to the historian Hesiod (eighth century B.C.), Nama was referred to as "the sweet wine of Cyprus," made from sun-exposed grapes. Worshipers of Aphrodite, the Goddess of Love who emerged from the waves off Cyprus, celebrated with "Cyprus Nama," said to be one of the oldest known wines in history.

Commandaria is reputed to be one of the longest-lived of all wines and will often display a *solera date* on its label.

COMMERCIANTE (ITALY)   See Broker.

COMMISSIONAIRE (FRANCE)   See Broker.

COMMON   Also known as *común, consumo, vinho consumo*, and *vino común*. *See* Ordinary.

COMMON CARRIER   See Carrier.

COMMUNE (FRANCE)   A town, village, district, vineyard area, or subdivision of a vineyard. Also known as *finage*.

COMPAGNONS DU BEAUJOLAIS (FRANCE)   The name of a wine brotherhood in Beaujolais that was formed in 1947 to promote its wines.

COMPLET (FRANCE)   See Complete.

COMPLETE   Describes a full, total, satisfying, and well-made beverage, with all the necessary constituents of quality. Also known as *complet, completo*, and *plein*.

COMPLETO (ITALY)   See Complete.

COMPLEX   Describes a wine that is multifaceted, containing many elements—acids, alcohols, fruits, tannins, and others—that harmonize, while each reveals its own subtle or difficult to detect character. Also known as *synthetos*.

COMPLEXITY   The various elements that make up bouquet, aroma, and taste in a wine. When a wine is described as having the aroma of fresh peaches or apples, it is displaying some of its complexities.

COMPOSITION CORK   *See* Agglomerated Cork.

COMPOUNDER   A machine that blends liqueurs.

COMPTE D'AGE (FRANCE)   On September 1, in the year following the harvest, cognac and armagnac receive the designation Zero (Compte 0); the following September 1, it receives the designation, One (Compte 1). Thus there are six registers of age for cognac and armagnac, from zero to five years. Cognac or armagnac that is more than five years old remain in the Compte 5 register.

COMPUTED COST   The adjusted cost of a product after trimming or fabrication.

COMTE (FRANCE)   Count.

COMTESSA (GERMANY)   A white grape variety developed in Siebeldingen from a cross of Madeleine Angevine and Gewürztraminer.

COMÚN (SPAIN)   *See* Ordinary.

COMUNE (ITALY)   A white grape variety.

COÑAC (SPAIN)   *See* Cognac.

CONCENTRATE   *See* Grape Concentrate.

CONCENTRATO (ITALY)   *See* Grape Concentrate.

CONCIA (ITALY)   A mixture of both cooked and fortified wines used in making some marsala wines. *See* Cooked Wine and Mistelle.

CONCIMAZIONE (ITALY)   Fertilizing.

CONCORD   A red grape variety with a rather tough skin that separates readily from the pulpy flesh (slipskin). It produces wines that are low in sugar content, with deep color and a fruity, *foxy*, grapy aroma and slightly tangy taste. The grapevine, named after Concord, Massachusetts, was first grown in September 1843 by Ephraim Wales Bull (1806–1895).

CONCORD SEEDLESS   A red grape variety developed at the New York State Experimental Station from an unknown origin.

CONDENSED MILK   A thick, sweetened milk made by evaporating part of the water from whole milk and adding a sweetener. Also known as *condensed sweetened milk*.

CONDENSED SWEETENED MILK   *See* Condensed Milk.

CONDENSER   A part of a distilling apparatus that converts the hot alcohol vapors into a liquid, called a *distillate*. Also known as *condenser coil*.

CONDENSER COIL   *See* Condenser.

CONDIMENTS   Seasonings, liquids, garnishes, or other ingredients used to *finish* or flavor a drink. Some examples are Tabasco sauce or other hot pepper sauce, Worcestershire sauce, bitters (Angostura and orange), olives, onions, nutmeg, vanilla, cloves, cinnamon, cinnamon sticks, and others.

CONDIMENT TRAY   A plastic, multicompartment tray with a plastic dust cover used for storage of most garnishes used in cocktails.

CONDITION   An assessment of a wine or beer by olfactory evaluation as well as chemical analyses to determine the relative health of the product.

CONDITIONING   A process by which new wooden barrels are thoroughly washed internally with mild alkaline solutions, such as soda ash, then rinsed with hot water. This is often done to lower or soften the tannin levels and to eliminate the raw taste often associated with wines aged in brand new wood.

CONDOM (FRANCE)   A city southeast of Bordeaux that is the center of the armagnac trade.

CONDRIEU (FRANCE)   A white-wine producing village located south of Côte Rôtie in the Rhône Valley.

CONEY ISLAND HEAD   A slang term for a beer that contains all or almost all foam. Characteristic of some beers poured by unscrupulous purveyors in Coney Island, Brooklyn, New York during the 1940s and 1950s. *See* Foam.

CONFRADÍAS (SPAIN)   Wine fraternities.

CONFRÉRIE (FRANCE)   A grape-growers' wine society.

CONFRÉRIE DES CHEVALIERS DU TASTEVIN (FRANCE)   Order of Burgundian Wine Lovers, founded in 1934 by George Faiveley and Camille Rodier. This world-famous Burgundy wine brotherhood has its headquarters at Clos de Vougeot.

CONGENERS   Trace-flavoring constituents vaporized off with the alcohol in distillation above 190 proof and developed and expanded during the aging process.

Congeners, which are produced during the fermenting process, are made up of fusel oils, esters, tannins, acids, aldehydes, and so on. In proper proportion with other elements, these components contribute to palatability and create the characteristic aroma, body, and taste of a particular distilled spirit. When the spirit is distilled at a lower proof, more congeners are present and the spirit will possess more character.

CONICAL   A grape cluster shaped with upper shoulders and an elongated apex.

CONIFERS   Any order of evergreen trees or shrubs, such as pine, spruce, fir, and so on, occasionally used for wine barrels.

CONQUISTADOR   A red grape variety released in 1983 by the University of Florida.

CON RETROGUSTO (ITALY)   With aftertaste.

CONSEIL INTERPROFESSIONNEL DU VIN DE BORDEAUX (CIVB) (FRANCE) (Professional Trade Council for Bordeaux Wine). Created on August 18, 1948, it acts in cooperation with wine growers and shippers to organize and direct the wine market, control quality, and promote Bordeaux wines.

CONSEJO REGULADOR (SPAIN)   The regulatory board (denominación de origen) of a specific region governing the production and quality control regulations and all wine produced within that region. It also helps in the promotion of its wines.

CONSOLIDATING BOTTLES   The practice of consolidating or mixing together similar types and brands of distilled spirits or wine in on-premise facilities. Federal law bars tampering with the contents of alcoholic beverages. Containers may not be refilled and contents of alcoholic beverages must remain exactly as received from the manufacturer or wholesaler. Partially emptied bottles may never be consolidated. Distilled spirits may only be kept in the licensed premises in the original containers as received from the wholesaler or manufacturer. Also known as *marrying bottles* or *refilling*.

CONSORTIA SEAL (ITALY)   Label of a growers consortium.

CONSORZIO (ITALY)   A consortium of wine producers.

CONSORZIO TUTELA (ITALY)   Local growers association.

CONSTANTIA   *See* Alexander.

CONSUMER COUPONS   Discounts available to customers by either a mail-in rebate coupon to a central clearing house or a cash discount at time of purchase (refund coupon), offered by retailer. *See* Rebate and Refund.

CONSUMER OFFER   Premium offer available for case and/or proof of purchase. Also known as *premium*.

CONSUMO (PORTUGAL)   *See* Common.

CONSUMPTION   The intake of beverages, either alcoholic or nonalcoholic.

CONTADINO (ITALY)   Peasant farmers, usually owning a few vineyards.

CONTAINER   A receptacle, regardless of the material from which it is made, used to store wine or to remove wine from wine premises. *See* Bulk Container.

CONTE (ITALY)   Count or earl.

CONTENTS   What is contained or how much liquid is inside a bottle, can, or other container used for beverages. Also known as *contenuto* and *inhalt*.

CONTENUTO (ITALY)   *See* Contents.

CONTINENTAL CLIMATE   One that has higher highs and lower lows and more extremes in temperature than does a maritime climate.

CONTINENTAL CONGRESS   The First Continental Congress (1774) met at the City Tavern in Philadelphia, Pennsylvania.

CONTINUOUS STILL   There are basically two types of stills used for distilling: the pot still and the continuous still. The continuous still is often referred to as a column still, Coffey still, and even erroneously as a patent still. The continuous still provides a continuous inflow of distilling liquid, which greatly boosts volume while saving considerable time. It generally does not produce the same high quality as the pot still. *See* Coffey Still, Column Still, and Still.

CONTRACT-BREWS   Beers made according to the specific recipes of the individual owners by established breweries. By contracting for a brewing, a microbrewery's costs are kept low. The major expenses for contract-brews are product packaging, marketing, and advertising.

CONTROLLED BY   Refers to property on which the bottling winery has the legal right to perform, and does perform, all of the acts common to viticulture under the terms of a lease or similar agreement of at least three years. *See* Estate Bottled.

CONTROLLED BY

CONTROLLABLE COSTS *See* Variable Costs.

CONTROLS Built-in methods for measuring performance or product against standards.

CONTROL STATE In the United States, a state in which all alcoholic beverages (retail off-premise) must be purchased from state-owned *liquor* stores. Currently, there are eighteen control states, plus Montgomery County, Maryland, that monopolize the wholesale function. Also known as a *monopoly state. See* License State.

CONTROL STATE PROFITS In the United States, revenue from the state sale of distilled spirits based on the state markup formula, but exclusive of state excise and sales taxes and less the costs of goods and operation.

CONVEX A leaf shape of a grape, with the outer edges turned downward.

CONVENTO *(ITALY)* Convent.

COOKED The odor or flavor exhibited by some wines, made from grapes, *must,* or wine, which have been exposed to heat, as in the cooking process known as *estufagem,* necessary for making madeira wines. Also known as *goût de cuit* and *gusto rancio. See* Baked, Cooked Wine, and Maderized.

COOKED WINE The concentrating of grape juice (*must*) by heating or boiling down. The cooking evaporates the water from the natural juice and enriches sugar and flavor content. During this time the must becomes thick, sweet, and caramel-like, and is often used to color or sweeten certain wines. Also known as *amuado, arrobo, arrope, calamich, cotto, cuit, defrutum, galant, hepsema, sancocho, sapa, vin cuit,* and *vino cotto. See* Concia, Cooked, Gusto Rancio, Maderized, Oxidation, and Surdo.

COOKER A vessel that allows heating and boiling of the mash in the making of beer.

COOKING WINES During Prohibition in the United States, wineries choosing to remain in business either sold bulk grapes, grape juice, wine tonics, or sacramental wines, or completely circumvented the law by producing cooking wines (taking perfectly sound wines and judiciously adding salt and other seasonings, rendering them unfit for consumption as a beverage). Since the repeal of Prohibition, cooking wines are still made and sold both to industry restaurants and supermarkets. Some restaurants actually made it a practice to add salt to wines designed to be used in cooking to discourage the help from consuming them. Also known as *kitchen wine.* According to the BATF, cooking wines must be labeled *Nonbeverage Cooking Wines* or *Not For Sale Or Consumption As Beverage Wines. See* Salted Wine.

COOLER ROOM *See* Cold Box.

COOLERS *See* Low-Alcohol Refreshers.

COOPER Experienced craftsman who makes wooden barrels by hand. Also known as *couper, cuper, tonelero,* and *tonnelier.*

COOPERAGE All containers, sizes, and materials, from wood to stainless steel, used for fermenting, holding, or aging beer, wine, brandy, and distilled spirits while in the cellar and prior to bottling.

COOPERATIVA *(SPAIN)* *See* Cooperative.

COOPERATIVE A winery or cellar owned and operated jointly by many small producers or growers. It is a method of pooling together resources such as labor, costs, vinification, storage, and so on. Also known as *cooperativa* and *cooperativo.*

COOPÉRATIVE DE MANIPULANT (FRANCE) Designates champagnes produced by cooperatives. Although many co-ops sell wines to négociants, some market their own labels. This appears on some champagne labels as the initials CM.

COOPERATIVE PROMOTION A promotion involving two or more suppliers of services or products joined together in a common promotion for their mutual benefit.

COOPERATIVO (ITALY) *See* Cooperative.

COPA (SPAIN) A long, tulip-shaped stem glass that contains six ounces and is traditionally used for the service of sherry wine. Also known as *sherry glass* and *whiskey sour glass*. *See* Copita.

COPITA (SPAIN) A long, tulip-shaped stem glass that contains four ounces and is traditionally used for the service of sherry wine. Also known as *a liqueur glass* and *sherry glass*. *See* Copa.

COPPER Reddish-brown color often associated with beers.

COPPER The brewing kettle in which hops and *wort* are boiled in the preparation of beer.

COPPER ALE (ENGLAND) A dark, copper-colored, bitter ale with a distinctive wine-like taste and aroma.

COPPER SULFATE A chemical used to clarify and stabilize wine by removing hydrogen sulfide and mercaptans.

COPPERY A metallic taste owing to bad distillation.

CORDIAL Derived from the Latin word *cor*, meaning heart, because the earliest cordials were administered to the sick to stimulate the heart and lighten the spirit. Cordials may be designated "dry" if the sugar, dextrose, or levulose, or a combination thereof, is less than ten percent by weight of the finished product. *See* Liqueur.

CORDIAL GLASS A small stemmed glass with a capacity of one to three ounces. Also known as *liqueur glass*. *See* Copa and Copita.

CORDON Extended trunk(s) and spurs of a grapevine are trained along a wire called a cordon wire. Also known as *cordone* and *spalliera*.

CORDON BLEU (FRANCE) A label designation used on cognac bottles that indicates that the youngest brandy used in the blend is at least 6-1/2 years old (although they contain a very high percentage of brandy that has been aged for twenty, thirty, or forty years or more).

CORDONE (ITALY) *See* Cordon.

CORDON TRAINING A training method of grapevines that takes its name from the French word for rope and is used to describe the appearance of the trunk. This system involves training the grapevine into roughly the shape of a T, which is to say the grapevine trunk has two arm-like extensions at approximately fifteen inches below the top wire. The arms are distributed to the left and the right and trained to a single wire, with spurs occurring at regular intervals along the length of the arms. Since cordons are on a lateral plane (unlike a bush), the grapevine's growth ensues around all parts of the grapevine and opens it up to the maximum amount of sunlight, yet at the same time the grapevine foliage is so situated that the grapes themselves are not exposed to direct sunlight, which can burn their delicate skins. When the grapevines are in full leaf, this system presents a somewhat wall-like or hedge-like appearance. This has the advantage of less complicated pruning, since all that is remaining for fruiting wood is a series of spurs. Finally, since growth occurs at only two locations along the length of both of the cordons, pruning is somewhat faster than with other forms of grapevine training and is considerably more precise. The grower also saves on labor costs in that no tying of canes to wires needs to be done. *See* Head Training, Shoot Positioning, and Training.

CORDS   Blemishes that occur during the glassmaking process. Discontinuities in the glass caused by improper mixing of the charge and so on. While these are not really impurities, they do produce lines in the glass that can disturb its clarity.

CORE SAMPLING   The extraction of a cross-section of earth to be analyzed for nutrients or the lack of them.

CORK   This spongy material, used as a stopper for bottles of wine, liqueurs, distilled spirits, or even beer, has been universal since about 1685. Cork, with its great elasticity, expands and contracts depending on temperature and atmospheric conditions, and makes the perfect tight seal for the neck of a bottle.

   Cork is actually the bark of an evergreen oak tree (*Quercus suber*) grown principally in Portugal and Spain, although the tree also grows in Algeria, France, Morocco, Tunisia, and Sardinia, Italy. Cork trees mature slowly; their outer bark, which is the cork, is harvested only when the tree reaches twenty-five years of age, and once every eight to eleven years thereafter for up to 150 years or more. It is only with the third harvest, when the tree is about forty years old, that the cork is of a quality suitable for wine closures.

   During the late summer, when the growth activity of the tree is at its highest, the outer bark (*phellem*) or cork layer actually separates from the *liber* (the inner live wood) making removal a relatively simple task and one that doesn't damage the living tree.

   After the bark is cut from the tree, it is processed and cut into circular shapes of various lengths. There is a very strict grading system that categorizes the corks according to color, smell, texture, the age of the tree, the number of imperfections and fissures (*lenticells*), its pliability, and so on.

   Most corks are 1.75 inches long and are graded by the number of holes in them (the fewer holes, the less chance for leakage). White wine corks are typically 1.5 to 2 inches long and red wine corks from 2 to 2.5 inches long. French Bordeaux wines traditionally use 2.25-inch corks, which often must be able to withstand decades of aging. For obvious reasons, the finest corks command the highest prices. Also known as *bouchon, rolha, stopfen, tapon*, and *tappo*. *See* Agglomerated Cork.

CORKAGE   A surcharge or fee charged by a restaurant for the opening and serving of a wine that a customer brings in with him or her. Also known as *corkage fee*.

CORKAGE FEE   *See* Corkage.

CORKED   Describes an unpleasant musty odor (mushrooms) or flavor imparted to wine by a defective (moldy, poor, soft, or disintegrating) cork or by chemicals used in the processing of corks. The chemical responsible for this corked odor and taste is 2,4,6-trichloroanisole. Also known as *bouché, bouchonné, corkiness, corky, goût de bouchon*, and *korkgeschmack*.

CORKINESS   *See* Corked.

CORKSCREW   A device used for removing the cork from a bottle. It usually consists of a knife, a screw, and depending on the model, a lever. Corkscrews should have a helical worm (like wire wrapped around a pencil) instead of a bore or screw, which "drills" a hole in the cork, rather than grasping it for extraction. Formerly known as *bottlescrew*. Also known as *cavatappi, sacacorcho, tire-bouchon*, and *wine key*.

The first mention in print of a corkscrew was in 1681; however, it was not until 1895 that Samuel Henshall obtained the first patent rights for a corkscrew. The waiter's lever was developed by a Mr. Dolberg in 1883. In 1978, Herbert Allen invented the "screwpull," dubbed history's easiest corkscrew.

CORKY *See* Corked.

CORN An integral ingredient of some alcoholic products such as Bourbon and corn whiskeys and American-made beers. The more corn added to the mash, the lighter in body the product.

CORNAS (FRANCE) A wine-producing village located in the Rhône Valley, famous for its red wine produced from the Syrah grape.

CORNICHON A red grape variety grown in parts of France and California.

CORNIFESTO (PORTUGAL) A red grape variety grown in the Douro region.

CORN SUGAR *See* Dextrose.

CORN WHISKEY Legally, corn whiskey is distilled at a proof not exceeding 160 from a fermented mash of at least 80 percent corn. Corn whiskey must be stored in uncharred oak barrels or used charred oak barrels at not more than 125 proof. It must be aged for a minimum of two years. Because of its dominant corn content, corn whiskey is extremely light in flavor.

COROLLA The petals of a flower. *See* Bud Break.

CORPO (ITALY AND PORTUGAL) *See* Body.

CORPOSO (ITALY) *See* Full-bodied.

CORPS (FRANCE) *See* Body.

CORQUETTE (SPAIN) *See* Grape Knife.

CORREDOR (SPAIN) *See* Broker.

CORSÉ (FRANCE) *See* Big.

CORTESE (ITALY) This traditional white grape variety of Piedmont produces wines of particular refinement. Once widely grown throughout southern Piedmont, its area of production is now limited to the Colli Tortonesi, Monferrato, and Novi Ligure zones of Alessandria. An extremely resilient grapevine, it thrives in vineyards that have good exposure to the sun. Wines made from the Cortese may be labeled *Cortese, Cortese di Gavi, Gavi*, or *Gavi dei Gavi*.

CORTESE DI GAVI (ITALY) *See* Cortese.

CORTO (ITALY) *See* Short.

CORTON-CHARLEMAGNE (FRANCE) A major white wine produced entirely from Chardonnay grapes on the steep slopes of the commune of Corton, located in the Côte de Beaune district of Burgundy.

The vineyards of Corton-Charlemagne were named after Emperor Charlemagne (742–814 A.D.), who owned vineyards and reigned in the mid-770s. Henry II

(1133–1189) and Charles the Bold (1433–1477), Burgundian Duke, also owned vineyards there.

CORVA *(ITALY)* A red grape variety.

CORVINA *(ITALY)* A red grape variety grown primarily in the Veneto region, where it is used as a blending grape in making Bardolino, Valpolicella, and Amarone wines. Corvina was first cited in literature as early as 1818. Also known as *Corvina Gentile, Corvina Rizza, Corvina Veronese, Corvinone,* and *Cruina.*

CORVINA GENTILE *(ITALY)* *See* Corvina.

CORVINA RIZZA *(ITALY)* *See* Corvina.

CORVINA VERONESE *(ITALY)* *See* Corvina.

CORVINONE *(ITALY)* *See* Corvina.

COSECHA *(SPAIN)* *See* Harvest.

COSECHEROS *(SPAIN)* Growers with relatively small vineyard holdings.

COST The price paid to acquire or produce an item.

COSTING Process of arriving at the actual cost, cost percentage, or selling price of a product by identifying the component costs of the product and then applying a percentage or formula.

COST PERCENTAGE *See* Beverage Cost Percentage.

COST PER PORTION The selling price per individual unit multiplied by the unit multiplier.

CO₂ TANK Container used to hold the CO_2 gas that is used in the dispensing of beer and carbonated nonalcoholic soft drinks.

COT *(FRANCE)* *See* Malbec.

COT *(FRANCE)* Wood on a grapevine from the previous vintage, pruned to just two buds.

CÔTE *(FRANCE)* Hill or slope in a grape-growing area.

CÔTEAU *(FRANCE)* Hillside.

COTEAUX CHAMPENOIS *(FRANCE)* Still wines produced in the region of Champagne, first authorized on August 21, 1974, rendering the term *vin nature de la champagne* obsolete.

CÔTE CHALONNAISE *(FRANCE)* A long, low line of hills that extends southward from the Côte de Beaune in Burgundy for about twenty miles. The grape varieties from which its classified red and white wines are made (Pinot Noir and Chardonnay) are the same as those grown in the Côte d'Or, but the wines of the Côte Chalonnaise are somewhat lighter and mature faster. The four most important villages in this area are Mercurey, Givry, Rully, and Montagny.

CÔTE D'OR *(FRANCE)* Literally, the golden slopes. This large area is twenty-five to thirty miles long and only one mile wide at its widest point. The greatest vineyards in Burgundy are in this district, which is traditionally divided into two wine-producing areas: Côte de Nuits in the north and Côte de Beaune in the south.

CÔTE DE BEAUNE (FRANCE)   In the southern half of the Côte d'Or of the Burgundy region lies the Côte de Beaune, which extends approximately fifteen miles from Nuits-Saint-Georges in the north to Santenay in the south. It is wider, longer, and has nearly twice the amount of land of its northern neighbor. The Côte de Beaune is known for its outstanding white wines, although there are also some very fine red wines produced.

CÔTE DE BROUILLY (FRANCE)   A *cru* commune in Beaujolais that possess a deeper color and somewhat livelier style than Brouilly and are considered to be better than those of Brouilly.

CÔTE DE NUITS (FRANCE)   The northern half of the Côte d'Or in the Burgundy region famous for its red wines, all of which utilize the Pinot Noir grape variety. The Côte de Nuits stretches for about twelve miles from the town of Fixin in the north to Nuits-Saint-Georges in the south. There are twenty-nine *appellation contrôlée* wines produced in this region. Several white wines are entitled to the *appellation contrôlée* designation in the Côte de Nuits: Musigny Blanc; Nuits-Saint-Georges Blanc; Morey-Saint-Denis; Monts-Luisants; and Clos Blanc de Vougeot.

CÔTE DES BLANCS (FRANCE)   Champagne's premium vineyard area for Chardonnay grapes.

CÔTE RÔTIE (FRANCE)   A famous red-wine-producing village in the northern part of the Rhône Valley. By law the wines must be made with a minimum of 80 percent Syrah grapes, with the other 20 percent being Viognier; it is only allowed to produce red wines.

In Côte Rôtie there are also the famous hillside vineyards of *Brune et Blonde*. At one time during the Middle Ages, these hills were owned by an aristocratic nobleman named Maugiron, who inhabited the château of Ampuis. According to legend, he gave the vineyards on these hills to his two daughters for their dowries. His two daughters, although different as day and night, were nevertheless both ravishing beauties. One possessed blonde hair while the other had long jet-black hair. Upon his death, his daughters' *hair color* determined the wines' future names—Côte Blonde (blonde-haired daughter) and Côte Brune (dark-haired daughter).

CÔTES DE PROVENCE (FRANCE)   A wine district in southern France situated along the Mediterranean coast, it produces ordinary red and white wines but is noted for its outstanding dry rosé wines. *See* Provence.

CÔTES-DU-RHÔNE (FRANCE)   *See* Rhône Valley.

CÔTES-DU-RHÔNE-VILLAGES (FRANCE)   Its *appellation contrôlée* was established in August 1967 for seventeen villages in the southern half of the Rhône. The red, white (dry or naturally sweet), and rosé wines of this area can be marketed either under the name of the village where they were produced or under the name of Côtes-du-Rhône-Villages, if the wine is a blend of wines from several villages. Most wines labeled Côtes-du-Rhône-Villages are usually fruity and a bit fuller than Beaujolais.

COTTAGE   A red grape variety developed in 1869 by Ephraim Wales Bull (1806–1895).

COTTO (ITALY)   *See* Cooked Wine.

COUDERC 7120   *See* Couderc Noir.

COUDERC 19-29935   *See* Muscat du Moulin.

COUDERC NOIR   A red grape variety. Formerly known as *Couderc 7120*.

COULAGE (FRANCE)   *See* Ullage.

COULANT (FRANCE)   Flowing, smooth, pleasant, and easy to drink. Generally used to describe light-bodied red and white wines that are low in tannin and alcohol.

COULEUR (FRANCE)   *See* Color.

COULEUSE (FRANCE)   *See* Leakage.

COULURE (FRANCE)   *See* Floral Abortion.

COUNOISE (FRANCE)   *See* Aubun.

COUNT   The number of units or items per pound, or the number of units or net pounds per container.

COUPAGE (FRANCE)   The blending of many wines in the making of cognac or champagne. *See* Blending.

COUPÉ (FRANCE)   A blended wine of little character.

COUPE (FRANCE)   *See* Saucer-Shaped Glass.

COUPER (FRANCE)   *See* Cooper.

COUPON   A rebate, often redeemable in-store.

COURBU NOIR (FRANCE)   A red grape variety grown in the southwest.

COURMI   An ancient Gaelic term for ale.

COURT (FRANCE)   *See* Short.

COURTIER (FRANCE)   *See* Broker.

COVER CHARGE   A basic charge or fixed fee added to the bill. It is usually for entertainment in night clubs or luxury restaurants, for some special feature that the establishment offers, or for seating, independent of charges for food or drink.

COVER COUNT   Records the number of patrons using the operation for specified time periods—hourly, daily, weekly, monthly, or even quarterly. *See* Covers.

COVER CROPS   Types of grass planted in between rows of vineyards late in the season to reduce erosion, soak up excess moisture, and compete for moisture with grapevines, which could be good with high vigor grapevines. In the spring, the cover crop is usually plowed or disked into the ground for needed nutrients. *See* Wild Mustard.

COVERS   Restaurant jargon for paying customers, place settings, or seats. It refers to the practice of having a cover on each customer's plate while in transit from the kitchen. A waiter who is able to serve ten covers is therefore serving ten people. The number of covers equals the number of customers for any given meal or time period, as when establishing an accurate customer count. Also known as *number of portions*. *See* Cover Count.

COWART   A red grape variety.

COWBOY COCKTAIL   A straight shot of whiskey.

CRABB'S BLACK BURGUNDY   A red grape variety named by Hiram W. Crabb of Napa Valley, California. The grape is actually the Mondeuse Noire. *See* Mondeuse Noire.

CRACHOIR (FRANCE)   A spittoon.

CRACK   A fissure on a cork caused by dryness or brittleness.

CRACKLING   Slightly sparkling wines produced in any manner that results in a carbonation of less than 2.7 atmospheres of pressure. Taxed at a lower rate than champagnes and sparkling wines, crackling wines are normally low-priced. *See* Spritz.

CRADLE   *See* Wine Cradle.

CRAIE (FRANCE)   Chalk soil.

CRANBERRY JUICE   A nonalcoholic and noncarbonated fruit juice made from the liquid constituent of cranberries. It may be sweetened or unsweetened.

CRANBERRY LIQUEUR   A sweetened and flavored liqueur consisting of a base of alcohol, minimum 2.5 percent sugar, flavored and colored with cranberries.

CRAYÈRES (FRANCE)   The chalk quarry pits where most bottles of champagne are produced and aged.

CREAM   A component of milk, whose butterfat content determines the form and style of the cream.

CREAM ALE   A blend of ale and lager beer. Cream ale is highly carbonated, which results in a rich foam and strong effervescence.

CREAM LIQUEURS   Mixtures of dairy cream and whiskey (usually Irish or Scotch), generally beige in color, with an alcoholic content usually between 17 and 20 percent by volume. Also known as *Irish cream liqueurs*.

CREAM OF TARTAR   A white powder or crystal substance obtained from deposits of tartaric acid in wine barrels. Also known as *tartar*. *See* Tartaric Acid.

CREAM SHERRY   A sherry that is rich, deep amber to golden brown in color and that usually displays an exquisite bouquet and a very sweet and "creamy" taste. An even sweeter cream sherry, made entirely from Pedro Ximénez (P.X.) grapes, is called "brown."

Cream sherry is made by blending sweet wines made from the juice of P.X. and Moscatel grapes to a sherry base wine. The P.X. grapes are left outside in the sun for twelve to fourteen hours to dry after harvesting, which concentrates their sugar levels. They are then placed on *esparto* mats (made of grass) to further dry. So intense is their sweetness that fermentation usually stops at about 14 percent alcohol, resulting in a high degree of residual sugar. Cream sherry should be served after dinner at cool room temperature.

CREAM SODA   A soft drink usually made with carbonated water, sugar or sweetener, caramel coloring, acids, and a syrup made from vanilla beans.

CREAMY   An impression conveyed by the taste of certain wines and beers. *See* Mellow.

CREATA (ROMANIA AND YUGOSLAVIA)   *See* Banat Riesling

CREEK   A red grape variety.

CREMA *(ITALY)*   Cream.

CRÉMANT *(FRANCE)*   A sparkling wine usually produced from a mixture of grapes, depending on where it is produced. Perhaps the biggest difference between crémant and champagne lies in the fact that during the secondary fermentation, less sugar is added, which in turn produces less alcohol and less carbon dioxide. In fact, crémant contains a minimum of 3.5 atmospheres of pressure, compared to the normal five to six atmospheres of pressure in champagne. It is appreciated for its lightness of flavor and less gassy taste. This term is no longer authorized by champagne producers since 1994.

CRÈME *(FRANCE)*   Cream.

CRÈME   A term, widely applied to liqueurs, which refers to a special sweetness and not to dairy creams. This term could in fact be used to describe most cordials or liqueurs.

CRÈME DE ALMOND   Almond-flavored liqueur.

CRÈME DE ANANAS   Pineapple-flavored liqueur.

CRÈME DE BANANA   Banana-flavored liqueur.

CRÈME DE CACAO   Cacao-flavored liqueur made from cocoa and vanilla beans.

CRÈME DE CAFE   Coffee-flavored liqueur.

CRÈME DE CASSIS   Black currant-flavored liqueur.

CRÈME DE CELERY   Celery-flavored liqueur.

CRÈME DE CHOCOLATE   Chocolate-flavored liqueur.

CRÈME DE FRAISE   Strawberry-flavored liqueur.

CRÈME DE FRAMBOISE   Raspberry-flavored liqueur.

CRÈME DE MANDARINE   Tangerine-flavored liqueur, made from the dried peel of tangerines.

CRÈME DE MENTHE   Mint-flavored liqueur, made from several varieties of mint, but principally peppermint.

CRÈME DE MOKA (CRÈME DE MOCCA)   Coffee-flavored liqueur.

CRÈME DE NOISETTE   Hazelnut-flavored liqueur.

CRÈME DE NOYAUX (CRÈME DE NOYA)   Almond-flavored liqueur, made from crushed apricots, cherries, peaches, and plums, with orange-peel flavor and a brandy base.

CRÈME DE PRUNELLE   Plum-flavored liqueur.

CRÈME DE ROSE   Liqueur made from essential oil of rose petals and vanilla.

CRÈME DE THÉ   Tea-flavored liqueur.

CRÈME DE VANILLA   Liqueur made from vanilla beans.

CRÈME DE VIOLETTE   Liqueur flavored with vanilla and violet petals. It is similar in color and taste to Crème Yvette and Parfait Amour.

Crème Yvette   Lavender-colored liqueur with hints of bubblegum; made from violet petals. It was named after French actress Yvette Gilbert from the 1890s. It is similar in color and taste to Crème de Violette and Parfait Amour.

Crescent Cube   *See* Ice Cubes.

Crescenz (Germany)   *See* Wachstrum.

Creux (France)   *See* Hollow.

Criadera (Spain)   The first or top aging *butts* utilized in the *solera* system of aging sherry wine.

Criado Por (Spain)   Produced by. Also known as *elaborado por*.

Criado y Embotellado Por (Spain)   Grown, produced, and bottled by.

Crianza (Spain)   Nursery; refers to the aging process in a sherry bodega or winery. The wine (red) must be aged for not less than two years, of which at least one must be in 225-liter oak barrels. Also known as *vino de crianza*.

Criolla (Spain)   *See* Mission.

Crisp   A term applied to wines and beers that are light, with a fairly high level of acidity making them clean and fresh-tasting.

Crno (Yugoslavia)   *See* Red.

Croatina   *See* Bonarda.

Crochet de Dégorger (France)   A specially shaped knife used to remove the metal *agrafe* after the secondary fermentation in making sparkling wine.

Crop   *See* Harvest.

Crop   The quantity of fruit borne on grapevines.

Crop Control   The management of the vineyard by various methods, including pruning, crop thinning, leaf thinning, fertilization, and spraying. *See* Crop Thinning and Leaf Thinning.

Crop Load   The quantity of crop in relation to the grapevine's leaf and overall bearing capacity.

Crop Recovery   The rate of crop produced from newly developed growth following an injury, usually spring frosts.

Crop Thinning   A method employed in vineyards to regulate the amount of fruit that can be brought to maturity. It consists of removing whole grape clusters (especially unsound fruit) so as to ensure that the number of remaining clusters is low and thus each has the best chance for optimum maturity. It often means the removal of as much as one-third of the crop from overproducing grapevines. Also known as *ausdünnen, cluster thinning, éclaircissage, thinning*, and *vendange verte*. *See* Crop Control and Leaf Thinning.

Crossbreeding   A new grape variety created by the mating or breeding of one grape variety with another in order to obtain a more desirable offspring. Also known as *hybridization*. *See* Hybrid.

Crouchen   *See* Cruchen Blanc.

CROUPE *(FRANCE)* A ridge or slight elevation in the ground.

CROWN *See* Head.

CROWN CAP A metal stopper whose edges are crimped over the mouth of a bottle. Often used on beer bottles or in the making sparkling wines for the secondary fermentation in a stoppered bottle.

CROWN SUCKERING The removal of extraneous shoots from grapevines to thin the vegetative canopy and avoid shading and excess crop loads. *See* Suckering and Leaf Thinning.

CROZE The carved or cut groove found at both ends of a barrel that accepts the "head." *See* Farine.

CROZES-HERMITAGE *(FRANCE)* *See* Hermitage.

CRU *(FRANCE)* Literally, growth, when applied to wines, but synonymous with a special vineyard or a vineyard of high quality, whether classified or not. It reflects the particular soil, climate, and grape varieties that give the wine its distinctive quality. *See* Growth.

CRU BOURGEOIS *(FRANCE)* A classification of Bordeaux wines (ranked just below the five classified growths) that were not classified in 1855, but were in 1966 by the Bordeaux Chamber of Commerce. The cru bourgeois classification is made up of first Grands Bourgeois (exceptionnels), second Grands Bourgeois, and third Bourgeois. Also known as *Bourgeois Growths*.

CRUCHEN BLANC *(SOUTH AFRICA)* A white grape variety. Also known as *Crouchen*.

CRU CLASSÉ *(FRANCE)* The classified growths. The dry red and sweet white wines of Bordeaux, which were classified or ranked in 1855, 1953, 1959, 1969, and 1985, according to potential quality and the prices the wines had been selling for prior to the classification.

CRU EXCEPTIONNEL *(FRANCE)* An unofficial classification of Bordeaux wines just below *classé* and above *bourgeois*. Common Market regulations, however, do not permit use of the word *exceptionnel* on labels.

CRUINA *(ITALY)* *See* Corvina.

CRUSH Another term for the harvest. *See* Harvest.

CRUSHER A mechanical device utilized for breaking or cracking of the skins of grapes in order to release the juice for fermentation. Also known as *fouloir*.

CRUSHER/DESTEMMER A mechanical device with a large hopper into which grapes are dumped. The first part of the operation cracks the berries, allowing the sugar-rich juice known as *free-run* to flow freely. The second part of this simultaneous crushing/destemming operation removes the stems from the grapes by centrifugal force with the use of a large auger that catches the stems, literally ripping off the berries. The stems exit at one side of the machine while the berries and juice usually exit at the bottom. The stems, which are a good source of nitrogen, are loaded into trucks and dumped between the vineyard rows to decompose during the winter and be disked into the soil in the spring. Also known as *fouloir-égrappoir* and *stemmer*. *See* Crusher, Destemmer, and Destemming.

CRUSHING The process whereby the skins of the grapes are cracked open by a machine, liberating the juice. Also known as *ammostare, ammostatura, esmagamento*, and *foulage*.

CRUST *See* Sediment.

CRUSTA An obscure American name for an elaborate cocktail containing lemon juice, aromatic bitters, curaçao, and a distilled spirit. It is often garnished with an orange slice, maraschino cherry, or lemon peel; frosted or rimmed with powdered sugar, and served in a tall wineglass over crushed ice.

CRUSTED PORTS *(PORTUGAL)* No longer produced. *See* Late-Bottled Vintage Ports.

CRUTIN *(ITALY)* *See* Infernotti.

CRUZETA *(SPAIN)* *See* Training.

CRYOMACERATION A winemaking technique wherein the skins and juice of freshly crushed grapes are held at extremely cold temperatures prior to fermentation.

CRYOEXTRACTION A process by which whole grape clusters that have been attacked by *Botrytis cinerea* are placed into cold storage (25 degrees Fahrenheit) for about twenty-four hours. The grapes are then pressed, with the juice (which does not freeze due to high sugar levels) freely running off into a fermentation tank. This method has proved successful for French Sauternes, German Eiswein, and some California selected late-harvest wines.

CRYPTOGAMIC DISEASES From the Greek *kryptos* (hidden) and *gamos* (marriage). They are fungal diseases such as *Uncinula necator* (powdery mildew), *Plasmopara viticola* (downy mildew), black rot, gray rot, and *Botrytis* bunch rot, which directly affect the grapevines, the leaves, or the grapes.

CRYPTOGAM A plant that bears no flowers or seeds, but propagates by means of spores.

CRYSTAL-CLEAR Also known as *kristallklar*. *See* Clear.

CRYSTALLINE DEPOSITS Crystal deposits (potassium bitartrate) that accumulate either at the bottom of a bottle or at the bottom of a cork. They do not dissolve in the wine, but also will not impair its quality, taste, luster, or color. Also known as *crystals* and *weinsteine*. *See* Cold Stabilization, Potassium Bitartrate, and Tartaric Acid.

CRYSTAL MALT *See* Caramel Malt.

CRYSTALS *See* Crystalline Deposits.

CUADRILLA FORESTERA *(SPAIN)* Grape pickers. *See* Chef de Troupe.

CUARTA (SPAIN) *See* Barrel.

CUBA *(SPAIN)* A fermentation tank.

CUBELETS *See* Ice Cubes.

CUBIC   A dimension expressing volume.

CUERPO (SPAIN)   See Body.

CUFEX   A proprietary fining agent used for the removal of excessive metal hazes, notably copper and iron. See Casse, Citric Acid, Ferrocyanide Compounds, Fining, and Fining Agents.

CUIT (FRANCE)   Also known as vin cuit. See Cooked Wine.

CULATTONE (ITALY)   See Sediment.

CULM   In brewing or distilling, barley is steeped in warm water and allowed to sprout or germinate. It is then put into a kiln where it becomes green malt and is often roasted. The kiln-dried malt is then screened or sieved to remove the dried rootlets or sprouts, which are known as culm.

CULTAVAR (FRANCE)   See Cultivar.

CULTIVAR   A cultivated variety of grape, produced horticulturally, rather than a naturally occurring variety. Also known as cultavar.

CULTIVATING   The turning or loosening of the soil by mechanical means in order to control weeds and aerate the soil.

CUNACHO (SPAIN)   See Grape-Picking Basket.

CUNNINGHAM   A red grape variety discovered by Jacob Cunningham of Prince Edward County, Virginia. Also known as Long.

CUP   A United States volumetric measure equal to eight ounces.

CUPADA (SPAIN)   See Cuvée.

CUPER (NETHERLANDS)   See Cooper.

CUP OF JAVA   A slang term for a cup of coffee.

CUP OF JOE   A slang term for a cup of coffee.

CUPPA (AUSTRALIA)   A cup of tea.

CUPS   Drinks containing wine, similar to punches. Ingredients include fruits, fruit juices, and carbonated mixes.

CURAÇAO   A clear or amber-colored liqueur first produced in the sixteenth century by the Dutch from the bitter peels of Dutch West Indies oranges. When curaçao was first produced (with less sugar), it was called "double curaçao," then "triple sec." Curaçao is usually lower in alcohol and is also available in a blue-colored version. See Triple Sec.

CUSPIDOR   See Spittoon.

CUSTOMER LEVEL GOAL DEPLETION WORKSHEET   A form used to allocate brand territorial depletion goals among distributors in a given territory.

CUT   To weaken a drink by the addition of water or a mixer.

CUT CASE CARD   A sign used to promote a product on a small case stacking, which attaches to a displayed cut case by fitting into the back edge of a case.

CUTICULA (ITALY)   The outer layer of the grape berry's skin. *See* Cutin.

CUTIN   The varnishlike material covering the surface of grapes and other fruits containing waxes and resins. *See* Bloom, Cuticula, and Micro-Flora.

CUTTING   *See* Reducing.

CUTTING   A severed portion of the cane on a grapevine used for propagation.

CUTTING WINE   *See* Blending.

CUVA (SPAIN)   A large barrel with a capacity of 25,000 liters (6,600 gallons), seldom used today. *See* Barrel.

CUVAISON (FRANCE)   The time spent by the *must* in contact with the skins in a fermentation tank.

CUVE (FRANCE)   A barrel or, literally, the contents of a barrel of wine.

CUVE CLOSE (ITALY)   *See* Charmat Method.

CUVE DE DÉBOURBAGE (FRANCE)   A settling tank. *See* Débourbage.

CUVÉE (FRANCE)   A blend of wines bottled as one lot. Any volume of wine produced and specially selected to be fermented a second time for sparkling wines. Also known as *cupada* and *uvaggio*.

CUVÉE DE PRESTIGE (FRANCE)   A winery's most thoughtfully conceived, carefully crafted, luxury sparkling wine or champagne.

CUVERIE (FRANCE)   *See* Winery.

CYATHI   An ancient Roman cup that held the equivalent of the modern quartino or quarter of a liter.

CYDER (AUSTRALIA AND ENGLAND)   *See* Cider.

CYLINDRICAL   Describes an elongated grape cluster lacking shoulders.

CYNTHIANA   A red grape variety discovered around 1850 growing in the woods of Arkansas. It is believed by some *ampelographers* that Cynthiana and Norton are the same grape variety.

CYSTER   Apple juice used with honey in place of water.

CYTRYNÓWKA (POLAND)   Lemon-flavored vodka.

DAILY ALCOHOLIC BEVERAGE ISSUE REPORT   A detailed report that specifies quantity of bottles, sizes of bottles, and names of beverages that were issued from storage to the bar or other departments for service.

DAILY BEVERAGE COST   The actual wholesale dollar value of all beverages used by an establishment in a given shift or day. This figure includes direct purchases as well as storeroom issues.

DAILY BEVERAGE COST PERCENTAGE   The beverage cost (for a shift or day) divided by the retail dollar amount of sales.

DAILY REPORT   A compilation of the costs and sales of the previous shift or day for all departments in the property.

DAIQUIRI   A cocktail invented in or about 1898 by Jennings S. Cox, an American, who served as chief engineer for the Spanish-American Iron Company near the village of Daiquiri in Cuba. It consists of light rum, sugar, and lime juice.

DAISY   A very large cocktail, usually made with distilled spirits, grenadine syrup (for color), lemon or lime juice, and soda.

DAMASCHINO (ITALY)   A white grape variety that appears to have been introduced to Sicily during the period of Arabic domination.

DAME-JEANNE (FRANCE)   A large glass bottle used for the transportation of wine. It contains anywhere from one to ten gallons and is usually wrapped with wicker or straw.

DAMENWEIN (GERMANY)   *See* Feminine.

DAMIGIANA (ITALY)   *See* Demijohn.

DAMINOZIDE   *See* Alar.

DAMSON PLUMS   A variety of small, oval, bluish-black plums, used to produce Britain's damson gin.

DANDELION WINE   A wine made from the fresh yellow flowers of wild dandelion plants. The other ingredients are sugar, citrus fruits (orange, lemon, and lime), yeast, and raisins.

DANK   A term often applied to wines or beers that display a moldy odor reminiscent of damp cellars.

DANUBE   The great river that connects Eastern and Western Europe. It flows through the classical wine regions in Lower Austria.

DANZIGWASSER (POLAND)   *See* Goldwasser.

DÃO (PORTUGAL)   A major red- and white-wine-producing region in north-central Portugal, just south of the Douro River.

DARJEELING TEA   A delicate, full-bodied flavored tea with an exquisite bouquet. The leaves are grown in the foothills of Darjeeling, high on the southern slopes of the Himalayas in northeastern India.

DARK   Describes the color of some red wines and beers.

DARK BEER   A beer characterized by a very deep, dark color, full-bodied flavor, and a creamy taste, with overtones of malt, bitterness, sweetness, and caramel. Its usual production involves the addition of roasted barley during the initial brewing stages.

DARKENING   The color of white wines that begin to darken with age and oxidation.

DARK RUM   A rum that derives its color from aging in lightly charred oak barrels for a period of five to seven years. The skimmings of sugar from the previous distillation are added to the sugarcane molasses and allowed to slowly ferment for twelve to twenty days. It is this special fermentation process that gives the dark rums a pungent bouquet and more pronounced flavor of butter and molasses. The mash is distilled twice in pot stills and is run off at between 140 to 160 proof. The rum is then aged and blended and at bottling the proof is adjusted with distilled water. Also, considerably more caramel is added than is the case for lighter rums, to give it a deep mahogany color. *See* Rum.

DASH   A measurement equivalent to one-sixth of a teaspoon or one forty-eighth of an ounce.

DATTIER DE SAINT-VALLIER   A white grape variety. Formerly known as *Seyve-Villard 20-365*.

DDP   *See* Delivered Duty Paid To Named Point.

DDU   *See* Delivered Duty Unpaid To Named Point.

DE   *See* Diatomaceous Earth.

DEAD   A beer or wine that is old and well past its peak or prime of drinkability. This condition could also occur due to improper handling or storage. Also known as *goût mauvais*. *See* Dried Out and Old.

DEAD MARINE   *See* Dead Soldier.

DEAD SOLDIER   A slang term for an empty bottle of beer, it originated sometime during World War I. Also known as a *dead marine*.

DEALER   *See* Broker.

DEARING   A white grape variety.

DEBOLE (ITALY)   *See* Thin.

DÉBOURBAGE (FRANCE)   Allowing the unfermented grape juice to settle, generally for twenty-four hours prior to fermentation. This method allows the heavier particles to settle to the bottom for later removal prior to fermentation. This method was developed by Denis Débourbage. *See* Cuve de Débourbage.

DÉBOURREMENT (FRANCE)   The moment when the scales on a grapevine that protect the bud during the winter open up.

DECAFFEINATION   The removal of caffeine from coffee beans with no significant change in natural flavor or character in coffee brewed from them. Different coffee beans have different caffeine contents, depending on their growing region and species. For example, *arabica* beans have about one-half the caffeine content of *robusta* coffee beans.
   The general methods of removing caffeine are *direct contact method, indirect contact method*, and *water process (Swiss water process)*. In order to qualify as a decaffeinated coffee, at least 97 percent of the caffeine naturally existing in the bean must be removed. Also known as *decaffeinato*.

DECAFFEINATO (ITALY)   *See* Decaffeination.

DECANT   To pour wine from the bottle into a serving container so that any sediment remains in the bottle.

DECANTER   A glass carafe or bottle into which mature wines (usually red) are decanted prior to service. *See* Carafe.

DECANTING   Pouring wine from a bottle. The purpose of decanting is twofold. First, aeration during the decanting process allows the wine to "breathe," to gain in bouquet, and to dissipate any off odors or gasses that may have accumulated under the cork. Second, separating the wine from its sediment allows it to be served perfectly bright and clear, thus enhancing its appearance. Decanting is recommended for full-bodied red wines and port but is unnecessary for white, rosé, and sparkling wines. Also known as *dépotage*. *See* Aeration and Breathing.

DECAVAILLONAGE (FRANCE)   A plowing method used along a row of grapevines. It employs a special plow that sidesteps at each grapevine stem. After the passage of the plow, the soil around each stem is tidied up. Also known as *tier le cavaillon*.

DÉCHARNÉ (FRANCE)   *See* Thin.

DÉCHAR/RECHAR   A process by which barrels are scraped down on the inside and recharred.

DECHAUNAC   A red grape variety developed from a cross of Seibel 5163 and Seibel 793 by Albert Seibel, but named after Adhemar deChaunac (the winemaker for the Canadian firm called Brights Wines Ltd. of Ontario, Canada) at a testimonial dinner in his honor in 1972. Originally called Cameo, the grape is one of the most popular varieties in the east, especially in the Finger Lakes district of New York. Formerly known as *Seibel 9549*.

DECIGRAM   A metric unit of weight; one-tenth of a gram; ten decigrams are equal to one gram.

DECIMETER   A metric unit of length; one-tenth of a meter; ten decimeters equals thirty-nine inches.

DECKROT *(GERMANY)*   A red grape variety developed in 1938 from a cross of Pinot Gris and Färbertraube, in Freiburg.

DECKWEIN *(GERMANY)*   Imported red wine, generally high in alcohol and color content, used to improve the color of German red wines. Seldom used today.

DECLASSIFICATION   When a wine does not meet or attain the standards (yield, production, alcohol, taste test, and so on) of law established by a district, region, or country, the wine is declassified, a retrogressive (sometimes voluntary) step in the hierarchy of the wine laws.

DECRECIPTO *(ITALY* AND *SPAIN)*   *See* Dead and Old.

DECRÉCIPTO *(PORTUGAL)*   *See* Dead and Old.

DÉCRÉPIT *(FRANCE)*   *See* Dead and Old.

DECREPIT   Also known as *decrecipto, decrécipto*, and *décrépit*. *See* Dead and Old.

DÉCUVAGE *(FRANCE)*   Draining the contents of a tank or the unloading of grapes from fermentation tanks immediately after fermentation for the pressing step. *See* Draining Off and Encuvage.

DEFECTIVE PRODUCT   Products that are unmarketable because of product deterioration, leaking containers, damaged bottles, or damaged labels.

DEFRUTUM   An ancient Roman wine made with concentrated *must*. *See* Cooked Wine.

DÉGORGEMENT *(FRANCE)*   The process of freezing the neck of a bottle that contains champagne and a small amount of riddled sediment. This ice plug of sediment and champagne is then forced out by pressure within the bottle when the temporary cap is removed, leaving the remaining champagne crystal-clear. Also known as *disgorging* and *sboccatura*.

DÉGORGER *(FRANCE)*   One who disgorges bottles of sparkling wines.

DÉGOUTANT *(FRANCE)*   A red grape variety.

DEGREE DAYS   When a vintner is deciding on a grape variety to plant, many factors must be considered: location, the soil and its composition, drainage, and the weather that will affect the crop and possibly bring it greatness. The most important criterion in the analysis, however, is *heat summation*: the geographic classification of regions in terms of heat degree days during the seven-month growing season.

In 1936, University of California, Davis, professor Albert Winkler decided that temperature was a basis for segregating the grape-growing areas of California into five climatic regions. For classification purposes, Winkler used 50 degrees Fahrenheit as a base temperature applied specifically to the grape-growing season (April 1 to October 31). (The baseline is set at 50 degrees because there is almost no shoot growth below this temperature.) Winkler then developed a formula for heat summation above this 50 degree base. Heat summation is defined as the mean temperature or average high and low, greater than 50 degrees, from April 1 through October 31. The resulting figure is expressed as degree days.

For example, if the mean for a day is 70 degrees (50 degrees low and 90 degrees high), the summation for the twenty-four hour period is twenty degree days (70 – 50 = 20). If this condition occurred every day for a thirty-day month, the summation would be six hundred degree days (twenty degree days times thirty calendar days). *See* Heat Summation.

DEGREES BALLING   *See* Brix.

DEGREES BRIX   *See* Brix.

DEGREES CELSIUS   To convert Fahrenheit into Celsius, subtract 32 from the Fahrenheit temperature, then divide by 1.8; *or* subtract 32 from Fahrenheit, then multiply by 0.55.
To convert Celsius into Fahrenheit, multiply the Celsius temperature by 1.8 and then add 32, *or* divide Celsius by 0.55, then add 32.

DEGREES FAHRENHEIT   *See* Degrees Celsius.

DEGUSTACION (*SPAIN*)   Wine-tasting.

DÉGUSTATION (*FRANCE*)   An old word or term that described a wine-tasting.

DEGUSTAZIONE (*ITALY*)   Wine-tasting. Also known as *assaggio*.

DEHARDENING   *See* Rest.

DEI (*ITALY*)   Of the (plural).

DEKUYPER (*NETHERLANDS*)   The cooper or barrel maker.

DEL (*ITALY*)   Of the.

DELAWARE   A red grape variety that was brought in 1849 from the garden of Paul Provost of Frenchtown, New Jersey, to Delaware, Ohio, by Abram Thompson, editor of the *Delaware Gazette*. Delaware is often used as a base for sparkling wines.

DELGADO (*SPAIN*)   *See* Thin.

DELICADO (*PORTUGAL* AND *SPAIN*)   *See* Delicate.

DÉLICAT (*FRANCE*)   *See* Delicate.

DELICATE   Describes wines that are soft, pleasing, and light in style, with lower intensity flavors, rarely assertive. Delicate would be the opposite of a big, robust, full-bodied wine. Usually reserved for young and fresh red wines or white wines, lower in alcohol. Also known as *delicado, délicat, delicato, delikat, fein*, and *zart*.

DELICATESSEN   A red grape variety developed by Thomas Volney Munson (1843–1913) of Denison, Texas. It was so named because many grape varieties went into making it.

DELICATO (*ITALY*)   *See* Delicate.

DELIGHT SEEDLESS   A white grape variety developed in 1946 by Dr. Harold P. Olmo at the University of California, Davis.

DELIKAT (*GERMANY*)   *See* Delicate.

DELIMITED   A word applied to a geographic area with specific borders within which a particular distilled spirit or wine may be legally made.

DELIVERED DUTY PAID TO NAMED POINT   Seller imports goods, pays duty, etc., bears risk, and pays freight to named point. Can include delivery into buyer's warehouse at seller's expense. Also known as *DDP*.

DELIVERED DUTY UNPAID TO NAMED POINT   Similar to *delivered duty paid to named point* except that buyer pays duty and any other taxes. Seller bears risk and pays freight to inland destination. Also known as *DDU*.

DELIVERED EX-QUAY   Seller pays for unloading of vessel; may include or exclude duty. Also known as *DEQ*.

DELIVERED EX-SHIP   Seller pays freight and retains risk until vessel arrives at destination port; buyer pays for unloading, duty, and so on. Also known as *DES*.

DELIZIO *(ITALY)*   Delicious.

DELLA *(ITALY)*   Of the.

DELMONICO GLASS   A cocktail glass that holds five to seven ounces of a cocktail or sour with a frothy head.

DEMERARA   Guyanese rums have long been known by the generic name Demerara, after the river that divides the country and runs past its once-proud capital, Georgetown, which was built by Dutch settlers in the seventeenth century. *See* Rum.

DEMI *(FRANCE)*   Half.

DEMIJOHN   A large glass (or plastic) container that usually holds five gallons of liquid and is often used for the transportation or storage of wine, spring water, or mineral water. It is a corruption by the British of the French Dame-Jeanne, which meant a large glass bottle used for the transportation of wine. It held anywhere from one to ten gallons of wine and was usually wrapped with wicker or straw. Also known as a *bombona*, *carboy*, and *damigiana*.

DEMI-MUID *(FRANCE)*   A large barrel with a capacity of 171 gallons. *See* Barrel.

DEMINERALIZED WATER   Water from which the mineral salts have been removed by passing it over a bed of *ion-exchange resins*. *See* Distilled Water.

DEMI-QUEUE *(FRANCE)*   A large barrel with a capacity of approximately sixty gallons (228 liters).

DEMISEC *(FRANCE)*   Semidry or half-dry; used mostly in the Champagne region. In the United States it is applied to rather sweet sparkling wines. *See* Semidry Wine.

DEMITASSE *(FRANCE)*   Literally, half cup; often used when requesting a cup of espresso coffee.

DENOMINACÃO DE ORIGEM *(PORTUGAL)*   The equivalent of Italy's DOC wine laws.

DENOMINACIÓN DE ORIGEN *(SPAIN)*   The equivalent of Italy's DOC wine laws.

DENOMINATION OF ORIGIN   *See* Appellation of Origin.

DENOMINAZIONE DI ORIGINE CONTROLLATA (DOC) *(ITALY)*   Italy's wine laws; translates as "controlled denomination of origin." These laws were enacted on July 12, 1963, when the president of the Republic of Italy, Antonio Segni, signed them under

Presidential Decree No. 930. On July 15, these laws were published in the *Gazzetta Ufficiale della Republica Italiana*, the official registry of the Italian government.

The basic aim of the wine laws was to protect the name of origin and the sources of *musts* (unfermented grape juice) and wines, and to provide measures to prevent fraud and unfair competition. These very comprehensive laws cover just about every phase of grape-growing and winemaking and provide strict controls at every step of the process.

As of 1994, there are more than 250 wines that have been granted DOC or DOCG status, which is only approximately 15 percent of the nation's production. The aim of the Italian government is to bring classified wines to more than 50 percent by the year 2000.

DENOMINAZIONE DI ORIGINE CONTROLLATA E GARANTITA (DOCG) *(ITALY)*
This designation is given to those wines that are considered to be of a higher quality than DOC wines and made under even stricter guidelines. There are currently thirteen wines that have received the DOCG status. They are Albana di Romagna, Asti (a spumante) and Moscato d'Asti, Barbaresco, Barolo, Brunello di Montalcino, Carmignano, Chianti, Gattinara, Sagrantino di Montefalco, Torgiano Rosso Riserva, Taurasi, Vernaccia di San Gimignano, and Vino Nobile di Montepulciano. For other wines, applications for the status have been made and are pending.

DENSIMÈTRE *(FRANCE)*   A seldom-employed glass instrument used in the 1830s to show the amount of natural grape sugar left in the wine after primary fermentation.

DENSITY   The compactness of a substance; referred to as its specific gravity. Also known as *pyknós*.

DEPLETION   A case of product shipped from the distributor to the retailer.

DEPLETION ALLOWANCE   Payments made to a distributor based on a rate per case depleted. This rate cannot lower the *FOB* in that territory below the minimum FOB as listed in the control states. Also known as *standard depletion allowance*.

DÉPOSÉE *(FRANCE)*   Registered. *See* Marque Déposée.

DEPOSIT   *See* Sediment.

DEPOSITO *(PORTUGAL AND SPAIN)*   A large tank or barrel used for the storage of wines. *See* Barrel.

DEPOSITO *(ITALY)*   *See* Sediment.

DEPÒSITO *(SPAIN)*   *See* Sediment.

DÉPOSITO *(PORTUGAL)*   *See* Sediment.

DÉPÔT *(FRANCE)*   *See* Sediment.

DÉPOTAGE *(FRANCE)*   *See* Decanting.

DEPRESSANTS   Drugs or alcohol that slow or reduce the activity of bodily systems.

DEPTH   A wine or beer with intense complex flavors that seem to fill the mouth from front to back is described as having depth. The subtle layers of flavor are generally long-lasting. Depth of flavor is expected of most premium wines and beers.

DEPTH CHARGE   A shotglass full of whiskey that is dropped (glass and all) into a large glass of beer; the beer is then consumed.

DEQ   *See* Delivered Ex-Quay.

DES   *See* Delivered Ex-Ship.

DESCARNADO *(PORTUGAL)*   *See* Thin.

DESENGAGE *(PORTUGAL)*   *See* Destemming.

DESERTO VINO *(YUGOSLAVIA)*   *See* Dessert Wine.

DESICCATED GRAPES   Cracked and shriveled grapes, resembling raisins, that result from being attacked by *Botrytis cinerea*, the "noble rot." *See Botrytis Cinerea*.

DESIGNATED DRIVER PROGRAM   Informal arrangement between a customer and the operator of a beverage facility. One person in a group voluntarily does not drink alcoholic beverages and serves as the driver for the group. The person acting as the designated driver is usually offered complimentary "mocktails" or soft drinks.

DESQUET *(FRANCE)*   *See* Bontemps.

DESSERT WINE   A sweet or very sweet wine often made from dried grapes or that has been fortified by adding grape brandy. These wines are meant for consumption after dinner. Also known as *deserto vino, licoroso, likörwein, liquoreux, liquoroso, vinho liquoroso*, and *vino liquoroso*. *See* Luscious.

DESSERT WINE   A still wine naturally having an alcoholic content in excess of 14 percent but not in excess of 24 percent by volume. Dessert wines can be dry or sweet. This category of wine is based on a higher tax rate; the name does not necessarily indicate a sweet beverage for after dinner consumption. *See* Wine Product.

DESTEMMER   A mechanical device utilized for separating the grapes from the stems. Also known as *égrappoir*.

DESTEMMING   The separation of the grapes from the stems prior to fermentation or pressing. Also known as *desengage* and *égrapper*. *See* Crusher/Destemmer.

DESTILLARE   The Latin term for *distillation*. *See* Distillation.

DESTINATION INSPECTION   The inspection performed at the receiving point of the consignee of material to ascertain whether or not the shipment is in conformance with purchase specifications and contractual documents.

DETERIORATION   Any impairment of quality, value, or usefulness. Includes damage caused by corrosion and contamination.

DETOXIFICATION   The process of weaning or removing the physiological effects of alcohol from an addicted individual. A reduction of the toxic properties of a poisonous substance in the body.

DEUTSCHE WEINSTRASSE *(GERMANY)*   German Wine Road.

DEVELOPED   This term describes a wine that has reached its point of maturity in all of its characteristics.

DEXTRIN   Soluble, partly degraded carbohydrate molecules formed from starch in its decomposition by acids, heat, or diastase (enzymes). It is in the intermediate state between starch and sugar. It is produced during mashing and although not fermentable, it contributes to the terminal body of the beer. Also spelled *dextrine*. *See* Diastase and Amylase.

DEXTROSE   A basic crystalline sugar produced commercially from corn starch and sometimes used as a substitute for malt in brewing. Also known as *corn sugar*.

DGN   *See* Dirección General de Normas.

DI (ITALY)   Of.

DI   *See* Direct Import.

DIABETIKER-WEINSIEGEL (GERMANY)   Diabetic Wine Seal. An official seal, affixed to the neck of a wine bottle, which guarantees that the wine adheres to limitations of wines suitable for people with diabetes. *See* Für Diabetiker Geeignet.

DIÄBIER (GERMANY)   Diet beer; generally very low in calories.

DIACETYL   An odor and flavor of butter present in some wines (Chardonnay) and even beers. Wines that undergo *malolactic fermentation* often display this odor and flavor in varying levels. Also known as *buttery*.

DIAMMONIUM PHOSPHATE   Yeast food that is contained in distilling ingredients.

DIAMOND   A white grape variety developed in 1879 from a cross of Concord and Iona grapes by Jacob Moore of Brighton, New York. It is grown primarily in Eastern United States vineyards, where it is widely used as a base for sparkling wines. Its popularity has dwindled greatly in recent years due to superior varieties and the fact that its yields are low. Also known as *Moore's Diamond*.

DIANA   A red grape variety, formerly used as a blending grape in an attempt to improve the quality of Catawba wines. Its name originates from Mrs. Diana Crehore of Milton, Massachusetts, who in 1834 planted a seed of an open pollinated Catawba grape variety. One red fruited seedling was unusually fine and was named in her honor by the Massachusetts Horticultural Society.

DIASTASE   An enzyme secreted by the embryo in barley when conditions of temperature and moisture favor germination. This acts to modify and make soluble the starch in the barley, thus preparing it for conversion at a later stage to maltose. However, this enzyme activity is halted by drying the malt. A preparation of amylase enzymes can also be added to the mash to enhance the conversion of starch to sugar. *See* Dextrin and Amylase.

DIATOMACEOUS EARTH (DE)   A filtering agent used in making some alcoholic beverages. It is essentially pure silica that is mined from the floor of the sea. It comes from the silicified cell wall or the fossilized skeletons of microscopic aquatic life called diatoms, of which the more well-known plankton forms a major part. Diatoms are the primary link in the sea's chain of life—in fact all life, for it is these tiny creatures that produce approximately 80 percent of the oxygen that humans breathe. Commercial deposits mined in the United States today are about fifteen million years old and collectively contain about ten thousand known species of diatoms. Their skeletons, almost pure calcium, are totally inert and therefore impart no flavor to wine. Also known as *infusorial earth, kieselguhr,* or *diatomite*.

DIATOMITE   *See* Diatomaceous Earth.

DICE   *See* Ice Cubes.

DICK (GERMANY)   *See* Cloying.

DI CORPO (ITALY)   Full-bodied, with a high alcoholic content.

DIETHYLENE GLYCOL   A chemical used in some industrial products such as antifreeze. It is not approved for use in food or beverages.

DIFFUSE   Describes wines and beers that taste unstructured and unfocused due to being served too warm or served in warm to hot weather.

DIGESTIVE   A beverage that contains moderate to high levels of bittering substances. Alcoholic products from France that have the letter "D" stamped on their labels are examples of digestives. Also known as *digestivo*. *See* Bitters.

DIGESTIVO (ITALY)   *See* Digestive.

DIMIAT (BULGARIA)   A white grape variety. It is known as *Smederevka* in Yugoslavia.

DINDARELLA (ITALY)   A white grape variety grown primarily in Veneto.

DINNER WINE   A still table wine, generally dry, with an alcoholic content from 7 to 14 percent by volume. Also known as *table wine*.

DIOECIOUS   In viticulture, having the male (staminate) on one grapevine and the female (pistillate) on another. *See* Hermaphroditic.

DIONYSUS   The Greek god of wine. *See* Bacchus.

DIRECCIÓN GENERAL DE NORMAS (DGN) (MEXICO)   In an effort to control the production and quality of tequila, the Mexican government has devised a set of strict regulations. These regulations have since become somewhat more restricted and defined and are now known as *Norma Oficial Mexicana de Calidad* (NOM).

DIRECT IMPORT   When a retailer purchases directly from a supplier (winery, brewery, or distillery), bypassing the middle level or distributor. This practice is illegal in most states. Also known as *DI*.

DIRECT ISSUES   *See* Direct Purchases.

DIRECT PRODUCER   Grape variety that grows on its own root system, not needing to be grafted to other root stock to thrive and produce. Seldom employed today.

DIRECT PURCHASES   Alcoholic beverages that are received and put directly into the beverage area (bar). These items never go through the storeroom, therefore there are no requisitions for them. A system of this nature opens itself up to employee pilferage. Also known as *direct issues*.

DISBUDDING   The removal of excess buds or very young shoots on a grapevine.

DISCOUNT PURCHASING   *See* Bulk Buying.

DISCUS   *See* Distilled Spirits Council of the United States.

DISERBANTE (ITALY)   *See* Herbicide.

DISGORGING   *See* Dégorgement.

DISPLAYED CONSUMER OFFER   Use of a consumer offer as part of a promotional in-store display.

DISPOSABLE INCOME   Income that households have left after the payment of taxes and household bills.

DISSOLVE   To mix a solid into a liquid solution.

DISTILLATE   The concentrated clear liquid obtained from distillation. Also known as *distillato*.

DISTILLATION   Distillation involves the separation of alcohol from the liquid in a fermented mash. Since alcohol boils at 173.1 degrees Fahrenheit and water boils at 212 degrees Fahrenheit, it is relatively easy to separate the alcohol and flavoring components from the mash. The higher the heat, the greater the volume of distilled *neutral* spirits. The lower the heat, the greater the amount of flavor (from the base grains) that is carried through distillation. The mash enters near the top of a continuous still or column still, while steam enters near the still's bottom chambers, thus vaporizing the alcohol and flavoring components. When the vapor is drawn off, it condenses into a liquid, known as *low wine*, with an alcoholic content of anywhere from 45 to 65 percent. The low wine is redistilled or further refined, allowing the alcohol to reach an even higher concentration and to further remove unwanted impurities and flavors. The resulting liquid is called *high wine* or new whiskey; it is crystal-clear and ready for maturing. Also known as *distillazione*. *See* destillare.

DISTILLATO (ITALY)   *See* Distillate.

DISTILLATORE (ITALY)   Distiller.

DISTILLAZIONE (ITALY)   *See* Distillation.

DISTILLED SPIRITS   Ethyl alcohol, hydrated oxide of ethyl, spirits of wine, whiskey, rum, brandy, gin, and other distilled spirits, including all dilutions and mixtures thereof, for nonindustrial use. Also known as *spiritueux*. *See* Spirits.

DISTILLED SPIRITS COUNCIL OF THE UNITED STATES (DISCUS)   The distilled spirits industry's trade association.

DISTILLED SPIRITS PLANT   An establishment qualified for producing, warehousing, or processing distilled spirits, including distilled denatured spirits.

DISTILLED WATER   Ordinary water from which minerals are removed by the process of distillation. *See* Demineralized Water.

DISTILLERIA (ITALY)   *See* Distillery.

DISTILLERS' BEER   The alcoholic beer or low wine ready for distillation.

DISTILLERS FEED GRAINS   Highly nutritious animal feed made from the processed grain residue left behind after fermentation and distillation. Although lower in bulk than unprocessed grain (because the starch is removed during mashing and fermentation), these feeds remain high in protein and are enriched beyond the food value of the unprocessed grain because of the presence of yeasts used in fermentation.

DISTILLERY   A building that houses the apparatus where distilling of alcoholic beverages is carried out. Also known as *distilleria*.

DISTILLING MATERIAL   Any fermented or other alcoholic substance capable of, or intended for use in, the original distillation or other original processing of distilled spirits.

DISTINCTIVE   A beverage that has recognizable qualities or characteristics that can immediately be distinguished.

DISTINGUÉ (*FRANCE*)   *See* Elegant.

DISTINGUIDO (*SPAIN*)   *See* Elegant.

DISTINGUISHED   Also known as *distingué* and *distinguido*. *See* Elegant.

DISTRIBUIDORES EXCLUSIVOS (*SPAIN*)   Exclusive distributors.

DISTRIBUTOR POST-OFF   A case price discount on alcoholic beverages that a distributor sometimes is permitted to offer to a retailer. Also known as *file-off*, *post down*, *post*, and *file down*.

DISTRIBUTORS   Wholesalers (the second level of the three-tier system) who purchase wholesale from suppliers and sell retail to retailers. *See* Wholesalers.

DISTRIBUZIONE (*ITALY*)   Distribution.

DITCH   A trench used for conveying water to saloons in the western part of the United States during the 1800s and early 1900s.

DITTA (*ITALY*)   Bottled at the premises of the firm or company.

DIVE   A dilapidated bar.

DIXIE   A white grape variety developed in 1976.

DO (*PORTUGAL* AND *SPAIN*)   *See* Denominación de Origen or Denominacão de Origem.

DOC (*ITALY*)   *See* Denominazione di Origine Controllata.

DOCE (*PORTUGAL*)   Also known as *adamado*. *See* Sweet.

DOCG (*ITALY*)   *See* Denominazione di Origine Controllata e Garantita.

DOCK GLASS (*PORTUGAL*)   A small, short-stemmed, elongated wineglass with a tulip-shaped bowl that holds two to three ounces. These glasses are used by professional port tasters for evaluation purposes. Also known as *port glass*.

DOG RIDGE   A grape variety developed by Thomas Volney Munson (1843–1913) of Denison, Texas.

DOLCE (*ITALY*)   *See* Sweet.

DOLCETTO (*ITALY*)   A red grape variety grown primarily in the Piedmont region, where it is produced in the Langhe Hills just south of the town of Alba. The Dolcetto grapevine is indigenous to the area and was subject to local government regulations as early as 1593. It is Piedmont's most widely grown grapevine after Barbera.

    Dolcetto differs from the more famous wines of Piedmont, like Barolo, in that it is lighter, with an intense purple color in its youth, and is intended to be drunk young.

    The name Dolcetto could be roughly translated to mean "little sweet one." The name, however, is misleading: Dolcetto is a dry red wine with a pleasing bitter aftertaste. Also known as *Dolsin, Dolsin Nero, Dolsin Raro*, and *Ormeasco* (in Liguria).

DÔLE (*SWITZERLAND*)   *See* Red Wine.

DOLOMIES (*FRANCE*)   Limestone rock rich in magnesium; used as a fertilizer.

DOLSIN (*ITALY*)   *See* Dolcetto.

DOLSIN NERO (*ITALY*)   *See* Dolcetto.

DOLSIN RARO *(ITALY)* *See* Dolcetto.

DOM *(GERMANY)* Cathedral.

DOMAINE *(FRANCE)* Wine estate; a synonym of *château, clos*, or *cru*.

DOMAINE BOTTLED *(FRANCE)* Same as château bottled, except as practiced in Burgundy. Also known as *Mise en bouteilles au domaine*.

DOMÄNE *(GERMANY)* A domain or vineyard estate.

DOMESTIC In the United States, a term often used to describe alcoholic beverages made in the country, as opposed to imported types. However, the term domestic should be avoided, because it has the connotation of a cheap replica or imitation. Instead, the term American should be substituted.

DOMINA *(GERMANY)* A red grape variety developed from a cross of Pinot Noir and Portugieser.

DOM PÉRIGNON *(FRANCE)* Dom Pierre Pérignon was born in January 1638 in Sainte-Ménehould near the Champagne-Lorraine border. As chief cellarmaster at Hautvillers (1668–1715), he perfected the technique for making champagne by blending grapes and wines from various vineyards to achieve a consistent and harmonious balance. He used an oil-soaked hemp rag, an ill-fitting wooden plug, or the bark of a tree as a temporary bottle stopper. In 1668, Dom Pérignon bottled the first bottle of champagne. He did not, however, discover, invent, or create the wine that is now called champagne. Dom Pérignon became blind during the latter stages of his life and died in September 1715.

DONA BRANCA *(PORTUGAL)* A white grape variety used mainly in the production of *Vinho Verde*.

DONZELHINO *(PORTUGAL)* A red grape variety grown in the Douro region.

DONZELHINO BRANCO *(PORTUGAL)* A white grape variety grown in the Douro region.

DOP BRANDY *(SOUTH AFRICA)* *See* Grappa.

DOPPLEBOCK *(GERMANY)* *See* Bock Beer.

DOPPLEOHM *(GERMANY)* A large barrel with a capacity of seventy-nine gallons. *See* Barrel.

DOPPLESTÜCK *(GERMANY)* A large barrel with a capacity of 634 gallons. *See* Barrel.

DORADILLO *(AUSTRALIA)* A white grape variety.

DORATO *(ITALY)* *See* Grecanico.

DORIN *(SWITZERLAND)* *See* Chasselas Doré.

DORMANCY The inactive, nonvegetative resting of a grapevine that occurs in winter and during which time the canes are pruned. *See* Rest and Quiescence.

DORNFELDER *(GERMANY)* A red grape variety developed in 1956 from a cross of Helfensteiner and Heroldrebe by August Herold at Weinsberg.

DORONA DI VENEZIA *(ITALY)* *See* Corvina.

DORTMUNDER BEER (GERMANY)   A golden-colored lager beer with a high level of malt and hops, traditionally brewed in Dortmund.

DOSAGE (FRANCE)   The addition of a mixture of sugar syrup, grape concentrate, and/or brandy to champagne or sparkling wines before recorking and eventual shipping, which establishes the level of sweetness in the finished product. Also known as *dosing, liqueur d'expédition*, and *süssung*. See Liqueur de Tirage.

DOSAGE ZÉRO   *See* Extra Brut.

DOSING   *See* Dosage.

DOSSER   *See* Grape-Picking Basket.

DOUBLE AUM (GERMANY)   A barrel with a capacity of approximately sixty gallons. *See* Barrel.

DOUBLE MAGNUM   An oversized bottle equivalent in capacity to four 750-milliliter bottles or three liters (101.4 ounces). It is also the largest sized bottle that French champagne is fermented in. *See* Jeroboam.

DOUBLE PRUNING   The cultural practice whereby twice the number of buds dictated by the balanced pruning formula are retained after an initial pruning in early to mid-winter. A second pruning is done after bud damage can be assessed and/or the threat of spring frost injury is minimal.

DOUBLER   A *pot still* used for doubling. *See* Doubling.

DOUBLING   In whiskeymaking, it is the redistilling of a spirit to help improve its strength and flavor. *See* Doubler.

DOUCEREUX (FRANCE)   *See* Cloying.

DOUIL (FRANCE)   A grape harvesting vat where picked grapes are dumped.

DOURO (PORTUGAL)   An important grape-growing region where port wine is produced. The production of port is limited to a strictly defined area of approximately 68,000 acres along the River Douro in northern Portugal. The slopes of the Douro, which have a slatelike soil known as schist, are cut out and terraced for planting with vineyards. These walled terraces prevent erosion of the precious soil. The Douro is the world's second legally demarcated wine region (Italy's Chianti Classico region was demarcated in 1716 by the grand duke of Tuscany). In 1756, during the era of the Marquês of Pombal (almost 200 years before France's *appellation contrôlée* regulations became law), the Douro region was defined to protect the quality and good name of port (known as *Porto* in Portugal). In that same year, Pombal reestablished the Oporto Wine Company.

DOUSICO (GREECE)   A distilled spirit that is flavored with anise-seed.

DOUX (FRANCE)   *See* Sweet.

DOUX (FRANCE)   The sweetest champagne produced; it is not available in the United States and only produced in limited quantities for Eastern Europe. According to the European Common Market, champagnes labeled "doux" must contain more than fifty grams of sugar per liter.

DOWNY MILDEW (PLASMOPARA VITICOLA)   A fungal disease native to North America that attacks most species of grapevines. The disease (then known as *Peronospora*) was inadvertently introduced in 1878 into European vineyards, where it devastated the grapevine species *Vitis vinifera*, which is generally more susceptible to the disease than native American grapevines. Today, the disease can be found on grapevines in most regions of the world that are wet during the growing season. The fungus causes direct yield losses by rotting inflorescences, clusters, and shoots, and indirect losses by prematurely defoliating grapevines, which increases their susceptibility to winter injury and delays ripening of the fruit. Also known as *blattfallkrankheit*.

DRAFF   The residue left from the mashing process in making beer (or whiskey), which is then strained to produce the *wort*.

DRAFT BEER   According to the United States government, draft beer may be so labeled on cans or bottles if it is unpasteurized or if it has been bottled under sterile filtration methods. It may not be labeled "draft beer" if it has been pasteurized, but it may use the terminology draft-brewed, old-time on tap taste, or draft beer flavor.

Draft beer is of a delicate and perishable nature and its flavor can change if it is not kept under constant refrigeration. The ideal storage temperature for draft beer is 38 degrees Fahrenheit. If the temperature is allowed to rise above 45 to 50 degrees Fahrenheit for an extended length of time, secondary fermentation may occur, making the beer unpalatable. Also spelled *draught beer*. Also known as *tap beer* and *keg beer*.

DRAGON'S MILK   An eighteenth-century term for strong ale.

DRAINED WEIGHT   Weight of contents of a package minus its liquid and container.

DRAINING OFF   After the primary fermentation (alcoholic fermentation) of red wines (which contain skins, seeds, and pulp) the juice is drained off (kept separate) and the skins, which are still heavily laden with juice, are immediately sent to a press for further juice extraction.

White wines are first allowed to settle, then drained off from the fermentation tank without disturbing the sediment that is at the bottom of the tank. From there, the white wine is transferred to another container where it remains until bottling. *See* Decuvage and Encuvage.

DRAKE TUBE   A cylindrical tube with a capacity of more than 100 milliliters that contains a hydrometer for measuring the specific gravity of beer or wine.

DRAM   A unit of avoirdupois weight equal to 0.0625 ounces.

DRAM SHOP ACTS   State acts that define liability for alcoholic beverage sales to patrons who injure or kill third parties.

DRAM SHOP LIABILITY   Liability to third parties created by the sale of alcoholic beverages to a patron.

DRAPEAU (FRANCE)   *See* Jacketed Tank.

DRAUGHT BEER   *See* Draft Beer.

DRAW-KNIFE   A sharp, two-handled instrument that is pulled toward the cooper in order to shave the staves of a wooden barrel to more or less their finished shape.

DRAW ONE   A slang term meaning to pour a beer.

DRAYAGE   Road transportation for a container between the nearest railway terminal and the shipper/receiver's facility, or between the ocean carriers and the terminal.

DREGS (PORTUGAL)   The extremely heavy sediment found in some bottles of port wine, especially *vintage port*. *See* Sediment.

DRIED FRUIT BRANDY   A brandy that conforms to the standards for fruit brandy, except that it has been derived from sound, dried fruit, or from the standard of wine of such fruit. Brandy derived from raisins or raisin wine are designated "raisin brandy." Other brandies are designated in the same manner as fruit brandy from the corresponding variety or varieties of fruit, except that the name of the fruit is qualified by the word "dried."

DRIED OUT   A wine or even beer lacking in fruit and flavor due to excessive dryness. Generally it is an indication that the beverage is past its peak of maturity and is getting old and tired. *See* Dead and Old.

DRIED WHOLE MILK   A milk product from which only the water has been removed, leaving the milk and cream content intact.

DRIMYS (GREECE)   *See* Pungent.

DRINKING WATER   Bottled water that comes from a government-approved source (municipal or state) and is filtered or treated in some manner before bottling. The water can come from the tap, a well, a lake, and so on. It can also be blended with water from other sources. The water is always processed in some way (e.g., the addition of chlorine or other chemicals, the addition or deletion of mineral salts).

DRIP IRRIGATION   The slow, frequent, precise application of irrigation water directly to the plant through devices known as emitters. Emitters are placed on the soil or just below the surface of the row crop soil.

Although there are usually a large number of emitters per acre, they wet only a small portion of the soil. Drip (or trickle) systems utilize the simple concept of supplying a plant's daily water requirements directly to the plant. These systems can be elaborate and sophisticated but are typically the most uniform, efficient, and manageable of all the types of irrigation systems. They are especially adapted to situations where water is expensive or of low quality or where crops of high value are grown.

DRIPPING ROD   A graduated rod (sometimes glass) that measures the contents of a barrel of wine.

DROSOPHILA MELANOGASTER   A strain of fruit flies that are drawn to grapes or fermenting grape juice by the smell of small quantities of vinegar formed during fermentation. The fruit flies lay eggs in the broken skins of the grapes, seriously contaminating the grapes or *must* and raising the level of volatile acidity, which could cause the wine to turn to vinegar.

DRU (FRANCE)   *See* Heavy.

DRUNK   *See* Intoxicated.

DRUPEGGIO (ITALY)   A white grape variety used in the blend of Orvieto wine, from Umbria. Also known as *Canaiolo Bianco*.

DRY   A wine with little or no noticeable residual sugar, usually containing less than 0.2 percent sugar; however, the range for a dry wine can be construed to be within the range of 0.2 to 0.6 percent sugar. Most wine tasters begin to perceive the presence of sugar at levels of 0.7 percent. On champagne and sparkling wines, *dry* only refers to faintly sweet—not as dry as brut. Also known as *sec, seco, secco, suho, trocken*, and *xirós*.

DRY   A designation of a liqueur, if the sugar, dextrose, or levulose, or a combination thereof, is less than 10 percent by weight of the finished product.

DRY BEER   Beers made to be drier to the taste with no aftertaste. Basically, during the cooking process, brewers extract as much sugar as possible from the malted barley and mixing grains (rice, corn, etc.), then allow the fermentation to last an additional seven to ten days. Another method is to allow more of the malt and adjunct cereals to be converted into fermentable sugars, which are used more efficiently during fermentation. This results in a beer with a higher alcoholic content.

Actually, dry beers originated in Germany with the brewing of *diäbier*, beers specially produced for people with diabetes. *See* Für Diabetiker Geeignet.

DRY BREAK   When a bottle is broken and left in its case untouched for several months. The cardboard will dry out and unless the case is shaken or the liquid was colored, the break will not be detected.

DRY COUNTY   County (or similar governmental jurisdiction) in the United States whose voters have not approved the sale of alcoholic beverages. Counties permitting sale only by private clubs are considered dry. *See* Wet County.

DRY GIN   *See* London Dry Gin.

DRY GOODS   Paper and so forth, behind a bar. *See* Dry Storage.

DRYING SHED   A shed where the malted barley necessary in the production of Scotch whisky is dried.

DRY SHERRY   *See* Amontillado and Cocktail Sherry.

DRY STORAGE   That portion of the bar or storeroom utilized for the storage of nonrefrigerated goods. *See* Dry Goods.

DRY VERMOUTH   *See* Vermouth.

DRY WHOLE MILK   Whole milk with all of its moisture evaporated.

DRY YEAR   A narrow, woody growth ring on a cork tree caused by lack of rain.

DUC (FRANCE)   Duke.

DUELA (SPAIN)   *See* Staves.

DUFT (GERMANY)   *See* Fragrance.

DUI   Driving under the influence of alcohol. *See* DWI.

DULCE (SPAIN)   *See* Sweet.

DULCE APAGADO (SPAIN)   *See* Mistelle.

DULCET   A red grape variety.

DULL   Describes a wine or beer that displays lack of brilliance in its appearance, or a wine that is uninteresting and lacks distinction or individuality because of low acidity. Also known as *breit* and *terne*.

DUMB   Describes a wine with potential, but not yet developed enough or not offering its full quality or character. Also used to describe wines with undeveloped aromas and flavors but that display full and hard levels of tannin. Often, the wine is too young or perhaps served too cold. Wines often go through certain stages of development called dumb where, for unexplained reasons, they "just don't taste right." Several reasons might be a full-bodied red wine served during warm weather, wines subjected to recent rough handling, freshly or newly bottled wine, and so on. Also known as *closed-in, fermé, muto, numb*, and *restrained*. *See* Numb.

DUMPING A closeout; alcoholic products are "dumped" onto the retail market at below list prices in order to eliminate all existing merchandise inventory.

DUNCAN TAVERN MUSEUM A tavern in Kentucky where pioneer Daniel Boone used to drink.

DUNDER The residue (sugar cane juice remains) left in the still after distillation, which is generally used in making full-bodied rums.

DUNKEL (GERMANY) Dark.

DUNKEL WEISSBIER (GERMANY) A dark wheat beer. *See* Wheat Beer.

DUNKIRK A white grape variety.

DÜNN (GERMANY) *See* Thin.

DUPE A shortened term or abbreviation for "duplicate." Each check has two parts: a hard copy, which is presented to the guest, and a soft copy, which is turned in at the bar for service. As the server writes on this check, a "dupe" or duplicate copy of the order is inscribed.

The duplicate check control system ensures management that each check is accounted for and properly priced. It also verifies the quantities of a beverage that has been ordered and served.

DUR (FRANCE) *See* Hard.

DURCHGEGOREN (GERMANY) Fully fermented.

DURELLA (ITALY) A white grape variety grown primarily in Veneto.

DURIF A red grape variety that flourishes in the Rhône Valley of southern France, where it is disallowed for use in *appellation contrôlée* wines but is commonly used as a blending grape for *vin ordinaire* wines. The grape is named after Dr. Durif, a nurseryman, who in 1880 propagated it mostly in the Rhône Valley. Incorrectly spelled *Duriff* and once believed to be the true name of the *Petite Sirah* grape. *See* Petite Sirah.

DURO (ITALY AND SPAIN) *See* Hard.

DUSTY *See* Chewy.

DUTCH GIN *See* Holland Gin.

DUTCHESS A white grape variety developed in 1868 from a natural crossing of a White Concord seedling pollinated by mixed pollen of Delaware and Walter, by Andrew Jackson Caywood of Marlboro, New York (Dutchess County).

DWI Driving while intoxicated. *See* DUI.

e \ '\=e \ *n, often cap, often attrib*

E A letter designation used on labels of armagnac, cognac, and some other brandies as an abbreviation for *extra*.

E A symbol that appears after the milliliter or liter content of the bottle, indicating it originated in Europe.

EARL GREY TEA A very delicate and mild tea that owes its perfumed fragrance to the oil of the *bergamot orange*. However, in high levels the odor of bergamot is intensely pinelike, reminiscent of a disinfectant. Earl Grey is made from a blend of teas from India and China.

In the eighteenth century, Charles, Earl Grey, a British statesman and representative to the Imperial court of China, tasted a special blend of tea destined for the Emperor. He became so fond of it that he bought the secret recipe and began selling the tea to the public.

EARLY BURGUNDY *See* Abouriou.

EARLY MUSCAT A white grape variety developed in 1958 by Dr. Harold P. Olmo of the University of California, Davis.

EARLY NIABELL A red grape variety developed in 1958 from a cross of Campbell Early and another seedling by Dr. Harold P. Olmo of the University of California, Davis.

EARTHY A term used to describe the odor or taste imparted to a wine by the soil in which the grapevine is grown. Also known as *bodengeschmack, erdig, goût de terroir*, and *yeódis*.

EAU (FRANCE) *See* Water.

EAU-DE-VIE Literally, "water of life." A clear distillate of fruit or grape wine, first produced by the Arabs in the seventh century, it is the origin of today's brandies. Grape brandies, which include armagnac and cognac, are known as *eau-de-vie* before barrel aging. Also known as *aguardente* and *aguardiente*. *See* Grappa and Alcools Blancs.

EBULLIOMETER   An instrument used in the United States to measure the alcoholic content of wine. Also known as *ebulliscope*. *See* Alcoholometer.

EBULLIOMETRY   This is the technique of precise determinations of boiling and condensation temperatures. The boiling (point) temperature is that temperature at which liquids or a solution boil under a certain constant pressure.

EBULLISCOPE   *See* Ebulliometer.

ECHELLE (FRANCE)   In the Champagne region, vineyards are rated according to the quality level of the grapes they produce. This official designation, called a "growth" or *cru*, can range from 80 (the least distinguished) to 100 percent. Vineyards that produce the best grapes because of the right consistency and drainage of the soil, the most ideal exposure to the sun, and other viticultural and climatic conditions, are rated 100 percent. The prices of grapes at harvest time are fixed in relation to the classification of each *cru* in this scale.

ECHT (GERMANY)   *See* Genuine.

ECHT (POLAND AND RUSSIA)   *See* Kümmel.

ÉCLAIRCISSAGE (FRANCE)   *See* Crop Thinning.

ECM   European Common Market.

EDEL (GERMANY)   *See* Noble.

EDELBEERENAUSLESE (GERMANY)   The term used prior to 1971 for wines of the *beerenauslese* category.

EDELFÄULE (GERMANY)   The noble mold responsible for Eiswein, Beerenauslese, and Trockenbeerenauslese wines. *See Botrytis Cinerea*.

EDELSÜSSE (GERMANY)   A great, sweet, noble wine.

EDELWEISS   A white grape variety developed by Elmer Swenson of the University of Minnesota and released in the 1960s.

EDELZWICKER (FRANCE)   A wine made in Alsace from a blend of *noble grape varieties*.

EDES (HUNGARY)   *See* Sweet.

EDIBLE PORTION (EP)   The portion remaining after trimming or fabrication that is used for consumption in a beverage facility. *Pouring costs* are sometimes referred to as EP costs.

EDUCACIÓN (SPAIN)   The maturing and/or blending of a new wine.

EDULCORÉ (FRANCE)   Artificially sweetened.

EEC   European Economic Community.

EFFERVESCENT WINE   *See* Sparkling Wine.

EFFEUILLAGE (FRANCE)   *See* Leaf Thinning.

EFKHÁRISTOS (GREECE)   *See* Pleasant.

EGALISAGE (FRANCE)   A further blending of wines from different barrels.

EGGNOG A rich, creamy, nonalcoholic dairy beverage made with egg yolks, cream, and sugar. The alcoholic version includes brandy or rum as well. The name *eggnog* is probably a corruption of "Egg-and-Grog." Also spelled *egg nog*. *See* Advokatt.

EGG WHITES Also known as *chiara*. *See* Albumen.

ÉGRAPPER *(FRANCE)* *See* Destemming.

ÉGRAPPOIR *(FRANCE)* *See* Destemmer.

EGRI BIKAVÉR *(HUNGARY)* A deep, rich, robust, dry red wine often referred to as "bull's blood," coming from the town of Eger, made primarily from the Kadarka grape.

EHRENFELSER *(GERMANY)* A white grape variety developed from a cross of Johannisberg Riesling and Sylvaner clones by Professor Birk at the Geisenheim Institute in the Rheingau. The Ehrenfelser, named for the Ehrenfels ruins near the village of Rüdesheim, was created in 1929, but did not receive a patent until 1969.

EHRWEIN (GERMANY) *See* High-Quality.

EIDETIC IMAGERY OR RECOLLECTION Commonly known as photographic memory. A persisting mental image of a visual scene that the subject sees as "outside his head" and is able to "read off" with unusual vividness by moving his eyes, as if scanning the original scene.

EINSET SEEDLESS A red grape variety developed at the State Experimental Station in Geneva, New York, and introduced in September 1985.

EINSPÄNNER *(AUSTRIA)* Strong black coffee with a *hat* of frothy cream, served in a glass.

EINZELLAGE *(GERMANY)* *See* Vineyard.

EISBOCK *(GERMANY)* An extra strong bock beer in which the alcoholic content has been raised by freezing. When the beer begins to melt, the water is drawn off, concentrating the taste as well as raising the alcohol level. *See* Ice Beer.

EISENBERG *(AUSTRIA)* A village and wine region near the Hungarian border in southern Burgenland. Mostly fruity red wines are produced in this area.

EISWEIN *(GERMANY)* A name reserved for wine made from grapes harvested frozen. These frozen grapes produce a wine that is both sweeter and more concentrated than the average sweet wine.

The practice of making wine from grapes naturally frozen on the grapevine has long been a part of the wine culture of Germany and Austria. However, eiswein is produced in many areas of the world, including the United States. With the Rhine and Mosel's best vineyards lying just about as far north as grapes can ripen, working with frozen grapes is not only a tradition but sometimes a necessity as well. German (and Austrian) winemakers have built their reputations by exploiting nature, allowing the grapes to hang on the grapevine past normal harvesting time to further ripen.

The adversary that the vintner faces late in the growing season is cold weather and the chance of an early frost or hard freeze. If the grapes are spared a freezing cold and can sufficiently dry before harvest, wines of incredible lusciousness and complexity can be produced. But if nature wins the battle and a hard freeze hits the vineyards, the winemaker has but one outside chance—to pick and crush the frozen grapes, hopefully producing the rare and unique eiswein. Although this was once a rare product (made only every second or third decade), eiswein is nowadays produced somewhat more frequently because new, colder vineyard sites are allowed to yield frozen grapes.

The making of eiswein is governed by a simple physical law. Water, which freezes at 32 degrees Fahrenheit, constitutes the major portion of the pulp and juice of grapes. As the grapes freeze, it is the water inside them that actually freezes, and not the other elements, of which sugar is the largest component. When these grapes are crushed, the frozen water is not pressed out, only the luscious, sugary nectar of the grapes, which is only a fraction of the juice. But while the freeze steals from juice quantity, the *must* weight gains in concentration. It becomes heavily laden with sugar, sometimes doubling its usual strength; it also has a high level of acidity. The resulting wines are characteristically rich in body with a fine natural sweetness and a mature, complex bouquet and flavor. All of the flavors of the grape are intensified and magnified, making this wine of considerable risk a prized success for the vintner.

In making eiswein, the grapevines are wrapped in large plastic covers to protect them from birds, wind, and snow. The grapes are then allowed to hang on the grapevines in the hope that cold weather will strike, hard freezing the grapes on the grapevines. Sustained day and night temperatures in the high teens to low twenties (Fahrenheit) will allow the grapes to freeze. Sometimes the winemakers will not harvest them until November, December, or even January. However, the longer they wait, the stronger the chance the grapes will shrivel up and fall from the grapevines.

When the grapes are sufficiently frozen, they are harvested (usually early in the morning before the sun can thaw them) and shipped to the winery. There they are pressed in small batches in a basket press, extracting a slight fifty gallons of juice per ton of grapes. The flow of the sweet juice from the press is pencil thin, the grapes yielding less than one-third the normal volume of juice. Also known as *ice wine*.

EKLEKTÓS *(GREECE)*   *See* Vinous.

ELABORADO POR *(SPAIN)*   *See* Criado Por.

ELBLING *(GERMANY)*   *See* Burger.

ELÉGANT *(FRANCE)*   *See* Elegant.

ELEGANT   A wine characterized by a dignified richness, class, grace, refinement, and exceptional character. A step above the rest, with good balance; however, not big and robust. Also known as *bonito, distinguished, elégant, elegante,* and *racé.*

ELEGANTE   *See* Elegant.

ÉLEVAGE *(FRANCE)*   The maturing or aging of wine or distilled spirits in a barrel.

ELEVENSES *(ENGLAND)*   A cup of coffee or tea generally taken around the middle of the morning.

ÉLEVEUR *(FRANCE)*   *See* Broker.

ELIXIR   Once, a term used by alchemists who sought out various recipes in search of love potions, cure-alls, everlasting life, rejuvenation, and aphrodisiacs. Today, the term elixir refers to alcoholic beverages that have medicinal value.

ELLAGIC ACID   A phenol present in grape skins, seeds, and stems that causes bitterness in wine. It is usually removed by gelatin fining. *See* Phenol.

ELLEN SCOTT A red grape variety developed by Thomas Volney Munson (1843–1913) of Denison, Texas, and named for Mrs. Munson.

ELONGATED WINE (ENGLAND) An old term for wine that was *stretched* by the addition of water, often used to reduce the alcohol for purposes of excise duty. *See* Watered-Down.

ELTINGER *See* Knipperlé.

ELVICAND A grape variety developed by Thomas Volney Munson (1843–1913) of Denison, Texas.

ELVIRA A white grape variety introduced in Missouri in 1869 by Jacob Rommel. Also known as *Missouri Riesling*.

EMBOTELLADO (SPAIN) Bottled.

EMBOTELLADO EN LA BODEGA (SPAIN) Bottled at the bodega.

EMBOTELLADO EN ORIGEN (SPAIN) *See* Estate Bottled.

EMBOTELLADO POR (SPAIN) Produced and Bottled by.

EMERALD RIESLING A white grape variety developed in 1946 from a cross of Muscadelle and Johannisberg Riesling by Dr. Harold P. Olmo of the University of California, Davis.

EMILIA-ROMAGNA (ITALY) One of twenty wine-producing regions, located north of Tuscany in north-central Italy. Emilia-Romagna is famous for its Lambrusco wine and for the city of Bologna, noted for its rich cuisine, which includes Parmigiano-Reggiano cheese, prosciutto ham, and Balsamic vinegar.

EMIR (TURKEY) A white grape variety.

EMPEROR A red grape variety grown in California.

EMPTY BOTTLE RETURN *See* Bottle-For-Bottle.

EN BLANC (FRANCE) *See* Blanc de Noirs.

ENCABEZADO (SPAIN) *See* Fortification.

ENCAPSULATED YEAST Beads, a few millimeters in diameter, consisting of an alginate that encapsulates the yeasts needed for the secondary fermentation of wine to produce sparkling wines. Also known as *calcium alginate beads*. *See* Alginate and Yeast.

ENCÉPAGEMENT (FRANCE) The varietal makeup of a vineyard.

ENCHERTOS (PORTUGAL) Grafts or scions for grafting onto rootstocks.

EN CLARO (SPAIN) When a newly fermented wine becomes bright, but prior to its being fortified.

ENCORCHADOR (SPAIN) Person responsible for the hand-corking of wine bottles.

ENCORPADO (PORTUGAL) *See* Full-Bodied.

ENCRUZADO (PORTUGAL) A white grape variety grown in the Dão region.

ENCUVAGE (FRANCE) The loading of tanks with grapes prior to pressing or fermentation. *See* Decuvage and Draining Off.

ENERGIZER   Nutrients and nitrogen in the form of phosphates added to fermentations to increase the efficiency of the yeast. *See* Ammonium Phosphate.

ENGARRAFADO NA ORIGEM (PORTUGAL)   *See* Estate Bottled.

ENGLISH BREAKFAST TEA   A black, full-bodied, and rich tea made from a blend of India and Ceylon teas.

ENGLISH CUVÉE   *See* Brut.

ENJAMBEUR (FRANCE)   A special tractor with two wheels on each side of the row of grapevines that is to be straddled.

EN MASSE (FRANCE)   *See* Mise en Masse.

ENOCIANINA (ITALY)   A concentrated, powdered pigment extract made from the coloring of black grapes. It is used in perfumes and in its liquid form it is used by the United States Department of Agriculture when stamping and labeling various cuts and grades of meat.

ENOLOGIA (ITALY AND SPAIN)   *See* Enology.

ENOLOGIST   A technician of the grapevine and of wine. Enologists' technical and practical know-how enable them to assume entire responsibility for the vinification and breeding of wines. They conduct all the analyses on the grape and the resultant wine and interpret the results. Also known as *enologo* and *enologue*. *See* Winemaker.

ENOLOGO (ITALY)   *See* Enologist.

ENOLOGUE (FRANCE)   *See* Enologist.

ENOLOGY   The science or the study of wine and winemaking; related to viticulture, which is the science of grape culture. Also spelled *enologia* and *oenology*.

ENOPHILE   Anyone who loves wine and wine lore to the point of exaltation and pays tribute to it. Also spelled *oenophile*.

ENOTECA (ITALY)   A wine library or wine bottle collection used for display and reference. A wine bar where wines may be sampled and/or purchased. Also spelled *oenoteca* and *vinothek*.

ENOTHÉQUE (FRANCE)   A wine library or wine bottle collection used for display and reference. A wine bar where wines may be sampled and/or purchased. Also spelled *oenothéque* and *vinothéque*.

ENOTRIA TELLUS (GREECE)   Land of Wine—the name given to Italy by ancient Greek writers. Also spelled *oenotria*.

ENOTRI VIRI (GREECE)   Men of Wineland—the name given to Italians by ancient Greek writers. Also spelled *oenotri*.

EN-PRIMEUR (FRANCE)   Wine sold prior to its being on the market. *See* Futures Market.

ENTERING TRADE CHANNELS   A term that depicts distilled spirits shipped in bottles by bottlers or importers to wholesalers, retailers, United States military installations, or to any other domestic market outlet. Generally, the federal excise tax is payable as the products enter trade channels. *See* Imports for Consumption and Withdrawals.

EN TIRAGE *(FRANCE)*   Literally, "on the yeast," used when discussing the secondary fermentation of sparkling wines.

ENTIRE   A grape leaf that has no lobes.

ENTRE-DEUX-MERS *(FRANCE)*   Literally, "between two seas." A large white-wine-producing district in the Bordeaux region.

ENTRÉE   The main or principal item of the meal; the meat or the fish are examples.

EN VASO *(SPAIN)*   *See* Gobelet.

ENVEJECIDO POR *(SPAIN)*   Aged by.

ENZIAN   A spirit distilled in most Scandinavian- and German-speaking countries, produced from the very long roots of the yellow mountain gentian plant. It is quite bitter to the taste and is usually served, well-chilled, after dinner.

ENZYMES   Small organic substances produced by yeast that serve as catalysts during fermentation.

EP   *See* Edible Portion.

EPERNAY *(FRANCE)*   A city in the Champagne region noted for its sparkling wine production and for commerce.

ÉPICÉ *(FRANCE)*   *See* Spicy.

EPIGEAL   That part of a grapevine consisting of the trunk, which has as its functions support, transport, and reserve; the arms, which are shoots of more than a year in age; the canes, which are shoots of one year of age; and the fruiting canes, those bearing buds opening in the current season. The latter, in turn, bear the leaves and the flowers from which the clusters develop.

ÉPINETTES *(FRANCE)*   *See* Grape Knife.

ÉPLUCHAGE *(FRANCE)*   A process of hand-sorting or picking over by hand of the newly harvested grapes to eliminate defective or immature bunches, berries, and material-other-than-grapes (MOG). Also known as *triage*.

EQUILIBRADO *(PORTUGAL AND SPAIN)*   *See* Balance.

EQUILIBRATO *(ITALY)*   *See* Balance.

ÉQUILIBRÉ *(FRANCE)*   *See* Balance.

EQUIPMENT   All functional items such as tap boxes, glassware, pouring racks, and similar items used in the conduct of a retailer's on-premise business.

ERBACEO *(ITALY)*   Tasting or smelling of herbs.

ERBALUCE *(ITALY)*   A white grape variety grown in Piedmont.

ERBEN *(GERMANY)*   Heirs.

ERDIG *(GERMANY)*   *See* Earthy.

EREDI *(ITALY)*   Heirs.

ERYTHRONEURA COMES   *See* Grape Leafhopper.

ERZEUGERABFÜLLUNG *(GERMANY)*   Estate bottled by a producer, not a shipper. *See* Originalabfüllung.

ESCALA *(SPAIN)*   Each series or group of barrels holding a similar wine from the same *solera* system.

ESCANCIADOR *(SPAIN)*   *See* Sommelier.

ESCANÇÃO *(PORTUGAL)*   *See* Sommelier.

ESGANA-CÃO *(PORTUGAL)*   A white grape variety grown in the Douro region.

ESMAGAMENTO *(PORTUGAL)*   *See* Crushing.

ESPAGNE *(FRANCE)*   *See* Cinsaut.

ESPALIER *(FRANCE)*   A method of pruning grapevines.

ESPARTO MATS   Straw mats utilized for the drying of grapes for the eventual making of sweet sherries. *See* Straw Mats.

ESPECIAL *(SPAIN)*   A specially selected vintage.

ESPORTARE *(ITALY)*   *See* Export.

ESPORTAZIONE *(ITALY)*   Exportation.

ESPRESSO *(ITALY)*   Speed.

ESPRESSO *(ITALY)*   A deep, dark, strong black coffee made in a machine that forces steam through finely ground, dark-roasted coffee grounds.

ESPRESSO CON GHIACCIO *(ITALY)*   Refrigerated or fresh espresso with fresh cold milk over ice. *See* Caffè Freddo.

ESPRESSO DOPPIO *(ITALY)*   A double espresso.

ESPRESSO MACCHIATO *(ITALY)*   A shot of espresso "marked" with a scoop of foamed milk on top.

ESPUMANTE   Term used in Brazil and Portugal for a sparkling wine. Also known as *vinho espumante*. *See* Sparkling Wine.

ESPUMOSA *(SPAIN)*   Term used in Spain for a sparkling wine. Also known as *vino espumosa*. *See* Sparkling Wine.

ESSENCE   An unofficial term used by some California winemakers during the 1960s and 1970s to describe late-harvested wines with intense varietal character and sweetness.

ESSENCE   Preparation of natural constituents extracted from fruit, herbs, flowers, berries, and so forth. They may not be used in the production of any formula wine except agricultural wine. The essences may be produced on wine premises or elsewhere. Where an essence contains distilled spirits, use of the essence may not increase the volume of the wine more than 10 percent nor its alcohol content more than 4 percent by volume.

ESSENTIAL OILS   Volatile oils that give distinctive odor or flavor to plants, flowers, and fruits. In wines they combine with the alcohol to help determine its bouquet.

ESSENZ *(HUNGARY)*   The measured level of unfermented sugar present in the *must*. *See* Brix.

ESTAGIO *(PORTUGAL)*   A period of time when the wine rests or ages after being put through the *estufa*.

ESTATE BOTTLED   A term that may be used by a bottling winery on a wine label only if the wine is labeled with a viticultural area appellation of origin and the bottling winery (1) is located in the labeled viticultural area; (2) grew all of the grapes used to make the wine on land owned or controlled by the winery within the boundaries of the labeled viticultural area; (3) crushed the grapes, fermented the resulting *must*, and finished, aged, and bottled the wine in a continuous process, the wine at no time having left the premises of the bottling winery. Also known as *embotellado en Origen* and *engarrafado Na Origem*. *See* Château Bottled, Controlled By, and Domaine Bottled.

ESTERS   Organic, volatile compounds that contribute fruity aromas to wines, beers, and distilled spirits. Esters are formed by reactions of alcohol and organic acids and sometimes contribute rather solvent-like smells such as those of vinegar or nail polish remover. Beers, too, are often described as having apple, banana, blueberry, grapefruit, pear, or strawberry esters.

ESTUFA *(PORTUGAL)*   A process used on the island of Madeira, where huge "hot houses" or heating chambers are used to give madeira, a fortified wine, its distinctive character. Also known as *baking*. *See* Caramelization, Estufagem, and Hydroxymethylfurfural.

ESTUFADO *(PORTUGAL)*   *See* Vinho Estufado.

ESTUFAGEM *(PORTUGAL)*   The process of heating or *baking* madeira wine in heating chambers called *estufas*. *See* Estufa.

ET *(FRANCE)*   And.

ÉTAMPÉ *(FRANCE)*   A branded or stamped cork.

ETEREO *(ITALY)*   *See* Ethereal.

ETHANOL   *See* Ethyl Alcohol.

ETHEREAL   Referring to smell; it is a scent depending on the presence of components of the "bouquet" of the ethers (high quality alcohols) developed in the course of aging. Also known as *etereo*.

ETHYL ACETATE   Sometimes a wine will smell vinegary but not taste acidic; this is the effect of ethyl acetate. In low concentrations it has a vaguely sweet, fruity odor, but in large amounts it smells like nail polish remover (it is an ester). Ethyl acetate exists in all wines to some degree and often complements many other odoriferous compounds. Oxidation (possibly in a barrel) or possible exposure to wild yeasts present on the grapes can cause a volatile acid or acetic acid to form. The esters of acetic acid and ethyl alcohol combine to form ethyl acetate.

ETHYL ALCOHOL   The principle alcohol found in all alcoholic beverages. Also known as *alcool éthylique* and *ethanol*. *See* Alcohol.

ETHYLENE GLYCOL   *See* Glycol.

ETICHETTA *(ITALY)*   *See* Label.

ETIQUETA (SPAIN)   *See* Label.

ÉTIQUETTE (FRANCE)   *See* Label.

ÉTOFFÉ (FRANCE)   *See* Rich.

ETTARO (ITALY)   *See* Hectare.

ETTOGRADO (ITALY)   *See* Hectograde.

ETTOLITRO (ITALY)   *See* Hectoliter.

EUCALYPTUS   The oil odor of an evergreen species, occasionally found in some California Cabernet Sauvignon or Pinot Noir wines.

EUMELAN   A red grape variety discovered in 1847 by Mr. Thorne at Fishkill Landing, New York.

EUROPEAN OAK   A general term given to all types of wooden barrels emanating from various forests, mostly in France and Yugoslavia.

EVAPORATED MILK   Whole milk that has approximately 50 to 55 percent of its water evaporated, but is not sweetened like *condensed milk.*

EVAPORATION   When a wine or distilled spirit is aging in a wooden barrel, a slight loss in the volume of the liquid occurs due to changes in temperature, humidity, soakage, and the porosity of the wooden barrels. The amount that evaporates is approximately 3 percent of annual production. In the Cognac and Armagnac regions of France, evaporation is known as the *angel's share* and *shrinkage.*

EVÁRMOSTOS (GREECE)   *See* Balance.

EVÓDIS (GREECE)   *See* Fragrance.

EVYENÍS (GREECE)   *See* Noble.

EX-CELLAR   Price of wine in the cellars without duty or importer's markup.

EXCISE MAN   Since 1651, a term for a British tax officer. *See* Revenuers.

EXCISE TAX   Indirect tax levied by the United States government on the alcohol content by volume of distilled spirits and on malt beverages and the various categories of wine. License and control states and the District of Columbia also levy excise taxes, either on the volume or value base of distilled spirits.

EXOTIC   A red grape variety developed from a cross of Flame Tokay and Ribier.

EXPANSIVE   Full of taste, body, and flavor; often used to describe full-bodied wines with mouth-filling capabilities.

EXPENSE   The cost of assets consumed or converted in generating income; an expired cost.

EXPORT   Goods or commodities sent or carried outside of a country's territorial borders for eventual sale or trade. Also known as *esportare* and *exportacion.*

EXPORTACIÓN   *(Spain) See* Export.

EXPORTADOR (SPAIN)   Exporter.

EXTENDED SKIN CONTACT   The process of allowing young red wines to stay in contact with their skins after fermentation has ceased (often up to two weeks), which softens the tannin, brightens the color, and enhances the fruitiness of the wine. Also known as *cappello galleggiante, extended skin maceration, long-vatted,* and *macération pelliculaire. See* Skin Contact and Vatting.

EXTENDED SKIN MACERATION   *See* Extended Skin Contact.

EXTRA   A red grape variety developed by Thomas Volney Munson (1843–1913) of Denison, Texas.

EXTRA (E)   A label designation used on armagnac, calvados, and cognac bottles to indicate an extra or extremely high quality product. It also indicates that the youngest brandy used in the blend is at least six years old (armagnac) and (calvados), and 6-1/2 years old (cognac), although larger amounts of older brandies have also been used.

EXTRA BRUT   A champagne or sparkling wine that contains less than six grams of sugar per liter or no *dosage.* Also known as *brut absolut, brut de brut, brut intégral, brut nondosage, brut sauvage, brut zéro, dosage zéro, pas dosé, natural, naturale, sans sucre,* and *ultra brut.*

EXTRACT   *See* Percolation.

EXTRACTABLES   Those elements that are extracted from oak barrels, including vanillin and other substances with desirable odors, lignin fragments, hydrolyzable tannins, and "bodying" factors that affect the flavor impression of the wine. Substances extracted from grape skins; anthocyanins (pigmentation), flavonoids, and tannins are also extractables.

EXTRACTS   The nonvolatile, soluble solids present in a wine. This includes everything left after water and alcohol have been removed and residual sugar subtracted (acids, proteins, tannins, pigments, etc.). Also known as *extrakt.*

EXTRA DRY   Term used for a champagne that is not as dry as brut but is drier than sec. According to the European Common Market, extra dry champagnes contain between twelve and twenty grams of sugar per liter.

EXTRAKT (GERMANY)   *See* Extracts.

EXTRA SEC   A slightly sweetened sparkling wine or champagne.

EYE OF THE PARTRIDGE   *See* Oeil de Perdrix.

EZERJÒ (HUNGARY)   A white grape variety.

E

EZERJÒ (HUNGARY)

f \'ef \ n, often cap, often attrib

FAA   *See* Federal Alcohol Administration Act.

FABBRICA DI BIRRA (ITALY)   *See* Brewery.

FABER (GERMANY)   A white grape variety with a slight Muscat bouquet, developed in 1929 from a cross of Pinot Blanc and Müller-Thurgau by George Scheu at the Alzey Research Station in the Rheinhessen. Also known as *Faberrebe*.

FABERREBE (GERMANY)   *See* Faber.

FABRICATED PRODUCT   An item after trimming, boning, and so on.

FABRICATED YIELD PERCENTAGE   The yield or edible portion expressed as a percentage of the amount as purchased.

FACINGS   The number of bottles on display of an item (linear width) on the front line of a store shelf.

FACTORIA (SPAIN)   *See* Fattoria.

FACTORIAL ANALYSIS   A statistical method to identify common factors in a set of strongly correlated variables.

FACTORY HOUSE   The name of a house in Oporto, Portugal, built around 1786 or 1790, used by the British Association of Port Wine Shippers as their headquarters. In addition to meetings, tastings, and luncheons, occasional festive harvest dinners also take place there.

FAD (GERMANY)   *See* Flat.

FADED   Describes a wine that has lost its bouquet, character, and definition, usually through age or excessive oxidation. When wines are exposed to the air for prolonged periods of time, their bouquet and taste appear to fade.

FAIBLE (FRANCE)   *See* Feeble.

FALANGHINA *(ITALY)* A white grape variety grown primarily in Apulia and Latium.

FALANGHINA FALSA *(ITALY)* A white grape variety grown primarily in Apulia and Latium.

FALANGHINA VERACE *(ITALY)* A white grape variety grown primarily in Apulia and Latium.

FALCETTA *(ITALY)* *See* Grape Knife.

FALERNIAN An ancient Roman wine.

FALERNUM A colorless, slightly alcoholic, spiced, almond-lime syrup originating in the Caribbean, used as a flavoring in rum drinks.

FALKENSTEIN *(AUSTRIA)* A village and one of the largest wine regions in Lower Austria. Here the Grüner Veltliner, Müller-Thurgau, and Welschriesling are grown. The grapes grow in the historical surroundings of mighty fortresses and beautiful castles.

FALLING BRIGHT A spontaneous, natural clearing of suspended material from a newly fermented wine or beer. Also known as *star bright*.

FALSE WINE Wines made from sources other than grapes. Also known as *second wine*.

FALUNS *(FRANCE)* Chalk deposits that are rich in fossilized shells.

FÄRBERTRAUBE *(GERMANY)* A red grape variety.

FARGUES *(FRANCE)* Sweet white wine made from a blend of Sauvignon Blanc, Sémillon, and Muscadelle grape varieties. It is also one of the five communes within Bordeaux's Sauternes district entitled to be called Sauternes.

FARINE *(FRANCE)* A flour paste mixture used to seal the *croze* on a wooden barrel.

FARO A *lambic-type* beer, often sweetened with fruit or seasoned with spices. *See* Lambic.

FASS *(GERMANY)* A barrel.

FASSGESHMACK *(GERMANY)* The smell or flavor imparted to wine by aging in wooden barrels.

FASSLE *(GERMANY)* *See* Porrón.

FAT Describes a heavy, intense wine that has a higher than average glycerin level. It is often rich but lacking in elegance, acidity, and complexity. Also known as *fett, pâteaux, pakhys, pastoso*, and *wuchtig*. *See* Gordo.

FATIGUE *(FRANCE)* *See* Tired.

FATIGUED Also known as *fatigue*. *See* Tired.

FATTE *See* Barrel.

FATTORIA *(ITALY)* Farm or estate. Also known as *factoria* and *feitoria*.

FAUCET *See* Spigot.

FAVORITA *(ITALY)* A white grape variety grown in Piedmont since the beginning of the nineteenth century.

FAVORITE A red grape variety released in 1973 by the USDA. It was developed from a cross of Lenoir and Herbemont and is grown primarily in Texas.

F AND B *See* Food and Beverage.

FDA *See* Food and Drug Administration.

FÉCONDATION *(FRANCE)* *See* Pollination.

FECUNDATION A growth of grapevines in early spring that leads to the formation of the seeds in each grape.

FEDERAL ALCOHOL ADMINISTRATION (FAA) ACT A law enacted by the United States Congress in 1935, intended to promote fair competition in the marketing of alcoholic beverages by prohibiting certain trade practices that result in the exclusion of competing products in interstate commerce. Among other things, it also regulates the labeling and advertising practices of the alcoholic beverage industry.

FEDERAL EXCISE TAX (FET) A tax imposed by the United States government on all types of alcoholic beverages, including imports and those that are American-produced.

FEDERAL STANDARDS OF IDENTITY *See* Standards of Identity.

FEDERWEISSER *(GERMANY)* *See* Nouveau.

FEEBLE Wines that are thin in color and faint in body, lacking character and distinction. Also known as *apagado* and *faible*. *See* Thin.

FEHÉR BOR *(HUNGARY)* *See* White Wine.

FEHÉRBURGUNDI *(HUNGARY)* *See* Pinot Blanc.

FEHÉR SZAGOS *(HUNGARY)* A white grape variety used in making California sherry.

FEIN, FEINE *(GERMANY)* *See* Delicate.

FEINSTE *(GERMANY)* The finest.

FEINTS *See* Tails.

FEITORIA *(PORTUGAL)* *See* Fattoria.

FELD *(GERMANY)* Field. Also known as *acker*.

FELS *(GERMANY)* Cliff.

FEMININE Describes wines that are soft and delicate. Also known as *damenwein*.

FENDANT *(SWITZERLAND)* *See* Chasselas Doré.

FERMÉ *(FRANCE)* *See* Dumb.

FERMENTAÇÃO *(PORTUGAL)* *See* Fermentation.

FERMENTACÍON *(SPAIN)* *See* Fermentation.

FERMENTACÍON TUMULTUOSA *(SPAIN)* *See* Tumultuous.

FERMENTATION The conversion (by the action of yeast) of sugar contained in the grapes into *ethyl alcohol* or *ethanol*. Yeasts are introduced into tanks of *must* to start the process; fermentation stops when the sugars are depleted or when the alcohol level reaches about 14 percent and kills the yeast. Secondary fermentation takes place in sparkling wines to give them their distinctive carbonation.

It was in 1789 that the famed French chemist Antoine-Laurent Lavoisier made one of the first studies on the natural phenomena or fermentation; he was followed in 1810 by Joseph-Louis Gay-Lussac, who correctly devised the overall equation for fermentation. In 1857, Louis Pasteur began the first scientific study of fermentation in the town of Arbois, in the Jura region of France.

Gay-Lussac's formula for fermentation is:

$$C_6H_{12}O_6 = 2C_2H_5OH + 2CO_2$$
(sugar glucose) (ethyl alcohol) (carbon dioxide)

The equation describes the following process: yeast "eat" (metabolize) sugar and in the process create, in approximate equal proportions, alcohol and carbon dioxide gas (CO_2), with heat as a by-product. If yeast is added to a sugar-water mixture, fermentation would produce only alcohol and CO_2, but when grapes and yeast are put together, the end product is wine.

The term also refers to the natural action of yeast in converting malted barley and hops into beer or converting rice into saké. Distilled spirits are also fermented and the resulting *liquor* is then distilled in the various methods characteristic to each type of spirit. Also known as *angegoren, fermentacão, fermentación, fermentazione, gärung*, and *moroni*.

FERMENTATION LOCK A low-pressure valve made of glass or plastic that seals a barrel or other container of fermenting wine from the outside air while permitting carbon dioxide gas given off during fermentation to escape through sulfited water. Also known as *airlock, bosador, bubble cap, ventilating bung, water bung, water seal*, and *water valve*.

FERMENTATION TANK A barrel, stainless steel tank, concrete vat, or other type of structure utilized for the primary fermentation of grapes and grape juice into wine. Also known as *tinas*.

FERMENTAZIONE (ITALY) *See* Fermentation.

FERMENTAZIONE NATURALE (ITALY) Naturally fermented, usually in reference to sparkling wines.

FERMENTED IN THE BOTTLE *See* Transfer Method.

FERMENTED IN THIS BOTTLE *See* Méthode Champenoise.

FERMENTER Any container that is used to ferment grape juice into wine. Formerly made of wood or concrete, it is now made mostly of glass or stainless steel.

FERMENTI (ITALY) *See* Yeast.

FERMENTING The time during which the wine or beer remains in the fermentation vats.

FERNÃO PIRÃO (PORTUGAL) *See* Fernão Pires.

FERNÃO PIRES (PORTUGAL) A white grape variety grown throughout Portugal. Also known as *Fernão Pirão* and *Maria Gomez*.

FERN MUNSON   A grape variety developed by Thomas Volney Munson (1843–1913) of Denison, Texas.

FERROCYANIDE COMPOUNDS   Used to remove trace metal and objectionable levels of sulfide and mercaptans from wine. The compound most often used is potassium ferrocyanide, which is not legal in the United States. Also known as *blue fining*. *See* Casse and Cufex.

FERROUS SULFATE   A compound used to clarify and stabilize wine.

FEST *(GERMANY)*   *See* Firm.

FESTBIER *(GERMANY)*   Beers made for traditional festivals (e.g., Oktoberfest), anniversaries, or special events. The styles as well as taste and alcoholic content of these beers vary. Also known as *jubiläumsbier* and *spezialitäten*.

FESTIVEE   A red grape variety developed in Canada.

FET   *See* Federal Excise Tax.

FETEASCA ALBA *(ROMANIA)*   A white grape variety with a strong aroma, somewhat reminiscent of Gewürztraminer or Muscat. Also known as *Leányka* and *Mädchentraube*.

FETEASCA NEAGRA *(ROMANIA)*   A red grape variety.

FETEASCA REGALA *(ROMANIA)*   A red grape variety.

FÉTE DE LA FLEUR *(FRANCE)*   Flower festival. Every year the wine fraternities celebrate the flowering of the grapevine, which occurs in May or June.

FETT *(GERMANY)*   *See* Fat.

FEUILLETTE *(FRANCE)*   A small barrel with a capacity ranging from 112 to approximately 144 liters (thirty-two to thirty-eight gallons), depending on the wine region. *See* Barrel.

FEURIG *(GERMANY)*   *See* Fiery.

FIACCO *(ITALY)*   *See* Tired.

FIANO *(ITALY)*   A white grape variety grown primarily in Campania.

FIASCO *(ITALY AND SPAIN)*   The name given to the straw-covered, bulbous-bodied, long-necked bottle that houses some Chianti and other wines. Its origin can be traced back to 1265, according to a document preserved at San Gimignano. Also known as *fiasque*.

FIASQUE *(FRANCE)*   *See* Fiasco.

FICELAGE *(FRANCE)*   *See* Wire Hood.

FIELD BLEND   Formerly a widespread practice in many parts of the world where several different red and/or white grape varieties were grown in the same vineyard area. They were harvested, crushed, and fermented together to produce a single wine; thus the wine was *blended in the field*.

FIELD BUDDING   A grafting technique, now rarely used. Instead, the more modern "bench grafting" is preferred. Also referred to as *chip budding*.

FIELD CRUSHING A method of crushing grapes in the vineyard, developed around 1969 or 1970 by the Mirassou Vineyards of San Jose, California. Grapes are crushed and sealed in a CO_2 atmosphere in tanks alongside the mechanical harvester within minutes of picking. By conventional methods, two to twenty hours may elapse between picking and crushing, during which oxidation can cause the loss of fresh flavor. *See* Mortl.

FIELD GRAFTING The native rootstock (*Vitis rupestris*) is planted in the vineyard and allowed to grow one season. It is then notched to accept a European (*Vitis vinifera*) grapevine bud, then the graft is loosely covered with soil to facilitate callousing. In spring the soil is removed and if the graft has taken, shoots will emerge from the budded vinifera portion of the grapevine. These are then protected by milk cartons against wind, frost, or pest damage. This technique was developed during the 1970s in California. Sometimes referred to as *budding*.

FIELD SELECTION *See* Mass Selection.

FIELD WATER CAPACITY The amount of water present in the soil several days after it has been saturated by rains.

FIERINESS Brandy or other distilled spirits that leave behind the sensation of burning. *See* Fiery.

FIERY Also known as *caliente, feurig*, and *fieriness*. *See* Hot.

FIESTA SEEDLESS A white grape variety released in 1965 by the USDA.

FIFO *See* First-In, First-Out.

FIFTH An old term (prior to 1978) denoting one-fifth of a gallon or 25.6 ounces. Also referred to as four-fifths.

FIGLIA (*ITALY*) Daughter.

FIGLIO (*ITALY*) Son.

FIGS A scent often characteristic of the Sémillon, a white grape variety.

FILANT (*FRANCE*) *See* Oily.

FILANTE (*ITALY* AND *SPAIN*) *See* Oily.

FILE DOWNS *See* Distributor Post-Off.

FILE-OFF *See* Distributor Post-Off.

FILLETTES (*FRANCE*) Half-bottles (375 milliliters) used in Alsace, Loire Valley, and Bordeaux; also known as *little girls*.

FILLINGS The new whiskey after it is removed from the still.

FILM YEAST *See* Flor.

FILS (*FRANCE*) Son.

FILTER To screen out solids in wine, beer, or distilled spirits by mechanical means. Also known as *filtre*.

FILTERING A mechanical process by which wine, beer, or distilled spirits is forced through a porous filter medium (paper, pads, or membranes) that traps suspended particles and thus removes them. Filtering is utilized to remove yeast and bacteria cells, making the beverage microbiologically stable. It is also used before fermentation to clarify press juice and to give beverages the highest possible clarity (for consumer acceptance). Also known as *filtrage, filtrate,* and *filtration. See* Clarifying, Fining, Microfiltration, Polishing Filter, Sterile Filtration, Ultrafiltration, and Unfiltered.

FILTRAGE (*FRANCE*) *See* Filtering.

FILTRATE (*ITALY*) *See* Filtering.

FILTRATION *See* Filtering.

FILTRATO (*ITALY*) A concentrated grape *must* that, when added to a wine, provokes a secondary fermentation. It is often used in making Lambrusco wine. *See* Back Blending and Governo.

FILTRE (*FRANCE*) *See* Filter.

FIN (*FRANCE*) High-quality. *See* Fine.

FINAGE (*FRANCE*) *See* Commune.

FIN BOIS (*FRANCE*) A district in the region of Cognac.

FINDLING (*GERMANY*) A white grape variety developed by F. Kimmig from a Müller-Thurgau mutant.

FINE *See* Fining.

FINE (*FRANCE*) A term that may be found on cognac labels, but has no legally defined meaning.

FINE (*ITALY*) *See* Marsala Fine.

FINE Also known as *fin, fine,* and *fino. See* High-Quality.

FINE (*ITALY*) *See* Fine.

FINE COGNAC (*FRANCE*) A term that may be found on cognac labels, but has no legally defined meaning.

FINESSE A term applied to a wine with subtlety of flavor; breed, class, and distinction.

FINGER LAKES The Finger Lakes vineyards are located approximately 350 miles northwest of New York City, along Lakes Canandaigua, Cayuga, Hemlock, Keuka, and Seneca. The clear, deep waters of the Finger Lakes of New York keep this region's climate temperate, and plentiful shale beds (similar to those in Champagne, France) help drain the soil. The slow-warming lakes retard spring growth, protecting it against the danger of frost, and keep the grapevines warmer on chilly fall nights. Although the Finger Lakes received their *appellation* in October 1982, grape-growing and winemaking date back to the 1820s.

FINING The process of "polishing" or clarifying a cloudy or hazy wine or beer to brilliancy by removing suspended particles. The selected fining agent is added to the beverage and as it settles to the bottom (by gravity), it attracts particles in suspension. Most wineries and breweries use positively charged fining agents to help clarify wines and beers by removing precipitates of excess pectin, peptides, iron compounds, or unstable protein. Other wineries and breweries use agents that carry a negative charge for the softening of excessive tannin levels in beers and red wines and the removal of browning agents. Also known as *affiné, chiarificare, collage, coller, fine*, and *schönen*. *See* Clarifying, Colloidal Suspension, Filtering, Fining Agents, Over-Fining, Particle Matter, Sterile Filtration, and Unfined.

FINING AGENTS   Substances used in the fining of wine or beer. Among them are activated carbon, activated charcoal, albumen (egg whites), bentonite, casein, Cufex, gelatin, isinglass, kieselsol, Spanish earth, Sparkolloid, and (in ancient times) animal blood. Also known as *chiarificante*. *See* Fining and Rousing.

FINISH   The tactile and flavor impressions left in the mouth while a beverage is being swallowed. Some beverages finish harsh, hot, and astringent, while others are smooth, soft, and elegant. *See* Aftertaste and Length.

FINKEL (NORWAY)   The name of a high-proof spirit distilled from potatoes.

FINO (ITALY)   Refined.

FINO (SPAIN)   High-quality. *See* Fine.

FINO (SPAIN)   A type of sherry made entirely from Palomino grapes. It is very dry, light, and pale in color, with a distinctive mild nutty-tangy taste.

FIOLERI (ITALY)   Glassblower.

FIORE (ITALY)   *See* Flowery.

FIORITURA (ITALY)   *See* Flowering.

FIRE-BREWED   In beermaking, the brewing kettle is heated directly by fire rather than by the more conventional high pressure, heated steam process. Contrary to some beliefs, the resulting beer does *not* taste any different.

FIRING GLASS   A glass used for drinking toasts; firing glasses were banged down hard on the dining table, simulating the sound of firing muskets, hence the need for a stout base, and the name.

FIRKIN   A beer barrel used in England that contains forty-one liters or 10.8 gallons. *See* Barrel and Pin.

FIRM   A wine with structure and backbone; opposite of "flabby." Also known as *fest* and *nevródis*.

FIRNE (GERMANY)   *See* Maderized.

FIRST GROWTHS (FRANCE)   The five red wines (four from the Médoc, one from Graves) officially classified in 1855 (Château Mouton-Rothschild since 1973) as being of the highest quality.

FIRST-IN, FIRST-OUT (FIFO)   A rotation procedure utilized mostly for those products that are perishable or semiperishable. It consists of issuing requisitions and ensures that products received first (existing stock that is the oldest) is utilized first. Also known as *rotate stock*.

FISCHLEIM (GERMANY)   *See* Isinglass.

FISH GLUE   *See* Isinglass.

FIVE-GALLON CANISTER   A metal canister with a capacity of 640 ounces that holds either premix beverage or postmix syrup used for soda systems.

FIXED ACIDITY   The total (titratable) acidity less the volatile acidity or the non-volatile acids of the wine. The major acids of wine include tartaric, citric, malic, lactic, succinic, and inorganic acids. Also known as *acidità fisse*.

FIXED COPPER AND LIME   The common name for a systemic fungicide effective against a host of grapevine diseases, among them Botrytis bunch rot, black rot, powdery mildew, and downy mildew. *See* Bordeaux Mixture.

FIXED COSTS   Costs or expenses that remain constant or are generally fixed in nature, regardless of the volume of business, such as rent, property taxes, and interest. These costs cannot be controlled by an individual (such as department head) in a company. Also referred to as *noncontrollable costs*.

FIXIN (FRANCE)   The northernmost village of the Côte de Nuits in Burgundy. Fixin was known as *Fiscinus* in the year 830 and *Fiscentiae* in 995.

FIZZ   A cocktail consisting of distilled spirits, citrus juices, and sugar, with carbonated water added at the end. It is often served as a morning-after "hangover cure-all" with a multitude of other ingredients, such as egg whites or yolks, various fruit juices, syrups, wines, and even beer.

FLABBY   Describes a wine lacking character, usually due to a low level of acidity. Also known as *flaccido* and *mou*.

FLACCIDO (ITALY)   *See* Flabby.

FLACH (GERMANY)   *See* Flat.

FLACO (SPAIN)   *See* Thin.

FLAG   A toothpick holding a cherry and orange slice as a garnish on a cocktail.

FLAGEY-ECHÉZEAUX (FRANCE)   A small red-wine village of the Côte de Nuits in Burgundy. In the year 1131, Flagey was known as *Flagiacum*; in 1886, the village of Flagey added to its name that of its most illustrious vineyard, Echézeaux.

FLAGON   A term for odd-shaped wine bottles of varying sizes and shapes, although it was a common term used to describe wine bottles of ordinary shape in earlier times.

FLAKE ICE   *See* Ice Cubes.

FLAKE STAND   *See* Worm.

FLAMBÉ (FRANCE)   *See* Flaming.

FLAMEADO (SPAIN)   *See* Flaming.

FLAMING   Burning off alcohol by igniting with a match. Usually, brandies or other distilled spirits to be flambéed are warmed first, then poured into a glass or dish and ignited. Also known as *flambé* and *flameado*.

FLAME SEEDLESS   A red grape variety developed in 1961 from a cross of (Cardinal and Thompson Seedless) and (Red Málaga and Tifafihi Ahmer) and (Muscat of Alexandria and Thompson Seedless) by Harmon and Weinberger in California.

FLAME TOKAY   A white table grape used principally in California for dessert wines.

FLAME UP   *See* Proof.

FLANZY   In the early 1950s, carbonic maceration was called "Flanzy" after Professor Michael Flanzy, an enologist who helped develop it. *See* Carbonic Maceration.

FLASCHE (*GERMANY*)   *See* Bottle.

FLASCHENREIF (*GERMANY*)   A wine that is ready for bottling.

FLASK   A flat-sided bottle with a capacity of 8 to 33.8 ounces.

FLAT   Describes a wine or beer that is dull, insipid, lacking in vigor, character, flavor, and liveliness due to low natural acidity or possibly from being open too long. Also known as *fad, flach, flat, goût d'évent, matt,* and *pesante.*

FLAT   Describes a sparkling wine, beer, or soft drink that has lost its effervescence.

FLAT BEER   Draft beer may become *flat* due to any of the following: greasy glasses, not enough pressure in the beer lines, the CO_2 pressure being shut off during the night, the precooler or coils being too cold, a leaky pressure line, loose tap or vent connections, a sluggish pressure regulator, or an obstruction in the beer lines.

FLAT CASE   The standard size case of product (e.g., four-bottle, three- or four-liter case; six-bottle, 1.5 or 1.75 liter case; twelve-bottle, 750-milliliter or one-liter case; twenty-four-bottle, 375-milliliter case, etc.). Flat cases can refer to either depletions or shipments, as appropriate.

FLAT CUBES   *See* Ice Cubes.

FLAVOR   Those complex impressions originating on the palate when the wine is swirled in the mouth. Also known as *geschmack, sabor, sapore,* and *saveur.*

FLAVONOIDS   Flavoring compounds, technically phenols, found in the skins of grapes, especially red. *See* Phenols and Tannin.

FLAVORED BRANDY   A mixture of brandy with a minimum of 2.5 percent sugar, flavored and colored with various types of fruit and/or herbs and that may or may not contain added sugar. By United States federal law (1992) it cannot be bottled at less than 60 proof (30 percent alcohol by volume).

FLAVORED GIN, VODKA, RUM, OR WHISKEY   A mixture of distilled neutral spirits that are flavored and colored with various types of fruit and/or herbs and may or may not contain added sugar. By United States federal law (1992) it cannot be bottled at less than 60 proof (30 percent alcohol by volume).

FLAVORED WINES   *See* Apéritif Wine and Low-Alcohol Refreshers.

FLEMA (*SPAIN*)   *See* Brouillis.

FLESHY   Also known as *charnu. See* Full-Bodied.

FLEUR (*FRANCE*)   *See* Flor.

FLEURIE (*FRANCE*)   A *cru* commune in Beaujolais, probably so named because the wine it produces is known for its delicate and flowery bouquet.

FLEX CARD   A cut case card that promotes a product and can be used any time of the year. This can be personalized for local promotions.

FLEXHOSE   A flexible metal hose attached to the beverage handgun used for the service of carbonated soft drinks. *See* Handgun.

FLIERS   Small particles occasionally observed floating in a glass of white wine.

FLINTY   Describes the odor or taste of a wine reminiscent of two flints being rubbed together or struck with steel. It is noticeable in some dry, hard, almost austere white wines, especially French Chablis and Pouilly Fumé. Also known as *goût de pierre-à-fusil* and *gun flint*.

FLIP   A popular drink in the United States during the early 1700s. It was made by combining rum, beer, cream, beaten eggs, and various spices, which were then heated by plunging a hot loggerhead (a long-handled tool with a ball or bulb at the end) into the mixture, causing it to foam and take on a burnt, bitter flavor. Also known as *beer flip*. *See* Hot Caudle, Rumfustian, and Sling.

FLOAT   Pouring a shot of distilled spirits on top of a finished cocktail without stirring or mixing.

FLOATING LIQUEURS   *See* Pousse-Café.

FLOCCULATION   When fermentation is complete, the dead yeast cells agglomerate—that is, clump up and form particles large enough to settle to the bottom, forming a firm deposit, rather than remaining in suspension. This makes racking easier and less wine is lost in the lees. Also known as *agglomeration* and *clumping*.

FLOGGING A CORK HOME   To drive the cork into the bottle by means of a wooden hammer; a practice no longer used today.

FLOOT   A slang term meaning a full eight-ounce glass of whiskey.

FLOR (SPAIN)   A yeast-like substance (*Saccharomyces cerevisiae*) that forms a whitish film on the surface of certain sherries when the temperature in the cellar is between 60 and 70 degrees Fahrenheit. After a year or so, the wine under the flor develops a distinctive yeasty taste, which is technically due to a large increase in the aldehyde content of the wine. The longer the sherry sits on the flor, the more flavor it extracts and the finer it becomes.

All types of sherry start out the same, but for some unknown reason flor forms on the surface of some barrels of sherry and not on others. When the flor forms a very thick white blanket, the sherry becomes a *fino*. If a thinner film forms, the sherry becomes an *amontillado*. If no film forms, the sherry becomes an *oloroso*.

After a period of eighteen to twenty-four months of aging undisturbed under the blanket of flor (if it forms), the wine is transferred to the winery's *solera* system. A fino will be sent to the fino solera, an amontillado to the amontillado solera, and so on. Also known as *film yeast* and *fleur*.

FLORA   A white grape variety developed in 1938 (released in 1958) from a cross of Gewürztraminer and Sémillon by Dr. Harold P. Olmo of the University of California, Davis.

FLORAISON (FRANCE)   *See* Flowering.

FLORAL   Also known as *odeur florale*. *See* Flowery.

FLORAL ABORTION   Absence of or defective fertilization of the blossoms of a grapevine, or a failure to develop or set at all, causing a malformation at time of flowering. This causes the blossoms or flowers to wither and fall from the grapevines, with no fruit-bearing ability. This malady, which is caused by bad weather or too early a spring, occurs in the springtime, leading to the loss of a potential bunch of grapes. Also known as *clorose* and *coulure*. *See* Berry Set, Shatter, and Shot Berries,

FLORAL GRAPPA *(ITALY)* Grappa infused and often bottled with flower petals. *See* Grappa.

FLORENTAL A red grape variety developed from a cross of Gamay Noir à Jus Blanc and Seibel 8365. Formerly known as *Burdin 7705*.

FLOWER CLUSTER *See* Inflorescence.

FLOWERING An indeterminate period in the grapevine development after bud break, when the flowers are pollinated and begin to yield small berries. Also known as *fioritura, floraison,* and *geschein*.

FLOWERS A red grape variety discovered in the early 1800s by William Flowers in a swamp near Lamberton, North Carolina.

FLOWERS OF WINE A malady of wine caused by film yeasts (*Candida mycoderma*). The wine, when exposed to prolonged air contact, develops small white patches that grow to complete surface coverage within days. It is a common but not a serious disorder that can be treated with sulfur dioxide. Also known as *Mycoderma vini* and *piqûre acétique*.

FLOWERY An organoleptic term desribing wines that display a pleasing perfume or floral fragrance akin to flowers in general. A term usually applied to young white wines such as Chenin Blanc, Gewürztraminer, Johannisberg Riesling, and Muscat. Flowery can also be detected in some beers and distilled spirits, especially liqueurs. Also known as *blumig, fiore, floral, nez fleuri, perfume,* and *profumo*. *See* Fragrance.

FLÜCHTIGE SÄURE *(GERMANY)* *See* Volatile Acidity.

FLUID OUNCE A United States measure of liquid volume, 128 fluid ounces being equal to one gallon.

FLURBEREINIGUNG *(GERMANY)* The process of consolidating groups of small vineyards on uneven terrain into large, more easily workable plots by improving access roads and drainage.

FLÛTE An elongated wine bottle used in Alsace, France, and near the Rhine River in Germany. Effective July 5, 1972, all Alsatian wines must be bottled in tall, elegant "flûte" bottles, and it is compulsory for wines sold under the Alsace appellation to have been bottled in Alsace, and not shipped in barrels.

FLUTE-SHAPED GLASS The proper glassware for champagne and sparkling wines, it is in the shape of an elongated **V**, with a capacity of approximately eight to ten ounces. *See* Tulip-Shaped Glass and Saucer-Shaped Glass.

FOAM A thick, rich, creamy collar of gas bubbles that clings to the top of a glass of beer. It is important to remember that for maximum profit, in addition to eye and taste appeal, beer should be served with a good foam head (3/4-inch). A perfect glass of beer shows a ring of foam after every sip. Foam is approximately 25 percent liquid beer. Also known as *head*. *See* Collar of Foam and Coney Island Head.

FOB *See* Free On Board.

FOB POST-OFF *See* Post-Offs.

FOJETTA *(ITALY)*   The name used in Rome to indicate generally a half liter of wine, but it once meant a special glass carafe. The glass container was substituted in 1589 by Pope Sixtus V for those of earthenware, pewter, or the like, since the opaque recipients quite often were used to mislead clients as to the quality and the quantity of the wine they were buying. *See* Cognitella.

FOLGASÃO *(PORTUGAL)*   A white grape variety grown in the Douro region.

FOLIAGE   The growing mass of leaves on a grapevine.

FOLIAGE WIRE   *See* Catch Wire.

FOLD   The ratio of the volume of the fruit *must* or juice to the volume of the volatile fruit-flavor concentrate produced from the fruit *must* or juice; for example, one gallon of volatile fruit-flavor concentrate of one hundred-fold would be the product from one hundred gallons of fruit *must* or juice.

FOLLATURA *(ITALY)*   *See* Punching Down.

FOLLE BLANCHE   A white grape variety grown primarily in France and California. Folle Blanche (called *Picpoul* or *Picpoule*) was for many years the principal grape of the Cognac and Armagnac regions of France. Though still used, it has been largely replaced by better producers and is now mostly found in the vineyards surrounding Nantes, in the Loire Valley of France, where it is called *Gros Plant*. Also known as *Avillo* in Catalonia, Spain.

FONCÉ *(FRANCE)*   Dark.

FOND DE TONNEAU *(FRANCE)*   *See* Head or Head Boards.

FOND DE VERRE *(FRANCE)*   A persistence of the bouquet in the glass for hours after it has been emptied.

FONDÉ *(FRANCE)*   Founded or established in.

FONDO *(ITALY)*   *See* Sediment.

FONDRE *(FRANCE)*   To blend (colors).

FONGICIDE *(FRANCE)*   *See* Fungicide.

FONTANA *(ITALY)*   Fountain.

FOOD AND BEVERAGE   A food and beverage department, in either a hotel or similar property. It is one of the most demanding areas in a hotel and one of the principle revenue producers. The food and beverage department is responsible for food and beverage activities in the property.

FOOD AND DRUG ACT   A United States law that required certain standards of identification for whiskey and imposed greater federal control on the production of distilled spirits. It was signed into law by President William Taft in 1909.

FOOD AND DRUG ADMINISTRATION (FDA)   The United States federal agency in charge of the enforcement of regulations relating to nonalcoholic beverages, some alcoholic beverages, and pesticides used in vineyards.

FOOT   *See* Base.

FOOTCANDLE   A unit of illumination equal to one lumen per square foot.

FOOTED PILSNER   A stemmed glass in the shape of an elongated **V**, with a capacity of eight to ten ounces; used to serve beer.

FORASTERA (ITALY)   A white grape variety grown in the south. Also known as *Forestiera, Frastera*, and *Furastera*.

FORECASTING   Predicting what will happen in the future on the basis of data from the past and present.

FOREIGN WINE   In the United States, wine produced outside the United States.

FORESHOT   *See* Heads.

FORESTIERA (ITALY)   *See* Forastera.

FORMOSA OOLONG TEA   A tea with an intensely pungent and penetrating bouquet reminiscent of ripened peaches. *See* Oolong Tea.

FORMULA   A recipe.

FORMULA WINE   Special natural wine, agricultural wine, and other than standard wine (except for distilling material and vinegar stock) produced on bonded wine premises under an approved formula.

FORSELINA (ITALY)   A white grape variety grown primarily in Veneto.

FORT (FRANCE)   *See* Strong.

FORTA (GERMANY)   A white grape variety developed from a cross of Madeleine Angevine and Sylvaner.

FORTANA (ITALY)   A red grape variety grown in the region of Lombardy. *See* Fortanella and Fortanina.

FORTANELLA (ITALY)   A subvariety of Fortana.

FORTANINA (ITALY)   A subvariety of Fortana.

FORTE (ITALY)   *See* Strong.

FORTE (PORTUGAL)   *See* Big.

FORTIFICATION   The addition of distilled spirits to a wine to arrest fermentation and leave some residual sugar, to give better keeping properties, or to make the wine stronger. Also known as *encabezado*.

FORTIFIED WINE   A table wine to which brandy or other distilled spirits have been added to raise the alcoholic content to somewhere between 16 and 22 percent alcohol by volume. Examples are *madeira, marsala, port,* and *sherry*.

FORTIFY   *See* Fortification.

FORWARD   A wine that matures early and is approachable in its youth.

FORZATO (ITALY)   A wine, made from very overripe grapes, that contains a high degree of alcohol.

FOUDRE (FRANCE)   A large barrel with a capacity of one thousand liters (264 gallons), mostly used in Alsace. *See* Barrel.

FOULAGE *(FRANCE)*   *See* Crushing.

FOULAGE À PIED *(FRANCE)*   *See* Treading.

FOULOIR *(FRANCE)*   *See* Crusher.

FOULOIR-ÉGRAPPOIR *(FRANCE)*   *See* Crusher/Destemmer.

FOUNTAIN INN   The pub in Baltimore, Maryland, where Francis Scott Key completed "The Star Spangled Banner."

FOURNEAU *(FRANCE)*   Furnace.

FOXÉ *(FRANCE)*   *See* Foxy.

FOX GRAPE   *See Vitis Labrusca*.

FOXTON   *See* Foxy.

FOXY   Describes the pronounced grapy aroma and flavor of many grapes (*Vitis labrusca*) native to the East Coast of the United States. The term foxy has no proved origin, although some winemakers feel that the name was given because foxes and deer enjoy eating the grapes. William Bartram, a journalist, influenced by the already existing name of the grape, wrote that "this name was due to the smell of the ripe fruit," which, he said, "was like the effluvia arising from the body of the fox."

Technically, a flavor substance called *methyl* (or *ethyl*) *anthranilate*, which is added to synthetic grape drinks, is responsible for this grapy aroma and flavor. Also known as *foxé, foxton, fuchsgeschmack, goût de fox, goût de renard, queue de renard*, and *volpino*. *See Vitis Labrusca*.

FRAGOLA *(ITALY)*   *See* Isabella.

FRAGRANCE   A term applied to a wine that has an amply scented and agreeable aroma or bouquet. Also known as *duft, evódis, fragrante*, and *oloroso*. *See* Flowery.

FRAGRANTE *(ITALY)*   *See* Fragrance.

FRAIS *(FRANCE)*   *See* Fresh.

FRAISE *(FRANCE)*   Strawberry; usually made into a liqueur or clear brandy.

FRAMBOISE *(FRANCE)*   Raspberry; usually made into a liqueur or clear brandy. It is known as *himbeergeist* in Germany and parts of Switzerland.

FRAMBOISE *(BELGIUM)*   A *lambic type* of wheat beer or sour brown ale to which raspberries have been added. *See* Lambic.

FRANCAVIDA *(ITALY)*   A white grape variety.

FRANC DE GOÛT *(FRANCE)*   *See* Vinous.

FRANC DE PIED *(FRANCE)*   Ungrafted grapevines.

FRANCO BORD *(FRANCE)*   *See* Free on Board.

FRANÇOIS *(FRANCE)*   In 1837, Professor André François, a pharmacist from Châlons-sur-Marne in the region of Champagne, invented the *glucometer*. With this instrument he was able to determine the precise amount of sugar to be added to still wines for the secondary fermentation into sparkling wines. Also known as *réduction françois*.

FRANCONIA (GERMANY) *See* Franken.

FRANDSDRUIFT *See* Palomino.

FRANKEN (GERMANY) One of thirteen qualitätswein (quality) grape-growing regions. The wines of Franken, made under the close scrutiny of the Frankischer Weinbauverband (Franken Wine Association founded in 1836), are pleasant, combining dryness with a certain mellowness but lacking somewhat in the varied aromas and bouquets of other German wines. Most Franken wine is made from Müller-Thurgau, Sylvaner, and Johannisberg Riesling grapes.

This is the only region from which wine is exported in a *bocksbeutel,* the distinctive, round flagon-style bottle first introduced in 1728. Also spelled *Franconia.*

FRANKENRIESLING (GERMANY) *See* Sylvaner.

FRANKEN RIESLING *See* Sylvaner.

FRANSDRUIF (SOUTH AFRICA) *See* Palomino.

FRAPPATO (ITALY) A red grape variety grown primarily in Sicily.

FRAPPÉ (FRANCE) A drink that is super-chilled by the addition of crushed or shaved ice, over which liqueurs are poured.

FRAPPER (FRANCE) To chill or ice, as in a bottle of champagne.

FRASCATI (ITALY) A dry (also semidry and sweet) white wine produced on the slopes of the Alban hills in the Castelli Romani district, approximately 12.5 miles south of Rome.

It is a blend of a blend of Malvasia Bianca di Candia and Trebbiano Toscano grapes with small amounts of other white grapes, including Malvasia del Lazio, Greco, Bellone, Bonvino, and Chardonnay.

FRASTERA (ITALY) *See* Forastera.

FRATELLI (ITALY) Brothers.

FRATELLO (ITALY) Brother.

FRAUNCES TAVERN The tavern in New York City where George Washington said farewell to his officers after a victory in 1783. It is one of the oldest taverns in America still in existence and was founded in 1762 by Samuel Fraunces at the corner of Pearl and Broad streets in Manhattan, New York.

FREDDO (ITALY) Cold.

FREDONIA A red grape variety developed in 1927 from a cross of Champion and Lucile at the State Experimental Station in Geneva, New York.

FREEBIE A slang term for services or items given or received gratis by some customers.

FREE ON BOARD (FOB) Costs agreed upon by the buyer and seller, where the seller delivers by train, ship, plane, etc., to the point of shipment, without charge and exclusive of freight, which must then be borne by the purchaser. Also known as *franco bord.*

FREE PORT A port, part of a port, or zone where cargo may be unloaded, stored, and reshipped without payment of customs or duties. Also known as *free zone.*

FREE POUR Pouring distilled spirits from a bottle without the aid of a measuring device.

FREE-RUN JUICE   The initial juice released by the grapes by the sheer weight or pressure of the mass, before the press is used. This juice is sometimes fermented separately (since it is thought to make better quality wine); other times it is combined with press juice. The people from ancient Greece called it *Prodomos* or *Protopos*. Also known as *vin de goutte* and *yema*. *See* Press Juice.

FREE ZONE   *See* Free Port.

FREIGHT DROP/SHIP   Freight, parcel post, or postage on drop shipments of *point of sale* (POS) material.

FREIGHT FORWARDER   Initiates a booking to secure vessel space and prepares export documentation.

FREIHERR (GERMANY)   Baron.

FREISA   A red grape variety grown primarily in the Piedmont region. Freisa d'Asti wine features on its neck label black grapes superimposed on a yellow tower in Asti.

FREISAMER (GERMANY)   A white grape variety developed in 1916 from a cross of Sylvaner and Ruländer at the State Viticultural Institute in Freiburg.

FREON   A trade name for a nonflammable gas used as a refrigerant and to cool stainless steel tanks used in making some beverages.

FRENCH 75   A cocktail consisting of champagne and cognac that became popular with the American soldiers based in France's Champagne region during World War II. The soldiers named the powerful drink after the French 75-millimeter artillery cannon known for its impact and accuracy.

FRENCH-AMERICAN HYBRIDS   Grape varieties developed from a cross of American grapevines with European *Vitis vinifera* grapevines. Also known as *French Hybrids*. *See* Hybrids.

FRENCH COLOMBARD   *See* Colombard.

FRENCH HYBRIDS   *See* French-American Hybrids.

FRENCH OAK   Refers to the wooden barrels constructed from trees located inside the forests of France. Among the more popular are Allier, Bourgogne, Limousin, Nevers, Tronçais, and Vosges.

FRENCH-TYPE VERMOUTH   A dry white vermouth. *See* Vermouth.

FRÈRES (FRANCE)   Brothers.

FRESCO (ITALY AND PORTUGAL)   *See* Fresh.

FRESCOR (SPAIN)   *See* Fresh.

FRESH   A term often applied to younger white or lighter red wines displaying a youthful, lively fruity aroma and clean, acidic taste. Also known as *frais, fresco, frescor,* and *frisch. See* Young.

FRESHLY BREWED COFFEE   Coffee that has just been freshly made and is less than one hour old (a generally accepted standard within the food and beverage industry). After that time, coffee begins to lose its aroma and its taste begins to deteriorate, turning flat and harsh.

FRINCUSA (ROMANIA)   A white grape variety.

FRÍO (*SPAIN*)   Cold.

FRISCH (*GERMANY*)   *See* Fresh.

FRIULARA (*ITALY*)   *See* Raboso.

FRIULI-VENEZIA GIULIA (*ITALY*)   One of the smallest of twenty wine-producing regions, Friuli-Venezia Giulia borders on Austria and Yugoslavia in the most northeastern region of Italy. Its terrain is predominantly rocky and hilly and the climate generally quite mild. Pordenone, Gorizia, and Udine are the important wine centers of this region.

There are six delimited zones within the Friuli region; from smallest to largest, they are Latisana, Aquileia, Isonzo, Collio, Colli Orientali del Friuli, and Grave del Friuli.

FRIZZANTE (*ITALY*)   *See* Spritz.

FROG EYES   The large, lazy bubbles, usually found in a glass of bulk process sparkling wine, that mercifully soon disappear. It is unaffectionately known as *oeil de crapaud*, meaning toad's eyes.

FROMENTIN (*ITALY*)   *See* Furmint.

FRONTERA (*SPAIN*)   Frontier.

FRONTIGNAN   *See* Muscat de Frontignan.

FRONT-OF-THE-BAR   The portion of the bar where the customer sits and is served drinks.

FRONT-OF-THE-HOUSE   Those areas of a hotel, restaurant, tavern, or any facility that is in the public eye. This includes the lobby, dining, sitting, and drinking areas where guests and customers have direct access.

FROSTING   The chilling of a glass in the freezer, with or without first wetting it, for the service of beer and some cocktails usually served straight up. Also known as a *frozen glass* or *mug* and *glass frosting*.

FROST POCKET   A grape-growing area that is susceptible to the collection of cool air or frost.

FROTHEE   A proprietary brand name product consisting of egg whites and other ingredients, used in cocktails to make an airy, foamy head.

FROZEN DRINK DISPENSER   A machine that dispenses a *frozen* drink in fairly large quantities. Usually relegated to daiquiris, piña coladas, and margaritas.

FROZEN GLASS OR MUG   *See* Frosting.

FRUCHTIG (*GERMANY*)   *See* Fruity.

FRUCTOSE   A simple sugar, predominantly found in fruits, that is almost twice as sweet as glucose. Also known as *fruit sugar*. Same as levulose.

FRÜHBURGUNDER (*GERMANY*)   A red grape variety.

FRÜHROTER VELTLINER (*AUSTRIA*)   A white grape variety.

FRUIT DESSERT WINE   This is fruit or berry wine having an alcoholic content in excess of 14 percent but not in excess of 24 percent by volume. Also known as *berry dessert wine*.

FRUITÉ *(FRANCE)* *See* Fruity.

FRUIT GRAPPA *(ITALY)* Grappa infused with or distilled from fresh fruit, similar to an eau-de-vie. *See* Grappa.

FRUIT JUICES The natural juices of any type of fruit, often with vitamin C, sugar, sugar substances, artificial sweeteners, citric acid, or water added.

FRUIT-LIKE Referring to smell and taste; it is said of a young wine, the taste of which is similar to ripe fruit.

FRUITS Those fruits that are utilized either as garnishes or ingredients in cocktails. Citrus fruits, such as lemons, limes, and oranges, are the principal fruits needed for many cocktails. They should be cut into three distinct shapes, depending on the kind and type of drink served: wheels, peels, and wedges.

FRUIT SQUEEZER A hand-held instrument used to squeeze citrus fruits, while at the same time straining away unwanted seeds and pulp.

FRUIT SUGAR *See* Fructose.

FRUIT TABLE WINE Fruit or berry wine having an alcoholic content not in excess of 14 percent by volume. Such wines may also be designated "light fruit wine" or "light berry wine." Also known as *berry table wine.*

FRUIT WINE Wine made from the juice of sound, ripe fruit (including wine made from berries or from a combination of grapes and other fruits or berries).

FRUITY An organoleptic term applied to wines that have a definite pleasant aroma and flavor of grapes or other fresh fruits. The fruitiness is never cloying; rather, it imparts a lively, refreshing quality to the wine. Also known as *afrutado, fruchtig, fruité, fruto, fruttato, nez fruité, odeur fruité,* and *würzig.*

FRUTO *(PORTUGAL)* *See* Fruity.

FRUTTATO *(ITALY)* *See* Fruity.

FRY A white grape variety named after B.O. Fry, a Georgia grape breeder.

FUCHAL *(PORTUGAL)* The major shipping port for madeira wine.

FUCHSGESCHMACK *(GERMANY)* *See* Foxy.

FUDER *(GERMANY)* A large barrel with a capacity of one thousand liters (264 gallons), mostly used in the Mosel region. *See* Barrel.

FUGACE *(ITALY)* *See* Short.

FULL Also known as *pieno. See* Full-Bodied.

FULL-BODIED A term relating to the body or mouth-filling capacity of a beverage. Additionally, it applies to beverages that are rich, powerful, fleshy, robust, intensely flavored, and comparatively high in extract, glycerin, possibly sugar, or alcohol content. Beers that have high levels of malt and hops are also referred to as full-bodied. Opposite of *light-bodied.* Also known as *big, charpenté, corposo, encorpado, fleshy, full, fülle, fullness, gras,* and *gehaltvoll. See* Heavy.

FULL CUBES *See* Ice Cubes.

FÜLLE *(GERMANY)* *See* Full-Bodied.

FULLNESS   *See* Full-Bodied.

FUMARIC ACID   Occasionally utilized to help prevent the growth of lactic acid bacteria, to stabilize wine, and to correct natural deficiencies in grape and fruit wine.

FUMÉ *(FRANCE)*   Smoke.

FUMÉ BLANC   *See* Sauvignon Blanc.

FUMET *(FRANCE)*   *See* Bouquet.

FUMIGATION   A procedure by which holes are drilled deep into the soil; then an insecticide or fungicide is injected. The land is then covered with plastic sheets for a period of about two months.

FUMIN *(ITALY)*   A red grape variety grown in the Valle d'Aosta region.

FUNCTION   Sales responsibility assigned to a person or group within a sales team (e.g., on-premise function, convenience store function).

FUNDADA *(SPAIN)*   Founded.

FUNGICIDA *(SPAIN)*   *See* Fungicide.

FUNGICIDE   Any substance that controls the growth, infection, and spread of fungi on plants. Also known as *anticrittogamico, fongicide, fungicida,* and *fungizid. See* Herbicide, Insecticide, and Pesticide.

FUNGIZID *(GERMANY)*   *See* Fungicide.

FUNGUS   Any of the simple, lower plants, including the yeasts, molds, and mushrooms, which lack chlorophyll and subsist on other life forms.

FURASTERA *(ITALY)*   *See* Forastera.

FÜR DIABETIKER GEEIGNET *(GERMANY)*   A wine suitable for people with diabetes. *See* Diabetiker-Weinsiegel and Dry Beer.

FURMENTIN *(ITALY)*   *See* Furmint.

FURMINT *(HUNGARY)*   A white grape variety that produces Hungary's classic Tokay wines. Its origins are actually Italian; it was brought to Hungary from the Friulan hills in 1632.

The Furmint grape variety is very susceptible to *Botrytis cinerea* and produces a range of Tokay wines from dry to extremely sweet in taste. Also known as *Fromentin, Furmentin, Posip,* and *Sipon.*

FURROW IRRIGATION   A seldom-used method that entails digging a trench in between rows of grapevines, then flooding it with water.

FÜRST *(GERMANY)*   Prince.

FUSEL *(GERMANY)*   A slang term meaning bad liquor.

FUSEL OIL   Actually a higher-boiling alcohol, noticeable in fermented beverages, especially distilled spirits. Fusel oil contributes to the flavor and overall quality of wine and distilled spirits, although in actuality it totals less than 0.1 percent of the beverages. It combines with esters, tannins, acids, and aldehydes to form what are commonly known as *congeners.*

FUSTO *(ITALY)*   A barrel of any size for the aging of wines. *See* Barrel.

FÛT *(FRANCE)*   *See* Barrel.

FÛT *(FRANCE)*   The trunk of a tree from just above the roots to the lower branches, giving nine to ten feet of clean, straight timber, easily sawn into staves for barrel-making.

FUTURES MARKET   An economic market in which contracts are undertaken today at prices specified today for fulfillment at some specified future time. *See* En-Primeur.

GAERUNG (AUSTRIA)   *See* Primary Fermentation.

GAGLIOPPO (ITALY)   A red grape variety grown in Calabria. Also known as *Gaioppo, Galaffa,* and *Uva Navarra.*

GAIOPPO (ITALY)   *See* Gaglioppo.

GALACTURONIC ACID   One of the components of the chemical composition of pectin.

GALAFFA (ITALY)   *See* Gaglioppo.

GALANT   *See* Cooked Wine.

GALEGO DOURADO (PORTUGAL)   A white grape variety grown in the Carcavelos region.

GALESTRO (ITALY)   A dry, non-DOC white wine first produced in 1979. The original idea was to find use for the Trebbiano grapes whose use in Chianti was on the decline. This delicate, light white wine takes its name from the ancient rocks of its native Tuscany. It owes its distinctive aroma to the presence of Trebbiano Toscano, Chardonnay, Vernaccia di San Gimignano, Malvasia del Chianti, Riesling Renano, and Pinot Bianco grapes.

GALL   An abnormal growth of plant tissue caused by stimuli external to the plant itself (generally, insects or parasitic fungi).

GALLIC ACID   A phenol present in grape skins, seeds, and stems that causes bitterness in wine. It is usually removed by gelatin fining. *See* Phenol.

GALLIZATION   A winemaking process named after Dr. Gall. *See* Amelioration.

GALLON   A United States measurement of liquid volume, one gallon being equivalent to 128 fluid ounces or to the volume of 231 cubic inches. Also known as a *wine gallon* or *bulk gallon.* An Imperial or British gallon equals 160 ounces or 1.2 gallons. Also known as *gallone.*

GALLONE (ITALY) *See* Gallon.

GAMAY The traditional red grape variety of the Beaujolais district of France; it produces a wine that is extremely fruity and berry-like, resembling cherries, blackberries, and raspberries.

On July 31, 1394, Philip the Bold, Duke of Burgundy, issued an edict banishing the "evil and disloyal" Gamay grape from his kingdom (the areas around Dijon, Beaune, and Chalon) in favor of the bigger and fruitier Pinot Noir grape which was in demand at that time. Also known as *Bourguignon Noir, Gamay Noir à Jus Blanc, Gamay Rond*, and *Petit Gamai*. *See* Gamay Beaujolais, Napa Gamay, and Valdiguié.

GAMAY BEAUJOLAIS A red grape variety, originally thought to be the true Gamay grape of the Beaujolais district of France, now identified as a strain of Pinot Noir. When used on United States wine labels, the name must be shown in direct conjunction with either Napa Gamay or Pinot Noir, as the case may be. *See* Gamay.

GAMAY NOIR À JUS BLANC (FRANCE) *See* Gamay.

GAMAY ROND *See* Gamay.

GAMAY ST-LAURENT *See* Abouriou.

GAMZA (BULGARIA) *See* Kadarka.

GARAFÃO (PORTUGAL) A wicker or straw-covered demijohn. *See* Garrafa.

GARBATO (ITALY) *See* Amiable.

GARGANEGA (ITALY) A white grape variety grown primarily in the Veneto region, where it produces Soave and Lugana. Known locally as *Terlano*. There are two varieties of Garganega: *Garganega Comune* and *Garganega Grossa*. Garganega Comune is also known as *Garganega Biforcuta, Garganega Frastagliata*, and *Garganega Rossa*. Garganega Grossa is also known as *Dorona di Venezia, Garganegona*, and *Garganega Piramidalis*.

GARGANEGA BIFORCUTA (ITALY) *See* Garganega.

GARGANEGA COMUNE (ITALY) *See* Garganega.

GARGANEGA FRASTAGLIATA (ITALY) *See* Garganega.

GARGANEGA GROSSA (ITALY) *See* Garganega.

GARGANEGA PIRAMIDALIS (ITALY) *See* Garganega.

GARGANEGA ROSSA (ITALY) *See* Garganega.

GARGANEGONA (ITALY) *See* Garganega.

GARIBALDI DOLCE (GD) (ITALY) A marsala designation, named after General Giuseppe Garibaldi, who in 1862 (according to legend) tasted and enjoyed a particular type of wine that has since been known as "Marsala G.D." *See* Marsala Superiore.

GARLIC *See* Paraffin.

GARNACHA (SPAIN) *See* Grenache.

GARNACHA BLANCA (SPAIN) *See* Grenache.

GARNACHA TINTA (SPAIN) *See* Grenache.

GARNACHO (SPAIN) *See* Grenache.

GARNISH   The finishing touch to a cocktail, usually consisting of citrus fruit in the shape of wheels or wedges added to a drink (generally for eye appeal) prior to serving. Other garnishes include maraschino cherries, pineapple wedges, and cocktail onions and olives, as well as certain vegetables.

GARRAFA (PORTUGAL)   *See* Bottle.

GARRAFA (SPAIN)   A wicker or straw-covered bottle containing approximately five liters. *See* Garafão.

GARRAFEIRA (PORTUGAL)   An outstanding wine from a single vintage that has additional wood and bottle aging prior to sale. In addition, both red and white wines must have an alcoholic strength that is at least one-half of one degree above the legal minimum set for the region in which the wine originates. In the case of red, it is aged at least two years in wood and an additional one year in bottle. White wines must be aged at least six months in wood, followed by a further six months in bottle. *See* Reserva (Portugal).

GARRONET   A red grape variety. Formerly known as *Seyve-Villard 18283.*

GARTEN (GERMANY)   Garden.

GÄRUNG (GERMANY)   *See* Fermentation.

GAS CHROMATOGRAPHY   A versatile analytic method for the efficient separation of volatile components in a wine sample so that each one can be identified and quantified.

GASCOGNE (FRANCE)   *See* Gascony.

GASCON JAR   An armagnac bottle of 250 milliliters, shaped like a claret bottle.

GASCONY (FRANCE)   The name given to the Bordeaux region during the Middle Ages, prior to it being called Aquitaine. Spelled *Gascogne* in France.

GASEOSO (SPAIN)   *See* Artificially Carbonated Wine.

GASIFICADO (SPAIN)   *See* Charmat Method.

GASSY   A table wine that displays excessive amounts of carbon dioxide. It could result from *malolactic fermentation* occurring in the bottle.

GATTINARA (ITALY)   A full-bodied (DOCG) red wine made in the Piedmont region from a blend of Nebbiolo (known locally as *Spanna*), Bonarda, and Vespolina grapes. The Gattinara *consorzio* features on its neck label towers standing among the vineyards.

GATTUNGSNAME (GERMANY)   *See* Generic Wine.

GAUGER   A seldom-used term for an official or customs officer who is in charge of gauging spirits to determine their relative alcoholic content.

GAVI (ITALY)   *See* Cortese.

GAY-LUSSAC, JOSEPH-LOUIS (1778–1850)   A French chemist and physicist who, in 1810, correctly devised the overall equation for fermentation. It is also, in France, the name for the standard metric measurement of alcoholic strengths contained in a beverage, often abbreviated "GL."

GAZÈIFIÈ (FRANCE)   *See* Artificially Carbonated Wine.

GD *(ITALY)*   Garibaldi Dolce. *See* Marsala Superiore.

GEBIET *(GERMANY)*   Wine-producing region.

GEBRÜDER *(GERMANY)*   Brothers.

GEERNTET DURCH *(GERMANY)*   Harvested or picked by.

GEFÄLLIG *(GERMANY)*   *See* Pleasant.

GEHALTVOLL *(AUSTRIA)*   *See* Full-Bodied.

GEISENHEIM   Germany's premier school of viticulture, founded in 1872 in the Rheingau region.

GELATIN   A long chain protein fining agent derived from beef or pork and from either fresh or dried egg whites from chicken eggs. It is produced by hydrolysis of collagen in animal cartilage and bones by boiling them in water. The jelly-like substance first extracted is gelatin, whose active component is gluten, upon which its actual fining power depends. On further treatment, more gelatin is extracted and concentrated, and finally glue is produced. Gelatin carries a positive charge. Also known as *gelatina, gélatine*, and *gelatine*. *See* Fining and Fining Agents.

GELATINA *(ITALY AND SPAIN)*   *See* Gelatin.

GÉLATINE *(FRANCE)*   *See* Gelatin.

GELATINE *(GERMANY)*   *See* Gelatin.

GEMARKUNG *(GERMANY)*   The geographic boundary of a viticultural region or district.

GEMEINDE *(GERMANY)*   A village or parish.

GEMMA *(ITALY)*   *See* Bud.

GEMULTICHKEIT *(GERMANY)*   The joyous atmosphere in a pub or tavern.

GENERALLY RECOGNIZED AS SAFE (GRAS)   The term means that the treating material so marked has an FDA listing in Title 21, Code of Federal Regulations, Part 182 or Part 184, or is considered to be generally recognized as safe by the United States Food and Drug Administration. It has no adverse effects when used as directed.

GÉNÉREUX *(FRANCE)*   *See* Generous.

GENERIC WINE   A designation of a particular class or type of wine, but such designations also may have geographic significance (the name of a district, commune, or region where the wine originates from). A simpler definition would be "place-name"— wines that are named after European wine-producing districts such as Burgundy, Chablis, Champagne, Chianti, Port, Rhine, Sauternes, Sherry, and so forth. Also known as *gattungsname* and *générique*.

GÉNÉRIQUE *(FRANCE)*   *See* Generic Wine.

GENEROSO *(ITALY, PORTUGAL, AND SPAIN)*   *See* Generous.

GENEROUS   Describes wines rich in color, body, alcohol, and extract. Also known as *généreux, generoso*, and *vino generoso*.

GENEVA GIN   *See* Holland Gin.

GENOTYPE   The gene stock of a grapevine inherited by a specimen from its parents.

GENTIL ROSÉ AROMATIQUE   *See* Gewürztraminer.

GENUINE   A legally meaningless term used to refer to beverages that are honestly made or produced. Also known as *echt, genuino*, and *schietto*.

GENUINO *(ITALY* AND *PORTUGAL)*   *See* Genuine.

GENUS   The various botanical groups of grapevine species.

GERANIUM   A pungent, grassy aroma so called because it really does smell like crushed stems and leaves of geraniums. It is a spoilage odor occasionally found in some wines that have undergone *malolactic fermentation* in the presence of sorbic acid, a stabilizer often added to some wines. The bacterial decomposition of sorbic acid causes this powerful volatile ester to form, making the wines unfit for consumption.

GÉRANT *(FRANCE)*   General manager of a property.

GERBAUDE *(FRANCE)*   The presentation of flowers to the lady of the house after the wine harvest.

GERENTE *(SPAIN)*   The manager of a bodega.

GERING *(GERMANY)*   *See* Little.

GERMINATION   To sprout or cause to sprout, as from a spore, seed, or bud.

GEROPIGA *(PORTUGAL)*   A mixture of brandy and a concentrate of unfermented grape juice (reduced by evaporation), used for blending to give added sweetness and body to some port wines. *See* Grape Concentrate.

GESCHEIN *(GERMANY)*   *See* Flowering.

GESCHMACK *(GERMANY)*   *See* Flavor.

GESCHMEIDIG *(GERMANY)*   *See* Supple.

GESPRITZER *(AUSTRIA)*   *See* Spritzer.

GESTOPPT *(GERMANY)*   A wine that has not completely finished fermenting; either due to a *stuck fermentation* or because the winemaker has intentionally stopped the fermentation in order to create a wine with residual sugar. *See* Stuck Fermentation.

GEVREY-CHAMBERTIN *(FRANCE)*   A famous red-wine village in the Côte de Nuits district of Burgundy; it first appeared in written records in 1895. In 1847, by ordinance of Louis Philippe, *Chambertin*, Gevrey's greatest vineyard, was added to the name. In the seventh century A.D. the vineyard of Gevrey-Chambertin was known as *Gibriacus*.

GEWÄCHS *(GERMANY)*   *See* Wachstrum.

GEWÜRZ *(GERMANY)*   Spicy.

GEWÜRZTRAMINER   A white grape variety with a slightly pinkish skin, originally from the Pfalz region of Germany, although grown in most regions of the world. The name *Traminer* is derived from the grape-growing village of Tramin (in Italy, Termeno)

G

GEWÜRZTRAMINER

in the South Tyrol area south of Bolzano, Italy. In Germany, the name *Gewürz* means "spicy." Gewürztraminer is a quintessentially Alsatian wine and very few if any countries produce a wine of equal distinction.

Its aroma is often assertive on the palate, finishing with a touch of bitterness. It is delicious, spicy, and fruity, with a pungent flavor and a highly perfumed and flowery bouquet that is strongly reminiscent of apricot, cinnamon, ginger, grapefruit, litchee, and peach. Formerly known as *Traminer*. Also known as *Gentil Rosé Aromatique, Red Traminer, Savagnin Rosé, Traminer Aromatico, Traminer Musqué,* and *Tramini Piros*.

GEZUCKERT (GERMANY)   A wine that has been *sugared*.

GHEMME (ITALY)   A medium-bodied, dry red wine produced in the Piedmont region from a blend of Nebbiolo, Vespolina, and Bonarda Novarese grape varieties.

GHIACCIO (ITALY)   *See* Ice.

GIALLO (ITALY)   Yellow.

GIANO (ITALY)   Roman God Janus.

GIBBERELLIC ACID   One of several compounds in a family of plant hormones or plant growth regulators called the *gibberellins*. Beginning in the late 1950s, researchers in California discovered that gibberellic acid can have a number of beneficial effects on grapevines. Applications of gibberellic acid on seedless table grapes at bloom generally reduce berry set, increase berry size, and promote growth of shoots.

GIBRIACUS (FRANCE)   *See* Gevrèy-Chambertin.

GIBSON   A cocktail consisting of gin or vodka, white dry vermouth, and garnished with a pearl cocktail onion. The drink was apparently named after the American illustrator Charles Dana Gibson (1867–1944), famous for his drawings of the turn-of-the-century "Gibson Girl." The story goes that Gibson ordered a martini—usually served with an olive—from the bartender Charley Connolly of the Players Club in New York City. Connolly found himself out of olives and instead served the drink with two tiny white onions. The cocktail is first mentioned in print in 1930.

GIFT CARTONS   Decorative boxes used to contain bottles of product for resale.

GIGONDAS (FRANCE)   A wine-producing village located in the southern half of the Rhône Valley. Its red wines, produced from the Grenache, Syrah, Cinsaut, and Mourvèdre grapes, are some of the most powerful wines of the Rhône Valley. A small quantity of rosé wine is made, but it is rarely exported to the United States.

GILL   An ancient drinking glass that held about one-quarter pint (four ounces).

GIMLET   A cocktail consisting of gin and Rose's lime juice. In the 1890s, a British naval surgeon, Sir T.O. Gimlette, was concerned with the heavy drinking his men were accustomed to. So he diluted the gin with lime juice and although it didn't dissuade them, he unintentionally created a new drink.

GIN   A distilled spirit made by the additional processing of distilled neutral spirits flavored primarily with juniper berries plus other seeds, roots, and barks.

In United States production, most often there is a *gin head* containing trays of herbs and other flavoring botanicals such as juniper, cassia bark, coriander seed, orange peel, cardamom, angelica, and so forth. The flavoring is picked up by the alcohol vapors as they rise; these accumulated vapors are then condensed.

The distilled neutral spirits can also be mixed or soaked with juniper berries and other flavoring materials and then strained and bottled, or the flavoring essences can simply be added. Normally, gin is not aged and is bottled at not less than 80 proof.

GIN FIZZ   A cocktail consisting of gin, lemon juice, and sugar, and topped with seltzer.

GINGER ALE   A carbonated soft drink made from water, sugar or corn syrup, drops of capsicum extract or essence of ginger flavor, organic acid, and caramel color. First produced in 1809.

GINGER BEER   A carbonated soft drink made from water, sugar or corn syrup, fermented ginger, organic acid, and caramel color. Ginger beer originated in England during the nineteenth century and was consumed in great quantities in the United States during Prohibition as a substitute for real beer.

GINGER-FLAVORED BRANDY   A mixture of brandy with a minimum of 2.5 percent sugar, flavored and colored with ginger. By federal law it cannot be bottled at less than 60 proof (30 percent alcohol by volume).

GIN HEAD   *See* Gin.

GIN LIQUEUR   A liqueur bottled at not less than 60 proof, in which the distilled spirit used is entirely gin, and that possesses a predominant characteristic gin flavor derived from the distilled spirit used.

GIN MILL   Slang term for a bar.

GIN RICKEY   A cocktail consisting of gin and lime juice. Civil War Colonel Joe Rickey had this drink named after him at the St. James Hotel in New York City in 1895. *See* Rickey.

GIONINA   A grape variety grown on a small scale in the midwestern United States.

GIOVANE (ITALY)   *See* Young.

GIRASOL (SPAIN)   *See* Gyropalette.

GIRÒ (ITALY)   A red grape variety grown in the region of Sardinia.

GIRONDE (FRANCE)   An important river in Bordeaux that crosses the Garonne and Dordogne rivers in the south and flows into the Atlantic Ocean in the north. The four most important communes that make up the Médoc district are located on the west side of the Gironde River.

GIRONE COMUNE (ITALY)   *See* Girò.

GIRONE DI SPAGNA (ITALY)   *See* Girò.

GIVRY (FRANCE)   A red-wine commune in the Côte Chalonnaise district of Burgundy. Givry was the favorite red wine of King Henry IV of England, who reigned from 1399 to 1413.

GL   *See* Gay-Lussac.

GLABROUS   Describes a grape leaf having very few or no hairs on its surface.

GLACÉ (FRANCE)   A drink chilled by refrigeration or immersion in ice, not with ice in it.

GLÄNZEND (GERMANY)   *See* Brilliant.

GLASS   As we know it today, glass was first produced by the Syrians in approximately 2000 B.C. The natural raw materials used to create glass—siliceous sand, sodium carbonate or Solvay soda (soda ash), and calcium carbonate limestone—are placed in huge furnaces where they are heated to about 2,700 degrees Fahrenheit and become molten.

GLASS CHILLER   A refrigerated box or container utilized for the quick chilling of glasses for beer and cocktails usually served straight up. *See* Chilling a Glass.

GLASS FROSTING   *See* Frosting.

GLASSWORKS   The first glassworks of France was established in 1723 in Bordeaux.

GLATT (GERMANY)   *See* Smooth.

GLENORA SEEDLESS   A red grape variety developed from a cross of Ontario and a Russian seedless and released through the New York State Experimental Station in September 1976. Formerly known as *NY 35814*.

GLOBULAR   This term describes the nearly round shape of a grape cluster.

GLÖGG   A traditional Swedish or Scandinavian hot spiced drink, similar to hot mulled wine, usually consumed during the cold weather. It is made from a combination of akvavit or brandy, wine, cardamom seeds, cloves, sugar, raisins, almonds, and other ingredients. Glögg is served warm in glasses containing a small cinnamon stick, raisins, currants, or almonds. *See* Mulled Wine.

GLORIA (GERMANY)   A white grape variety developed from a cross of Sylvaner and Müller-Thurgau.

GLUCOMETER (PORTUGAL)   The device used to measure the unfermented sugar in the *must* for making port wine. *See* Brix.

GLUCOSE   The simple sugar used by the body; other sugars are usually converted into glucose by enzymes in the body before they can be used as energy sources. It is a monosaccharide hexose sugar. *See* Grape Sugar.

GLÜHWEIN (GERMANY)   *See* Mulled Wine.

GLYCERIN   A by-product of the fermentation of grapes into wine. Glycerin increases the feeling of fatness in the mouth, giving the wine a soft, almost oily tinge on the tongue and palate. Glycerin coats the surface of the mouth and obscures acidity or tartness, so sometimes acid needs to be added to the wine to compensate. Also known as *glycerol*.

GLYCEROL   A thick, syrupy liquid that is a component of fat. *See* Glycerin.

GLYCOL   Same as *ethylene glycol*. Any of a group of alcohols of which ethylene glycol is the type.

GLYKYS (GREECE)   *See* Sweet.

GNÔLE (FRANCE)   Brandy.

GOAL   Target case volume in a territory for a specified time period. Must specify either shipments or depletions, nine-liter or flat cases. Also known as *quota*.

GOAL DEPLETION REPORT   Monthly report from sales statistics that provides current month and year-to-date territorial brand depletion information compared to last year and to goal.

GOBELET *(FRANCE)*   A pruning method used in the Beaujolais district of Burgundy that trains the grapevine in the shape of a *goblet*. Also known as *en vaso*.

GOBLET   A bowl-shaped drinking vessel with a stem and base, ordinarily made of glass.

GOLD   A white grape variety developed in 1958 by Dr. Harold P. Olmo at the University of California, Davis.

GOLD COIN   A grape variety developed by Thomas Volney Munson (1843–1913) of Denison, Texas.

GOLDEN CHASSELAS   A white grape variety.

GOLDEN GINS   These gins are aged in wood for a short period of time and have a light golden-brown color extracted from the barrel. Golden gin is quite difficult to find today.

GOLDEN MUSCAT   A white grape variety released in 1927 and developed from a cross of Muscat Hamburg and Diamond at the State Experimental Station in Geneva, New York.

GOLDRIESLING   *See* Riesling Doré.

GOLDWASSER   (Also known as *Danzigwasser*, named for Danzig, now Gdansk, Poland, the town where it was first produced.) An orange-based liqueur that can also be made with the addition of anise, caraway seeds, or even fennel. Alchemists believed for many centuries that, by mixing pure gold with alcohol, they could create "liquid gold" or the elixir of passion, stamina, and good health, for use as an aphrodisiac, or even as a guarantee of immortality. By the end of the sixteenth century, a beverage was made in Europe in which flakes of gold were combined with alcohol; it was called *goldwasser*. The current production uses 23-karat gold leaf, which is quite pure and harmless to ingest. In fact, it is so thin and light (technically, it is classified as of double-X thinness) that, when the bottle is shaken, the flakes appear to be suspended and float indefinitely. The gold is purchased in thin sheets resembling tissue paper; in fact, they cost more than gold in solid form. The reason is simple: the labor needed to prepare this paper-thin gold leaf is considerable. The gold is added to the liqueur and immediately blended with rapid movements. As the liquid is agitated, the gold breaks up into tiny flecks.

GÖNC *(HUNGARY)*   A small, thirty-six-gallon barrel in which Tokay wine is aged. *See* Barrel.

GONDOLA   A wheeled, open-topped horizontal tank used to collect grapes after harvesting. Also known as *ballonges*.

GO-OUT   Full fiscal year forecast made during the current year for the next fiscal year.

GORDO *(SPAIN)*   Name given to a full-bodied wine and also applied when its organoleptic characteristics show a high alcoholic strength. *See* Fat.

GORDO BLANCO   *See* Muscat of Alexandria.

GORZALE WINO (POLAND)   Scorched or distilled wine. Term used for vodka until the sixteenth century to distinguish the beverage from medicinal vodkas.

GORZALKA (POLAND)   Ancient term for vodka, used until the sixteenth century.

GOUDRON   *See* Tarry.

GOULEYANT (FRANCE)   Describes a wine that is easy to drink.

GOURMET CUBES   *See* Ice Cubes.

GOÛT (FRANCE)   Taste; used to describe the taste of a wine.

GOÛT AMÉRICAIN (FRANCE)   Describes a fairly sweet wine, chiefly demisec or doux champagnes, generally exported to South America or Eastern Europe.

GOÛT ANGLAIS (FRANCE)   Describes a fairly dry wine, chiefly brut champagnes for the English market.

GOÛT DE BOISÉ (FRANCE)   *See* Oaky.

GOÛT DE BOUCHON (FRANCE)   *See* Corked.

GOÛT DE CUIT (FRANCE)   *See* Cooked.

GOÛT D'ÉVENT (FRANCE)   *See* Flat.

GOÛT DE FERMENT (FRANCE)   Taste of a wine still fermenting, or in a bottle, having recently undergone a secondary fermentation.

GOÛT DE FOX (FRANCE)   *See* Foxy.

GOÛT DE GOUDRON (FRANCE)   *See* Tarry.

GOÛT FRANCAIS (FRANCE)   This term describes a sweet champagne.

GOÛT DE LUMIÈRE (FRANCE)   Light rays close to the UV wavelength are responsible for the "light stroke" that is detrimental to wine and beer.

GOÛT DE PAILLE (FRANCE)   A wine with a taste of wet straw that is quite objectionable.

GOÛT DE PIERRE-À-FUSIL (FRANCE)   Also known as *pierre-à-fusil*. *See* Flinty.

GOÛT DE PIQUÉ (FRANCE)   *See* Acescence.

GOÛT DE POURRI (FRANCE)   A wine or beer with a rotted taste. *See* Rot.

GOÛT DE RANCE (FRANCE)   *See* Butyric Acid.

GOÛT DE RANCIO (FRANCE)   *See* Rancio.

GOÛT DE RENARD (FRANCE)   *See* Foxy.

GOÛT DE SAUVAGE (FRANCE)   Taste imparted by native American grapevines and some hybrids.

GOÛT DE TERROIR (FRANCE)   *See* Earthy.

GOÛT DE VIEUX (FRANCE)   The distinctive smell and taste of an old wine.

GOÛT MAUVAIS (FRANCE)   *See* Dead.

GOUVEIO *(PORTUGAL)* *See* Verdelho.

GOVERNO *(ITALY)* A process occasionally used to produce Chianti wine meant for early consumption. It consists of inducing a secondary fermentation by the addition of 5 to 10 percent *must*, pressed from selected grapes partly dried on wicker frames. This process adds roundness and liveliness to the wine, along with a certain prickliness, noticeable on the tip of the tongue. The governo method was introduced in 1364 by Ruberto Bernardi, a Tuscan goldsmith. Also known as *governo Toscano. See* Cannici, Filtrato, and Straw Mats.

GOVERNO TOSCANO *(ITALY)* *See* Governo.

GOYURA *(AUSTRALIA)* A white grape variety developed from a cross of Muscat of Alexandria and Sultana.

GRAACH *(GERMANY)* A vineyard town located on the right bank of the Mittelmosel.

GRACIANO *(SPAIN)* A red grape variety grown in the Rioja region. Also known as *Morrastal.*

GRADAZIONE ALCOOLICA *(ITALY)* Alcoholic grade; percentage of alcohol by volume.

GRADEVOLE *(ITALY)* *See* Pleasant.

GRADI ALCOOL *(ITALY)* Percentage or degrees of alcohol.

GRAF *(GERMANY)* Earl or count.

GRAFTING A viticultural technique that joins a bud (part of the grapevine that produces grapes) or other part of one grapevine to a portion of another so that their tissues unite. Also known as *greffe* and *injerto.*

GRAIN Small, hard seeds of cereal grass, such as wheat, oats, rye, rice, barley, and others, necessary for making beer and most distilled spirits.

GRAIN ALCOHOL *See* Ethyl Alcohol.

GRAIN NEUTRAL SPIRITS *See* Neutral Spirits.

GRAIN SPIRITS Spirits distilled from a fermented mash of grain and stored in oak containers. By recognizing the qualities developed by storage, grain spirits are distinguished from grain neutral spirits.

GRAIN WHISKIES Whiskies made in a continuous distillation process from a mash of cereals, including malted barley and other unmalted cereals, yeast, and water. Grain whiskies used to make Scotch whisky are mostly made in the Lowlands of Scotland, although some come from the Highlands.

GRAINY A negative term often applied to beers with an excessive use or corn or rice adjuncts.

GRAM A metric unit of weight, 28.349 grams being equal to one ounce, one thousand grams to a kilogram, which is equal to 2.2 pounds.

GRAMS PER LITER The unit of measure equivalent to the parts per thousand unit of measure prescribed in the Internal Revenue Code of 1986.

GRANACHA *(FRANCE)* *See* Grenache.

GRANATO *(ITALY)* Garnet.

GRAND CRU *(FRANCE)* A great growth that is a legal grade of quality. It is authorized for certain superior wines from classified Bordeaux, Burgundy, or Alsatian vineyards.

GRAND CRU *(FRANCE)* A Champagne vineyard rated at 100 percent.

GRAND CRU CLASSÉ *(FRANCE)* A great growth that is a legal grade of quality. It is authorized for certain superior wines from classified (1855) Bordeaux vineyards.

GRANDE CHAMPAGNE *(FRANCE)* Not a sparkling wine, but rather the premier grape-growing area of the Cognac region. Cognacs identified as Grande Champagne must be made exclusively from grapes grown in the Grande Champagne section of Cognac. Also known as *Grande Fine Champagne*.

GRANDE FINE CHAMPAGNE *(FRANCE)* *See* Grande Champagne.

GRANDE MARQUE *(FRANCE)* An unofficial designation used to identify the best producers located in the Champagne region.

GRANDE RÉSERVE *(FRANCE)* A label designation used on calvados and cognac bottles to indicate that the youngest brandy used in the blend is at least five years old (calvados) and 6-1/2 years old (cognac), although they contain a very high percentage of brandy that has been aged for twenty, thirty, or forty years or more.

GRAND FORMAT A term loosely used in France to denote large bottles of wine.

GRAND NOIR *See* Grand Noir de la Calmette.

GRAND NOIR DE LA CALMETTE A red grape variety grown primarily in California, where it is utilized as a blending grape due to its high juice yields. Also known as *Grand Noir*.

GRANDS ECHÉZEAUX *(FRANCE)* A red *grand cru* vineyard located in the commune of Flagey-Echézeaux.

GRAND VIN *(FRANCE)* Great wine. An unofficial term utilized quite freely by many wineries.

GRAND VIN ORDINAIRE *(FRANCE)* A term with absolutely no legal meaning.

GRANEL *(SPAIN)* Wine in bulk.

GRANITE SHOTTING A procedure, unused in many years, that involved roughening up or scoring the inside of bottles by use of granite chips so that the crust formed by port wine is provided with a grip, thus rendering decanting much easier.

GRANO *(SPAIN)* *See* Seeds.

GRAN RESERVA *(SPAIN)* Red wines that have been aged in oak barrels (225 liter) for a minimum of two years, followed by three years in the bottle; they may not leave the *bodega* until the sixth year after the vintage. Whites and rosés must be aged for four years, six months of which must be in oak barrels. In practice, many wineries age the wines far longer than the minimum. Gran Reservas are usually only laid down in exceptional years.

GRANULAR CORK   Used to treat wines stored in redwood and concrete tanks to help smooth them out.

GRANVAS (SPAIN)   *See* Charmat Method.

GRAPA (SPAIN)   *See* Agrafe.

GRAPE   Any of various juicy, round, smooth-skinned, edible fruit, generally green or red-purple, borne in clusters on a woody vine. Also known as *rebe, traube, uva*, and *weinbeere*.

GRAPE   Grape was originally not the name of the fruit, but rather the name of the small hook with which bunches of grapes and grapefruit were cut and gathered. This tool we would refer to as a "grapple," related to the word "grab." The original name for the grape itself, often used in Old English, was wineberry.

GRAPE BRICK   During Prohibition you could buy a package containing dehydrated grape juice that had a warning label on its wrapper that stated, "Do Not Mix This Package With Warm Water, Yeast, And Keep In A Warm Location For Two Weeks, for This Will Make Wine, And That Is Illegal!"

GRAPE CONCENTRATE   Strained, dehydrated grape juice or extract, or grape juice that has been boiled down to a very sweet syrup. Also known as *concentrate* and *concentrato*. *See* Geropiga.

GRAPEFRUIT JUICE   The liquid constituent of a grapefruit.

GRAPEFRUITY   An odor or characteristic taste often identified with certain cold-climate grape varieties (e.g., Gewürztraminer and Johannisberg-Riesling).

GRAPE JUICE   The liquid constituent of a grape that accounts for more than 85 percent of the grape. Also known as *traubensaft*.

GRAPE LEAFHOPPER   (*Erythroneura comes*) The adult grape leafhopper is about one-eighth inch long, pale in color, and its back and wings are marked with yellow and red. Grape leafhoppers are abundant during the summer on the undersides of grape leaves. They suck juice from the leaves and cause white blotches that later change to brown. As a result, many leaves fall from the grapevines prematurely. This damage prevents normal grapevine growth and interferes with proper ripening of the fruit.

GRAPE KNIFE   A hand-held knife used to cut bunches of grapes during harvest. Also known as *corquette, épinettes, falcetta*, and *serpette*.

GRAPE-PICKING BASKET   A wicker, wooden, or plastic basket with shoulder straps, carried on the backs of grape-pickers, and used to transport freshly picked grapes during the harvest.

Also a small tank with shoulder straps, carried on the back, that is filled with wine or *must*, and then carried and dumped into another barrel. It is seldom used in today's winery. Also known as *bailhot, beneau, brenta, caque, cesto vindimo, cunacho, dosser, hotte de vendange, mannequin, osier baskets, panier à vendange, pannier, portador*, and *tineta*. *See* Lug Boxes.

GRAPE POMACE BRANDY   *See* Grappa.

GRAPE PRESS   *See* Wine Press.

GRAPES Although there are more than eight thousand grape varieties in the world, most of them are not suitable for making fine wine, nor are their parent grapevine species highly regarded. In making fine wine, the most prominent grapevine species are *Vitis vinifera*, *Vitis labrusca*, and French-American hybrids.

Each grape variety has its own individual color, aroma, taste, and flavor—sort of a "fingerprint" that identifies it either by minute and subtle nuances, or by a wide and marked margin.

GRAPE SUGAR The natural sugar contained in ripe grapes, which is primarily glucose. *See* Glucose.

GRAPE VARIETY The name of a grape or grapes used in winemaking. Also known as *casta, cépage, rebsorte, variety,* and *vitigno.*

GRAPEVINE Any of the species of woody vines that bear edible fruit. Grapevines are hermaphroditic or monoecious, which means that they are self-pollinating. Also known as *ampelos, vid, videira, vigne, vite,* and *weinreb.*

GRAPE WINE Wine produced by the normal alcoholic fermentation of the juice of sound, ripe grapes (including restored or unrestored pure condensed grape *must*) with or without the addition, after fermentation, of pure condensed grape *must,* and with or without added grape brandy or alcohol, but without other addition or abstraction except as may occur in cellar treatment. The product may be ameliorated before, during, or after fermentation by either the use of dry sugar and/or water. *See* Wine.

GRAPPA (ITALY) Grappa is a distillate made primarily from the skins, pulp, and seeds (collectively known as *pomace* or *vinaccia* in Italian) of grapes—the remains from the pressing of the grapes for winemaking. The pomace utilized in the production of grappa is generally still quite moist, which adds flavor and varietal character. In Italy grappa is made by distillers collectively known as *grappaioli.*

The origin of the name grappa comes from a town called *Bassano del Grappa* in the Veneto region of Italy, where grappa was originally produced. Northern Italy accounts for approximately 90 percent of the grappa sold in Italy.

In Italy, grappa is divided into two types: *pregiate* (premium) and *correnta* (standard or normal). The only *consorzi* in Italy that have developed any type of regulation relative to grappa exist in the region of Trentino–Alto Adige. Elsewhere, the only guarantee of quality a consumer has is the producer's name and reputation.

In the production process, water is added to the pomace (which may be from either red or white grapes), along with yeast and sugar. After the pomace finishes refermenting, the resulting liquid is distilled in either the traditional small *pot still* or the more modern *continuous still*. It is generally removed from the still at between 100 to 130 proof. As with other distilled spirits, only the *heart* or center of the distillate is utilized in the final product.

It is estimated that 225 pounds of pomace yields approximately five liters of pure alcohol. The pomace utilized in making grappa should be fresh and not more than one day old. The pomace of pressed fruit such as apples, apricots, and pears can also be used.

Grappa can be a blend of many different grape varieties or be made from a single grape variety (known as *Grappa di Monovitigno*).

Specialty types of grappa include *Floral Grappa,* which is infused and often bottled with flower petals. *Fruit Grappa* is infused with or distilled from fresh fruit, similar to an eau-de-vie. *Ùe* is a distillate from a mixture of pomace and wine. *Grappa*

Aromatizzata is grappa infused and often bottled with herbs; it is also known as *herbal grappa*. *Grappa Con Ruta* develops its characteristic odor and taste from *rue*. Rue is a strongly scented herb from the *ruta graveolens* family, with yellow flowers and bitter-tasting leaves, formerly used for medicinal purposes but now used occasionally as a flavoring for grappa.

This collected distillate is usually stored in ceramic, stainless steel, or glass containers; it is bottled when quite young. However, if it is determined that the distillate should be aged, then oak barrels are used.

Old-style grappa, which was rough- or coarse-tasting (depending on raw material and production methods utilized), was usually wood aged several years before it smoothed out. Modern distillation, which utilizes better raw materials, results in a higher quality grappa that is considerably smoother and more refined. Nowadays, grappa is rarely aged in wooden barrels.

In addition to a considerably higher quality grappa, hand-blown glass bottles and flasks have become an important part of the overall packing of grappa.

Grappa Giovane is young, unaged grappa, generally about six months old. *Grappa Invecchiata* is grappa that has been aged for months or even years, generally in wooden barrels, hence its amber color.

Grappa is traditionally served after dinner as a digestive; it is consumed straight, either at cool room temperature, or well chilled in a small glass or brandy snifter. Grappa is occasionally added to espresso coffee to make *caffè corretto*.

Grappa is also known as *alcools blancs, eau-de-vie, grape pomace brandy*, or *pomace brandy* (for short). Grappa is produced in many countries under other names: *aguardiente de orujo* (or *orujo*) in Spain; *aguardente de bagaceira* (or *bagaceira*) in Portugal; *dop brandy* in South Africa; *marc* in France; *trester* in Germany; and *tsigouthia* in Greece.

GRAPPA AROMATIZZATA (*ITALY*) Grappa infused and often bottled with herbs. Also known as *herbal grappa. See* Grappa, Grappa Con Ruta, and Rue.

GRAPPA BRANDY *See* Grappa.

GRAPPA CON RUTA (*ITALY*) Grappa that develops its characteristic odor and taste from *rue. See* Grappa, Grappa Aromatizzata, and Rue.

GRAPPA DI MONOVITIGNO (*ITALY*) Grappa from a single grape variety. *See* Grappa.

GRAPPA GIOVANE (*ITALY*) Young, unaged grappa, generally about six months old. *See* Grappa.

GRAPPA INVECCHIATA (*ITALY*) Grappa that has been aged for months or even years, generally in wooden barrels, hence its amber color. *See* Grappa.

GRAPPAIOLI (*ITALY*) Distillers who make grappa.

GRAPPE (*FRANCE*) *See* Cluster.

GRAPY Similar to fruity, with a characteristic smell of a young, often immature fruity wine with fresh grape overtones. A taste almost of fresh-picked grapes. Most *Vitis labrusca* grape varieties display this characteristic. Also known as *sappy*.

GRAS An acronym for "generally recognized as safe." *See* Generally Recognized As Safe.

GRAS (*FRANCE*) *See* Full-Bodied.

GRASA *(ROMANIA)* A white grape variety, generally used to make sweet wines. *See* Som.

GRASIG *(GERMANY)* *See* Green.

GRASSY A term applied to certain white wines, especially Sauvignon Blanc and Sémillon, which display a vegetal, herbaceous odor, often reminiscent of freshly mowed grass. In low levels, it adds character to the wine, but in the extreme, it becomes unappealing to most consumers. *See* Herbaceous and Vegetal.

GRAU *(GERMANY)* Gray.

GRAUER BURGUNDER *(GERMANY)* *See* Pinot Gris.

GRAVE *(ITALY)* Gravel.

GRAVE DEL FRIULI *(ITALY)* A wine-producing area within the region of Friuli-Venezia Giulia. *See* Friuli-Venezia Giulia.

GRAVELLEUX *(FRANCE)* Gravelly.

GRAVES *(FRANCE)* Gravel.

GRAVES *(FRANCE)* An important wine district in the southern part of Bordeaux, along the Garonne River, that produces both dry red and white wines. Graves and Sauternes are the only districts in Bordeaux that produce AOC white wines. Only three grape varieties are permitted: Sémillon (about 70 percent of total plantings), Sauvignon Blanc, and Muscadelle. Graves translated means *gravel*, which is the composite makeup of the soil.

On March 4, 1937, the wines of Graves were officially granted their AOC designation. In 1953, a classification of the wines of Graves was begun by the INAO, which completed the task in 1959.

GRAY RIESLING *See* Chauché Gris.

GRECANICO *(ITALY)* A white grape variety grown in the region of Sicily. Also known as *Dorato*.

GRECHETTO *(ITALY)* A white grape variety grown primarily in the region of Umbria, where it produces Orvieto and Torgiano Bianco.

GRECO *(ITALY)* *See* Albana.

GRECO DI ANCONA *(ITALY)* *See* Albana.

GRECO DI TUFO *(ITALY)* A white grape variety grown primarily in Campania.

GREEN Describes an immature, undeveloped wine that usually displays an austere, somewhat sour taste. Green wines are usually unbalanced and are characterized by a high level of malic or tartaric acid. Also known as *grasig, green wine, grün, verde, verdoso,* and *vert. See* Sour, Tart, Unripe, and Young.

GREEN BEER A term generally applied to young or immature beers that have just finished fermenting and are still cloudy.

GREEN DRAGON TAVERN A pub located in Boston where Paul Revere and his fellow patriots held their meetings.

GREEN-GRAFTING   A viticultural practice that entails the mounting of a variety (scion) on a rootstock while the stems of the two partners are still in a herbaceous (green) rather than a ligneous (brown) state.

GREEN HUNGARIAN   A white grape variety grown in California, where it is used primarily as a blending grape, although several wineries do make a varietal wine from it. In 1949, J. Leland Stewart of Souverain Vineyards, California, became the first winery to bottle Green Hungarian as a separate varietal.

GREEN MALT   Malt that has germinated but has not yet been dried or kilned.

GREENNESS   A form of green.

GREEN OLIVE   A term applied to certain red wines, especially Cabernet Franc, Cabernet Sauvignon, and Sauvignon Blanc, that display a distinct aroma and taste of green olives. In low levels, it adds character to the wine, but in the extreme, it becomes unappealing to most consumers.

GREEN TEA   An unfermented tea that comes mainly from China, Japan, and Taiwan. The green tea leaves are steamed, rolled, and dried over hot air to inactivate fermentation.

GREEN WINE   *See* Green and Vinho Verde.

GREENWOOD   Undulations in the surface of a cork caused by moisture conditions.

GREFFE (FRANCE)   *See* Grafting.

GREFFE-SOUDE (FRANCE)   Nursery-prepared plant that is grafted onto American rootstocks.

GRÊLE (FRANCE)   *See* Hail.

GRENACHE   A red grape variety used mostly in the United States for rosé wines or as a blending grape. It is widely grown throughout the Mediterranean, especially in France's southern regions, where it is partly responsible for Châteauneuf-du-Pape and Tavel rosés. In Spain it produces the reds from Rioja and Catalonia.

Grenache is of Spanish origin and was first introduced as a California varietal wine by Almadén Vineyards in 1941. Also known as *Carignane Rousse, Garnacha, Garnacho, Granacha,* and *Grenache Noir.*

GRENACHE NOIR   *See* Grenache.

GRENADINE   A red syrup (either alcoholic or nonalcoholic) with an unusual flavor derived from pomegranate or red currants.

GREY RIESLING   Also spelled *Gray Riesling. See* Chauché Gris.

GREY ROT   *See* Rot.

GRIGNOLINO (ITALY)   A red grape variety grown primarily in the Piedmont region. The Grignolino grapevine is indigenous to the Asti area and its presence there can be traced back to 1252.

GRILLO (ITALY)   A white grape variety grown in Sicily, often used to make table wines or marsala. Also known as *Riddu.*

G

GRILLO (ITALY)

GRIND   To crush or pulverize coffee beans into fine particles by use of mechanical or, rarely, hand mills.

GRIP   A seldom-used term used to describe the manner in which wine holds onto the insides of a glass. Also its mouth-filling capabilities, which are firm and rich.

GRIS (FRANCE)   *See* Vin Gris.

GRIS (FRANCE)   Grey.

GRIST   Grain, necessary for making whiskey or malt beverages, that must be ground or already has been ground.

GRITS   Coarsely chopped corn or other hulled grains used as an adjunct in the brewing of beer.

GROG (AUSTRALIA)   Term for any alcoholic drink.

GROG   A name for rum, derived from the nickname of Admiral Edward Vernon (1684–1757), the English naval officer for whom George Washington's estate was named. The admiral was known as "Old Grog" because he wore a shabby boat coat made out of grogram, a coarse fabric woven from silk and wool and often stiffened with gum. He ordered his men to take a daily drink of rum and water as a caution against scurvy, and until September 1, 1862, seagoing sailors from the United States were served grog. Also known as *Navy Grog*.

GROG BLOSSOM   The British, during World Wars I and II, were occasionally said to have a Grog Blossom, which meant a rosy nose, presumably from years of drinking.

GROLLEAU (FRANCE)   A red grape variety grown in the Loire Valley, where it is often referred to as *Groslot*. It is often used in making rosé wines of Anjou.

GROPELLO (ITALY)   A red grape variety grown in the region of Lombardy.

GROSLOT   *See* Grolleau.

GROS MANSENG (FRANCE)   A white grape variety grown in the southwest.

GROS PLANT   *See* Folle Blanche.

GROSS DOLLAR PROFIT   The total dollar sales minus the cost of goods sold.

GROSSIER (FRANCE)   *See* Rough.

GROSSLAGE (GERMANY)   A composite vineyard made up of numbers of individual vineyards with subregions.

GROSS MARGIN   Revenues minus direct product costs.

GROS VERT   A white grape variety grown in California.

GROSS WEIGHT   Weight of a container plus its contents.

GROUND WATER   Water beneath the earth's surface between saturated soil and rock that supplies wells and springs; necessary for proper growing of grapevines.

GROWING DEGREE DAYS   *See* Heat Summation.

GROWLERS   A slang, seldom-used term for "pails of beer to go."

GROWTH (FRANCE)   A standard of quality applied to wines of France; also known as *cru*.

GROWTH CYCLE   Used to denote the annually recurrent events that mark growth, development, and fruiting of the grapevines.

GRUMELLO (ITALY)   A full-bodied red wine produced primarily from the Nebbiolo grape variety in the Valtellina district of Lombardy.

GRÜN (GERMANY)   *See* Green.

GRÜNER SYLVANER (GERMANY)   *See* Sylvaner.

GRÜNER VELTLINER (AUSTRIA)   A white grape variety grown extensively in areas of Lower Austria and Vienna.

GUARNACCIA (ITALY)   A red grape variety grown primarily in Campania. Also known as *Cannamelu, Tintore,* and *Uarnaccia.*

GUÉRITE (FRANCE)   The receptacle used to catch the temporary cork and sediment during *disgorging*.

GUEUZE (BELGIUM)   A *lambic-type* beer, made from a blend of various aged *lambics*, that is quite effervescent with aromas of apple or even rhubarb. However, all beers produced from lambics are quite sour. It is also brewed in Berlin, Germany. *See* Lambic.

GUIGNARDIA BIDWELLII   *See* Black Rot.

GUINGETTE (FRANCE)   A local tavern or roadside inn that features live music and dancing.

GUM ARABIC   A substance obtained from various species of acacia trees or shrubs and occasionally used to clarify and stabilize wine.

GUN FLINT   *See* Flinty.

GUNPOWDER PROOF   *See* Proof.

GUSTO RANCIO (ITALY)   The so-called cooked taste or flavor of marsala wines, often imparted from *cotto*, a cooked wine. *See* Cooked and Cooked Wine.

GUT (GERMANY)   Good.

GUTEDEL (GERMANY)   A white grape variety brought to Baden by Karl Friedrich from Lake Geneva in 1780. It is thought to have come from Turkey or even Egypt, where it was mentioned as early as 2,800 B.C.; later imported into France. It is correctly known as *Chasselas Doré*.

GUTENBORNER (GERMANY)   A white grape variety developed from a cross of Müller-Thurgau and Chasselas Napoléon.

GUTTURNIUM (ITALY)   The name of an ancient silver Roman drinking vessel, which was a precursor of the modern *tastevin*. The word *gutturnium* is probably the source of the name of a local red, DOC wine from Emilia-Romagna. *See* Tastevin.

GUYOT (FRANCE)   A pruning method (named after Dr. Jules Guyot) used in the Beaujolais district of Burgundy that consists of training grapevines on a single vertical axis.

GW-7   *See* Horizon.

GYPSUM   *See* Calcium Sulfate and Plastering.

GYROPALETTE   An automated riddling machine used for making sparkling wines. There have been many variations and modifications of this automated riddling system, often dubbed "VLM" (very large machine). Older models stood approximately four feet high, wasted thirteen feet of airspace, and were capable of riddling 504 bottles at once. The newer machine, which stands seventeen feet high, once described as a "cubist gyroscope," can riddle 4,032 bottles at once! It can also be programmed to turn and/or tilt three times in twenty-four hours. A bottle of sparkling wine can be machine riddled in twelve days (three movements a day) as opposed to the approximately thirty days of a traditional hand-riddling cycle. Also known as *girasol. See* Remuage.

HA *See* Hectare.

HABILLAGE (FRANCE) A bottle-dressing (combination of label and foil capsule), when referring to champagne bottles.

HABZÓ (HUNGARY) *See* Sparkling Wine.

HAIL Precipitation in the form of pellets of ice and hard snow; it is detrimental to grapevines. During heavy hailstorms, the hail damages clusters of berries as well as breaking the delicate canes and other parts of the grapevine. Also known as *grêle*.

HALBROT (SWITZERLAND) *See* Rosé Wine.

HALBFUDER (GERMANY) A large barrel with a capacity of five hundred liters (132 gallons), mostly used in the Mosel region. *See* Barrel.

HALBSTÜCK (GERMANY) A large barrel with a capacity of six hundred liters (158.5 gallons). *See* Barrel.

HALBTROCKEN (GERMANY) A wine designation that was put into effect by the wine authority of the Common Market in Brussels on August 1, 1977. The reason for this designation was that some people prefer wines drier than most of the German wines on the market.

Halbtrocken wines contain a maximum of eighteen grams per liter of residual sugar (which can also be expressed as 1.8 grams per hundred milliliters or 1.8 percent residual sugar). The variance here can be ten grams per liter. For example, if the wine contains five grams per liter of acidity, the maximum sugar level can only be fifteen grams per liter.

HALB UND HALB (GERMANY) A light-brown citrus liqueur made from a base of alcohol and flavored with cloves and other spices.

HALF AND HALF (ENGLAND) A drink consisting of equal parts stout and ale.

HALF AND HALF A commercial mixture of half 18-percent cream and half 3.5-percent milk.

HALF-BARREL   *See* Keg.

HALF-BOTTLE   A bottle with a capacity of 12.7 ounces or 375 milliliters.

HALF-CUBE   *See* Ice Cubes.

HALF-DICE   *See* Ice Cubes.

HALF-KEG   A container with a capacity of seven and three-quarters gallons of beer.

HAMMONDSPORT   A wine-producing district in the Finger Lakes region of New York State.

HANDGUN   A hand-held dispensing head with a flexible metal hose, connected to the postmix or premix portion of the automatic soda system utilized in some bars. *See* Flexhose.

HAND SHAKER   A combination of a large mixing glass and a stainless steel container that fits over it. It is used for cocktails that need to be hand shaken for incorporation of ingredients. Also known as *mixing cup, mixing glass,* or *mixing steel*.

HANEPOOT (SOUTH AFRICA)   *See* Muscat of Alexandria.

HAPPY HOUR   A limited period of the day, usually one to two hours before dinner, during which patrons can enjoy extra-large drinks or alcoholic beverages whose prices have been discounted. Also known as *attitude adjustment hour*.

HARD   Describes a wine (generally red) with excessive tannin that usually dissipates with age. Not necessarily a fault in a young, immature wine, because it may indicate a long maturity period. Similar to *green*. Also known as *âpreté, dur, duro, hart,* and *sklirós*.

HARD CIDER   The result of fermentation of cider without the addition of sugar. It is relatively low in alcohol (about 5 to 8 percent) and has a very limited shelf-life. *See* Apple Juice, Apple Wine, Cider, and Sweet Cider.

HARDENING   The process by which a plant or tissue is made more resistant to environmental extremes, such as low temperature.

HARD LIQUOR   A term commonly taken to mean distilled spirits; beverages that contain at least 40 percent alcohol (80 proof). Also known as *liquor*.

HARDPAN   A compacted and often clayey layer of soil that hampers root penetration; it results from accumulation of cementing materials or may be caused by repeated plowing to the same depth. *See* Plow Pan.

HARDWOOD   Surface hardness caused by cutting cork too close to the wood of the tree.

HARDY   Unless qualified, this descriptive term means the indicated grape variety has performed well in hardiness trials in many vineyard sites and is not subject to damage by extremes in temperature.

HARMONICA (SPAIN)   *See* Balance.

HARMONIOUS   Also known as *evármostos* and *harmonisch. See* Balance.

HARMONISCH (GERMANY)   *See* Balance.

HARO (SPAIN)   The primary wine-producing town of Rio Alta.

HARRIAGUE (URUGUAY)   *See* Tannat.

HARSH   *See* Astringency.

HÁRSLEVELÜ (HUNGARY)   A white grape variety used in making Tokay wines.

HART (GERMANY)   *See* Hard.

HARTFORD   An ancient grape grown in the 1840s by Paphro Steele in West Hartford, Connecticut.

HARVEST   The annual gathering or picking of the grapes for the making of wine. Also known as *añada, annata, année, ano de colheita cosecha, crop, crush, lese, picking, recolta, weinlese,* and *year of the harvest. See* Vintage and Vintage Wine.

HARVEST CYCLE   Although ice-making machines vary considerably in methods of forming and releasing ice, the operating cycles are similar in most cases. The water-contact or water-container surfaces are chilled to below the freezing point in the ice-making cycle. When the ice reaches a certain thickness, the water-contact or water-container surface is heated briefly to release the ice; this is the harvest cycle.

HARVEY WALLBANGER   A cocktail consisting of orange juice, vodka, and Galliano liqueur. It seems that in southern California (according to legend), Tom Harvey would arrive at his favorite pub after a day's surfing and order an "Italian Screwdriver"; then, after consuming several of them, he would attempt to leave and start banging into walls! Hence the name.

HASANDEDE (TURKEY)   A white grape variety.

HAT   *See* Cap.

HAUT (FRANCE)   High. In the United States this term means "sweet" when referring to certain white, *generic* wines. *See* Haut Sauterne.

HAUTAIN (FRANCE)   A pruning method by which the grapevines are trained, often with *espaliers* (posts larger than standard size), in an upward manner for greater sun exposure.

HAUT-MÉDOC (FRANCE)   The southern portion of the Médoc, famous for the red wines of Saint-Estèphe, Pauillac, Saint-Julien, and Margaux.

HAUT SAUTERNE   A generic United States white wine of medium sweetness. Rarely produced nowadays. *See* Haut.

HAZY   *See* Cloudy.

HDP   *See* Hybrid Direct Producers.

HEAD   The upper portion of a grapevine, consisting of the top of the trunk and upper arms. Also known as the *crown*.

HEAD   *See* Foam and Coney Island Head.

HEAD OR HEAD BOARDS   The ends of a barrel. Each head is made of at least three or more pieces of oak held together by wooden dowels and usually caulked with straw. Also known as *fond de tonneau*.

HEADLIGHT   A grape variety developed by Thomas Volney Munson (1843–1913) of Denison, Texas.

HEADING LIQUID   A liquid formula that, when added to beer, increases the head retention and produces a thick, foamy head. Need for this procedure exists when insufficient malt is used in making the beer. It is seldom used nowadays.

HEAD PRUNING   A classic nineteenth-century pruning method consisting of cutting the grapevine back to the main stock every winter, leaving two bud branches or longer canes with eight to sixteen bud branches. These form a classic goblet shape, open in the center to allow plenty of sun to get to the grapes and good air circulation. *See* Pruning.

HEADS   In distillation, the first crude spirit to appear from the still; it is collected and redistilled. Also known as *foreshot, produit de tête*, and *singlings*.

HEADSPACE   In a barrel or tank, the space of air between the top of the wine and the top of the container. This space is the result of evaporation or leakage. *See* Ullage.

HEADSPACE   A distilled spirits bottle of a capacity of two hundred milliliters or more is held to be filled so as to mislead the purchaser if it has a headspace in excess of 8 percent of the total capacity of the bottle after closure.

HEAD TRAINING   The oldest form of grapevine training, which has been used for centuries, can still be found in California's older vineyards. With the head system, the grapevine is kept rather low to the ground. In the early stages of its growth, it is allowed to develop "arms" that radiate from the main trunk, somewhat like the spokes of a wheel. The leaf and fruit-bearing canes or grapevine branches emanate from these arms. On each of the arms are "spurs" or year-old segments of growth that generate tiny buds that in turn produce new growth and bear the next year's grapes. By controlling the number of buds left on the grapevine through pruning, the number of grape clusters produced can be controlled.

This technique, however, has some problems. The low position of the grapevine makes soil cultivation, pruning, and harvesting quite difficult. Head-trained grapevines give low yields and not necessarily the best quality. Although the radial configuration of the grapevine arms does allow fairly good air circulation around the grapevine and exposure to the sun, more modern training techniques have demonstrated a clear improvement in both of these factors. *See* Cordon Training, Shoot Positioning, and Training.

HEADY   A term that usually refers to wines with excessive alcohol content. Roughly equivalent to *strong* wines. Also, used loosely as a term for sparkling wines that show a persistent foam on their surface. Also known as *capiteux*.

HEART ROOTS   *See* Tap Roots.

HEARTS   In distillation, elements that vaporize between the heads and tails and are utilized in the final product. Also known as *madilla, middle cuts*, and *middle liquors*.

HEARTY   A term generally used to describe full-bodied red wines with strong scents and high alcohol and extract levels. Also known as *herzhaft*.

HEATER   *See* Brandy Heater.

HEAT INSTABILITY   Used to denote protein precipitation in a wine that causes cloudiness or haziness.

HEAT SUMMATION   The geographic classification of regions in terms of heat degree days during the seven-month growing season; the mean temperature or average high and low, greater than 50 degrees, from April 1 through October 31. The resulting figure is expressed as degree days. Also known as *growing degree days*. *See* Degree Days.

HEAT-TREATED VINES   The products of a process in which samples from the best grapevines are taken from the vineyard and tested against an index plant to isolate viruses. Most virus-free grapevines are raised in a hothouse, where the heat causes the grapevines to grow faster than the viruses. The top three inches of the grapevines are then cut off. The process is repeated and the heat-treated vines are then vineyard planted.

HEAVY   A term used to describe a wine that is high in alcohol but hasn't the flavor or acidity to balance it, or an excessively full-bodied wine of little distinction that lacks finesse and, because of this, is tiring to drink. Also known as *dru, lourd, ponderous, schwer*, and *varys*. *See* Full-Bodied.

HEAVY-BODIED BLENDING WINE   Wine made from fruit without added sugar, with or without added distilled wine spirits, and conforming to the definition of natural wine in all respects except maximum total solids content.

HEAVY GOBLET   A stemmed glass with a large, round bowl with a capacity of eight to ten ounces; used to serve beer.

HEAVY SOIL   Finely textured soils that contain high levels of clay and silt.

HECHO EN MEXICO (SPAIN)   Made in Mexico.

HECTARE (HA)   A metric measure equal to ten thousand square meters of land or 2.471 acres. Also known as *ettaro* and *hectarea*.

HECTAREA (SPAIN)   *See* Hectare.

HECTOGRADE (HG)   The metric system for measuring the alcoholic content of wine. Also known as *ettogrado*.

HECTOLITER (HL)   A metric measurement equal to one hundred liters, 26.418 gallons, or 11.12 cases of twelve 750-milliliter bottles. In the European Economic Community, wine production is referred to in hectoliters per hectare (hl/ha), 65.28 gallons, or 27.47 cases. Also known as *ettolitro* and *hectolitro*.

HECTOLITRO (SPAIN)   *See* Hectoliter.

HECTOR   A white grape variety grown in the United States.

HEFE (GERMANY)   *See* Yeast.

HEFE WEIZEN (GERMANY)   Wheat beer that still has the yeast in the bottle. *See* Wheat Beer.

HEFIG (GERMANY)   *See* Yeasty.

HEIDA   *See* Paien.

HELBON (GREECE)   An ancient wine.

HELENA   A white grape variety developed in 1958 by Dr. Harold P. Olmo of the University of California, Davis.

HELFENSTEINER (GERMANY)   A red grape variety developed in Weinsberg from a cross of Frühburgunder and Trollinger.

HELIX-TYPE CORKSCREW   A corkscrew with an open-core design and usually manufactured as either a wire helix or from a solid round bar of steel in which the metal is cut away to form the helix. In the latter case, the helix is generally more web-shaped than the wire helix and somewhat resembles an auger type. The only apparent disadvantage of the helix is that the point, pitch, and alignment can be damaged by heavy-handed use.

HELL (*GERMANY*)   Pale; the color of some beers.

HELLES BIER (*GERMANY*)   *See* Light Beer.

HEPSEMA (*GREECE*)   An ancient wine made by concentrated *must. See* Cooked Wine.

HERBACEOUS   Describes the odor or taste of herbs (undefined as to species) such as parsley, rosemary, sage, or thyme, occasionally found in a wine or beer. This grassy or vegetal smell may be contributed by hops (beermaking) or the varietal character of certain grape varieties such as Cabernet Sauvignon, Cabernet Franc, Merlot, and Sauvignon Blanc. *See* Grassy, Stemmy, and Vegetal.

HERBAL GRAPPA (*ITALY*)   *See* Grappa Aromatizzata.

HERBEMONT   A red grape variety developed in 1819 by Nicholas Herbemont of Georgia. Some Herbemont is grown in the midwestern United States as well as in South Carolina.

HERBERT   A red grape variety.

HERBICIDE   Any chemical substance used to destroy plants or weeds or to inhibit their growth. Some are selective and kill only certain plants. Also known as *diserbante. See* Fungicide, Insecticide, and Pesticide.

HERBS   Aromatic plants that are utilized in making vermouth and other aromatized wines, certain liqueurs, and flavored wines.

HERB TEA   Technically not real tea, but an infusion of dried buds, leaves, and flowers in boiling water. There are more than four hundred different herbs that are suitable for use in herb teas and do not contain caffeine. Only one herbal tea, the South American *maté*, contains caffeine. Also known as *tè alle erbe*.

HERMANN   A white grape variety first grown in 1863 by F. Langendoerfer of Hermann, Missouri.

HERMAPHRODITIC   Grapevines are self-pollinating; therefore, they contain both the male (staminate) and female (pistillate) reproductive sex organs. Also known as *monoecious. See* Dioecious.

HERMITAGE (*SOUTH AFRICA*)   *See* Cinsaut.

HERMITAGE (*FRANCE*)   The name of a village in the southern part of the Rhône Valley famous for its full-bodied red wines. Hermitage red wine is produced from 100 percent Syrah grapes, while the white Hermitage is produced from a blend of Roussanne and Marsanne grapes. It is difficult to obtain due to its small production. The wines of Crozes-Hermitage are lighter than those of Hermitage.

Hermitage or hermit was a name supposedly given to Henri Gaspard de Stérimberg, a valiant knight in Pope Innocent III's crusade. As the story goes, upon his return in 1225, he spent his remaining thirty years at the top of a hill as a hermit, dedicating his life to viticulture.

HEROLDREBE *(GERMANY)*   A red grape variety developed in 1956 from a cross of Portugieser and Limberger and grown primarily in Württemberg. It was named for August Herold of the State Agricultural Institute of Weinsberg.

HERREN *(GERMANY)*   Lords.

HERSTELLER *(GERMANY)*   A manufacturer or producer of alcoholic beverages.

HERZHAFT *(GERMANY)*   *See* Hearty.

HESSISCHE BERGSTRASSE *(GERMANY)*   One of thirteen qualitätswein (quality) grape-growing regions; its wines are produced primarily for local consumption. Johannisberg Riesling and Müller-Thurgau are its primary grape varieties.

HETEROZYGOTE   A grapevine not breeding true to type for its particular characteristics.

HEURIGE *(AUSTRIA)*   A wine of the new year.

HEXENE   A green taste some grapes have if picked unripe.

HEXOSE   Any of the simple sugars, like fructose, galactose, glucose, or mannose, with molecules that contain six carbon atoms each.

HG   *See* Hectograde.

HIDALGO   A grape variety developed by Thomas Volney Munson (1843–1913) of Denison, Texas.

HIGGINS   A white grape variety grown primarily in Florida and Texas.

HIGHBALL   A cocktail containing blended whiskey (or any type of whiskey) and ginger ale (or other carbonated mixer). Originally in St. Louis in the 1880s, early railroaders used a ball on a high pole as a signal for railroad trains to go ahead or speed up. This signaling device was called a highball. The trainmen, always on a fast schedule, had time only for a quick drink. Hence, when bartenders found that ice, whiskey, and water could be speedily mixed into a delightful drink, they called it a highball.

HIGHLAND MALTS   Barley is grown in the Scottish highlands. The whiskies produced there (highland malts) are full of body and flavor, noted for their sweet oak and intensely smoky *(peaty)* characteristics and great balance.

HIGH-PROOF CONCENTRATE   A volatile fruit-flavor concentrate (essence) that has an alcohol content of more than 24 percent by volume and is unfit for beverage use (nonpotable) because of its natural constituents (e.g., without the addition of other substances).

HIGH QUALITY   A loosely used term for those beverages that are exceptionally well-made, exquisite, at their peak, or superior in quality and character. Also known as *ehrwein, fine, hochfein, köstlich,* and *spitzen.*

HIGH WINE   When the vapor is drawn off during the distillation process, it condenses into a liquid known as *low wine,* which has an alcoholic content of anywhere from 45 to 65 percent. The low wine is redistilled, or further refined, which allows the alcohol to reach an even higher concentration and further remove unwanted impurities and flavors. The resulting liquid is called *high wine* or new whiskey; it is crystal-clear and ready for maturing.

HIJAS *(SPAIN)* Daughters.

HIJOS *(SPAIN)* Sons.

HIMBEERGEIST *(GERMANY)* *See* Framboise.

HIMROD SEEDLESS A white grape variety developed in 1952 from a cross of Thompson Seedless and Ontario at the State Experimental Station in Geneva, New York.

HIPPOCRAS An ancient, highly spiced honey wine that was made more than 2,300 years ago by Hippocrates, a Greek physician. He wrote about a certain Roman liqueur called Hydromel that was made of wine, honey, cinnamon, and other aromatic herbs and botanicals. Hippocras was quite popular in Europe until the time of Louis XV. *See* Mead.

HISTAMINES Crystalline base compounds found in various molds, grape skins (especially red) and other plants; they are usually held responsible for the dilation and increased permeability of blood vessels, a major part of allergic reactions.

HL *See* Hectoliter.

HOCHFARBIG *(GERMANY)* A wine that is deeply colored.

HOCHFEIN *(GERMANY)* *See* High-Quality.

HOCHGEWÄCHS *(GERMANY)* A superior vineyard.

HOCHHEIM *(GERMANY)* The easternmost vineyard village of the Rheingau.

HOCK For many years the wines from Hochheim, Germany (which contains five vineyards between Mainz and Wiesbaden), were referred to, mainly by the British, as *hock*; earlier, the British called them *Rhenish* wines.

HOF *(GERMANY)* A court or manor house.

HOGSHEAD A barrel used in many wine-producing countries; its capacity varies from region to region. It is occasionally also used for storing or shipping distilled spirits and beer. *See* Barrel.

HÖHE *(GERMANY)* High, as in altitude.

HOIST A FEW A slang term for drinking a glass of beer.

HOLANDAS *(SPAIN)* An old, seldom-used term for distilled grape wine spirits. The name is taken from the country of Holland, which in the past was a great importer of distilled spirits.

HOLDING POWER The total number of bottles or display boxes (usually of a given size or type) that a shelf will hold, given the current facing set or schematic.

HOLLAND OR DUTCH GIN A gin produced primarily in Holland from a low-proof, distilled malt spirit to which juniper and other botanicals are added, resulting in a heavier body than the dry gins produced in the United States and England. Another general characteristic of Holland gin is that it retains and imparts some of the taste and odor of the grain. Also known as *Geneva* or *Schiedam*. Geneva is spelled *jenever* in Belgium.

HOLLEJO (SPAIN)   Grape skin.

HOLLOW   A term sometimes applied to a wine that has a beginning and an end, but no middle. It lacks a positive center impression or middle body. Also known as *creux*.

HOLZIG (GERMANY)   *See* Oaky.

HOME BREW   Illegal or illicit beer that was made at home in the United States during Prohibition.

HOMOGENIZED   A process by which milk is spun at very high speeds in order to break down the fat globules, transforming them into a stable emulsion; otherwise, they would rise to the surface, requiring the milk to be shaken prior to use. Pasteurization of milk is required by law, whereas homogenization is not.

HONEST   A term occasionally used to describe a simple but well-made wine.

HONEY   The odor or taste of honey often detected in sweet wines made from grapes that have been attacked by *Botrytis cinerea*. Also known as *honigartig*.

HONEY WINE   *See* Mead.

HONIGARTIG (GERMANY)   *See* Honey.

HONOR BARS   Drinking establishments in which guests are expected to keep track of the amount of alcoholic beverages they have consumed and then pay the appropriate sum of money. Also known as the *honor system*.

HONOR SYSTEM   *See* Honor Bars.

HOOCH   A home-concocted drink made of boiled ferns and flour by the Alaskan Indians of the Hutsnuwu tribe, who called it "hoochino." Soldiers who were sent from the United States to Alaska after the territory was purchased from Russia in 1867 added molasses and distilled it, shortening the name to "hooch." Hooch was the Army's term for distilled spirits during the first and second World Wars.

HOOP DRIVER   A tool used for driving the hoops on a barrel to tighten them.

HOOPS   The metal rings that surround a wooden barrel. They are needed to hold the wooden staves together and give support to the barrel.

HOP EXTRACT   The result of the processing of hops to isolate their bittering oils, often used in brewing beer.

HOPFEN (GERMANY)   *See* Hops.

HOP JACKET   A stainless steel tank where the *wort* is filtered (removing the hops) and stored after brewing.

HOPKINS EARLY RED   *See* Wyoming.

HOP LEAF   The flowers of the hop plant in a loose, dried form.

HOP PELLETS   The dried flowers of the hop plant, formed and pressed into pellets for later use in beermaking.

HOPPY   Describes an odor detected in some ales; it is caused by a high level of hops used in the brewing process.

HOPS   The dried, cone-like flowering blossoms from the unfertilized female hop plant called "catkin," which is a perennial, herb-like climbing vine (*Humulus lupulus*) of the cannabis family. The hops contain a naturally occurring amount of resin, plus various oils that are the perfect bittering agents for beer. There are many varieties of hops, all of which lend variety to beer bitterness, flavor, and bouquet. The taste of hops is generally characterized by a slight bitterness in some beers to a distinctive bitter, almost astringent taste in others.

Hops also possess antiseptic properties that inhibit the growth of bacteria. This is particularly important in the brewing of the nonpasteurized draft beers. Also known as *hopfen*.

HORCHATA (SPAIN)   An unusual alcoholic beverage made from either almonds or pumpkin seeds.

HORGAZUELA (SPAIN)   *See* Palomino.

HORIZON   A white grape variety developed at the State Experimental Station in Geneva, New York. Formerly known as *GW-7*.

HORIZONTAL BACK CARD   Large display card used to promote a product on large case stackings.

HORIZONTAL SET   The practice of stocking a line, type, or variety of product lengthwise on a shelf. Also known as *billboard*.

HORIZONTAL TASTING   An organized tasting (generally of wines) that refers to the *breadth* of a selection of alcoholic beverages. For example, a tasting of ten 1990 Chianti Classico wines from various producers.

HORS D'AGE (FRANCE)   A label designation used on armagnac and calvados bottles that indicates that the youngest brandy used in the blend is at least ten years old (armagnac) and six years old (calvados), although they contain a very high percentage of brandy that has been aged for twenty, thirty, or forty years or more.

HOSPICES DE BEAUNE (FRANCE)   A charity hospital located in Burgundy that hosts an annual wine auction to raise money. The Hospices de Beaune (which was designed by Flemish architect Jacques Viscrere) was established by Nicolas Rolin and his wife, Guigone de Salins, in 1443. Rolin was a tax collector for the Grand Chancellor, Philippe le Bon, of the Duchy of Burgundy, in 1395, during the reign of King Louis XI. There were no wine auctions held at the Hospices de Beaune in 1956 and 1968 due to poor wine vintages.

HOST BAR   A feature of a private party or function with unlimited drinks, where guests do not pay for individual drinks. The host or sponsoring organization pays the final tab, calculated by each bottle opened, regardless of whether or not the contents have been totally consumed. Some state liquor laws permit the organization to claim any opened bottles (often referred to as "stubs"), while other states prohibit such actions. Also known as *sponsored bar* or *open bar*.

HOT   An unpleasant pain sensation generally caused by an excess of alcohol in a beverage, making it out of balance. The sensation usually affects nerve endings at the bottom of the nose or is felt in the back of the throat when the beverage is swallowed. It is also characteristic of certain dessert wines lacking substantial fruit. Also known as *burning, fiery*, and *schnapsig*. *See* Alcoholic.

HOT BOTTLING   Bottling wine or beer immediately after pasteurization, while it is still hot. *See* Pasteurization.

HOT CAUDLE   A cocktail made with spiced and sweetened hot wine or ale, bread or gruel, spices, and a beaten egg yolk. Also known as *caudle*. *See* Flip, Rumfustian, and Sling.

HOT PRESSED   Describes crushed grapes that are heated to a temperature of approximately 160 degrees Fahrenheit and held at that temperature for a period of thirty minutes to one hour prior to pressing. This helps to extract additional pigments from the skins.

HOTTE DE VENDANGE *(FRANCE)*   *See* Grape-Picking Basket.

HOT TODDY   A drink of brandy, whiskey, or other distilled spirits, with hot water, sugar, lemon juice, cloves, cinnamon, and other spices. Also known as *toddy*.

HOUR GLASS   A glass in the shape of an hourglass, generally with a capacity of eight to ten ounces, used to serve beer.

HOUSE BRANDS   *See* Well Brands.

HOUSE STYLE   *See* Blending.

HOUSE WHISKEY   *See* Well Brands.

HOUSE WINE   The wine of the "house" or restaurant that typically comes in large bottles (three or four liters or larger) and is served in half- or full carafes. Also, a wine specially blended or bottled for the restaurant or bar. Also known as *vin de carafe*. *See* Jug Wine.

HOUX *(FRANCE)*   A fruit brandy made from holly berries in Alsace.

HUBBARD   A white grape variety.

HÜBSCH *(GERMANY)*   *See* Pleasant.

HUDSON RIVER VALLEY   The oldest wine-producing region in the United States, located in New York State, with a history that dates from the late 1500s, when immigrant French Huguenots planted grapes on Mohonk Mountain. The Hudson River Valley received its *appellation* in July 1982.

HUE   Usually the separation of colors of wine seen at the edge of the glass.

HULL   The outer covering or shell of cereal grains. Also known as *husk*.

HUMAGNE *(SWITZERLAND)*   A white grape variety.

HUMBERT 3   A red grape variety.

HUNT   A red grape variety grown primarily in the Carolinas, Georgia, and eastern Texas.

HUNTER RIVER RIESLING *(AUSTRALIA)*   *See* Sémillon.

HUSK   *See* Hull.

HÜXELREBE *(GERMANY)*   A white grape variety developed in 1927 from a cross of Chasselas Doré and Courtillier Musqué in the Rheinhessen. It was developed by George Scheu and named for Fritz Huxel, a vintner at Westhofen.

HYBRID   The group of grape varieties referred to as hybrids, French-American hybrids, or French hybrids. They are crosses (and sometimes recrosses) of native American grapevine species such as *Vitis labrusca, Vitis riparia*, and *Vitis rupestris*, with *Vitis vinifera*, the European grapevine species. In France and several other wine-producing countries, the growing of hybrids in wine districts entitled to the *appellation contrôlée* is banned.

Much hybridization took place during the 1870s as a result of the *phylloxera* epidemic, in order to develop grapevines resistant to its ravages. Other hybridization has developed grape varieties that have the ability to withstand severe cold winters, are disease resistant, and yield balanced wines in shortened growing seasons. Also known as *hybride* and *incrocio. See* Crossbreeding.

HYBRID DIRECT PRODUCERS (HDP)   Hybrid grape varieties, developed in France during the 1870s, which grow and produce crops on their own roots.

HYBRIDE (GERMANY)   *See* Hybrid.

HYBRIDIZATION   *See* Crossbreeding.

HYDROGEN ION EXCHANGE   A process that utilizes hydrochloric acid as a regenerator to eliminate sediment from wine.

HYDROGEN SULFIDE (H_2S)   The source of a smell of rotten eggs, it results from a variety of causes, most commonly from the reduction of elemental sulfur during fermentation. Most yeast strains will produce some amount of it. The presence of metal ions such as aluminum, zinc, iron, or tin seems to promote H_2S formation. Vineyard spraying with elemental sulfur or sulfur containing compounds close to harvest time is often a cause. Removal of this undesirable volatile component is possible with limited aeration during racking and before bottling. Also known as *böckser*.

HYDROMEL   The Roman equivalent of mead, which was weak and watered. *See* Mead.

HYDROMETER   A cylindrical glass instrument with a scale running along its length and a bulbous weighted end. It is used in winemaking or beermaking to measure the unfermented sugar content prior to fermentation. Usually, a small sample of grapes is crushed and the liquid is strained and immediately placed into a graduated cylindrical tube. A hydrometer is placed into the tube and allowed to bounce around freely until the weight of the displaced liquid equals the weight of the hydrometer and its movement ceases. The point where the hydrometer meets the surface of the grape juice (*meniscus*) is noted and a reading of the hydrometer is taken.

Other hydrometers measure specific gravity, potential of alcohol, and sugar levels. Also known as *areometer, mustimeter, mustimètre*, and *saccharometer. See* Meniscus and Twadell.

HYDROMETER TESTING JAR   A tall glass or plastic cylinder (graduated or ungraduated) that holds liquids to be read by a hydrometer.

HYDROXYMETHYLFURFURAL   A chemical compound that gives wines that have been baked (madeira and some California sherry) a caramel-like odor. *See* Baked, Caramelization, and Estufa.

HYGROMETER   An instrument used for measuring the humidity of the atmosphere, especially indoors.

IBU   *See* International Bittering Units.

ICE   Water that has been frozen by submitting it to temperatures below its freezing point, 32 degrees Fahrenheit. Also known as *ghiaccio*.

ICE (ITALY)   *See* Instituto Commercio Estero.

ICE BEER   A beer that has been brewed at a colder-than-usual temperature, then immediately chilled to below freezing (32 degrees Fahrenheit), which forms ice crystals. The crystals are then filtered out of the beer, resulting in a slightly higher alcohol content than regular beers. Some brewers claim that this process eliminates bitter-tasting proteins, resulting in a smoother-tasting beer. Contrary to popular belief, this process did not originate in the United States or even Canada, but rather in Germany, where a beer called *eisbock* is brewed utilizing this method. *See* Eisbock.

ICE BREAKER   *See* Ice Crusher.

ICE BUCKET   A container used for temporary storage of ice cubes, made available to guests for cocktails. A metal vessel that contains ice and water for the chilling of bottles of white wine and sparkling wine. Also known as a *wine bucket*.

ICE CHEST   *See* Ice Storage Bin.

ICE CRUSHER   A motor-driven machine with spiked rollers to crush large pieces of ice or ice cubes. Also known as *ice breaker*.

ICE CUBES   Water that has been frozen in the shape of a cube by metal or plastic trays with partitions.
    Commercial ice-making machines can produce different shapes and sizes of ice cubes; some of them have been dubbed crescent cubes, cubelets, flake ice, flat cubes, gourmet cubes, full cubes (also called dice), half-cubes (also called half-dice), ice nuggets, and regular and square cubes. Of these, the standard sizes are:

regular (1-1/8" x 1-1/8" x 7/8"; thirty cubes per pound)

full (also called dice) (7/8" x 7/8" x 7/8"; forty-eight cubes per pound)

half-cubes (also called half-dice) (3/8" x 7/8" x 7/8"; ninety-six cubes per pound)

ICED COFFEE   Freshly brewed coffee with sugar and/or milk and ice, either in cube or crystal form, added for chilling.

ICED TEA   Freshly brewed tea with sugar, lemon juice, and ice, either in cube or crystal form, added for chilling.

Iced tea was first made by an English tea concessionaire at the 1904 St. Louis World's Fair who decided to combat a slump in sales of hot tea caused by a heat wave; he poured the tea over ice and his customers loved it.

ICED TEA GLASS   A tall, cylindrical glass with a capacity of twelve to fourteen ounces. Also known as a *Tom Collins* glass.

ICED TEA SPOON   A long-handled spoon with a shallow bowl used for stirring iced tea.

ICE HARDNESS   A scale that measures the ratio of true ice to entrained water per pound of ice, which determines the relative hardness of various shaped ice cubes.

ICE-MAKING MACHINE   Modern ice-making machines can produce from one hundred to 3,300 pounds of ice per hour, depending on the make and model of the machine. There are basically two types of machines: one produces cubes; the other, flakes. The capacity of an ice-making machine is generally expressed in production per twenty-four hours. It is important to note that most ice-making machines give varying production ratings for different temperature levels of the air-cooled or water-cooled condenser unit, as well as for different temperatures of water used.

ICE NUGGETS   *See* Ice Cubes.

ICE SCOOP   Plastic or metal scoop used to remove ice from ice-making machines.

ICE STORAGE BIN   An insulated container, usually made of foamed polystyrene and featuring a hinged or sliding door, used for the storage of ice. Also known as *ice chest*.

ICE TUB   A rectangular, shallow rubber or plastic tub used behind the bar to hold ice cubes and/or bottled beer for fast chilling and service.

ICE WATER JACKET   *See* Jacketed Tank.

ICE WINE   *See* Eiswein.

IDVDM   *See* Instituto do Vinho da Madeira.

IDYS (GREECE)   *See* Pleasant.

IGT (ITALY)   *See* Indicazione Geografica Tipica.

IL (ITALY)   The masculine definite article.

ILLINOIS 179–1   A white grape variety developed from a cross of Dattier de Saint-Villier and Seibel 11342.

IMBOTTIGLIARE (ITALY)   To bottle.

IMBOTTIGLIATO (ITALY)   Bottled.

IMBOTTIGLIATO AL CASTELLO (ITALY)   Bottled at the castle.

IMBOTTIGLIATO ALLA CANTINA (ITALY)   Bottled at the winery.

IMBOTTIGLIATO ALLA FATTORIA *(ITALY)* Bottled at the farm or estate.

IMBOTTIGLIATO ALL'ORIGINE *(ITALY)* Bottled at the source or estate bottled.

IMBOTTIGLIATO DAL PRODUTTORE ALL'ORIGINE-DAL VITICOLTORE *(ITALY)* Estate-bottled.

IMBOTTIGLIATO NELLA ZONA DI PRODUZIONE *(ITALY)* Bottled in the production zone, but presumably not at the estate.

IMMATURE Also known as *ápsitos* and *immaturo*. *See* Young.

IMMATURO *(ITALY)* *See* Young.

IMPAIRED *See* Intoxicated.

IMP AND AN IRON *See* Puddler and His Helper.

IMPERIAL An oversized bottle equivalent in capacity to eight 750-milliliter bottles or six liters (202.8 ounces). Although it has the same capacity as a Methuselah, it is not used for champagne or port wine.

IMPERIAL GALLON A measurement of liquid volume, one gallon being equal to 160 ounces or 1.2 United States gallons. Also known as *British Gallon*. *See* Gallon.

IMPERIAL STOUT A very strong dark fruity brew originally made in the Czarist Russian Empire. Nowadays it is brewed mostly in Great Britain, Denmark, and Finland. *See* Stout.

IMPIGNO *(ITALY)* A white grape variety grown primarily in the south.

IMPORTATORE *(ITALY)* Importer.

IMPORTAZIONE *(ITALY)* Importation.

IMPORT DUTY Levy on distilled spirit products imported to the United States. Import duties are assessed on a *proof gallon*.

IMPORTS Goods or services, acquired or purchased from a foreign nation, necessary for continuation of business or a way of life.

IMPORTS FOR CONSUMPTION Alcohol beverages for which United States custom duties have been paid, regardless of whether or not they are stored in government-supervised warehouses before being shipped for resale. The federal excise tax is payable on entering trade channels. *See* Entering Trade Channels and Withdrawals.

INAO *(FRANCE)* *See* Institut National des Appellations d'Origine.

IN BIANCO *(ITALY)* *See* Vinificato in Bianco.

IN BOND Refers to wine or distilled spirits possessed under bond to secure the payment of the taxes and on which such taxes have not been determined. The term includes any wine or distilled spirits on the bonded wine premises or a distilled spirits plant, or in transit between bonded premises (including, in the case of wine, bonded wine premises). Additionally, it refers to wine and distilled spirits withdrawn without payment of tax or with respect to which relief from liability has not yet occurred. Also known as *all-in-bond*. *See* Bonded Wine Premises and Bottled-in-Bond.

INCROCIO *(ITALY)* *See* Hybrid.

INDEXING   Identification of viral infections in grape varieties that do not display any obvious symptoms by grafting buds or other parts of the grapevine onto other, very susceptible varieties.

INDIAN QUEEN TAVERN   The name of the tavern in Philadelphia where Thomas Jefferson penned his first draft of the Declaration of Independence.

INDIA PALE ALE   A very bitter ale with a hoppy aroma and taste. It was the kegged ale that the British sent to their troops serving in India in the past century.

INDICAZIONE GEOGRAFICA TIPICA (IGT) *(ITALY)*   A segment of Italy's wine law, enacted in 1992, which translates to "typical geographic indications." It refers to the area (often a large one) in which the grapes are grown and vinified. The designation is less restrictive than *DOC*.

INE *(ITALY)*   *See* Instituto Nazionale Esportazione.

INEBRIATED   *See* Intoxicated.

INFERNO *(ITALY)*   A full-bodied red wine produced from the Nebbiolo grape variety in the Valtellina district of Lombardy, located in the northern part of Italy.

INFERNOTTI *(ITALY)*   The traditional name for very secret wine cellars that have often been hidden for decades. Also known as *crutin* in Piedmont.

INFESTATION   What occurs when undesirable elements inhabit, spread in, or overrun in large numbers, so as to be harmful, unpleasant, or bothersome. The situation occurs in vineyards that are infested with insects, animals, or even disease to the point of danger to the grapevines.

INFLORESCENCE   The flowering cluster of a grapevine. Also known as *flower cluster*.

INFUSE   To steep in boiling liquid until the liquid absorbs the flavor of the seasoning agent. A process used in making tea, coffee, and many liqueurs. Also known as *infusion*.

INFUSION   *See* Infuse and Maceration.

INFUSORIAL EARTH   *See* Diatomaceous Earth.

INHALT *(GERMANY)*   *See* Contents.

INJERTO *(SPAIN)*   *See* Grafting.

INKY   Describes an intensely dark, almost black color in some red wines.

INN   A place of repose for travelers that usually offers both lodging and liquid refreshments. *See* Bar, Cocktail Lounge, Pub, Saloon, and Tavern.

INNKEEPER   One who manages an inn.

INOCULATING   The action of adding yeast or bacteria to a biological environment in order to trigger development or fermentation.

INÓDIS *(GREECE)*   *See* Vinosity.

IN-ROOM BAR   In-room refrigerator and storage cabinet stocked with a variety of drinks and snacks and refilled daily; all items consumed are charged to the guest's hotel bill. In some types of in-room bars, charges are instantly transferred for addition to the room charge. In such computerized systems, printouts are instantaneous and provide a wealth of information, from restocking reports to usage tracked by room type. Also known as *mini-bar*.

INSECTICIDE A chemical substance used for killing insects. *See* Fungicide, Herbicide, and Pesticide.

INSIPID A term describing tasteless, thin, characterless wine or beer, lacking in firmness and structure. Also known as *insipido* and *vapid*.

INSIPIDO *(ITALY* AND *SPAIN)* *See* Insipid.

INSTITUT NATIONAL DES APPELLATIONS D'ORIGINE (INAO) *(FRANCE)* On July 30, 1935, a French law established the Institut National des Appellations d'Origine for wines and distilled spirits, and decrees governing each wine appellation were laid down by the minister of agriculture.

INSTITUTO COMMERCIO ESTERO (ICE) *(ITALY)* A governmental organization based in Rome and known in the United States as the Italian Trade Commission; it is the Italian government's foreign trade promotion organization. It has offices throughout Italy and in more than eighty cities around the world.

INSTITUTO DO VINHO DA MADEIRA (IDVDM) *(PORTUGAL)* The Madeira Wine Institute, an official governing body regulating all laws and matter to do with madeira wine.

INSTITUTO NAZIONALE ESPORTAZIONE (INSTITUTE NATIONAL EXPORTATION) (INE) *(ITALY)* A round red seal with the words "Marchio Nazionale" appears on the neck of many Italian wine bottles exported to North America. It indicates compliance with governmental quality control procedures.

INSTITUTO SPUMANTE ITALIANO METODO CHAMPENOISE (ISIMC) *(ITALY)* An organization of Italian wineries making spumante using the champagne method.

INTEGRATED PEST MANAGEMENT (IPM) An ecologically based pest management strategy that focuses on long-term prevention or suppression of pests through a combination of techniques such as biological control, alternative cultural practices, and use of resistant grape varieties. Pesticides are used only when careful field monitoring indicates they are needed and are selected and applied in a manner least disruptive to the environment. *See* Organically Grown Wine.

INTENSE A term describing a wine or beer with highly concentrated qualities (e.g., bouquet and display of a well-defined flavor).

INTERLAKEN SEEDLESS A white grape variety developed in 1947 from a cross of Thompson Seedless and Ontario grapes at the State Experimental Station in Geneva, New York.

INTERMODAL A term describing transportation involving different modes of travel (e.g., vessel/rail/truck).

INTERNATIONAL BITTERING UNITS (IBU) A scale used to measure the relative quantity of bitterness contained in beer. *See* Bitter.

INTERNODE On a grapevine, the portion on the shoot or cane between two nodes (buds).

INTERPLANTING   A viticultural technique that consists of bending canes from a parent grapevine to ground level and burying them. The buried cane draws energy from the parent grapevine while it sends down its own roots. When it is established, it is then cut loose from the parent vine and a new grapevine with a genetic structure exactly the same as the original old vine is formed. This method is especially desirable for reestablishing an existing vineyard. Also known as *provignage*.

INTERPROFESSION *(FRANCE)*   An interprofessional syndicate or lobby of grapegrowers, winemakers (vintners), or producers who combine their efforts and money in an organized manner to protect their wines and reputation, and, at the same time, form a promotional arm. Synonymous with *Comité Interprofessionnel*.

INTERVEINAL   The tissue located between the veins of a leaf on a grapevine.

INTOXICATED   Significantly or legally under the influence of excessive alcohol consumption and being incapable of complete control of one's actions. Some slang terms for a person who is under the influence of alcoholic beverages are *alky, bitten by the brewer's horse, blind, bombed, borracho, drunk, inebriated, impaired, juiced, lit up, loaded, looped, lush, oiled, pickled, pissed, plastered, ripped, sloshed, smashed, soused, stewed, stoned, three sheets to the wind, under the table, waffled,* and *zonked*.

INVAIATURA *(ITALY)*   *See* Véraison.

INVECCHIAMENTO *(ITALY)*   *See* Aging.

INVECCHIATO *(ITALY)*   Aged.

INVENTORIES   Stocks of raw materials, intermediate products, and finished goods held by producers or marketing organizations.

INVERNENGA *(ITALY)*   A white grape variety.

INVERT SUGAR   A mixture of glucose and levulose (fructose) in approximately equal proportions, found in some fruits. It is produced artificially by the hydrolysis of sucrose.

INVERT SUGAR SYRUP   A substantially colorless solution of invert sugar that has been prepared by recognized methods of inversion from pure dry sugar and contains not less than 60 percent sugar by weight (60 degrees Brix).

INVERTASE   The enzyme responsible for converting sucrose into roughly equal parts of fructose and glucose in order for fermentation to occur.

IN VINO VERITAS   The expression "in wine there is truth," coined by the Roman scholar Gaius Plinius (better known as Pliny the Elder) between 33 and 79 A.D.

IN VITRO   Literally, "in glass." Plants are multiplied under controlled conditions (light, temperature, and hygrometry) inside a jar or a tube in a synthetic culture medium.

INZOLIA *(ITALY)*   A white grape variety native to Sicily. Also spelled *Insolia* and known as *Ansonica* in Tuscany.

IODINE SOLUTION   A test indicator that detects the presence of starch in a wine as the possible source of a haze.

IONA   A red grape variety that is a seedling of the Diana grape (itself a seedling of Catawba), grown primarily in the eastern United States. It was named after Iona Island, located in the Hudson River near Peekskill, New York, by Dr. C. W. Grant in 1859.

IPM   *See* Integrated Pest Management.

IRISH COFFEE   A drink often served to celebrate Saint Patrick's Day (March 17) consisting of cube sugar, Irish whiskey, and strong black coffee (not espresso), with whipped heavy cream floated on top.

Like many other drinks whose origins are clouded in mystery, Irish coffee (according to some) was introduced by Joe Sheridan in 1938 to airline passengers who braved cold planes and bumpy flights. Flight attendants would ease the pain by adding a shot of whiskey to hot coffee. They used Irish whiskey when the flights arrived or departed from Shannon Airport in Ireland.

Another story, which takes place in 1952, has the owner of the lounge at Shannon Airport offering customers strong, hot coffee laced with Irish whiskey to ease the long waits in between flights.

IRISH CREAM LIQUEURS   *See* Cream Liqueurs.

IRISH STOUT   *See* Stout.

IRISH WHISKEY   A distinctive product of Ireland, manufactured in compliance with the guidelines of Irish Distillers, Ltd. It is commonly thought that Irish whiskey is produced from potatoes, mainly because of the general association between the Irish and potatoes; this is not true. Irish whiskey is not a single malt or pure malt whiskey—it is a blend made from a mash of cereal grains, mostly barley (malted and unmalted), wheat, oats, corn, and rye. Most Irish whiskey is produced in pot stills, which help give it a distinctive taste, although the use of continuous stills is increasing in popularity.

Irish whiskey must be aged a minimum of three years, but it is usually aged five to eight years prior to shipping. Aging generally takes place in used Bourbon or sherry barrels or a combination of the two. Irish whiskey has a delicate odor of honey, vanilla, and orange peel, with a light and mild flavor.

IRON HAZE   *See* Casse, Citric Acid, and Cufex.

IRREGULARITY   A slight abnormality not serious enough to be classed a defect.

IRRIGATION   A controlled system that applies the right amount of water at the right time to the grapevines. Each variety of grape requires water in different quantities and at different periods of growth. Prior to irrigation, a determination is made as to how much water is needed in a forty-eight-hour period, and how much the ground (which can be thought of as a reservoir) can hold and drain through.

ISABELLA   A red grape variety used mostly for sparkling wines, although its popularity in the eastern part of the United States has dwindled. Its origin is unknown, but it has been traced back to 1815 in the Prince Nurseries at Flushing, New York. The grape was named after Mrs. Isabella Gibbs of Brooklyn in 1816. Also known as *Fragola* and *Uva Americana*.

ISIMC *(ITALY)*   *See* Instituto Spumante Italiano Metodo Champenoise.

ISINGLASS   A protein fining agent derived from dried sturgeon air bladder (viscera). It contains a large amount of gelatin and carries a positive charge. Russian isinglass is a superior grade obtained chiefly from the sturgeon. Also known as *cola de pescado, colla di pesce, fischleim*, and *fish glue*. *See* Fining and Fining Agents.

ISKRIASHTO *(BULGARIA)* *See* Sparkling Wine.

ISLAND BELLE *See* Campbell Early.

ISLAY MALTS Whiskies from a barley-growing and Scotch-producing area, noted for their very full-bodied, peaty, pungent, and salty characteristics and distinct flavor.

ISONZO *(ITALY)* A wine-producing area within the region of Friuli-Venezia Giulia. *See* Friuli-Venezia Giulia.

ITALIA *(ITALY)* A white grape variety developed in 1911 from a cross of Bicane and Muscat Hamburg by Pirovano. Some is also grown in California.

ITALIA PARTICOLARE (IP) *(ITALY)* *See* Marsala Fine.

ITALIAN-TYPE VERMOUTH A sweet white or red vermouth. *See* Vermouth.

IVES A red grape variety that produces wine with a *foxy* taste. Ives is an accidental seedling, first discovered by Henry Ives in Cincinnati, Ohio, in 1840.

JACKETED TANK   Apparatus that circulates hot and cold water, enabling the grape *must* or *wort* to be heated up when the fermentation is too slow, or cooled down if the temperature is too high. Also known as *drapeau, ice water jacket, steel jacketed tank*, and *water jacket*.

JACK ROSE COCKTAIL   A cocktail named after a gangster who turned state's evidence after the killing of Herman Rosenthal in a bar in Times Square in 1912.

JACQUEZ   *See* Lenoir.

JAEGER   A grape variety developed by Thomas Volney Munson (1843–1913) of Denison, Texas.

JAEN (PORTUGAL AND SPAIN)   A white grape variety.

JAHRGANG (GERMANY)   *See* Vintage.

JAMAICAN RUM   A dark, full-bodied, pungent rum, distilled from molasses and used almost exclusively in cocktails.

JAMES   A red grape variety, which dates from about 1890 and was named for B.W.M. James of Pitt County, North Carolina.

JAMLIKE   *See* Jammy.

JAMMY   Desribes an odor and taste sensation often associated with fruity red wines that have concentrated flavors and a grapy, berrylike taste reminiscent of jam. Also known as *jamlike*.

JARRA (SPAIN)   A wooden or stainless steel pail with a capacity of approximately twelve liters (about four gallons) used in the blending of sherry wines.

JARZEBIAK (POLAND)   Vodka flavored with rowanberries.

JASMINE TEA   A light and flowery tea made from a blend of green and black teas scented with dried jasmine flowers.

JAVA A slang term for coffee.

JEFFERSON A red grape variety developed in 1870 from a cross of Concord and Iona by James H. Ricketts in Newburgh, New York.

JENEVER GIN (BELGIUM) *See* Holland Gin.

JERK WINE The product of a seldom-employed practice whereby water is added to grape remains after pressing to extract additional "tainted" juice, which, after fermentation, is then sold at very low prices. *See* Watered Down.

JEREZ DE LA FRONTERA (SPAIN) The city in southwest Andalusía, about ninety miles inland, where sherry wine is produced. The Jerez area is triangular in shape and lies between the Guadalquivir and Guadalete rivers in southwest Spain, with the Atlantic Ocean on the west. The official sherry-producing zone, known as the *zone de Jerez superiore* or "zone of superior sherry," is bounded by three major towns: Puerto de Santa María, Sanlúcar de Barrameda, and Jerez de la Frontera. The entire Jerez area consists of some 28,325 acres of vineyards (1991).

JEROBOAM An oversized bottle equal in capacity to four 750-milliliter bottles or three liters (101.4 ounces). *See* Double Magnum.

Jeroboam was the king of the newly formed Northern Kingdom of Israel who led the ten northern tribes of ancient Israel in revolt against King Rehoboam, the son and successor to King Solomon.

JIGGER A double-edged (usually stainless steel) measuring cup, with each end containing a different capacity of liquid. *See* Shot Glass.

JIMA (SPAIN) The harvest of agave plants for making tequila.

JIMADOR (SPAIN) The person in charge of the harvest of agave plants for making tequila.

JNDV (PORTUGAL) *See* Junta Nacional do Vinho.

JOANNES-SEYVE 12428 A white grape variety.

JOANNES-SEYVE 23416 A white grape variety.

JOANNES-SEYVE 26205 *See* Chambourcin.

JOANNES-SEYVE 26627 A white grape variety.

JOÃO DE SANTARÉM (PORTUGAL) *See* Periquita.

JOB SPECIFICATION A job analysis resulting from the specification of what kind of traits and experience are needed to perform the job.

JOCKEY BOX An underbar cocktail station unit typically containing ice bins, speed rail, bottle wells, and cold plate for a postmix system.

JOE A slang term for coffee.

JOHANNISBERG (GERMANY) A vineyard town in the Rheingau region.

JOHANNISBERG RIESLING A white grape variety, which is the predominant grape of Germany, producing the best of the distinctive wines of the Rhine and Mosel regions. Johannisberg Riesling also flourishes in Alsace, France, Australia, Austria, and the United States, as well as other parts of the world. Johannisberg Riesling was probably derived from a wild grapevine, *Vitis vinifera silvestris*, still found growing naturally in woods in the upper Rhine of Germany.

Johannisberg Riesling produces wines characteristically smelling quite floral, with aromas of tropical fruits (pineapple), apple, apricots, peaches, and Muscat grapes, balanced by good acidity. *Botrytis cinerea* can add the odor and flavor of honey.

The thick aromatic skins are susceptible to sunburn and infection by *Botrytis cinerea*. In favorable seasons this tendency can be taken advantage of to produce a late-harvest sweet wine. The fruit picks easily by hand but juices with mechanical harvesting. Also known as *Riesling*, *Riesling Renano*, *Rheinriesling*, *Klingelberger*, *Rizling*, and *White Riesling*.

JOHN COLLINS   A cocktail consisting of vodka, lemon juice, sugar, and soda water. *See* Tom Collins.

JONICO (*ITALY*)   *See* Negro Amaro.

JOURNAL   An old Burgundian (French) measurement of land equivalent to anywhere from one-third to five-sixths of an acre.

JOURNAL   Summary of daily transactions as they occur; book of original entry.

JOVEN (*SPAIN*)   *See* Young.

JUBILÄUMSBIER (*GERMANY*)   A beer brewed for an anniversary or special event. *See* Festbier.

JUGER   An ancient Roman unit of land, equivalent to about half an acre.

JUGO (*SPAIN*)   *See* Juice.

JUG WINE   Inexpensive wine of no particular breed or quality (often sweet), usually sold in quantity (carafes, jugs). Also known as *bulk wine* and *suffig*. *See* House Wine and Ordinary.

JUHFARK (*HUNGARY*)   A white grape variety.

JUICE   The unfermented liquid (concentrated or unconcentrated) from fruit, berries, grapes, and authorized agricultural products, exclusive of pulp, skins, or seeds. Also known as *jugo*.

JUICED   *See* Intoxicated.

JULEP   The name of a southern American drink consisting of bourbon whiskey, sugar, water, and spearmint leaves, along with an abundance of crushed ice. The name *julep* itself can be traced back more than six hundred years and stems from the Arabic *julab* or Persian *jul-ab*, meaning rose water. The word is cited in English as early as the year 1400 and indicated "a syrup made only of water and sugar." In actuality, mint and sugar were being blended with distilled spirits before the birth of America. The true Southern-style mint julep coincided with the discovery of Kentucky straight bourbon whiskey around the late 1700's. Also known as *mint julep*. Also spelled *julip*.

JULIÉNAS (*FRANCE*)   A *cru* commune in Beaujolais, supposedly named after Julius Caesar. The wine produced here is sometimes harsh in its youth, but softens with one to two years of bottle aging. In a normal year, the fresh, fruity wine of Juliénas is more assertive and longer-lasting than that of Saint-Amour.

JULIP   *See* Julep.

JUNG *(GERMANY)* *See* Young.

JUNGWEIN *(AUSTRIA)* *See* Young.

JUNIPER BERRIES Aromatic berries of a cypress tree whose oils are used in the making of gin and some liqueurs.

JUNTA NACIONAL DO VINHO (JNDV) *(PORTUGAL)* The national official body governing all Portuguese wines and to which the Instituto do Vinho da Madeira is answerable.

JURAÇON BLANC *(FRANCE)* A white grape variety.

JURADE DE SAINT-ÉMILION *(FRANCE)* To help promote the wines of Saint-Émilion (Bordeaux), John Lackland, on July 8, 1199, established the Jurade de Saint-Émilion, a wine brotherhood still in existence today.

J

JULIP

k \\'kā \\ *n, often cap, often attrib*

KABINETT (GERMANY) The most basic Qualitätswein mit Prädikat (QMP) grade of wines, which indicates a quality wine that must be sold under a geographic designation: the wine province, region, district, or village where it was produced. These wines are dry, generally the lightest, and may not be *chaptalized*.

KADARKA (HUNGARY) A red grape variety. Also known as *Gamza* and *Skadarska*.

KAFFEE (GERMANY AND NORWAY) *See* Coffee.

KAHMIG (GERMANY) *See* Yeasty.

KAHVE (TURKEY) *See* Coffee.

KALECIK (TURKEY) A red grape variety.

KANDAHAR A white grape variety grown in the United States.

KANZLER (GERMANY) A white grape variety developed in 1927 from a cross of Müller-Thurgau and Sylvaner by George Scheu at the Alzey Research Station in the Rheinhessen.

KAPUZINER (AUSTRIA) Coffee with a little milk; the mixture resembles the color of a Capuchin monk's robe. *See* Cappuccino.

KASU (JAPAN) The *lees* that remain after rice has fermented into saké. *See* Lees.

KAY GRAY A white grape variety developed by Elmer Swenson of the University of Minnesota.

KEEMUN TEA An elegant, smooth, flowery tasting black tea from the province of Anwhei in northern China.

KEG A container of beer with a capacity of 15.5 gallons; also known as a *half-barrel* of beer. A small barrel with a capacity of less than ten gallons. *See* Barrel.

KEG BEER *See* Draft Beer.

KEG PARTY   *See* Beer Bash.

KEG REFRIGERATOR   *See* Cold Box.

KÉKFRANKOS (HUNGARY)   *See* Blaufränkisch.

KÉKNYELÜ (HUNGARY)   A white grape variety.

KELLER (GERMANY)   *See* Wine Cellar.

KELLERABFÜLLUNG (GERMANY)   Cellar bottling by the shipper.

KELLERBIER (GERMANY)   An unfiltered lager beer with a high hop content.

KELLERGASSE (AUSTRIA)   *See* Wine Cellar.

KELLERMEISTER (GERMANY)   *See* Cellarmaster.

KELTER (GERMANY)   *See* Wine Press.

KENNZEICHNUNG (GERMANY)   Any statement on a bottle of alcoholic beverages; some are obligatory, others optional.

KENTUCKY COFFEE TREE   A large tree (*Gymnocladus dioica*) of the legume family with brown curved pods containing seeds sometimes used as a substitute for coffee.

KERNER (GERMANY)   A white grape variety developed in 1969 from a cross of Trollinger (red) and Johannisberg Riesling (white) by grapevine breeder August Herold in Weinsberg, located in Württemberg. Kerner was named after Justinus Kerner (1786–1862), a poet, song librettist, and senior official of the town of Weinsberg.

KERNIG (GERMANY)   *See* Big.

KHADI (AFRICA)   An alcoholic beverage brewed from honey and wild berries.

KHARAKTÍR (GREECE)   *See* Character.

KHONDRÓS (GREECE)   *See* Rough.

KICK   *See* Punt.

KICKER   A chemical additive used to speed fermentation of the mash for making beer or distilled spirits.

KICKER   A method of determining the price of a drink; for example, adding five or ten cents to the base cost of the drink instead of figuring out the cost of every ingredient.

KIEBAER (DENMARK)   Cherry.

KIESELGUHR (GERMANY)   An early name for diatomaceous earth. *See* Diatomaceous Earth.

KIESELSOL   A generic term for aqueous suspension of silicon dioxide, developed in Germany during World War II as a tannin substitute during gelatin fining. Kieselsols are used in the juice and wine industries. *See* Fining and Fining Agents.

KILDERKIN   A barrel, used in eighteenth-century England, with a liquid measure of eighteen imperial gallons. *See* Barrel.

KILL-DEVIL   *See* Rum.

KILN A mesh-type flooring used to dry malt by means of a fire underneath. In the older floor malting method, the barley, after being soaked in water for two to three days, was spread on a kiln floor for germination or sprouting, which generally took eight to twelve days. The venue has been largely replaced by large drums that mechanically heat the barley, but the principle of the process remains the same.

KILO *See* Kilogram.

KILOGRAM A metric unit of weight equivalent to one thousand grams or about 2.2046 pounds. Also known as *chilogrammo* and *kilo*.

KING RUBY A red grape variety grown in California.

KIPPERLÉ *See* Knipperlé.

KIR (FRANCE) A popular apéritif drink made with *crème de cassis* and dry white wine, named after the late mayor of the city of Dijon, Canon Félix Kir. Kir was the favorite drink of the mayor from the 1940s until his death in 1968 at age 92. Originally, Kir was made by mixing Aligoté wine (a highly acidic white wine from Burgundy) with a tablespoon or so of crème de cassis, served chilled. Today, just about any white wine is used and mixed with anywhere from several teaspoons to one-third of a glass of crème de cassis. Cassis is a black currant liqueur.

KIRCHE (GERMANY) Church.

KIRMISI (TURKEY) *See* Red.

KIRSCH (FRANCE) A fruit brandy made from small, semi-wild black cherries that generally come from the Black Forest (*Germany*), the Vosges (*France*), or parts of Switzerland.

KIRSCHWASSER (GERMANY AND SWITZERLAND) *See* Kirsch.

KISLAV (RUSSIA) A distilled spirit produced from watermelons.

KITCHEN WINE *See* Cooking Wines.

KIU (CHINA) Third century B.C. name for beer. *See* Beer.

KLAPOTETZ A windmill with huge clappers that sounds like a carbine gun with a high pitched whistle or shrill, used to frighten birds away. Although the exact origin of the klapotetz is lost in antiquity, it is believed to have been introduced into the Lower Styria in Austria by the Romans (circa 100 B.C.), who were the first to plant vineyards there.

KLAR (AUSTRIA) *See* Clear.

KLASSISCH (GERMANY) Classic.

KLEIN (GERMANY) *See* Little.

KLEINBERGER (GERMANY) *See* Burger.

KLEINER RÄUSCHLING *See* Knipperlé.

KLEVNER (SWITZERLAND) *See* Pinot Noir.

KLINGELBERGER *See* Johannisberg Riesling

KLIPPE (GERMANY)   Cliff.

KLOSTER (GERMANY)   Monastery or church.

KLOSTERNEUBURG (AUSTRIA)   (KMW for Klosterneuburg Mostwaage Scale) The unit used to measure the level of unfermented sugar present in the *must*. The KMW was devised by Freiherr von Babo. One degree KMW = 5 degrees Öechsle. To determine degrees Brix, multiply KMW degrees by 1.25. To determine KMW degrees, divide Brix by 1.25. *See* Brix.

Klosterneuburg, which was established in 1860, is also the name of the Vocational School of Viniculture and Viticulture, located near Vienna.

KNIPPERLÉ (FRANCE)   A red grape variety native to Alsace. Also known as *Eltinger, Kipperlé, Kleiner Räuschling*, and *Ortlieber*.

KNOCHIG (GERMANY)   *See* Bone Dry.

KNOCKDOWNS   Gift cartons packed separately from product.

KOERPER (AUSTRIA)   *See* Body.

KOKUR (RUSSIA)   A white grape variety.

KOLA (COLA ACUMINATA)   *See* Cola.

KOLOR (GERMANY)   A red grape variety developed in 1938 from a cross of Spätburgunder and Färbertraube.

KÖLSCH (GERMANY)   A pale, golden-colored, top-fermented beer traditionally brewed in Cologne.

KONSHU (JAPAN)   *See* Koshu.

KONSUMWEIN (GERMANY)   *See* Ordinary.

KOPF (GERMANY)   Summit or hilltop. Also known as *kupp*.

KÖPPEN-GEIER SYSTEM   A climatic classification system based on monthly and annual averages of temperature and precipitation of the earth's five climatic regions. Named after Vladimir Köppen and Rudolf Geier, German meteorologists and climatologists.

KORKGESCHMACK (GERMANY)   *See* Corked.

KORNBRANNTWEIN (GERMANY AND NETHERLANDS)   A distilled spirit produced from cereal grains and considered the German/Dutch version of rye whiskey.

KÖRPER (GERMANY)   *See* Body.

KÖRPERARM (GERMANY)   *See* Light-Bodied.

KOSHER SALT   *See* Coarse Salt.

KOSHER WINE   Wines made under strict rabbinical supervision, suitable for Jewish religious practice. These wines are so labeled.

KOSHIKI (JAPAN)   A rice-steaming tub used in the making of saké.

KOSHU (JAPAN)   A white grape variety first grown in 1186. Also known as *Konshu*.

KÖSTLICH (GERMANY)   *See* High-Quality.

KOTSIFALI (GREECE) A red grape variety.

KOÚFOS (GREECE) *See* Light-Bodied.

KOUMISS *See* Kumiss.

KÖVIDINKA (HUNGARY) A white grape variety.

KRÄFTIG (GERMANY) *See* Big.

KRÄUSENING (GERMANY) A fermentation process where new, actively fermenting beer from a different fermenting batch is added to encourage a complete fermentation and add a natural carbonation. *See* Wort.

KRESZENZ (GERMANY) *See* Wachstrum.

KREUZ (GERMANY) Crucifix.

KRIEK (BELGIUM) A *lambic-type* beer that has been further fermented by the addition of sour or bitter black cherries to produce a dry brew with an unusual cherry flavor. *See* Lambic.

KRISTALLKLAR (GERMANY) *See* Clear.

KRISTALL WEIZEN (GERMANY) Wheat beer that has been filtered. *See* Wheat Beer.

KRUPNIK (POLAND) A honey-flavored liqueur.

KUHLMANN 188–2 *See* Maréchal Foch.

KUHLMANN 194–2 *See* Léon Millot.

KULMBACHER BEER (GERMANY) Beer that is brewed in the town of Kulmbach. Some Kulmbacher beers are reported to have as much as 14 percent alcohol by weight, but those exported to the United States have far less.

KUMISS A drink made from sour mare's or camel's milk that has fermented; it is consumed by the Tartar nomads of Asia. Also known as *arjan* and *koumiss*. *See* Skhou.

KÜMMEL A clear liqueur made with a distilled spirit base and flavored with caraway seeds, cumin, anise, and other aromatics. It was first produced in the sixteenth century in Europe; the Netherlands, Poland, Germany, and the Baltic countries all claim it as their own. Also known as *echt*.

KUPER (GERMANY) *See* Cooper.

KUPP (GERMANY) *See* Kopf.

KURZ (GERMANY) *See* Short.

KVASS (RUSSIA) A fermented drink made from rye and barley, flavored with herbs or cranberries. Also spelled *kwas*.

LA (FRANCE, ITALY, AND SPAIN)   The feminine definite article.

LABARDE (FRANCE)   One of the five communes entitled to the appellation *Margaux* in the Bordeaux region.

LABEL   A piece of paper attached to a bottle that identifies its country or place of origin, ownership, contents, classification, identifying brand, and type of product. In the United States, labels for wine and distilled spirits must be approved by BATF.

In 1903, the routine use of paper labels closely followed the invention of the fully automatic bottle-making machines by Michael J. Owen, plant manager of Libbey Glass Company, Inc., of Toledo, Ohio. Also known as *etichetta, etiqueta, étiquette*, and *rotula*.

LABOR COST   The payroll cost incurred as a result of employing full- or part-time people to prepare and provide the products and services utilized or consumed by guests. Labor costs may be fixed or variable.

LABORATORY TESTING   The scientific method of determining enological, viticultural, distillation, or brewing practices, experiments, samples, procedures, and so forth, which are necessary for making most alcoholic beverages. Also referred to as *bench testing*.

LABRUSCA   *See Vitis Labrusca.*

LACCASE   An enzyme found in grapes affected by the mold *Botrytis cinerea* that consumes oxygen and results in browning of *musts*.

LACQUER   A term applied to the *odor* of many very old fortified wines. Also known as *varnish*.

LACROSSE   A white grape variety developed by Elmer Swenson of the University of Minnesota.

LACTIC ACID   An organic acid that appears during the *malolactic fermentation* of wine, when malic acid changes into carbon dioxide and lactic acid. Eventually, this fades and becomes imperceptible in tasting. It is the principal acid of milk; its name derives from the Latin word for milk, "lic." It is also used to stabilize and correct natural deficiencies in wine. *See* Malolactic Fermentation.

LACTOSE   A white crystalline sugar made from whey, which is found in milk.

LADY   A white grape variety first identified in 1870 by Mr. Imlay of Muskingum, Ohio, and sold to George Campbell, a nurseryman in Delaware, Ohio.

LADY FINGERS   *See* Olivette Blanche and Rish Baba.

LADY WASHINGTON   A white grape variety developed from a cross of Golden Chasselas and Isabella by James H. Ricketts in Newburgh, New York.

LAGAR *(PORTUGAL AND SPAIN)*   Large, shallow stone tanks into which boxes of grapes are dumped prior to crushing.

LAGARINO *(ITALY)*   *See* Lagrein.

LAGE *(GERMANY)*   A small vineyard.

LAGER   Lager, a type of beer, was developed in Germany in about the seventh century. It was first introduced into the United States by the Germans in 1840. Lager comes from the German word *lagern* (to store) and is applied to bottom-fermented beer in particular because it must be stored at low temperatures for prolonged periods of time. Lagers were traditionally stored in cellars or caves for completion of fermentation. They are bright gold to yellow in color, with a light to medium body, and are usually well carbonated. Unless stated otherwise, virtually every beer made in the United States (more than 90 percent of them) is a lager.

LAGERING   Storing beer to mellow or ripen it.

LAGERN *(GERMANY)*   To store.

LAGERN BIER *(GERMANY)*   A storehouse for beer.

LAGRAIN *(ITALY)*   *See* Lagrein.

LAGREIN *(ITALY)*   A red grape variety grown primarily in Trentino-Alto Adige. Prior to 1919 it was called *Lagreinkretzer*; it is also known as *Lagarino* and *Lagrain*.

LAGREINKRETZER *(ITALY)*   *See* Lagrein.

LAGRIMA *(ITALY)*   A red grape variety.

LÁGRIMA   *See* Málaga.

LAIRÉN *(SPAIN)*   *See* Airén.

LAIT *(FRANCE)*   *See* Milk.

LAKE EMERALD   A white grape variety developed in 1945 (named in 1954) from a cross of Pixiola and Golden Muscat by Professor Loren Stover of the Florida Agricultural Experimental Station.

LAKE ERIE   A wine-producing region in northwest New York State; it received its *appellation* in November 1983.

LAKE GARDA *(ITALY)* A famous lake located in the northern region of Lombardy, famous for its white Lugana wines.

LAKE KEUKA The "thumb" of the Finger Lakes region in upstate New York.

LAKEMONT SEEDLESS A white grape variety introduced in 1972 from a cross of Ontario and Thompson Seedless at the State Experimental Station in Geneva, New York.

LA MANCHA *(SPAIN)* A wine district in central Spain, around Madrid, famous for Valdepeñas wines.

LAMBIC A family of wild-fermented beers, generally brewed near Brussels. Some of the ingredients added during the brewing process are cranberries, peaches, raspberries, sour cherries, and wheat. Most of the beers are winy and somewhat acidic, almost resembling vermouth rather than beer. Some examples of lambic beers are Faro, Framboise, Gueuze, and Kriek.

LAMBRUSCO *(ITALY)* A red grape variety indigenous to the Emilia-Romagna region; it typically makes *frizzante* wines, although a *spumante* version can be found. The Lambrusco grape produces lively, light-bodied wines that are ruby red in color, with a cherry-strawberry odor and taste.

There are many strains of the Lambrusco grape variety; among them are di Sorbara (also known as *Sorbarese*), Grasparossa, Maestri, Marani, Montericcio, Reggiano, Salamino, and Viadanese.

In Italy, local growers formed a *consorzio* to help protect and promote their wines. These consorzios give member wineries special labels for attachment to the bottle's neck. Each neck label depicts a different scene, insignia, or emblem. The labels on Lambrusco wines show a white cock and grapes on a red ground, or a man and woman treading grapes.

LAMBSWOOD An ale flavored with roasted or baked apples.

LAMPIA *(ITALY)* A red subvariety of the Nebbiolo grape variety, widely grown throughout the Piedmont region.

LANDAL A red grape variety developed from a cross of Plantet and Seibel 8216. Formerly known as *Landot 244*.

LANDED-AGE A formerly used British term for champagne kept an extra year or two after *landing* (being shipped) before it was considered fit for drinking.

LANDOT 244 *See* Landal.

LANDOT 2281 A red grape variety developed from a blend of Seyval and Plantet; used primarily in the midwestern and northeastern United States for blending.

LANDOT 4511 *See* Landot Noir.

LANDOT NOIR A red grape variety developed from a cross of Landal and Villard Blanc. Formerly known as *Landot 4511*.

LANDWEIN *(GERMANY)* A category of wines, defined according to the 1982 wine laws, that is a step above *Tafelwein* in quality and may be *chaptalized*. Less than 10 percent of Landwein is exported to the United States.

LANGE (GERMANY)   *See* Length.

LANGUEDOC (FRANCE)   A wine-producing province in the south, west of the Rhône River, which produces mostly *vin ordinaires*. *See* Midi and Roussillon.

LAPSANG SOUCHONG TEA   A dark tea with a smoky flavor that comes from drying the leaves over camphor logs. The leaves are grown in the southern Chinese province of Fukien.

LATE-BOTTLED VINTAGE PORTS (LBV)   These are ports of a single vintage, declared by the shipper during the fourth year after the vintage. The port is bottled between July 1 of that year and December 31 of the sixth year after harvest. Generally, late-bottled vintage ports are vintages not declared as vintage ports and are usually ready to drink when released. Late-bottled vintage port replaced what was known as *crusted ports*.

LATE HARVEST   A term used mainly in California to denote wines made from especially ripe grapes picked or harvested later than usual. These grapes are often shriveled, resembling raisins. Also known as *récolte tardive* and *vendange tardive*.

LATERAL   A branch of a shoot on a grapevine.

LATISANA (ITALY)   A wine-producing area in the region of Friuli-Venezia Giulia. *See* Friuli-Venezia Giulia.

LATIUM (ITALY)   One of twenty wine-producing regions located in the central part of Italy. It is bordered in the north by Umbria and Tuscany, in the south by Molise and Campania, in the east by Abruzzo, and in the west by the Tyrrhenian Sea.

The wine produced in Latium is approximately 90 percent white, with the remaining 10 percent mostly devoted to non-DOC reds. Some of the best wines of this region are in fact not DOC wines and are bottled under the name of Castelli Romani. Known as *Lazio* in Italy.

LATTE (ITALY)   *See* Milk.

LATTE MACCHIATO (ITALY)   A mug of steamed milk "marked" with a bit of espresso poured through the center of the foam.

LAUTERN (GERMANY)   To make clear. *See* Clear.

LAUTER TUN   A large circular copper or stainless steel vessel with perforations at the bottom, used in brewing to separate the grain from the liquid (*wort*) by straining. *See* Mash Tun.

LAY (GERMANY)   Slate rock.

LAYER   A long cane from an adjacent grapevine that is utilized to replace a missing grapevine.

LAYERING   A technique whereby liqueurs are slowly poured over the back of a teaspoon into a straight-sided liqueur glass so that they will remain separated according to their density. *See* Pousse-Café.

LAZIO (ITALY)   *See* Latium.

LBV   *See* Late-Bottled Vintage Ports.

LDS   *See* Liquor Dispensing System.

LEACHING   Filtering of raw, newly distilled whiskey through a cistern or vat filled with finely ground and tamped-down charcoal. *See* Activated Charcoal and Charcoal Mellowed.

LEACHING   The downward removal of soluble salts from the soil by the application of water or by heavy, drenching rains.

LEAFHOPPER   *See* Grape Leafhopper.

LEAF THINNING   A method employed in the vineyards to regulate the balance between leaf surface and sun exposure. Thinning consists of removing excess leaves, which increases sunlight and air circulation, limiting the formation of some mold types. Also known as *ausdünnen, effeuillage*, and *thinning*. *See* Crop Control, Crop Thinning, and Crown Suckering.

LEAFY   An odor and/or taste sensation of some wines that display a green, vegetative, or herbaceous quality analogous to the smell of leaves.

LEAKAGE   What occurs when wine leaks past a cork due to improper storage or a faulty cork. The correct level of humidity for a wine cellar is between 55 and 65 percent. If the humidity begins to rise, reaching 80 percent or more, corks may leak as the wine in the bottle expands.

Some wine racks are designed so that the neck of the bottle is pointed down. This leads to trouble, for it is not uncommon for wine bottles to leak at the neck or through the cork. Also known as *barrel leak, couleuse*, and *weeper*. *See* Ullage.

LEÁNYKA (HUNGARY)   *See* Feteasca Alba.

LEATHERY   Describes an odor occasionally found in red wines rich in tannin, reminiscent of rawhide.

LEBENDIG (GERMANY)   *See* Lively.

LECHE (SPAIN)   *See* Milk.

LEER (GERMANY)   *See* Thin.

LEES   Dead yeast cells, pulp, skins, seeds, and other solids that settle to the bottom of a barrel or tank during and after fermentation. The lees are left behind during racking or filtering. Also known as *bottoms, kasu, lias, lie*, and *pé*.

LEES BRANDY   Brandy distilled from the lees of standard grape, citrus, or other fruit wine, designated as "lees brandy" qualified by the name of the fruit from which the lees are derived.

LÉGER (FRANCE)   *See* Light-Bodied.

LEGGERO (ITALY)   *See* Light.

LEGS   The usually narrow trails or streaks of a transparent liquid (primarily water) apparent on the inner walls of a wine or brandy glass that run downward after it has been swirled. Legs are *not* glycerin, but are rather due to a phenomena called *surface-tension pump*, which, due to the evaporation of ethyl alcohol at the surface, draws up a small quantity of wine in "capillary-looking" tubes. Legs are usually found in rich, full-bodied wines or brandies with high extract and alcoholic content. Also known as *arches, church windows, rivulets, ropes, sheets*, and *tears*.

LEHRE BUBE (GERMANY)   An apprentice brewer. *See* Brewmaster.

LEICHT (GERMANY)   *See* Light-Bodied.

LEITE (PORTUGAL)   *See* Milk.

LEMBERGER   *See* Limberger.

LEMONADE   A nonalcoholic drink made from lemon juice and water, usually sweetened. Also known as *limonata*.

LEMON JUICE   The liquid constituent of a freshly squeezed lemon.

LEMON AND LIME SODA   A soft drink usually made with carbonated water, sugar or sweetener, acids, and a lemon- and lime-flavored syrup.

LEMONY   Describes a condition in a wine, especially white, where there is an excess of acidity.

LEN DE L'ELH (FRANCE)   A white grape variety grown in the southwest.

LE NEZ DU VIN (FRANCE)   Literally, the nose of wine, referring to the scent or odor of wines.

LENGTH   The continuation or persistence of flavor that lingers in the mouth, during tasting and after swallowing a beverage. Also known as *long* and *longueur*. *See* Aftertaste and Finish.

LENOIR   A red grape variety of unknown origin, grown in Texas. Formerly grown in quantity in France and Madeira, Portugal; however, its acreage worldwide is shrinking. Also known as *Black Spanish* and *Jacquez*.

LENTICEL   A tiny, round, slightly raised pore-like spot found on stalks and grape berries.

LENTICELS   Cork cells; they run horizontally and contain air.

LÉON MILLOT   A red grape variety that is similar in character to Maréchal Foch. Formerly known as *Kuhlmann 194-2* and *Millot*.

LES (FRANCE)   The plural definite article.

LESBIAN (GREECE)   An ancient sweet, red wine.

LESE (GERMANY)   *See* Harvest.

LESEGUTAUTBESSERUNG (AUSTRIA)   *See* Chaptalization.

LES PILIERS CHABLISIENS (FRANCE)   The wine brotherhood, founded in 1953, that is responsible for promoting the wines of Chablis.

LEUCONOSTOC OENOS   A strain of bacteria responsible for the formulation of *malolactic* fermentation.

LEVADURA (SPAIN)   *See* Yeast.

LEVE (PORTUGAL)   *See* Light-Bodied.

LEVER   The part of a corkscrew that is attached to the lip on top of a bottle of wine. While the bottle is held, the handle of the corkscrew is gently lifted up in a straight motion until the cork comes completely out of the bottle.

LEVER *(FRANCE)* A viticultural procedure where the young shoots on a grapevine are passed between the trellis wires and fastened with clips or wicker.

LEVULOSE *See* Fructose.

LEVURE *(FRANCE)* *See* Yeast.

LIAS *(SPAIN)* *See* Lees.

LIATIKO *(GREECE)* A white grape variety.

LIBATION A beverage, usually alcoholic.

LIBERTY A red grape variety developed in 1961 and named in 1976.

LICENSEE Any person holding a basic permit issued under the United States Federal Alcohol Administration Act. Also known as *permittee*.

LICENSE STATE In the United States, a state in which all alcoholic beverages (retail off-premise) can be purchased directly from licensed, "uncontrolled" retailers rather than from state-owned liquor stores only. States where private individuals can secure licenses to conduct all phases of the wholesale or retain sale of alcoholic beverages. Currently, thirty-two states and the District of Columbia authorize distribution by wholesalers. Also known as *open state*. *See* Control State.

LICOR *(SPAIN)* *See* Liqueur.

LICOR DE EXPEDICIÓN *(SPAIN)* *See* Liqueur d'Expédition.

LICOR DE TIRAJE *(SPAIN)* *See* Liqueur de Tirage.

LICOROSO *(SPAIN)* *See* Dessert Wine.

LIE *(FRANCE)* *See* Lees.

LIEBFRAUMILCH *(GERMANY)* An off-dry white wine from the Rheinhessen region whose name, translated, means "milk of the blessed mother."

Liebfraumilch was at one time produced from a blend of grapes grown in Rheingau, Rheinhessen, Pfalz, and Nahe. However, with changes in the German wine law (1990), vintners no longer can blend grapes from the four regions for Liebfraumilch. Only one of the four regions can be shown as a source for Liebfraumilch, and the region must be stated on the label. No single vineyard site, district, or grape variety designations are allowed on the label. The word "Liebfraumilch" cannot be shown in type larger than that used to identify the region. The law further specifies that all Liebfraumilch must be made at least 70 percent from one of the following grape varieties: Johannisberg Riesling, Sylvaner, Müller-Thurgau, or Kerner. Additionally, the wine law restricts residual sugar to a range of 1.8 to 4.5 percent. It is estimated that 60 percent of all wines from Germany are exported under the Liebfraumilch appellation.

LIEBLICH *(GERMANY)* *See* Sapid.

LIENS *(FRANCE)* The tying of the shoots and canes during the year for training the grapevine along the wires.

LIES FINE *(FRANCE)* Fine lees

LIEVITO *(ITALY)* *See* Yeast.

LIGERO *(SPAIN)*   *See* Light-Bodied.

LIGHT   Also known as *leggero*. *See* Little.

LIGHT   When referring to beer, it often means the opposite of dark in color.

LIGHT BEER   Beer having less alcohol and fewer calories than traditional lager beers.

Light beer is usually produced by the dilution of regular beers that have been brewed with the use of high-extract grains or barley and have been allowed to ferment dry. Another method of production involves the addition of enzymes, which reduce the number of calories and the beer's alcoholic content; its flavor is also considerably lighter. The purpose of producing light beer is to make a lower-calorie beer. A regular twelve-ounce beer has 135 to 170 calories; a light beer usually has under one hundred calories. There are no current BATF rulings on minimum or maximum calorie levels. Also known as *helles bier*.

LIGHT-BODIED   Describes a pleasant, refreshing wine or beer, lacking in body, color, or alcohol; opposite of *full-bodied*. Also known as *körperarm, koúfas, léger, leicht, leve*, and *ligero*.

LIGHT RUM   (also labeled *white* or *silver*) Rum that is clear in color and displays either a very light molasses flavor or the neutrality of vodka. It must be aged a minimum of one year in either glass or stainless steel containers, but more traditionally is aged in uncharred barrels. If aged in barrels, it is further treated through carbon filtration systems, which eliminates any color that may have been picked up from the barrel.

Light-bodied rums are generally produced in Puerto Rico, Virgin Islands, Cuba, Dominican Republic, and Haiti.

LIGHT WHIPPING CREAM   Cream that contains between 30 and 35 percent milkfat.

LIGHT WHISKEY   Whiskey produced in the United States from various cereal grains. It is distilled at 160 to 189 proof and stored in used or uncharred new oak barrels. If light whiskey is mixed with less than 20 percent of straight whiskey on a proof gallon basis, the mixture is designated "blended light whiskey." It is lighter than other whiskies in flavor, aroma, and taste because the flavor congeners are removed during the distillation at a high proof. This whiskey was first authorized for production after January 26, 1968, and on July 1, 1972, the first bottles were ready for sale.

LIGHT WINE   A category of table wines that was spawned in 1981 to meet the strong demand for wines with a lower caloric and alcohol content that could satisfy their consumers' wine needs and simultaneously decrease their caloric intake by as much as one-third.

According to regulations under the United States Federal Alcohol Administration Act, Title 27 Code of Federal regulations, wine under 14 percent alcohol should be designated as table (or light) wine or the alcohol content should be stated.

The category never really got started and, although more than a dozen wineries did market light wines, it is now almost nonexistent.

LIGNIFICATION   The hardening of the wood of grapevine branches, which takes place at the same time as the fruit matures.

LIGURIA (ITALY)   The second-smallest of the twenty wine-producing regions (Valle d'Aosta is the smallest), it is located along a narrow strip of land on the Italian Riviera in the northwest. The region is best known for its Cinqueterre, a white wine named after the five communes in which it is produced.

LIKÖRWEIN (GERMANY)   *See* Dessert Wine.

LIMBERGER   A red grape variety grown in Washington State. Formerly spelled *Lemberger*. *See* Blaufränkisch.

LIMEADE   A nonalcoholic drink made from lime juice and water, usually sweetened.

LIME JUICE   The liquid constituent of a freshly squeezed lime.

LIMITED BOTTLING   A wine term with no legal definition, used to denote a reserve-type wine where there is only a limited quantity produced or, actually, the entire lot of a single wine that the winery has to offer. *See* Reserve.

LIMÓN   A light green citrus fruit with a taste quite similar to lemon and lime, with the flavor of lemon predominating. It is indigenous to Mexico and the southwestern United States, where it is traditionally served with tequila drinks. Although limes are the customary citrus fruit used in the United States for margaritas, lemons would offer a more authentic taste.

LIMONATA (ITALY)   *See* Lemonade.

LIMONE (ITALY)   Lemon.

LIMOUSIN OAK (FRANCE)   (Technically known as *Quercus sessilis*.) Wooden barrels made from wood grown in the Limousin forest near Limoges in central France. Limousin oak is soft with a loose grain, allowing rapid extraction of flavor and tannin. Limousin adds vanilla and lemon flavors, which tend to emphasize wine's acidity. Traditionally used for cognac and white French Burgundies, Limousin oak is being used extensively in California for aging Chardonnay wines.

LIMPID   Also known as *limpide, limpido,* and *limpio*. *See* Clear.

LIMPIDE (FRANCE)   *See* Clear.

LIMPIDO (ITALY)   *See* Clear.

LIMPIO (SPAIN)   *See* Clear.

LINALOOL   A terpene alcohol with a pronounced floral odor present in varying levels in Flora, Gewürztraminer, Johannisberg Riesling, Malvasia Bianca, Müller-Thurgau, and Muscat grapes.

LINDLEY   A red grape variety, named in 1869 for English botanist John Lindley, developed from a cross of Mammoth Sage and Golden Chasselas by Edward S. Rogers of Salem, Massachusetts. Formerly known as *Rogers 9*.

LINEAR FEET OF SHELF SPACE   A measurement of the length of shelf space occupancy expressed in inches or feet.

LINE (FRANCE)   A seldom-used measurement (equivalent to one-tenth of an inch) for the thickness of staves on a wooden barrel. Staves were measured in lines, a measure also used for corks.

LINGERING   *See* Aftertaste.

LIPARÓS (*GREECE*)   *See* Oily.

LIQUEUR   Derived from the Latin word *liquefacere* meaning to dissolve or melt; a fitting term, since the entire process of making liqueurs involves dissolving selected ingredients in a neutral distilled spirit. The words "cordial" and "liqueur" are identical in meaning and are so indistinguishable that they are always mentioned together in United States federal and state laws and regulations. Liqueur is generally accepted as the European name and *cordial* as the American.

Liqueurs are products obtained by mixing or redistilling distilled spirits with or over fruits, flowers, plants, or pure juices therefrom, or other natural flavoring materials, or with extracts derived from infusion, percolation, or maceration of such materials, and containing sugar, dextrose, or levulose, or a combination thereof, in an amount not less than 2.5 percent by weight of the finished product. This amounts to about one and one-half tablespoon of sugar (simply syrup) per liter. In practice, most liqueurs contain large percentages (up to 35 percent) of some sweetening agent. While there is no minimum alcohol level mandated by the federal government, most liqueurs are between 34 to 60 proof, while others are as high as 100 proof. Liqueurs may be designated "dry" if the sugar, dextrose, or levulose, or combination thereof is less than 10 percent by weight of the finished product. Also known as *licor. See* Cordial.

LIQUEUR DE TIRAGE (*FRANCE*)   The sugar or sweetener added to still wine to induce yeast cells to begin secondary fermentation, producing a sparkling wine. Also known as *licor de tiraje. See* Dosage and Liqueur d'Expédition.

LIQUEUR D'EXPÉDITION (*FRANCE*)   The shipping dosage in making champagne that determines its relative dryness. Also known as *dosage, licor de expedición*, and *rabboccatura. See* Liqueur de Tirage.

LIQUEUR GLASS   *See* Cordial Glass.

LIQUIDO (*ITALY*)   Liquid.

LIQUID SUGAR   A substantially colorless refined sugar and water solution containing not less than the equivalent of 60 percent pure dry sugar by weight (60 degrees Brix).

LIQUOR   A term commonly taken to mean distilled spirits. Also known as *hard liquor* and *liquore*.

LIQUOR DISPENSING SYSTEM (LDS)   An automatic dispensing system for distilled spirits, used for on-premise alcoholic beverage service. This system can be set to dispense a predetermined quantity of distilled spirit each and every time it is activated. It provides a consistent, standardized drink and controls inventory, eliminating over- and underpouring, spillage, and free drinks. Its major drawback is that it is impersonal and most customers want to see the drinks being poured from the bottle at the bar rail, rather than watching the drink being dispensed from a tube.

LIQUORE (*ITALY*)   *See* Liquor.

LIQUOREUX (*FRANCE*)   *See* Dessert Wine.

LIQUOR LICENSE   A state permit to sell and/or serve alcoholic beverages.

LIQUOROSO (*ITALY* AND *PORTUGAL*)   *See* Dessert Wine.

LIRAC (FRANCE)   A wine commune in the Rhône Valley that produces red, white, and rosé wines. The grape varieties grown are Grenache, Mourvèdre, Cinsaut, and Syrah, for the red and rosé wines, and Clairette, Ugni Blanc, and Bourboulenc, for the white wines.

LISTA DEI VINI (ITALY)   Wine list.

LISTÁN (SPAIN)   *See* Palomino.

LISTOFKA (RUSSIA)   A black-currant-flavored liqueur.

LITER   A metric unit of capacity equal to one thousand cubic centimeters, of alcoholic beverage at 20 degrees Celsius or 33.814 ounces (1.0567 quarts) at 68 degrees Fahrenheit. One gallon equals 3.78541 liters. One liter equals 0.264172 gallons. Also known as *litro*.

LITRO (ITALY AND SPAIN)   *See* Liter.

LITTLE   Describes a wine or beer with a scant smell, flavor, body, or aftertaste. It features no particular characteristics, substance, or distinction. Also known as *gering, klein, light, naive, petit*, and *small*.

LITTLE GIRLS   *See* Fillettes.

LIT UP   *See* Intoxicated.

LIVELY   Describes young wines that are fresh, with plenty of zestiness, acidity, fruit, and possibly a little carbon dioxide, making them spritzy. Also known as *lebendig, racy, sprightly, vif, vigorous*, and *zesty. See* Vivacious.

LIVRE (FRANCE)   A former unit of value (money, vineyard land, and so on).

LOADED   *See* Intoxicated.

LOAM   A type of soil that is a mixture of sand, silt, and clay particles. *See* Sandy Loam.

LOBE   The rounded or angular projection of a grape leaf.

LOCALLY DISPOSABLE   Brand-identified funds designated for use for local promotional efforts, such as custom-made signs.

LOCAL OPTION   Choice of whether or not to permit sale of distilled spirits, wine, or beer.

LODGE   The British term for a Portuguese port firm or producer.

LOGGERHEAD   A long-handled tool with a ball or bulb at the end, often used to heat beer or rum-based drinks. *See* Mulled Wine and Poker Beer.

LOGO   Short for logogram, a term that refers to a proprietary brand name or trademark that represents a company. *See* Brand Name and Trademark.

LOGROÑO (SPAIN)   A province in the Rioja-Alta, situated to the north of the River Ebro, it is the business and financial hub of the wine district. The majority of Rioja wineries or *bodegas* are to be found along the roads that run between Logroño and Haro.

LOIRE VALLEY (FRANCE)   One of the six major wine-producing regions, located along the Loire River in north-central France. The Loire Valley produces mostly dry white wines (75 percent of the total production), the rest being rosé and red wines.

Like Alsace the region lies very far north and doesn't receive sufficient sunshine to fully ripen red grapes.

Most of the wines of the Loire Valley are sold under district or village appellations such as Anjou, Pouilly Fumé, Saumur, and Vouvray. There is one notable exception: Muscadet, which is sold under its grape varietal name. Technically speaking, the Muscadet grape is actually the Melon de Bourgogne.

The river Loire has a double distinction: it is the longest river in France (625 miles) and the longest of all the world's great rivers that nurture wine grapes along their banks.

LOMANTO   A red grape variety developed by Thomas Volney Munson (1843–1913) of Denison, Texas.

LOMBARDIA (ITALY)   *See* Lombardy.

LOMBARDY (ITALY)   One of twenty wine-producing regions located in the center of northern Italy; borders on Switzerland to the north, Veneto and Trentino-Alto Adige to the east, Emilia-Romagna to the south, and Piedmont to the west. Three of Italy's largest freshwater lakes—Maggiore, Como, and Garda—are in Lombardy. The Po, Italy's longest river, flows through the region's premier agricultural zone, the Po River Valley. Milan, Italy's industrial capital and largest city, after Rome, is in Lombardy.

There are three major areas of wine production in Lombardy: Oltrepò Pavese, Valtellina, and Brescia, which includes the area south of Lake Iseo and the Lake Garda district. Two smaller areas of production also contribute to the regional output: the Colli Morenici Mantovani del Garda, located in the hills just south of Lake Garda in the province of Mantua, and the area north of Bergamo, in central Lombardy. Known as *Lombardia* in Italy.

LONDON DRY GIN OR DRY GIN   A generic name for gin lacking sweetness. None of the grain tasted or odor is retained. In England, gin mash usually contains less corn and more barley, because English distillers feel that this produces a distilled spirit of extraordinary smoothness. Their gins are distilled at a high proof, then redistilled in the presence of juniper berries. English gins have a lightly balanced, aromatic juniper bouquet and flavor; they are light, dry, crisp, and clean, with the delicate flavoring of the juniper berry, although this is slightly toned down. These gins are ideal for drinking straight, in martinis, or mixed in cocktails. London dry gins, although originally produced only in or near London, are now produced all over the world, and the term presently has little meaning.

LONDON PARTICULAR (LP) (ITALY)   *See* Marsala Superiore.

LONG   *See* Cunningham.

LONG   Also known as *lange* and *lungo*. *See* Length.

LONG DRINK   A cocktail served in a larger-than-usual glass, which permits the addition of more mixer (carbonated beverage, fruit juice, etc.). Also known as *tall drink*.

LONG ISLAND   A major wine-producing region located east of New York City, noted for its production of high-quality wines made almost exclusively from *Vitis vinifera* grape varieties.

LONGUEUR (FRANCE)   *See* Length.

LONG-VATTED   *See* Extended Skin Contact.

LOONYIEN *(CHINA)*   A white grape variety.

LOOPED   *See* Intoxicated.

LOSS LEADER   An item that an establishment offers for sale at cost or less than cost to attract customers. *See* Price Leader.

LOTE *(PORTUGAL)*   Newly fermented wine prior to aging or blending.

LOT   Wine of the same type. When used with reference to a "lot of wine bottled," lot means the same type of wine bottled or packed into containers on the same date.

A LOT OF BOTTLED WINE   Wine of the same type bottled on the same date into bottles or consumer units of the same measure on the same bottling line.

LOUCHE *(FRANCE)*   *See* Cloudy.

LOURD *(FRANCE)*   *See* Heavy.

LOUREIRO   A white grape variety grown mainly in Portugal and Spain.

LOW-ALCOHOL REFRESHERS   A blend of fruit juices, carbonated water, and sugar, with an alcohol base (6 percent or less) of wine, distilled spirits, or malt. Some producers also bottle flavored low-alcohol refreshers. This category also includes *coolers, wine coolers,* and certain *flavored wines. See* Apéritif Wine.

LOWFAT MILK   Milk that has sufficient milkfat removed to bring that level to between 0.5 and 2 percent. It also contains at least 8.25 percent nonfat solids. Milk in this category is labeled lowfat, 2 percent, or 1 percent milk. If nonfat milk solids are added to reach the 10 percent solids-nonfat level, the product must be labeled "protein-fortified" or "fortified with protein."

LOW-INPUT SUSTAINABLE AGRICULTURE   *See* Sustainable Agriculture.

LOWLAND MALTS   Barley is grown in the Scottish lowlands. The whiskies produced there (lowland malts) are mild and light in body, with little smokiness.

LOW WINE   During distillation, when the vapor is drawn off, it condenses into a liquid known as low wine, with an alcoholic content of anywhere from 45 to 65 percent. The low wine is redistilled or further refined, so that the alcohol reaches an even higher concentration and unwanted impurities and flavors are further removed.

LOZIA *(BULGARIA)*   *See* Vineyard.

LP *(ITALY)*   London Particular. *See* Marsala Superiore.

LUCIDO *(ITALY)*   A white grape variety.

LUCILE   A red grape variety.

LUFTGESCHMACK *(GERMANY)*   *See* Oxidation.

LUG BOXES   Boxes made of heavy gauge plastic, metal, or even wood, used by pickers during grape harvest. After the grapes are picked they are placed in the lug boxes, which hold from thirty-five to fifty pounds. The name is derived from the task of lugging the heavy box around. *See* Grape-Picking Basket.

LUMIÈRE *(FRANCE)* Particular taste caused by the effect of direct sunlight on sparkling wines such as champagne. It often happens with bottles that have not been given anti-ultraviolet treatment. This can also sometimes happen with still wines.

LUMINEUX *(FRANCE)* *See* Bright.

LUNGO *(ITALY)* *See* Length.

LUPULIN A yellow resinous powder obtained from the strobiles of hops used to flavor beer.

LUSCIOUS Soft, sweet, fat, fruity. A term often used when referring to naturally sweet wines of extremely high sugar content (e.g., Sauternes, Trockenbeerenauslese). Also known as *aveludado* and *lush*. *See* Dessert Wine.

LUSH *See* Intoxicated.

LUSH *See* Luscious.

LUXURY CHAMPAGNE An overused term with little meaning that describes the highest quality French champagnes.

MA *(FRANCE)* *See* Marque d'Acheteur.

MACABEO *(SPAIN)* A white grape variety grown throughout the Rioja Region, used to produce sparkling wines. Also known as *Viura*.

MACACOS *(PORTUGAL)* Long wooden paddles that are employed to punch down or submerge the *cap* in fermentation tanks. *See* Punching Down.

MACERATION A method of extracting color and flavor from fruits, seeds, flowers, herbs, spices, or grape skins by leaving them in contact with the fermenting juice and/or a neutral distilled spirit. Also a production method employed in making liqueurs and some brandies. It is also known as the *cold method*, because the flavoring materials are sensitive to heat and would be damaged by it. The cold method is a lengthy process that can take as long as a year.

Maceration is not unlike the brewing of tea. Fruit or other ingredients destined to be made into liqueurs are placed directly into the distilled spirit or brandy and allowed to steep until sufficient amounts of the aroma and flavor have been extracted. Each ingredient has its own unique aroma and taste. After the steeping is complete, the distilled spirit (liqueur) is drawn off and filtered; water is added and the color adjusted, and it is finally blended with sugar syrup or occasionally honey for consistency of taste. The liqueur is then allowed to age or marry from several months to one year, in order to blend the flavors before bottling. Also known as *infusion*.

MACÉRATION CARBONIQUE *(FRANCE)* *See* Carbonic Maceration.

MACÉRATION PELLICULAIRE *(FRANCE)* *See* Extended Skin Contact.

MACERAZIONE CARBONICA *(ITALY)* *See* Carbonic Maceration.

MÂCHÉ *(FRANCE)* *See* Chewy.

MAÇIO *(PORTUGAL)* *See* Mellow.

MÂCON (FRANCE) A town in the Côte Mâconnaise on the Sâone River in southern Burgundy, just north of Beaujolais. The local red wine is fruity and very pleasant when young, but the predominant wine (approximately 70 percent of total production) is white. The region's slopes are covered with vineyards that produce light, dry white wines, such as the world-renowned Pouilly-Fuissé.

MACROCLIMATE The climate of a viticultural region as determined by heat summation or other determining factors.

MÄDCHENTRAUBE (HUNGARY) *See* Feteasca Alba.

MADD *See* Mothers Against Drunk Driving.

MADE AND BOTTLED BY *See* Produced and Bottled By.

MADEIRA (PORTUGAL) An island off Portugal in the Atlantic Ocean, some 360 miles from the coast of Morocco, famous for its fortified wines. Madeira is a fortified wine (beginning in 1753) with an alcoholic content of 17 to 20 percent by volume due to the addition of a 96 proof brandy. The five styles of madeira (driest to sweetest) are Sercial, Verdelho, Rainwater, Bual, and Malmsey.

MADEIRIZADO (PORTUGAL) *See* Maderized.

MADELEINE ANGEVINE A white grape variety developed from a cross of Précoce de Malingre and Madeleine Royale. It is grown primarily in England, where it produces light wines with a sort of *Muscat* aroma.

MADERISATION (PORTUGAL) *See* Maderized.

MADÉRISÉ (FRANCE) *See* Maderized.

MADERIZATION The condition of being maderized.

MADERIZED Term applied to a wine that is past its prime, flat, somewhat oxidized, and has acquired a brownish tinge. Directly applied to wines that have been poorly stored and subjected to excessive heat. Usually has a baked smell and flavor reminiscent of madeira wine. Also known as *firne, madeirizado, maderisation, madérisé, maderization,* and *maderizzato. See* Baked, Caramelization, Cooked, Estufa, and Oxidation.

MADERIZZATO (ITALY AND SPAIN) *See* Maderized.

MADILLA (SPAIN) *See* Hearts.

MADURO (PORTUGAL AND SPAIN) *See* Maturity.

MAGER (GERMANY) *See* Thin.

MAGLIOCCO CANINO (ITALY) A red grape variety grown in the south. Also known as *Arvino*.

MAGNOLIA A white grape variety introduced in 1961 by the North Carolina Agricultural Experimental Station. Magnolia, along with Carlos and Dixie, are supplanting Scuppernong in the southeast vineyards of the United States.

MAGNUM Bottle of wine equal in capacity to 50.8 ounces or two 750-milliliter bottles. Also referred to as 1.5 liter.

MAGOON A red grape variety.

MAGRO (ITALY)   *See* Thin.

MAGUEY (SPAIN)   The agave plant used to produce tequila and mezcal. *See* Agave.

MAIBOCK   A bock beer brewed in the spring. *See* Bock Beer.

MAI CHIU (CHINA)   *See* Beer.

MAIGRE (FRANCE)   *See* Thin.

MAIN (GERMANY)   An important river in Franken.

MAINRIESLING   *See* Rieslaner.

MAIPO (SPAIN)   An important wine-producing region in Chile.

MAISCHE (GERMANY)   *See* Mash and Must

MAISCHBOTTICH (GERMANY)   A mash tub used in the making of beer or some distilled spirits. *See* Mash Tun.

MAISON (FRANCE)   Business or firm.

MAISON DU VIN (FRANCE)   A wine house.

MAI TAI   A cocktail consisting of light rum, dark rum, orgeat syrup, triple sec, pineapple juice, grenadine syrup, and lime juice. This world-famous drink, created in 1944 by Trader Vic, translates from Polynesian as "the best, out of this world."

MAÎTRE DE CHAIS (FRANCE)   Also known as *caviste*. *See* Cellarmaster.

MAIWEIN (GERMANY)   *See* May Wine.

MAIUELO (SPAIN)   Wine made from young grapevines, generally under seven years of age.

MAKE LOVE TO A BLONDE IN A BLACK SKIRT   An expression used when drinking a pint of stout (a dark beer from Ireland). Using a stirrer, you carve the shape of a shamrock in the head of the stout. If the stout is fresh and you carve the figure correctly, you should be able to see the shamrock in the bottom of the glass in the remaining head when the stout is finished.

MAKIN'   The process of making or producing non-taxpaid or illicit distilled spirits for use or resale.

MÁLAGA (SPAIN)   A wine district in the south of Spain, named after the shipping port in the province of Eastern Andalucía. Málaga is also a walnut-colored wine, generally sweet or very sweet, made from Pedro Ximénez and Moscatel grapes, in the city it is named after. There is a sweeter version known as *lágrima*, made only from free-run juice. Málaga was once known as *Mountain* in old English writings.

MALATO (ITALY)   *See* Spoiled.

MALBEC   A red grape variety, imported into Bordeaux from Cahors at the end of the eighteenth century by M. Malbeck. Malbec is generally blended with Cabernet Sauvignon and Merlot in the red wines of Bordeaux, France. Malbec is an abundant producer, contributing color and tannin to the wine. It generally has a fruity bouquet of plums and berries—blackberries, cherries, and raspberries. In the Médoc of Bordeaux,

M

MALBEC

it is known locally as *Pressac*. In southwestern France it is known locally as *Cot* or *Auxerrois*.

MALIC ACID A fixed acid that derives from the Latin for apple, *malum*. It is the principal acid of apples (hence its name) and the second important major acid found in grapes. Its tart, astringent taste makes it easily recognizable. It can be found in apples, apricots, blackberries, cherries, gooseberries, nectarines, peaches, pears, and plums.

As grapes ripen, the malic acid present at high levels in the green grapes decreases. The hotter the year, the faster it decreases. This is why it is more apparent when the weather has been colder. *See* Malolactic Fermentation.

MALMSEY (PORTUGAL) The sweetest of all madeira wines, quite dark in color, with similarities to a cream sherry. It is also a white grape variety, transplanted by Prince Henry the Navigator from Crete to the Portuguese Island of Madeira in the 1400s. *See* Malvasia.

There is an interesting story that the Duke of Clarence, the brother of England's King Edward IV, was reputedly drowned in a barrel of malmsey.

MALOLACTIC ORGANISM *Leuconostoc oenos* strains ML-34 and PSU-1 were isolated and grown in the early 1960s for use in inoculating *musts* or wines for *malolactic fermentation*.

MALOLACTIC BACTERIA A strain of bacteria responsible for the formulation of a *malolactic fermentation*. It has been recognized and studied by an impressive list of famous microbiologists, including Louis Pasteur, who in 1858 demonstrated that lactic acid in wine was caused by organisms that he called "new yeasts." In 1889, Kulisch, a German, used pasteurized cider to prove the biological nature of malolactic fermentation, though he thought the causative agent was yeast.

MALOLACTIC FERMENTATION (Incorrectly referred to a "secondary fermentation.") The term comes from the Latin *malum*, apple. It is a bacterial fermentation, converting malic acid to lactic acid while releasing carbon dioxide. This action is caused by the metabolic activity of certain strains of bacteria. The bacteria genus most often responsible for this fermentation in wine are strains of *Leuconostoc oenos*. This conversion of malic acid is often to be desired in wines from cooler climates where there is an excess of acidity in the grapes and the wine. It usually happens after or simultaneously with the alcoholic fermentation. Malolactic fermentation occurring after bottling is considered spoilage, since unwanted turbidity and effervescence result from the bacterial growth.

Malolactic fermentation offers some advantages to wine: 1) it reduces the fixed acidity by converting a dicarboxylic acid (a two acid group) to a monocarboxylic acid (a one acid group), making the wine softer and more pleasant to drink when young; 2) it increases biological stability in the wine by assuring that a malolactic fermentation will not take place in the bottle; 3) it allows early marketing; 4) it permits the use of smaller amounts of SO_2; and 5) it increases the sensory quality and flavor complexity of the wine. Also known as *malolattica fermentazione* and abbreviated *M-L*. *See* Lactic Acid.

MALOLATTICA FERMENTAZIONE (ITALY) *See* Malolactic Fermentation.

MALT Sprouted or germinated barley (unless otherwise specified) used in beer and distilled spirit-making. The three main types are pale, crystal or caramel, and black.

Barley is soaked in water and kept damp until it begins to sprout. When the sprouting has proceeded for a short time so that organic agents called enzymes are formed, the barley is dried and the process halted. Also known as *barley malt*.

MALT ADJUNCTS   Various cereal grains, such as corn and rice, that are added to the mash either in substitution of or in conjunction with barley in order to provide additional sources of starch and certain desired characteristics in the beer.

MALT BEVERAGE   A beverage made by the alcoholic fermentation of an infusion in potable brewing water or malted barley with hops, or their parts, or their products, and with or without other malted cereals, and with or without the addition of unmalted or prepared cereals, other carbohydrates or products prepared therefrom, and with or without the addition of carbon dioxide, and with or without other wholesome products suitable for human food consumption.

MALTED MILK   A highly concentrated beverage that has less than 3.5 percent moisture and a butterfat content of 7.5 to 10 percent. Also, the name of a sweetened milk beverage that combines malted cereals, milk, ice cream, and a flavoring.

MALT EXTRACTS   Extracts produced by mashing malted barley together with warm water and then either concentrating it into a syrup or dehydrating it into powder form. Commercially produced malt extracts (syrups or powders) are packaged in cans or plastic bags and are usually available either hopped or unhopped.

MALTING   The process by which barley is germinated and kiln-dried in order to develop a high level of enzyme power and desired physical characteristics for use in mashes. Also known as *mälzerei*.

MALT KILN   A heated room where barley malt can be dried after its sprouting period.

MALT LIQUOR   An American term for a lager beer with a considerably higher level of alcohol (usually above 5 percent) than most lager beers or ales. Tastes vary from brewery to brewery and brand to brand, with some even sweetened with fruit syrup. The name comes from the beer's malty flavor, which has overtones of bitterness. Its color is typically darker than that of regular beers and its taste is correspondingly heavier and fuller-bodied.

MALTOSE   A fermentable sugar (malt sugar) that can be converted to alcohol and carbon dioxide gas by the action of the yeast during fermentation.

MALT SCOTCH   Often referred to as single-malt Scotch, it is produced by the pot still method from a mash consisting of only malted barley. A *single-malt* whisky means a malt whisky produced by a single distillery. By way of contrast, *blended* Scotch means a blend of pot-stilled malt whiskies with whiskies produced in Scotland by the column still method from a cereal mix that may contain unmalted as well as malted barley and other grains.

Malt Scotches are generally darker in color than blended Scotches and because of increased aging in the barrel, they are traditionally served at room temperature. Also known as *malt whisky*.

MALTSTER   One who is in control of the malting process utilized in the making of beer and some distilled spirits.

MALT WHISKY   *See* Malt Scotch.

MALTY   Describes the caramel taste of germinated and roasted barley.

MALVASIA   A white grape variety of Greek heritage that produces wines with a Muscat flavor. Malvasia is grown extensively throughout Italy (as well as Spain, Portugal, France, and others) where it is used either as a blending grape (with Chianti and Frascati) or exclusively in making sweet dessert wines. Wines made from Malvasia grapes can have problems with premature oxidation. Also known as *Malmsey, Malvasia Bianca del Chianti, Malvasia Bianca di Candia, Malvasia del Lazio*, and *Malvoisie*.

MALVASIA BIANCA DEL CHIANTI (ITALY) Also known as *Malvasia Toscana* and *Malvasia Bianca Lunga. See* Malvasia.

MALVASIA BIANCA DI CANDIA (ITALY) *See* Malvasia.

MALVASIA CORADA (PORTUGAL) A white grape variety grown in the Douro region.

MALVASIA DEL LAZIO (ITALY) Also known as *Puntinata. See* Malvasia.

MALVASIA FINA (PORTUGAL) A white grape variety used in the making of white port wine.

MALVASIA GROSSO (PORTUGAL) A white grape variety grown in the Douro region.

MALVASIA PARDA (PORTUGAL) A white grape variety grown in the Douro region.

MALVASIA REI (PORTUGAL) A white grape variety grown in the Douro region.

MALVOISIE (FRANCE) *See* Malvasia.

MALVOISIE (SWITZERLAND) *See* Pinot Gris.

MALZ (GERMANY) *See* Malt.

MÄLZBIER (GERMANY) A dark, sweet, malty beer that is low in alcohol.

MÄLZEREI (GERMANY) *See* Malting.

MAMERTINE An ancient wine of Rome.

MAMMOLO (ITALY) A red grape variety occasionally used in the blend of certain Chianti wines from Tuscany.

MAMMOTH SAGE A red grape variety.

MANCHE (FRANCE) The upper portion of a champagne cork, it often consists of scraps of cork glued together (*agglomerated*). *See* Miroir and Rondelle.

MANDARINE LIQUEUR A sweetened alcoholic beverage consisting of a base of alcohol, minimum 2.5 percent sugar, flavored and colored with dried peels of mandarins (tangerines).

MANDARINO (ITALY) An almond-flavored wine no longer legally known as Marsala.

MANDELBITTE (GERMANY) A bitter, almond-like flavor.

MANDILARIA (GREECE) A red grape variety occasionally used as a *mistelle* in the making of vermouth-type wines.

MANGARA (PORTUGAL) *See* Powdery Mildew.

MANHATTAN A cocktail consisting of bourbon or blended whiskey, sweet red vermouth, dash of bitters, and a cherry garnish.

The former Manhattan Club, a six-story building erected on Madison Avenue in New York City in 1859, was originally a residence for Leonard Jerome, the father of Jennie Jerome (1854–1921). In 1874, she married Lord Randolph Churchill and two years later she bore a son, Sir Winston, who would later figure heavily in English politics. It was this same Lady Churchill who first persuaded a reluctant bartender to mix bourbon "with a lesser portion of sweet vermouth and aromatic bitters" to please a guest of honor. As one of New York's leading socialites, she was giving a party in honor of Samuel J. Tilden's election as a reform governor. She named the drink "Manhattan" after the club where the celebration was being held; it is still one of the world's most popular cocktails.

MANITO   A red grape variety developed by Thomas Volney Munson (1843–1913) of Denison, Texas.

MANNE (FRANCE)   The part of the shoot on a grapevine that flowers.

MANNEQUIN (FRANCE)   *See* Grape-Picking Basket.

MANSENG (FRANCE)   A white grape variety native to the Juraçon region, where it produces full-bodied dessert wines.

MANTA (PORTUGAL)   *See* Cap.

MANTEY   A white grape variety.

MANTONACO (ITALY)   A white grape variety.

MANZANILLA (SPAIN)   The palest, lightest, and driest *fino*-style sherry made. Manzanilla sherries are produced in the town of Sanlúcar de Barrameda, near the coast, at the mouth of the Guadalquivir River, ten to fifteen miles outside of Jerez. Manzanillas are also more astringent or "tonic" in taste than *fino* sherries, which is probably due to both the ocean breezes and the unique soil content of the vineyards where the grapes are grown.

MANZANITA   A type of soil consisting of moderately well-drained, gravelly silt loam with a heavy clam loam subsoil. This soil is formed in alluvium, derived dominantly from basic igneous rock sources (volcanic rock materials), and is characterized by a rich brick-red color caused by high iron content.

MAP   *See* Marketing Action Plan.

MARADELLA (ITALY)   A red grape variety.

MARASTINA (YUGOSLAVIA)   A white grape variety.

MARASCHINO LIQUEUR   A sweetened alcoholic beverage consisting of a base of alcohol, minimum 2.5 percent sugar, flavored and colored with Dalmatian marasa cherries, rose petals, and spices.

MARC (FRANCE)   *See* Grappa.

MARCA (ITALY)   Of marked character (of grape, type, and district).

MARCHAND DE VIN (FRANCE)   A wine merchant (generally a wine shop proprietor or restaurateur).

MARCHE (ITALY)   *See* Marches.

M

MARCHE (ITALY)

MARCHES (ITALY)   One of twenty wine-producing regions, located in the north-central part of Italy; its eastern boundary is the Adriatic Sea. It is bordered to the west by Umbria, to the south by Abruzzo, and to the north by Emilia-Romagna and Tuscany. Marches' most famous wine is Verdicchio, a white dry wine. Known as *Marche* in Italy.

MARCHIO (ITALY)   Mark; generally used when referring to "trademark." *See* Trademark.

MARCHIO DEPOSITATO (ITALY)   A registered trademark.

MARCHIO NAZIONALE (ITALY)   *See* Instituto Nazionale Esportazione.

MARCHIO REGISTRATO (ITALY)   A registered trademark.

MARC OF GRAPES (FRANCE)   The capacity of a traditional champagne press, four thousand kilograms or 8,800 pounds of grapes, yielding a total of 2,550 liters (673 gallons) of juice. *See* Cocquard.

MARÉCHAL FOCH   A red grape variety originally developed in Alsace, France, by Eugene Kuhlmann. Formerly known as *Foch* and *Kuhlmann 188-2*.

MARGARITA   A cocktail consisting of tequila, triple sec, and freshly squeezed lemon juice, with the rim of the glass coated with coarse salt. It was purportedly concocted by a Virginia City bartender in memory of his girlfriend, who was accidentally shot during a barroom brawl. Another story has the margarita created in 1948 in Acapulco, Mexico, by socialite Margarita Sames.

MARGAUX (FRANCE)   A commune in the Haut-Médoc district of Bordeaux that produces almost exclusively red wines, noted for their bouquet, finesse, and silky texture. Margaux also includes the townships of Arsac, Cantenac, Labarde, and Soussans, comprising some 2,800 acres of vineyards.

On August 10, 1954, the wines of Margaux were officially granted their *appellation contrôlée* designation.

MARGIN   The edge of a leaf blade on a grapevine.

MARGUERITE   A grape variety developed by Thomas Volney Munson (1843–1913) of Denison, Texas.

MARIA GOMEZ (PORTUGAL)   *See* Fernão Pires.

MARIE-JEANNE (FRANCE)   A bottle, formerly used in Bordeaux, which contained approximately 84.53 ounces or the contents of about three regular-sized (750-milliliter) bottles.

MARIENSTEINER (GERMANY)   A white grape variety developed in 1971 from a cross of Sylvaner and Rieslaner in Würzburg. It is grown primarily in Germany and Switzerland.

MARKANT (GERMANY)   *See* Breed.

MARKENWEIN (GERMANY)   A registered brand name. *See* Trademark.

MARKET   A center of business within a territory.

MARKET   The potential number of guests who could frequent an establishment serving alcoholic beverages. Also the group that the establishment would like to attract.

MARKETING   The performance of business activities that direct the flow of goods and services from producer to consumer or user. Also, a social process by which individuals and groups obtain what they need and want through creating and exchanging products and value with others.

MARKETING ACTION PLAN (MAP)   A clear and concise communication from a sales promotion department to field sales persons regarding marketing plans for each product.

MARKETING PLAN   A detailed set of marketing objectives for a particular product and programs for achieving them. Wider in scope than an advertising plan because it contains programs for all marketing functional areas including personal selling, product development, and pricing.

MARKET SEGMENTS   Subgroups of consumers, each with some common characteristic that influences that group's demand for a product.

MARKET SHARE   A product's or service's piece of the total market for that product or service. Usually expressed in a percentage basis or on a point scale. Percentage of an industry's sales accounted for by a single firm. The percentage of product category sales realized by a specified product or brand.

MARKET TEST   *See* Test Market.

MARKUP   The amount added to the raw cost to cover overhead and profit in arriving at the selling price; the cost of doing business.

MARL   Sedimentary rock consisting of a mixture of clay and carbonate.

MARQUE *(FRANCE)*   Mark; generally used when referring to "trademark." *See* Trademark.

MARQUE D'ACHETEUR *(FRANCE)*   Used for private-label champagne, called "buyer's own brand" in the trade. This appears on some champagne labels as the initials **MA**.

MARQUE DÉPOSÉE *(FRANCE)*   A registered brand name. Also known as *déposée*. *See* Trademark.

MARRYING BOTTLES   *See* Consolidating Bottles.

MARRYING WINES   *See* Blending.

MARS SEEDLESS   A red grape variety developed in 1972 from a cross of Island Belle and Arkansas 1339. The flavor is strong and typically *Vitis labrusca* in character, resembling somewhat that of Campbell Early.

MARSALA *(ITALY)*   Marsala is both the name of a city in northwest Sicily and the name of a fortified wine made from a blend of grapes indigenous to Sicily.

Like sherry and port, marsala is a fortified wine; it bears some resemblance to madeira in that one or more of its constituents are cooked or heated during the processing.

The DOC law has set production rules for three versions of marsala. They are: *Marsala Fine, Marsala Superiore*, and *Marsala Vergine* or *Vergine Soleras*.

MARSALA FINE *(ITALY)*   A type of marsala wine that may be labeled as *oro, ambra*, or *rubino*, and made in the *secco, semisecco*, or *dolce* versions. This marsala must be aged for a minimum of one year in a barrel and have a minimum alcoholic content of 17 percent. It is the most heavily advertised and consumed of all marsala in the United States. It is often labeled I.P. for *Italia Particolare* or *Italia*.

MARSALA SUPERIORE (ITALY)   A type of marsala wine that may be labeled as *oro, ambra*, or *rubino*, and made in the *secco, semisecco*, or *dolce* versions. This marsala must be aged a minimum of two years in a barrel (if aged four years, may be labeled *riserva*) and have a minimum alcoholic content of 18 percent. It is made in basically two styles, dry and sweet. It is produced with the addition of a heated or cooked *must* (*cotto*), which gives the wine a delicate bitterness or caramel-like taste. This type of marsala is occasionally labeled as follows: L.P. (London Particular); S.O.M. (Superior Old Marsala); G.D. (Garibaldi Dolce).

MARSALA VERGINE OR VERGINE SOLERAS (ITALY)   A type of marsala wine that may be labeled as *oro, ambra*, or *rubino*, and made in the *secco* version. This is considered to be the finest marsala and is made by the *solera* system. By law, it cannot contain less than 18 percent alcohol. What makes marsala vergine so special is that it is made from the best wines of the vintage and must be aged a minimum of five years in a barrel before it can be sold by the producer (if aged ten years it may be labeled *riserva* or *stravecchio*). When properly stored, marsala *vergine* can be cellared for ten to fifteen years.

MARSANNE (FRANCE)   A white grape variety grown extensively in the Rhône Valley, where it is used in making some red Hermitage wines. It is also the solo grape in white Hermitage and white Saint-Joseph wines.

MARSIGLIANA (ITALY)   A red grape variety.

MARTHA   A white grape variety introduced in 1868 by Samuel Miller of Calmdale, Pennsylvania.

MARTIN METHOD   A device that detects fraudulent substances used in *chaptalization* of wines by means of nuclear magnetic resonance. *See* Chaptalization.

MARTINI   A cocktail consisting of gin or vodka and white dry vermouth, garnished with a lemon peel or green cocktail olive.

Martinez was the original name of this popular drink, first introduced in 1860 by Jerry Thomas in San Francisco's Occidental Hotel. The original recipe was considerably different from what we know today. It consisted of one jigger of gin, one wineglass of sweet red vermouth, a dash of bitters, and two dashes of maraschino liqueur. It was then shaken well and garnished with a lemon slice.

The drink was really popularized by James Bond movies in which the super spy requested his vodka martini be served to him "shaken, not stirred."

MARZEMINO (ITALY)   A red grape variety grown primarily in the Trentino-Alto Adige and Lombardy regions.

MÄRZENBIER (GERMANY)   A medium-strong, amber-colored beer originally brewed in March (hence its name), laid to rest during summer's heat, and generally drunk before October, with any remaining beer consumed at Oktoberfest.

MASCALISU (ITALY)   *See* Nerello Mascalese.

MASCULINE   Akin to big and full-bodied; opposite of feminine.

MASH   Produced when ground malt (sprouted barley) or any other material (including rice) capable of or intended for use in the fermenting process is soaked and then cooked in water to convert the soluble starches into sugar. The mash is then utilized in the making of beer, saké, and whiskey. Also known as *maische* and *moto*.

MASHING   The preparation of base ingredients for fermenting through the addition of water and sometimes heat. After cleaning and milling, coarse ground grain (meal) is mixed with water. This suspension is heated to bring the starch into solution (extraction), where the enzymes of the malt can break it down into grain sugar. This may be done by infusion mashing—the heating of uncooked grain with malt to conversion temperature—or, as in the United States, by cooking and then conversion. The grains in solution are cooked, often under pressure, to break down the cellulose walls and gelatinize and liquefy the starch for conversion to grain sugars by adding malt. The converted mash is pumped to the fermenter or, in the case of Scotch or malt beverages, the screened solution (*wort*) is drawn off for the addition of yeast in the fermentation process. The fermented mash yields distiller's beer, the low-alcohol solution distilled for beverage spirits.

MASH RAKE   A tool occasionally used in beer- or whiskey-making as a stirring rod or device to stir or mix the mash and break up solid matter.

MASH TUN   A large copper or stainless steel vessel where hot water and malt (adjunct cereals are often used) are mixed together. A precisely controlled time and temperature cycle converts the starches in the malt to fermentable sugars. When complete, the liquid is called *wort*. *See* Lauter Tun and Maischbottich.

MASSASOIT   A red grape variety developed by Edward S. Rogers of Salem, Massachusetts. Formerly known as *Rogers 3*.

MASSERIA (ITALY)   Similar to a *fattoria*. *See* Fattoria.

MASS SELECTION   Consists of visually identifying and marking healthy and productive grapevine stumps in the vineyards and removing stems to serve as reproductive material. Also known as *field selection*.

MASTER BLENDER   One whose responsibility it is to maintain the integrity of a company's signature taste. In order to keep his nose and taste buds in top form, the master blender lives under the rigid routine of an athlete. His is a difficult job: he must be able to discern, by taste and smell, the year that the grapes of a certain wine were grown and from which sections of the region the grapes came—even from which section within a section. Since the same section may produce quite a different variety of wines in different years, the taster's job is as much an art as a science. He must, in effect, analyze with one sniff the life history of each sample brought to him.

MASTIC   *See* Masticha.

MASTICHA (GREECE)   A sweetened aniseed liqueur with a distilled spirit base, flavored with *mastic*, a sap or resin from the mastic bush or shrub (or sap from trees of the cashew family). It is made primarily on the island of Chios; however, it originated on the mainland of Greece. *See* Anise-Based Spirits and Ouzo.

MATARO   *See* Mourvèdre.

MATCHSTICK   An undesirable odor and/or taste reminiscent of burnt matches, derived from an excess of sulfur dioxide added to a wine. Fairly common with newly bottled wines, with time it will usually dissipate. *See* Sulfur Dioxide.

M

MATCHSTICK

MATHASER BIERSTADT   The world's largest beer garden, founded in 1901 in Munich. It contains sixteen restaurants and has room for 5,200 people.

MATT (GERMANY)   *See* Flat.

MATTONE (ITALY)   Brick-red.

MATURE   *See* Maturity.

MATURE WINE   *See* Maturity.

MATURING   The process of aging a wine, beer, or distilled spirit, either in wooden barrels, stainless steel, or glass, until it is in peak condition and ready for consumption. *See* Maturity.

MATURING CELLAR   *See* Wine Cellar.

MATURITY   The stage in the aging of wines, beers, or distilled spirits when they have developed all of their characteristic qualities to full perfection. Also known as *ausgebaut, maduro, mature, mature wine, maturing, maturo, mûr,* and *vinho maduro. See* Aging, Barrel Aging, Ripe, and Ripe for Bottling.

MATURITY   The stage of fruit development when it has reached the maximum quality point and is ready for harvest. *See* Ripeness.

MATURO (ITALY)   *See* Maturity.

MAUER (GERMANY)   Wall.

MAURY   A red grape variety.

MÄUSELN (GERMANY)   *See* Mousy.

MAUZAC BLANC (FRANCE)   A white grape variety grown primarily in Languedoc.

MAVRO (GREECE)   Black.

MAVRODAPHNE (GREECE)   A red grape variety responsible for the ever-popular red sweet dessert wine of the same name that has some similarities to port.

MAVRON   A red grape variety native to Cypress.

MAVRUD (BULGARIA)   A red grape variety that produces wines that are fairly robust, but unfortunately tend to oxidize easily.

MAYOLET (ITALY)   A red grape variety grown in the Valle d'Aosta region.

MAYORAL (SPAIN)   *See* Chef de Troupe.

MAY WINE   A festive German white wine punch, often sweetened, containing strawberries and perhaps other fruit, that is flavored with woodruff, an aromatic herb. Also known as *maiwein. See* Woodruff.

MAZER   An ancient wooden drinking vessel traditionally used throughout the fourteenth and fifteenth centuries for the consumption of mead. The container was frequently carved from hard wood, such as maple or oak, and featured two handles.

MAZUELO (SPAIN)   *See* Carignan.

MEAD   A clear, pale, or golden-colored wine, made from heather or clover honey, that can be dry or sweet. It cannot contain more than 14 percent alcohol, but in practice most mead is between 8 and 12 percent alcohol by volume. It may not be flavored or colored and distilled spirits cannot be used. Mead is a very ancient, mildly intoxicating beverage that was quite popular in England and northern Europe during the fifth and sixth centuries A.D. Also known as *beeswine, honey wine, pyments*, and *sack mead*. *See* Hippocras, Hydromel, Mazer, Metheglin, and Melomel.

MEATY   *See* Chewy.

MECHAGE (FRANCE)   *See* Sulfur Stick.

MECHANICAL BEVERAGE CONTROL SYSTEM   An automated distilled spirit system that is programmed to record the number of drinks dispensed from a bottle as well as to regulate the size of each drink. Also known as *metered pour*.

MECHANICAL HARVESTER   A mechanical harvester is approximately eighteen feet in length, twelve feet in width, and weighs about 18,000 pounds. The driver of this machine sits on the top and expertly guides the gentle giant through the vineyards, straddling each row of grapevines as the *pivotal pulsator* (or beater arm) removes the ripe grapes from the grapevines. As the harvester moves down the rows of grapevines, the pulsator or *trunk shaker* vigorously shakes the trunks on the grapevines, causing the grapes at the top of the grapevines to drop into the machine below. At the same time, the curved tips of the four to six pivotal strikers, which consist of a double bank of flexible horizontal rods, reach up under the foliage canopy of the grapevine and strike the ends of the cordon, or cane, ejecting the fruit from the ends of the canes. The combination of the pulsator and the pivotal strikers gives maximum efficiency in harvesting all of the ripe grapes on each grapevine.

When the grapes drop into the harvester, they travel along a conveyor belt past suction blowers that expel any leaves that may have entered the machine along with the grapes. This minimizes possible green leaf off-flavors and bitterness, which characterized some of the earliest mechanical harvester experiments. The grapes then move up the conveyor to the top of the machine, where an extension of the conveyor carries them across the row to a gondola moving parallel to the harvester. The mechanical harvester picks an average of one acre of grapes (three to five tons) per hour. The daily tonnage of grapes picked by one machine is equal to that of thirty manual laborers.

The mechanical harvester was first developed in the early 1950s by University of California, Davis, agricultural engineer Lloyd Lamouria while working with viticulturist Albert Winkler. However, it wasn't until 1969 or 1970 that Mirassou Vineyards of San Jose, California, became the first winery to use the harvester on a commercial scale.

MECHANICAL IMPACT   Mechanical impact is contact of a glass with another object—a spoon, a beer tap, or another glass. This contact can cause minute abrasions that are invisible to the eye. These abrasions weaken the glass and make it more susceptible to breakage from further impact or thermal shock. Any severely abraded glass must be removed from service.

MEDAGLIA (ITALY)   Medal. *See* Medallions.

MEDALLA (SPAIN)   Medal. *See* Medallions.

MEDALLIONS   Tiny oval or circular designs (medals) embossed on the necks of some wine bottles or carafes. Originally, Italian winemakers used lead medallions to certify the proper volume of a bottle. The glass version serves no official function today, except perhaps to provide a better grip. Also known as *medaglia* and *medalla*.

M

MEDALLIONS

MEDIA *(SPAIN)*   A barrel equal to one-half butt. *See* Barrel.

MEDICINAL   Describes a wine, beer, or distilled spirit having the odor or taste of medicine.

MEDIO SECO *(SPAIN)*   *See* Semidry Wine.

MEDIUM-BODIED   A loosely defined descriptor meaning average in extract, alcohol, aroma, and flavor.

MEDIUM-DRY   *See* Semidry Wine.

MEDIUM-SWEET   *See* Semisweet.

MÉDOC *(FRANCE)*   The largest and most important wine district of Bordeaux and possibly the greatest producer of red wines in the world. Médoc is named after an ancient Celtic tribe that once lived there.

Bordeaux is divided into many districts, most of which are called *communes*. The four most important communes, those that make up the Médoc district, are located on the west side of the Gironde River. The Médoc produces dry red wines, with only one exception: a white wine of Château Margaux. The communes from north to south are Saint-Estèphe, Pauillac, Saint-Julien, and Margaux. On the right bank of the Dordogne River are the districts of Saint-Émilion and Pomerol, both of which produce only dry red wines. South of Médoc, along the Garonne River in the capital of Bordeaux lies the Graves district, where dry red and white wines are produced. Farther south is the district of Sauternes, noted for its extremely sweet white wines and a few dry white wines as well.

MÉDOC NOIR *(HUNGARY)*   *See* Merlot.

MEIODOCE *(PORTUGAL)*   *See* Semisweet.

MEIOSECO *(PORTUGAL)*   *See* Semidry Wine.

MELANCONIUM FULIGINEAUM   *See* Bitter Rot.

MÉLANGE *(AUSTRIA)*   Half coffee, half milk.

MELK *(NORWAY)*   *See* Milk.

MELLOW   An organoleptic term that refers to the way an alcoholic beverage feels in the mouth; pleasant, soft, and smooth, without any harsh edges. Also known as *amaduré-cido, blando, creamy, maçio, milde, moelleux, myelódis*, and *soft*.

MELLOW   A term with no legal meaning, often used to describe some red jug table wines from California that usually display distinct sweetness.

MELNIK *(BULGARIA)*   *See* Shiroka Melnishka Losa.

MELODY   A white grape variety developed in 1965 from a cross of Seyval and Geneva White 5 (Pinot Blanc and Ontario) at the State Experimental Station in Geneva, New York.

MELOMEL   Mead that is blended with fruit juices other than apple. *See* Mead.

MELON D'ARBOIS *(FRANCE)*   The local name in the Jura region for the Chardonnay grape.

MELON DE BOURGOGNE *(FRANCE)*   A white grape variety grown primarily in the Loire Valley. Most of the wines of the Loire are sold under district or village appellations such as Anjou, Pouilly Fumé, Saumur, and Vouvray. There is one notable exception and that is Muscadet, which is sold under its grape varietal name. Technically speaking, the Muscadet grape is the Melon de Bourgogne, which was transplanted from Burgundy by order of King Louis XIV in 1639. In 1709 a severe frost decimated the vineyards around Nantes. A search for a new grapevine that would withstand the killing winter frosts resulted in the importation from Burgundy of a hardier grape, Melon de Bourgogne, later renamed Muscadet. *See* Muscadet.

MEMBRANE   The surface covering the inner wall of a cell. It plays an active part in exchanges between cells and their surrounding medium.

MENCIA *(SPAIN)*   A red grape variety.

MENDOCINO   A wine-producing region located north of San Francisco, California, near Ukiah, noted for its production of Cabernet Sauvignon, Zinfandel, and other red wines.

MENDOZA   An important wine-producing region in Argentina.

MENISCUS   Dividing line between water and air. It is the curved upper surface of a column of liquid; as a result of capillary action. It is convex when the walls of the container are dry, concave when they are wet. The lowest point on this curve is always read as the volume, never the upper edge. *See* Hydrometer.

MENTHES *(FRANCE)*   Mint; especially crème de menthe. *See* Mint.

MERAGUS *(ITALY)*   *See* Nuragus.

MERCAPTANS   A slightly sour, particularly objectionable, onion- or garlic-like, skunky, or even rubbery smell of ethyl and methyl alcohol reacting with hydrogen sulfide. It is also reminiscent of H_2S (hydrogen sulfide) or a gas leak. The odor is due to the breakdown of sulfur dioxide, originally used as a preservative.

MERCHANDISING   Sales promotion as a comprehensive function including market research, development of new products, coordination of manufacture and marketing, and effective advertising and selling.

MERCHANDISING ALLOWANCE   Where legal, promotional funds used to support distributor programs such as shelf improvement, increased distribution efforts, special on-premise programs, and other programs.

MERCURIALES *(FRANCE)*   Opening wine prices offered by growers to *négociants* or other parties, particularly in the Bordeaux trade.

MERCUREY *(FRANCE)*   A commune in the Côte Chalonnaise district of Burgundy immediately to the south of the Côte d'Or. It yields some good wines that resemble those from farther north. Most Mercurey is red and is produced entirely from the Pinot Noir grape.

The name Mercurey originates from a Roman temple dedicated to the god Mercury (557 A.D.), the site of which is now occupied by a windmill.

MERITAGE   A term, originating in California, denoting those wines made entirely from a blend of the traditional Bordeaux grape varieties. It can be the winery's best wine of its type.

No single variety may make up more than 90 percent of the blend.

Both red and white Meritage wines must contain a minimum of two or more of the accepted grape types listed below.

Meritage red grape varieties are Cabernet Sauvignon, Merlot, Cabernet Franc, Petit Verdot, Malbec, Carmenère, Gros Verdot, and St-Macaire.

Meritage white grape varieties are Sauvignon Blanc, Sémillon, and Muscadelle (also known as *Sauvignon Vert*).

MERLOT   A red grape variety grown worldwide. It is one of the predominant grape varieties of the Bordeaux region of France. In the Médoc and Graves district, it is blended in significant amounts with Cabernet Sauvignon and Cabernet Franc; in the districts of Pomerol and Saint-Émilion it constitutes the predominant grape in the wines. Merlot is also used straight as a varietal in many parts of the world.

Merlot gives scented, fruity wines, smelling very much of raspberries and cherries, with hints of green olive and cinnamon. It is a silky and soft, medium-bodied wine with a good varietal character of spicy cherries, raspberries, and plums, which is responsible for much of the softness and suppleness of the wines in which it appears. Merlot is used extensively to soften and tame the more assertive bitter and tannic Cabernet Sauvignon. Merlot has less tannin than Cabernet Sauvignon berries and thinner skins, and because they are low in malic acid, the resulting wine is softer. When blended with Cabernet Sauvignon, the resulting wine develops faster, shortening aging requirements. In 1968 Louis M. Martini Winery of California bottled the first Merlot as a separate varietal. Also known as *Médoc Noir*.

MERLOT BLANC (FRANCE)   A white grape variety grown primarily in Fronsac, Bourg, and especially Blaye, in Bordeaux.

MERSIN (TURKEY)   An orange-based liqueur, white in color.

MESCAL   *See* Tequila.

MESEGUERA (SPAIN)   A white grape variety grown primarily in Valencia.

MESO-CLIMATE   The climate of a viticultural zone or subzone, generally determined by conditions other than heat summation.

MESSWEIN (GERMANY)   *See* Sacramental Wines.

METABISULFITE   Either in potassium or sodium form, when mixed with water, produces sulfur dioxide gas, which is used in wine- and beer-making as a sterilant and antioxidant. *See* Sulfur Dioxide.

METABOLISM   The sum of the processes by which food is manufactured and broken down for energy gain.

METALLIC   Describes an acrid, tinny, unpleasant taste or sensation detected in some beers or in low-alcohol wines. The taste is sometimes acquired through contact with metal during the fermenting or aging process. Sometimes beer will take on metallic flavors, even in a bottle. Also known as *metallico*.

METALLICO (ITALY)   *See* Metallic.

METAMERISM   A change in the observed color of wine, depending on the nature of the illuminating light.

METER   A metric unit of length, one meter being equal to 39.37 inches.

M

M E R L O T

METERED POUR *See* Mechanical Beverage Control System.

METHANOL *See* Methyl Alcohol.

METHEGLIN A Welsh mead spiced with aromatic herbs. *See* Mead.

MÉTHODE CARBONIQUE *(FRANCE)* *See* Carbonic Maceration.

MÉTHODE CHAMPENOISE *(FRANCE)* A secondary fermentation method utilized to produce perhaps the finest quality sparkling wines and champagnes. It was pioneered in France during the nineteenth century and is the only method that can legally be used to produce French champagnes. The entire process of a *secondary fermentation* takes place in the same stoppered bottle, followed by the time-honored method of *riddling* and *disgorging.* Following this, a shipping *dosage* is added; then the champagne is additionally aged prior to final shipment. It is also known as *fermented in* **this bottle,** *méthode traditionnelle,* and *metodo classico.*

MÉTHODE TRADITIONNELLE *(SPAIN)* A synonym for *méthode champenoise.*

METHUEN TREATY A treaty made between Great Britain and Portugal in 1703. It provided preferential treatment for Portuguese wines by requiring French wine producers to pay one-third more duty than the Portuguese. In return, the English were permitted to export wool into Portugal free of duty. The treaty was terminated in 1866.

METHUSELAH An oversized bottle equal in capacity to eight 750-milliliter bottles or six liters (202.8 ounces). It has the same capacity as an Imperial and is used exclusively for champagne.

Methuselah was an ancient patriarch of Babylonia who distinguished himself by his incredible longevity, living 969 years. In addition (according to legend), he sired many sons and daughters and was Noah's grandfather.

METHYL ALCOHOL A colorless, volatile, flammable, and poisonous liquid obtained by the destructive distillation of wood and synthesized chiefly from carbon monoxide and hydrogen. It is mainly used in fuels, solvents, antifreeze, and so on. Also known as *methanol* and *wood alcohol.*

METHYL ANTHRANILATE *See* Foxy and *Vitis Labrusca.*

METHYLATED SPIRITS Ethyl alcohol made unfit for consumption by the addition of methyl alcohol.

METODO CHARMAT *(ITALY)* *See* Charmat Method.

METODO CLASSICO *(ITALY)* The official name by which all *méthode champenoise*-produced sparkling wines are known. It became effective with the release of the 1991 vintage. *See* Méthode Champenoise.

METRIC SYSTEM A universal system of measure, the units being multiples or divisions of ten, one hundred, one thousand, and so on.

METRIC TON The equivalent of one thousand kilograms, 2,204.62 pounds, or approximately ten quintals of wine. Also known as *tonelada.*

MEUNIER A red grape variety grown primarily in Champagne, France, where, due to its neutral character, it is blended with Chardonnay and Pinot Noir to form the basis of most champagnes. Also known as *Müllerrebe, Pinot Meunier,* and *Schwarzriesling.*

M

MEUNIER

MEUNEL OAK   Oak, suitable for use in barrels, from Poland and Lithuania.

MEURSAULT *(FRANCE)*   A white wine made from the Chardonnay grape in the heart of the Côte de Beaune in Burgundy. Meursault is the second largest wine-producing commune of the Côte de Beaune, covering more than one thousand acres. Meursault gets its name from the Roman Legions, who dubbed it *muris saltus*, "the mouse's jump" in Latin. Time and the Gallic accent corrupted *muris saltus* to Meursault.

MEYNIEU 6   A white grape variety, originally developed in Bordeaux, now grown to a small degree in the Upper Midwest of the United States.

MEZCAL   Also spelled *mescal*. *See* Tequila.

MÉZESFEHÉR *(HUNGARY)*   A white grape variety.

MEZZO SECCO *(ITALY)*   *See* Semidry Wine.

MEZZULA *(ITALY)*   The small opening in a large barrel or tank used for cleaning the container.

MG   Abbreviation for milligram, a metric unit of weight; one thousand milligrams equals one gram.

MICHET *(ITALY)*   A red grape variety, a subvariety of the Nebbiolo grape, grown primarily in the Piedmont region.

MICKEY   *See* Mickey Finn.

MICKEY FINN   Whiskey or other distilled spirits to which a powerful narcotic or purgative knockout drop has been added. It is given to unsuspecting persons so that they can be robbed. Mickey Finn was a Chicago bartender famous for this concoction. Also known as a *mickey*.

MICROBREWERY   A small brewery of modest size and production, at one time brewing less than fifteen thousand barrels. Microbreweries produce small, hand-crafted batches of beer. *See* Brewpub.

MICROCLIMATE   The climate of a small distinct area that has either slightly or greatly varying degrees of elevation, fog intrusion, humidity, proximity to water, susceptibility to frost, precipitation, temperature changes, and wind. Individually or collectively, these elements affect the quality of a wine to a lesser or greater degree.

MICROCUTTING   A fragment of a stem containing a preexistent bud; the microcutting is removed from a mini-plant grown *in vitro* and planted in an aseptic nutrient medium to produce an identical mini-plant.

MICROFILTRATION   Very low pressure (generally from five to fifteen psi) semipermeable membrane process used in the separation of particles in the .05 to 5.0 micrometer range from aqueous solutions such as wine. *See* Filtering.

MICRO-FLORA   Colonies of wine yeast and smaller quantities of other yeast and bacteria that collect on the skins of the grape before harvest, often referred to as *bloom*. *See* Bloom and Cutin.

MICRON   A millionth of a meter (about 0.00004 inch).

MICROPOROUS   Describes a type of membrane or other material able to filter out yeast.

MIDDLE CUTS   *See* Hearts.

MIDDLE LIQUORS   *See* Hearts.

MIDDLE RHINE *(GERMANY)*   *See* Mittelrhein.

MIDI *(FRANCE)*   A major grape-growing area in the south along the Mediterranean Sea; it produces mostly coarse, highly alcoholic wines. This vast area is now known as the Languedoc-Roussillon. *See* Languedoc and Roussillon.

MILCH *(GERMANY)*   *See* Milk.

MILDE *(GERMANY)*   *See* Mellow.

MILDEW   A serious cryptogamic (fungal) disease that attacks grapevines in rainy or damp seasons, crippling both green tissue and fruit. Mildew must be treated with fungicide sprays. The two most basic types are *downy* and *powdery* mildew.

MILK   A liquid beverage coming from cows, goats, sheep, mares, camels, yaks, lamas, and even reindeer, that is meant for human consumption. Also known as *lait, latte, leche, leite, melk, milch*, and *süt*.

MILK SHAKE   A drink containing milk, flavored ice cream, and ice.

MILK STOUT   A low-alcohol, medium-sweet beer with a high lactic acid content and dark color. *See* Stout.

MILLÉRANDAGE *(FRANCE)*   *See* Shot Berries.

MILLESIMATO *(ITALY)*   A sparkling wine from a favorable harvest, vintage dated.

MILLÉSIME *(FRANCE)*   *See* Année.

MILLÉSIMÉ *(FRANCE)*   *See* Vintage Wine.

MILLIGRAM (MG)   A metric unit of weight; one thousand milligrams equal one gram.

MILLILITERS (ML)   A metric unit of volume; one thousand milliliters equal one liter.

MILLING   The mechanical process by which whole grain is reduced to suitable size, with the outer cellulosic wall broken to expose more starch surface to the cooking and conversion of starch to sugars.

MILLOT   *See* Léon Millot.

MIND YOUR PS AND QS   In the old alehouses before cash registers were invented, there was a chalkboard where the barkeep would put chalk marks to keep track of how many pints (p's) and quarts (q's) you consumed. When you were ready to leave the pub, the barkeep would add up the chalk marks and tell you how much you owed. To make sure that the barkeep remembered this task, the owner would often tell him to mind his p's and q's.

MINERAL OIL   An oil spread on the surface of wine in storage tanks to prevent the access of air that would cause oxidation. Rarely used today.

MINERAL WATER   Natural still or sparkling water that comes from the earth. All mineral water contains some minerals, but to be classified a "natural mineral water" in Europe (the standards were set by the European Common Market in 1980 and took effect in 1984) the water must have at least five hundred milligrams of minerals per liter *as it flows from the ground*. The minerals are collected in the water as it travels over great distances through geological formations. The minerals are thus dissolved and become an integral part of the water. Minerals are thought to be more readily absorbed by the body when in solution than as a component of solid food.

In most countries of Western Europe where bottled mineral waters are a common household beverage, no drinking water can be classified as a "natural mineral water" unless it contains dissolved minerals in its natural state. Italian law requires that mineral water be bottled only at its source. In Italy, if the mineral water has a mineral content under five hundred milligrams per liter, it is considered to be of low mineral content and must be classified as *oligominerale*.

The United States federal government has not established a formal definition for mineral water. In 1979, however, California set a minimum standard of total dissolved solids for mineral water sold in that state at five hundred milligrams per liter. This means that a water cannot be called a mineral water unless it has at least five hundred milligrams of minerals dissolved in it.

The mineral content of bottled waters varies from state to state, country to country, and producer to producer. In addition to being basically low in sodium and virtually calorie- and carbohydrate-free, mineral water contains many trace elements and minerals, which also vary in their interest to consumers. Some producers are even flavoring their mineral waters with natural citrus extracts such as mandarin orange, lemon, and lime.

Among the elements and minerals in mineral water are aluminum, ammonia, bicarbonate, boron, bromide, calcium, carbonate, chloride, chromium, cobalt, copper, fluoride, iodine, iron, lithium, magnesium, manganese, nickel, nitrate, phosphorus, potassium, selenium, silica, sodium, strontium, sulfates, and zinc. Also known as *acqua minerale* and *sprudel*.

MINIATURE BOTTLE   A small bottle usually containing less than two ounces. Also known as *airline bottles* or *nips*.

MINI-BAR   *See* In-Room Bar.

MINNELLA BIANCA (ITALY)   A white grape variety grown primarily in Sicily.

MINOR   Any person under the legal drinking or purchasing age.

MINOR'S SEEDLING   *See* Venango.

MINT   A term suggesting the odor or taste of fresh green mint, noted especially in some Cabernet Sauvignon and Zinfandel wines. The odor and flavor of mint can range in intensity and type from eucalyptus to peppermint, spearmint, or wintergreen. In the case of wintergreen, the odor is *methyl salicylate* (methyl alcohol + salicylic acid). Also known as *menthe* and *minty*.

MINT JULEP   *See* Julep.

MINTY   Suggesting the odor or taste of fresh mint. *See* Mint.

MINUIT, PETER   After purchasing New Amsterdam, he established America's first public brewery there in 1622. *See* New Amsterdam.

MIRABELLE (FRANCE)   A fruit brandy made from small, golden-yellow plums with a highly aromatic perfume that generally come from Alsace as well as some Central European countries.

MIROIR (FRANCE)   The bottom of a champagne cork, often stamped with the name of the Champagne house. *See* Manche and Rondelle.

MISE (FRANCE)   The bottling.

MISE D'ORIGINE (FRANCE)   Bottled by the shipper.

MISE EN BOUTEILLES AU CHÂTEAU (FRANCE)   Estate bottled at the designated château. *See* Château-Bottled.

MISE EN BOUTEILLES AU DOMAINE (FRANCE)   Estate bottled at the designated château. *See* Château-Bottled.

MISE EN BOUTEILLES DANS NOS CAVES (FRANCE)   A term which means that the wine was bottled "in our cellar"; however, it is not a legally defined term and has no real significance.

MISE EN BOUTEILLES DANS LA REGION DE PRODUCTION (FRANCE)   An ambiguous term, literally meaning "bottled in the production region," that is not legally defined and has no real significance.

MISE EN BOUTEILLES À LA PROPRIÉTÉ (FRANCE)   Bottled by the proprietor, shipper, or négociant.

MISE EN MASSE (FRANCE)   The arrangement of sparkling wine bottles neck down after the riddling process for longer aging "on the yeast." Also known as *en masse*.

MISE EN PLACE (FRANCE)   A place for everything and everything in its place. Everything set up and ready for business.

MISE SUR POINTE (FRANCE)   *See* Sur Pointe.

MISH   A red grape variety named for W.M. Mish, who found it growing near Washington, North Carolina, in 1846.

MISKET DE SLIVEN (BULGARIA)   *See* Red Misket.

MISSION   A white grape variety that was extensively grown in California during the eighteenth and nineteenth centuries, when it was used primarily to make sweet table wines, notably angelica. It was originally planted by the Jesuit priest Father Juan Ugarte at a mission in southern California in 1697. Although the grape is grown extensively in Argentina, Chile, and other Spanish-speaking countries, where it is known as *Criolla* or *País*, it is believed that grapevine cuttings were brought to South America from Europe in the 1500s.

MISSOURI RIESLING   *See* Elvira.

MISTELA (SPAIN)   *See* Mistelle.

MISTELLA (ITALY)   *See* Mistelle.

MISTELLE   Grape juice in which fermentation has been arrested or prevented by the addition of brandy or other distilled spirits. The result is a wine with a natural residual sugar and alcoholic content of approximately 15 percent. The process is called *mutage*. Some mistelles are used for sweetening wines in making apéritifs and vermouths; others stand alone as apéritifs. Some examples of mistelles are Pineau des Charentes and Ratafia de Champagne. Also known as *dulce apagado*, *mistela*, *mistella*, *muté*, *muting*, and *sifone*. *See* Back Blending, Concia, Ratafia, and Surdo.

MIT DOPPELSCHLAG (AUSTRIA)   Coffee with double whipped cream.

MIT SCHLAGOBERS (AUSTRIA)   Coffee with whipped cream.

MITTELRHEIN (GERMANY)   One of thirteen qualitätswein (quality) grape-growing regions, located along the Rhine River in the northwestern part of Germany. The region is famous for its spectacular vineyards on the steep Rhine slopes. Its wines, almost exclusively white, are hearty and stylish. Major grape varieties are Johannisberg Riesling, Müller-Thurgau, and Kerner. Also known as *Middle Rhine*.

MIX   To put or blend together ingredients into a single mass or compound.

MIXED DRINK   *See* Cocktail.

MIXER   An electric appliance used to mix or blend together ingredients for certain types of cocktails instead of hand-shaking them.

MIXING CUP   *See* Hand Shaker.

MIXING GLASS   *See* Hand Shaker.

MIXING STEEL   *See* Hand Shaker.

MIXOLOGIST   *See* Bartender.

MIXOLOGY   The art of following a recipe or formula to produce a standard and consistent drink according to specifications. An experienced mixologist can be compared to a chemist or a chef, producing perfect-tasting and eye-appealing drinks every time. Unfortunately, mixology is slowly becoming a lost art, for most cocktails are premixed and the popularity of "standard drinks" is also fading.

ML   Abbreviation for milliliter, a metric unit of volume; one thousand milliliters equal one liter.

M-L   An abbreviation for malolactic fermentation. *See* Malolactic Fermentation.

MOCKTAILS   Any cocktail or other type of beverage that is prepared without the addition of an alcoholic beverage. Also known as *virgin drinks*.

MOELLEUX (FRANCE)   *See* Mellow.

MOG   Material other than grapes (birds, bird nests, excessive leaves, stems, canes, etc.).

MOKKA (AUSTRIA)   Strong black coffee served in *demitasse* cups.

MOLAR BLANCO (SPAIN)   A white grape variety.

MOLAR NEGRO (SPAIN)   A red grape variety.

MOLASSES   A thick, usually dark brown syrup produced by boiling sugar, which evaporates the water, crystallizing the sugar. Also known as *blackstrap molasses*.

MOLDS   Filamentous fungi that are found both in the vineyard and in the winery. They commonly produce large numbers of spores, which explains their wide distribution in nature. Mold growth often is observed on walls, wooden barrels, and other damp surfaces in the winery. Their development in wine or on wine contact surfaces may result in off-flavors. *See* Mycelia and Torula.

MOLDY   An organoleptic term desribing to undesirable odors (mustiness) or flavors, usually among wines made from grapes infected with mold, or wines that have been stored or aged in stale, unclean wooden barrels that have harbored mold. Also known as *schimmelgeschmack*. *See* Bottle Stink, Mousy, and Musty.

MOLECULE The smallest particle of a compound that can exist in a free state and still retain the characteristics of the compound.

MOLETTE (FRANCE) A white grape variety grown primarily in Seyssel, where it is mainly used in making sparkling wines.

MOLINARA (ITALY) A red grape variety grown primarily in the Veneto region, where it is used (along with several other grape varieties) in making Bardolino and Valpolicella wines. The name Molinara, derived from the vernacular *Mulinara*, means that when the grapes are in bloom they seem pruinose, or dusted with flour. Molinara is also known as *Brepon, Rossanella*, and *Rossara*. In the Bardolino area, it also bears the name *Rossone*.

MOLINERA GORDA *See* Red Málaga.

MOLISE (ITALY) The youngest wine-producing region; originally it was part of Abruzzo, but a change in the laws in 1963 made it a separate region. Molise is bordered to the north by Abruzzo, to the west by Latium and Campania, and to the south by Apulia. Its east coast border is the Adriatic Sea.

In 1983 these wines gained DOC status: Biferno Bianco, Biferno Rosso, Biferno Rosato, Pentro di Isernia Rosato, Pentro di Isernia Bianco, and Pentro di Isernia Rosso.

MONACA (ITALY) *See* Monica.

MONASTRELL (SPAIN) A red grape variety. Also known as *Morastel*.

MONBADON (FRANCE) *See* Burger.

MONBAZILLAC (FRANCE) A fairly sweet, golden-colored dessert wine produced in the Bergerac region in the southwest.

MONDEUSE NOIRE A red grape variety grown primarily in Savoie, France. In Veneto and Friuli-Venezia Giulia, Italy, the Mondeuse Noire is known as *Refosco*. Also known as *Crabb's Black Burgundy, Petite Pinot*, and *Refsko*.

MONFERRATO (ITALY) A major wine-producing district south of the Po Valley in Piedmont, noted for its production of Barbera wines.

MONICA (ITALY) A red grape variety grown in Sardinia. Among the wines produced from it are Monica di Sardegna and Monica di Cagliari. Also known as *Monaca, Munica, Niedda, Pascali*, and *Passale*.

MONOECIOUS *See* Hermaphroditic.

MONOPOLE (FRANCE) A wine blended by a merchant-shipper and given a brand or trademark name. It is the French term for *monopoly*.

MONOPOLY STATE *See* Control State.

MONTAGNE A tavern on Lower Broadway in Manhattan, New York, which was the headquarters of the Sons of Liberty and the site where the Revolutionary War was planned.

MONTAGNE DE REIMS (FRANCE) The premium vineyard zone for growing of Pinot Noir grapes in the Champagne region.

M

MONTAGNY *(FRANCE)*   A commune in the Côte Chalonnaise of Burgundy that produces very fine white wines from the Chardonnay and Pinot Blanc grapes.

MONTALCINO *(ITALY)*   A picturesque and very hilly section of Tuscany situated approximately twenty-five miles southeast of Siena and Chianti Classico, approximately 1,600 feet above sea level. It is bordered by the Orcia River to the south and the Ombrone River to the west. The terrain is comprised of a variety of soil types, mainly a mixture of clay with some carbonate, lime, and gravel. Montalcino is best known for its long-lived red DOCG wine, Brunello di Montalcino, made from the Sangiovese Grosso grape variety. Montalcino also grows some Moscadello di Montalcino grapes. Famous in ancient times, this was one of the most distinguished wines of Tuscany; slightly sparkling, straw-colored, with an intense aromatic bouquet and the sweet and distinctive characteristic flavor of the Moscato grape. *See* Brunello di Montalcino, Rosso di Montalcino, and Sangiovese Grosso.

MONTEFIASCONE *(ITALY)*   A vineyard town on Lake Bolsena in Latium, famous for its production of Est! Est!! Est!!! di Montefiascone, a dry or semidry white wine made from a blend of Trebbiano Toscano, Malvasia, and Rossetto grapes.

MONTEFIORE   A red grape variety.

MONTELLATO *(ITALY)*   A red grape variety.

MONTEPULCIANO *(ITALY)*   A red grape variety grown primarily in Abruzzo; some is also grown in Apulia, Marches, and Umbria. Also the name of a province in Tuscany famous for its production of Vino Nobile di Montepulciano, a red wine.

MONTEPULCIANO D'ABRUZZO *(ITALY)*   A red DOC wine made from a blend of Montepulciano and Sangiovese grape varieties, produced in the South-central regions of Abruzzo.

MONTEREY RIESLING   *See* Sylvaner.

MONTHÉLIE *(FRANCE)*   A small red wine commune in the Côte de Beaune, just above Volnay.

MONTICELLO   A red grape variety introduced in 1973 from a cross of (Fredonia and Niagara) and (Fredonia and Athens) at the Virginia Polytechnic Institute.

MONTILLA *(SPAIN)*   An unfortified sherry-style wine produced primarily from Pedro Ximénez grapes in the villages of Montilla and Los Moriles in the hills south of Córdoba, one hundred miles inland from Jerez. Although most Montillas are dry, some small amounts of sweeter Montilla are made. The three basic styles of Montilla are *fino, amontillado,* and *oloroso.*

MONTLOUIS *(FRANCE)*   A wine-producing commune located along the Loire Valley, which produces wines exclusively from the Chenin Blanc grape. Sparkling wines are also made.

MONTONICO BIANCO *(ITALY)*   A white grape variety grown primarily in Sicily.

MONTRACHET *(FRANCE)*   The most noted vineyard of the Côte de Beaune in Burgundy, straddling the communes of Puligny and Chassagne. Montrachet, made entirely from the Chardonnay grape, is considered by many to be the finest dry white wine in the world.

Translated, its name means "bald hill," because the barren hilltop is uncovered and literally bald today. Originally, one man owned the entire vineyard and called it *Le Montrachet*. Upon his death the land was divided up among his survivors. His eldest son or "chevalier" received a part renamed Chevalier-Montrachet. Another part went to his illegitimate son (whom he acknowledged as a youthful discretion), hence the name Bâtard-Montrachet, and finally the last part to his unmarried daughters (whom he believed were still virgins), Les Pucelles.

French novelist and dramatist Alexandre Dumas (1802–1870) was known to have declared that "Le Montrachet should be drunk kneeling, with one's head bared."

MONTU (ITALY)   A white grape variety.

MOONSHINE   A homemade distilled product, made from virtually any ingredients, which is extremely high in alcohol and quite rough; originally from the southern part of the United States. Moonshine is also a group of non-tax paid distilled spirits that are sold illicitly.

As early as 1796, *white brandy* smuggled on the coasts of Kent and Sussex, England, and gin smuggled on the north of Yorkshire were known as *moonshine*. Brought to the United States by immigrants from the British Isles, the term came into general usage with the passing of the years and the spread of the illicit distiller's art. Also known as *shine* or *white lightning*.

MOONSHINER   One who produces *moonshine*.

MOORED   A red grape variety developed from a cross of Fredonia and Athens, introduced in 1973.

MOORE'S DIAMOND   *See* Diamond.

MOOR'S HEAD   The collecting coil on a pot still; it collects the vapors prior to the cooling process.

MORASTEL (SPAIN)   *See* Monastrell.

MORBIDO (ITALY)   *See* Supple.

MORDANT (FRANCE)   *See* Acrid.

MOREL   A seldom-used process in which the grapes are fermented unstemmed and are gradually pressed by means of a cross-peg stirrer. Named after a French-born winemaker who made wines in St. Helena, California, in the late 1880s. *See* Carbonic Maceration.

MORELLO (ITALY)   A red grape variety.

MORELLONE (ITALY)   *See* Primitivo di Gioia.

MORETO (PORTUGAL)   A red grape variety grown in the Douro region.

MOREY-SAINT-DENIS (FRANCE)   A small red wine commune located in the northern end of the Côte de Nuits in Burgundy, noted for its production of robust and fleshy red wines. On January 19, 1927, Morey added its name to one of its smallest vineyards, Clos Saint-Denis.

MORGEN (GERMANY)   An acre of land. *See* Acre.

MORGON (FRANCE)   A *cru* commune in Beaujolais that produces a full-bodied but not coarse wine that usually requires nearly a year in the barrel and another year in the bottle before it is ready to drink. It takes three years to actually reach its prime.

MORIO-MUSKAT (GERMANY)   A white grape variety developed in the 1930s from a cross of Sylvaner and Pinot Blanc, with no Muscat in its parentage, by Peter Morio of the Bavarian Institute for Wine and Grape Development in Würzburg.

MORONEAN *(GREECE)* An ancient wine.

MORONI *(JAPAN)* *See* Fermentation.

MORRASTAL *(SPAIN)* *See* Graciano.

MORTL There are a number of different types of field crushing equipment used throughout the world. One is the German-made Mortl system, which crushes the grapes in the field right after they are picked. The Mortl holds approximately five tons of grapes and is pulled through the vineyard by a tractor. This process provides the ultimate in freshness preservation between the time the grapes are picked and the juice is processed. *See* Field Crushing.

MOSCATEL DE MÁLAGA *(SPAIN)* *See* Muscat of Alexandria.

MOSCATEL DE SETÚBAL *(PORTUGAL)* A very long-lived, sweet, fortified wine made from the Muscat of Alexandria grape variety.

MOSCATEL GALEGO *(PORTUGAL)* A white grape variety grown in the Douro region.

MOSCATEL GORDO BLANCO *(SPAIN)* *See* Muscat of Alexandria.

MOSCATEL ROMANO *(SPAIN)* *See* Muscat of Alexandria.

MOSCATEL ROXO *(PORTUGAL)* A black strain of the Muscat of Alexandria grape variety.

MOSCATO BIANCO *(ITALY)* *See* Muscat Blanc.

MOSCATO CANELLI *(ITALY)* *See* Muscat Blanc.

MOSCATO D'ASTI *(ITALY)* *See* Muscat Blanc.

MOSCATO ROSA *(ITALY)* A red grape variety grown primarily in the Trentino-Alto Adige region.

MOSCOPHILERO *(GREECE)* A white grape variety.

MOSCOW MULE A cocktail created and popularized in 1946 at Jack Morgan's Cock N' Bull Restaurant in Los Angeles, California. It consists of vodka and ginger beer, with a wedge of a fresh lime.

MOSELBLÜMCHEN *(GERMANY)* A white wine, light in body, with some residual sugar, theoretically from the Mosel. Its name translates as "little flower of the Mosel."

MOSELLE *(GERMANY)* *See* Mosel-Saar-Ruwer.

MOSEL-SAAR-RUWER *(GERMANY)* One of thirteen Qualitätswein (quality) grape-growing regions located along the Mosel River. The grapes of this region, which have been producing wine for more than two thousand years, are grown mainly on slate ground covering the exceedingly steep hillsides of the valleys watered by the Mosel River and its tributaries, the Saar and Ruwer. Wines here are made primarily from the Johannisberg Riesling grape. They are the lightest (lowest in alcohol) of the German wines, being fragrant and flowery, refreshing and clean, with an almost peachy taste. Also spelled *Moselle*.

MOSELTALER *(GERMANY)* A generic light white wine generally produced in the Mosel region.

MOSKHÁTOS (GREECE)   *See* Musky.

MOSLAVAC (YUGOSLAVIA)   A white grape variety.

MOST (GERMANY)   *See* Must.

MOSTO (ITALY AND SPAIN)   *See* Must.

MÔSTO (PORTUGAL)   *See* Must.

MOSTGEWICHT (GERMANY)   The *must* (or sugar) weight of grape juice, usually expressed in degrees Öechsle.

MOSTWAAGE (AUSTRIA)   The *must* (or sugar) weight of grape juice, usually expressed in degrees Klosterneuburger.

MOTHERS AGAINST DRUNK DRIVING (MADD)   A national coalition of concerned citizens whose aim is to increase public awareness and knowledge regarding alcohol abuse or misuse by disseminating information to the public, the alcoholic beverage industry, and local and state legislators.

MOTO (JAPAN)   *See* Mash.

MOU (FRANCE)   *See* Flabby.

MOUILLÉ (FRANCE)   *See* Watered Down.

MOULIN-À-VENT (FRANCE)   A *cru* commune in Beaujolais (south of Chénas) that produces the best-known and probably the finest of all Beaujolais wine. First written mention of this wine was in 1757. A nearby seventeenth century windmill (*moulin-à-vent*)—still standing, minus its sails—is the source of its name. The character and taste of the wine are due to the granite-like quality of the local soil. Moulin-à-Vent is a dark-colored, full-bodied wine that takes a long time to mature; it lasts up to four or five years, but peaks in about three.

MOUNTAIN   *See* Málaga.

MOUNTAIN   A loosely-used term with no legal meaning, often used on California jug wine labels—for example, Mountain Chablis, Mountain Burgundy, and so on. According to BATF, there is no legal requirement that grapes used in these jug wines come from vineyards located in mountainous areas. In addition, it is not necessarily true that mountain-grown grapes are superior to grapes grown in flat areas or in valleys.

MOURISCO BRANCO (PORTUGAL)   A white grape variety grown in the Douro region.

MOURISCO DE SEMENTE (PORTUGAL)   A red grape variety grown in the Douro region.

MOURISCO TINTO (PORTUGAL)   A red grape variety used in the making of port wine.

MOURVAISON (FRANCE)   A red grape variety grown in the southeast near Provence.

MOURVÈDRE   A red grape variety used primarily as a blending grape in the Rhône Valley of France as well as in Australia, Spain, California, and Algeria. Also known as *Mataro*.

M

MOURVÈDRE

MOUSEY   *See* Mousy.

MOUSINESS   *See* Mousy.

MOUSSE *(FRANCE)*   The froth or foam on the surface of a glass of sparkling wine or beer.

MOUSSEC *(ENGLAND)*   *See* Sparkling Wine.

MOUSSEUX *(FRANCE)*   *See* Sparkling Wine.

MOUSY   A term for a disagreeable, acetic-acid-like odor or taste produced by a bacteria called *acetamide*. It usually occurs when newly fermented wines are left too long on their lees. Also spelled *mousey*. Also known as *mäuseln* and *mousiness*. *See* Bottle Stink, Moldy, and Musty.

MOÛT *(FRANCE)*   *See* Must.

MOUTERIJ *(NETHERLANDS)*   A malt house.

MOUTWIJN   The base distilled spirit utilized for Holland (Dutch) gin, produced by three passes (runs) through pot stills.

MOUTWIJN GENEVER   A Holland (Dutch) gin that has been twice redistilled through various botanicals, primarily juniper berries.

MOUTHFILLING   Describes wines or beers that display intense, full flavors that can be markedly fruity and fairly high in extract and possibly alcoholic content. Also known as *vollmundig*.

MOUTON *(FRANCE)*   A linguistic corruption of *motte* (mound) and not of the word for sheep, as some believe.

MR. & MRS. T.   The *T* stands for Taylor, who in 1962 developed the original recipes for Bloody Mary Mix, Piña Colada Mix, Margarita Mix, Sweet N' Sour Mix, Lemon X, and Sour Mix.

MTSVANE *(RUSSIA)*   A white grape variety.

MUDDLER   A hardwood instrument, hand-held, used for crushing ice, fruit, cube sugar, fresh mint leaves, or other herbs.

MUFFA NOBILE *(ITALY)*   *See Botrytis Cinerea*.

MUG   A heavy, flat-bottomed beer glass, generally with a capacity of twelve to fourteen ounces and having a handle. *See* Stein and Tankard.

MUG HOUSE   A slang term for a bar or tavern.

MUI QUAI LU *(CHINA)*   A liqueur made from fermented rose petals.

MULLED WINE   A sweetened and spiced red wine drink to which sugar, lemon peel, and spices such as nutmeg, cloves, and cinnamon are added. It is then heated by a *loggerhead* and served very warm to hot. Also known as *glühwein*. *See* Bishop, Glögg, Loggerhead, Poker Beer, and Wassail.

MÜLLERREBE *(GERMANY)*   *See* Meunier.

MÜLLER-THURGAU   A white grape variety developed in 1882 by Professor Hermann Müller (1850–1927), a Swiss ampelographer from Thurgau. For many years it was thought to be a cross between the Johannisberg Riesling and Sylvaner grapes, but there is no evidence to support this theory. Also known as *Rivaner*.

MULTANER (GERMANY)   A white grape variety developed from a cross of Johannisberg Riesling and Sylvaner grapes.

MULTICOUNTY APPELLATIONS   An appellation of origin comprising two or no more than three counties in the same state, which may be used if all of the grapes were grown in the counties indicated and the percentage of the wine derived from grapes grown in each county is shown on the label, with a tolerance of plus or minus 2 percent.

MULTISTATE APPELLATION   An appellation of origin comprising two or no more than three states that are all contiguous may be used if 1) all of the grapes were grown in the states indicated and the percentage of the wine derived from grapes grown in each state is shown on the label, with a tolerance of plus or minus 2 percent; 2) the wine has been fully finished and blended and the appellation does not result in an alteration of class or type in one of the labeled appellation states; and 3) the wine conforms to the laws and regulations governing the composition, method of manufacture, and designation of wines in all the states listed in the appellation.

MULTIUSE WINE BRAND   A wine that is capable of being merchandised as an apéritif, to be sold by the glass, as well as fitting nicely into a standard wine list.

MUM (ENGLAND)   An alcoholic beverage brewed from fir bark and herbs.

MÜNCH   A red grape variety developed in the late 1800s by Thomas Volney Munson (1843–1913) of Denison, Texas.

MÜNCHENER (GERMANY)   *See* Munich Beer.

MUNICA (ITALY)   *See* Monica.

MUNICH BEER (GERMANY)   Literally from Munich. This type of beer was originally produced in Bavaria, although it is currently brewed in many parts of the world. It is slightly darker in color than Pilsner-type beers, although milder and less bitter than other German types. It also has a more pronounced malty aroma and taste, with a sweet finish and aftertaste. Also known as *Münchener*.

MUNSON, THOMAS VOLNEY (1843–1913)   A local hybridizer who developed many grape varieties suitable for planting in the hot and dry Texas sun. He was also instrumental in helping the French to reestablish their vineyards after the devastating effects of the *phylloxera* plague. Because of his work, he was awarded the Legion of Honor by the French Government in 1888.

MUNSON RED   A generic name given to a group of red *hybrids* developed by Thomas Volney Munson (1843-1913) in Denison, Texas.

MÛR (FRANCE)   *See* Maturity.

MÛRE (FRANCE)   A fruit brandy made from blackberries.

MURETO DO ALENTEJO (PORTUGAL)   A red grape variety.

MURKY   A term used to describe some red wines that appear to be turbid or muddy, often with a high pH (around 4.0).

MUSCADELLE   A white grape variety, generally blended in small proportions with the Sémillon and Sauvignon Blanc, which gives intense fruit and a faint Muscat flavor to the wine. Muscadelle is grown mostly in Graves and Sauternes in the Bordeaux region of France. Also known as *Muscadelle de Bordelais*; in France and some parts of California it is known as *Sauvignon Vert*. It is argued that the Muscadelle is the same grape variety as the Tocai of Italy. *See* Tocai.

MUSCADELLE DE BORDELAIS *(FRANCE)*   *See* Muscadelle.

MUSCADET *(FRANCE)*   A bone-dry, steely, clean, light white wine, usually high in acidity. Muscadet, which is made from the Melon de Bourgogne grape variety, is produced in the far western part of the Loire Valley. *See* Melon de Bourgogne.

MUSCADINE   A native American grape of the grapevine species *Vitis rotundifolia*. Muscadines are indigenous to the south Atlantic states and produce heavily aromatic, sweet, liqueur-type wines. The best known type of Muscadine is Scuppernong, a white grape variety. Also known as *Muscadinia*.

MUSCARDIN *(FRANCE)*   A red grape variety grown primarily in the Rhône Valley.

MUSCAT   A white grape variety widely grown throughout the Mediterranean area as well as in parts of northern Europe and California. There are many varieties, subvarieties, and styles of the Muscat that vary from region to region and country to country.

MUSCAT À PETITS GRAINS   *See* Muscat Blanc.

MUSCAT BLANC   A white grape variety that produces wines with an intense spice-perfumed aroma and a grapy taste that resembles a fresh fruit salad. It is prolifically grown in the Piedmont region of Italy, where it forms the base of many Muscat-type wines. Among them are Asti (a *spumante*), Moscato Bianco, and others. Although its correct name is *Muscat à Petits Grains*, it is known by a host of other names that include *Moscato Bianco, Moscato Canelli, Moscato d'Asti, Muscat de Frontignan, Muskateller*, and *Sargamuskotaly*.

In 1906, Molon wrote that "the name Moscato—which must be derived from *muschio* or *mosca* (or musk)—appeared for the first time in the writings of Pier de'Crescenzio (thirteenth century)."

MUSCAT DE FRONTIGNAN *(FRANCE)*   A white grape variety grown in parts of southern France and California, where it produces mostly fortified dessert wines. *See* Muscat Blanc.

MUSCAT DU MOULIN   A white grape variety. Formerly known as *Couderc 19-29935*.

MUSCATEL   A sweetened, amber-colored, fortified wine, generally produced in California from the Muscat grape. Although quite popular during the 1940s to 1960s, its popularity has dwindled.

MUSCAT GORDO BLANCO *(AUSTRALIA)*   *See* Muscat of Alexandria.

MUSCAT HAMBURG   A red grape variety grown in California. It produces light-colored, intensely spicy wines that are often fortified or allowed to contain some residual sugar. Also known as *Black Muscat*.

MUSCAT OF ALEXANDRIA   A white grape variety widely grown throughout the Mediterranean area as well as in California. It produces mostly table wines that are quite varietal in character, with some underlying bitterness, and are often sweet or slightly sweet. Also known as *Gordo Blanco, Hanepoot, Moscatel de Málaga* in Málaga; *Moscatel Gordo Blanco, Moscatel Romano, Muscat Gordo Blanco*, and *Zibibbo*.

MUSCAT OTTONEL   A white grape variety with an exceptionally strong but pleasant Muscat aroma, grown in central and eastern Europe. Also known as *Muskotály*.

MUSCULAR   Describes robust, full-bodied, and assertive wines, generally displaying good acidity and great texture. Also known as *nerbo, nervig*, and *sinewy. See* Brawny and Powerful.

MUSELET (FRANCE)   *See* Wire Hood.

MUSHROOM   Some very old red Bordeaux and Cabernet Sauvignon wines occasionally have an odor that reminds one of fresh-picked, dirt-laden mushrooms.

MUSIGNY (FRANCE)   A red-wine-producing vineyard located in the commune of Chambolle-Musigny in the Côte de Nuits of Burgundy. Its wines, made from the Pinot Noir grape, can be described as fleshy and seductive.

MUSKATELLER (GERMANY)   *See* Muscat Blanc.

MUSKAT-SYLVANER (GERMANY)   *See* Sauvignon Blanc.

MUSKOTÁLY (HUNGARY)   *See* Muscat Ottonel.

MUSKY   Describes a peculiar odor characteristic of wines made with the Muscat grape as the base, especially during fermentation, when the odor can be detected. Also known as *moskhátos*.

MUSQUÉ (FRANCE)   The heavily perfumed odor often associated with wines made from the Muscat grape variety.

MUST   The unfermented juice or any mixture of juice, pulp, skins, and seeds prepared from fruit, berries, or grapes. The term is derived from the Latin term *mustum*. Also known as *maische, most, mosto, môsto, moût*, and *stum wine*.

MUSTIMÈTRE (FRANCE)   *See* Hydrometer.

MUST WEIGHT   The quantifiably measurable amount of sugar in ripe grapes or *must*. Also known as *mostgewicht* and *mostwaage*.

MUSTARD   *See* Wild Mustard.

MUSTIMETER   *See* Hydrometer.

MUSTY   Describes an unpleasant odor or flavor in wine similar to a moldy smell, often due to an unclean cellar. It can also result from aging wine in wooden barrels that have decayed or become waterlogged. Also known as *ammuffito. See* Bottle Stink, Moldy, and Mousy.

MUTAGE (FRANCE)   *See* Mistelle.

MUTÉ   Also known as *muto. See* Back Blending and Mistelle.

MUTING   *See* Mistelle.

MUTO (ITALY)   *See* Back Blending and Mistelle.

MUY AÑEJO (SPAIN)   Well-aged, longer than *añejo*; used in reference to rum and tequila.

MYCELIA   A concentration of fungus filaments. *See* Molds.

MYCODERMA   A spoilage bacteria, mold, or yeast that consumes alcohol, impairing the odor and flavor of wine. It is taken from the Greek words *mykes*, meaning fungi, and *derma*, meaning skin.

MYCODERMA ACETI   The name given for *acetobacter* by Louis Pasteur that was accepted for a long time but is incorrect. *See* Acetobacter.

MYCODERMA VINI   *See* Flowers of Wine.

MYELÓDIS (GREECE)   *See* Mellow.

MYRTILLE (FRANCE)   *See* Myrtle.

MYRTLE   An evergreen bush whose berries (blueberry) are often used to make fruit brandy or fruit-flavored brandy. Also known as *myrtille*. *See* Airelle.

MYSLIWSKA (POLAND)   A hunter's vodka.

NABI   National Association of Beverage Importers.

NACKENHEIM *(GERMANY)*   A wine-producing town located in the Rheinhessen, overlooking the Rhine River just south of Mainz. Nackenheim produces fruity white wines from Johannisberg Riesling and Sylvaner grape varieties.

NACHGESCHMACK *(GERMANY)*   *See* Aftertaste.

NÁGYBURGUNDI *(HUNGARY)*   *See* Pinot Noir.

NAHE *(GERMANY)*   One of thirteen Qualitätswein (quality) grape-growing regions, located near the Rhine River. This region is planted with Riesling, Sylvaner, and Müller-Thurgau grapes, and produces wines of varying taste and quality, some of which are not unlike Rheingau wines.

NAIVE   *See* Little.

NAMA   *See* Commandaria.

NAME BRAND   *See* Call Liquor.

NANOMETER   A unit of wave length, one nanometer being equal to one-billionth of a meter. Abbreviated *nm*.

NAPA GAMAY   A red grape variety, originally thought to be the true Gamay of the Beaujolais district; now identified as Valdiguié, a very heavy producer of "ordinary" wines in the Midi Region of southern France. However, it may continue to be called Napa Gamay in California. *See* Gamay.

NAPA VALLEY   A grape-growing region in California, located northeast of San Francisco, which many consider the most celebrated wine region in the United States. It is almost twenty-five miles long and at most, a few miles wide, about one-sixth the size of Bordeaux.

NAPLES   A red grape variety developed in 1952 from a cross of Delaware and (Mills and Iona).

NAPOLÉON _(FRANCE)_   A label designation used on armagnac, calvados, and cognac bottles to indicate that the youngest brandy used in the blend is at least six years old (armagnac), six years (calvados), and 6-1/2 years old (cognac), although they contain a very high percentage of brandy that has been aged for twenty, thirty, or forty years or more.

NARIZ _(SPAIN)_   A wine-taster's term for comparing the relative pungency of two or more similar wines or _musts._

NASE _(GERMANY)_   _See_ Nose.

NASCO _(ITALY)_   A white grape variety grown in the region of Sardinia.

NATIONAL LIQUOR BEVERAGE ASSOCIATION (NLBA)   In the United States, a trade association of the alcoholic beverage industry whose goal is the promotion of distilled spirits through consumer awareness.

NATIVE AMERICAN GRAPE VARIETIES   Native American grapes and grapevines, mostly found east of the Mississippi River. The grapevines, properly identified as _Vitis labrusca_ species, have a pronounced grapy or foxy odor and flavor that characterizes them as well as wine made from the grapes.

Around 1000 A.D., explorer Leif Ericson first discovered these wild grapevines growing when he landed on the east coast of North America near Newfoundland. In fact, he found so many grapevines that he named the place "Vineland the Good." _See Vitis Labrusca_ and Wild Grapevines.

NATIVE PRODUCT   In the United States, a term sometimes used by state legislatures to distinguish goods produced within a state from out-of-state ("imported") goods.

NATUR _(GERMANY)_   A term, illegal since 1971, meaning a natural wine.

NATURAL   _See_ Extra Brut.

NATURALE _(ITALY)_   _See_ Extra Brut.

NATURALLY SPARKLING   _See_ Sparkling Water.

NATURAL SPRING WATER   _See_ Spring Water.

NATURAL WATER   A colorless, transparent, odorless, liquid suitable for human consumption. Drinking water comes either from an underground spring or from a well. No adulteration of the water is permitted; however, filtering may be permissible. _See_ Drinking Water and Water.

NATURAL WINE   The product of the juice or _must_ of sound, ripe grapes or other sound, ripe fruit (including berries) that contains not more than 21 percent by weight (21 degrees Brix dealcoholized wine) of total solids.

NATURAL WINE   A term without legal meaning that refers to wines made without additives or preservatives that would change the taste or alcohol content.

NATURE _(FRANCE)_   _See_ Vin Nature.

NATURGEWÄCHS _(GERMANY)_   A term, illegal since 1971, meaning a natural growth.

NATURREIN _(GERMANY)_   A term, illegal since 1971, meaning a naturally pure wine.

NAVY GROG   *See* Grog.

NBWA   National Beer Wholesalers Association.

NCADD   National Commission Against Drunk Driving.

NCPID   National Coalition to Prevent Impaired Driving.

NEAR BEER   A beer-like malt beverage made from cereals; it was first brewed during Prohibition as a substitute for beer. *See* Needled Beer and Nonalcoholic Malt Beverage.

NEAT   *See* Straight.

NEBBIOLO *(ITALY)*   A red grape variety grown primarily in the Piedmont region. The Nebbiolo produces wines that are usually rough and tannic when young but with age evolve into wines of extraordinary power, depth, and complexity. When blended with other varieties, the Nebbiolo grape gives the resultant wine body and substance.

The Nebbiolo in fact is not one grape but a family of grapes whose variations probably arrived through mutation. There are two subvarieties: Michet, which is the most prized, and Lampia, which is widely grown throughout the area. Nebbiolo is used to produce Barolo, Barbaresco, Gattinara, Ghemme, and many other wines.

Originally called *Vitis vinifera Pedemontana* (the grapevine of Piedmont), the grape is referred to as *Nubiola, Nebiola, Nibiol,* and *Nebiolium* in documents dating back to the Middle Ages. Its present name and spelling, officially sanctioned in 1962, are derived from the word *nebbia* (fog). Some say that it was given this name because of the persistent fog found in the area of cultivation, while others believe that it alludes to the thick bloom that forms on the grape skins, making them look as if they were surrounded by tiny patches of fog.

Nebbiolo is known by several other names including Spanna (in the provinces of Vercelli and Novara, a term that reflects the method of cultivation), Chiavennasca (in the province of Sondrio in Lombardy); in Valle d'Aosta and around Carema, it is called *Picotener, Picultener,* or *Pugnet.*

NEBBIOLO BIANCO *(ITALY)*   *See* Arneis.

NEBUCHADNEZZAR   An oversized bottle equal in capacity to twenty 750-milliliter bottles or fifteen liters (507 ounces). It weighs approximately sixty-five pounds when full.

Nebuchadnezzar (605–562 B.C.) was a warring king of Babylon who sacked Jerusalem around 600 B.C. His exploits are described in the Bible in II Kings 24 and 25 and Daniel 4.

NECTAR   A very sweet, often thick juice of one or more fruits, especially apricot and pear.

NEEDLED BEER   A slang term that refers to near beer as brewed during Prohibition; it often contained illegal distilled spirits. *See* Near Beer.

NEEDLING   The process of inserting an electric probe (often called a needle) into a tank of fermenting beer, which stimulates and hastens the aging process.

NEFLE *(FRANCE)*   A fruit brandy made from medlar fruit in Alsace.

NÉGOCIANT *(FRANCE)*   Also known as *negoziante*. *See* Broker.

NÉGOCIANT-ELEVEUR (FRANCE) A shipper who buys wine in barrels from growers and then ages and bottles it in his or her own cellars. *See* Broker.

NÉGOCIANT-MANIPULANT (FRANCE) One who sells champagnes produced under his or her complete control. This appears on some champagne labels as the initials *NM*. *See* Broker.

NÉGOCIANT-NON-MANIPULANT (FRANCE) One who sells champagne under his or her own name but is not its producer.

NEGOZIANTE (ITALY) *See* Broker.

NEGRA MOLE (PORTUGAL) A red grape variety often used in a blend to produce madeira wines. Also known as *Tinta Negra Mole*.

NEGRARA (ITALY) A red grape variety grown primarily in the northeast, where it is used in the blend of Bardolino, Valpolicella, Amarone della Valpolicella, and other wines.

NEGRO AMARO (ITALY) A red grape variety grown in Apulia, where it produces dark-colored, full-bodied wines such as Matino Rosso and Rosato. Also known as *Albese, Jonico, Nero Leccese,* and *Uva Cane.*

NEGRO D'AVOLA (ITALY) A red grape variety.

NEGRONI A cocktail consisting of Campari, gin, and sweet red vermouth, with a splash of seltzer and twist of lemon. Purportedly conceived by a pub-crawling Count Negroni who demanded that the bartender at his favorite Florentine bar add a shot of gin to his usual Americano cocktail.

NEGUS A hot wine (generally port or sherry) drink, often sweetened and flavored with various spices; named after Colonel Francis Negus, an eighteenth-century aristocrat.

NEMATODE A soil-borne vineyard parasitic pest (worm) that has a long, cylindrical, unsegmented body and a heavy cuticle. It generally lives in the soil and feeds on roots of grapevines.

NERBO (ITALY) *See* Muscular.

NERELLO CAPPUCCIO (ITALY) A red grape variety grown in Sicily.

NERELLO MANTELLATO (ITALY) A red grape variety grown in Sicily. Also known as *Nero Cappuccio.*

NERELLO MASCALESE (ITALY) A red grape variety grown in Sicily. Also known as *Mascalisu, Niereddu Mascalese, Nirello Mascalese,* and *Niuru Mascalisu.*

NERO (ITALY) Very dark red, to the point of almost being black.

NERO BUONO DI CORI (ITALY) A red grape variety.

NERO D'AVOLA (ITALY) A red grape variety native to Sicily, used specifically in Cerasuolo di Vittoria and Regaleali Rosso. Also known as *Calabrese.*

NERO DI TROIA (ITALY) *See* Uva di Troia.

NERO GROSSO (ITALY) A red grape variety grown primarily in Sicily.

NERO LECCESE (ITALY) *See* Negro Amaro.

NERVIG (GERMANY)   *See* Muscular.

NET (FRANCE)   *See* Clean.

NET PROFIT   Sales of products minus expenses and costs.

NET RATE   A wholesale rate to be marked up for eventual resale to the consumer.

NETT (GERMANY)   *See* Clean.

NETTLE BEER (ENGLAND)   An alcoholic beverage brewed from nettles.

NETTO (ITALY)   *See* Clean.

NET WEIGHT   Weight of a container's contents, not including the container itself (gross less tare).

NEU (GERMANY)   New.

NEUBURGER (AUSTRIA)   A white grape variety developed from a cross of Pinot Blanc and Sylvaner in the Wachau district of Lower Austria.

NEUCHÂTEL (SWITZERLAND)   A dry, tart white wine produced on the northern shore of Lake Neuchâtel from the Chasselas grape. The vineyards of Neuchâtel are also the source of a light-colored, intriguingly fragrant red wine, and of one of Switzerland's celebrated rosés, *oeil de perdrix* (an ancient wine term meaning the pink color of a partridge's eye); both are made from the Pinot Noir grape.

NEUF (FRANCE)   New, as in Châteauneuf-du-Pape.

NEUTRAL   Describes an alcoholic beverage exhibiting low intensity in olfactory, tactile, and taste sensations. Also known as *neutre* and *neutro*.

NEUTRAL BRANDY   Brandy produced at more than 170 proof.

NEUTRAL SPIRITS   Distilled spirits, distilled from any material at or above 190 proof, that lack any distinctive taste, color, and odor and thus are neutral in character. These distilled spirits are used for blending with straight whiskey and for making gin, vodka, and liqueurs. Also known as *cologne spirits, grain neutral spirits, pure alcohol*, and *silent spirit*.

NEUTRE (FRANCE)   *See* Neutral.

NEUTRO (ITALY, PORTUGAL, AND SPAIN)   *See* Neutral.

NEUTRON PROBE   A moisture-reading device that measures the amount of water in the soil and monitors the uptake of water by the grapevines. In a sense, this allows the viticulturist to "see" underground. The neutron probe is a tube about one foot long and one inch in diameter. The tip contains an isotope of *Americium Beryllium*, which sends out atoms that have an affinity for the hydrogen ions in water. To utilize the device, a two-inch-diameter hole is drilled in the soil, usually to a depth of five feet. An aluminum tube is then placed in the hole and this becomes a monitoring station.

To check soil moisture content, the probe is inserted into the tube at various depths. As the ions are discharged into the soil, they are deflected by the hydrogen atoms and then counted by a sensor as they bounce back to the probe. A microprocessor built into the unit converts these bulk readings into a calibrated reading of inches of water per foot.

The neutron probe is able to measure minute differences in the amount of soil moisture in hundreds of an inch. This means viticulturists cannot only tell what part of a grapevine's root zone is utilizing the water but also determine how much water has been used. Also known as *tensiometere*.

NEVERS OAK *(FRANCE)* (Technically known as *Quercus robur.*) Named after the city of Nevers in central France. Its relatively hard wood and fine to medium grain make it suitable for aging both red and white wines without overpowering flavors. Nevers oak has a moderate tannin extraction and a rich, buttery oak flavor that greatly softens wine's acidity. Nevers is used extensively for Cabernet Sauvignon and Merlot as well as red and white wines in Burgundy.

NEVOEIRA *(PORTUGAL)* A red grape variety grown in the Douro region.

NEVRÓDIS *(GREECE)* *See* Firm.

NEW AMSTERDAM The site of the first American brewery. *See* Minuit, Peter.

NEW SOUTH WALES *(AUSTRALIA)* A wine-producing state located west of Sydney; it is the second largest in terms of production after South Australia. The most popular grape-growing areas are Canberra District, Hunter Valley, Mudgee, and Riverina.

NEW YORK MUSCAT A red grape variety developed in 1961 from a cross of Muscat Hamburg and Hubbard, at the State Experimental Station in Geneva, New York.

NEW YORK STATE The United States' second-largest producer of grapes and wines (thirty-six thousand acres and more than thirty-five million gallons [1994]). There is a wine for every taste, with white, red, sparkling, and dessert wines produced from *Vitis labrusca*, French-American hybrids, and *Vitis vinifera* grapes. Wines that carry the New York State appellation, regardless of whether or not they are estate bottled, must have a minimum of 75 percent of their volume derived from grapes grown in New York State.

The major wine-producing regions are Finger Lakes, Hudson Valley, Long Island, and Lake Erie.

NEYRET *(ITALY)* A red grape variety grown in the Valle d'Aosta region.

NEZ *(FRANCE)* *See* Nose.

NEZ FLEURI *(FRANCE)* *See* Flowery.

NEZ FRUITÉ *(FRANCE)* *See* Fruity.

NEZ SUBTIL *(FRANCE)* *See* Subtle.

NIAAA National Institute on Alcohol Abuse and Alcoholism.

NIABELL A red grape variety developed in 1958 from a cross of Niagara and Campbell Early by Dr. Harold P. Olmo of the University of California, Davis.

NIAGARA A white grape variety developed in 1868 from a cross of Concord and Cassady by C. L. Hoag and B. W. Clark of Lockport in Niagara County in upstate New York.

NICHE MARKETING A marketing plan that creates a narrow or select market that is highly desired by a small segment of the population.

NIEDDA *(ITALY)* *See* Monica.

NIEDER *(GERMANY)* Lower.

NIELLUCCIO   A red grape variety native to Corsica.

NIEREDDU MASCALESE (ITALY)   *See* Nerello Mascalese.

NIERSTEIN (GERMANY)   The foremost vineyard village of the Rheinhessen region, located on the Rhine River; it is noted for its production of high quality white wines, primarily from the Johannisberg Riesling grape variety.

NIGHTCAP   A slang term for a drink (alcoholic beverage) taken before retiring to bed.

NILGIRI TEA   A relatively mild tea made from leaves grown on the mountain ranges in southern India.

NINETEENTH HOLE (19TH HOLE)   Any place, as the bar or lounge of a clubhouse, where golfers meet for drinks, light snacks, and conviviality after playing a round of golf.

NINE-LITER CASE   The industry standard size case. One hundred flat cases of 1.75 liters contain 1,050 liters, equal to 117 nine-liter cases.

NIP   The British term for a quarter of a bottle; also the name of the smallest bottle in which champagne is sold (usually six ounces). A term often used in reference to miniature bottles.

NIRELLO MASCALESE (ITALY)   *See* Nerello Mascalese.

NITROGEN   An important plant nutrient necessary for yeast cells to multiply. Although fruit juices contain some nitrogen, when diluted there is usually an insufficient amount for a satisfactory fermentation. For this reason, ammonium salts (sulfate or phosphate) are usually added, as they are a rich source of nitrogen. The salts are conveniently sold as yeast nutrients. *See* Nutrients.

NITROGEN GAS   An inert gas often used in the making of alcoholic beverages to maintain pressure during filtering and bottling of sparkling wine. It is also utilized in some "wine-by-the-glass programs" in conjunction with a "nitrogen system." In this system, the inert nitrogen gas, injected under gentle pressure through a sealed stopper, replaces the wine as it is removed from the bottle and preserves the remaining wine by keeping it oxygen free. The wine may be quickly dispensed and the remainder easily stored after use.

NIURU MASCALISU (ITALY)   *See* Nerello Mascalese.

NLSA   National Liquor Stores Association.

NM (FRANCE)   *See* Négociant-Manipulant.

NOAH   A white grape variety developed in the late 1860s by Otto Wasserzieher of Nauvoo, Illinois.

NOBILE (ITALY)   *See* Noble.

NOBLE   Describes a wine that displays the ultimate combination of elegance, breed, body, structure, and maturity as well as great balance and character. Also, a wine made from noble grapes—the best varietals, such as Cabernet Sauvignon, Pinot Noir, Chardonnay, or Sauvignon Blanc. Also known as *edel, evyenís, nobile*, and *vornehm*.

NOBLE   A red grape variety developed in 1946 at the North Carolina Agricultural Experimental Station. It is primarily grown in Florida, North Carolina, and other parts of the southeast United States.

NOBLE EXPERIMENT, THE   A slang term for Prohibition.

NOBLE ROT   *See* Botrytis Cinerea.

NOBLESSA *(GERMANY)*   A white grape variety developed in 1975 from a cross of Madeleine Angevine and Sylvaner.

NOBLING *(GERMANY)*   A white grape variety developed in 1939 from a cross of Gutedel and Sylvaner in Freiburg, located in Baden.

NOCERA *(ITALY)*   A red grape variety grown in Sicily.

NODE   The enlarged or thickened part of the grapevine cane or shoot where leaves, clusters, tendrils, and buds begin to grow.

NOGGIN   An English measure for beer equaling one-quarter pint or four ounces.

NOIR *(FRANCE)*   Black.

NOIRIEN *(FRANCE)*   *See* Pinot Noir.

NO-HOST BAR   *See* Cash Bar.

NOM   *See* Norma Oficial Mexicana de Calidad.

NOMENCLATURE   A set or system of official names or titles.

NONALCOHOLIC MALT BEVERAGE   A "beer-like" malt beverage made from various cereals that is *not* alcohol free but rather contains less than 0.5 percent alcohol by volume. Nonalcoholic malt beverages cannot be labeled or advertised as beer, lager, ale, porter, stout, or any other designation commonly associated with malt beverages. They may, however, be labeled as "malt beverage," "cereal beverage," or "near beer." *See* Near Beer.

NONBEVERAGE WINE   Wine or products made from wine that is rendered unfit for beverage use. Can also be labeled as *Not For Sale or Consumption As Beverage Wines. See* Cooking Wines.

NONCONTROLLABLE COSTS   *See* Fixed Costs.

NONFAT DRIED MILK   Skim milk that has been pasteurized and homogenized and the water content removed through heat and evaporation.

NONFERMENTABLE REDUCING SUGAR   *See* Reducing Sugar.

NONFERMENTABLES   *See* Reducing Sugar.

NONREFUNDABLE   A specified condition on the terms of purchasing a commodity whereby the item purchased may not be returned for cash, credit, or replacement.

NONPERISHABLE   Distilled spirits and some other alcoholic beverages that do not spoil or deteriorate readily.

NONVINTAGE (NV)   A term that applies to those sparkling wines whose *cuvées* contain wine from previous vintages. The term can also be applied to some table wines that do not display a vintage date on their label. Also known as *sans année. See* Blending and Reserve Wine.

NORMALWEIN (AUSTRIA) *See* Vino da Tavola.

NORMANDY (FRANCE) A northern province famous for its production of calvados, an apple brandy. *See* Calvados.

NORMA OFICIAL MEXICANA DE CALIDAD (NOM) A designation marked by an individualized number on the label of every bottle of classified tequila; it is the official Mexican seal of quality and authenticity. *See* Dirección General de Normas.

NORTON A red grape variety whose name derives from Dr. Daniel Norborne Norton of Richmond, Virginia, a grape breeder who found it growing wild on Cedar Island near the James River in about 1815. Formerly known as *Norton Seedless*; also known as *Virginia Seedling*. *See* Cynthiana.

NORTON SEEDLESS *See* Norton.

NOSE The combination of aroma and bouquet. Also known as *nase* and *nez*. *See* Aroma and Bouquet.

NOSIOLA (ITALY) A white grape variety grown in Trentino-Alto Adige.

NOTARDOMENICO (ITALY) A red grape variety grown in the central regions.

NOT STOCKED An item available or authorized for retail sale in a particular location but not carried by the store as a regular item.

NOUAISON (FRANCE) Fertilization of the flower and the beginning of the fruit.

NOUVEAU (FRANCE) A term used to indicate a new wine (of the year) that has been fermented to capture the ultimate in lightness and freshness in addition to its intense grapy aromas and flavors. This youthful red wine seldom has any aging potential; therefore, it is meant to be enjoyed within a short time after vinification. The term is often used in conjunction with Beaujolais. Also known as *federweisser, primeur, vin de l'année, vin de primeur,* and *vin nouveau. See* Beaujolais Nouveau, Carbonic Maceration, and Vino Novello.

NOVELLO (ITALY) *See* Vino Novello.

NSF National Sanitation Foundation.

NU (FRANCE) Bare; the raw cost of wine prior to bottling.

NUANCE *See* Subtle.

NUBE (SPAIN) *See* Cloudy.

NUCLEUS The central, usually spherical or oval mass of protoplasm present in most plant cells, containing most of the hereditary material, it is necessary to such functions as growth and reproduction.

NUITS-SAINT-GEORGES (FRANCE) A red and white wine village on the Côte de Nuits in the region of Burgundy. The red wines of the Côte de Nuits are velvety, round, smooth, full, and usually not high in tannin. Only one white wine is produced, called Nuits-Saint-Georges Blanc.

The name *Nuits* was derived from the tribe of *Nuithons* who were closely associated with the Burgundians and lived there at one time. In 1892, the village of Nuits added its name to that of its most illustrious vineyard, Saint-Georges.

NUMB A still wine, sparkling wine, or beer that has been overly chilled, to the point that very little odor or taste can be detected. *See* Dumb and Closed In.

NUMBER OF PORTIONS   The number of servings. *See* Covers.

NURAGUS *(ITALY)*   A white grape variety grown in the region of Sardinia. Also known as *Abbondosa, Axina de Margiai, Axina de Poporus*, and *Nuragus Trebbiana*.

NURAGUS TREBBIANA *(ITALY)*   *See* Nuragus.

NUT BROWN ALE   *See* Brown Ale.

NUTRA-SWEET   *See* Aspartame.

NUTRIENTS   A yeast food or energizer, largely made up of vitamin B_1, magnesium sulfate, potassium phosphate, urea, and ammonium phosphate, which supplies the *must* with a suitable source of nitrogen and phosphorous. Its use keeps yeasts healthy throughout fermentation and maximizes alcohol content by preventing premature cessation of fermentation (often referred to as a stuck fermentation). Also known as *seed yeast, yeast energizers, yeast nutrients*, and *yeast starter*. *See* Nitrogen, Starter, and Stuck Fermentation.

NUTTY   Describes the characteristic nut-like odor and flavor of madeira, marsala, sherry, or vin santo. Wines exposed to excess oxygen will often display a similar oxidized or *rancio* odor.

NV   *See* Nonvintage.

NY 35814   *See* Glenora Seedless.

O   A letter designation used on labels of armagnac, cognac, and some other brandies as an abbreviation for *old*.

OAK   Any large hardwood tree of the genus *Quercus* that is suitable for the aging of wines and distilled spirits. It is a ring-porous wood having relatively large pores or tubes in the spring portion of each annual ring. These are part of the pattern of oak lumber and are easily seen with the naked eye in the end grain. Oak is also the preferred wood for the aging and storage of wines and distilled spirits because it adds and develops greater complexity in the taste and odor. Also known as *rovere*.

OAK CHIPS   Chopped, split, or ground pieces of oak that are often used to give wine and distilled spirits an *oaked* odor and/or flavor without the necessity of using wooden barrels.

OAKY   The odor and/or flavor of wines or distilled spirits aged in small oak barrels. Some oak barrels impart a toasty or spicy vanillin odor and taste, which is desirable in moderation but undesirable if exaggerated. Delicate use of oak aging can add subtle complexity to full-bodied wines. Also known as *boisé, goût de boisé, odeur boisé*, and *holzig*. *See* Over-Aged and Woody.

OAST   A kiln used for the drying of hops or malt to be used in beer or distilled spirits.

OAT   A hardy, widely grown cereal grass often used in making distilled spirits and some beers.

OATMEAL STOUT   A brewed beverage, rich, flavorful, and quite dark in color, in which oatmeal is added to the roasted malt. *See* Stout.

OBER (GERMANY)   Upper.

OBERLIN 595   *See* Oberlin Noir.

OBERLIN NOIR   A red grape variety grown in the south of France. Formerly known as *Oberlin 595*.

OBJECTIVE   Relating to information that is independent, factual, real, and often measurable.

OBLATE   Describes spherical grapes with ends flattened much like a pumpkin.

OBSCURA (SPAIN)   *See* Candling.

OCHA (JAPAN)   A green tea. *See* Green Tea.

OCCUPATIONAL TAX   In the United States, a fee charged for one of the federal permits authorizing an individual to deal as manufacturer, wholesaler, or retailer in distilled spirits, wine, or beer.

OCHA (JAPAN)   *See* Green Tea.

OCHOKO (JAPAN)   Small porcelain cups traditionally used for serving *saké*. Also known as *sakazuki*.

OCHŌSHI (JAPAN)   *See* Tokkuri.

ÖCHSLE (GERMANY)   *See* Öechsle.

OCKFEN (GERMANY)   One of the very best white-wine-producing villages located along the Saar River.

OCTAVE (SPAIN)   A barrel with a capacity of approximately sixteen gallons, used for sherry wine. *See* Barrel.

ODEUR (FRANCE)   *See* Odor.

ODEUR BALSAMIQUE (FRANCE)   The odor or smell of balsam or incense.

ODEUR BOISÉ (FRANCE)   *See* Oaky.

ODEUR D'IODE (FRANCE)   An iodine smell often associated with Scotch whisky.

ODEUR DE RÉSINE (FRANCE)   *See* Retsina.

ODEUR DE SUIE (FRANCE)   *See* Smoky.

ODEUR EMPYREUMATIQUE (FRANCE)   The smell or odor reminiscent of something burning.

ODEUR ÉPICÉ (FRANCE)   *See* Spicy.

ODEUR FLORALE (FRANCE)   *See* Floral.

ODEUR FRUITÉ (FRANCE)   *See* Fruity.

ODEURS PRIMAIRES (FRANCE)   The primary smells emanating from the grape itself, often found in young wines.

ODEURS SECONDAIRES (FRANCE)   The secondary smells emanating from fermentation, caused by the yeasts.

ODEURS TERTIAIRES (FRANCE)   Tertiary or aging smells that develop as the wine ages either in wood or in the bottle.

ODOR   Also known as *odeur*. *See* Smell.

ODORE DE FUSTO (ITALY)   A barrel smell; this odor can be positive and pleasing if moderate, or unpleasant if excessive or if the barrel is in poor condition.

ÖECHSLE (GERMANY AND SWITZERLAND)   A term derived from the name of Christian Ferdinand Öechsle (1774–1852), a chemist who lived in the town of Pforzheim in Baden, Germany. He devised the method used to measure the level of sugar present in the *must*.

Öechsle is a measurement of the specific gravity of must (it refers to the number of grams by which one liter of grape must is heavier than one liter of water). Each quality category of German wine (spätlese, auslese, etc.) has to have a certain minimum Öechsle level to justify its title. When you divide by eight, you get the future alcoholic content of the wine. You must remember, however, that the Öechsle level includes the sweetness of unfermented sugar of a spätlese or auslese wine. Therefore, the actual alcoholic strength is likely to be less, since part of the sugar remains in the wine as unfermented residual sugar. To determine Brix, take Öechsle, divide by four, and subtract one. To determine Öechsle, take Brix, add one, and multiply by four. Also spelled *Öchsle*. *See* Brix.

OEIL DE PERDRIX (FRANCE)   A term that literally means "eye of the partridge." In the nineteenth century it was the common name for a wine that had a slight pinkish or copper tint in its color; often applied to pink or rosé-colored champagne. Also known as *ojo de gallo*. *See* Vin Gris.

OEILLADE (AUSTRALIA)   *See* Cinsaut.

OENOLOGY   *See* Enology.

OENOPHILE   *See* Enophile.

OENOTECA (ITALY)   *See* Enoteca.

OENOTHÈQUE (FRANCE)   *See* Enothèque.

OENOTRI (GREECE)   *See* Enotri Viri.

OENOTRIA (GREECE)   *See* Enotria Tellus.

OESTERREICHER   *See* Sylvaner.

OFC   Old Fine Canadian; used when referring to whisky.

OFF   Describes wines or beers that do not show their true character in smell and/or taste or that display undesirable attributes. It is often due to improper storage or aging and, in advanced cases, the seriously negative odor or taste is a result of some type of spoilage. Also referred to as *off-odors* or *off-flavors*.

OFF-DRY   *See* Semidry Wine.

OFF-FLAVORS   *See* Off.

OFFICE INTERNATIONAL DE LA VIGNE ET DU VIN (OIV) (FRANCE)   An organization, established in 1924, that carries out studies and investigations on a world-wide scale in technical, economic, scientific, and legal areas relative to grape-growing and wine.

OFF-ODORS   *See* Off.

OFF-LICENSE   *See* Off-Premise Outlets.

OFF-PREMISE OUTLETS   (Off-Sale) Retail establishments specializing in the sale of alcohol beverages, usually package stores, in which alcohol beverages are sold in bottles or cans to be consumed elsewhere. Also known as *off-license.*

OFIQUE *(SPAIN)*   A method of refrigeration that stabilizes the wine and prevents it from becoming cloudy.

OHANEZ *(SPAIN)*   *See* Almeria.

OÏDIUM   *See* Powdery Mildew.

OIL CAN   A slang term that refers to a thirty-two-ounce beer can.

OILED   *See* Intoxicated.

OILER   A slang term for a person who drinks alcoholic beverages excessively.

OILINESS   *See* Oily.

OILY   Describes a tactile impression of fat, roundness, or slipperiness created by the combination of high glycerin and slightly low acidity. It is found in some wines, most noticeably Chardonnay, as well as in sweet, late-harvest wines. Also known as *filant, filante, liparós, oleoso, oiliness, ölig,* and *ropy. See* Unctuous.

OIML   International Organization of Legal Metrology. *See* Sikes Scale.

OINOCHOE *(GREECE)*   A pitcher-like vessel with a three-lobed rim, for dipping wine from the crater or bowl and pouring it into the drinking cup. Also known as *olpe.*

OINOS *(GREECE)*   *See* Wine.

OIV *(FRANCE)*   *See* Office International de la Vigne et du Vin.

OJEN *(SPAIN)*   *See* Anise-Based Spirits.

OJO DE GALLO *(SPAIN)*   Eye of the partridge. *See* Oeil de Perdrix.

OJO DE LIEBRE *(SPAIN)*   Eye of the hare; the local name in Catalonia for the Tempranillo grape variety. *See* Tempranillo.

OKTOBERFEST *(GERMANY)*   A beer festival held each year in Germany that begins the end of September and lasts into the beginning of October. An estimated 1.2 million gallons of beer are consumed by five million visitors during this sixteen-day festival.

In 1810, when Prince Ludwig, the Crown Prince, married Theresia of Sachsen-Hildburghausen in Munich, his father, Max Joseph, the royal Wittelsbach of Bavaria, threw a large and massive wedding. The party was so successful that the meadow where it was held was renamed "Theresia's Meadow." The annual tradition or party, which actually started out as a wedding ceremony, continues to this day, except it is known as the Oktoberfest.

OKOLEHAO   In Hawaii, an 80-proof distilled spirit made from cooked *ti roots* (taro or kalo plants).

OKOWITA *(POLAND)*   *See* Aqua Ardens and Aqua Vitae.

OKUZ GOZU *(TURKEY)*   A red grape variety.

ÖL *(DENMARK, ICELAND, NORWAY, AND SWEDEN)*   *See* Beer.

OLASZRIESLING *(HUNGARY)*   *See* Welschriesling.

OLASZ RIZLING (HUNGARY)   *See* Welschriesling.

OLD (O)   A designation used on labels of armagnac, cognac, and some other brandies to indicate a well-aged product (not a negative term).

OLD   A wine or beer that is faded and past its prime or peak of drinkability. Also known as *over the hill, over the top, passé, pasado, shot, tot*, and *velhissimo*. Also known as *decrepit*. *See* Dead and Dried Out.

OLD BOTTLED SHERRY   A seldom-used term that describes an amontillado-type sherry that is slightly sweetened and often meant to be aged in the bottle.

OLD EAST SHERRY   A seldom-used term that describes an oloroso-type sherry that is full-bodied and sweet.

OLD-FASHIONED   A cocktail containing whiskey, bitters, and a dash of soda, garnished with fruit. The origin of the old-fashioned is traced back to one Thomas Louis Witcomb, a respected bartender at the Pendennis Club in Louisville, Kentucky, which first opened its doors in 1881. Many older recipes called for a sprig of mint, making it similar to the Mint Julep. Some papers in the 1800s make reference to Juleps made "the old-fashioned way." The drink was first introduced in the eastern United States at the original Waldorf bar some time in the 1890s.

OLD-FASHIONED GLASS   An ordinary short, squat bar glass without a base (foot) or stem, with a capacity of six to eight ounces. Also known as *on the rocks glass, rocks glass*, and *tumbler*.

OLD TALBOTT TAVERN, THE   A tavern located in Bardstown, Kentucky; it is the oldest tavern in continuous use west of the Alleghenies since 1779.

OLD TOM GIN   A British dry gin usually sweetened by the addition of sugar syrup; it was quite popular during the eighteenth century but it is rarely seen today.

OLD VINES   A loosely used grape-growers' term to indicate those grapevines that are more than thirty years of age. The term is occasionally used on wine labels to indicate the use of such grapevines in the making of the wine.

OLEOSO (ITALY AND PORTUGAL)   *See* Oily.

ÖLIG (GERMANY)   *See* Oily.

OLFACTION   The sense of smell (perception of aroma and bouquet) and the act of smelling. Also known as *olfacto*.

OLFACTO (PORTUGAL)   *See* Olfaction.

OLFACTORY   To do with the sense of smell.

OLIGOMINERALE (ITALY)   *See* Mineral Water.

OLIVELLA (ITALY)   A red grape variety grown in the central regions.

OLIVETTE BLANCHE   A white seedless grape variety often referred to as Lady Fingers, it is grown primarily in California.

OLOROSO (SPAIN)   *See* Fragrance.

OLOROSO (SPAIN)   One of two basic types of sherry; it is dark amber to walnut in color, semisweet, and full-bodied.

OLPE (GREECE)   A small, pitcher-like vessel used for serving wine. Also known as *oinochoe*.

OLTREPÒ PAVESE (ITALY)   One of three major wine-producing areas located in the northern region of Lombardy. Oltrepò Pavese was once part of Piedmont and is also referred to as Vecchio Piemonte, or Old Piedmont. This area has for the past century been Milan's chief supplier of Barbera and Bonarda wines.

The principal grape varieties of the area, grown exclusively in hillside vineyards, are both red: Barbera and Bonarda (also known as *Croatina*). Increasing amounts of vineyard space, however, are being devoted to such white varieties as Riesling Italico, Riesling Renano, Moscato Bianco, Pinot Grigio, Chardonnay, and Müller-Thurgau. Pinot Nero and Uva Rara (red grapes) are also grown.

OLUTEZA (FINLAND)   *See* Beer.

ONCTUEUX (FRANCE)   *See* Unctuous.

ONDENC (FRANCE)   A white grape variety grown primarily near Bordeaux; its total acreage has dwindled significantly in recent years.

ON-OFF SALES   A retail establishment licensed not only to sell and serve alcoholic beverages for on-premise consumption but also to offer certain types of alcoholic beverages for off-premise consumption.

ON-PREMISE RETAIL DEALER   *See* On-Premise Outlets.

ON-PREMISE OUTLETS   (On Sale) In the United States, retail establishments where alcoholic beverages are consumed on the premises—generally taverns, bars and grills, restaurants, clubs, and so forth. In some states these outlets also have licenses to sell for off-premise consumption. Also known as *on-premise retail dealer*.

ONTARIO   A white grape variety developed in 1908 from a cross of Winchell and Diamond at the State Experimental Station in Geneva, New York.

ON-THE-ROCKS   Wine or a cocktail served over ice cubes.

ON-THE-ROCKS GLASS   *See* Old-Fashioned Glass.

ON THE YEAST   Period during secondary fermentation when yeast cells are allowed to remain in contact with the wine, thereby contributing to the traditional "yeasty" nose of champagne. The process may last anywhere from three weeks to several years, depending on the producer.

OOLONG TEA   A dark, semifermented tea, a cross between black fermented tea and green unfermented tea. Almost all oolong tea comes from China and Taiwan (Formosa). *See* Formosa Oolong Tea.

OPAQUE   Absence of light; often used when referring to dark red wines or stout.

OLD PARTICULAR (OP) (ITALY)   A type of marsala *superiore* wine.

OPEN BAR   *See* Host Bar.

OPEN CONTAINER LAW   Ordinance in some communities that prohibits the drinking of alcoholic beverages on sidewalks and in public areas.

OPENING INVENTORY   The dollar value of the amount of goods on hand at the beginning of a given period.

OPENING OFFER   The prices of wines, generally announced in March the year following the harvest.

OPEN STATE   *See* License State.

OPORTO *(PORTUGAL)*   A seaport city in northern Portugal, on the Douro River, famous for its production of *port*, a fortified wine.

OPÓS *(GREECE)*   Sap.

OPPENHEIM *(GERMANY)*   An important vineyard village of the Rheinhessen famous for its production of white wines made primarily from the Sylvaner grape.

OPTIMA *(GERMANY)*   A white grape variety developed in 1970 from a cross of (Sylvaner and Johannisberg Riesling) and Müller-Thurgau at the Geilweilerhof Research Station in the Pfalz.

ORANGEADE   A drink made with orange juice, water, and a sweetener. Also known as *orange crush*.

ORANGE BITTERS   Concentrated orange-flavored bitters containing herbs, used in cocktails.

ORANGE BLOSSOM   A cocktail that is the same as a screwdriver, except that gin is substituted for the vodka.

ORANGE CRUSH   *See* Orangeade.

ORANGE FLOWER WATER   A flavoring extract from an orange zest, often used in cocktails.

ORANGE JUICE   The liquid constituent of an orange.

ORANGE MUSCAT   A white grape variety grown primarily in California, where it is utilized in making dessert wines.

ORANGE PEKOE TEA   A fine grade of black tea of China, Sri Lanka (Ceylon), and India, made from delicate, medium-sized leaves. The term does not refer to a type or flavor of tea but rather a leaf grade or size. The dried tea leaves are cut, sifted, and sorted into various grades. The finest to the coarsest quality are orange pekoe (from the finest leaves), pekoe, souchong, broken orange pekoe, broken pekoe, broken pekoe souchong, fannings, and fines ("dust"). There is even a Darjeeling Orange pekoe and Assam Orange Pekoe. The term "orange" is from an ancient Chinese custom of scenting the tea leaves with orange blossoms.

ORANGE SODA   A soft drink usually made with carbonated water, sugar or sweetener, caramel coloring, acids, and a syrup made from oils of oranges.

ORANGE SPICE TEA   A fragrant tea scented with oranges and spices, it is a blend of various black teas.

ORANIENSTEINER *(GERMANY)*   A white grape variety developed from a cross of Johannisberg Riesling and Sylvaner at the Geisenheim Institute in the Rheingau.

ORCAE *(SPAIN)*   A large earthenware jar used to store wine.

ORDER FORM   A form used to record items ordered from each purveyor, acting as a check for verification when items are received.

ORDINAIRE *(FRANCE)*   *See* Ordinary.

ORDINARY   Describes a simple, common wine, beer, or distilled spirit without any special breed or distinction, however soundly made it may be. Generally applied to wines and beers meant for everyday consumption. Also known as *common, konsumwein, ordinaire, simple, tischwein, vino corriente, vino da pasto, vino de pasto*, and *vin ordinaire. See* Jug Wine.

ORGANIC   Grown without synthetic fertilizers or pesticides, with some exceptions. Organic farmers substitute composts, crop rotation, mechanical cultivation, botanical pesticides, and biological pest controls. Under pending federal law, prohibited materials must be discontinued three years before a crop can be labeled organic. Products labeled organic must meet specific requirements of the California Organic Foods Act of 1990. *See* Organically Grown Wine.

ORGANICALLY GROWN WINE   Wines made from organically grown grapes, traditionally vinified, which have had sulfites added to the *must* and/or finished wine. Also known as *coltivazione biologica. See* Certified Organic, Integrated Pest Management, Organic, Organic Wine, and Sustainable Agriculture.

ORGANIC WINE   Wine made from organically grown grapes, traditionally vinified but without the addition of sulfites to the *must* and/or finished wine. *See* Organically Grown Wine.

ORGANOLEPTIC   Describes the evaluation of all types of beverages in an analytical context by utilization of the senses: sight, smell, taste, and tactile or viscous perceptions. Also known as *organoleptique* and *sensory evaluation*.

ORGANOLEPTIQUE *(FRANCE)*   *See* Organoleptic.

ORGEAT   A sweet-almond-flavored nonalcoholic syrup used in certain cocktails. It is a combination of almond flavoring, orange flower water, and barley water.

ORIGINALABFÜLLUNG *(GERMANY)*   Label terminology used prior to 1971 to indicate an estate-bottled wine. The term was replaced with *erzeugerabfüllung*.

ORIGINAL GRAVITY   The extract of *wort* before fermentation in the making of beer.

ORLANDO SEEDLESS   A white grape variety.

ORMEASCO *(ITALY)*   *See* Dolcetto.

ORO *(ITALY)*   Gold.

ORRIS ROOT   A root sometimes used in the nineteenth century by the French to restore to Bordeaux wines the perfume destroyed by blending or mixing.

ORTEGA *(GERMANY)*   A white grape variety developed in 1971 from a cross of Müller-Thurgau and Siegerrebe in Würzburg; it was reportedly named after the Spanish philosopher José Ortega y Gasset.

ORTLIEBER   *See* Knipperlé.

ORTRUGO *(ITALY)*   A white grape variety.

ORTSTEIL *(GERMANY)*   A geographic portion of a wine-producing commune.

ORUJO *(SPAIN)*   *See* Grappa.

ORVIETO (ITALY)   The name of a city in southwestern Umbria, where wines are produced in the Paglia and Upper Tiber valleys as well as throughout the province of Terni. The Orvieto Classico area is in the heart of this DOC zone.

Orvieto is made primarily from Procanico (also known as Trebbiano Toscano) and Verdello grapes, with the rest a blend of Grechetto, Drupeggio, and Malvasia Toscana. It is produced in *secco* (dry), *abboccato* (semidry), and *dolce* (sweet) styles.

OSAP   Office of Substance Abuse Prevention.

OSELETA (ITALY)   A red grape variety grown in Veneto.

OSIER BASKETS (FRANCE)   *See* Grape-Picking Basket.

OSIRIS (GERMANY)   A white grape variety developed from a cross of Johannisberg Riesling and Rieslaner. It was named after the ancient Egyptian deity who, among other functions, presided over the growing of grapes.

OSMOSIS   The tendency of a solution to pass through a semipermeable membrane from areas of weaker to higher concentrations in an effort to equalize the concentrations.

OSSIDATO (ITALY)   *See* Oxidized.

OSTEINER (GERMANY)   A white grape variety developed from a cross of Johannisberg Riesling and Sylvaner.

OSTERIA (ITALY)   An inn or tavern. *See* Tavern.

OSTERREICHER (GERMANY)   *See* Sylvaner.

OTHELLO   A red grape variety developed in 1859 from a cross of Clinton and Black Hamburg by Charles Arnold in Paris, Ontario, Canada. The grapes contain a high level of *methyl anthranilate*.

OTRE (ITALY)   *See* Wine Skin.

OTTAVIANELLO (ITALY)   *See* Cinsaut.

OUILLAGE (FRANCE)   *See* Topping.

OUNCE   A United States liquid measurement, sixteen ounces being equal to one pint.

OUNCE BEVERAGE CONTROL SYSTEM   An automated system that is programmed to analyze and record beverage sales by number and type of drinks dispensed as well as to calculate the actual consumption of each type of beverage through the use of figures generated by physical inventories and issues. Also known as *ounce beverage control technique* and *ounce control method*.

OUNCE BEVERAGE CONTROL TECHNIQUE   *See* Ounce Beverage Control System.

OUNCE CONTROL METHOD   *See* Ounce Beverage Control System.

OUT OF STOCK   Item(s) usually carried or available at an individual retail location, but currently not present on the shelf for purchase.

OUTRAS CASTAS (PORTUGAL)   Varieties of grapevines that are not *Vitis vinifera*

OUVRÉE *(FRANCE)*   An old Burgundian vineyard term for a measure of 0.0428 hectares or one-tenth of an acre.

OUZO *(GREECE)*   A liqueur with a licorice-like flavor. It has a distilled spirits base and its sweet fragrant flavor comes from either cold flavoring the distilled spirit with aniseed (*Pimpinella anisum*) or by distilling pure aniseed-flavored distilled spirit with gentian root and other herbs. It is drier than anisette and is higher in alcohol—mostly in the 90-proof range. Found in all the Mediterranean countries, where it is usually taken with water or served on rocks, which turns it an opalescent, milky, yellowish-white. *See* Anise-Based Spirits and Masticha.

OVER-AGED   Beverages that have been aged in wooden barrels or glass containers longer than necessary. *See* Oaky and Woody.

OVERCROPPING   The growing of more grape clusters than a grapevine can bring to maturity at normal harvest time, or can yield and have remain healthy. This can result from disease, insects, light pruning, or water stress.

OVER-FINING   A condition that exists when a fining agent is used in excess, which actually causes further hazing instead of clearing wine. *See* Fining.

OVERPOURING   The pouring of an excessive quantity of an alcoholic beverage so that the drink does not adhere to a standardized recipe. *See* Burned Drinks.

OVERPRODUCTION   The production of a quantity that exceeds normal needs or demands.

OVERPROOF   A distilled spirit whose alcoholic content is more than 100 proof.

OVERRIPE   Describes grapes left on the grapevine beyond normal maturity, causing the berries to dry out, concentrating their flavor. Generally, wines made from these grapes tend to be heavy, unbalanced, and lacking acidity. However, some grapes, notably Zinfandel, often benefit from some overripeness during harvest. Also known as *surma-turité*.

OVER-THE-HILL   *See* Old.

OVER-THE-TOP   *See* Old.

OVOID   Describes egg-shaped grapes.

OWN PRODUCTION   When used with reference to wine in a bonded winery, the term means wine produced by fermentation in the same bonded winery, whether or not produced by a predecessor in interest. The term includes wine produced by fermentation in bonded wineries owned or controlled by the same or affiliated persons or firms when located within the same state.

OWN-ROOTED   A grapevine grown from a cutting on its own root system that develops its own root system, as opposed to grafted or budded rootstocks.

OXIDASE   Any of a group of enzymes that cause the browning of fresh fruit, particularly damaged or moldy fruit. It is easily destroyed by heat, sulfur dioxide, or Vitamin C. Fruits high in Vitamin C do not brown easily or only after the vitamin has been destroyed during the course of fermentation.

OXIDATION   A chemical change in alcoholic beverages due to exposure to excessive oxygen during aging in barrel, while in glass, or from a bad cork. Oxidation causes a loss of freshness in both smell and taste while causing a browning of the color. Also known as *luftgeschmack* and *oxydation*. *See* Maderized and Oxidized.

OXIDIZED   A condition of oxidation. *See* Oxidation.

OXYDATION *(FRANCE)* *See* Oxidation.

O

p \ˈpē\ *n, often cap, often attrib*

P   A letter designation used on labels of armagnac, cognac, and some other brandies as an abbreviation for *pale.*

PA   *See* Promotional Allowance.

PAARL (*SOUTH AFRICA*)   An important wine-producing region.

PACKAGE   The container that holds beer, wine, or distilled spirits.

PACKER   A proprietor of wine premises who fills wine into a container larger than four liters.

PAGEDEBIT (*ITALY*)   A white grape variety.

PAGLIERINO (*ITALY*)   *See* Straw.

PAGO (*SPAIN*)   The area of a vineyard or a distinctly named vineyard.

PAID BAR   A private room bar setup where all drinks are prepaid and tickets for drinks are sometimes used.

PAIEN (*SWITZERLAND*)   A white grape variety. Also known as *Heida.*

PAÍS (*SPAIN*)   *See* Mission.

PAKHYS (*GREECE*)   *See* Fat.

PALACIO (*SPAIN*)   Palace.

PALATE   In organoleptic evaluation, the sense of taste in the mouth as an entity.

PALATINATE (*GERMANY*)   *See* Pfalz.

PALE (P)   A designation used on labels of armagnac, cognac, and some other brandies to indicate a pale color (not in a negative sense).

PALE   Describes the lighter color of ale (or some other types of beer) in comparison to porter or stout.

PALE   Describes a wine that is deficient in color or intensity of color. Also known as *blass, pallid*, and *pallido*.

PALE ALE (ENGLAND)   A copper-colored ale, usually full-bodied, highly hopped, and quite bitter.

PALE CREAM (SPAIN)   A pale-colored cream sherry.

PALE DRY   A loosely-used term meaning dry and light-colored.

PALHETE (PORTUGAL)   Rainwater madeira, a very pale, light, fortified wine. The term is derived from the word *palha*, meaning straw. Also spelled *palhetinho*. *See* Rainwater Madeira.

PALHETINHO (PORTUGAL)   *See* Palhete.

PALLAGRELLO (ITALY)   A white grape variety from Southern Italy. Also known as *Coda di Volpe*.

PALLET   Low-set, portable stand, generally made of wood, on which supplies can be stacked to keep them off the floor.

PALLID   *See* Pale.

PALLIDO (ITALY)   *See* Pale.

PALMA (SPAIN)   A high-quality fino sherry.

PALMA (SPAIN)   Special chalk marks placed on wooden barrels containing sherry wine that denote a developing fino sherry.

PALMCHAM (SOUTH AFRICA)   A carbonated wine produced from the juice of the adoka tree in Ghana.

PALM TODDY   An alcoholic beverage brewed from the sap of coconut or palm trees.

PALO CORTADO (SPAIN)   A true rarity among sherries. Although there is no literal translation for *Palo Cortado*, these sherries have been described as an intermediate classification—they are the lightest of the *olorosos*.

Like all fine sherries, the Palo Cortados are produced from Palomino grapes that are grown in the chalky *albariza* soil unique to the Sherry region. They do not develop any type of *flor* and are quite rare. Of a thousand barrels of wine, perhaps only one will develop the distinctive color of brushed gold, the bouquet of almonds, and the *amontillado* nose and *oloroso* body, which are characteristic of Palo Cortados. Therefore, a sherry producer cannot produce this style of sherry every year and its production amounts to less than 1 percent of the total. The production of Palo Cortado was greatly cut by the *phylloxera* devastation during the 1880s.

PALOMBINA (ITALY)   A red grape variety.

PALOMINO (SPAIN)   A white grape variety that grows primarily in *albariza* soil. This grape is used in the production of 85 percent of all sherry wine and is also grown in South Africa and California, where it is used to produce sherry-type wines.

The grape is also known locally by many different names: *Listán* in Sanlúcar, *Horgazuela* in Puerto de Santa Maria, and *Alban, Temprana*, and *Tempranilla* in other areas. In South Africa it is known as *Fransdruif*.

PAMID (BULGARIA)   A red grape variety.

PAMLICO   A white grape variety developed from a cross of Lucida and Burgaw; it is grown primarily in the southeastern United States.

PAMPANUTO (ITALY)   A white grape variety grown in the south.

PANIER À VENDANGE (FRANCE)   *See* Grape-Picking Basket.

PANNIER   *See* Grape-Picking Basket.

PANSA BLANCA (SPAIN)   *See* Xarel-lo.

PANSA ROJO (SPAIN)   A white grape variety.

PAPAZHARASI (TURKEY)   A red grape variety.

PAPYRI   A 1300 B.C. Egyptian regulation of beer shops to prevent people from overindulging.

PAR   *See* Par Stock.

PARADIS (FRANCE)   Warehouses utilized for the storage of the oldest of cognacs, often up to one hundred years of age.

PARAFFIN   A white, waxy, odorless, colorless, tasteless solid substance used for sealing small holes in leaking wooden barrels. In addition to paraffin, garlic and tooth-picks are occasionally utilized. Also known as *waxing* and *wax lined. See* Typha Latifoglia.

PARASITE   An organism that lives on or in the body of another organism and obtains food from it.

PARCELLE (FRANCE)   A small parcel of land within a vineyard, usually belonging to one individual.

PARDINA (SPAIN)   A white grape variety.

PARELLADA (SPAIN)   A white grape variety that forms the basis for much of the still and sparkling wines produced.

PARFAIT AMOUR LIQUEUR   A sweetened alcoholic beverage consisting of a base of alcohol, minimum 2.5 percent sugar, with various flavorings including anisette, citrus peels, coriander, flower petals, lemon, orange, rose petals, vanilla, and violets. It is made in several colors, mainly bright violet. It is similar in color and taste to *Crème de Violette* and *Crème Yvette*.

PARFUM (FRANCE)   *See* Flowery.

PARING KNIFE   A small, sharp-pointed knife with a 2.5- to 3.5-inch blade, used for peeling and cutting lemons, limes, oranges, and other citrus fruit for garnishes.

PARROCO (ITALY)   Parish priest.

PAR STOCK   The minimum or maximum specified amount of a product on hand to satisfy customers' needs for a specific period of time. Usually refers to the amount of alcoholic beverages needed during a shift or business day at the bar. Also known as *bar pars* and *par. See* Safety Stock.

PAR STOCK LIST   An inventory of all items kept in supply, along with the quantity of each item that should always be available in stock.

PARLOR CAR   A railroad car, often with individual swivel seats or tables, that serves alcoholic beverages as well as some food.

PARTICLE CORK   *See* Agglomerated Cork.

PARTICLE MATTER   Minute particles in a liquid that are held in suspension, such as dead yeast cells, grain fragments, grape pulp or skin fragments, protein matter, and so on. They are generally eliminated by means of fining agents. *See* Colloidal Suspension and Fining.

PARTIDISTA (PORTUGAL)   *See* Broker.

PARTS PER MILLION (PPM)   The number of units existing per a total of one million units. It is the same as milligrams per liter and is often written as mg/liter or 0.000000.

PASADO (SPAIN)   *See* Old.

PASCAL BLANC (FRANCE)   A white grape variety grown in the southeast.

PASCALI (ITALY)   *See* Monica.

PAS DOSÉ (ITALY)   *See* Extra Brut.

PASSAGEM (PORTUGAL)   *See* Racking.

PASSALE (ITALY)   *See* Monica.

PASSÉ (FRANCE)   *See* Old.

PASSERINA (ITALY)   A white grape variety grown in Abruzzo.

PASSION FRUIT LIQUEUR   A sweetened alcoholic beverage consisting of a base of alcohol, minimum 2.5 percent sugar, flavored with a mixture of tropical juices and the fruit of a passion flower.

PASSERILLAGE (FRANCE)   *See* Passito.

PASSITO (ITALY)   A sweet wine made from overripe grapes that have been allowed to dry or shrivel in the sun, causing higher sugar levels; they are then pressed. Also known as *passerillage* or *roti*.

PASSOVER WINE   Wine specially made for the springtime Jewish holiday of Passover.

PASS-THROUGH   A post-off that is passed through to the consumer. *See* Distributor Post-Off.

PASTEUR, LOUIS (FRANCE)   A chemist and bacteriologist (1822–1895) born in a town called Arbois, in the Jura region, and credited as conducting the first scientific study of fermentation (1857).

PASTEURISÉ (FRANCE)   *See* Pasteurization.

PASTEURIZATION   The process by which a liquid or substance is heated to a minimum of 160 degrees Fahrenheit and held at that temperature for a specified period of time to destroy bacteria and microorganisms while stabilizing the product. In the case of beer or wine (if needed), the liquids are pasteurized after bottling, then cooled rapidly.

In the 1870s pasteurization was introduced to the brewing industry by Adolphus Busch. Pasteurization is also known as *hot bottling, pasteurisé, pasteurizzato,* and *thermolization.*

PASTEURIZZATO *(ITALY)* *See* Pasteurization.

PASTIS *(FRANCE)* A category of *anise-based distilled spirits* produced in France; its leading brands are Pernod and Ricard. *See* Anise-Based Spirits.

PASTOSO *(ITALY, PORTUGAL, AND SPAIN)* *See* Fat.

PÂTEAUX *(FRANCE)* *See* Fat.

PATENT STILL An erroneous name for the continuously-fed *column still*, invented by Aeneas Coffey, who was granted a patent for it in 1832. *See* Coffey Still.

PATRONS Another term for customers who frequent an establishment.

PAUILLAC *(FRANCE)* A renowned wine-producing commune in the Haut-Médoc, north of the city of Bordeaux, where some of the greatest red-wine-producing vineyards lie.

On November 14, 1936, the wines of Pauillac were officially granted their *appellation contrôlée* designation.

PAUVRE *(FRANCE)* *See* Poor.

PAUVRETÉ *(FRANCE)* Poverty; a quality of thin brandy with little to recommend it.

PAVILLON *(FRANCE)* Small house.

PAXERETE *(FRANCE)* A sweet wine made partly from the Pedro Ximénez grape variety, often used as a sweetener for sherry.

PÉ *(PORTUGAL)* *See* Lees.

PEABODY A white grape variety grown in the United States.

PEACH-FLAVORED BRANDY A mixture of brandy with a minimum of 2.5 percent sugar, flavored and colored with fresh and dried peaches. By United States federal law it cannot be bottled at less than 60 proof (30 percent alcohol by volume).

PEACH LIQUEUR A sweetened alcoholic beverage consisting of a base of alcohol, minimum 2.5 percent sugar, flavored and colored with fresh and dried peaches. It is sweeter and lower in proof than peach-flavored brandy.

PEACHES An odor reminiscent of peaches, occasionally detected in some young white wines like Johannisberg Riesling, Muscat, and Gewürztraminer as well as some fruity, late-picked white grape varieties that have been affected by *Botrytis cinerea*.

PEAK A wine or beer that reached its apex for drinking (e.g., neither too young nor too old). *See* Shelf Life.

PEAR BRANDY *See* Poire.

PEAR LIQUEUR A sweetened alcoholic beverage consisting of a base of alcohol, minimum 2.5 percent sugar, flavored and colored with pears.

PEAR WILLIAMS *See* Poire.

PEAT A soft, not fully formed coal in a primary state. Peat is made up of decomposed, compacted, and carbonized vegetal material, mainly sphagnum moss mixed with mud and roots, often found in swamps covering some 1.7 million acres in Scotland.

During the smoking process of Scotch whisky, the barley lies above the smoking peat on screens, which allows the burning vapors to permeate the barley, swirling around and under it. This not only dries out the barley but infuses it with a unique smoky aroma and taste.

PEAT REEK   The dark, oily, almost acrid smoke emanating from the burning or smoldering dried peat, utilized to dry and impart a flavor to green malt in the making of Scotch whisky.

PÊCHE (FRANCE)   A fruit brandy made from peaches.

PÉCOUI-TOUAR (FRANCE)   A red grape variety grown in the southeast.

PECTIN   A water-soluble carbohydrate, obtained from the pith and peel of certain ripe fruits, that in excess tends to cause cloudiness in wine. *See* Pectolytic Enzyme.

PECTINASE   A type of *pectolytic enzyme*. *See* Pectolytic Enzyme.

PECTIN HAZE   A haze, occasionally encountered in wine, caused by excessive levels of pectin. *See* Pectolytic Enzyme.

PECTOLYTIC ENZYME   A group of enzymes used to clarify wine, aid in filtration, and reduce pectin content. *See* Pectin, Pectinase, and Pectin Haze.

PÉ DE CUBA (PORTUGAL)   *See* Starter.

PEDERNÃO (PORTUGAL)   *See* Arinto.

PEDICEL   The stalk or small stem of a grapevine that attaches the grape berry to the cluster structure.

PEDRO XIMÉNEZ (SPAIN)   A white grape variety used in making sweet wines, especially sherry. The Pedro Ximénez grapes that grow on the lower slopes of the *albariza* and *barro* soils are left outside to dry in the sun for twelve to fourteen hours after harvesting, which concentrates their sugar levels. They are then placed on *esparto* mats (made of grass) to further dry. So intense is their sweetness that fermentation usually stops at about 14 percent alcohol, resulting in a high degree of residual sugar. The color is usually rich and dark brown and liqueur-like in its concentration. It is traditionally served after meals in place of a brandy or liqueur. Abbreviated *PX*.

PEDUNCLE   The botanical term for the thick stalk by which a bunch of grapes is attached to the cane of a grapevine. This stalk is a valuable source of tannin for red wine.

PEEL   The part of a citrus fruit that contains the outer layer (zest) and the inner, bitter layer (pith). Also known as *skin*.

PEG   A small glass used for whiskey that holds the equivalent of about 1.5 ounces. In England, it is a drink usually made with brandy or whiskey and soda water.

PEGGED   The name given to a champagne cork that is partially or totally molded to the interior diameter of the bottle. It lacks resilience, thus producing the thin stem mushroom shape.

PEKOE   *See* Orange Pekoe Tea.

PELAVERGA (ITALY)   An ancient red grape variety from Piedmont.

PELLAGRELLO (ITALY)   *See* Pallagrello.

PELLAGRELLO ROSSO (ITALY)   A red grape variety.

PELLEJO (SPAIN)   *See* Wine Skin.

PELOURSIN (FRANCE)   A red grape variety grown primarily in the southwest.

PELURE D'OIGNON (FRANCE)   A wine whose light color is similar to that of an onion skin.

PENN, WILLIAM   The famous American statesman was probably the first in the future United States to operate a brewery on a large commercial scale; it was located in Pennsbury, Bucks County, Pennsylvania (1638).

PENTOSE   Any of a group of monosaccharides (simple sugars) with five atoms of carbon in the molecule, including ribose, arabinose, and so on. *See* Reducing Sugar.

PEPPERMINT LIQUEUR   A sweetened alcoholic beverage consisting of a base of alcohol, minimum 2.5 percent sugar, flavored and colored with peppermint.

PEPPERMINT SCHNAPPS   A colorless, mint-flavored liqueur, with the sugar content about half that of white crème de menthe. It is also higher in proof.

PEPPERY   An aromatic smell or taste evocative of black pepper, herbs, or spices, with a pungent flavor. A biting harshness, possibly due to hard tannins and high alcohol, that may dissipate or become smoother with additional age. Noticeable in young ruby and vintage ports and many young, full-bodied red wines.

PEPTONIZE   To digest, dissolve, or metabolize through fermentation.

PERCEIVED COST   The customer's perception of how much money an alcoholic or nonalcoholic beverage should cost, distinct from what the producer may believe it should.

PERCEIVED VALUE   The customer's perception of how much money an alcoholic or nonalcoholic beverage is worth, distinct from what the producer may believe it is.

PERCENTAGE METHOD   A method of calculating a figure (wholesale or selling price), using percentages rather than dollar values.

PERCEPTION   The complete process of receiving information through one of the senses, comparing this information with past experiences, identifying, and evaluating it, and storing it for future reference.

PERCOLATION   The percolation method of producing liqueurs is similar to the percolation of coffee. Distilled spirits are put into the bottom of a tank and the botanicals (fruits, flowers, etc.) are placed in a basket-like container, tray, or bag at the top of the tank. The distilled spirits from the bottom of the tank are then pumped to the top, where they are sprayed over the botanicals, dripping back to the bottom to be percolated over and over until the desired flavor has been extracted. The final product is called an *extract*.

PERCOLATION   The downward movement of water through soil.

PERFUME   Also known as *parfum*. *See* Flowery.

PERGOLINA (ITALY)   *See* Regina.

PERIQUITA (PORTUGAL)   A red grape variety grown in the Algarve and Bairrada regions. Also known as *Castelão Frances* and *João do Santarém*.

PERISHABLE   Describes a substance that deteriorates readily if not properly treated or refrigerated.

PERKINS   A white grape variety discovered in 1830 by Jacob Perkins in Bridgewater, Massachusetts.

PERLAGE   The bubbles in a glass of sparkling wine and how long they persist. Also known as *perlaggio*.

PERLAGGIO *(ITALY)*   *See* Perlage.

PERLANT *(FRANCE)*   A wine that sparkles slightly—less so than *pétillant* and *crémant*, and much less than *mousseux*. In France, the wine usually contains 1.5 to 2.5 atmospheres of pressure.

PERLE *(GERMANY)*   A white grape variety developed from a cross of Gewürztraminer and Müller-Thurgau at the Alzey Research Station in the Rheinhessen.

PERLETTE SEEDLESS   A white grape variety developed in 1936 from a cross of Muscat Reine des Vignes and Thompson Seedless by Dr. Harold P. Olmo of the University of California, Davis.

PERLE OF CSABA   A white grape variety grown since the early 1900s.

PERLWEIN *(GERMANY)*   *See* Artificially Carbonated Wine.

PERMITTEE   *See* Licensee.

PERNAND-VERGELESSES *(FRANCE)*   A small village just north of Aloxe-Corton and adjacent to Corton-Charlemagne in Burgundy's Côte de Beaune; it produces good quality red and white wines.

PERONOSPORA   *See* Downy Mildew.

PERPETUAL INVENTORY   A daily, ongoing bookkeeping system that adds to and subtracts from the inventory as bottles enter and leave the storeroom.

PERRICONE *(ITALY)*   A red grape variety grown in Sicily. Also known as *Pignatello*.

PERRY *(ENGLAND)*   A sparkling wine made from pears.

PERSISTANCE *(FRANCE)*   *See* Persistence.

PERSISTENCE   One of the characteristics of a very good wine—the length of time that the bouquet and the flavor of a wine or beer remains after being swallowed. Also known as *persistance* and *persistenza*.

PERSISTENZA *(ITALY)*   *See* Persistence.

PERSONAL SELLING   The person-to-person or one-on-one communication by which the attributes or benefits of a given product or service are conveyed.

PESANTE *(ITALY)*   *See* Flat.

PESSAC-LÉOGNAN *(FRANCE)*   An *appellation contrôlée* established on September 9, 1987, which applies only to those red and white wines produced in the northern ten communes of Graves, located southwest of the city of Bordeaux. It was recognized that these ten communes consistently produced superior quality wines than those further south. The red wines must contain a minimum of 25 percent Cabernet Sauvignon and the white wines a minimum of 25 percent Sauvignon Blanc.

PESTICIDE   Any substance that controls the spread of harmful or destructive organisms, especially a fungicide, herbicide, or insecticide. *See* Fungicide, Herbicide, and Insecticide.

PETER MINUIT   *See* Minuit, Peter.

PÉTILLANT *(FRANCE)*   *See* Spritz.

PETIOLAR SINUS   On a grapevine, the sinus formed by the basal leaf lobes at the petiolar attachment.

PETIOLE   The stem portion of a leaf that attaches the leaf blade to the shoot on a grapevine.

PETIOLE ANALYSIS   By taking a sample of the *petiole* and analyzing it, viticulturists can determine the current nutritional status of the entire grapevine.

PETIT *(FRANCE)*   *See* Little.

PETIT BOUSCHET *(FRANCE)*   A red grape variety developed in 1828 from a crossing of Aramon and Teinturier du Cher by Louis Bouschet

PETIT CHABLIS *(FRANCE)*   A lesser appellation of Chablis made from the Chardonnay grape variety; according to AOC regulations, the wine must attain 9.5 percent alcohol. It is the simplest of the four classifications, accounting for less than 10 percent of production, and is rarely exported to the United States. The other three chablis wines are *grand cru, premier cru*, and *chablis*.

PETIT CHÂTEAU *(FRANCE)*   A term with many meanings that depends on where it is used. In Bordeaux it denotes some of the lesser properties (not from the 1855 Classification); in the United States it is used when referring to *cru bourgeois* wines or other wines from Bordeaux.

PETITE CHAMPAGNE *(FRANCE)*   This cognac is a blend made from grapes grown in the Grande Champagne and Petite Champagne sections of Cognac; at least 50 percent of it must be from grapes grown in the Grande Champagne section. Also known as *petite fine champagne*.

PETITE FINE CHAMPAGNE *(FRANCE)*   *See* Petite Champagne.

PETITE PINOT   *See* Mondeuse Noire.

PETITE SIRAH   A red grape variety grown in California, where it has mistakenly been known for decades as *Durif*. Traditionally, it has been used as a blending grape, adding inky black color, richness, body, and a somewhat spicy-peppery character to wines. Petite Sirah has no lineage to the *Syrah* grape variety grown in the Rhône Valley of southern France.

In 1964, Concannon Vineyards of California became the first winery to bottle Petite Sirah as a separate varietal. *See* Durif and Syrah.

PETITE SYRAH *(FRANCE)*   *See* Syrah.

PETIT GAMAI   *See* Gamay.

PETIT MANSENG (FRANCE)   A white grape variety native to Juraçon.

PETIT ROUGE (ITALY)   A red grape variety grown in the region of Valle d'Aosta.

PETIT VERDOT   A red grape variety grown primarily in the Médoc in the Bordeaux region of France, where it is used in small amounts as a blending grape, along with Cabernet Sauvignon and Merlot. Small parcels of Petit Verdot are planted in California and Chile; it is utilized as a blending grape there as well. Also known as *Verdot*.

PETTY CASH   A small cash fund used in a beverage operation for small incidental expenses that do not warrant a formal purchase order.

PEVERELLA   A white grape variety grown in California.

PEYCHAUD'S BITTERS   A type of bitters produced in New Orleans, used almost exclusively in the Sazerac cocktail.

PEZSGO (HUNGARY)   *See* Sparkling Wine.

PFALZ (GERMANY)   One of thirteen Qualitätswein (quality) grape-growing regions, bordered by the Rhine River to the east, France to the south and southwest, the Mosel-Saar-Ruwer to the west, and the Rheinhessen to the north. The majority of its high-quality wines are made from the Sylvaner and Müller-Thurgau grapes, with a small portion of Johannisberg Riesling. Climate and soil combine to aid in making not only the common wine of the German *Weinstube* or local pub but also some outstanding wines. Wines from the villages of Forst and Deidesheim are among the finest of the Pfalz, being fuller and sweeter than Mosels, Rheingaus, and even Rheinhessens. Other major Pfalz winemaking towns are Wachenheim, Ruppertsberg, Duerkheim, and Ungstein. Formerly called *Rheinpfalz*. Also known as *Palatinate*.

PFEFFRIG (AUSTRIA)   *See* Spicy.

PFLÜMLI (SWITZERLAND)   A brandy made from prunes.

PH   The potential of hydrogen. The concept of pH was introduced in 1909 by the Danish chemist Sorensen as an expedient means of expressing the hydrogen ion concentration in a solution. *P* symbolized the Danish word *potenz* (power) and *H* represented hydrogen. pH serves, therefore, as shorthand for "acid power." The definition is the logarithm of the reciprocal of the hydrogen-ion concentration in gram equivalents per liter of solution, on a scale whose values run from 0 to 14, with 7 representing neutrality; numbers less than 7 indicate increasing acidity and numbers greater than 7 indicate increasing alkalinity.

PHENOL   A group of more than one hundred related compounds that occur naturally in wine grapes, mostly in the skins, seeds, and stems. Although winemakers often use "tannin" and "phenol" interchangeably, tannin is a subclass of phenol—admittedly, a very large and important one. About 65 percent of the phenols of grapes are contained in the seeds, while about 22 percent are in the stems, 12 percent in the skins, and only 1 percent in the pulp. These numbers are only generalizations at best, for the numbers will vary between varieties and also red and white grapes. *See* Anthocyanin, Astringency, Ellagic Acid, Gallic Acid, Phenolic, Seeds, Skin, Stems, and Tannin.

PHENOLIC   A term that describes any compound with a phenol-type structure. Such compounds are generally categorized into two major groups: flavonoids and non-flavonoids. The flavonoid group consists of *tannin* (often expressed as gallic acid) and a number of *catechin* compounds, which are bitter and often involved with browning. Among other subgroups, the flavonoids also include the anthocyanin (red) and leucoanthocyanin (white) color pigment compounds. The non-flavonoids are a much smaller and less important group of phenolics, existing primarily as derivatives of the aromatic compound cinnamic acid.

When complex structures are formed from primary phenols, such as in grapes during maturation and in winemaking processes, such compounds are called *phenolics*. *See* Phenol.

PHLOEM   Living plant tissue located just beneath the bark and outside of the cambium layer on a grapevine or cork oak tree.

PHOSPHATES   *See* Nutrients.

PHOTOSYNTHESIS   The process by which grapevines are able to manufacture carbohydrates. It involves combining carbon dioxide from the air and water from the soil, utilizing light energy in the presence of chlorophyll in the leaves. This in turn nourishes both the grapevine and the fruit it bears. *See* Chlorophyll and Chloroplasts.

PHYLLOXERA VASTATRIX   This species name comes from the Greek *phyllon*, meaning leaf, and *xeros*, meaning dry. A native eastern and southern United States (Mississippi River Valley) aphid-like pest, it lives on wild grapevine species that have varying levels of tolerance or resistance to it. It is a parasitic, microscopic, burrowing plant louse, yellowish in color, which eats away at the roots of grapevines. The name *Phylloxera vastatrix* was given to this insect in 1864 by J.E. Planchon, professor of pharmacy and entomology at Montpellier. *Phylloxera* was identified as *Daktulosphaira vitifoliae* as early as 1856 by Dr. Asa Fitch, American entomologist, in his book "The Noxious, Beneficial, and Other Insects of the State of New York." It is speculated that *phylloxera* was accidentally exported to Europe during the last century on grapevine cuttings that were actually sent to help control the spread of powdery mildew. Another theory, however, suggests that *phylloxera* was inadvertently brought to Europe by horticulturists who had intended to study American grapevines. Regardless of which is fact, grapevine cuttings have been sent from America to Europe since 1629; however, the lack of swift ocean transportation provided a natural biological barrier prior to the advent of clipper ships and steamers in the 1850s. The transportation advances, which cut ocean travel from several months to merely one month, made it possible for the *phylloxera* to survive the ocean voyage.

Phylloxera decimated vineyards in Europe, beginning in the 1860s, because the grapevine *Vitis vinifera* is highly susceptible to infestation. Between 1870 and the turn of the century almost every grape-growing area in Europe as well as in California was destroyed. In Europe, the insect was first found in 1863 on English grapevines at a greenhouse in Hammersmith, near London. It then spread to the Department of Gard, west of Avignon, and the seaport of Marseilles in the south of France in 1864. European catastrophe soon followed. Among the most devastated areas were the Rhône Valley of France in 1863, followed by Saint-Rémy in 1868, the Midi and Bordeaux in 1869, and Alsace in 1870; Pfalz, Germany, and Burgundy, France in 1874; Portugal (Madeira) and Málaga, Spain, in 1880; Capetown, South Africa, in 1886; Jerez, Spain, in 1894; and Melbourne, Australia, in 1899, just to name a few major areas.

At the Beaune Congress of 1869, M. Gaston Bazille, professor of science at the Society of Agriculture of Herault, advanced his idea that American rootstocks be grafted to French grapevines to defeat the *phylloxera* plague. His work on this project began in about 1871.

The rootstock almost universally accepted (and grafted onto in the United States) was AxR #1 (cross of a *Vitis vinifera* Aramon (southern France) and an American *Vitis rupestris*). This cross was developed by the French viticulturist Victor Ganzin in 1876. Unfortunately, with a new strain of *phylloxera* (biotype B), this miracle rootstock's reputation, not to mention its effectiveness, has vanished. Nowadays, most new grapevines worldwide are grafted onto a *phylloxera*-resistant American rootstock to ensure proper grapevine health and adequate bearing. Also known as *reblaus*.

PHYSICAL INVENTORY   A physical, bottle-by-bottle count of stock physically on the premises at the end of an accounting period.

PHYTOTOXIC   Causing injury or death of grapevines or parts of grapevines.

PICARDAN NOIR *(FRANCE)*   The local name for the Cinsaut grape variety in the Rhône Valley.

PICHET *(FRANCE)*   A small, opaque carafe, decanter, or jug popular in restaurants.

PICKING   *See* Harvest.

PICKLED   *See* Intoxicated.

PICK-ME-UP   Any of a number of concoctions designed to alleviate the effects of overconsumption of alcohol.

PICK-UP STATION   A section of the front of the bar where servers place orders for drinks, receive drinks, turn in collected moneys, and return empty glasses.

PICOLIT *(ITALY)*   A white grape variety grown exclusively in the region of Friuli-Venezia Giulia. Picolit grapevines thrived during the late 1700s and by the mid-nineteenth century produced the most prestigious wines of Italy, bottles of which graced the tables of royalty throughout England, France, Russia, and Austria.

Unfortunately, the grapevine in later years produced very few grapes and was thought to have a genetic disease called *floral abortion*. Modern research conducted by Dr. Giovanni Cargnello at the Conegliano Institute, however, discovered that the Picolit grape variety is not self-pollinating because it is purely female and not, as is usual, hermaphroditic. Technically, Picolit is known as *Picolit Giallo*.

Picolit grapes produce a brightly golden-colored dessert wine in dry, semidry, and sweet versions (without the help of *Botrytis cinerea*, known as *muffa nobile*). The sweet version is made from dried grapes (called *passito*).

PICOTENER *(ITALY)*   *See* Nebbiolo.

PICPOUL   *See* Folle Blanche.

PICPOULE   *See* Folle Blanche.

PICULTENER *(ITALY)*   *See* Nebbiolo.

PIÈCE *(FRANCE)*   A barrel with a capacity of fifty-five to sixty gallons, used in various parts of France for the storage of wines. *See* Barrel.

PIECE   During the early 1800s, a term used to denote 250 bottles of wine.

PIED *(FRANCE)*   Individual grapevines.

PIED DE CUVE *(FRANCE)*   *See* Starter.

PIEDE DI PALUMBO *(ITALY)*   A red grape variety.

PIEDILUNGO (*ITALY*)   A red grape variety.

PIEDIROSSO (*ITALY*)   A red grape variety grown in the south.

PIEDMONT (*ITALY*)   One of twenty wine-producing regions, located in the north-west, bordered by France to the west and Switzerland to the north. The Ligurian Apennines and the Alps surround Piedmont to the south, west, and north.

Piedmont is actually a contraction of the dialectical words "A Pie' di Monte" (at the foot of the mountains). The area has been producing good to excellent wines for well over a century using the most underrated wine grape in the world, the Nebbiolo.

Piedmont produces the greatest number of superb red wines in Italy. The production of DOCG, DOC, and non-DOC wines is concentrated in the southern part of Piedmont in the provinces of Cuneo, Asti, and Alessandria. This area of exclusively hilly vineyards accounts for 90 percent of the total regional output. Other areas of production are the hills between the towns of Novara and Vercelli and the zone around the regional capital of Turin. Known as *Piemonte* in Italy.

PIEDS DE VIGNE (*FRANCE*)   *See* Rootstock.

PIED TENDRE (*FRANCE*)   *See* Colombard.

PIEMONTE (*ITALY*)   *See* Piedmont.

PIENO (*ITALY*)   *See* Full-Bodied.

PIEPRZÓWKA (*POLAND*)   A pepper-flavored vodka.

PIERCE   A red grape variety grown in the United States.

PIERCE'S DISEASE   A bacteria transmitted by the sharpshooter, a large leafhopper, that destroys grapevines. At one time it was called Anaheim Disease and California Vine Disease. It was first discovered by Newton B. Pierce, a United States Department of Agriculture plant pathologist assigned to the West Coast to study the problem, who reported in 1892 on detailed studies and observations that are the basis of our present-day understanding of this serious disease.

PIERRE-À-FUSIL (*FRANCE*)   *See* Flinty.

PIESPORT (*GERMANY*)   A famous vineyard town located in the Mittelmosel, noted for its production of light and delicate white wines.

PIGIARE (*ITALY*)   *See* Pressing.

PIGIATURA (*ITALY*)   *See* Pressing.

PIGIATRICE (*ITALY*)   *See* Wine Press.

PIGMENT   *See* Anthocyanin.

PIGMENTAZIONE (*ITALY*)   Pigmentation. *See* Anthocyanin.

PIGMENTO (*ITALY*)   Pigment. *See* Anthocyanin.

PIGNATELLO (*ITALY*)   *See* Perricone.

PIGNOLA VALTELLINESE (*ITALY*)   A red grape variety grown in the region of Lombardy.

PIGNOLETTO (*ITALY*)   A white grape variety grown in Emilia-Romagna, producing a wine of the same name.

PIKANT (GERMANY)   *See* Piquant.

PIKRÓS (GREECE)   *See* Bitter.

PILFERAGE   Stealing, especially in small quantities.

PILONGO (PORTUGAL)   *See* Alvarelhão.

PILS   *See* Pilsner.

PILSENER   *See* Pilsner.

PILSNER   This is the most popular type or style of beer produced. The word *Pilsner* is taken from the Czechoslovakian town of Pilsen. Characteristically, these beers are light golden in color, with a highly pronounced hops flavor (referred to as *Bohemian*) and a clean, crispy taste that refreshes and leaves the palate clean. Pilsner-style beers are usually dry to very dry in taste, although there are some slightly sweet pilsners produced. Also spelled *pils* and *pilsener*.

PILSNER GLASS   A tall, conical beer glass with a short stem and a full funnel-shaped bowl.

PIN   A barrel, used in eighteenth-century England, with a capacity of approximately 5.4 gallons. *See* Barrel.

PIÑA (SPAIN)   The heart of the agave plant, used in making tequila and mezcal.

PIÑA COLADA   A cocktail consisting of rum, pineapple juice, and coconut milk. Purportedly concocted in 1963 by Don Ramos Portas Mingot, a bartender at the Barrachina Restaurant in San Juan, Puerto Rico. However, one Ramon "Monchito" Marrero of Monchito's Bar in the San Juan Hilton, claims he created it in 1954.

PINARD (FRANCE)   Slang for an ordinary red wine.

PINEAPPLE   An odor occasionally encountered in some white wines, notably Johannisberg Riesling and Chenin Blanc, which is an ester, chemically formed from *ethyl butyrate* (ethyl alcohol + butyric acid).

PINEAPPLE JUICE   The liquid constituent of a pineapple.

PINEAU DES CHARENTES (FRANCE)   *See* Mistelle and Ratafia.

PINEAU D'AUNIS (FRANCE)   A red grape variety used to make rosé and red wines in Anjou.

PINEAU DE LA LOIRE (FRANCE)   *See* Chenin Blanc.

PINK CHAMPAGNE   *See* Rosé Champagne.

PINOT   A great grape wine family that includes such subdivisions as Blanc, Gris, Noir, St.-George, and others.

PINOTAGE (SOUTH AFRICA)   A red grape variety developed on November 17, 1924 from a cross of Pinot Noir and Cinsaut by Professor Abraham Izak. Perold at the Stellenbosch University.

PINOT AUXERROIS (FRANCE)   *See* Auxerrois Blanc.

PINOT BEUROT (FRANCE)   *See* Pinot Gris.

PINOT BIANCO (ITALY)   *See* Pinot Blanc.

PINOT BLANC   A white grape variety with some similarities of Chardonnay. Pinot Blanc is grown in some parts of California, where it is used in sparkling winemaking; however, it is grown prolifically in Alsace, France, and the northern regions in Italy. Also known as *Clevner, Fehérburgundi, Pinot Bianco*, and *Weissburgunder*.

PINOT CHARDONNAY   *See* Chardonnay.

PINOT GRIGIO (ITALY)   *See* Pinot Gris.

PINOT GRIS   A white grape variety that produces well-balanced, full-bodied wines. They can be fruity, but that sensation on the palate is followed by a luscious, slightly smoky, absolutely dry finish. Pinot Gris, which is also called *Tokay d'Alsace*, is not to be confused with Hungarian Tokay; with that in mind, the European Economic Community (EEC) banned the use of the name Tokay in Alsace, France. Also known as *Auxerrois Gris, Szürkebarát, Grauer Burgunder, Malvoisie* (it stems from pre-thirteenth-century words derived from Monemvasia, a small Greek village), *Pinot Beurot*, and *Pinot Grigio*; in Baden, Germany, *Ruländer*.

PINOT MEUNIER   *See* Meunier.

PINOT NERO (ITALY)   *See* Pinot Noir.

PINOT NOIR   A red grape variety grown mostly in Burgundy, France, where it produces some of the finest wines in the world, and is also vinified, along with Meunier and Chardonnay, to produce champagne. In addition, Pinot Noir is extensively grown throughout the world, especially in Italy and California.

Pinot Noir wines are medium to deep ruby-red, with a distinctive aroma and taste of black cherry, black currant, black pepper, dried fruits, jam, mint, plum, raspberry, spice, and strawberry. The wines are silky and soft, with a velvety texture and rich, full finish. Also known as *Blauburgunder, Blauer Klevner, Blauer Spätburgunder, Borgogno Nero, Nágyburgundi, Noirien, Klevner, Pinot Nero, Plant Doré, Spätburgunder*, and *Savagnin Noir*.

PINOT ST-GEORGE   A red grape variety grown almost exclusively in parts of France where it is used mostly for blending. Small quantities are grown in California, where it produces fairly good wines approaching Pinot Noir in style. Correctly known as *Negrétte*.

PINPOINT BUBBLES   Tiny bubbles resembling continuous chains of beads emanating from a glass of sparkling wine or even beer. Fine, small bubbles usually indicate a superior quality product. *See* Beads.

PINT   A United States liquid measurement of volume; equal to sixteen ounces (one-eighth of a gallon or 0.568 liters).

PINTA (ITALY)   A bottle with a capacity of two liters, used in the Piedmont region.

PIPA (SPAIN)   *See* Pips.

PIPE   A barrel used to store or ship madeira, marsala, port, and other fortified wines. Its proportions vary with the area in which it is used. Its capacity ranges from 418 to 550 liters (110 to 141 gallons). *See* Barrel.

PIPE   An English wine measure of 1497 stated that a pipe had a capacity of two hogsheads or 126 gallons. *See* Barrel.

PIPELING   Part of the three-tier distribution network of alcoholic beverages where a producer sells to a wholesaler (distributor) of a certain product, without the necessity of that wholesaler distributing said merchandise to retailers.

PIPS   An antiquated term for the seeds or pits contained in a grape berry. Also known as *pipa*. *See* Seeds.

PIQUANT   Describes a wine that is agreeably pungent, tart, or stimulating to the taste; pleasantly sharp or biting due to its lively acidity. Also known as *pikant*.

PIQUÉ (FRANCE)   *See* Volatile Acidity.

PIQUERA (SPAIN)   An open hole in the middle of the frontal side of the lagar (primary fermentation tank) through which the *must* flows out.

PIQUETTE (FRANCE)   A term applied to any poor, thin, acid wine, usually produced by adding water to the pomace, then repressing. This wine is generally sold locally in large jugs. *See* Watered Down.

PIQÛRE ACÉTIQUE (FRANCE)   *See* Flowers of Wine.

PIRODNO (YUGOSLAVIA)   Natural.

PIS   *See* Profit Investment Statement.

PISADOR (SPAIN)   *See* Treading.

PISCO   A brandy from Chile or Peru, distilled from Muscat of Alexandria and/or Mission grapes. The name Pisco is taken from the name of a port in southern Peru whence the brandy was shipped to the United States prior to Prohibition.

PISSED   *See* Intoxicated.

PITH   The bitter, white, fibrous inner layer of a citrus fruit that lies directly beneath the outer skin. It is a good source of pectin.

PITS   *See* Seeds.

PIVO (CZECHOSLOVAKIA AND RUSSIA)   *See* Beer.

PIWO (POLAND)   *See* Beer.

PIXIOLA   A white grape variety.

PLANT D'ARLES (FRANCE)   *See* Cinsaut.

PLANT DE GRAISSE (FRANCE)   A white grape variety once quite popular in the Armagnac region, although its acreage is now fading fast. Also known as *Président*.

PLANT DORÉ (FRANCE)   *See* Pinot Noir.

PLANTES NOBLES (FRANCE)   Noble grape varieties.

PLANTET   A red grape variety. Formerly known as *Seibel 5455*.

PLANT GRIS (FRANCE)   *See* Aligoté.

PLANT PROPAGATION   The reproduction of grapevines by seeds, cuttings, and so on.

PLANT POUZIN   *See* Clinton.

PLAQUE *(FRANCE)* The metal cap that prevents the cork from being severed by the wire hood on bottles of sparkling wine.

PLASMOPARA VITICOLA *See* Downy Mildew.

PLASTERED *See* Intoxicated.

PLASTERING A practice formerly used extensively in the Sherry region of Spain, where gypsum or *yeso*, also known as *plaster of Paris* (calcium sulfate), was added to grapes or the *must* prior to fermentation to increase the total acidity and lower the pH of the resulting wine. Also known as *plâtré*.

PLAT *(FRANCE)* *See* Flat.

PLATINO *(ITALY)* Platinum.

PLATO The term often used in brewing to designate the percent of fermentable solids in the mash. *See* Brix.

PLÂTRÉ *(FRANCE)* *See* Plastering.

PLAVAC MALI *(YUGOSLAVIA)* A red grape variety, believed by some to be identical to the Zinfandel or Primitivo grape.

PLEIN *(FRANCE)* *See* Complete.

PLEASANT A loosely used term generally applied to wines or beers that are appealing, agreeable, and delightful to the senses. Also known as *agreeable, amiable, charm, efkháristos, gefällig, gradevole, lovely, nice*, and *pleasing*.

PLEASING *See* Pleasant.

PLECHISTIK *(RUSSIA)* A red grape variety.

PLIAGE *(FRANCE)* A process by which the shoots are tied to the trellis wire after pruning of the grapevine has taken place.

PLONK *See* Swill.

PLOVDINA *(YUGOSLAVIA)* A red grape variety.

PLOWPAN A compacted layer of earth at the bottom of the furrow at the same depth. *See* Hardpan.

PLUM BRANDY *See* Mirabelle, Quetsch, Schwarzwälder, and Slivovitz.

PLUMMY A term generally applied to red wines that are full of or tasting of plums.

PLUMP *(GERMANY)* *See* Awkward.

PLUMS An odor and taste occasionally detected in some late-harvested red grape varieties of higher than average sugar at harvest. A trait of some red wines, such as Zinfandel, Pinot Noir, Petite Sirah, and even some Portuguese port.

PLYMOUTH GIN This is actually an *appellation* and is only produced by the Coates firm of Plymouth, England, which was founded in 1798. It is an aromatic gin, sometimes pink in color from the addition of angostura bitters. Its taste lies somewhere between that of Dutch and London dry gin. Plymouth gin was originally associated with the British Royal Navy, which, as legend has it, invented this gin as a tolerable way of drinking bitters, which helped control intestinal disorders. They often mixed it with lime juice; hence the nickname "limey," which is frequently applied to the British. Unfortunately, the production of Plymouth gin has dwindled in recent years.

PO   *See* Purchase Order.

POCHEEN   *See* Poteen.

PODERE *(ITALY)*   Farm, agricultural holding.

PODRIDÃO DOS CACHOS *(PORTUGAL)*   *See Botrytis Cinerea.*

POGGIO *(ITALY)*   Hill.

POIGNETAGE *(FRANCE)*   The shaking of sparkling wine bottles while they are undergoing secondary fermentation, to keep the sediment suspended and to aid in riddling. Not to be confused with the riddling process.

POINTE *(FRANCE)*   *See* Punt.

POINT OF PURCHASE (POP)   A display or in-house piece of advertising (e.g., table tent, menu board) that is intended to encourage impulse on-premise sales.

POINT OF SALE (POS)   A piece of advertising posted within an establishment designed for customers' viewing and related sales.

POIO *(PORTUGAL)*   A terraced vineyard.

POIRE   A brandy made from pears in Switzerland, Austria, Germany, France, and occasionally Canada. The best known is Poire Williams, each bottle of which contains a fully mature pear—not an easy accomplishment. After the pear has flowered and is about the size of a grape, it is placed, still on the branch, in the bottle. When the pear is mature, the branch is cut away, the pear washed, and the bottle filled with pear brandy.

Poire is a dry, high-proof brandy, usually clear or slightly amber-tinged in color. Also known as *Pear Williams* or *pear brandy*.

POKER BEER   Beer heated with a red-hot poker, often served as a winter drink. *See* Loggerhead and Mulled Wine.

POLE UNIT   Display piece supported by a cardboard pole, which can be free-standing or attached to the display.

POLISHING FILTER   The final filtering step in winemaking or brewing where the product is directed through an ultra-fine filtering medium designed to totally clear the liquid to a shimmering brilliance. *See* Filtering.

POLLINATION   During bloom, pollen is deposited on the stigma at the top of the pistil. Each pollen grain may produce a tube that grows downward through the pistil to the embryo sac in the ovule. The male cells from the pollen tube are discharged into the embryo sac, resulting in the fertilization of the egg. This is necessary for the formation of a normal seed and eventual development of grapes. Also known as *fécondation*.

POLSUHO *(YUGOSLAVIA)*   *See* Semidry Wine.

POLYMERIZATION   The joining together of phenol compounds.

POLYSACCHARIDE   Any of a group of complex carbohydrates, such as starch, that upon hydrolysis yield more than two molecules of monosaccharides (simple sugars).

POMACE   The residual skins, pulp, and seeds remaining after the grapes have been pressed. The pomace is often utilized in the making of *grappa*.

The skins and seeds, which are a good source of nitrogen, are loaded into trucks and dumped between the vineyard rows to decompose during the winter and be disked into the soil in the spring. Pomace is also known as *bagaço, cake*, and *vinaccia*. *See* Grappa.

POMACE BRANDY   *See* Grappa.

POMEROL (FRANCE)   A major red-wine-producing district on the right bank of the Dordogne River in Bordeaux, just northwest of Saint-Émilion. Most Pomerols are made with a predominance of the Merlot grape, which yields soft and velvety wines with a fullness, warmth, and depth of flavor.

Although the wines of Pomerol were never officially classified, several of them would rank with the finest from Médoc. On December 8, 1936, the wines of Pomerol were officially given their *appellation contrôlée* designation.

To help promote the wines of Pomerol, the La Confrérie des Hospitaliers de Pomerol, a wine brotherhood, was established.

POMMARD (FRANCE)   A red wine commune in Burgundy's Côte de Beaune district, which lies between Beaune in the north and Volnay to the south. Pommard is noted for its production of fine quality red wines, which have been extremely popular in the United States, mostly because the name Pommard is easy for Americans to pronounce.

PONDEROUS   *See* Heavy.

PONIENTE (SPAIN)   The cool, humid winds that often blow in the Sherry region.

PONY GLASS   A small, short-stemmed glass with a tubular bowl that holds approximately 1.5 ounces.

POOR   Describes a barely drinkable wine or beer with little or no merit, character, or quality. Also known as *pauvre*.

POP   *See* Soda Pop.

POP WINES   The term usually refers to inexpensive, light-bodied wines that appear under proprietary labels with creative names. These wines, carbonated or slightly effervescent and low in alcohol, are made from an infusion of grape or other fruit flavors to produce a "soda pop" type of wine.

PORES   Tubes or canals in the lenticel structure of a cork.

POROSITY   A term that refers to the size limitation of materials that may pass through a medium. It is the ratio of the volume of a material's pores to its total volume.

PORPORA (ITALY)   *See* Purple.

PORRÓN (SPAIN)   A round-bellied bottle with a long spout. Usually during a contest, people bet to see from how far away wine can be poured (generally at arm's length) into one's mouth without splashing one's face or spilling any wine. It is known as Fassle in Germany. *See* Bota.

PORT   A heavy, full-bodied, sweet red or white fortified wine, traditionally served after dinner; it is named for the city of Oporto in northern Portugal. The production of port is limited to a strictly defined area of approximately sixty-eight thousand acres along the River Douro in the Alto Douro (Upper Douro) region. The slopes of the

Douro, which have a slate-like soil known as schist, are cut out and terraced for planting with vineyards. These walled terraces prevent erosion of the precious soil.

The production and marketing of port are strictly controlled by the *Instituto do Vinho do Porto* (Port Wine Institute), set up in June 1933. Stringent laws govern the production of all port from the grapevine to the final product. An official certificate of origin is issued by the Port Wine Institute after careful tasting and examination of each lot. The official seal of guarantee over the neck of the bottle indicates approval by the Institute.

The name *Porto* is also specifically protected by law in the United States. Since 1968, the only wine in the United States that can be called Porto is the fortified wine produced in Portugal's Douro region. Therefore, if an American wine producer decided to produce a port-like wine, he or she may not call it Porto; it must simply be labeled a port.

PORTADOR (SPAIN)   *See* Grape-Picking Basket.

PORTAINJERTO (SPAIN)   *See* Resistant Rootstocks.

PORTER   The predecessor of stout; it is characterized by its intense deep dark color, its often smoky or fruity bouquet, and a persistent bittersweet taste. This top-fermented beer is usually lower in alcohol than stout and should ideally be served at 55 degrees Fahrenheit. It was invented in 1722 by Ralph Harwood, a London brewer, who named it after the porters who enjoyed drinking it. *See* Stout.

PORTEUR (FRANCE)   A grape picker. *See* Chef de Troupe.

PORT GLASS (PORTUGAL)   *See* Dock Glasses.

PORTION   A standardized, measured part of a drink or quantity of drink served to one person.

PORTION CONTROL   The establishment of standards for the size, volume, and ingredients that are to be served, through procedures used to control beverage costs throughout the various steps of production.

PORTION CONTROL MEASUREMENT   Proper utilization of various devices such as automatic pourers, shot glasses, and so on, to ensure that each drink item will be measured out accurately, according to the relevant standard portion.

PORTION COST   The raw, wholesale ingredient cost per drink, derived by dividing total yield by drink size to determine the number of drinks. The number of drinks is then divided into the total cost to obtain the individual drink cost. Also known as *prime ingredient cost*.

PORTION SIZE   A specified drink size to be served to a single customer. The drink size should be controlled or standardized to offer customers a consistent drink, but it also makes planning purchases and calculating profits easier.

PORTLAND   A white grape variety developed in 1912 by the State Experimental Station in Geneva, New York.

PORTO (PORTUGAL)   The shortened name for the city of Oporto.

PORT-OF-THE-VINTAGE   A term formerly used in Portugal, now no longer permitted.

PORT OF (YEAR) In Portugal, a port of a single vintage; this is actually a tawny port, aged in wood rather than the bottle.

PORTS Those places and activities normally associated with sea or aerial transportation services.

PORTUGUISER (GERMANY) *See* Blauer Portugieser.

PORT WITH AN INDICATION OF AGE In Portugal, a tawny port with age (average) specified on the bottle (e.g., ten, twenty, thirty years, and so on).

POSIP (YUGOSLAVIA) *See* Furmint.

POS PLANNING FORM A document utilized to determine the quantity and cost of national promotions for a brand in a given territory.

POSSET A hot drink made of milk curdled with ale, wines, and so forth, usually spiced with nutmeg. The drink was popular in England from the Renaissance through the eighteenth century.

POST-DOWNS *See* Distributor Post-Off.

POSTES-GREFFES (FRANCE) *Phylloxera*-resistant American rootstocks on which European grapevines are grafted.

POSTMIX SODA SYSTEM A carbonated beverage system in which water, tanks of carbon dioxide, and concentrated syrups are bulk-purchased separately. One five-gallon canister of postmix syrup yields approximately 3,840 ounces of product at five parts carbonated water to one part syrup.

The ingredients are blended together in a beverage establishment by the use of a mechanical device (carbonator) and dispensed to customers by use of a push-button handgun. A postmix system is normally less expensive to operate than either premix or bottles. *See* Premix.

POST-OFF *See* Distributor Post-Off.

POSTS *See* Distributor Post-Off.

POT (FRANCE) In Beaujolais, a bottle that contains approximately 16.9 fluid ounces or a two-thirds bottle of wine.

POTABLE Drinkable.

POTABLE SPIRIT Distilled spirits fit for human consumption.

POT ALE The residue left in the wash still after the first distillation in a pot still or continuous still. Also known as *burnt ale*.

POTASSIUM BENZOATE A chemical used in carbonated soft drinks, fruit drinks, cocktail mixers, beverage syrups, cider, and wine coolers as a preservative. Its use in wine is not permitted.

POTASSIUM BITARTRATE A combination of potassium, derived from the soil in which a grapevine lives, and tartaric acid, the principal acid component of grapes. During fermentation, potassium and tartaric acid combine to form potassium bitartrate in solution form. Much of the potassium bitartrate is removed during fermentation because it is less soluble in alcohol than it is in water or grape juice, so that, as the percentage of alcohol increases, more of the potassium bitartrate crystallizes and precipitates out. Also known as *argols*. *See* Cold Stabilization, Crystalline Deposits, and Tartaric Acid.

POTASSIUM FERROCYANIDE   *See* Ferrocyanide Compounds.

POTASSIUM METABISULPHITE   A white crystalline powder, soluble in water, that contains approximately 57 percent by weight of sulfur dioxide SO_2. It is commonly used for sterilizing and preserving wine. *See* Campden Tablet and Sulfur Dioxide.

POTASSIUM SORBATE   Generically recognized as safe (GRAS) as a chemical preservative when used in accordance with good manufacturing practices. It is allowed in wine as a sterilizing and preservative agent and to inhibit mold growth and secondary fermentation. *See* Sorbic Acid.

POTATURA (ITALY)   *See* Pruning.

POTEEN   Illicit Irish whiskey, similar to moonshine. Also spelled *pocheen* and *potheen*.

POTENTIAL ALCOHOL   An estimate, based on the Brix readings at harvest, of the percentage of alcohol the finished wine will contain after fermentation, provided that all sugar is metabolized. Also known as *alcol da svolgere*.

POTENTIAL BEVERAGE COST   The estimated or projected cost of a particular volume of alcoholic beverages, which will generate a given amount of sales volume. However, it must be kept in mind that the actual cost may differ.

POTENTIAL SALES VOLUME   The actual sales dollar an individual bottle of wine, beer, or distilled spirits would earn if all contents were sold.

POTHEEN   *See* Poteen.

POT STILL   The pot still resembles a large copper pot or kettle with a broad rounded base topped by a long column. The shape and size of the still, even the way it is fired (flame or steam), the speed of heating the liquid, the temperature of the still, and the volume of the *heart* are all believed to affect the quality of the distillate. Initially, anywhere from 250 to 2,600 gallons of liquid to be distilled (depending on the still's size) are loaded into the base of the pot still. The liquid is then heated and kept simmering until the alcohol is vaporized and rises up into the column, taking with it flavors from the base liquid; this gives the distillate its characteristic aroma and taste. When the vapor rises to a certain point in the column, it comes into contact with a cold condenser, which turns the vapor into liquid alcohol. Pot stills produce only single batches of distilled spirits. After each batch has been distilled, the pot still must be refilled. Pot stills produce the finest quality as well as the highest priced distilled spirits, but the process is laborious and time-consuming. *See* Alembic and Still.

POTTLE   An obsolete English wine measurement equivalent to one-half gallon.

POUILLY-FUISSÉ (FRANCE)   A dry, full-bodied white wine made exclusively from the Chardonnay grape in the region of Burgundy, west of Mâcon and north of Beaujolais.

POUILLY FUMÉ (FRANCE)   A dry, full-bodied white wine made from the Sauvignon Blanc grape in the village of Pouilly-Sur-Loire, located in the Loire Valley. Its name comes from the bloom of yeast on the grape's surface, which looks gray (fumé means smoked).

POUILLY-SUR-LOIRE *(FRANCE)* A small white-wine vineyard town in the Loire Valley producing wines mostly from the Sauvignon Blanc grape, labeled *Pouilly Fumé*.

POUILLY-VINZELLES *(FRANCE)* A white wine commune from the southern Côte Mâconnais in Burgundy; it adjoins Pouilly-Fuissé and produces white wines from the Chardonnay grape variety.

POULSARD *(FRANCE)* A red grape variety grown in the Jura region.

POUND A United States measure of weight. Sixteen ounces equal one pound; two thousand pounds is called a *ton*.

POUNDS PER SQUARE INCH (PSI) A measure of pressure.

POURER A plastic or stainless steel device that can be fitted into the neck of a bottle; it permits the pouring of a free or predetermined amount of liquid. *See* Free Pour

POURING COSTS *See* Edible Portion.

POURRITURE *(FRANCE)* Rotting of the grapes.

POURRITURE NOBLE *(FRANCE)* *See Botrytis Cinerea.*

POUSSE-CAFÉ A specialty after-dinner drink consisting of liqueurs floated on top of one another in layers, creating a rainbow effect. Also known as *floating liqueurs*. *See* Layering.

POUSSE-CAFÉ GLASS Straight-sided liqueur glass.

POWDERY MILDEW *(UNCINULA NECATOR)* A fungal disease that was first recognized in California in 1859; however, it probably originated in Japan in the early 1800s. Powdery mildew gained notoriety when it was introduced into European vineyards (where it was called *oïdium*) in 1845 and spread rapidly throughout the continent. Uncontrolled, powdery mildew can cause reduced grapevine growth, yield, quality, and winter hardiness. The disease is characterized by a powdery film of spores that attacks and mildews the grapes and leaves. Also known as *ächerich, ceniza*, and *mangara*.

POWERFUL A full-bodied wine, high in alcohol (hard tannins for red wines), extracts, and generous flavor, that seems to fill the mouth. Powerful could also apply to some big, full-bodied white wines, especially if they have been fermented and/or aged in oak barrels. Also known as *puissant* and *viril*. *See* Brawny and Muscular.

PPM *See* Parts per Million.

PRAÇA *(PORTUGAL)* A white grape variety grown in the Douro region.

PRÄDIKAT *(GERMANY)* *See* Qualitätswein mit Prädikat.

PRAMNIAN *(GREECE)* An ancient wine that was purportedly the favorite wine of Nestor.

PRECHECK The ringing up of a check prior to drinks being dispensed or offered.

PRECIOUS ROOM A locked or otherwise secured storage area within a larger locked storage area.

PRECIPITATION The separation out of solution of small, crystalline particles, usually bitartrate of potassium (cream of tartar), in a beer or wine, usually accomplished through chilling.

PRÉCOCE (FRANCE) *See* Precocious.

PRECOCIOUS A loosely used term for wines that are forward and mature quickly, and therefore should be consumed young. Also known as *précoce*.

PRÉCOCE DE MALINGRE A white grape variety.

PRECOSTING A method by which sales projections and ingredients costs are utilized to calculate actual beverage costs for a given drink item in advance of sales.

PREDATORY PRICING The act of pricing products below cost to drive out competition and then jacking prices up when the action succeeds.

PREDETERMINED COST Any cost calculated prior to it actually being incurred.

PREDICATO (ITALY) *See* Capitolare Wines.

PREIGNAC (FRANCE) A sweet white wine made from a blend of Sauvignon Blanc, Sémillon, and Muscadelle grape varieties. It is also one of the five communes within Bordeaux's Sauternes district entitled to be called "Sauternes."

PRÉMEAUX (FRANCE) A red-wine-producing village located in Burgundy's Côte de Nuits district, entitled to the *appellation* Nuits-Saint-Georges.

PREMIER-CHAUFFE (FRANCE) The first distillation in the making of cognac.

PREMIER CRU (FRANCE) Refers to a first or top-growth wine from the finest vineyards under the 1855 classification in Bordeaux; in Burgundy it follows Grand Cru.

PREMIÈRES CÔTES DE BORDEAUX (FRANCE) A wine-producing district that covers a strip of land some thirty-five miles long and three miles wide along the right bank of the Garonne from Bordeaux to Saint-Macaire. Here both red and white wines are produced, with the red mostly from the north where the southern exposure receives long hours of sunshine. A renaissance château in Cadillac known as the Dukes of Epernon is the home of the Connétablie de Guyenne, a famous wine fraternity.

PREMIÈRES CÔTES DE BLAYE (FRANCE) A wine-producing district that extends north of Bourg along the right bank of the Gironde opposite the Médoc. The district of Blaye is the main producer of the red Côtes de Blaye.

PREMIÈRE TAILLE (FRANCE) The second pressing of grapes used to produce champagne.

PREMIUM *See* Consumer Offer.

PREMIUM A subjective term, not officially recognized, generally applied by winemakers, brewmasters, or marketers to indicate a superior quality or their top-of-the-line beverages. Also known as *private reserve, proprietor's reserve, reserve,* or *réserve.*

PREMIUM BRANDS Those brands of alcoholic beverages that are top quality, have brand recognition, are positioned well in the customer's mind, and generally command the highest prices. Also known as *premium pour, super call,* and *top shelf.*

PREMIUM POUR *See* Premium Brands.

PREMIUM WELL A *premium brand* of an alcoholic beverage that beverage service operators utilize as their *house brand* for all beverages ordered without a call name.

PREMIX To mix ingredients prior to use.

PREMIX SODA SYSTEM   A carbonated beverage system in which all ingredients (water, concentrated syrups, and carbon dioxide) are mixed at a fixed ratio prior to being purchased by the beverage facility. The carbonated water and syrup are mixed in pressurized canisters (usually five gallons) and then dispensed directly out of these containers. A premix system is normally more expensive to operate than postmix. *See* Postmix.

PRENSA (SPAIN)   *See* Wine Press.

PRENTISS   A white grape variety developed in 1870 by J.W. Prentiss of Pultney, New York.

PRENZAS (SPAIN)   Wine made from the third pressing of the grapes.

PREPARED AND BOTTLED BY   *See* Cellared and Bottled By.

PRE-PHYLLOXERA WINES   Wines made prior to the devastation by *phylloxera* (a root-louse) of most of Europe's grapevines in the 1870s. Some wine purists believe that these wines were superior to wines made post-*phylloxera*; however, there is no scientific evidence to support their theory.

PRESA DI SPUMA (ITALY)   *See* Secondary Fermentation.

PRESIDENT   A grape variety developed by Thomas Volney Munson (1843–1913) of Denison, Texas.

PRÉSIDENT (FRANCE)   *See* Plant de Graisse.

PRESS   *See* Wine Press.

PRESSAC (FRANCE)   *See* Malbec.

PRESSING   The act of pressing grapes, either prior to or after fermentation, to liberate the juice or wine contained inside. Also known as *pigiare, pigiatura*, and *pressurage*.

PRESS JUICE   That portion of the wine that is pressed from the skins, pulp, and so forth, under pressure after draining off the free-run juice. Press juice has more aroma and flavor, deeper color, and is usually richer in extract, tannin, and other flavoring compounds than free-run juice. It is blended back, in varying degrees, with the free-run juice. Also known as *vin de presse. See* Free-Run Juice.

PRESSOIR (FRANCE)   *See* Wine Press.

PRESSURAGE (FRANCE)   *See* Pressing.

PRESTIGE CUVÉE (FRANCE)   Top-of-the-line champagnes, made from the pressings of grapes grown in the top-rated villages in vintage years, aged on the yeast longer than standard champagnes, and aged in the bottle for between eight to nine years.

PRETTO (ITALY)   *See* Vino Pretto.

PREUVE (FRANCE)   A small glass cup that is lowered into cognac barrels for a sample for evaluation and testing. *See* Wine Thief.

PRICE AFFIRMATION   In the United States, statutes in varying open states in which the supplier guarantees without reservation that the price of the merchandise listed is the lowest price, FOB distillery, winery, or any of the suppliers' other shipping points, offered to and paid by any other customer anywhere in the United States, regardless of the size or type of customer, and that this price includes the same quantity discounts, cash rebates, and all other forms of discounts, allowances, and rebates as are offered any other customer in the United States for the same merchandise.

PRICE EXTENSIONS   A process by which the selling price of one particular unit is multiplied by the number of units in an order or projected order in order to arrive at a total cost figure (number of units times unit price).

PRICE LEADER   An item that an establishment offers for sale with an especially low price, often temporarily, meant to attract customers; it is hoped they will also buy other items at the regular price. *See* Loss Leader.

PRICE MARGIN   The amount by which the selling price of a particular item exceeds the basic raw cost to the establishment of the item sold.

PRICE-OFF   A temporary price reduction, widely used as a basic offer in sales promotion.

PRICER   A sign that is designed to put a feature price on display.

PRICE-VALUE RELATIONSHIP   *See* Perceived Cost and Perceived Value.

PRICING POLICY   A standardized pricing structure utilized by most beverage facilities that determines the retail sales value of their product(s).

PRICKED WINE   *See* Spritz.

PRICKLY   *See* Spritz.

PRICKLY   Describes an unpleasant, sharp quality of wine, noticed in the odor and on the palate, that creates a sharp-edged, raw, possibly almost effervescent quality caused by an excess of volatile acidity. A prickly wine may be just drinkable, for it might not have reached the final vinegary state. Also known as *pricked wine*.

PRIÉ ROUGE (ITALY)   A red grape variety grown in the Valle d'Aosta region.

PRIMARY   The largest bud or shoot at each normal node of the cane or spur on a grapevine.

PRIMARY FERMENTATION   The first stage of fermentation, in which the added yeast begins to metabolize the sugar, converting it into carbon dioxide and alcohol. Also known as *alcohol fermentation* and *gaerung*.

PRIMARY FERMENTER   An open-topped vessel, usually made of stainless steel, wood, concrete, or fiberglass, in which the primary fermentation takes place.

PRIME COST   *See* Product Cost.

PRIME COST PRICING   The basing of a selling price on beverage cost and direct labor cost.

PRIME INGREDIENT COST   *See* Portion Cost.

PRIMEUR (FRANCE)   *See* Nouveau.

PRIMING   The addition of cane sugar, corn sugar, or other sweet solutions to beer just prior to bottling to promote additional fermentation in the bottle.

PRIMITIVO DI GIOIA (ITALY)   A very dark red grape variety grown almost exclusively in southern Italy, where it produces dark, intensely colored wines, often with some residual sugar and high alcoholic content. Some *ampelographers* believe that the elusive Zinfandel grape variety of California may be genetically linked to the Primitivo. Also known as *Morellone, Uva di Corato*, and *Zagarése. See* Zinfandel.

PRINCE, WILLIAM ROBERT (1795–1869) A nurseryman and heir to the Botanical Gardens at Flushing, Queens, New York, who in his time had the largest collection of *Vitis vinifera* varieties in America. He experimented extensively with many varieties of grapes and even offered Zinfandel, a red grape variety of unknown origin, in his catalog, listed as "Black St. Peters." *See* Zinfandel.

PRISE DE MOUSSE *(FRANCE)* The secondary fermentation of a still wine into a sparkling wine.

PRIVATE LABEL A shop's own label, usually carrying the shop's name on a particular item or line of wines, beers, or distilled spirits. Often good values, they are not always consistent, shipment to shipment.

PRIVATE RESERVE Also known as *proprietors reserve. See* Premium.

PROCANICO *(ITALY)* *See* Trebbiano.

PROCESSED A loosely used term often applied to jug wines or other similar types that have been pasteurized, over-filtered, or processed by other means to strip away most of the odor and/or flavor, making the wine bland to the palate.

PROCESSING Distilled spirits are blended together or otherwise processed by the addition of distilled spirits or flavoring or coloring material. For example, straight whiskeys are processed by blending them with distilled neutral spirits; distilled spirits are redistilled for flavoring as in making gin; distilled neutral spirits, with the aid of flavoring essences and other materials, are transformed into liqueurs. Formerly known as *rectifying*.

PRODOMOS *(GREECE)* The name given by the ancient Greeks to free-run grape juice. Also known as *protopos. See* Free-Run Juice.

PRODOTTO *(ITALY)* *See* Product.

PRODUCED AND BOTTLED BY Means that the named winery (a) fermented not less than 75 percent of such wine at the stated address, or (b) changed the class or type of the wine by the addition of alcohol, brandy, flavors, colors, or artificial carbonation at the stated address, or (c) produced sparkling wine by secondary fermentation at the stated address. The term is synonymous with *made and bottled by*. Also known as *producido por*.

PRODUCIDO POR *(SPAIN)* *See* Produced and Bottled By.

PRODUCT Distilled spirits, wine, or malt beverages, as defined in the United States Federal Alcohol Administration Act. Also known as *prodotto* and *produit*.

PRODUCT COST The combined total of the beverage and labor costs for a given beverage item or set of beverage items. Also known as *prime cost*.

PRODUCT DISPLAY Any wine rack, bin, barrel, shelving, and the like from which distilled spirits, wine, or malt beverages are displayed and sold.

PRODUCT-SERVICE MIX The combination of product and services offered to perspective customers in a beverage facility.

PRODUCT SHEET   A full-color page of pictures of product(s) that includes product information.

PRODUIT *(FRANCE)*   *See* Product.

PRODUIT DE QUEUE *(FRANCE)*   *See* Tails.

PRODUIT DE TÊTE *(FRANCE)*   *See* Heads.

PRODUTTORE *(ITALY)*   Producer.

PRODUTTORE RIUNITI *(ITALY)*   United producers.

PRODUTTORI *(ITALY)*   Producers.

PRODUZIONE *(ITALY)*   Production.

PROFIT INVESTMENT STATEMENT (PIS)   A brand's basic financial planning document. This document is basically a profit and loss statement (P & L) for the brand that also includes a *return on investment* (ROI) analysis. The PIS can either be short- or long-term in nature.

PROFUMO *(ITALY)*   *See* Flowery.

PROHIBITION   The Eighteenth Amendment to the Constitution of the United States went into effect on January 16, 1920 (during the administration of President Woodrow Wilson, 1913–1921), and was repealed on Tuesday, December 5, 1933 (during the administration of President Franklin D. Roosevelt, 1933–1945), by the Twenty-first Amendment, which was signed at 6:55 P.M. It lasted thirteen years, ten months, nineteen days, seventeen hours, and 32-1/2 minutes. It was referred to by many as "The Noble Experiment," or the "Volstead Act," named after Andrew J. Volstead, a Minnesota representative, the author of the Eighteenth Amendment. Prohibition forbade the manufacture, sale, or transportation of intoxicating liquors within, the importation thereof into, or exportation thereof from the United States and all territory subject to the jurisdiction thereof for beverage purposes. Intoxicating liquors were defined as those containing one-half of one percent or more alcohol by volume and fit for use for beverage purposes. It did not, however, actually prohibit the consumption of alcoholic beverages. In fact, the act provided for certain exemptions, including wine for sacramental purposes, homemade wine, salted wines for cooking, and liquor for medicinal and certain nonbeverage purposes, such as toilet preparations.

Other prohibitions have been enacted. From 1736 to 1742, the Gin Act or Gin Prohibition was put into enforcement in England. From 1735 to 1742, in the state of Georgia, a prohibition against hard liquor was imposed. From 1908 to 1934 (twenty-six years), there was a prohibition against drinking in Iceland; it is considered the longest in modern time. From 1914 to 1924, there was a prohibition against drinking in Russia. Also known as the *Volstead Act*.

PROKUPAC *(YUGOSLAVIA)*   A red grape variety.

PROMOTION   An act, technique, or method that stimulates or helps bring about growth of sales or consumer acceptance.

PROMOTIONAL ALLOWANCE (PA)   Refers to either financial or marketing promotional allowance to aid the distributor or retailer.

PROMOTIONAL EXPENSE   Advertising or other expenses incurred as a result of a newly established brand or a new activity with an already established brand.

PRONTA BEVA (ITALY)   A quickly maturing young wine; ready to drink.

PROOF   An old English term that was once called "gunpowder proof." To test the strength of the distilled spirit, old-time distillers poured it on gunpowder or black powder and struck a match. If the distilled spirit blazed up, it was too strong. Distilled spirits at proper strength mixed with the powder would burn slowly in a blue flame. If it did not burn well, it was too high in water. Mixing 50 percent alcohol with 50 percent water gave a slow, steady flame. That strength was considered perfect and was called "100 proof." Today, the same scale is applied to the alcoholic content of distilled spirits on the following basis: pure 100 percent alcohol (at 60 degrees Fahrenheit) is 200 proof; 1 degree of proof is equal to 0.5 percent alcohol. Divide the proof by two and you get the percentage of alcohol in the bottle. Also known as *gunpowder proof* and *flame up.*

PROOF GALLON   A United States gallon of liquid at 60 degrees Fahrenheit that contains 50 percent by volume (100 proof) ethyl alcohol and has a specific gravity of 0.7939 at 60 degrees Fahrenheit. *See* Tax Gallon.

PROPAGATION   The process of causing a grapevine to reproduce itself by a natural reproduction or, as most commonly practiced by viticulturists, by rooting a cutting from the mother plant.

PROPIONIC ACID   A spoiling acid caused by micro-infection (bacteria), which causes a highly undesirable "goaty" odor and bitterness in the wine. The bacteria break down the tartaric acid to propionic acid. Fortunately, its occurrence is now rare.

PROPORTIONED   *See* Balance.

PROPRIETÀ (ITALY)   Property of.

PROPRIÉTAIRE (FRANCE)   *See* Proprietor.

PROPRIÉTAIRE-NÉGOCIANT (FRANCE)   A vineyard owner who supplements his wincholding by buying other people's grapes or wines.

PROPRIÉTAIRE-RÉCOLTANT (FRANCE)   Owner or manager of a winery.

PROPRIETARIO (ITALY)   *See* Proprietor.

PROPRIETARY BRAND NAME   *See* Brand Name.

PROPRIETARY NAME   *See* Brand Name.

PROPRIETARY WINE   Wines carrying a made-up name originated by a specific winery or proprietor. *See* Brand Name.

PROPRIÉTE (FRANCE)   Property or estate.

PROPRIETOR   The person qualified to operate a wine premises. The meaning includes the concept of "winemaker" when the context so requires. Also known as *propriétaire* and *proprietario.*

PROPRIETORS RESERVE   *See* Premium.

PROSECCO (ITALY)   A white grape variety often used in making sparkling wines.

PROTEASE   A protein-splitting enzyme used in winemaking and brewing.

PROTEIN HAZE   A haze often encountered in wines and beer due not only to precipitation of heat-sensitive protein fractions but also to complex formations between wine proteins and reactive phenols.

PROTEINS   A class of complex nitrogenous compounds that occur naturally in grapevines and yield amino acids when hydrolyzed. Proteins provide the amino acids essential for the growth and repair of tissue.

PROTOPOS (GREECE)   *See* Prodomos.

PROVENCE (FRANCE)   A vineyard region in the French Riviera, near the Mediterranean Sea. *See* Côtes de Provence.

PROVIGNAGE (FRANCE)   *See* Interplanting.

PROVINCIA (ITALY)   Province.

PRUFÜNGSNUMMER (GERMANY)   *See* Amtliche Prufüngsnummer.

PRUGNOLO (ITALY)   *See* Sangiovese Grosso.

PRUGNOLO GENTILE (ITALY)   *See* Sangiovese Grosso.

PRUINA (FRANCE)   *See* Bloom.

PRUINOSE (FRANCE)   *See* Bloom.

PRUNE   An organoleptic term often associated with very overripe, dried-out grapes that give a pruney, pungent quality that is undesirable in some wines. The odor and/or taste is sometimes prevalent in old port wines. *See* Pflümli.

PRUNE JUICE   The liquid constituent of a prune.

PRUNELLE   A fruit brandy made from blackthorn or sloe berries.

PRUNELLE SAUVAGE   A fruit brandy made from wild plums.

PRUNING   The cutting-off or removal of the excess portion of grapevines to increase the vigor of the plant and to produce finer quality grapes. It is a complex and highly judgmental operation that controls grapevine shape, stretches grapevines over a larger portion of guide wires, regulates the crop size grapevines will bear, and controls the quality that the particular crop will make to the wine. It is generally performed during the winter dormant period. Also known as *potatura* and *taille*. *See* Balanced Pruning, Brush Weight, Cane Pruning, Head Pruning, and Spur Pruning.

PSI   *See* Pounds per Square Inch.

PUB (ENGLAND)   A shortened term for "public house," a licensed bar where beer and distilled spirits are offered for sale; often a center of social activity for a community. Also known as *public house* and *publik house*. *See* Bar, Cocktail Lounge, Inn, Saloon, and Tavern.

PUB CRAWL   A slang term for the visitation of many bars or other alcoholic-beverage-serving establishments in one night.

PUBLICAN   A bartender in an English pub.

PUBLIC BAR   A bar that is open to the general public for the sale and service of alcoholic beverages.

PUBLIC HOUSE   *See* Pub.

PUBLIK HOUSE   *See* Pub.

PUCKERY   *See* Astringency.

PUDDING WINE *(ENGLAND)*   A slang term for any white wine that is more or less sweet.

PUDDLER AND HIS HELPER   Slang term for a shot of whiskey accompanied by a glass of beer; a "puddler" was a job in the old steel mills of Pittsburgh. The drink (also known as an "Imp and an Iron") consisted of a shot of Imperial whiskey followed by a glass of Iron City beer. *See* Bat and a Ball.

PUFF   A cocktail consisting of equal parts distilled spirits and milk, topped with soda water.

PUGLIA *(ITALY)*   *See* Apulia.

PUGNET *(ITALY)*   *See* Nebbiolo.

PUISSANT *(FRANCE)*   *See* Powerful.

PUKHLYAKOVSKY *(RUSSIA)*   A white grape variety.

PULCIANELLA *(ITALY)*   An often-used bottle for the white wines of Orvieto, from the region of Umbria. Also known as *toscanello*.

PULIGNY-MONTRACHET *(FRANCE)*   A wine-producing village in the Côte de Beaune district of Burgundy, noted for its production of excellent dry white wines made entirely from Chardonnay grapes. Puligny-Montrachet extends for some 575 acres, with Chassagne-Montrachet as its neighbor directly south. Puligny was known as *Puliniacus* in 1095. In 1879, the commune of Puligny added its name to that of its most illustrious vineyard, Montrachet.

PULITO *(ITALY)*   *See* Clean.

PULL DATE   The date a product should be pulled off the shelves, after which time it begins to deteriorate.

PULP   The inner soft, moist, and fleshy part of a grape. Also known as *pulpe*.

PULPE *(FRANCE)*   *See* Pulp.

PULQUE *(SPAIN)*   A viscous, milky-white alcoholic beverage fermented (not distilled) from the juice of agave plants; it was enjoyed for centuries before the art of distilling came to Mexico from Spain. Because of its rather low alcoholic content and susceptibility to spoilage, it is consumed locally and rarely reaches the United States.

PUMPED   Describes what happens when sustained high humidity causes corks to swell; it is not uncommon to find them partially out of the bottle.

PUMPING OVER   In wine fermentation *on the skins*, the grape skins float to the surface and harden, forming what is known as the *cap* or *hat*. Several times a day this cap must be broken up to allow the carbon dioxide gas to escape. It is also important for the skins to stay in contact with the fermenting juice, to aid in color extraction. To accomplish this, the wine may be pumped from the bottom of the tank over the cap of floating skins and seeds at the top of the tank several times daily. Also known as *remontado, remontage, remontagem,* and *remontagio. See* Punching Down.

PUNCH   Any drink of many ingredients; its name is derived from Hindustani and Sanskrit words meaning five. Punches were first introduced into England in about 1655, after Jamaica had been conquered from the Spanish.

PUNCHEON   A barrel, used in the West Indies for the storage of rum, with a capacity of 115 to 136 gallons. *See* Barrel.

PUNCHING DOWN   In wine fermentation *on the skins*, the skins float to the surface and harden, forming what is known as the *cap* or *hat*. Several times a day this cap must be broken up to allow the carbon dioxide gas to escape. It is also important for the skins to stay in contact with the fermenting juice, to aid in color extraction. To accomplish this, long paddles or oars may be used to break up (*punch down*) the cap and stir the skins back into the juice. Also known as *follatura* and *retrousse le gâteau*. *See* Macacos and Pumping Over.

PUNGENT   A term that implies a powerful, assertive, heavily scented odor that is quite strong and penetrating. It usually indicates a high degree of volatile acidity in a wine. Also known as *drimys*. *See* Volatile Acidity.

PUNT   The dome-shaped indentation in the bottom of certain bottles that serves to strengthen them. This type of bottle is used especially for carbonated wines and champagnes; the punt helps to collect sediment in aged wines. Also, it will accommodate a wooden peg to hold bottles in place during shipping. Back when bottles were hand-made, glass blowers would support the bottom of a bottle with an iron rod (called a "punty," from the Italian word *puntello* or point) while they formed the neck. Naturally this rod left a ragged mark in the still soft glass. In order to finish the bottle neatly, a little bit of glass was pushed into the bottom to form a rounded hollow and a smoother resting surface (the circumference of the indentation). Also known as *kick, pointe, puntello,* or *push-up*. *See* Champagne Bottle.

PUNTELLO (ITALY)   *See* Punt.

PUNTINATA (ITALY)   *See* Malvasia.

PUNZANTE (SPAIN)   *See* Sharp.

PUPÎTRES (FRANCE)   The hinged, A-framed wooden racks that normally hold sixty bottles on each side in ten rows of six bottles each. They are drilled with large angled holes; these openings hold champagne and sparkling wine bottles for *riddling*, the shaking and turning of each bottle to move the sediment to the neck of the bottle. The racks were invented in 1818 by Antoine Müller, an employee of the French champagne house of Veuve Clicquot. Also known as *riddling racks*.

PURCHASE ORDER (PO)   A written order form from the buyer specifying merchandise ordered from a purveyor; it is filled out in quadruplicate: one copy to the purveyor, one copy to the department head, one copy to the accounting department, and one copy to the receiving clerk.

PURCHASE REQUISITION   A form used to request the purchasing agent to order certain goods.

PURCHASE SPECIFICATION   A standard, detailed specification established to ensure proper quality, quantity, weight, and size of products procured from purveyors. Also known as *standard purchase specification*.

PURCHASE STANDARD   A criterion, a gauge, a yardstick; the goals of quality set by management.

PURCHASING   The acquisition of goods and services through a purchase order and by the payment of money or its equivalent for them.

PURE BAR   A beverage facility that serves a wide range of nonalcoholic beverages only in a sophisticated and highly social environment.

PURE ALCOHOL   *See* Neutral Spirits.

PURE CONDENSED MUST   The dehydrated juice or *must* of sound, ripe grapes, or other fruit or agricultural products, concentrated to not more than 80 degrees Brix, the composition thereof remaining unaltered except for removal of water.

PURE DRY SUGAR   Refined sugar 95 percent or more by dry weight, having a dextrose equivalent of not less than 95 percent on a dry basis, and produced from cane, beets, or fruit, or from grain or other sources of starch.

PURPLE   A color characteristic, also called violet, of some very young red wines; it fades as the wine matures. Also known as *porpora* and *violaceo*.

PURVEYOR   A seller or vendor who supplies a product or service to customer firms, whether at the wholesale or retail level.

PUSH-UP   *See* Punt.

PUTRID   Describes an awful odor of a bacterially spoiled beverage.

PUTTONYO (HUNGARY)   During harvest, baskets or vats (with a capacity of eight to ten gallons) are filled with overripe grapes affected with *Botrytis cinerea*, which are used to make the sweet, Aszú style of wine. The baskets are then added to fermenting tanks of wine, usually between three (being the lightest) and six (being the sweetest). The number of baskets is ultimately indicated on the label—for example, "Tokaji Aszú 3 Puttonyos." The more puttonyos added to a tank, the sweeter, richer, and naturally more expensive the wine.

PX (SPAIN)   *See* Pedro Ximénez.

PYKNÓS (GREECE)   *See* Density.

PYMENTS   *See* Mead.

P

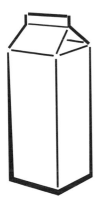

q \ˈkyü\ n, often cap, often attrib

QBA (GERMANY)   *See* Qualitätswein bestimmter Anbaugebiete.

QMP (GERMANY)   *See* Qualitätswein mit Prädikat.

QUAFF   To drink beer or wine in large gulps. *See* Chug.

QUAFFING WINE   A wine that is without nuance but is pleasant and refreshing when drunk alone or with food.

QUAGLIANO (ITALY)   A red grape variety grown in Piedmont.

QUAICH (SCOTLAND)   A small, shallow drinking vessel with ears for use as handles. Also spelled *quaigh*.

QUAIGH (SCOTLAND)   *See* Quaich.

QUALITÄTSWEIN BESTIMMTER ANBAUGEBIETE (QBA) (GERMANY)   A label classification for "quality" table wines that meet certain requirements for alcohol content, region of origin (must come from one of thirteen specified wine regions), and grape variety, and is subject to examination by authorities. Qualitätswein wines may be *chaptalized*.

QUALITÄTSWEIN MIT PRÄDIKAT (QMP) (GERMANY)   A wine designation that traditionally includes Germany's finest and most expensive wines. None of these can be *chaptalized*. *Prädikat* wines must come from a specific area or *Bereich*. This category has six subdivisions that correlate the successively higher levels of sugar produced by the German custom of late and selective picking. (The drawback to this custom is that the riper the grapes—and thus the higher the sugar level—the smaller the quantity of wine produced, as selectivity increases with lateness of harvest.) Also known as *prädikat*.

QUANTITY DISCOUNT   A discount provided by the vendor to the seller that allows huge volume purchases in return for a lower dollar amount assigned to said purchase. Also known as *volume discount*.

QUANTITY PURCHASING   *See* Bulk Buying.

QUART   A United States measure of volume. Thirty-two fluid ounces equal one quart; four quarts equal one gallon.

QUART HOUSE   The oldest retail liquor store in the United States (Marion County, Kentucky), where neighbors would bring quart jars to fill from the miller's barrels.

QUARTAUT (FRANCE)   A barrel used for storage of wine that varies in its capacity from fourteen to fifteen gallons. *See* Barrel.

QUARTER BOTTLE   A bottle with a capacity of 6.4 fluid ounces.

QUARTIER (FRANCE)   A section of a vineyard.

QUARTINO (ITALY)   A quarter of a liter. *See* Cyathi.

QUARTS-DE-CHAUME (FRANCE)   A small, white-wine-producing vineyard in the Coteaux du Layon district of Anjou, located in the Loire Valley. It is noted for its rich, sweet dessert wines produced from overripe grapes affected by *Botrytis cinerea*.

QUEEN OF THE VINEYARDS   A white grape variety grown in the United States.

QUEEN SEEDLESS   A red grape variety developed in 1954 from a cross of Muscat Hamburg and Thompson Seedless by Dr. Harold P. Olmo of the University of California, Davis.

QUEIMAR (PORTUGAL)   To distill a wine.

QUENTE (PORTUGAL)   *See* Warmth.

QUERCUS ALBA   American white oak from Arkansas, Kentucky, Minnesota, Missouri, Ohio, Tennessee, Virginia, and Wisconsin, utilized in the making of wooden barrels for the aging and/or storage of alcoholic beverages.

QUERCUS BICOLOR   American white oak from Arkansas, Kentucky, Missouri, Ohio, Tennessee, and Wisconsin, utilized in the making of wooden barrels for the aging and/or storage of alcoholic beverages.

QUERCUS GARRYANA   American white oak from Oregon, utilized in the making of wooden barrels for the aging and/or storage of alcoholic beverages.

QUERCUS GERIANA   American white oak from Oregon, utilized in the making of wooden barrels for the aging and/or storage of alcoholic beverages.

QUERCUS LYRATA   American white oak from Arkansas, Kentucky, Missouri, Ohio, Tennessee, and Wisconsin, utilized in the making of wooden barrels for the aging and/or storage of alcoholic beverages.

QUERCUS PRINUS   American white oak from Arkansas, Kentucky, Missouri, Ohio, Tennessee, and Wisconsin, utilized in the making of wooden barrels for the aging and/or storage of alcoholic beverages.

QUERCUS ROBUR   *See* Nevers Oak.

QUERCUS SESSILIS   *See* Limousin Oak.

QUETSCH (FRANCE)   A fruit brandy made from small, blue plums with a highly aromatic perfume. It is generally produced in Alsace as well as in some Central European countries.

QUEUE *(FRANCE)*   *See* Barrel.

QUEUE DE RENARD *(FRANCE)*   *See* Foxy.

QUIESCENCE   The state of a plant that is nongrowing because of existing environmental conditions (e.g., very low or high temperature), but that will grow when placed in conditions favorable for growth. *See* Dormancy and Rest.

QUILLAJA   The bark of the *Quillaja saponaria* tree from South America, occasionally utilized in certain soft drinks to make them foam.

QUINCY *(FRANCE)*   A small vineyard town in the lower Loire Valley near Sancerre and Pouilly Fumé, noted for its dry white wines produced from the Sauvignon Blanc grape.

QUININE   A bitter, white, crystalline alkaloid derived from the bark of the cinchona tree. It is the bittering flavor agent used in making *quinine water* or *tonic water* and some bitter-lemon carbonated soft drinks. Quinine is often used in making bitter apéritifs, especially from France and Italy. Also known as *quinquina*.

QUININE WATER   *See* Tonic Water.

QUINQUINA *(FRANCE)*   *See* Quinine.

QUINTA *(PORTUGAL)*   A wine estate, equivalent to a French château; or a single-vineyard designation.

QUINTAL   A metric measurement of weight equal to one hundred kilograms or 220.46 pounds. Also known as *quintale*.

QUINTALE *(ITALY)*   *See* Quintal.

QUOTA   *See* Goal.

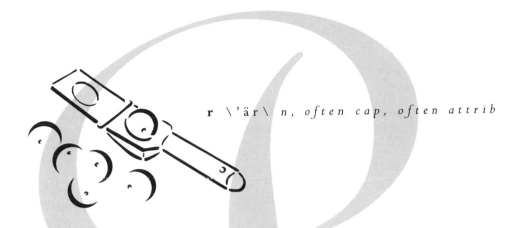

r \ ' är \ *n, often cap, often attrib*

RABADI   A thickened or reduced milk, popular in India.

RABANER (GERMANY)   A white grape variety developed from a cross of Johannisberg Riesling and Johannisberg Riesling (different types and strains). The name celebrates the scholastic theologian Hrabanus Maurus, archbishop of Mainz from 847 to 956.

RABBOCCATURA (ITALY)   *See* Liqueur d'Expédition.

RABIGATO (PORTUGAL)   A white grape variety used in the making of white port wine.

RABO DE OVELHA (PORTUGAL)   A white grape variety grown in the Dão region.

RABOSA (ITALY)   *See* Raboso.

RABOSO (ITALY)   A red grape variety grown in the region of Veneto. Also known as *Friulara, Raboso del Piave*, and *Raboso Veronese*. Also spelled *Rabosa*.

RABOSO DEL PIAVE (ITALY)   *See* Raboso.

RABOSO VERONESE (ITALY)   *See* Raboso.

RACÉ (FRANCE)   *See* Elegant.

RACHIS   The bunch without its grapes; actually, just the stems. Also known as *rafle*.

RACIMO (SPAIN)   *See* Cluster.

RACK   A slang term, often used in breweries, that means to fill a container with beer.

RACKING   The process in which wine or beer is carefully moved from one barrel or tank to another in order to separate it from the *lees* or solids, mainly yeast sediment. This helps to clarify the wine or beer and also serves to aerate the wine if desired. Also known as *abstich, passagem, soutirage, svinatura, trasfega*, and *trasiego*.

RACOTER (FRANCE)   The replacement of dead stems by new grapevine plantings.

RACY   Also known as *rassig*. *See* Lively.

RADIATION FROST   A type of frost that is characterized by light winds, temperature inversions, clear skies, and daytime temperatures above 32 degrees Fahrenheit.

RADLMASS   *See* Shandy.

RAFLE (FRANCE)   *See* Rachis.

RAHM (GERMANY)   Cream.

RAIL   That recessed portion of a bar closest to the bartender where drinks are poured, mixed, and served from. Also utilized for soiled glasses prior to washing.

RAIL   The metal (formerly brass) pipe or bar, which forms the front part of a bar, utilized as a footrest.

RAINES LAW   In 1896, in New York, there was a Sabbath Law named after Senator John Raines, author of the bill, that forbade the sale of liquor and closed the saloons on Sunday.

RAINWATER (PORTUGAL)   A type of madeira, a fortified wine, believed to have been created by Mr. William Neyle Habersham, a local madeira shipper from Savannah, Georgia. Mr. Habersham made very special blends of Sercial and Verdelho that were lighter and quite a bit paler (almost like rainwater) than most of the madeiras that were consumed during the mid-1800s. However, another account states that wines destined for sale in Savannah, Georgia, were accidentally left unbunged overnight during a heavy rain storm. The resulting diluted madeira was dubbed by wine merchant Andrew Newton "as soft as rainwater." Rainwater is mostly a blend of Tinta Negra Mole with at least 15 percent Verdelho grape varieties. *See* Palhete.

RAISIN BLANC (SOUTH AFRICA)   *See* Servin Blanc.

RAISIN BRANDY   *See* Dried Fruit Brandy.

RAISINS   A cluster of grapes or individual grape berries that have been dried in the sun or by artificial heat. Also known as *uva pasas*.

RAISIN WINE   A wine made from dried grapes.

RAISINY   Describes an odor and/or flavor occasionally detected in wines made from grapes that have more or less dried (shriveled or raisined) on the grapevine; often encountered in hot climate wines.

RAKI   *See* Arrack.

RAMADA (PORTUGAL)   A special method of planting and pruning grapevines, utilized in colder regions prone to spring frosts. The grapevines are trained and pruned on wires strung along posts, rather like a pergola system.

RAMATO (ITALY)   A white wine that is copper-colored, due to the fact that it is vinified in contact with the grape skins, causing greater depth of color and flavor.

RAMISCO (PORTUGAL)   A red grape variety grown in the Colares region.

RAMOS GIN FIZZ   A cocktail consisting of gin, lemon juice, lime juice, sugar, egg white, cream, and soda water. Supposedly invented by Henry C. Ramos in 1888 at his famous Imperial Cabinet Bar and Saloon in New Orleans, during the Mardi Gras.

RAMSEY   A grape variety developed by Thomas Volney Munson (1843–1913) of Denison, Texas.

RANCID   *See* Butyric Acid.

RANCIO (SPAIN)   A nutty odor or flavor in a wine, often used to describe a sherry-like taste occasionally displayed in wines that have prolonged air exposure. Also known as *goût de rancio* and *vino de rancio*.

RANINA (YUGOSLAVIA)   *See* Bouvier.

RAPÉ (FRANCE)   Discarded or rejected clusters of grapes normally found during the harvest.

RÂPEUX (FRANCE)   *See* Rough.

RASPBERRY-FLAVORED BRANDY   A mixture of brandy with a minimum of 2.5 percent sugar, flavored and colored with raspberries. By United States federal law it cannot be bottled at less than 60 proof (30 percent alcohol by volume).

RASPBERRY LIQUEUR   A sweetened alcoholic beverage consisting of a base of alcohol, minimum 2.5 percent sugar, flavored and colored with raspberries. It is sweeter and lower in proof than raspberry-flavored brandy.

RASPBERRIES   A fruity or zesty nuance or aroma reminiscent of raspberries, generally found in some light-bodied red wines, especially Beaujolais, some Zinfandel, and Bourgueil.

RASPON (SPAIN)   *See* Stems.

RASSIG (GERMANY)   *See* Lively.

RASTEAU   A sweet, fortified wine, similar in color to a white port.

RATAFIA (FRANCE)   A sweet, fruity apéritif made with *mistelles* in the Champagne region. Ratafias are generally aged for one year in wooden barrels, which gives the final product an oxidized color and taste. United States federal regulations prohibit use of the name for an American-produced product; however, a French-made ratafia called Pineau des Charentes is available in the marketplace.

The first written reference to ratafia appears in the eighteenth-century records of the French champagne house of Veuve Clicquot, although there is speculation that it was produced much earlier. *See* Mistelle.

RAUCHBIER (GERMANY)   An amber to dark-colored beer, brewed with the addition of malt that was dried over smoking beechwood; it is mostly found in Bamberg or Hamburg.

RAUENTHAL (GERMANY)   An important wine town, located in the Rheingau, producing white wines that display considerable fruit and spice; these wines are generally well balanced.

RAUH (GERMANY)   *See* Rough.

RAULÍ   A type of beechwood formerly used for barrelmaking in Chile.

RÄUSCHLING (SWITZERLAND)   A white grape variety grown almost exclusively near Lake Zurich.

RAVELLO BIANCO (ITALY) A local white wine produced near the Amalfi Drive in Campania, noted for its delicate fragrance and taste.

RAWHIDE A taster's term for a wine that displays a leathery texture, occasionally found in some red wines that have been aged in oak barrels.

RAW MATERIAL COST The wholesale price of raw materials utilized in making alcoholic and nonalcoholic beverages.

RAVAT 6 *See* Ravat Blanc.

RAVAT 51 *See* Vignoles.

RAVAT 262 *See* Ravat Noir.

RAVAT BLANC A white grape variety developed from a cross of Chardonnay and Seibel 5474; it is grown primarily in the eastern and midwestern United States. Formerly known as *Ravat 6*.

RAVAT NOIR A red grape variety developed from a cross of Seibel 8365 and Pinot Noir; it is grown primarily in the eastern and midwestern United States. Formerly known as *Ravat 262*.

RAYA (SPAIN) A vertical line or trace made with chalk on the head of a sherry butt (barrel) to identify and classify wines that will become *finos* or *amontillados*. The butts of the palest and finest sherry wines will be marked with one stroke / (raya), destined to be used for fino sherry; the fuller or heavier wines will be marked with two strokes // (dos rayas), for oloroso-type sherries. This word is also used for a coarse, oloroso-type sherry.

RAYON D'OR A white grape variety developed from a cross of Seibel 405 and Seibel 2007; it is grown primarily in the eastern and midwestern United States. Formerly known as *Seibel 4986*.

RAZZA (ITALY) *See* Breed.

REAL MCCOY, THE An expression that derives its name from Captain Bill McCoy, a Florida boatmaker who built yachts for Carnegie and the Vanderbilts. During Prohibition (1920–1933), he ran "rum row" consignments from Nassau in the Bahamas to the Florida coast and Scotch whisky from Scotland. The distilled spirits were sold just outside the United States' territorial waters from his tall ship, the "Arethusa," to motor launches and other vessels. He was a man of integrity who shipped to the United States nothing but "genuine." The reputation of his Scotch whisky and rum was so high that the expression the Real McCoy became a byword for quality.

REBATE The practice of returning a portion of an amount paid, as for goods or services, serving as a reduction or discount. *See* Consumer Coupons and Refunds.

REBE (GERMANY) *See* Grape.

REBECCA A white grape variety grown around 1850 in New York State.

REBÈCHE (FRANCE) A term formerly used to denote the final pressing of the grapes in the making of champagne. This is no longer permitted under AOC regulations (1994).

REBLAUS (GERMANY) *See* Phylloxera Vastatrix.

REBO (ITALY) A red grape variety grown primarily in the Trentino-Alto Adige region in the north; it was developed by Rebo Rigotti in 1948 from a cross of Merlot and Marzemino grape varieties at the Experimental Research Station and School of Enology at San Michele all'Adige.

REBSORTE (GERMANY) *See* Grape Variety.

REBSORTEN SEKTS (GERMANY) Sparkling wines produced from a particular variety of grape type.

RECEIVING The act of accepting delivery (receiving) of beverages that have been ordered, checking beverages and other merchandise from purveyors, and recording such transactions.

RECEIVING CLERK An employee who is in charge of receiving beverages or other types of merchandise and who performs the receiving function.

RECEIVING SHEET A daily form (record) on which the receiving clerk lists all merchandise accepted as delivered, noting the invoice number and ascertaining which department the goods should be delivered to.

RÉCEMMENT DÉGORGÉ (FRANCE) Recently disgorged.

RÉCHE (FRANCE) *See* Rough.

RECIOTO DELLA VALPOLICELLA (ITALY) A single bunch or cluster of the best and ripest grapes that have received the most direct sunshine is called *recie* or *orecchie* (ears) (*recioto* is a word from the old Veronese dialect of the area). These grapes are utilized in the process of making Recioto della Valpolicella wine.

Recioto wines are sometimes labeled Recioto della Valpolicella; Recioto della Valpolicella Spumante; Recioto della Valpolicella Liquoroso, or simply Recioto. Reciotos without the suffix Amarone are *amabile* (semisweet to sweet) and contain more than 1 percent residual sugar (the maximum that Amarone can have under DOC regulations). The *liquoroso* designation is for a very sweet dessert wine (with a minimum of 16 percent alcohol). There is also a *spumante*, which is *amabile*, with a remarkable amount of body and finesse.

To produce an *amabile* or *spumante*, fermentation is halted before all of the sugar is metabolized, and the wine is immediately filtered to eliminate the yeast. The *spumante* is made by inducing a secondary fermentation that creates effervescence (less of it, however, than in French champagne). *See* Amarone della Valpolicella.

RECIOTO DI SOAVE (ITALY) A white wine from the province of Verona, made from partially dried grapes. It is sweet to the taste, with overtones of pears, apricots, and bananas.

RECIPE A formula used to produce beverage items for consumption.

RECIPE COSTING The practice of calculating the exact cost for every ingredient in a recipe in order to ascertain the total recipe cost and the portion cost.

RECIPE FORECASTING The practice of estimating, prior to sales, how many portions will be yielded from a standardized recipe.

RECIPE YIELD The count, weight, or volume that a standardized formula (recipe) will produce.

RECOLTA *(ROMANIA)*   *See* Harvest.

RÉCOLTE *(FRANCE)*   *See* Année.

RÉCOLTE TARDIVE *(FRANCE)*   *See* Late Harvest.

RÉCOLTE-MANIPULANT *(FRANCE)*   Identifies champagnes produced by one of the fifteen thousand growers in the Champagne region. Includes wines that are partially produced by cooperatives but finished by the growers. Appears on some champagne labels as the initials *RM*.

RECONDITIONING   The conduct of operations, after original bottling or packing, to restore wine to a merchantable condition. The term includes relabeling or recasing operations.

RECTIFIED AND BOTTLED BY   No longer a legal term. *See* Processing.

RECTIFYING   No longer a legal term. *See* Processing.

RED   A term used to describe the color of some alcoholic and nonalcoholic beverages. Also known as *cherveno, crno, kirmisi, rosso, rosu, rot, rouge, tinto*, and *vörös*.

RED AMBER   A red grape variety.

RED CACO   A red grape variety.

RED CRIMSON   A red grape variety grown in the United States.

RED EAGLE   A grape variety developed by Thomas Volney Munson (1843–1913) of Denison, Texas.

RED LAYER   In a wooden barrel, beneath the charred layers of wood (pure carbon), is the red layer of caramelized wood sugars that give whiskey and brandy their rich, dark color. Also, the deep charred layers yield tannin and vanillin. At high external temperatures (above 90 degrees Fahrenheit), the whiskey or brandy in the barrel expands and penetrates the caramelized or "red layer" of wood behind the char, making the whiskey or brandy smoother and somewhat more flavorful.

RED MÁLAGA   A red grape variety grown primarily in California. Also known as *Molinera Gorda*.

RED MISKET *(BULGARIA)*   A white grape variety, unrelated to the Muscat grape family. Also known as *Misket de Sliven*.

REDONDO *(PORTUGAL* AND *SPAIN)*   *See* Round.

RED SUMOLL *(SPAIN)*   A red grape variety.

RED TRAMINER   *See* Gewürztraminer.

REDUCE   To cook down; to evaporate some of the liquid, thus obtaining a stronger brew.

REDUCING   Prior to bottling, the proof or alcohol content of distilled spirits is lowered or adjusted, usually by the addition of demineralized or distilled water. Also known as *cutting*.

REDUCING SUGAR   The amount of unfermentable sugar that will not ferment and that remains in a wine. The most common reducing sugars are glucose and fructose, along with pentose. Also known as *nonfermentable reducing sugar* or *nonfermentables*. *See* Pentose and Residual Sugar.

RÉDUCTION FRANÇOIS *(FRANCE)* The system of measuring the *liqueur de tirage* necessary for making sparkling wine. *See* François.

RED VELTLINER A red grape variety grown in California.

RED VERMOUTH *See* Vermouth.

RED WINE A wine made with coloration derived from contact with the skin of the grape, as opposed to a white wine, which is either made entirely from white grapes or from black grapes without prolonged skin contact. Also known as *rotwein, vinho tinto, vino rosso, vino tinto, vin rouge*, and *vörösbor*.

REDWOOD BARRELS *See* Sequoia Sempervirens.

REEDY A term that infers a woody or slightly herbaceous taste in wine.

REFERENCIA *(SPAIN)* A sample of a wine blend retained by the shipper.

REFILLING *See* Consolidating Bottles.

REFINED A loosely defined term for a wine that is free from crudeness or coarseness and is cultivated and elegant, with great subtleness.

REFOSCO *(ITALY)* *See* Mondeuse Noire.

REFRACTOMETER A hand-held optical instrument that measures the amount of light bent as it passes through grape juice; one views this through an eye piece. This measurement gives the percent of sugar weight in the grapes and helps viticulturists determine when they are ready for harvest.

REFRESH To refresh a barrel of aging wine or distilled spirits by the addition of a newer or younger type. This is often practiced in the making of sherry wine and some distilled spirits. Also known as *rociar*.

REFRESHMENT BAR OR STAND A commercial food and/or beverage establishment in transportation terminals, sports arenas, or other high-volume, fast-food areas that cater to fast-paced individuals. These facilities offer patrons limited fast-food menus and alcoholic beverages, which are consumed either while standing or seated on stools.

REFRIGERATION *See* Cold Stabilization.

REFSKO *(YUGOSLAVIA)* *See* Mondeuse Noire.

REFUNDS Mail-in rebate sent to the consumer upon presentation of refund slip and proof-of-purchase and/or cash register receipt. *See* Consumer Coupons and Rebate.

REGALE A red grape variety developed in 1982.

REGE *(FRANCE)* Rows of grapevines.

REGINA *(ITALY)* A white grape variety grown in Sardinia, where it is also known as *Pergolina*.

REGIONAL A wine that takes its name from a geographical area where grapes are grown or wine made, rather than from a specific town or vineyard.

RÉGISSEUR (FRANCE)   Estate manager.

REGNER (GERMANY)   A white grape variety developed in 1929 from a cross of Luglienca Bianca and Gamay Früh at the Alzey Research Station in the Rheinhessen. It was named in honor of a member of the viticultural institute's staff.

RÉGNIÉ (FRANCE)   A *cru* commune in Beaujolais, near the communes of Brouilly and Morgon, producing distinctive and appealing fruity wines reminiscent of strawberries. Régnié officially received its AOC designation in 1988, making it the tenth cru in Beaujolais.

REGULAR CUBES   *See* Ice Cubes.

REGULATOR   That part of a tap beer system that maintains the carbon dioxide pressure at a constant level.

REHOBOAM   A formerly used oversized bottle equal in capacity to six 750-milliliter bottles or 4.5 liters (152.1 ounces), used exclusively for champagne.
    Rehoboam (952 B.C.), a son of King Solomon (and grandson of King David), was the first king of the southern kingdom of Judah and the last king of David's united monarchy.

REICHENSTEINER (GERMANY)   A white grape variety developed in 1978 from a cross of Müller-Thurgau and (Madeleine Angevine and Calabrese) by Dr. Helmut Becker at the Geisenheim Institute in the Rheingau.

REIF (GERMANY)   *See* Ripe.

REIMS (FRANCE)   A city located on the Marne River; it is the capital of the Champagne region. Formerly spelled *Rheims*.

REIN (GERMANY)   Pure.

REINTÖNIG (GERMANY)   *See* Clean.

REINHEITSGEBOT (GERMANY)   The so-called German brewing purification law or the Bavarian Purity Order. It was enacted in 1516 by Bavaria's Duke Wilhelm IV, who decreed that beer could be brewed only from malt, hops, and water, with no other additives except for yeast. This law is also followed in other countries, including Norway and Switzerland.

RELIANCE SEEDLESS   A red grape variety developed in 1983 from a cross of Ontario and Suffolk Red by Dr. James N. Moore at the Arkansas Agricultural Experiment Station.

RELISH FORK   A small, narrow fork, usually with two or three tines, utilized for spearing the cocktail olives or onions necessary for certain cocktails.

REMAILY SEEDLESS   A white grape variety developed in 1965 from a cross of Lady Patricia and N.Y. 33979 by George Remaily, a commercial artist, at the State Agricultural Experimental Station in Geneva, New York.

REMONTADO (SPAIN)   *See* Pumping Over.

REMONTAGE (FRANCE)   *See* Pumping Over.

REMONTAGEM (PORTUGAL)   *See* Pumping Over.

REMONTAGIO *(ITALY)* *See* Pumping Over.

REMPLISSAGE *(FRANCE)* *See* Topping.

REMUAGE *(FRANCE)* The process in which the sediment contained in a bottle of sparkling wine or champagne is carefully worked down to the neck by gentle turning (riddling) of the bottle on a regular basis. This is accomplished by a rotative twisting movement, while the bottle is placed in an increasingly downward position, which aids in the eventual settling and collection of sediment in the bottle's neck. Also known as *riddling, ruetteln,* and *scuotimento.*

REMUEUR *(FRANCE)* Riddler.

RENEWAL SPUR *See* Spur.

RENTAMT *(GERMANY)* The revenue office.

REORDER POINT The point at which beverages and other supplies must be ordered (with sufficient lead time) in order to maintain minimum stock so that customers can still be satisfied with what is on hand.

REP Short for representative. An individual or company authorized to represent a business organization (supplier) and to provide goods and/or services in return for monetary transactions.

REPEAL *See* Prohibition.

REPISA *(PORTUGAL)* The second pressing of the grapes.

REPOSADO *(SPAIN)* A designation that indicates that the tequila has been aged at least one year.

REPRODUCING APPARATUS A stainless steel tank equipped with various devices specially designed for yeast reproduction, necessary in making all types of alcoholic beverages.

REQUISITION A written order (usually on preprinted forms) requesting the beverage storeroom to withdraw items from stock and to issue them to the requester.

RESA *(ITALY)* Yield, as in either grapes or wine.

RESALE AT WHOLESALE A sale to any trade buyer.

RESERVA *(PORTUGAL)* A wine that represents an exceptional harvest, set aside for extra-long aging to develop a depth of character and delicacy of bouquet. *See* Garrafeira.

RESERVA *(SPAIN)* Red wines that have been aged in 225-liter oak barrels for a minimum of one year, followed by two years in the bottle; they may not leave the *bodega* until the fourth year after the harvest. White wines must be aged a minimum of two years, six months of which must be in oak barrels. In practice, many wineries age the wines far longer than the minimum. Reservas are usually laid down only in very fine years.

RESERVE A term often found on wine labels of United States wines; it has no legal or real meaning. *See* Limited Bottling.

RESERVE *See* Premium.

RÉSERVE *(FRANCE)*   *See* Premium.

RÉSERVE *(FRANCE)*   A label designation used on armagnac, calvados, and cognac bottles to indicate that the youngest brandy used in the blend is at least five years old (armagnac), three years old (calvados), and 4-1/2 years old (cognac) although they contain a very high percentage of brandy that has been aged for twelve to twenty years or more.

RESERVED FOR ENGLAND   *See* Brut.

RESERVE WINE   Wine from previous vintages added to the *cuvée* of nonvintage wines to produce a wine with consistent quality and style. *See* Blending and Nonvintage.

RÉSIDU *(FRANCE)*   Residue.

RESIDUI *(ITALY)*   *See* Residual Sugar.

RESIDUAL SUGAR   The measure of natural grape sugar intentionally left in the wine after fermentation. Sweetness is balanced by acidity, creating a harmonious taste experience. Sweetness is a function of style, not quality. Some rare and expensive sweet wines have sugar levels as high as 20, 25, and even 30 percent. More and more United States wineries are listing the residual sugar on their back labels as an aid to the consumer. Also known as *residui, restsuesse, restsüsse,* and *zuckerrest. See* Reducing Sugar.

RESIN   *See* Retsina.

RÉSINE *(FRANCE)*   *See* Retsina.

RESINOUS   *See* Retsina.

RESINATED WINES   *See* Retsina.

RESISTANT ROOTSTOCKS   Special types of grapevine roots that are more resistant to the attack of certain root parasites than others. Also known as *portainjerto.*

RESPIRATION   The release of stored energy and sugars in a plant for use in synthesizing enzymes, colors, aromas, flavors, tannins, glucosides, and vitamins; it is largely controlled by temperature. The loss of malic and tartaric acids as grapes begin to change color and ripen is also due to respiration and is mostly affected by temperature.

RESSAIBO *(PORTUGAL)*   *See* Aftertaste.

REST   A state of suspended growth due to internal physiological blocks. Rest is fulfilled by exposure to temperatures of 45 degrees Fahrenheit or less for an extended period (chilling requirement). After the rest period is satisfied, a plant may either break dormancy and begin to grow if conditions allow, or may remain dormant if conditions do not favor growth. Often known as *dehardening. See* Dormancy and Quiescence.

REST   The practice of allowing bottles of wine to rest or lay quietly, untouched, in one location for several days after purchase.

RESTORED PURE CONDENSED MUST   Pure condensed *must* to which has been added an amount of water not exceeding the amount removed in the dehydration process.

RESTRAINED   *See* Dumb.

RESTSUESSE *(AUSTRIA)*   *See* Residual Sugar.

RESTSÜSSE *(GERMANY)*   *See* Residual Sugar.

RETAIL Package stores, supermarkets, and so forth, that purchase alcoholic and nonalcoholic beverages from wholesalers and then sell to consumers at retail price.

RETAILER Any person engaged in the sale and/or service of distilled spirits, wine, or malt beverages directly to consumers.

RETAIL ESTABLISHMENT Any premises where distilled spirits, wine, or malt beverages are sold or offered for sale to consumers, whether for consumption on- or off-premises.

RETICENT A wine that seems to be holding back its bouquet or taste, possible due to youth or a *dumb* stage it is passing through.

RETROGUSTO (*ITALY* AND *SPAIN*) *See* Aftertaste.

RETROUSSE LE GÂTEAU (*FRANCE*) *See* Punching Down.

RETSINA (*GREECE*) A white table wine that has been adulterated by addition of 0.15 to 1 kilogram of dried and powdered pine resin (along with aromatic gums and spices) to one hectoliter of wine; these are added to either the *must* or finished wine, contributing to Restina's unique flavor.

The resin is actually sap (technically called *sandarac*, a type of resin used in the production of varnish) obtained from the bark of several types of Aleppo tree *(Tetraclinis articulata)* from Africa and Australia. In ancient Greece, resin was used in the preparation of wine to impart flavor and act as a preservative.

Retsina, which is produced mainly in Attica from the Rhoditis, Savatianó, and Assyrtiko grape varieties, has a turpentine-like odor which may offend the novice drinker. There is also a rosé Retsina wine called Kokkinélli. Also known as *odeur de résine, resin, resinated wines, résine,* and *resinous.*

RETURN The transfer of distilled spirits, wine, or malt beverages from a trade buyer to the industry member from whom they were purchased, for cash or credit.

RETURN ON INVESTMENT (ROI) The gain or share of profit associated with the investment of capital, usually expressed as a percentage.

REUILLY (*FRANCE*) A dry white wine made from the Sauvignon Blanc grape variety in the upper Loire Valley.

REVENUE Money received by an establishment from consumers for either goods sold or services rendered.

REVENUERS In the United States, Alcohol Tax Unit men who enforced taxation of alcoholic beverages during Prohibition. *See* Excise Man.

RHEIMS (*FRANCE*) *See* Reims.

RHEIN (*GERMANY*) The local name for the Rhine River.

RHEINGAU (*GERMANY*) One of thirteen Qualitätswein (quality) grape-growing regions, it produces the greatest of all German wines. It is almost all one large hillside, facing south and protected against the northern climate by the Taunus mountain chain. The wines made in this area are noble indeed, combining elegance with style and delicacy and yet with substance and fruit as well. Almost every village and vineyard produces a wine whose quality is distinctive and that an expert can identify. The Johannisberg Riesling is the primary grape variety planted in the Rheingau. Some of

Germany's better-known winemaking estates, including Schloss Johannisberg, Steinberg, and Schloss Vollrads, are in this area. The main Rheingau villages in which wines are made are Rüdesheim, Johannisberg, Rauenthal, Kiedrich, Erbach, Hattenheim, Oestrich, Hallgarten, Eltville, Geisenheim, and Hochheim. For many years the wines of Hochheim, which contains five vineyards between Mainz and Wiesbaden, were referred to, mainly by the British, as *hock*; earlier, the British called them *Rhenish* wines.

RHEINHESSEN (*GERMANY*)   One of thirteen Qualitätswein (quality) grape-growing regions. Most of Germany's wine that is exported is made in this region; it produces even larger quantities than Mosel-Saar-Ruwer and Rheingau. Its wines, profiting from a warmer climate, are softer, rounder, and a little fuller than the aristocratic wines of the Rheingau. The main grape varieties of Rheinhessen are the Sylvaner and Müller-Thurgau, which produce very soft, sometimes fairly sweet wines with a delicate bouquet. Because this is a large area, Rheinhessen's wines vary a great deal in their characteristics. In good years, some of the finest, if not *the* finest, *Prädikat* wines of Germany are made here. Some towns with well-known vineyards are Nierstein, Oppenheim, Bodenheim, Nackenheim, Bingen, Worms, and Guntersblum. It is in Rheinhessen that most of the better *Liebfraumilch* wine is produced.

RHEINPFALZ (*GERMANY*)   *See* Pfalz.

RHEINRIESLING   *See* Johannisberg Riesling.

RHENISH   The English name for Rhine wines of Germany, from the earliest days of their import to the eighteenth century, when the term *hock* replaced it.

RHINE WINE   A generic term for any number of white wines produced in the Rhine regions of Germany.

RHINE WINE   A generic wine term used in the United States for a white table wine, generally semidry to sweet, and somewhat bland-tasting.

RHODITIS (*GREECE*)   A white grape variety often blended with *Savatianó* to produce the famous *retsina* wine. Also spelled *Roditis*.

RHÔNE VALLEY (*FRANCE*)   A major grape-growing region located below Burgundy in the southeast. Rhône Valley's wine production is more than 90 percent red, with some fine whites and even rosé wines. It is the second-largest AOC wine-producing region (Bordeaux is the largest). The Rhône region, which is the southernmost of France's six major fine-wine regions, received its AOC status in 1937.

The vineyards—totaling nearly 150,000 acres—stretch along both sides of the Rhône River for about 125 miles, beginning in the south around the famous papal stronghold of Avignon and extending north to the outskirts of the city of Lyon. In the south the grapevines work hard to survive in chalky, stone-covered soil; in the northern area they scale palisades towering over the river.

Rhône wines are robust and full-bodied, with plenty of bouquet and taste. They are generally higher in alcohol (minimum 11 percent) than red Burgundies or Bordeaux due to their geographic location. The general name for wines produced in the Rhône Valley is *Côtes-du-Rhône*.

RHUM (*FRANCE*)   *See* Rum.

RIBEAUVILLÉ (*FRANCE*)   A wine-producing town in the region of Alsace, noted for its Johannisberg Riesling wines.

RIBIER   A red grape variety grown primarily in California. Also known as *Alphonse Lavalée*.

RIBOLLA GIALLA *(ITALY)*   A white grape variety grown primarily in Friuli-Venezia Giulia.

RIBOLLA NERA *(ITALY)*   *See* Schioppettino.

RICE   An integral ingredient of some alcoholic beverages including saké and American-made beers. The more rice added to the mash, the lighter in body the product.

RICE WINE   A wine made from grain with an alcoholic content of 12 to 15 percent by volume. *Saké*, although technically a brewed product, is erroneously referred to as rice wine. *See* Saké.

RICCO *(ITALY)*   *See* Rich.

RICH   A term that describes wines or even beers that display a generous bouquet and substantial body; mouthfilling fullness in taste, with fruity flavors and good acidity. Also known as *étoffé, riche, ricco,* and *saftig.*

RICHARD'S BLACK   A red grape variety grown primarily in California.

RICHE *(FRANCE)*   *See* Rich.

RICK   A framed, open warehouse where barrels of distilled spirits are stored for aging and maturing.

RICKEY   From the Hindustani word "rekhta" meaning poured out, scattered, or mixed.

RICKEY   A drink family name given to those cocktails (a cross between Collins and sours) made with distilled spirits and lemon or lime juice, with a sweetening agent and soda water or ginger ale added. *See* Gin Rickey.

RICOLMATURA *(ITALY)*   A procedure of topping off of a bottle of wine with wine from the same vintage, usually performed when the wine is about twenty-five years old, the approximate life of a cork.

RIDDLING   *See* Remuage.

RIDDLING RACKS   *See* Pupîtres.

RIDDU *(ITALY)*   *See* Grillo.

RIESLANER *(GERMANY)*   A white grape variety developed in 1929 from a cross of Sylvaner and Johannisberg Riesling by Dr. Ziegler at the Alzey Research Station. Incorrectly referred to as *Mainriesling.*

RIESLING   *See* Johannisberg Riesling.

RIESLING DORÉ   A white grape variety supposedly developed from a cross of Johannisberg Riesling and Courtiller Musque. It is grown in Alsace, France, and the western part of the United States. Also known as *Goldriesling.*

RIESLING RENANO *(ITALY)*   *See* Johannisberg Riesling.

RIESLING ITALICO *(ITALY)*   *See* Welschriesling.

RIM   The outer edge or lip of the bowl on a wine or beer glass, where the drinker's lips touch it. Generally, the smaller and thinner the rim, the finer the quality of the glass. Also known as *bead*.

RIM   The outer edge of a wine (especially red), when viewed against a white background as the glass is tipped to a 45-degree angle, presents a good indication of how the wine is aging. A brick-red color generally indicates maturity, whereas a brown color indicates that the wine has deteriorated or is too old for consumption.

RIMMING   Decorating the rim of a glass with either salt, celery salt, or sugar by first placing the glass upside down on the liquid tray, which usually contains lemon or lime juice, and then immediately into the salt or sugar tray, which leaves a thin layer of either on the rim of the glass. Rimming is necessary when serving drinks such as Bloody Mary, Margarita, Salty Dog, Gimlet, Pink Squirrel, and Sours.

RIOJA *(SPAIN)*   A major grape-growing region producing mostly red wines in the Bordeaux style. Some fine quality white wines are also produced there.

Rioja encompasses some 110,000 acres of vineyards in the northeastern part of Spain in an eighty-mile stretch of land along the Ebro River, not far from the western Pyrenees and only two hundred miles south of Bordeaux, France.

The average elevation of the Rioja's vineyards is more than fifteen hundred feet above sea level. These heights produce lighter wines than those that are made from grapes grown in lower and warmer sections of the country. Most of the vineyards are situated on either side of the Ebro River, which flows east from the Pyrenees toward the Mediterranean.

Seven tributaries cross the Rioja; one of them that lies towards the western end is called the "Rio Oja." Actually, the name Rio, which means "river," is joined with Oja. Rio Oja is the name of a mountain stream that flows into the River Ebro, some 165 miles northeast of Madrid.

Rioja is divided into three viticultural subzones: Rioja Alta, Rioja Alavesa, and Rioja Baja. Rioja Baja is in the southeastern portion of the *DO*. The wines from Rioja Baja are heartier, fuller-bodied, with higher alcohol and lower acid than those produced in the other two subzones. Rioja Alavesa, to the west, north of the Ebro River, is higher in altitude, cooler and wetter. Rioja Alavesa produces wines that are light and delicate, with excellent flavor and color, but not usually possessing sufficient body, alcohol, and acid to permit beneficial aging. Rioja Alta is the largest of the three subzones, located in the hilly western part of Spain south of the Ebro River; it enjoys a mild continental climate. Its wines are elegant and fruity in style with good acidity, and age well.

RIOJA ALAVESA *(SPAIN)*   *See* Rioja.

RIOJA ALTA *(SPAIN)*   *See* Rioja.

RIOJA BAJA *(SPAIN)*   *See* Rioja.

RIPARIA   *See Vitis Riparia.*

RIPASSO *(ITALY)*   A process used in Verona for some Valpolicella wine that has some similarity to the Tuscan *governo*. Immediately after the Valpolicella wine ferments, the juice is poured into barrels containing the wine-soaked skins and seeds from Amarone or *Recioto* wines. These skins, which still contain some unfermented sugar, cause the wine to undergo a second alcoholic fermentation. This process increases the alcoholic content of the wine about 2 percent and gives the wine more structure, tannin, extract, glycerin, color, and bouquet. *See* Appassimento.

RIPE   Describes wines, beers, or distilled spirits that have reached their full term of aging or have achieved a proper state of bouquet and flavor development. They are full, soft, and mature. Also known as *reif*. *See* Aging, Barrel Aging, Bottle Aging, Maturity, and Ripe for Bottling.

RIPE FOR BOTTLING   A term that means that the wine, beer, or distilled spirit has improved in the barrel to the highest point possible, after which aging usually is completed in glass or stainless steel. *See* Aging, Barrel Aging, Bottle Aging, Maturity, and Ripe.

RIPENESS   A term referring to flavor and a proper balance between sugar, acid, and pH in a grape. Sugar is thus only one component of ripeness and cannot alone define ripeness. In fact, there are no tests to measure ripeness or flavor, which is an essentially subjective, relative concept. Ripeness exists as a potential affected by individual vineyard characteristics and weather patterns. *See* Maturity.

RIPLEY   A white grape variety developed in 1912 at the State Experimental Station in Geneva, New York.

RIPPED   *See* Intoxicated.

RIPPING   A process that tears the soil to a depth of three to five feet, to loosen it so that the grapevine can spread its roots.

RIQUEWIHR (FRANCE)   One of the finest wine-producing villages located in the Alsace region, noted for its Johannisberg Riesling wines.

RISERS   The name of the metal pipes often used in vineyards to support the sprinkler heads above the level of foliage in an overhead water sprinkler system.

RISERVA (ITALY)   A DOC or DOCG wine with extra barrel-aging at the winery. The minimum number of months or years required is solely determined by the individual DOC or DOCG.

RISERVA SPECIALE (ITALY)   A rarely used term denoting an extra year of aging, longer than *riserva*.

RISH BABA   A white grape variety often referred to as Lady Fingers, originally from Iran.

RITOCCHINO (ITALY)   A vertical method of pruning grapevines utilized in Piedmont. This method increases the sunlight exposure of the leaf system with a slightly increased risk of landslide after heavy rainfall.

RIVULETS   *See* Legs.

RIVANER (YUGOSLAVIA)   *See* Müller-Thurgau.

RIZLING   *See* Johannisberg Riesling.

RKATSITELI (RUSSIA)   A white grape variety used primarily in making sparkling wines and for dry or semidry table wines. Some is sparsely grown since 1963 in the Livermore Valley of California as well as in New York and New Jersey, and even in China and eastern Europe. Also known as *Sunshine Coast*.

RM (FRANCE)   *See* Récolte-Manipulant.

ROAD HOUSE   An old slang expression for a pub or bar located alongside a roadway.

ROANOKE   A white grape variety.

ROASTED   A smell often found in wines made from grapes exposed to intense sunshine; slightly oxidative character reminiscent of sherry wine.

ROASTED MALT   Grain (usually barley) that has been exposed to great heat, causing a browning of its sugars and a chocolate brown-black color. Roasted grains are often used in the brewing of dark beers, especially stout and porter.

ROBE (*FRANCE*)   Refers to the color and other visual aspects of a wine. It is generally used to describe a fine red wine.

ROBE CHATOYANTE (*FRANCE*)   A glistening color.

ROBIN CARDINAL   *See* Thornsburg Robin.

ROB ROY   A cocktail consisting of Scotch whisky, sweet vermouth, and bitters, although dry vermouth is often substituted for sweet when making a "dry" Rob Roy.
    Robert MacGregor, a character immortalized in a novel by Sir Walter Scott (1817), was said to have hidden from the law in an oak tree, where now only a stump remains, four hundred yards along the road from the Glengoyne distillery in Scotland. The drink Rob Roy was named after MacGregor because of his red hair.

ROBOLO (*GREECE*)   A white grape variety.

ROBUST   Also known as *corsé, forte, kernig, kräftig, robusto*, and *romaléos*. *See* Big.

ROBUSTA   One of two types of coffee beans, the other being *arabica*.

ROBUSTO (*ITALY*)   *See* Robust.

ROCCA (*ITALY*)   A rock fortress.

ROCIAR (*SPAIN*)   *See* Refresh.

ROCK AND RYE   A liqueur bottled at not less than 60 proof (in which not less than 51 percent on a proof gallon basis of the distilled spirits used is rye whiskey) which possesses a predominant characteristic rye flavor derived from such whiskey. It must contain rock candy or sugar syrup, with or without the addition of fruit, fruit juices, or other natural flavoring materials. Some producers of rock and rye feature pieces of fruit such as lemons, oranges, or even cherries floating in the bottle. Rock and rye was originally sold as a sore throat remedy.

ROCKS   Slang term for ice cubes, as in the expression "on-the-rocks." Also the name of a glass—an on the rocks glass.

ROCKS GLASS   *See* Old-Fashioned Glass.

ROCKY   A term occasionally applied to the surface texture of the head on a glass of beer.

RODITIS (*GREECE*)   *See* Rhoditis.

ROEMER (*GERMANY*)   Green-tinted stemware used for wine service.

ROGERS 3   *See* Massasoit.

ROGERS 4   *See* Wilder.

ROGERS 9   *See* Lindley.

ROGNER (FRANCE)   To cut off the end of young tendrils on a grapevine with a knife in order to shape the foliage into a hedge.

ROI   *See* Return On Investment.

ROLHA (PORTUGAL)   *See* Cork.

ROLLE (FRANCE)   A white grape variety grown in the southeast.

ROLLING BAR   A portable service bar used in hotels, catering halls, banquets, or other locations where the bar must be mobile. Each rolling bar is equipped with ice bins and only the most-called-for brands of alcoholic as well as nonalcoholic beverages and mixes. Also known as *portable bar*.

ROLLO (ITALY)   A white grape variety.

ROMALÉOS (GREECE)   *See* Robust.

ROMANÉE-CONTI (FRANCE)   A *grand cru* vineyard in the village of Vosne-Romanée in the Côte de Nuits district of Burgundy, producing what is often regarded as the finest and most expensive of all red Burgundy wines. Romanée-Conti takes its name from the Prince de Conti, who owned it from 1760 to 1795, during the rule of Louis XV.

The vineyards of Romanée-Conti are quite small, measuring about 4-1/2 acres, producing an average of five hundred cases per year.

ROMANESCO (ITALY)   A white grape variety.

ROMEIKO (GREECE)   A red grape variety.

RÖMER (AUSTRIA)   Special wine glasses; it is also the German word for Romans.

ROMMEL   A grape variety developed by Thomas Volney Munson (1843–1913) of Denison, Texas.

ROMULUS SEEDLESS   A white grape variety developed in 1952 from a cross of Ontario and Thompson Seedless at the State Agricultural Experimental Station in Geneva, New York.

RON (SPAIN)   *See* Rum.

RONDE (FRANCE)   *See* Round.

RONDELLE (FRANCE)   A disk made from the best quality cork bark, used in the making of champagne corks. *See* Manche and Miroir.

RONDINELLA (ITALY)   A red grape variety grown primarily in the Veneto region, where it is used as a blending grape to produce Bardolino and Valpolicella wines. Rondinella, which is dark violet in color, was first mentioned in documents dating back to 1882.

ROOD   *See* Barrel.

ROOM TEMPERATURE   A synonym for the proper temperature for the service of red wines—65 to 68 degrees Fahrenheit, not 72 degrees, as practiced in the United States.

ROOSTERS   The term often associated with cocktails during the seventeenth through the nineteenth centuries. *See* Cocktails.

ROOT BEER   A carbonated, nonalcoholic drink prepared from potable water, carbon dioxide, sugar syrup, with or without harmless organic acid, flavored with extracts from the roots and bark of certain plants, and with or without the addition of caramel color.

Root beer was initially called "birch beer" and was first introduced as a soda flavored with various roots and herbs. Later, Charles E. Hires changed the name to root beer and advertised it as "The National Temperance Drink."

ROOT ENVIRONMENT   The nature of the soil, including root parasites, microorganisms, nutrients, and water surrounding the roots of a grapevine.

ROOTING   A young grapevine, produced from a cutting grown for one season, that is developing both roots and shoots.

ROOT PARASITES   Destructive organisms living in or on roots of grapevines.

ROOTS   The underground parts of a grapevine. Their primary function is to anchor the grapevine to the land and to absorb water and the nutrients dissolved in it; these will later be transported to the rest of the plant. Also, roots store up reserve sustenance.

ROOTSTOCK   Specialized stock material to which fruiting varieties of grapes are grafted to produce a commercially acceptable grapevine. Grape rootstock varieties are used for their tolerance or resistance to root parasites such as *phylloxera* and nematodes, or for vigor. Also known as *pieds de vigne* and *Souche*.

ROPES   *See* Legs.

ROPY   *See* Oily.

ROSADO (*PORTUGAL* AND *SPAIN*)   *See* Rosé Wine.

ROSATO (*ITALY*)   *See* Rosé Wine.

ROSÉ CHAMPAGNE   A sparkling wine generally made by the addition of a small quantity of red wine to the white champagne, which gives it the right degree of color. The addition of red wine usually takes place prior to the secondary fermentation in the bottle. Other methods include allowing the *must* to have limited skin contact with the red grapes; starting from a mixture of red and white grapes; or by blending red and white wines. Also known as *pink champagne*.

ROSÉ CLAIR (*FRANCE*)   Light rosé.

ROSEWEIN (*GERMANY*)   *See* Rosé Wine.

ROSÉ FONCÉ (*FRANCE*)   Deep rosé.

ROSETTE   A red grape variety, mostly used in making rosé wines. It was brought to New York by Charles Fournier in the late 1930s. Formerly known as *Seibel 1000*.

ROSÉ WINE   A wine made from red grapes that has a light pink color, acquired by only short contact with the skins; wine made from a mixture of red and white grapes; or wine made by blending red and white wines. Also known as *bleichert, blush wine, clarete, halbrot, rosado, rosato, rosewein, ruzica, vinho rosado, vino rosado, vino rosato*, and *vin rosé*.

ROSSANELLA (*ITALY*)   *See* Molinara.

Rossara *(Italy)* *See* Molinara.

Rossese *(Italy)* A red grape variety grown in the Liguria region.

Rossetto *(Italy)* *See* Trebbiano.

Rossignola *(Italy)* A red grape variety grown primarily in the Veneto region, where it is used as a blending grape to produce Bardolino and Valpolicella wines; it is also grown in Liguria. Rossignola was first mentioned in documents dating to the beginning of the nineteenth century.

Rosso *(Italy)* *See* Red.

Rosso di Montalcino *(Italy)* A red wine produced from the same vineyards that produce the world-famous Brunello di Montalcino. Rosso di Montalcino was granted its DOC status in 1983 and is made solely from Brunello grapes (also called Sangiovese Grosso). Rosso di Montalcino can be made from very young grapevines not considered suitable for Brunello di Montalcino or from a Brunello wine aged for a shorter period of time than required under DOCG. *See* Brunello di Montalcino, Montalcino, and Sangiovese Grosso.

Rossola *(Italy)* *See* Trebbiano.

Rossola Nera *(Italy)* A red grape variety grown in Lombardy.

Rossone *(Italy)* *See* Molinara.

Rosu *(Romania)* *See* Red.

Rot *(Germany)* *See* Red.

Rot A gradual decomposition of alcoholic or nonalcoholic beverages by the action of bacteria or fungi. Also the action of mold, parasites, or bacteria on grapevines, eventually causing their destruction.

Rotate Stock *See* First-In, First-Out.

Rotberger *(Germany)* A white grape variety developed from a cross of Trollinger and Johannisberg Riesling.

Roter Veltliner *(Austria)* A red grape variety.

Rotgipfler *(Austria)* A white grape variety usually blended with Zierfandler to produce Gumpoldskirchner.

Rothrock of Prince *See* Alexander.

Roti *(France)* *See* Passito.

Rotling *(Germany)* A pale red wine made from a blend of red and white wines.

Rotondo *(Italy)* *See* Round.

Rotten Egg Smell *See* Hydrogen Sulfide.

Rotula *(Portugal)* *See* Label.

Rotwein *(Germany)* *See* Red wine.

Rotgut A slang term for a low grade wine, beer, or distilled spirit, usually consumed by derelicts.

ROTUNDIFOLIA   *See Vitis Rotundifolia.*

ROUCANEUF   A red grape variety developed in 1924 and grown primarily in the south and southwestern parts of the United States. Formerly known as *Seyve-Villard 12309.*

ROUGE (FRANCE)   *See* Red.

ROUGEON   A red grape variety developed from a cross of Seibel 880 and Seibel 4202. Formerly known as *Seibel 5898.*

ROUGH   Describes a coarse, astringent tactile sensation (not a bitter taste) often found in red wines with high tannin levels. The term also applies to immature, out-of-balance wines that display a harsh finish and possibly aftertaste. The term is also used to describe beers that are overly hopped. Also known as *âpre, aspro, basto, coarse, grossier, khondrós, râpeux, rauh, réche, ruvido, selvatico,* and *trakhys.*

ROUND   Describes a wine that is harmonious, full, and well balanced, with no major defects or rawness. Also known as *ample, redondo, ronde, rotondo, rund,* and *strongylós. See* Balance.

ROUNDED-OUT   Describes the results of maturing process of red wines and some distilled spirits during which they precipitate out the harsh *tannin* and become softer.

ROUSING   The vigorous stirring (in a tank or barrel) by means of a *rousing stick* to incorporate fining agents after they have been added to wine or beer. Also known as *agitador. See* Fining, Fining Agents, and Rousing Stick.

ROUSING STICK   A wooden stick or stainless steel paddle used for *rousing.* Also known as *apaleador. See* Rousing.

ROUSSANNE (FRANCE)   A white grape variety grown primarily in the Rhône Valley, where it used to produce Châteauneuf-du-Pape, Hermitage, Croze-Hermitage, Saint-Joseph, and other famous wines.

ROUSSETTE (FRANCE)   *See* Altesse.

ROUSSILLON (FRANCE)   A wine-producing region located in the southern part of the country, mostly producing ordinary table wines of no particular regard. *See* Languedoc and Midi.

ROVERE (ITALY)   *See* Oak.

ROVIFERM   *See* Actiferm.

ROYAL (FRANCE)   A label designation on cognac bottles that indicates that the youngest brandy used in the blend is at least 6-1/2 years old although such cognac contains a very high percentage of brandy that has been aged for twenty, thirty, or forty years or more.

ROYALTY   A red grape variety developed in 1938 from a cross of Alicante Ganzin and Trousseau by Dr. Harold P. Olmo of the University of California, Davis.

RUBBERY   Describes an undesirable odor of *mercaptans,* occasionally detected in some white wines, probably due to the breakdown of high levels of sulfur dioxide. *See* Mercaptans.

RUBILANDE   A white grape variety developed from a cross of Seibel 2859 and Seibel 4643. Formerly known as *Seibel 11803.*

RUBINO *(ITALY)* *See* Ruby.

RUBIRED A red grape variety developed in 1938 from a cross of Alicante Ganzin and Tinto Cão by Dr. Harold P. Olmo of the University of California, Davis.

RUBIS *(FRANCE)* *See* Ruby.

RUBY A color displayed by many young red wines. Also known as *rubino* and *rubis*. *See* Ruby Port.

RUBY CABERNET A red grape variety developed in 1948 from a cross of Carignan and Cabernet Sauvignon by Dr. Harold P. Olmo of the University of California, Davis.

RUBY SEEDLESS A red grape variety developed in 1968 from a cross of Emperor and Pirovano by Dr. Harold P. Olmo of the University of California, Davis.

RUBY PORT *(PORTUGAL)* Traditionally, this is the very youngest port; it takes its name from its ruby color. Ruby port, by law, must be aged in wood a minimum of three years or so and bottled while it still retains its deep red color and vigorous taste. It is usually rich and fruity and is best consumed when young.

RUCHÈ *(ITALY)* An ancient red grape variety grown primarily in Piedmont.

RÜCKGRAT *(GERMANY)* *See* Backbone.

RUDE *(FRANCE)* *See* Astringency.

RÜDESHEIM *(GERMANY)* An important wine-producing village located in the Rheingau region, famous for its full-bodied and fruity wines.

RUE A strongly scented herb from the *Ruta graveolens* family, with yellow flowers and bitter-tasting leaves, formerly used for medicinal purposes, but now used occasionally as a flavoring for *grappa*. *See* Grappa, Grappa Aromatizzata, and Grappa Con Ruta.

RUETTELN *(GERMANY)* *See* Remuage.

RUFETE A red grape variety grown primarily in Portugal and Spain.

RUHE *(GERMANY)* The storage of beer after fermentation, prior to bottling or shipping.

RULÄNDER *(GERMANY)* The German name for the Pinot Gris, a white grape variety. Pinot Gris was first grown in 1711 by a merchant named Johann Seger Ruländ from Speyer, in the Pfalz region, who discovered the grapevine in 1689 in the dilapidated garden of an official of the Speyer law courts named Seuffert.

RULLY *(FRANCE)* A commune in the Côte Chalonnaise of Burgundy, noted for its fine white wines made from Chardonnay and Pinot Blanc grapes.

RUM An alcoholic distillate from the fermented juice of sugar cane, sugar cane syrup, sugar cane molasses, or other sugar cane by-products, produced at less than 190 proof in such manner that the distillate possesses the taste, aroma, and characteristics generally attributed to rum, and bottled at not less than 80 proof. It also includes mixtures solely of such distillates. In ancient times, rum was called Barbados brandy, Barbados water, or kill-devil.

There are three main types: 1) light-bodied, dry rums, characterized by those of Puerto Rico; 2) full-bodied, rich rums, exemplified by the rums of Jamaica, Barbados, Martinique, Trinidad, and Guyana's Demerara; and 3) the pungently aromatic Batavia Arak from Java. Also known as *rhum* and *ron*. *See* Rumbullion.

RUMBULLION   A popular seventeenth century-term for rum that originated either from the English or in the West Indies. *See* Rum.

RUMBUSTION   *See* Rumfustian.

RUMFUSTIAN   A popular Colonial drink made from strong beer (or rum), wine, gin, egg yolks, sugar, and spices; it was then heated. Also known as *rumbustion*. *See* Flip, Hot Caudle, and Sling.

RUM LIQUEUR   A liqueur bottled at not less than 60 proof, in which the distilled spirit used is entirely rum, and that possesses a predominant characteristic rum flavor derived from the distilled spirit used.

RUMMER   A glass or other vessel used for drinking toasts in praise of someone or something.

RUMMY   An old slang term for a person who drinks too much alcohol.

RUN   The completed distillation of one batch of low wine.

RUND (GERMANY)   *See* Round.

RUNDLET   *See* Barrel.

RUNNING TAB   A guest check system of dispensing and serving drinks, but not collecting any money until the guest is ready to leave the premises.

RUPESTRIS   *See Vitis Rupestris.*

RUSSIAN ISINGLASS   *See* Isinglass.

RUSSIAN TEA   Tea traditionally served with lemon juice or slices rather than with cream or milk.

RUVIDO (ITALY)   *See* Rough.

RUWER (GERMANY)   *See* Mosel-Saar-Ruwer.

RUZICA (YUGOSLAVIA)   *See* Rosé Wine.

RYE   A small, dark cereal grain often utilized in making certain distilled spirits, especially *rye whiskey.*

RYE LIQUEUR   A liqueur bottled at not less than 60 proof, in which not less than 51 percent, on a proof gallon basis, of the distilled spirits used is rye whiskey, that possesses a predominant characteristic rye flavor derived from such whiskey.

RYE MALT WHISKEY   *See* Rye Whiskey.

RYE WHISKEY   A distilled spirit distilled at not more than 160 proof from a fermented mash of grain containing at least 51 percent rye grain. It is stored at not more than 125 proof in charred new oak barrels for a minimum of two years, although four years is the standard. Straight rye whiskey is seldom sold today, although very often American blended whiskey or Canadian whisky is incorrectly referred to as "rye." Rye whiskey—real rye—is not to everyone's taste, for it has a strong and distinctive flavor of caraway seeds. Also known as *rye malt whiskey.*

RYUMOCHKI (RUSSIA)   Small shot glasses used for drinking vodka straight.

S \'es\ n, *often cap, often attrib*

SAALE-UNSTRUT (GERMANY) One of thirteen Qualitätswein (quality) grape-growing regions located in the north. Müller-Thurgau, Sylvaner, and Weissburgunder grape varieties are widely planted here.

SAAR (GERMANY) *See* Mosel-Saar-Ruwer.

SABOR (PORTUGAL AND SPAIN) *See* Flavor.

SABOROSO (PORTUGAL) *See* Sapid.

SABROSO (SPAIN) *See* Sapid.

SACA (SPAIN) The action of drawing out a specific quantity of wine from the *solera* for consumption.

SACACORCHO (SPAIN) *See* Corkscrew.

SACAR (SPAIN) *See* Sack.

SACCHARIFY To convert starch or dextrin into sugar by chemical means. In whiskey distilling it refers to the process that takes place during the malting and mash-tun stages by which the enzyme diastase turns the starch in cereals into sugar; it is then ready for the fermenting action of the yeast.

SACCHARIN A sweet, white, powdery, synthetic product derived from crystalline coal tar, three to five hundred times as sweet as sugar. It was discovered accidentally by Ira Remsen and C. Fahlberg in 1879 and introduced as a substitute for sugar. It has been primarily utilized since as an artificial sweetener in some nonalcoholic carbonated beverages.

SACCHAROMETER An instrument used to quantifiably measure the amount of sugar in a solution. *See* Hydrometer.

SACCHAROMYCES A genus of fungi, reproducing by budding, necessary for the production of certain types of alcoholic beverages.

SACCHAROMYCES CARLSBERGENSIS   The name of the first pure beer yeast culture; it was isolated in 1883 by Professor Emil Hansen of the Carlsberg Brewery in Denmark.

SACCHAROMYCES CEREVISIAE   The name of the principal yeast strain used in the fermentation of grapes into wine.

SACCHARUM OFFICINARUM (SPAIN)   The type of cane sugar from which rum is derived.

SACHSEN (GERMANY)   One of thirteen Qualitätswein (quality) grape-growing regions located in the east. Müller-Thurgau, Weissburgunder, and Gewürztraminer grape varieties are widely planted here.

SACK   An obsolete English term originating in Elizabethan England (1558–1603); it means a sweet fortified wine, mostly sherry, from Spain. It is believed that *sack* is derived from the Spanish *sacar*, to "withdraw" or "export." It is also reported that sack was the favorite drink of the English dramatist William Shakespeare (1564–1616). Also known as *canary sack*.

SACK MEAD   *See* Mead.

SACRAMENTAL WINES   Wines used during religious ceremonies and produced under the strictest regulations and requirements of a particular faith. Making these was permitted during Prohibition. Also known as *altar wine, messwein, vin de messe,* and *vinos de misa.*

SACRAMENTO   A wine-producing district in California, north of San Francisco.

SACY (FRANCE)   A white grape variety grown primarily in the Yonne district of Chablis. Also known as *Tresallier.*

SADD   Students Against Drunk Driving.

SADON (FRANCE)   A measurement unit typical of the Saint-Estèphe commune in Bordeaux; it corresponds to ten rows of one hundred grapevines.

SAFETY STOCK   The minimum stock needed to function for a shift or day. *See* Par Stock.

SAFTIG (GERMANY)   *See* Rich.

SAGGIAVINO (ITALY)   *See* Wine Thief.

SAGRANTINO (ITALY)   A red grape variety grown in Umbria, where it produces Sagrantino di Montefalco, a DOCG wine.

SAIGNÉE (FRANCE)   *See* Bleeding.

SAINT-AMOUR (FRANCE)   A *cru* commune in Beaujolais whose grapes are made into a rich red wine that is tinged with violet and has a spicy aroma, with hints of kirsch. In parts of Saint-Amour, the soil contains some limestone, which produces Beaujolais Blanc—a drier and more delicate wine than Mâcon Blanc, and with slightly less body.

SAINT-AUBIN (FRANCE)   One of the less known red- and white-wine-producing villages, situated behind Chassagne-Montrachet in the Côte de Beaune district of Burgundy.

SAINT BERNARD Those dogs that are usually identified with the carrying of a small keg of brandy or other distilled spirits around their necks to give relief and warmth to stranded skiers in Scandinavian countries.

SAINT CROIX A red grape variety developed by Elmer Swenson of the University of Minnesota.

SAINT-EMILION *(FRANCE)* The local name for the Trebbiano grape variety in the Cognac region. *See* Trebbiano.

SAINT-ÉMILION *(FRANCE)* A major red-wine-producing district located on the right bank of the Dordogne River in Bordeaux. The wines produced are primarily from the Merlot grape, with some Cabernet Sauvignon in the blend.

On November 14, 1936, the wines of Saint-Émilion were officially given their *appellation contrôlée* designation. On October 7, 1954, the INAO laid down a classification for Saint-Émilion that divided the seventy-six great vineyards into two classes: *premier grand cru* and *grand cru*. To help promote the wines of Saint-Émilion, John Lackland, on July 8, 1199, established the Jurade de Saint-Émilion, a wine brotherhood still in existence today.

SAINT-ESTÈPHE *(FRANCE)* A notable red wine commune located in the northern part of the Médoc in the Bordeaux region, noted for its robust, full-bodied red wines made primarily from the Cabernet Sauvignon grape, with some Merlot, Malbec, Cabernet Franc, and Petit Verdot in the blend. On November 14, 1936, the wines of Saint-Estèphe were officially given their *appellation contrôlée* designation.

SAINT-JOSEPH *(FRANCE)* A wine-producing district located in the northern part of the Rhône Valley, noted for its production of red, white, and rosé wines. The red wine is made solely from the Syrah grape, which yields a somewhat full-bodied wine. The white wines, also full-bodied, are produced from the Roussanne and Marsanne grapes.

SAINT-JULIEN *(FRANCE)* A famous red wine commune located between Pauillac and Margaux in the Médoc district of Bordeaux, noted for its refined, high-quality red wines made primarily from the Cabernet Sauvignon grape, with some Merlot, Malbec, Cabernet Franc, and Petit Verdot in the blend. On November 14, 1936, the wines of Saint-Julien were officially given their *appellation contrôlée* designation.

SAINT MARTIN The patron saint of the wines of Portugal, whose birthday is celebrated around the middle of November each year.

SAINT-PÉRAY *(FRANCE)* A wine-producing village in the northern Rhône Valley, known mostly for its white wine made primarily from the Marsanne grape. Since 1929, some of its production also goes into the making of *brut* and *demisec méthode champenoise* sparkling wines.

SAINT-VÉRAN *(FRANCE)* A white-wine-producing village located in southern Mâcon in the Burgundy region, producing wines similar to those of Pouilly-Fuissé.

SAINT VINCENT The patron saint of Champagne, whose birthday is celebrated on January 22 of each year; used to be the patron saint of Burgundy, France.

SAISON *(BELGIUM)* A sharply refreshing, amber-colored ale that displays a faintly sour taste.

SAKAZUKI *(JAPAN)* *See* Ochoko.

SAKÉ　A colorless brewed alcoholic beverage made from rice that is legally defined as a rice beer. Saké is an ancient fermented beverage known to have been made since about the third century A.D. in China, but it was not until about six hundred years ago that saké as we know it today was produced. *Saké* means "the essence of the spirit of rice" and, although it is native to China and Japan, it is produced in other parts of the world, including California.

In China there is a similar rice beer called *samshu* and in Korea, *suk*.

SALADO (SPAIN)　*See* Salty.

SALATO (ITALY)　*See* Salty.

SALÉ (FRANCE)　*See* Salty.

SALE　A transaction involving the delivery of goods or services for an agreed sum of money or other valuable consideration.

SALEM　A red grape variety.

SALES BROCHURE　A brochure featuring current or upcoming promotions for specific brands of alcoholic beverages.

SALES INCOME　The amount of money received from customers for goods and services rendered.

SALES JOURNAL　A business record used for posting all sales transactions by type.

SALES MIX　The total number of drink items on the menu, considered in relation to one another, that is sold during a specified period of time.

SALES VALUE　The value of the item at a certain selling price.

SALGADO (PORTUGAL)　*See* Salty.

SALINITY　The amount of soluble salts in a soil, generally expressed in a percentage.

SALMANAZAR　An oversized bottle equal in capacity to twelve 750-milliliter bottles or nine liters (304.2 ounces).

Salmanazar was a king of Assyria who ruled over the Judean kingdom from 732 to 734 B.C.

SALOON　An old western term for a bar. *See* Bar, Cocktail Lounge, Inn, Pub, and Tavern.

SALT　Used for rimming glasses as necessary for certain cocktails. *See* Coarse Salt and Rimming.

SALTED WINE　A wine or wine product, not for beverage use, that contains not less than 1.5 grams of salt per one hundred milliliters of wine. *See* Cooking Wines.

SALTY　Describes a taste that comes from the salts of certain acids found in wine. It can be detected on the middle front sides of the tongue. Also known as *salado, salato, salé, salgado*, and *salzig*.

SALVADOR　A red grape variety (*teinturier*) grown in California. Formerly known as *Seibel 128*. *See Teinturier*.

SALZIG (GERMANY)　*See* Salty.

SAMARINHO (PORTUGAL)   A white grape variety grown in the Douro region.

SAMBUCA   A generic anise- or licorice-flavored liqueur that is obtained from the white flowers of the *Sambucus nigra*, a kind of elderberry bush of the honeysuckle family. Sambuca is clear in color and similar to anisette, with more flavor and a higher alcoholic content; it is also much drier. Sambuca is primarily produced in Italy.

SAMOGON (RUSSIA)   Bootlegged vodka.

SAMPANJAC (YUGOSLAVIA)   *See* Sparkling Wine.

SAMSHU (CHINA)   *See* Saké.

SAMTIG (GERMANY)   *See* Velvety.

SANCERRE (FRANCE)   A small village located in the Loire Valley that produces a dry white wine made from the Sauvignon Blanc grape; bone dry, with striking acidity, but lacking the richness and full-bodied quality of Pouilly Fumé.

SANCOCHO (SPAIN)   *See* Arrope and Cooked Wine.

SANDARAC   *See* Retsina.

SANDY LOAM   A type of soil that is a mixture predominantly of sand, with the remainder silt and clay particles. *See* Loam.

SANGAREE   A tall drink served in the southwestern United States. The name is a corruption of the Spanish word *Sangría*, a similar drink of Spain and Spanish America.

SANGIOVESE DI ROMAGNA (ITALY)   A medium-bodied, dry red wine made from 100 percent Sangiovese grapes in the Emilia-Romagna region. *See* Sangiovese Piccolo.

SANGIOVESE GROSSO (ITALY)   A red grape variety grown primarily in the region of Tuscany, where it is used to produce Chianti, Brunello di Montalcino, and Vino Nobile di Montepulciano wines. The grape is also grown in many other regions including Abruzzo, Campania, Emilia-Romagna, Lombardy, Marches, Sicily, Veneto, and Umbria.

The Sangiovese grape is one of Italy's most noble varieties, believed to have originated from Tuscany where it is widely grown. Its name is believed to come from "Sanguis Jovis," Latin for "Jupiter's Blood." Also known as *Sangiovese Grosso (Brunello), Prugnolo*, and *Prugnolo Gentile*. *See* Brunello di Montalcino, Montalcino, Rosso di Montalcino, and Sangiovese Piccolo.

SANGIOVESE PICCOLO (ITALY)   The lesser clonal selection of the famous *Sangiovese Grosso*, a red grape variety noted for its production of extremely full-bodied, dry red wines. Also known as *Sangiavettoe, Sangioveto, San Gioveto*, and *Sangiovese di Romagna*. *See* Sangiovese Grosso.

SANGIAVETTOE (SPAIN)   The local name in Argentina for the Sangiovese Piccolo grape variety. *See* Sangiovese Piccolo.

SANGINELLA (ITALY)   A white grape variety.

SAN GIOVETO (ITALY)   *See* Sangiovese Piccolo.

SANGIOVETO (ITALY)   *See* Sangiovese Piccolo.

SANGRÍA (SPAIN)   A refreshing sort of wine punch made from a mixture of wine (red or white), slices of citrus fruits (lemon and orange), sugar, and sometimes soda water.

SAN JOAQUIN   A grape-growing district located in the Central Valley of California.

SANS ANNÉE (FRANCE)   *See* Nonvintage.

SANS SUCRE (FRANCE)   *See* Extra Brut.

SANTA CLARA   A grape-growing district in California, south of San Francisco.

SANTA MARIA (ITALY)   A grape variety from Piacenza.

SANTCHOO   *See* Alaai.

SANTÉ (FRANCE)   Health.

SANTENAY (FRANCE)   The southernmost village of the Côte de Beaune, located below Chassagne-Montrachet in Burgundy, producing good quality red and white wines. Santenay was known as *Sentennacum* during the Gallo-Roman occupation.

SAÔNE (FRANCE)   A river located in the southeast, flowing south into the Rhône River at Lyon.

SAPA   An ancient Roman wine made with concentrated *must*. *See* Cooked Wine.

SAPERAVI   A red grape variety from Russia grown in New York State.

SAPID   A term used to describe wines that are savory and luscious-tasting, as opposed to insipid. Also known as *lieblich, sapido, saboroso, sabroso,* and *savoureux.*

SAP IS DOWN   The dormant period when the sap is not running and trees can be cut for use as wine or whiskey barrels.

SAPIDO (ITALY)   *See* Sapid.

SAPORE (ITALY)   *See* Flavor.

SAPPY   *See* Grapy.

SARAP (TURKEY)   *See* Wine.

SARDEGNA (ITALY)   *See* Sardinia.

SARDINIA (ITALY)   The second-largest island in the Mediterranean; it has for centuries been a little-known wine-producing region, unknown even to most Italians from the mainland and Sicily. It is located across the Tyrrhenian Sea, south of Corsica, about 125 miles west of Rome.

Sardinia produces dry white, dry red, and sweet dessert wines, although very little reaches the United States. In ancient times, Sardinia was referred to as "Ichnusa," from the Greek word "ichnos," which meant "footprint." Known as *Sardegna* in Italy.

SARGADOZ (SPAIN)   *See* Calvados.

SARGAMUSKOTALY (HUNGARY)   *See* Muscat.

SARI-KABAK (RUSSIA)   A white grape variety.

SARI-PANDAS (RUSSIA)   A white grape variety.

SARMENTER (FRANCE)   To rake and burn the grapevine shoots cut during pruning.

SARSAPARILLA   Any of a number of tropical American, spiny, woody vines (genus *Smilax aristolochiaefolia*) of the lily family with large, fragrant roots and toothed, heart-shaped leaves. The name comes from the Spanish word for a bramble (*zarza*) and a small vine (*parrilla*). The dried roots of any of these plants and birch oil or sassafras is used to make a carbonated, flavored drink. Sarsaparilla first appeared in the United States in the 1840s and, although it is still found today, it is not as popular as it was years ago. Incorrectly spelled *sasparilla* or *sarsaprilla*.

SASSELLA (*ITALY*)   A full-bodied red wine produced primarily from the Nebbiolo grape variety in the Valtellina district of Lombardy, located in the north.

SATURATION   The degree of intensity of a color detected in wine or beer.

SATURN   A red grape variety developed from a cross of Dunstan 210 and NY 445791, by the Arkansas Agricultural Experimental Station.

SAUBER (*GERMANY*)   *See* Clean.

SAUCER-SHAPED GLASS   A flat, saucer-shaped stemmed glass with a large surface area, often used for the service of sparkling wines and champagne. Due to this glass's large surface area, sparkling wines served in it lose their aroma, send a shower of foam into the mouth, and prematurely go flat. The proper glassware to use is either a *flute-shaped* or *tulip-shaped* glass. Also known as *bird-bath glass*.

During the time of Helen of Troy, milk was served from glasses in the shape of a woman's breast. Today's popular flat saucer-shaped or bird-bath champagne glass allegedly derives its shape from a mold of Marie-Antoinette's breasts (1755–1793). However, the saucer-shaped glass or *coupe* was created on June 30, 1663, by Venetian glassmakers at the Duke of Buckingham's glass factory in Greenwich, England. Marie-Antoinette adored champagne and the glass was viewed as a salute to her good taste. Also known as *Coupe*.

SAUERKRAUT   An undesirable odor of bacterially spoiled wines, due to high levels of lactic acid. The odor may be encountered in wines that have undergone an excessive *malolactic fermentation*.

SÄUERLICH (*GERMANY*)   *See* Acidulous.

SAUMUR (*FRANCE*)   A wine-producing town along the south bank of the Loire Valley in the Anjou province; it makes dry white wines from the Chenin Blanc grape, which is sometimes also made into a sparkling wine via the *méthode champenoise*.

SÄURE (*GERMANY*)   *See* Acidity.

SAUTERNE   A white generic table wine produced in the United States that can range from dry to semisweet. There are no federal regulations that stipulate the grape varieties that American produced sauterne wine may contain.

SAUTERNES (*FRANCE*)   A district in the southern part of Bordeaux noted for its extremely sweet white wines and a few dry white wines as well. Sauternes, along with German *trockenbeerenauslese*, is among the sweetest wines in the world and among the most expensive. It is produced from three white grape varieties: Sauvignon Blanc, Sémillon, and Muscadelle.

Sauternes are made by exploiting a mold called the "noble rot" (technically *Botrytis cinerea*). This mold is present as spores at all times in most vineyards. Depending on the grape variety, the time of year, and climatic conditions, it can greatly enhance or severely damage the grapes in a vineyard.

S

The five communes entitled to be called "Sauternes" are Sauternes, Barsac, Preignac, Fargues, and Bommes. (Only wines from the commune of Barsac are entitled to the Barsac *appellation contrôlée*; however, a decree of 1936 gave this commune the right to the illustrious Sauternes appellation as well.) On September 11, 1936, the wines of Sauternes were officially given their *appellation contrôlée* designation. The Sauternes appellation requires a minimum alcoholic content of 13 percent and *chaptalization* is permitted. The sweet wines of Sauternes and Barsac were among those ranked by the 1855 classification of Bordeaux wines.

To help promote the sweet wines of Sauternes, a wine brotherhood, La Commanderie du Bontemps de Sauternes et Barsac, was established and is active today. *See Botrytis Cinerea*.

SAUVIGNON BLANC   A white grape variety grown in many parts of the world, including France, Italy, Spain, the United States, Austria, Australia, South Africa, Germany, South America, and eastern Europe. It produces mostly dry wines, although semidry and even sweet wines are produced.

Sauvignon Blanc produces dry wines, anywhere from light- to full-bodied, that display a fresh aroma of apricot, bell pepper, citrus, flint, gooseberry, grapefruit, green olive, hay, lemon, melon (cantaloupe), passion fruit, peach, pineapple, smoke, vanilla, and new-mown grass that can sometimes be quite herbaceous.

In Bordeaux, France, Sauvignon Blanc is blended with Sémillon and Muscadelle to produce either the dry white wines of Graves or the luscious sweet dessert wines of Sauternes. In the Loire Valley, Sauvignon Blanc is used in making Pouilly Fumé, Sancerre, and Quincy, which are often described as being "flinty."

In California, it is speculated that Sauvignon Blanc was first grown around the 1850s, although it made its first appearance in 1878 in the Livermore Valley and wasn't bottled as a separate varietal until Wente Brothers' 1935 vintage. The wines produced in California are generally made in the dry or semidry style; they display wondrous varietal fruit and character, with plenty of acidity. In California, Sauvignon Blanc is also known as and can legally be labeled as *Fumé Blanc*. Also known in other parts of the world as *Blanc Fumé, Muskat-Sylvaner, Sauvignon Jaune, Savagnin Musqué,* and *Surin*.

SAUVIGNON JAUNE (*FRANCE*)   *See* Sauvignon Blanc.

SAUVIGNON VERT   *See* Muscadelle and Tocai.

SAVAGNIN MUSQUÉ   A name occasionally used in California to denote the Sauvignon Blanc grape variety. *See* Sauvignon Blanc.

SAVAGNIN (*FRANCE*)   A white grape variety.

SAVAGNIN NOIR (*FRANCE*)   The local name in the Jura region for the Pinot Noir grape variety. *See* Pinot Noir.

SAVAGNIN ROSÉ   *See* Gewürztraminer.

SAVATIANÓ (*GREECE*)   A white grape variety often blended with *Rhoditis* and *Assyrtiko* in making *Retsina*. *See* Retsina.

SAVIGNY-LES-BEAUNE (*FRANCE*)   A red-wine-producing village in the Côte de Beaune producing light-bodied wines with good fruit and flavor.

SAVEUR (*FRANCE*)   *See* Flavor.

SAVOUREUX (*FRANCE*)   *See* Sapid.

SAXON   A type of old English beer named after the section of England where it originated.

SAZERAC   A cocktail created in 1859 at 13 Exchange Alley in a bar owned by John B. Schiller. It consists of Bourbon whiskey, Peychaud's bitters, Pernod, and sugar.

SBOCCATURA (ITALY)   *See* Dégorgement.

SCANT   Just barely (for example, "one scant teaspoon").

SCANTLING   Wooden beams, timber, scaffolds, or metal supports used to hold wooden barrels in a winery or distillery. Also known as *wedges*.

SCANTLING PIPE (PORTUGAL)   A barrel with a capacity of approximately 138 gallons or 627 liters.

SCARNO (ITALY)   *See* Thin.

SCELTO (ITALY)   Choice or specially selected.

SCENT   An agreeable odor or smell of a wine, beer, or even some distilled spirits, evocative of perfume. Also known as *senteur*.

SCHAL (GERMANY)   *See* Stale.

SCHARZHOFBERG (GERMANY)   A white-wine-producing vineyard located on a very steep hillside in Wiltingen on the Saar, famous for its superb wines made from the Johannisberg Riesling grape.

SCHAUMWEIN (GERMANY)   A sparkling wine containing a minimum of 3.5 atmospheres of pressure and 8.5 percent alcohol by volume. This designation is for the lowest quality (usually bulk-produced) sparkling wines. *See* Charmat Method.

SCHEMATIC   A written or pictorial layout indicating precisely where products are to be positioned on the shelf or in the cold box. Schematics are common in chain stores.

SCHEUREBE (GERMANY)   A white grape variety developed in 1916 by George Scheu at the Alzey Research Station in the Rheinhessen. He genetically cross-pollinated Johannisberg Riesling with Sylvaner in an effort to combine the elegance and fine flavor of the former with the early ripening characteristics of the latter. In 1956 the variety was officially named Scheu-Rebe in honor of its breeder; it was released commercially in 1959.

SCHIAVA GENTILE (ITALY)   *See* Schiava Grossa.

SCHIAVA GRIGIA (ITALY)   *See* Schiava Grossa.

SCHIAVA GROSSA (ITALY)   A red grape variety grown primarily in the northern region of Trentino-Alto Adige. Its subvarieties include *Schiava Gentile, Schiava Grigia, Schiava Meranese,* and *Schiavone*. Also known as *Black Hamburg* in England, *Trollinger* in Württemberg, Germany, and *Vernatsch* in the northern Italian region of Trentino-Alto Adige.

SCHIAVA MERANESE (ITALY)   *See* Schiava Grossa.

SCHIAVONE (ITALY)   *See* Schiava Grossa.

SCHIEDAM GIN   A type of gin named after one of the Dutch towns where it is distilled. *See* Holland Gin.

SCHIETTO (ITALY)   *See* Genuine.

SCHIMMELGESCHMACK (GERMANY)   *See* Moldy.

SCHIOPPETTINO (ITALY)   A red grape variety grown at Albana di Prepotto in the heart of the Colli Orientali del Friuli. Also known as *Ribolla Nera*.

SCHIUMA (ITALY)   The froth or smoke that emanates from the neck of a sparkling wine bottle when it is opened and poured. *See* Spuma.

SCHLEGELFLASCHEN (GERMANY)   The slender, swan-necked bottles in which most German wines are bottled.

SCHLOSS (GERMANY)   Castle; equivalent of the French word *château*. Also known as *burg*.

SCHLOSS BÖCKELHEIM (GERMANY)   An important white-wine-producing village located on the Nahe River, mostly planted in Johannisberg Riesling grapes.

SCHNAPPS   A northern European generic term for alcoholic beverages, especially the clear, unaged distilled spirits such as vodka, gin, and akvavit. A clear, white distilled spirit whose distinctive aroma or taste (similar to vodka), made from grain or potatoes, is popular in northern Europe. Usually consumed neat. Often flavored with fruit essences. Also spelled *snaps*.

SCHNAPPS   When used in conjunction with the term "flavored," schnapps indicates a liqueur that contains a minimum of 2.5 percent sugar.

SCHNAPSIG (GERMANY)   *See* Hot.

SCHÖN (GERMANY)   *See* Pleasant.

SCHÖNBURGER (GERMANY)   A white grape variety developed from a cross of Spätburgunder and (Gutedel and Muscat Hamburg) at the Geisenheim Institute in the Rheingau. The name is taken from Schönburg, a ruined castle at Oberwesel, Mittelrhine.

SCHÖNEN (GERMANY)   *See* Fining.

SCHOONER   A tall drinking glass that holds about sixteen ounces of beer.

SCHÖPPCHEN (GERMANY)   A glass of wine.

SCHORLEMORLE (GERMANY)   *See* Spritzer.

SCHUYLER   A red grape variety developed in 1947 from a cross of Zinfandel and Ontario at the State Experimental Station in Geneva, New York.

SCHUYLKILL MUSCADELLE   *See* Alexander.

SCHWANZ (GERMANY)   *See* Aftertaste.

SCHWARZ (GERMANY)   Black.

SCHWARZER (AUSTRIA)   Black coffee.

SCHWARZRIESLING (GERMANY)   *See* Meunier.

SCHWARZWÄLDER (GERMANY)   A fruit brandy made from small plums with a highly aromatic perfume; it is generally produced in Germany as well as in some central European countries.

SCHWEFEL (*GERMANY*) Sulfur smell.

SCHWEIF (*GERMANY*) *See* Aftertaste.

SCHWER (*GERMANY*) *See* Heavy.

SCIACARELLO (*FRANCE*) A red grape variety grown in Corsica.

SCIASCINOSO (*ITALY*) A red grape variety grown in the south.

SCIBELLITA (*ITALY*) *See* Zibibbo.

SCION The shoot or bud that is grafted onto the stock of a grapevine; it contains the leaf and fruit-bearing parts of the variety the grower desires.

SCIOTO A red grape variety grown primarily in Ohio.

SCOBICIA DECLIVIS Commonly known as the "lead cable borer." This tiny beetle tunnels a hole about the size of a pencil lead into wooden barrels.

SCOOPER A tall, long-handled grain shovel often used to turn or flip over barley during the kilning process.

SCOTCH ALE A medium-dark, full-bodied ale with a rich malty taste, generally produced in Scotland.

SCOTCH WHISKY A distinctive product of Scotland, made in compliance with the 1909 laws of Great Britain. Scotch's unique flavor and character come from the water used in its production and the type and amount of malt whisky used. Its distinctive smoky taste comes from the peat fires over which the barley malt is dried. Its primary base grain is barley (distilled by pot stills for heavy-bodied whisky) or corn (distilled by continuous or Coffey stills for lighter-bodied whisky). Most Scotch whisky is a blend of malt and grain whiskies.

After distillation is completed, Scotch is put into uncharred oak barrels, American oak bourbon whiskey or sherry wine barrels, where it ages for a minimum (by law) of three years. However, in practice most whiskies mature for much longer, often five to ten years or more, depending on the distiller. Scotch sold in the United States is generally aged a minimum of four years; if it is less than four years old, the bottle must carry an age label. In practice, however, Scotch is generally allowed to remain in wood for five years or more before bottling. When there is an age stated on the label of a Scotch whisky, it identifies the youngest whisky in the blend.

Scotch can be distilled in Scotland and bottled in the United States, which saves large sums of money for the importer with little or no sacrifice to the product's quality.

SCREW *See* Worm.

SCREWDRIVER A cocktail consisting of vodka (or gin) and orange juice. This very popular drink was supposedly created by oilmen or oil riggers, who would use their tools to stir it

SCUD A slang term used to describe mold that may develop on wines that are low in alcohol content.

SCUOLA DI OENOLOGIA DI CONEGLIANO (*ITALY*) Italy's premier enological and viticultural school, established in 1876, located in the northeast region of Veneto.

SCUOTIMENTO (*ITALY*) *See* Remuage.

SCUPPERNONG   A grape variety of the *Vitis rotundifolia* (Muscadine) family, native to southeastern United States. Scuppernong was named after a stream of this name in North Carolina where it was first found growing as early as 1524 by Giovanni da Verrazanno, the Florentine explorer.

SEC (FRANCE)   Dry, but when used on champagne or sparkling wine labels, indicates a semidry sparkling wine.

SECAILLER (FRANCE)   To replace the acacia stakes in a vineyard when they are in poor condition.

SECATEUR (FRANCE)   Shears or snippers used for pruning and for cutting grapes from grapevines.

SÉCHÉ (FRANCE)   *See* Dried Out.

SECCO (ITALY)   *See* Dry.

SECO (PORTUGAL AND SPAIN)   *See* Dry.

SECONDARY   The basal and the second largest bud or shoot at each node of the cane or spur on a grapevine.

SECONDARY FERMENTATION   An induced fermentation in a stoppered bottle, utilized in making sparkling wines. It is accomplished by adding sugar and yeast to a base wine already present in champagne bottles. The secondary fermentation generally lasts about six weeks, but the wines are usually aged a minimum of one year. Also known as *presa di spumante*.

SECOND WINE   *See* False Wine.

SEDIMENT   The slow reaction and eventual precipitation of fruit, tannin, tartrates, pigment, mineral salts, and other compounds, as the wine matures in a bottle. A brown deposit known as sediment settles on the side or bottom of the bottle. Sediment is quite harmless, although aesthetically unpleasant; it tastes like sand. Generally found in red wines. Also known as *beeswing, chemise, crust, culattone, deposit, deposito, depòsito, déposito, dépôt, dregs,* and *fondo*.

SEEDLING   A grapevine grown from a seed rather than a cutting. Also known as *semis*.

SEEDS   The pits contained in a grape berry. They comprise about 5 percent of the grape; there are usually two to four seeds per berry depending upon the variety of grape. The seeds are very high in tannin and astringent oils, containing roughly 65 percent of all phenols found in wine. Also known as *grano, pips,* and *pits*. *See* Phenol.

SEED YEAST   *See* Nutrients.

SEHR FEIN (GERMANY)   Very fine.

SEIBEL 128   *See* Salvador.

SEIBEL 1000   *See* Rosette.

SEIBEL 4986   *See* Rayon d'Or.

SEIBEL 5279   *See* Aurore.

SEIBEL 5455   *See* Plantet.

SEIBEL 5898   *See* Rougeon.

SEIBEL 7053   *See* Chancellor.

SEIBEL 8357   *See* Colobel.

SEIBEL 8745   *See* Seinoir.

SEIBEL 9110   *See* Verdelet.

SEIBEL 9549   *See* DeChaunac.

SEIBEL 10713   *See* Ambros.

SEIBEL 10878   *See* Chelois.

SEIBEL 11803   *See* Rubilande.

SEIBEL 13053   *See* Cascade.

SEIBEL 14596   *See* Bellandais.

SEINOIR   A red grape variety developed from a cross of Seibel 5163 and Seibel 880. Formerly known as *Seibel 8745*.

SEIT (GERMANY)   Since, when referring to the year a brewery was founded.

SEKT (AUSTRIA AND GERMANY)   From the Latin word *siccus*, meaning dry. It has been used officially in German wine law since 1925. *See* Sparkling Wine.

SELECT   A term that implies the alcoholic beverage contains certain qualities or attributes that set it apart from the rest. The term, however, carries no legal definition or application.

SELECTED LATE HARVEST   A term generally used in the United States to imply that the individual cluster or berries within a cluster were hand selected because of certain attributes. The term, however, carries no legal definition or application. *See* Select Harvest.

SELECT HARVEST   A term that implies that the harvest was picked out from the rest or other such connotation. It has no legal definition or application. *See* Selected Late Harvest.

SÉLECTION DE GRAINS NOBLES (FRANCE)   A designation of wines from Alsace, recognized as a classification in the wine laws of April 1, 1983; these wines are subject to the same restrictions as the *vendanges tardives*, with even higher minimum levels of natural sugar and alcohol. Only produced in truly great years from individually selected grapes affected by the "noble rot" (*Botrytis cinerea*), *sélection de grains nobles* wines are pure nectar, highly concentrated, with a lingering flavor. Produced in very small quantities, these wines are very difficult to obtain in the United States.

SELF WHISKIES   A term used in Scotland to denote a straight or unblended Scotch malt whisky.

SELO DE GARANTIA (PORTUGAL)   The official seal of guaranteed origin and authenticity for wines, used on bottles from demarcated regions such as Bairrada, the Dão, the Douro, or Vinho Verde.

SELTZER   Ordinary water that has been filtered and artificially carbonated. It contains no added minerals or salts. In most cases, it is salt free. Seltzer is named after *Niederselters*, a village near Wiesbaden, Germany. *See* Club Soda.

SELVATICO *(ITALY)* *See* Rough.

SEMIDRY WINE A wine that contains between 0.6 and 2.2 percent sugar. Also known as *abocado, abboccato, amabile, demisec, medio seco, medium-dry, meioseco, mezzo secco, off-dry, polsuho, semiseco, semisecco,* and *vino abocado. See* Sugar In Wine.

SEMIDULCE *(SPAIN)* *See* Semisweet.

SEMIFREDDO *(ITALY)* Chilled.

SÉMILLON A white grape variety grown in many parts of the world including France, California, Washington State, Australia, New Zealand, Chile, Argentina, and South Africa. Sémillon produces wines that smell like fresh figs or of freshly laundered bed sheets drying in the sun; they have a steely, spicy aroma and crisp herbaceous flavor, with underlying hints of citrus.

In the Sauternes district of France, it is blended with Sauvignon Blanc and Muscadelle to produce luscious, sweet dessert wines, while in the Graves district it produces dry, crisp wines. In California, it occasionally stands as a single varietal, but more often is blended with Sauvignon Blanc or even used in jug wine blends. Also known as *Blanc Doux, Chevrier, Colombier,* and *Hunter River Riesling.*

SEMIPERISHABLE Substance that is canned, dried, dehydrated, or otherwise processed to the extent that it may, under normal conditions, be stored in nonrefrigerated spaces. Semiperishable substances are not to be confused with nonperishable substances, which do not require care or protection in storage.

SEMIS *(FRANCE)* *See* Seedling.

SEMISECO *(SPAIN)* *See* Semidry Wine.

SEMISECCO *(ITALY)* *See* Semidry Wine.

SEMISWEET An often-used term that translates as half dry or half sweet. Also known as *medium-sweet, meiodoce,* and *semidulce.*

SEMPLICE *(ITALY)* *See* Ordinary.

SENECA A white grape variety developed in 1930 from a cross of Lignan Blanc and Ontario at the State Experimental Station in Geneva, New York.

SENOIA A red grape variety developed from a cross of Higgins and Carlos by B.O. Fry, a Georgia grape breeder.

SENSORIEL *(FRANCE)* *See* Organoleptic.

SENSORY EVALUATION Also known as *sensoriel. See* Organoleptic.

SENSUOUS The rich, alluring odor and/or taste of a silky, soft, and elegant wine; the term is generally reserved for full-bodied red wines.

SENTEUR *(FRANCE)* *See* Scent.

SEPARATOR A machine used in dairies for the separation of cream from milk.

SEPTIMER *(GERMANY)* A white grape variety developed in 1927 from a cross of Müller-Thurgau and Gewürztraminer by George Scheu at the Alzey Research Station in the Rheinhessen.

SEQUOIA SEMPERVIRENS   California redwood, utilized in the making of wooden barrels for the aging and/or storage of alcoholic beverages.

SERBESA *(PHILIPPINES)*   *See* Beer.

SERCIAL *(PORTUGAL)*   A fortified wine and also a white grape variety from the island of Madeira. The Sercial grape variety is viticulturally similar to the German Johannisberg Riesling and was in fact brought to Madeira from Germany. In reality, it bears absolutely no resemblance to the Johannisberg Riesling in taste. Sercial is the driest madeira; it is similar to a *fino* sherry, although slightly sweeter.

SERGIKARASI *(TURKEY)*   A red grape variety.

SERINE *(FRANCE)*   *See* Durif and Syrah.

SERIOUSNESS OF COLD INJURY   The amount of a grapevine's decrease in fruit production and/or quality resulting from cold injury.

SERPENTIN   The serpentine condenser coil found on a still.

SERPETTE *(FRANCE)*   *See* Grape Knife.

SERRATE   A grape leaf that has numerous distinct notches or teeth.

SERVER   A waiter or waitress in a beverage facility who takes orders and serves drinks to customers.

SERVICE   The act or manner of serving beverages to customers.

SERVICE BAR   A bar that provides alcoholic beverages exclusively to service personnel for the benefit of patrons seated elsewhere.

SERVICE CONTRACT   A contract between a shipper and an ocean carrier or conference. The shipper commits to a minimum quantity of cargo over a fixed time period. The carrier commits to a certain rate as well as a defined service level such as assured space, transit time, port rotation, etc. The contract must specify penalty provisions in the event of non-performance.

SERVIN BLANC *(SOUTH AFRICA)*   A white grape variety. Also known as *Raisin Blanc*.

SERVING TEMPERATURE   The optimum temperature for the service of wines and beers are as follows:

SERVING TEMPERATURES (FAHRENHEIT) FOR WINES AND BEERS

Dry, full-bodied red wines	65–68 degrees
Dry, light-bodied red wines	60–65 degrees
Dry white wines	50–55 degrees
Sparkling wines and champagne	42–46 degrees
Sweet red and sweet white wines	42–46 degrees
Dry, light-bodied beers	38–45 degrees
Dry, full-bodied beers	55–60 degrees

SERVIR *(FRANCE)*   To serve.

SET   *See* Berry Set.

SETINE   An ancient Roman wine.

SETÚBAL *(PORTUGAL)*   *See* Moscatel de Setúbal.

SETUP   Bottles of nonalcoholic mixes, ice, and glasses, usually provided free to customers who either bring in or separately purchase bottles of distilled spirits.

SÈVE *(FRANCE)*   Sap.

SEVERE   *See* Austere.

SEYVAL   A white grape variety introduced into the United States Finger Lakes district in 1949. In 1921, at Bouge-Chambalud in the Midi region of France, Bertille Seyve and Victor Villard developed this grape variety by crossing Seibel 5656 and Rayon d'Or. The grape is grown primarily in the eastern part of the United States. Formerly known as *Seyve-Villard 5276* and called *Seyval Blanc*.

SEYVAL BLANC   *See* Seyval.

SEYVE-VILLARD 5276   *See* Seyval.

SEYVE-VILLARD 12309   *See* Roucaneuf.

SEYVE-VILLARD 12375   *See* Villard Blanc.

SEYVE-VILLARD 18283   *See* Garronet.

SEYVE-VILLARD 18315   *See* Villard Noir.

SEYVE-VILLARD 20365   *See* Dattier de Saint-Vallier.

SEYVE-VILLARD 23410   *See* Valérien.

SEYVE-VILLARD 23657   *See* Varousset.

SFORZATO *(ITALY)*   *See* Sfurzat.

SFUGGENTE *(ITALY)*   Fleeting; describes a wine whose bouquet and taste are receding, elusive, and quite short. *See* Short.

SFURZAT *(ITALY)*   A full-bodied red wine produced in the northern region of Lombardy from a blend of predominantly Nebbiolo grapes. The wine, which is made from partly dried grapes that have been allowed to dry on racks from the harvest until December, is reminiscent of Amarone della Valpolicella. Also spelled *Sfurzato*.

SG   *See* Specific Gravity.

SGRADEVOLE *(ITALY)*   Describes a wine or beer that is unpleasant or disagreeable to drink.

SHAFT AND GLOBE   The name used by bottle collectors for long-necked wine bottles that were in use in the early seventeenth century.

SHAKER   The combination of a twelve-to fourteen-ounce mixing glass and a stainless steel container that fits over the glass.

SHAKING   One of the three methods utilized for making cocktails, the other two being stirring and blending.

SHALLOW Describes wines that are empty, lacking depth or character. Also known as *superficial* and *vuoto*.

SHAM PILSNER GLASS A tall, conical beer glass with a narrow bottom.

SHANDY A drink in which beer is mixed with either lemonade or ginger beer. It is quite popular in England and Germany, where it is often consumed by cyclists. Also known as *alsterwasser* and *radlmass*.

SHARE OF MARKET The relative percent of one brand's volume (in cases or dollars) compared to the total market movement. Also applies to items within the brand set.

SHARP Describes a wine that displays an unpleasant, excessive amount of acidity (or acetic acid) that becomes almost piercing and biting to the taste. Also known as *punzante*.

SHATTER The drying up and falling off of many of the grapevine's flowers, or the falling off of the tiny berries, depending of course, on the stage of development. Shatter is caused by extreme heat early in the growing season when the grape berries are quite small or, worse yet, still in the period of bloom, when the grapevine's flowers are in the process of transforming themselves into grape berries. If temperature extremes are experienced during this critical time, shatter occurs. *See* Berry Set and Shot Berries.

SHEETS *See* Legs.

SHEKAR A Hebrew word meaning strong drink from which our word *cider* is derived. *See* Cider.

SHELF IMAGE The relative impact of displayed bottles on a retail shelf as they appear to the consumer.

SHELF LIFE The length of time a beverage can be stored, maintaining optimum flavor and drinkability, before losing quality. *See* Peak.

SHELF LOCATION The actual site (on the shelf or floor) within a retail store where an item appears.

SHELF MARKERS *See* Shelf Talker.

SHELF POSITION The physical location on a shelf where a product is located, e.g., within eye scan, on the top shelf, on the bottom shelf, and so on.

SHELF SPACE The area currently occupied by an item or category on a retail store shelf.

SHELF TALKER A small display that attaches to a shelf and promotes the product and/or price. It can also include a refund or product information pad. Also known as *shelf markers*.

SHELL A type of drinking glass, generally for the service of beer or cocktails, that is shaped like a tall, tapered plain cylinder.

SHERIDAN A red grape variety developed in 1921 from a cross of Herbert and Worden at the State Experimental Station in Geneva, New York.

SHERMAT A winemaker's name for "sherry material"—the base wine or *cuvée* prior to being fortified, as in the making of sherry wine.

SHERRY (SPAIN)   A fortified and blended nonvintage wine (although some vintage-dated sherry is produced) made via the *solera system* and containing 17 to 22 percent alcohol. It is traditionally produced in Spain, although certain other countries produce a similar product they call sherry.

Sherry originated in southwest Andalusía in the region of Jerez. The town of Jerez was founded by the Phoenicians in 1100 B.C.; they brought their sailing ships to an inland city near the Bay of Cádiz on the Atlantic coast and named it *Xera*. After the Roman conquest, Xera was Latinized to *Ceret*, which the Moors pronounced as *Scherris*. This was subsequently Hispanicized to *Jerez* and anglicized, in reference to the beverage, into *sherry*.

SHERRY GLASS   *See* Copa and Copita.

SHINE   *See* Moonshine.

SHIPMENT   A case of product shipped from the producer or importer to the distributor.

SHIPPER'S ASSOCIATION   A group of shippers that consolidates or distributes freight on a nonprofit basis for members of the group in order to secure volume discount rates or service contracts from common carriers or conferences.

SHIRAZ (AUSTRALIA AND SOUTH AFRICA)   *See* Syrah.

SHIRLEY TEMPLE   A nonalcoholic cocktail consisting of ginger ale and grenadine syrup, named after the child actress Shirley Temple.

SHIROKA MELNISHKA LOSA (BULGARIA)   A red grape variety. Also known as *Melnik*.

SHŌCHŪ (JAPAN)   *See* Sochu.

SHOE PEGS   *See* Paraffin.

SHOOT   A green growth from a bud of a spur, arm, or trunk on a grapevine. A shoot always bears leaves and tendrils, and it may have fruit clusters. Its name is changed to "cane" in the fall when the leaves drop and the wood hardens. *See* Canes.

SHOOTER   A slang term for a shot of liquor.

SHOOT POSITIONING   A viticultural term for the positioning of shoots on grapevines to ensure they grow vertically between two narrowly spaced wires that hold the shoots upright. This vertical training guarantees adequate sun exposure for the grapes, which is essential for achieving full color and flavor development. *See* Cordon Training, Head Training, and Training.

SHORT   Describes a wine or beer that lacks a good finish and a long, lingering aftertaste. Opposite of *long*. Also known as *bref, corto, court, fugace,* and *kurz. See* Sfuggente.

SHORTAGE   The amount by which quantity supplied is less than quantity demanded at the existing price; the opposite of a surplus.

SHORT DRINK   A cocktail served in a smaller than normal glass. *See* Burned Drinks.

SHOT   *See* Old.

SHOT   *See* Straight.

SHOT BERRIES   If a temperature extreme is encountered midway in the flower-to-berry transformation, successful pollination called "berry set" usually does not take place, which prevents the berry from maturing and developing. Instead, small grapes of good quality, which unfortunately contain very little juice, are formed. These are called shot berries due to their size relationship to BBs or buckshot. Also known as *millérandage*. *See* Berry Set and Shatter.

SHOT GLASS   A small glass used for pouring a specific amount of a distilled spirit. Shot glasses come in varying capacities; they are incorrectly believed to contain 1.5 ounces. *See* Jigger.

SHOULDERED   Describes a grape cluster with one or more distinct branches closely attached to the main stem.

SHOUT (AUSTRALIA)   To buy a round of drinks.

SHRINKAGE   *See* Evaporation.

SHRUB   A fruit drink made from citrus juice, rum, and sugar; it was quite popular in eighteenth-century England.

SICERA   *See* Cider.

SICILIA (ITALY)   *See* Sicily.

SICILY (ITALY)   The largest island in the Mediterranean, off Italy's southern coast; it is also one of twenty wine-producing regions.

Sicily produces not only marsala, a fortified wine from its southern shores, but also a host of red, white, and rosé wines. Some Sicilian wines tend to be of a higher alcoholic nature due to the fact that they receive a great deal of sunshine throughout the year. This heat, which oftentimes actually bakes the grapes or causes them to become "sunburnt," is noticeable in white wines. Because of the higher concentration of coloring matter in the skins, a slightly deeper color is attained. Wines produced from grapes with very high sugar levels also tend to be flat, lacking a sufficient acid backbone to support the high sugar and alcohol levels. Credit must be given to the skills of the modern Sicilian winemakers, who in spite of difficult working conditions have produced wines that display lightness of body, freshness of taste, and a good balance between fruit and acidity. Known as *Sicilia* in Italy.

SICK   Also known as *malato*. *See* Spoiled.

SIDECAR   A cocktail consisting of brandy, triple sec, and lemon juice. The recipe was first created in 1935 at Harry's Bar in Paris from a combination of Cointreau and cognac.

SIDRA (SPAIN)   *See* Cider.

SIDRE (FRANCE)   *See* Cider.

SIEGER (GERMANY)   A white grape variety developed in the Rheinhessen from a cross of Madeleine Angevine and Gewürztraminer.

SIEGERREBE (GERMANY)   A white grape variety developed in 1929 from a cross of Madeleine Angevine and Gewürztraminer by George Scheu at the Alzey Research Station in the Rheinhessen.

SIEGERREBE (GERMANY)

S

SIEGFRIED *(GERMANY)* A white grape variety developed in the 1960s from a cross of Johannisberg Riesling and a seedling of Oberlin Noir at the Geilweilerhof Research Station in the Pfalz. Also known as *Siegfriedrebe*.

SIEGFRIEDREBE *(GERMANY)* *See* Siegfried.

SIFON *(SPAIN)* *See* Siphon.

SIFONE *(ITALY)* *See* Mistelle.

SIGNATURE DRINK A drink specialty of the house; it is designed and/or prepared in some novel manner so as to make it almost a "designer drink." Signature drinks are unique to the establishment and is what they are often known for.

SIKES SCALE The former English method of measuring the alcoholic strength of beverages by use of a hydrometer. Bartholomew Sikes was a British excise officer whose method of measurement was the one adopted by the government in the Hydrometer Act of 1818. On January 1, 1980, Britain adopted the system of measurement recommended by the International Organization of Legal Metrology (OIML). The OIML system measures alcoholic strength as a percentage of alcohol by volume at a temperature of 20 degrees Celsius. Incorrectly spelled *Sykes*.

SIKERA *(GREECE)* *See* Cider.

SILENT SPIRIT *See* Neutral Spirits.

SILICACEOUS EARTH *See* Spanish Earth.

SILKY Describes a wine that is significantly velvety smooth, soft, and finely textured on the palate. Also known as *soyeux*. *See* Velvety.

SILLERY *(FRANCE)* The name given to the region of Champagne during the Middle Ages, many years before a sparkling wine was made.

SILVANER *See* Sylvaner.

SILVER BULLET The name given to an extremely ice-cold, dry vodka martini during the 1950s and 1960s.

SILVER RUM *See* Light Rum.

SIMPLE Also known as *semplice*. *See* Ordinary.

SIMPLE SUGAR OR SYRUP A syrup made by mixing equal parts of sugar and water, then boiling the mixture until all the sugar dissolves.

SIN CRIANZA *(SPAIN)* A regional wine that is not aged in wood.

SINEWY *See* Muscular.

SINGAPORE GIN SLING A cocktail consisting of gin, cherry-flavored brandy, lemon and orange juice, and seltzer. This drink, originally called a "Straits Sling," was created in 1915 by Ngiam Tong Boon, a bartender of the Long Bar at the Raffles Hotel in Singapore.

SINGLE BARREL Whiskey from one individual barrel in a warehouse. Depending on the producer, it may or may not be mixed with distilled water to reduce the proof.

SINGLE MALT SCOTCH WHISKY A single malt Scotch whisky is the product of one particular distillery. *See* Malt Scotch.

SINGLES BAR   An establishment licensed to serve alcoholic beverages that caters specifically to single men and women. This clientele is cultivated by promotions, interaction, and so on.

SINGLE-SINGLE   A term applied to a Scotch whisky produced from a single distillation by a single distillery.

SINGLE-VILLAGE   A designation for grapes that come from a single village or town within the geographic area of production for that wine type. In this situation, there can be more than one winery producing this type of wine. The grapes from a single village have pronounced characteristics of that growing site.

SINGLE-VINEYARD   A designation for a specially delimited growing area within a selected vineyard site, where the grapes possess more intense characteristics than those grown in adjoining parts of the vineyard. This is often due to optimum soil and ideal climatic conditions that result in a wine with more varietal character and concentrated flavors. A limited release wine produced from grapes grown in these selected vineyards is designated "single-vineyard" on the label. Also known as *vigna, vigneti,* or *vigneto.*

SINGLE WHISKEY   A whiskey that is the product of one particular distillery.

SINGLINGS   *See* Heads.

SINKER   A heavy, perforated stainless steel or wooden plate utilized for keeping the *cap* of grape skins below the surface during fermentation.

SINK WORKBOARD   *See* Bar Workboard.

SINUS   The depression on a grape leaf between adjoining lobes.

SIPHON   An apparatus consisting of a bent tube used for carrying liquids out over the top edge of a container through the force of gravity and atmospheric pressure exerted upon the surface of the liquid. Also known as *sifon.*

SIPON (YUGOSLAVIA)   *See* Furmint.

SISTEM DE SOLERA (SPAIN)   *See* Solera.

SITE   Point of origin; shipping point.

SITE SELECTION   The area selected for planting and propagation of grapevines; the choice is as important as grape variety selection. It is a complex of above-ground environment, root environment, and management characteristics. The above-ground environment of a grapevine can be restrictive by its low temperature. The root environment is critical with respect to root pests and to availability of water. Management characteristics are relatively minor; they include the site's size, slope, and nearness to both market and to other vineyards. The selection must be made rationally and scientifically.

SIZZANO (ITALY)   A dry, red wine produced in the northwest region of Piedmont from a blend of Nebbiolo, Bonarda, and Vespolina grape varieties.

SKADARSKA (YUGOSLAVIA)   *See* Kadarka.

SKHOU   Distilled *kumiss. See* Kumiss.

SKIM MILK   Fresh fluid milk that has been almost entirely defatted by means of centrifugal force, leaving approximately 0.5 percent butterfat.

SKIN The outer covering or surface of a grape; it accounts for 5 to 12 percent of the grape and is composed of six to ten layers of cells. Approximately 12 percent of all phenols are contained in the skins. From the skin and the layers of cells immediately beneath the skin come the color of wine (particularly red wine) and much of the flavor characteristics. As the grape size increases, these flavor constituents decrease in their relationship to the rest of the grape; therefore, the best wine grapes are small. They have a higher ratio of flavor-rich components that contribute to varietal character in a wine. *See* Phenol.

SKIN *See* Peel.

SKIN CONTACT A winemaking technique whereby the grape skins (usually red) remain in contact with the fermenting juice for color and flavor extraction. Many flavor components are found in grape skins rather than the juice. To get these components into the wine, many wineries crush the grapes and leave the skins, juice, and seeds (collectively called *must*) together in a tank for hours or days before fermentation and/or pressing. *See* Extended Skin Contact.

SKLIRÓS (GREECE) *See* Hard.

SKU Stock-keeping units.

SKUNKY Describes a particularly unpleasant odor occasionally detected in beers left for prolonged periods of time in direct sunlight, or in unpasteurized keg beer that has been left unrefrigerated.

SLA State Liquor Authority.

SLADKO (BULGARIA) *See* Sweet.

SLATKO (YUGOSLAVIA) *See* Sweet.

SLING A cocktail for which a mug is filled two-thirds with strong beer and sweetened with sugar, molasses, or dried pumpkin. Rum is then added to this mixture and stirred with a loggerhead. It also is the name of a family of cocktails, often with gin as its base. *See* Flip, Hot Caudle, and Rumfustian.

SLIPSKIN A term applied to those grape varieties that possess a rather tough skin that separates readily from the pulpy flesh, hence *slipskin*.

SLIVOVITZ A fruit brandy made from small, blue plums with a highly aromatic perfume; usually produced in central Europe and Hungary.

SLOE GIN Not actually a gin but rather a red liqueur made from sloe berries (blackthorn berries), which give it a rather tart plum flavor.

SLOE GIN FIZZ A cocktail consisting of sloe gin, lemon juice, sugar, and soda water.

SLOP The spent grains and fluids that are drawn off from the bottom of the continuous still after distillation; they are dried and used as high-protein feed supplements for both livestock and poultry.

SLOSHED *See* Intoxicated.

SLURRY Mashed apples used in the making of apple brandy.

SMALL *See* Little.

SMALL BATCH   Whiskies made in lots of less than one thousand gallons (approximately twenty barrels), instead of up to millions of gallons a batch. Small batches suggest a more carefully made, less industrial product and generally command a higher price.

SMALL BEER   An old English term, dating back to about 1568, for a weak beer (low alcohol); in Colonial times, a thin ale was dubbed "small beer."

SMASH   A short drink made from brandy, bourbon, or other distilled spirits, mixed with sugar and mint. Another name for a small mint julep.

SMASHED   *See* Intoxicated.

SMEDEREVKA (YUGOSLAVIA)   A white grape variety known as *Dimiat* in Bulgaria.

SMELL   An olfactory sensation noticed directly by the nose; it is present in virtually every beverage. Smell also covers the odor from yeast, wooden barrels, corks, and so on. Also known as *odor*.

SMOKY   Describes an elusive, tactile impression evoking smoke, noticed either in the bouquet or on the palate, that some wines or beers leave. Often found in wines made from the Sauvignon Blanc grape variety in the Loire Valley of France (e.g., Pouilly Fumé). Also, the odor given off by wines or beers that have been fermented or aged in charred or toasted oak barrels. Also known as *odeur de suie*.

SMOOTH   Describes alcoholic beverages that display on the palate a soft, silky, and well-rounded texture, absent of roughness or harshness. Opposite of astringent. Also known as *glatt*.

SNAKE-HEAD WHISKEY   A slang cowboy term denoting a cheap whiskey.

SNAPS   The Scandinavian spelling of *schnapps*, referring to akvavit.

SNERVATO (ITALY)   *See* Thin.

SNIFTER   The traditional balloon-shaped, wide-brimmed brandy glass. The main consideration is to select a glass that will enhance the beverage's bouquet. The glass should be large enough (ten to twelve ounces) to enable the liquid to move around with ease, spreading the bouquet over a wide surface area. Unfortunately, most brandy snifters resemble footed aquariums, minus the water and goldfish. Ideally, the neck should be slightly indented to help the spirit retain its bouquet. Also known as *brandy glass* and *brandy snifter*.

SNOWBALLS   A distillers' term for the bubbles appearing inside vats of fermenting mash, due to fermentation.

SOAPY   Describes those wines and beers that are low in acidity, making them flat and uninteresting.

SOAVE (ITALY)   A famous dry white wine produced northeast of Verona in the region of Veneto from a grape blend predominantly of Garganega and Trebbiano di Soave, with small additions of Trebbiano Toscano, Chardonnay, Sauvignon Blanc, and Pinot Bianco.

SHŌCHŪ (JAPAN)   A 70-proof clear grain spirit distilled from a combination of barley, corn, wheat, sugar cane, or sweet potatoes, although occasionally rice will also be used. It is triple distilled and aged in white oak barrels, which creates its slightly sweet, smooth, distinctive taste and aroma. Also known as *shochu*.

SOCHU (JAPAN)

S

SODA   A nonalcoholic soft drink containing carbonated water, flavored with syrup and fruit. Also known as *soude*.

SODA OUT   A cocktail that is finished by topping with soda.

SODA POP   Any carbonated, nonalcoholic beverage consisting of sugar syrup or other sweeteners, natural or synthetic acids, flavoring agents, carbonated water, and natural and artificial colors.

In 1812, English author Robert Southey wrote that the name "pop" is derived from the sound produced when the cork or cap is removed from the bottle, which contains carbon dioxide. Also known as *pop* and *soft drink*.

SODA SYSTEM   *See* Post-Mix Soda System and Premix Soda System.

SODA WATER   *See* Carbonated Water.

SODIC   Describes a soil that contains an excess level of sodium in relation to calcium and magnesium.

SODIUM CARBONATE   A chemical used to reduce excess natural acidity in wine.

SODIUM CASEINATE   A chemical used to clarify wine.

SODIUM METABISULPHITE   A chemical used for sterilizing wine.

SODIUM SALT OR SORBIC ACID   A compound used as a sterilizing and preserving agent and to inhibit mold growth and secondary fermentation. *See* Sorbic Acid.

SOFT   *See* Mellow.

SOFT DRINK   A nonalcoholic, carbonated beverage. *See* Soda.

SOIL   Earth. There are countless types of soil throughout the world suitable for the growing of grapes. Winemakers and grape-growers constantly strive for the best soil for their grapevines, but, unfortunately, the best type of soil is often in dispute. What is accepted by all sides is that grapevines do best on well-drained soils that are able to supply adequate amounts of nutrients and water. Some elements that must be considered are drainage, soil structure, access to water, nourishment or lack of it, microclimate of the grapevine, soil acidity, presence of minerals, depth, slope, and exposure to sunlight.

SOIL MANAGEMENT   A viticultural term referring to the process of achieving a balance in the soil between the minerals and nutrients essential to growing healthy grapes.

SOIL MATRIX   The major soil type that encloses other *soil profiles*.

SOIL PROFILE   A vertical section or view of soil (generally up to six feet) depicting changes in color, moisture, structure, and texture.

SOLEAR (SPAIN)   The actual sunning or drying of grapes in the sun, for later use in sweetening some sherry types.

SOLERA (SPAIN)   A system of fractional blending, which produces a consistent style of fortified wine. According to some sherry producers, *solera* comes from the word *suelo*, meaning ground or land, and refers to the butts (barrels) nearest to the ground. Others say it comes from the Spanish word *solar*, which refers to the tradition that holds a family together. Still others believe it derives from the Latin *solum*, meaning floor, as it is the bottommost tier in the aging system.

The solera system involves a series of white American oak barrels, generally containing 130 gallons, arranged in rows or tiers, usually four barrels high. However, some soleras utilize as many as fourteen barrels. The arranging of barrels in tiers is not a requirement of the system or of law. The original or bottom row of barrels is called the *solera*, while the upper, or younger rows are called the *criaderas* (cradles). Each row is known as a scale and moving the wine from tier to tier is often referred to as "playing the scales."

The wine first sold is that on the bottom row, which is then replaced with wine from the second tier, and so on up through as many as fourteen tiers. The wine from the most recent vintage is poured into the barrels on the top tier, which were not completely filled; thus the youngest wine is blended with a slightly older wine of the same type, which has in turn been blended with a still older wine, and so on down through the tiers. Wines of a superior quality are created through this fractional blending.

Wine is not siphoned from tier to tier but rather is transferred into containers so that wine from various barrels on the same level can be blended for even further standardization. By law, the maximum that can be drawn out of a barrel of fully mature sherry is 33 percent. Sherry wines must age a minimum of three years in oak barrels before bottling; some, however, are much older when they are bottled.

One of the reasons for the blending is to tame the young, rough wine. The key to the solera system is that the aged sherries in the bottom "educate" the younger ones by giving them character and taste. The wine is also aerated as it passes from tier to tier and, in addition, picks up subtle nuances from the oak barrels. During this process, approximately 10 percent of the wine is lost through evaporation, whereas in an aging cellar, where the barrels are tightly bunged, the amount would be only 1.5 to 2 percent. Also known as *sistem de solera*.

SOLERA DATE (SPAIN)   The date that appears on the label of some sherries identifies the year the solera was established and has nothing to do with when the grapes were harvested or when the sherry was bottled. If, for example, a sherry from a producer states on the label "Solera 1908," this means that the solera was established in 1908. The chances of having any of the original wine remaining in the current system is quite remote.

SOLID   Describes a wine that has a firm and sound foundation and backbone, which allows it to improve with age. Also known as *solide*.

SOLIDE (FRANCE)   *See* Solid.

SOM (ITALY)   Superior Old Marsala. *See* Marsala Superiore.

SOM (ROMANIA)   *See* Grasa.

SOMATIC EMBRYOGENESIS   *In vitro* culture technique for production of plantlets that are normally produced by seeds. The method allows scientists to modify existing plants—only one or two agronomic characteristics—without using sexual crossing.

SOMMELIER (FRANCE)   One who is in charge of the service of wine and the wine cellar in a restaurant. The traditional uniform is a black and gray striped apron with a cellar key and wine-tasting cup on a silver chain dangling from the neck. Also known as *escancão, escanciador, weinkellner, wine butler, wine captain, wine steward,* and *wine waiter*. *See* Tastevin.

SONOMA RIESLING   *See* Sylvaner.

SONNE (GERMANY) Sun.

SONOMA VALLEY An important viticultural area north of San Francisco and west of Napa Valley, noted for its many fine vineyards.

SOPLICA (POLAND) A dry and very fine golden-colored vodka.

SOR (HUNGARY) *See* Beer.

SORBATES *See* Potassium Sorbate and Sorbic Acid.

SORBIC ACID A short-chain fatty acid that, together with its salt, potassium sorbate, exhibits antimicrobial properties. During *malolactic fermentation*, if the growth of lactic acid bacteria is in the presence of sorbic acid, heat, bacteria, a high pH, and low alcohol, a powerful odorous compound (2-ethoxyhexa-3, 5-diene) will form, which is responsible for the so-called geranium smell. *See* Potassium Sorbate, Sodium Salt or Sorbic Acid, and Stabilizing.

SORBITOL A white, sweet, odorless, crystalline alcohol present in some berries and fruits. It has no relation to either sorbates or sorbic acid.

SORÌ (ITALY) A term utilized in Piedmont to denote a southern exposure, a characteristic of the best vineyards.

SORICELLA (ITALY) A red grape variety. Also known as *Cavalla*.

SORRENTINE An ancient Roman wine.

SORTENBUKETT (GERMANY) *See* Varietal Character.

SOTTILE (ITALY) *See* Subtle.

SOUCHE (FRANCE) *See* Rootstock.

SOUCHONG TEA A pungent black tea from India or Ceylon. *See* Lapsang Souchong.

SOUDE (FRANCE) *See* Soda.

SOUND Describes a healthy, good-smelling, clean-tasting, well-made wine or beer with no major flaws or defects.

SOUPLE (FRANCE) *See* Supple.

SOUR Describes the disagreeable acid taste of all the volatile and nonvolatile acids of wine. Not to be confused with *acetic*. Wines made from immature grapes will have the taste. Also known as *asprigno* and *sourness. See* Green and Tart.

SOUR The name of the largest drink family; a sour consists of a distilled spirit (generally whiskey), lemon juice, and sugar, and is garnished with a cherry or orange slice. Also known as *whiskey sour*.

SOUR BEER *See* Spoiled.

SOUR GLASS A medium-sized, short-stemmed glass with a tubular bowl that holds approximately six ounces.

SOURING *See* Spoiled.

SOUR MASH A type of whiskey produced by using spent distiller's beer (residue from a previous distillation) to aid in fermenting a new batch of mash. The lactic acid present permits pH adjustment and suppresses the reproduction of undesired bacteria. Sour mash acquired its name because the spent distiller's mash has a slightly acid taste, although the resulting distilled spirits are anything but sour. Most bourbon and Tennessee whiskey is *sour mash* whiskey.

SOUR MILK   Milk that has gone sour due to bacterial contamination.

SOUR MIX   A premixed, nonalcoholic beverage mixer consisting of sugar syrup, lemon and/or lime juice, egg whites, and often a preservative. Sour mix is generally utilized in beverage facilities as a bar substitute for sugar and lemon or lime juice in cocktails. Also known as *sweet and sour mix*.

SOURNESS   *See* Sour.

SOUSÃO (PORTUGAL)   A red grape variety grown in the Dão and Minho regions.

SOUSED   *See* Intoxicated.

SOUSSANS (FRANCE)   One of the five communes entitled to the appellation *Margaux* in the Bordeaux region.

SOUTH AUSTRALIA   A major grape-growing state producing more than 50 percent of all Australian wine. Its most popular grape-growing areas are Adelaide, Barossa Valley, Clare Valley, and Coonawarra.

SOUTIRAGE (FRANCE)   *See* Racking.

SOVEREIGN ROSÉ   A white grape variety developed from a cross of Bath and Perle of Csaba.

SOYEUX (FRANCE)   *See* Silky.

SPA (ITALY)   Società Per Azioni. Joint-stock company.

SPA   *See* Standard Price Allowance.

SPACER (ENGLAND)   A term used in pubs for a nonalcoholic beer.

SPAGNOLA (ITALY)   A red grape variety.

SPALLIERA (ITALY)   A pruning method for grapevines, used in Sicily. *See* Cordon.

SPANISH CLAY   *See* Spanish Earth.

SPANISH EARTH   A complex silicate or clay, originally found only in certain types of soil in Spain, although some has been discovered in certain parts of the United States. It is used as a fining agent for wine and beer. Also known as *silicaceous earth*, *Spanish clay*, and *tierra de vino*. *See* Fining and Fining Agents.

SPANNA (ITALY)   The local name for the Nebbiolo grape variety in the provinces of Vercelli and Novara in the region of Piedmont. *See* Nebbiolo.

SPARGING   The spraying and distribution of hot water over the spent grains and hops in the mash tun to recover sugars and other extracts that might be remaining.

SPARKLETS   Small capsules containing carbon dioxide that dissolve upon contact with a liquid; used to carbonate certain nonalcoholic beverages.

SPARKLING BURGUNDY   A sweetish red sparkling wine generally produced in the eastern United States.

SPARKLING WATER   A generic term for any carbonated water. It may be naturally carbonated from its source and may be labeled *naturally sparkling*, or carbonation may be added.

SPARKLING WINE   An effervescent wine containing more than 0.392 grams of carbon dioxide per hundred milliliters of wine, resulting solely from the secondary fermentation of wine within a closed container. Most champagne and sparkling wines contain seventy to one hundred pounds per square inch when finished. Also known as *biser, cap classique, cava, champanski, effervescent wine, espumante, espumosa, habzó, iskriashto, moussec, mousseux, pezsgo, sampanjac, sekt, spumante, vinho do rodo, vinho espumante, vin mousseux, vino espumosa, vino spumante, vonkelwyn*, and *Xampan*.

SPARKOLLOID   A proprietary fining agent made up of refined polysaccharides (carbohydrate sugar compounds) and diatomaceous earth. It forms a coagulum due to the normal inorganic ions present in wine. It has little absorption capacity and acts mainly by entrapping haze particles; it finds its principle usage in cases of particularly difficult haze problems. *See* Fining and Fining Agents.

SPÄT (GERMANY)   Late.

SPÄTBURGUNDER (GERMANY)   *See* Pinot Noir.

SPÄTLESE (GERMANY)   A term that means late picking or late harvesting of the grapes. The official date for the end of the normal harvest, which is set by the wine commissioners of each village, usually takes place at least seven days after the normal harvest.

SPÄTROT (AUSTRIA)   *See* Zierfandler.

SPEAKEASY   A term applied to illicit saloons in New York City in 1899 (which predated Prohibition). Speakeasies served alcoholic beverages only to persons who would appear at the door and softly speak the password in order to enter. Also, an old Irish term for a place where illicit whiskey was sold.

SPECIAL INVENTORY   A physical counting of stock on hand at irregular periods of time, due to extraordinary circumstances.

SPECIALLY SWEETENED NATURAL WINE   A wine product made with a base of natural wine and having a total solids content in excess of 17 percent by weight (17 degrees Brix dealcoholized wine) and an alcohol content of not more than 14 percent by volume.

SPECIAL NATURAL WINE   A product produced from a base of natural wine (including heavy-bodied blending wine) to which natural flavorings are added.

SPECIALTY MALT   *See* Caramel Malt.

SPECIES   A member of a botanical genus family.

SPECIFICATION   An exact, detailed, accurate description of the quality and type of beverage to be supplied to an establishment. Specifications are used to ensure consistent quality.

SPECIFIC GRAVITY (SG)   The ratio of the weight or density of a given volume of liquid as compared to the weight or density of an equal volume of water at the same temperature. Water has a density of 1.00; a substance less dense than water will regis-ter less than 1.00, while a substance more dense than water will register over 1.00. *See* Density.

SPEED POUR   A pouring device inserted into the neck of a bottle of distilled spir-its that aids in its dispensing.

SPEED RACK   A stainless steel trough, either suspended from or attached to the underbar directly in front of a bartender, usually at the cocktail station, that contains bottles of distilled spirits or mixes that have the greatest consumer demand. Also known as *bottle trough* and *speed rail*.

SPEED RAIL   *See* Speed Rack.

SPENT BEER   The *stillage* or residue material remaining after distillation in the making of distilled spirits.

SPENT LEES   The *stillage* or residue in the distilled spirits still after the distillation of the *heads* and *tails*. Also known as *spent liquor*. *See* Stillage.

SPENT LIQUOR   *See* Spent Lees.

SPERONE (ITALY)   The spur of a grapevine.

SPEYSIDE MALTS   Speyside is a barley-growing and a Scotch-producing area noted for whiskies (Speyside Malts) that are quite mild, with a sherry-like odor and flavor.

SPEZIALITÄTEN (GERMANY)   *See* Festbier.

SPICY   An organoleptic term that evokes an impression of spices, either through odor, taste, or both, which can be reminiscent of various spices (e.g., cinnamon, cloves, nutmeg, black pepper). "Spicy" can also be used to describe the odor and/or taste of certain types of wine, such as Muscat, Gewurztraminer, and even some Zinfandels. Also known as *épicé, odeur épicé*, and *pfeffrig*.

SPIEL (GERMANY)   Flexible; balanced.

SPIGOT   A metal faucet or wooden tap utilized for drawing liquids from a barrel or tank, or to draw off the contents of a barrel. Also known as *faucet* and *tap*. *See* Zwickel.

SPILE   *See* Bung.

SPILLAGE ALLOWANCE   A discretionary portion of a distilled spirits bottle (e.g., one or two ounces) that management may assume will be lost accidentally. This *spillage allowance* is not factored into the calculation of the number of drinks per bottle.

SPINNER   A *capsule* on the neck of a wine bottle that is not set properly and there-fore is able to rotate.

SPIRITS   That substance known as ethyl alcohol, ethanol, or spirits of wine in any form (including all dilutions or mixtures thereof, from whatever source or by whatev-er process produced), but not denatured spirits unless specifically stated. *See* Distilled Spirits.

SPIRITS STILL   The third still used for the final run in making distilled spirits.

SPIRITUEUX (FRANCE)   *See* Distilled Spirits.

SPIRITUEUX (FRANCE)

S

SPIRIT WHISKEY   A mixture of neutral spirits of not less than 5 percent on a proof gallon basis of whiskey, or straight whiskey, or straight whiskey and whiskey, if the straight whiskey component is less than 20 percent on a proof gallon basis.

SPITTOON   A receptacle with a funnel-shaped top, made of brass, ceramic, glass, or even plastic, used for the spitting-out of wines, beers, or distilled spirits during a tasting. Also known as a *cuspidor* or *sputacchiere*.

SPITZEN (GERMANY)   *See* High-Quality.

SPITZENJAHR (GERMANY)   An excellent vintage.

SPITZENWEIN (GERMANY)   An excellent wine.

SPLASH   A small quantity of an ingredient added to a drink.

SPLICE THE MAIN BRACE   An old Navy term meaning to drink whiskey. The term often appears in Herman Melville's writings.

SPLIT   A small wine or champagne bottle containing a single serving of approximately 6.4 ounces.

SPLIT CASE   *See* Broken Case.

SPOGLIA (ITALY)   *See* Spoiled.

SPOILED   Describes a decayed wine or beer. Spoilage is caused by poor vinification, bacterial contamination, improper storage, or poor handling. The beverage usually displays cloudiness, murkiness, or an off-taste. Also known as *alterato, sick, spoglia, sour beer,* and *souring*. *See* Adulterated Wine and Bacterial Spoilage.

SPOLETINO (ITALY)   *See* Trebbiano.

SPONSORED BAR   *See* Host Bar.

SPORTS BAR   An establishment licensed to sell and serve alcoholic beverages in an environment permeated by sports paraphernalia, often including a large screen television and satellite television reception capable of picking up various local, national, and international sporting events.

SPOUDÉOS (GREECE)   Excellent.

SPRAYING   The treatment of grapevines by the application of liquid fungicides and insecticides as needed.

SPREADING GROWTH   The growth habit of certain grape varieties in which shoots extend upward and outward from the grapevine trunk.

SPRIGHTLY   *See* Lively.

SPRING-MILL CONSTANTIA   *See* Alexander.

SPRING WATER   A term used to indicate water from a deep underground source that flows naturally to the surface. If that water remains unprocessed and unchanged—nothing added or taken away—the term "natural" may be used and the product is called "natural Spring water."

SPRINKLER IRRIGATION   The irrigation of vineyards by means of surface pipes and sprinkler heads. Also utilized in some instances as frost protection.

SPRITIG (GERMANY)   *See* Burning.

SPRITZ   A slight effervescence in a wine or prickle on the tongue that may be caused by leaving some dissolved carbon dioxide in the wine, but it is more often the result of the addition of carbon dioxide gas to certain table wines. Also known as *crackling, frizzante, pétillant, prickly, spritzig, spritzy, vino de aguja*, and *vino frizzante*.

SPRITZER   A tall drink made with a base of wine (white, red, or rosé) and filled with a carbonated mixer. Also known as *gespritzer* and *schorlemorle*.

SPRITZIG (GERMANY)   *See* Spritz.

SPRITZY   *See* Spritz.

SPRUCE BEER   Beer or nonalcoholic malt beverages, famous during the Revolutionary War, produced by the addition of tops of spruce trees or spruce boughs to the fermenting liquid.

SPRUDEL (GERMANY)   *See* Mineral Water.

SPUMA (ITALY)   Foam, froth, effervescence. *See* Schiuma.

SPUMANTE (ITALY)   *See* Sparkling Wine.

SPUND (GERMANY)   *See* Bung.

SPUR   A short fruiting unit of one years' growth on a grapevine, usually consisting of one or two nodes that are retained at pruning. Also known as *Renewal spur*.

SPUR PRUNING   A practice that is common in very old vineyards where there is no trellising of stakes and wires. It is a method whereby the spurs are retained as fruiting units with the canes tied to the support wires. *See* Pruning and Cane Pruning.

SPUTACCHIERE (ITALY)   *See* Spittoon.

SQUARE CUBES   *See* Ice Cubes.

SQUEEZIN'S   A slang term for the end product or *tails* of a distillation. *See* Tails.

STAATSWEINGÜT (GERMANY)   State wine estate or domain.

STABILIMENTO (ITALY)   A bottling plant.

STABILIZER   Any additive used in winemaking and brewing for stability and to retard deterioration. *See* Sorbic Acid.

STABILIZING   The application of various treatments, including additives, used in making alcoholic and nonalcoholic beverages to keep them stable, thereby retarding deterioration. Among these treatments are ascorbic acid, cold stabilization, filtering, fining, pasteurization, refrigeration, sorbic acid, and sulfur dioxide.

STABLE   A wine or beer is said to be stable if there is no chance of refermentation taking place.

STAGIONATO (ITALY)   A wine that is correctly aged or matured.

STAHLIG (GERMANY)   *See* Steely.

STAINLESS STEEL   A type of metal used in winemaking because it is neutral (does not impart odor, taste, or add metal ions to the wine), is inert to acids and alcohols, is durable, cleans easily, can withstand severe temperature changes, is basically corrosion proof, and is unaffected by chemical cleaners. Also known as *acciaio inossidabile*.

STAINLESS STEEL

S

STAKE   A post made of wood, metal, or even cement, utilized as a support for grapevines and/or wires utilized for training of grapevines.

STALE   Describes a wine or beer that has lost its lively, fresh, youthful character and become dull and tasteless, with a musty, cardboard taste. Often the result of the beverage being kept too long. Also known as *schal*.

STALKS   *See* Stems.

STALKY   *See* Stemmy.

STAMPING   The process of marking a wine (on its capsule, cork, barrel, or cardboard box) to identify it.

STANDARD   An approved criterion, measure, or basis for comparison that is used to evaluate quantity, quality, and volume.

STANDARD BEVERAGE COST   *See* Beverage Cost.

STANDARD COST   *See* Beverage Cost.

STANDARD COST PERCENTAGE   *See* Cost Percentage.

STANDARD DEPLETION ALLOWANCE   *See* Depletion Allowance.

STANDARD DISTILLED SPIRITS BOTTLE   A standard distilled spirits bottle that is so made and formed, and so filled, as not to mislead the purchaser. An individual carton or other container of a bottle may not be so designed so as to mislead purchasers regarding the capacity of the bottle.

STANDARD DRINK LIST   A list of the alcoholic beverages or cocktails offered for sale in a retail, on-premise establishment.

STANDARD DRINK RECIPE   *See* Standard Recipe.

STANDARD DRINK SIZE   *See* Standard Portion.

STANDARD GLASSWARE   Glassware of a specific quality, quantity, type, and size for a given drink.

STANDARDIZED DRINK   *See* Standard Recipe.

STANDARDIZED RECIPE   *See* Standard Recipe.

STANDARD OF PERFORMANCE   In a performance-based objective, that part of the objective stating, in terms of measurable or observable performance, the standard for carrying out a given unit of work.

STANDARD PORTION   A carefully regulated measurement of each individual serving of a beverage, made in accordance with a standardized drink recipe. Also known as *standard drink size*.

STANDARD PRICE ALLOWANCE (SPA)   A general term used to denote any number of discounting or promotional activities.

STANDARD PURCHASE SPECIFICATION   *See* Purchase Specification.

STANDARD RECIPE   A written, regulated formula, established by management, that has been systematically tested for preparing any particular type of alcoholic drink and that yields a consistent, known quality and quantity of product each and every time it is used. A standard recipe includes a listing of ingredients, quantity, procedures, and equipment needed. Also known as *standard drink recipe, standardized drink*, and *standardized recipe*.

STANDARD-SIZED BOTTLE   A bottle with a capacity of 750 milliliters or 25.4 ounces.

STANDARDS OF FILL   Set standards, according to the BATF, as to the exact quantity of alcoholic beverage that an accepted size bottle must contain.

STANDARDS OF IDENTITY   The United States federal government's definition of the various classes and types of distilled spirits, wines, and malt beverages. Also known as *Federal Standards of Identity*.

STANDARD WINE   Natural wine, specially sweetened natural wine, special natural wine, and standard agricultural wine.

STANDARD YIELD   The total number of portions that are produced by a standard recipe.

STANDING PLAN   An established routine, formula, or set of procedures used in a recurring situation.

STAR BRIGHT   *See* Falling Bright.

STARCH   A white, tasteless, odorless food substance of the polysaccharide group, found in plants, as in the various grains utilized in making distilled spirits and malt beverages.

STARKA   A vodka flavored with brandy, port, honey, and vanilla, plus the leaves of several different types of Crimean apple and pear trees; it is produced in the Slavic countries.

STARKBIER (GERMANY)   A beer that has the highest alcohol level (up to 7 percent) of any beer in Germany. It was first brewed in the early seventeenth century by the Franciscan monks of the Paulaner Abbey, for the sole reason that it helped them through the long forty-day fast of Easter. However, it was not until the middle of the eighteenth century that its reputation spread to Duke Wilhelm V, who ordered the building of beer halls, called "Hofbrauhaus" in 1589.

STARTER   A highly concentrated and previously fermenting yeast culture, added to large volume *musts* to help start fermentations. Also known as *pé de cuba, pied de cuve*, and *yeast starter*. *See* Nutrients.

STATE STORES   In the United States, those retail premises operated by some states from which alcoholic beverages are purchased. *See* Control State.

STATION   A work area in a bar that is set up with all the essentials for the service of alcoholic beverages. Also known as *cocktail station* and *pouring station*.

STATIONARY BAR   *See* Cocktail Mix Station.

STAVES   The arched or curved lengths of wood, generally one inch in thickness and made of oak, that in greater or smaller quantities constitute the contour of barrels. The individual staves vary in width from two to four inches. Also known as *duela*.

STEAM BEER   A highly carbonated, deep brown-gold-colored beer, with an aromatic odor of cloves, orange peels, and peaches, and a tangy-bitter taste with a dry finish. The name *steam* originates from the final *kräusening* stage of fermentation, during which a partially fermented *wort* is added to speed the fermentation; at this point the active head produced by this process releases a steam. Steam beer is a bottom-fermented beer, like *lager*, yet with a taste of ale. Steam beer originated in San Francisco, California, during the Gold Rush.

STEAMSHIP CONFERENCE   An association of common carriers permitted to engage in concerted activity and to utilize a common tariff.

STEEL JACKETED TANK   *See* Jacketed Tank.

STEELY   Describes the taste of stony, gravelly, rocky, acidic, or mineral flavors or nuances found in some white wines, such as French Chablis and Puligny-Montrachet. Also known as *stahlig*.

STEEN   The local name in South Africa for the Chenin Blanc grape variety. *See* Chenin Blanc.

STEEP   To soak or infuse in liquid; a process by which grain is soaked in water in huge cisterns to begin the germination process. This is a necessary step in making distilled spirits, malt beverages, and tea.

STEIN (GERMANY)   Stone.

STEIN   A large, often ornately painted drinking vessel with a handle and lid, made of porcelain, earthenware, crystal, or pewter. The Germans have been producing steins for more than six hundred years; however, the reason steins have hinged lids on them is due to a sixteenth-century German law. When the bubonic plague ravaged most of Europe, it was believed that the disease came from filth and was carried by swarms of flies. Lawmakers then required that all food and drinking vessels be covered, thus the origin of lids. By the seventeenth century the plague had vanished; however, the powerful pewter guilds made certain the laws remained in effect until at the least the nineteenth century, when the law was repealed. By this time, steins with lids had become the standard, and such vessels were viewed as incomplete without lids. *See* Mug and Tankard.

STEINHÄGER GIN (GERMANY)   Gin produced in Westphalia; it is similar to London dry types, but with slightly more of a juniper taste. Also spelled *Steinhäeger*.

STEINSCHILLER (ROMANIA)   A white grape variety.

STEINWEIN (GERMANY)   A name used for many years to describe Franken wines.

STELLENBOSCH (SOUTH AFRICA)   An important wine-producing region.

ST. ÉMILION (FRANCE)   *See* Saint-Émilion.

STEMMY   Describes a green wood effect or the smell and taste of damp twigs, often displayed in wines fermented in contact with the stems for prolonged periods of time. The taste sensation is similar to that of chewing on dried grape stems. Also known as *stalky, stemminess, twiggy*, and *weedy*. *See* Herbaceous.

STEMMINESS   *See* Stemmy.

STEMMER   *See* Crusher/Destemmer.

STEMMED CHERRY   A cherry (generally maraschino) with a stem.

STEMMED GLASS   A glass used in beverage service (primarily wine), which features a base or foot and a bowl.

STEMS The thick stalks by which bunches of grapes are attached to the cane on a grapevine. These stalks are a valuable source of *tannin* in red wine. Approximately 22 percent of all phenols present in wine are contained in the stems, which have a pH over 4.0. Also known as *raspon* and *stalks*. *See* Phenol.

STENOSPERMOCARPY The technical term for producing grapes that are seedless, either by natural reproduction or through hybridization.

STERILANTS Sterilizing agents as heat, steam, sulfur dioxide, ascorbic acid, and other chemicals, that inhibit wild yeasts and spoilage bacteria in *musts* or on bottles and equipment.

STERILE BOTTLING The removal of yeast cells from a wine, usually at 0.45 microns or smaller. *See* Sterile Filtration.

STERILE FILTRATION A process for treating certain wines that have a small amount of residual sugar and, if any yeast were present, might begin a fermentation in the bottle. The wine is passed through a special filter (0.45 microns) that is so fine that even microscopic yeast cells are removed. *See* Clarifying, Filtering, Fining, and Sterile Bottling.

STERNEWIRT (GERMANY) A taproom located inside a brewery.

ST. ESTÈPHE (FRANCE) *See* Saint-Estèphe.

STEUBEN A red grape variety developed in 1947 from a cross of Wayne and Sheridan at the State Experimental Station in Geneva, New York.

STEWARD The person in charge of the storeroom where alcoholic beverages are stored.

STEWED *See* Intoxicated.

STIFF Similar to *dumb*.

STILL Apparatus used to concentrate and produce distilled spirits. Stills may be classified by the method of introducing fermented mixture. *See* Alembic, Coffey Still, Column Still, Continuous Still, and Pot Still.

STILLAGE The residue in the still after the distillation of the alcohol. It is drawn off for making distillers' feed. *See* Spent Lees.

STILL HOUSE A building where the actual process of distilling takes place and that houses the various pieces of equipment necessary for distilling.

STILL WINE A table wine containing not more than 0.392 grams of carbon dioxide per hundred milliliters. The opposite of a sparkling wine. Also known as *tranquillo*.

STIMULANTS Agents that temporarily increase functional activity, such as drugs, caffeine, and alcohol.

STIMULUS An agent or factor capable of inciting or provoking a sensory response.

STINGER A cocktail consisting of brandy and white crème de menthe.

STIR One of three methods of mixing a drink and incorporating its ingredients, the other two being shaking and blending.

STIRRER *See* Swizzle Stick.

STIRRUP CUP   A cup used for serving the parting drink or last drink served to a welcome guest. The name comes from an old custom of having a last drink with a departing guest after he had mounted his horse and had his feet firmly in the stirrups.

Also, the name of a drink consisting of whiskey and boiling water, to which a dollop of butter was added, and that was drunk immediately. Although the drink is obsolete and its origin lost in antiquity, it was at one time served in Louisville, Kentucky.

ST. JULIEN (FRANCE)   *See* Saint-Julien.

ST-LAURENT   A red grape variety grown primarily in Austria, although at one time it flourished in Alsace, France.

ST-MACAIRE   A red grape variety formerly grown in the Médoc in France; some is now grown in California.

STOCK   The underground portion of the root system of a grapevine, onto which the scion is grafted.

STOCKLESS PURCHASE   When the buyer purchases a large quantity of product but arranges for the supplier to store it and to deliver it a little at a time, as needed. This procedure is illegal in certain states.

STOFFA (ITALY)   *See* Stuffing.

STOFFIG (GERMANY)   *See* Stuffing.

STOLNO VINO (YUGOSLAVIA)   *See* Vino da Tavola.

STONED   *See* Intoxicated.

STOPFEN (GERMANY)   *See* Cork.

STOP FERMENTATION   A winemaking procedure where a little pure grape brandy is added to a sweet dessert wine to stop the fermentation. This prevents complete conversion of the natural grape sugar into wine alcohol and carbon dioxide so that the wine is sweeter than if fermentation had run its course.

STOPPEL   A glass stopper, carefully ground to fit a particular bottle using emery powder and oil. The stoppel is tied to the bottle by a piece of packthread around a button on top. As late as 1825, stoppels were considered the best stoppers for bottles. However, due to the fact that they were usually impossible to extract without breaking the bottle, their use declined.

STORING   The process of aging or laying away barrels, bottles of wine, or other items for future use.

STOUP   An obsolete term for a drinking vessel (cup, flagon, glass, or tankard) used for the service of wine or beer at the table.

STOUT   The word "stout" evolved from the term *extra stout porter*, a darker and stronger version of porter. A top-fermenting beer that obtains its dark (almost black) color from roasted barley, with a very high extract level. It contains mostly roasted barley, which is rendered sterile before germination, and a small amount of malt for added flavor. It is quite thick and malty, with an intense bitterness and underlying sweet taste. Stout is relatively low in carbonation and should be served at 55 degrees Fahrenheit.

Specific types of stout are Bitter Stout, Imperial Stout, Irish Stout, Milk Stout, Oatmeal Stout, and Porter.

STOVER   A white grape variety developed in 1956 (released in 1968) from a cross of Mantey and Roucaneuf by Professor Loren Stover of the Florida Agricultural Experimental Station.

STRAIGHT   Distilled spirits poured straight from the bottle without ice, soda, water, and so forth. Also known as *neat* and *shot*.

STRAIGHTFORWARD   A term that describes a wine that is simple, honest, and direct, without any pretense or subtleness.

STRAIGHT UP   A cocktail that is strained and served "up off the ice" in a stemware glass. Some examples are the martini, the Manhattan, and sours. Also known as *up*.

STRAIGHT WHISKEY   Alcohol distillate from a fermented mash of grain, distilled at 160 proof or less and stored during aging at between 80 to 125 proof. Straight whiskey must be aged for not less than twenty-four calendar months in new charred white oak barrels. Its proof is reduced to a level of not less than 80 by the addition of distilled water.

Straight whiskies must be made with a minimum of 51 percent of the grain that identifies that particular whiskey. Bourbon, for example, is made with at least 51 percent corn. Other straight whiskies are rye, bottled-in-bond whiskey, straight corn whiskey, and straight whiskey without an identifying grain tag, which simply means it was produced from a mash that contained less than 51 percent of any one grain type. A blend of straight rye whiskeys or a blend of straight bourbon whiskeys is a mixture of only straight rye whiskeys or straight bourbon whiskeys, respectively.

STRAINER   *See* Cocktail Strainer.

STRATEGIC PLANNING   Long-range planning to set organizational goals, objectives, and policies and to determine strategies, tactics, and programs for achieving them.

STRAVECCHIO (*ITALY*)   A very old wine or brandy.

STRAW   A term often used to describe the color of young white wines that range in color from pale yellow to greenish gold. Also known as *paglierino*.

STRAWBERRY-FLAVORED BRANDY   A mixture of brandy, minimum of 2.5 percent sugar, flavored and colored with strawberries. By federal law it cannot be bottled at less than 60 proof (30 percent alcohol by volume).

STRAWBERRY LIQUEUR   A sweetened alcoholic beverage consisting of a base of alcohol and minimum 2.5 percent sugar, flavored and colored with raspberries. It is sweeter and lower in proof than strawberry-flavored brandy.

STRAW MATS   Mats generally made of straw, cane, or wicker, where whole clusters of grapes are allowed to dry in the sun, concentrating their sugar levels. Also known as *canna, cane, castelli, straw wine, vin de paille,* and *wicker. See* Cannici, Esparto Mats, Governo, and Strohwein.

STRAW WINE   Wine made from grapes dried on straw mats. *See* Straw Mats.

STRAW WINE

STRENCHERB (GERMANY)   *See* Brut.

STREPPAROSSA (ITALY)   A red grape variety.

STRIPPER   A hand-held tool used to obtain twists or peels from citrus fruits.

STRIP STAMP   Tax stamp of the United States Internal Revenue Service, affixed over the closure of bottles of distilled spirits. Green stamps are used for bottled-in-bond distilled spirits and red stamps are used for most other distilled spirits. The strip stamps are required in only a few states.

STROHWEIN (GERMANY)   A seventeenth-century name given to a wine made from grapes dried on straw. *See* Straw Mats.

STRONG   A term that refers to wines, beers, or distilled spirits that display a high level of alcohol. The alcohol can be detected in the odor as well as in the taste, which often is harsh, hot, or has burning qualities. Also known as *fort* and *forte*.

STRONG   Describes wines that are full in flavor, with good acidity, extract, body, and level of alcohol.

STRONGYLÓS (GREECE)   *See* Round.

STRUCTURE   A term that describes a wine's "framework," which is determined by the interaction of essential components that create tactile impressions in the mouth (e.g., acid, tannin, fruit, and alcohol).

STRYFNÓS (GREECE)   *See* Astringency.

STUBS   *See* Hosted Bar.

STUCCHEVOLE (ITALY)   *See* Cloying.

STÜCK (GERMANY)   A barrel containing approximately three hundred gallons. *See* Barrel.

STUCK FERMENTATION   The gradual and premature cessation of fermentation prior to all the sugar being metabolized by the yeast into alcohol and carbon dioxide. This can be caused by many factors: 1) excessive heat, cold, or death of yeast cells; 2) low rate of heat dissipation during fermentation pasteurizing the yeasts; 3) low levels of yeast food, i.e., nutrients, largely made up of vitamin B_1, magnesium sulfate, potassium phosphate, urea, and ammonium phosphate, which supply the *must* with a suitable source of nitrogen and phosphorous. *See* Gestoppt and Nutrients.

STUFFING   A term that refers to the body, character, and extract of certain red wines. Also known as *stoffa* and *stoffig*.

STUM WINE   *See* Must.

STURDY   Describes a solid, substantial, and full-bodied wine with good structure and that can stand considerable aging.

STYLAR SCAR   A scar at the grape's apex left by the character of the flower.

STYLE   Originates in the winemaker's vision of the grape's potential expression. Wine styles vary because of the diversity and intensity of aromas and flavors, the wine emphasis (fruit or wood predominating in the aroma or flavor), and balance (toward tannin, acidity, or sweetness). Winemakers affect style by their selection of grapes, vineyard management techniques, and winemaking methods and equipment.

Suave *(Spain)* *See* Supple.

Subirat Parent *(Spain)* A white grape variety used for sparkling wines.

Subjective Describes a state of mind where personal reaction, opinion, and judgment are the mode of thinking.

Subsoil The general term for the layer of soil that underlies the surface layer of approximately two feet and continues downward for another two to three feet.

Subtle Describes a slight gentle or delicate nuance of smell or flavors, not easily detected, which is found in some wines and beers. Also known as *nez subtil* and *sottile*.

Sucaryl A trademark name for a compound used as low-calorie sweetener.

Succinic Acid One of the more prominent by-products of fermentation. It is one of the principal acids utilized in the formation of esters that helps to promote vinous character (winy aroma and flavor of wine).

Suckering Removing water sprouts and tendrils from grapevines that originate either below the ground surface or on the trunk of the grapevine and are not fruit-bearing. These suckers siphon off nutritive material that should be directed to the production of grapes. *See* Crown Suckering.

Suckers Shoots that spring from a bud at the base of a grapevine.

Sucrage *(France)* *See* Chaptalization.

Sucré *(France)* *See* Sweet.

Sucrose The form of sugar that occurs in sugar cane and sugar beets and is commonly known as table sugar. Each molecule contains one molecule each of glucose and fructose.

Sucrosity The impression of sweetness on the palate, with or without the actual presence of sugar.

Suds In the late 1800s and early 1900s it was customary to carry home a bucket of beer from a local tavern. To prevent the beer from foaming over, lard or other fats were rubbed on the inner surface, which assured the purchaser of a full bucket of what humorously was called "suds." Also referred to as a "bucket of suds."

Südtirol *(Italy)* South Tyrol, a viticultural area in the region of Trentino-Alto Adige.

Süffig *(Germany)* *See* Jug Wine.

Suffolk Red Seedless A red grape variety introduced in 1972 from a cross of Fredonia and Russian Seedless by the State Experimental Station in Geneva, New York.

Sugar Pure dry sugar, liquid sugar, and invert sugar syrup, used in the making of some alcoholic and nonalcoholic beverages.

Sugaring of Wine *See* Chaptalization.

Sugar in Wine Wines are often placed in three categories of sweetness: dry, semidry, and sweet. A wine below 0.6 percent is considered dry (truly dry wines con-

SUGAR IN WINE

S

tain less than 0.2 percent sugar); between 0.6 and 2.2 percent, semidry; while wine with greater than 2.2 percent sugar is generally considered sweet.

SUHO *(YUGOSLAVIA)* *See* Dry.

SUK *(KOREA)* *See* Saké.

SULFITE EXEMPT The status of wines made from organically grown grapes, vinified naturally, made without added sulfites, and exempt from sulfite notice label requirements.

SULFUR DIOXIDE (SO$_2$) A naturally appearing substance used worldwide for its antimicrobial and antioxidative activity. All fermenting yeasts produce SO$_2$ from inorganic sulfates that occur naturally in grape juice. The amount produced can vary from 16 to 125 milligrams per liter depending on the yeast strain, nutrient balance of the juice, and fermentation conditions.

Sulfur dioxide is used in grape juice destined to become wine for two reasons: as an antioxidant (to inhibit or prevent the enzymatic action that causes browning of white grape juice; the way cut apple slices turn brown when exposed to air), and as an antimicrobial (to wipe out natural bacteria and wild yeasts clinging to the grapes in order to have a controlled fermentation).

Normally a gas, it exists in solution through a complex set of equilibrium reactions that result in the transformation of the gas into dissolved free and bound forms. Sulfur dioxide is effective as a sterilant and antioxidant agent only when present in the solution form ("free"). The total sulfur dioxide is the sum of the free, bound, and chemical transforms. Since sulfur dioxide is not usually destroyed in wine, the total represents the sum of all sulfur dioxide in the wine at all stages of processing. The amount of sulfur dioxide in wine varies with time (aging after bottling), temperature, aeration in the glass or carafe, and the pH of the wine, among other factors, making accurate measurement difficult.

Excessive levels of free sulfur dioxide are sensory disadvantages (creating a disagreeable irritant to the nose) and the total sulfur dioxide content is subject to federal and state regulations.

No chemical substitute for sulfur dioxide exists anywhere in the world at the present time, although a worldwide search for an SO$_2$ substitute for wine has been ongoing since 1910. The French government has even offered to pay a royalty to anyone who can find a substitute. Also known as *anidride solforso* and *zolfo*. *See* Campden Tablet, Matchstick, Metabisulfite, Sodium Metabisulfite, and Sulfur Stick.

SULFURIC ACID A heavy corrosive acid derived from sulfur. In Europe and other countries it is used as the measurement of the total acidity in wine.

SULFUR STICK A flat, yellow stick or wick made of sulfur. It is burned to clean or disinfect the inside of a wooden barrel. Also known as *mechage*. *See* Sulfur Dioxide.

SULTANA *See* Thompson Seedless.

SULTANINA *See* Thompson Seedless.

SUMOLL *(SPAIN)* A red grape variety.

SUNBURNED A condition that grapes take on when grown in extremely hot climates; it causes a general loss of acidity and shriveling of exposed fruit. This sunburned characteristic generally carries through to the taste.

SUN IN SACKS   *See* Chaptalization.

SUNSHINE COAST   *See* Rkatsiteli.

SUPER CALL   *See* Premium Brands.

SUPERFICIAL   *See* Shallow.

SUPERFINE SUGAR   Sugar that rapidly dissolves in cocktails. Also known as *bar sugar*.

SUPÉRIEUR *(FRANCE)*   Superior.

SUPERIORE *(ITALY)*   A wine that contains a higher percentage (generally one-half of one degree or more) of alcohol than the minimum regulation required under DOC or DOCG law. Under some laws, additional bottle aging is also a requirement for use of the term.

SUPERIORE *(ITALY)*   *See* Marsala Superiore.

SUPERIOR OLD MARSALA (SOM) *(ITALY)*   *See* Marsala Superiore.

SUPERIOR SEEDLESS   A white grape variety grown primarily in California.

SUPPLE   Describes a wine or beer that has smoothness and softness on the palate and is easy to drink; acidity and alcohol are balanced. Also known as *geschmeidig, morbido, souple*, and *suave*.

SUPPLIER   Firms that bottle domestic or foreign-produced alcoholic beverages or that import bottled alcoholic beverages for resale. Frequently, "vendor" and "supplier" are used interchangeably.

SURDO *(PORTUGAL)*   A mixture of both cooked and fortified wines. It is used in making some madeira wines. *See* Cooked Wine and Mistelle.

SUREAU *(FRANCE)*   A fruit brandy made from elderberries in Alsace.

SURFACE TENSION   *See* Legs.

SURIN *(FRANCE)*   *See* Sauvignon Blanc.

SUR LATTES *(FRANCE)*   Champagne bottles stacked on thin strips of wood called laths (*lattes*); these are placed between each row of bottles, making the stacks quite firm during secondary fermentation.

SUR LIE *(FRANCE)*   A wine that is fermented and aged on the *lees*, which adds an extra dimension of aroma and flavor to the wine. *See* Autolysis.

SURMATURITÉ *(FRANCE)*   *See* Overripe.

SURPLUS   The amount by which quantity supplied exceeds quantity demanded at the existing price. Any excess or amount left over.

SUR POINTE *(FRANCE)*   Describes the position of bottles of champagne placed neck down so as to collect the deposits in one place, this operation follows the riddling stage. Also known as *mise sur pointe*.

SÜSS *(GERMANY)*   *See* Sweet.

SÜSSRESERVE *(GERMANY)*   *See* Back Blending.

SÜSSUNG *(GERMANY)*   *See* Dosage.

S

SUSTAINABLE AGRICULTURE   What farming systems that can maintain their productivity indefinitely practice. Such farms must be resource-conserving, environmentally compatible, socially supportive, and commercially competitive. They generally rely on biological processes such as soil-improving crops and biological pest control rather than external inputs such as synthetic fertilizers and pesticides, but often require higher levels of trained labor and management skill. Also known as *low-input sustainable agriculture*. *See* Organically Grown Wine.

SÜT (TURKEY)   *See* Milk.

SUWANNEE   A white grape variety introduced in 1983 by the University of Florida Agricultural Experimental Station.

SVINATURA (ITALY)   *See* Racking.

SWAMPY   Describes an extremely unpleasant odor, occasionally found in some beers or even wines, that is reminiscent of the odor of rotting vegetation frequently encountered in a swamp.

SWEET   Describes a basic taste sensation dependent upon the level of residual sugar in a wine. A sweet (as opposed to dry) wine is one that usually retains some sugar after fermentation has ceased. Sweetness is also derived to a lesser degree from alcohol and glycerin, both present in wine. Also known as *adamado, doce, dolce, doux, dulce, edes, glykys, sladko, slatko, sucré*, and *süss*. *See* Dessert Wine.

SWEET AND SOUR MIX   *See* Sour Mix.

SWEET CIDER   Freshly squeezed apple juice that is not fermented. *See* Apple Juice, Apple Wine, Cider, and Hard Cider.

SWEETENING   The addition of juice, concentrated juice, or sugar to wine after the completion of fermentation and before tax payment.

SWEET LIGHTNIN'   Moonshine that has honey, maple syrup, or other sugary substances added to help make it palatable.

SWEET MASH   Sweet mash is similar to sour mash except that neither a lactic acid culture nor a stillage has been added.

SWEET VERMOUTH   *See* Vermouth.

SWEET WINE   A wine that contains more than 2.2 percent sugar. *See* Dessert Wine and Sugar in Wine.

SWENSON RED   A red grape variety developed by Elmer Swenson of the University of Minnesota.

SWILL   A slang term for the lowest quality of wine. Also known as *plonk*.

SWIZZLE STICK   Another name for a drink stirrer.

SYKES   *See* Sikes Scale.

SYLLABUB   A drink made of hot, but not curdled, sweetened milk or cream mixed with brandy, wine (table or fortified), beer, or hard cider, and sugar, and beaten to a froth. Whipped cream is then floated on top. The drink was popular from the Renaissance through the eighteenth century.

SYLVANER   A white grape variety grown primarily in Germany and in Alsace, France, although it is said to have originated in Austria; its actual origin cannot be reliably ascertained. Sylvaner produces a light, fragrant (somewhat neutral), fresh and tart (high in acidity) white wine of steelish color.

Sylvaner is also spelled *Silvaner* and is also known as *Frankenriesling, Franken Riesling, Grüner Sylvaner, Monterey Riesling, Oesterreicher, Sonoma Riesling*, and *Zöldsilváni*.

SYLVOZ   A grapevine training and pruning method utilized in Europe, especially in Italy and France.

SYMPHONY   A white grape variety developed from a cross of Grenache and Muscat of Alexandria by Dr. Harold P. Olmo at the University of California, Davis.

SYMPOSIUM   In ancient Greece (around 400 B.C.), a social-drinking gathering during which individuals expressed judgment and compared wines of similar origin while simultaneously creating a glossary for the less knowledgeable.

SYNDICAT DES VIGNERONS *(FRANCE)*   A grape-growers' union.

SYNTHETOS *(GREECE)*   *See* Complex.

SYRAH   A red grape variety grown primarily in the Rhône Valley of southern France, where it produces dark, full-bodied, and long-lived wines, with fruit flavors of wild blackberries, plums, and cassis. It is the major grape in the blend of such great wines as Hermitage, Cornas, and Côte Rôtie, to name just a few. It is also grown prolifically in Australia, where it is known as *Shiraz*, while some is also grown in California, where for years it was mistakenly identified as *Petite Sirah* or *Petite Syrah*.

Syrah is known locally in the Rhône Valley as *Serine*; in Australia, it is often incorrectly referred to as *Hermitage*, the name of a great red-wine-producing village in the Rhône Valley as well as the local name for the Cinsaut grape variety in South Africa. *See* Durif and Petite Sirah.

SYRUPY   The tactile sensation of a very sweet wine that is low in total acidity.

SYSTEMIC FUNGICIDES OR PESTICIDES   Any of a group of fungicides or pesticides that are absorbed into the tissues of the plants, which in consequence become poisonous to fungi and insects that feed on them.

SZARAZ *(HUNGARY)*   *See* Dry.

SZEMELT *(HUNGARY)*   *See* Auslese.

SZÜRKEBARÁT *(HUNGARY)*   *See* Pinot Gris.

S

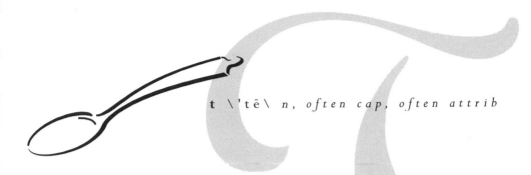

t \'tē\ *n, often cap, often attrib*

TA *See* Total Acidity.

TABLESPOON(T) A United States measure of volume equal to three teaspoons or half an ounce. Sixteen tablespoons is equal to one cup (eight ounces).

TABLE TENT A small folded paper flyer (often tent-shaped) that promotes alcoholic or nonalcoholic beverages; placed on restaurant tables.

TABLE WINE A still white, red, or rosé wine having an alcoholic content between 7 and 14 percent by volume. Such wine may also be designated as "light." Also known as *dinner wine*. *See* Vino da Tavola.

TAFELWEIN *(GERMANY)* A term that literally means "table wine." According to the 1971 German wine law, Tafelwein is a separate category of wines, one step below Qualitätswein. Tafelweins, which may be *chaptalized*, represent a small portion of German wines, and very few are exported to the United States. *See* Table Wine and Vino da Tavola.

TAGLIO *(ITALY)* *See* Blending.

TAILLE *(FRANCE)* *See* Pruning.

TAILS In distillation, the last run of a distillate; it contains a high percent of congeners (impurities), which are not used but rather are collected and redistilled. Also known as *backings, feints, produit de queue*, and *squeezin's*.

TALL BOY A slang term for a sixteen-ounce can of beer.

TALL DRINK *See* Long Drink.

TAM *See* Territorial Allocation Model.

TAMIÎOASA ROMANEASCA *(ROMANIA)* A white grape variety.

TANK A large container used for the fermentation or storage of alcoholic beverages. *See* Barrel.

TANKARD   A tall, one-handled drinking vessel used for serving beer; usually made of glass, pewter, or silver. *See* Mug and Stein.

TANK METHOD   *See* Charmat Method.

TANNAT (FRANCE)   A red grape variety grown primarily in the Jura Region. Also known as *Harriague*.

TANNIC   Also known as *tannico*. *See* Tannin.

TANNIC ACID   An astringent acid usually added to *must* or wine to increase the wine's longevity by slowing down the aging process. Not to be confused with *tannin*.

TANNICO (ITALY)   *See* Tannin.

TANNIN   One of a group of organic bitter compounds, better known as phenolics. Tannins are "large" phenols with astringent, leather-forming, protein-precipitating properties. They are considered phenolic polymers (giant molecules formed when thousands of the same initial molecule are linked together), which have the gustatory effect of astringency and/or bitterness. Tannin content is popularly referred to as a group of phenolic compounds—primarily anthocyanin pigments, flavonoids, and flavonols, among others. The pigments impart density and richness to wine, while flavonoids and flavonols are responsible for bitterness, astringency, and antioxidative properties.

Tannin is found in the seeds, stems, and skins of grapes, and is extracted from wooden barrels. It is quite astringent and causes a puckering sensation in the front of the mouth. Tannin, which is more concentrated in red wines than in white, contributes to the aging capacity of wine. One of the five elements that gives wine longevity, the others being sugar, alcohol, acidity, and carbonation. Also known as *tannic*. *See* Anthocyanin, Astringency, Phenol, and Phenolic.

TAP   *See* Spigot.

TAP BEER   *See* Draft Beer.

TAP BOX   *See* Beer Box.

TAPHOUSE   *See* Tavern

TAPMAN   *See* Bartender.

TAPPING CABINET   *See* Beer Standard.

TAPON (SPAIN)   *See* Cork.

TAPPO (ITALY)   *See* Cork.

TAPROOM   Same as barroom.

TAP ROOTS   The deepest penetrating roots, whence emanate feeder roots and, from these, very fine roots called "hair" roots. Roots grow somewhat laterally, extending the absorption area for water, minerals, and other nutrients from the soil. The greatest concentration of roots is within a radius of six feet of the trunk of a grapevine to a depth of eight feet. Also known as *heart roots*.

TAPPIT-HEN   An old Scottish bottle size, originally with a capacity of 76.84 ounces or the equivalent of three bottles of Portuguese port wine; no longer used. Also known as *tregnum*.

TAR BEER (ENGLAND)   An alcoholic beverage brewed from pine resin.

TAREFA DE BARRO (SPAIN) A large earthenware container or small barrel utilized for fermenting small batches of wine.

TARE WEIGHT The weight of a container or package less its contents.

TARIFF A publication containing the actual rates, charges, and rules of a common carrier or conference.

TARRANGO (AUSTRALIA) A red grape variety developed from a cross of Touriga and Sultana at Merbein in 1965 and released in 1975.

TARRY A term applied to certain Cabernet Sauvignon, Zinfandel, Barolo, and other full-bodied red wines that are said to have the odor and/or taste of *melting road tar* on a hot summer day. The wine is quite palatable, much more so than one would expect. Also known as *catrame, goudron*, and *goût de goudron*.

TART Describes the sharp, astringent, sour taste of acid that, when present in a moderate amount, lends a pleasant freshness to a wine. *See* Green and Sour.

TARTAR *See* Cream of Tartar.

TARTARIC ACID A colorless, crystalline acid, which is the principle natural fixed acid found in grapes and wine. Tartaric acid often occurs in such high levels in wine grapes that it crystallizes out as *cream of tartar* when the wine is cold stabilized. Also known as *acide tartrique*. *See* Bitartrate, Cold Stabilization, Crystalline Deposits, Potassium Bitartrate, and Tartrate.

TARTRATE A salt of tartaric acid. *See* Tartaric Acid.

TASHLI (RUSSIA) A white grape variety.

TASKER'S GRAPE *See* Alexander.

TASSE (FRANCE) Cup.

TASTE The overall flavor impression of an alcoholic or nonalcoholic beverage.

TASTE BUDS Any of the small papilla (nipple-like projections) embedded principally in the epithelium of the tongue that contain *taste receptors*, which function as the sense organs of taste. Each person has approximately ten thousand of these papilla cells, which regenerate every ten to eleven days.

TASTEVIN (FRANCE) A shallow, saucer-like silver cup, about three-quarters of an inch in depth by three inches across, with a handle. Its surface is indented with dimples, both on the bottom and sides, in order to refract the light when tasting young wines. It is often used by a *sommelier* to examine wine prior to its being served. It has given its name to the celebrated Burgundian confraternity of wine, the Confrérie des Chevaliers du Tastevin. *See* Gutturnium and Sommelier.

TAURASI (ITALY) A DOCG red wine produced in the southern region of Campania from a blend of Aglianico and other red grapes including Piedirosso (red feet), Sangiovese, and Barbera.

TAVEL (FRANCE) A village best known for its rosé wines; located on the right bank of the Rhône River in the Rhône Valley. The wines are produced from a blend of Grenache, Cinsaut, Clairette, Picpoul, and Bourboulenc grapes.

TAVERN The word "tavern" derives from *taberna*, Greek for hut, and from the old French *taverne*, meaning a place where alcoholic beverages are sold for consumption on the premises. Also known as *osteria, taphouse*, and *taverna*. *See* Bar, Cocktail Lounge, Inn, Pub, and Saloon.

TAVERNA (ITALY)   *See* Tavern.

TAWNY   Brownish-colored. A term applied to ports and other red wines that have a brownish or golden tinge instead of the customary ruby. This results from the loss of pigment by oxidation and through long aging, filtering, or fining, or from the use of grapes not heavy in color.

TAWNY PORT (PORTUGAL)   A port wine whose name is derived from the tawny color of the wine; this comes from long maturing in barrels, which causes the wine to lose some of its redness. Much smoother than ruby port, tawny port usually spends a minimum of six to eight years in the barrel (which helps round out the fieriness of the alcohol), resulting in a wine with a smooth texture and a touch of sweetness. Some tawny ports are described as having a nutty smell and taste. Tawny ports do not improve significantly in the bottle, for they have already matured in the barrel and are ready to consume. Tawny ports that state they are ten, twenty, or even thirty years of age are referred to as *Port with an Indication of Age.*

TAX DETERMINATION   Fixing the amount of United States federal excise tax as the distilled spirits leave the distilled spirits plant. Actual payment is made within thirty days of the end of the half-month tax period, not the calendar shipping date. *See* Tax Liability and Tax Period.

TAX GALLON   Unit of distilled spirits subject to the United States federal excise tax. Since the federal excise tax is based on a proof gallon, a tax gallon is synonymous with a proof gallon. *See* Proof Gallon.

TAX LIABILITY   On production of distilled spirits, producers incur liability for the United States federal excise tax. The distilled spirits and tax liability are transferable under government supervision. *See* Tax Determination and Tax Period.

TAXPAID WINE   Wine on which the tax imposed by law has been determined, regardless of whether the tax has actually been paid or the payment of tax has been deferred.

TAXPAID WINE BOTTLING HOUSE   Premises established primarily for bottling or packing taxpaid wine.

TAXPAID WINE PREMISES   Premises on which taxpaid wine operations other than bottling are authorized to be conducted.

TAX PERIOD   In the United States, each month consists of two tax periods of about one-half month; the first to fifteenth and the sixteenth to the end of the month. *See* Tax Determination and Tax Liability.

TAYLOR   A white grape variety. Also known as *Black Taylor, Bullitt*, and *Taylor's Bullitt.*

TAYLOR'S BULLITT   *See* Taylor.

TAZA (SPAIN)   Cup.

TAZZA (ITALY)   Cup.

T-BUDDING   A grafting procedure that involves cutting off the upper portion of a mature grapevine. A T-shaped incision is knifed into the remaining trunk and the outer layer is peeled back to make a pocket for a dormant bud of the desired new grape variety. A white bandage is wrapped tightly around the graft and, if all goes well, the bud will draw nourishment from the parent plant. Utilizing this procedure almost ensures full production of the new grape variety by the second harvest after conversion, instead of the normal five- to seven-year period. This technique was developed during the 1970s in California.

TE (NORWAY)   *See* Tea.

TÉ (SPAIN)   *See* Tea.

TÈ (ITALY)   *See* Tea.

TEA   A beverage made from an infusion of the dried and processed leaves of a flowering, tropical evergreen bush (*Camellia sinensis*) in hot water. The tea plant grows mostly in China, India, Africa, Argentina, and many Southeast Asian countries. All teas (there are more than three thousand varieties that take their names from the district where they are grown) are harvested from the same type of bush, which is fond of growing on hillsides (up to ten thousand feet), protected from direct sun, in warm, wet climates. The color and flavor of tea is ultimately dependent upon the fermentation of the leaves. It takes 4 to 4-1/2 pounds of leaves and buds to produce one pound of finished tea leaves, which yields 175 to 200 cups of tea. Tea varieties include green, oolong, black, and pekoe, among others.

The Chinese credit a legendary emperor named Shen Nung with the discovery of tea in 2737 B.C. According to legend, he only drank water that had been boiled and one day leaves from a nearby bush, *Thea sinensis*, fell into his boiling drinking water. Also known as çay, chá, chah, te, té, tè, tee, and thé.

TÈ ALLE ERBE (ITALY)   *See* Herb Tea.

TEARS   *See* Legs.

TEASPOON (TSP)   A United States measure of volume equal to one-third of a tablespoon or one-sixth of an ounce.

TEE (GERMANY)   *See* Tea.

TEEDUM BARREL   Barrel or other storage vessel where moonshiners kept their private drinking liquor.

TEETH   Small angular or rounded indentations on a grape leaf.

TEETOTALER   The term is found in the records of the Laingsburg, Michigan, Temperance Society of the 1830s. Two forms of pledges had been offered members: the first one called for moderate drinking, and a later type advocated total abstinence from "ardent spirits."

Members were identified on the rosters as "O.P.—Old Pledge" and "T.—Total." The latter were soon known as "teetotalers" and in time the term was applied to those who abstained from all beverages containing alcohol.

TEINTURIER (FRANCE)   A generic name for those grape varieties with color in the flesh as well as the skin of the berry (as opposed to most varieties, whose juice is colorless).

TELEGRAPH   A red grape variety developed by Mr. Christine of Westchester, Pennsylvania; in 1865 it was introduced by P.R. Freas, editor of the Germantown Telegraph. Also known as *Christine*.

TEMPRANA (SPAIN)   *See* Palomino.

TEMPRANA (SPAIN)

TEMPRANILLA (SPAIN) *See* Palomino.

TEMPRANILLO (SPAIN) The premier red grape variety of Rioja; it may be regarded in the same context as the Cabernet Sauvignon in Bordeaux of California, although it is not related to that particular variety. Also known as *Aragonez, Cencibel, Ojo de Liebre (eye of the hare), Tinta del País, Tinta Roriz, Tinto Fino, Tinto de Toro*, and *Ull de Llebre*.

TENDER Describes young, light-bodied, not especially long-lived wines that are easy to drink. Also known as *tendre*.

TENDONE (ITALY) A modern pruning method employed in Sicily that is a more economical and rapid method than others traditionally employed because it lends itself to mechanical harvesting. It also causes an increase in the per-plant yield, which approaches two times that formerly harvested from the same varieties of grapes. With grapevines supported on tensioned wires held high by intermittent stakes, the sun is better able to bathe the grape and leaf in its golden endowments. The result is invariably a better wine.

TENDRE (FRANCE) *See* Tender.

TENDRIL A long, slender, curled structure borne at some of the nodes of a shoot on a grapevine. This coil-like appendage can firmly attach itself to any object to help support the grapevine.

TENEDDU (ITALY) *See* Biancolella.

TENIMENTO (ITALY) Farm, agricultural estate.

TENNESSEE WHISKEY Proprietary whiskey from the state of Tennessee that has gone through the leaching process before aging in new, charred oak barrels. It is distilled at not exceeding 160 proof from a fermented mash of not less than 51 percent corn.

TENSIOMETER *See* Neutron Probe.

TENTH A half-bottle, equal in capacity to 375 milliliters or 12.8 ounces.

TENUTA (ITALY) Estate or farm.

TENUTA VINICOLA (ITALY) A wine estate, similar to a château.

TEQUILA An alcoholic distillate from a fermented mash (juice and/or sap) derived primarily from a blue variety of the genus plant *Agave tequilana weber* (named by Swedish botanist Carolus Linnaeus), with or without additional fermented substances. It is bottled at not less than 80 proof. The agave species (actually, there are more than four hundred), occasionally called the *maguey*, is often confused with cacti. The agave is known in the United States as the American aloe or century plant, because it was mistakenly believed to bloom only once every hundred years. The agave plant takes between eight and twelve years to mature before it can be used. Only the heart of the plant, often called the *piña*, or "head," is used. *See* Agave.

TEQUILA SUNRISE A cocktail consisting of tequila, orange juice, and grenadine syrup. It was purportedly served as a dawn pick-me-up at the race track Agua Caliente, Mexican, where the bars never closed.

TEQUILERO (SPAIN) One who produces tequila.

TERCERO (SPAIN) A barrel with a capacity of one-third of a pipe. *See* Barrel.

TERLANO (*ITALY*)   *See* Garganega.

TERLANO (*ITALY*)   A light-bodied, dry white wine produced in the Italian region of Trentino-Alto Adige principally from the Chardonnay and Pinot Blanc grape varieties.

TERNE (*FRANCE*)   *See* Dull.

TEROLDEGO (*ITALY*)   A red grape variety grown primarily in the northern region of Trentino-Alto Adige.

TERRA PROMESSA (*ITALY*)   A white grape variety grown in Veneto.

TERRET BLANC (*FRANCE*)   A white grape variety grown primarily in Provence and the Rhône Valley.

TERRET NOIR (*FRANCE*)   A red grape variety grown primarily in the Rhône Valley.

TERRITORIAL ALLOCATION MODEL (TAM)   A standard model for territorial allocations based on quantification of brand strategy, against which to measure marketing plans before they are implemented.

TERRITORY   A specified area, usually but not always a state, in which wholesalers conduct business. Goals and promotional spending are established within this area.

TERROIR   A viticultural term that cannot be translated into a specific English word. It is used in a viticultural sense to describe all of the unique environmental factors that affect the grapevine and its fruit at a particular location. Those factors include the soil's depth, temperature and nutrients; the amount of water the soil holds; and the area's temperature, rainfall, and temperature cycles. These factors determine the grape quality and therefore, the wine's quality.
   It is also used as a tasting term to describe a wine that is earthy-tasting.

TERZO (*ITALY*)   A barrel with a capacity of one-third of a pipe. *See* Barrel.

TESTA AND CODA (*ITALY*)   The *heads* and *tails*, as used in the distillation process.

TEST MARKET   A field experiment that introduces new products or programs into a limited number of representative markets; used to evaluate products or program elements or to evaluate the interactions in a total marketing plan. Also known as *market test*.

TÊTE DE CUVÉE (*FRANCE*)   Top or outstanding growth; generally used in Burgundy and Champagne. Also known as *vin de tête*.

TEXTURE   The feel of a wine or beer as it enters the mouth; it is sensed on the palate. The relative smoothness and taste of a sound, well-made, and round beverage. *See* Body.

THASIAN (*GREECE*)   An ancient wine.

THÉ (*FRANCE*)   Tea.

THERMAL SHOCK   A result of temperature change. Glass holds temperature and quick temperature changes can cause enough stress in the glass to cause breakage. For example, a glass with ice in it should not be emptied and put directly into the dishwasher. Similarly, a hot glass coming out of the dishwasher cannot be put directly into service. In both cases the glass must be given time to reach room temperature. Never put cold water or ice into a warm or hot glass. Cracks that result from thermal shock usually form around abrasions caused by mechanical impact. The thicker the glass, the more time it needs to reach room temperature.

THERMOLIZATION   *See* Pasteurization.

THERMOREGULATION   The process of controlling the temperature of stainless steel tanks during fermentation.

THIEF   *See* Wine Thief.

THIN   A term that describes a wine or beer that is lacking body and character. It can also be watery, weak, light, neutral-tasting, and possibly low in alcohol. Also known as *arm, debole, décharné, delgado, descarnado, dünn, flaco, leer, maigre, mager, magro, scarno, snerva-to, watery, weak, weich*, and *welch. See* Feeble.

THINNING   *See* Crop Thinning and Leaf Thinning.

THOMAS   A red grape variety.

THOMPSON SEEDLESS   A white grape variety named after William Thompson, an Englishman who first planted the grape variety in Sacramento Valley, California, in 1872. It is used predominantly in jug wine blends because it is considered a juice grape. Thompson Seedless is also the predominant grape variety used in raisin production. Also known as *Sultana* and *Sultanina*.

THORNSBURG ROBIN   A red grape variety developed by W. Thornburg in Arizona and grown in California. Also known as *Robin Cardinal*.

THREE SHEETS TO THE WIND   *See* Intoxicated.

THREE STAR (FRANCE)   A label designation on armagnac, calvados, or cognac bottles that indicates that the youngest brandy used in the blend is at least two years old (calvados) and three years old (armagnac and cognac), although they contain a blend of brandies five to nine years old.

THREE-TIER SYSTEM   In the United States, a system for the distribution of alcoholic beverages that involves separate and distinct manufacturers, wholesalers, and retailers, with alcoholic beverages passing from one level to the next and ultimately to the consumer. This system has historical significance and is supported by most state laws.

THRESHOLD LEVEL   The minimum detectable amount of a substance, whether by smell or taste.

TIBOUREN (FRANCE)   A red grape variety grown primarily in Provence.

TIED-HOUSE   The United States Federal Alcohol Administration (FAA) Act (1934), which prohibits a supplier (manufacturer, importer, or wholesaler) from having "any interest, direct or indirect" in a retail operation, and vice versa. Tied-House is a violation of many state laws as well.

TIERCE (FRANCE)   A barrel with a capacity of one-third of a pipe. *See* Barrel.

TIER LE CAVAILLON (FRANCE)   *See* Decavaillonage.

TIERRA DE VINO (SPAIN)   *See* Spanish Earth.

TIGHT   *See* Closed In.

TIME-VOLUME CONTRACT   Similar to a service contract except the carrier publishes two rates. If the shipper fails to fulfill the volume commitment, it must pay the higher rate on all containers shipped.

TIMORASSO (ITALY)   A white grape variety from the Alessandria district of Piedmont. Also known as *Timuassa, Timorosso, Timorazza*, and *Morasso*.

TINA (SPAIN)   *See* Barrel.

TINAIA (ITALY)   *See* Wine Cellar.

TINAJA (SPAIN)   A large earthenware container or vessel utilized for the fermentation and aging of wine.

TINAS (SPAIN)   *See* Fermentation Tank.

TINETA (SPAIN)   *See* Grape-Picking Basket.

TINI (ITALY)   Open-topped barrels for fermentation of wine.

TINNY   Describes a metallic taste occasionally found in canned beer, as if from the tin or can. Contrary to popular belief, there is absolutely no difference in taste between canned and bottled beer. The cans used today do not give off a metallic taste as they once did when they were made of tin or steel. The tinny off-taste is attributable to the flavor of old beer.

TINTA AMARELLA (PORTUGAL)   A red grape variety used in the making of port wine.

TINTA BARROCA (PORTUGAL)   A red grape variety used in the making of port wine.

TINTA CARVALHA (PORTUGAL)   A red grape variety grown in the Douro region.

TINTA DEL PAÍS (SPAIN)   *See* Tempranillo.

TINTA FRANCISCA (PORTUGAL)   A red grape variety used in the making of port wine.

TINTA LAMEIRA (PORTUGAL)   A red grape variety grown in the Douro region.

TINTA MADEIRA   A red grape variety grown in the Central Valley of California.

TINTA MARTINS (PORTUGAL)   A red grape variety.

TINTA NEGRA MOLE (PORTUGAL)   *See* Negra Mole.

TINTA PINHEIRA (PORTUGAL)   A red grape variety grown in the Dão and Bairrada regions.

TINTA POMAR (PORTUGAL)   A red grape variety grown in the Douro region.

TINTA RORIZ (PORTUGAL)   *See* Tempranillo.

TINTO (PORTUGAL AND SPAIN)   *See* Red.

TINTO BASTO (SPAIN)   *See* Tinto de Madrid.

TINTO CÃO (PORTUGAL)   A red grape variety used in the making of port wine.

TINTO DE MADRID *(SPAIN)* A red grape variety. Also known as *Tinto Basto*.

TINTO DE TORO *(SPAIN)* *See* Tempranillo.

TINTO FINO *(SPAIN)* *See* Tempranillo.

TINTOMETER An instrument utilized for measuring the color of wine.

TINTORE *(ITALY)* *See* Guarnaccia.

TINTORERA *(SPAIN)* A red grape variety.

TIO *(SPAIN)* Uncle.

TIPICITÀ *(ITALY)* A wine with a classic character.

TIPO VINTAGE *(PORTUGAL)* *See* Vintage Character Port.

TIQUIRA A distilled product made from tapioca roots, produced in Brazil.

TIRAGE *(FRANCE)* The laying of bottles on their sides in large stacks for the secondary fermentation, which changes the still wine into a sparkling wine.

TIRE-BOUCHON *(FRANCE)* *See* Corkscrew.

TIRED Describes a wine or beer that is fatigued, lifeless, and worn out, showing signs of age, and lacking freshness. A tired wine can be slightly oxidized or beginning to dry out—that is, losing its fruit. Also known as *fatigued, fiacco*, and *usé*.

TISCHWEIN *(GERMANY)* *See* Ordinary.

TITRATABLE ACIDITY *See* Total Acidity.

TOASTED BARRELS *See* Charring.

TOASTING The custom of honoring people by drinking to their health, wealth, or good fortune.

TOASTY Describes the agreeable odor of grilled or toasted bread, detected in some wines. It is derived from: 1) the charred or toasted wood inside of a wooden barrel; 2) *autolysis* (prolonged contact with the yeast); 3) barrel-fermentation of some wines, most notably Chardonnay; or 4) an oxidized odor detected in some old wines, especially whites.

TOBACCO The scent of fresh, burning tobacco detected in some red wines, especially Graves, from France.

TOCAI *(ITALY)* A white grape variety grown almost exclusively in the Friuli-Venezia Giulia region, in the northeast, where it has been grown for centuries; it produces dry, white wines with an underlying bitterness.

In the 1950s, the Hungarian Government attempted to stop Italian use of the name Tocai, arguing that Hungarian Tokay was the original. In 1954, after extensive studies by a panel of experts, an International Court in Trieste decided that Hungary did not have exclusive rights to the name Tocai and that the Hungarian grape Furmint (used to make Tokay) is a different grape variety entirely. According to the panel's findings, both these grapevines actually originated in Italy. It is believed that the Italian missionaries to the court of King Steven the Saint brought them to Hungary in the eleventh century.

Also known as *Sauvignon Vert, Tocai Friulano*, and *Tokai*. It is argued that the Tocai is the same grape variety as the Muscadelle of France. *See* Muscadelle.

TOCAI FRIULANO (ITALY)   *See* Tocai.

TO DROWN A SHAMROCK   An old Irish term meaning to have a drink in every bar or pub in town.

TODDY   *See* Hot Toddy.

TODDY   An intoxicating alcoholic beverage made from the sweet sap of various East Indian palm trees.

TŌJI (JAPAN)   The term given in ancient times to experienced women who were in charge of the brewing and serving of saké.

TOKAI (ITALY)   *See* Tocai.

TOKAJI ÉDES (HUNGARY)   A sweet Tokay wine. *See* Tokay.

TOKAJI SZAMORODNI (HUNGARY)   A simple Tokay wine made with or without the addition of *aszú* berries. *See* Tokay.

TOKAJI SZÁRAZ (HUNGARY)   A dry Tokay wine. *See* Tokay.

TOKAY   A generic United States wine that remotely resembles the famed dessert wine of Hungary.

TOKAY (HUNGARY)   A very popular dessert wine from the region of Tokaji-Hegyalja in the northeast corner of the country. Tokay is made from the Furmint, Hárslevelü, and Muscat Lunel grapes, which are harvested at various degrees of ripeness. Tokay wines range from bone dry to exquisitely sweet.

When a sweet Tokay wine is to be produced, the grapes are left to hang on the grapevines until they begin to shrivel and resemble raisins. It is at this point that a beneficial *Botrytis cinerea* mold attacks the grapes, adding a rich scent of honey and increasing the viscosity of their juice. After harvest these grapes (called *aszú*, meaning dried-out grapes) are placed into buckets, called *puttony*, with a capacity of about five gallons. The grapes are crushed and the juice is added, one bucket at a time, to newly fermented wine contained in small thirty-six gallon barrels called *gönc*. The number of *puttonyos* (generally up to six), which appears on the label indicates how many have been added to the wine. Generally the wine is aged for two years plus one additional year for each *puttony* added.

Among the rarest of all wines is the legendary Tokaji Eszencia, made from the unpressed juice of the *aszú*. This wine is rarely produced nowadays, perhaps only fifty barrels having been made within the last ten years. *See* Tokaji Édes, Tokaji Szamorodni, and Tokaji Száraz.

TOKAY D'ALSACE   *See* Pinot Gris.

TOKKURI (JAPAN)   The decanter that is traditionally used for the heating of saké. Also known as *ochōshi*.

TOLERANCE   The lawful limit of toxic residue allowable by law in or on edible substances.

TOM AND JERRY   A cocktail consisting of an egg yolk, an egg white, sugar, allspice, white rum, and milk. The Tom and Jerry was created from Edan's *Life in London*, also known as *Days and Nights of Jerry Hawthorne and his Elegant Friend, Corinthian Tom*, in 1928.

TOM COLLINS   A cocktail consisting of gin, lemon juice, sugar, and soda water. *See* John Collins.

TOM COLLINS GLASS   *See* Iced Tea Glass.

TOMATO JUICE   The liquid constituent of a tomato.

TONEL (*PORTUGAL* AND *SPAIN*)   *See* Barrel.

TONELADA (*SPAIN*)   *See* Metric Ton.

TONELERO (*SPAIN*)   *See* Cooper.

TOMENTOSE   Describes grape leaves with hair on their surfaces. *See* Tomentum.

TOMENTUM   The hairs on a grape leaf surface; they may be single upright hairs or a dense downy covering.

TONIC WATER   A carbonated water flavored with quinine, an alkaloid of the cinchona bark. Originally introduced to bring down tropical fevers, it is now a widely used mixer, usually with gin or vodka. Also known as *quinine water*.

TONNE   An English wine measure from 1497; a tonne had a capacity of two pipes or 252 gallons. *See* Barrel.

TONNEAU (*FRANCE*)   A large Bordeaux barrel equivalent in capacity to four barrels or nine hundred liters (237 gallons). *See* Barrel.

TONNELERIE (*FRANCE*)   Factory where barrels are made.

TONNELIER (*FRANCE*)   *See* Cooper.

TONSIL PAINT   In old western movies, the name given to whiskey by cowboys.

TOOTHPICKS   Also known as *shoe pegs*. *See* Paraffin.

TOP FERMENTATION   The use of a type of added yeast that floats to the top during fermentation. The yeast converts sugar to alcohol and CO_2 at warmer temperatures, usually between 60 and 70 degrees Fahrenheit. Most top-fermented beers are analogous to red wine, with a richer flavor and more body. Some top-fermented beers include ale, cream ale, porter, stout, and weisse beer.

TOP HAT   A slang term or phrase denoting a container (usually made of white cardboard with a waxed inner lining) of beer, much like a take-out container, which is taken out of a bar for future drinking.

TOPPING   A winery practice of adding wine or distilled spirits to wooden barrels (to fill them to the top) to replace what was lost through evaporation and soakage. Also known as *colmatura, ouillage, remplissage, topping off*, and *topping up*.

TOPPING OFF   *See* Topping.

TOPPING UP   *See* Topping.

TOPSAIL   A white grape variety.

TOP SHELF   *See* Premium Brands.

TORBATO *(ITALY)*   A white grape variety grown in the region of Sardinia.

TORBIDO *(ITALY)*   *See* Turbid.

TORCHIO *(ITALY)*   *See* Wine Press.

TORGIANO *(ITALY)*   A small medieval town in the region of Umbria, known for its production of two DOC wines, Torgiano Bianco and Torgiano Rosso, and one DOCG wine, Torgiano Rosso Riserva.

TORPID   Describes yeast that has lost motion, vigor, and the ability to bud due to low fermentation temperatures.

TORRE *(ITALY)*   Tower.

TORREFACTION   The act or process by which an alcoholic beverage (or *must*) is subjected to high levels of heat that sufficiently burn off or vaporize most or all of the volatile ingredients.

TORRONTES *(SPAIN)*   A white grape variety.

TORULA   Any of a group of yeast-like fungi that reproduce by budding. In some wine and distilled spirits aging cellars, the walls and ceilings are covered with this microscopic gray mold, which feeds on the alcohol vapors. Also known as *Cladosporium cellare*. *See* Molds.

TOSCA *(ITALY)*   A red grape variety.

TOSCANELLO *(ITALY)*   *See* Pulcianella.

TOSCANO *(ITALY)*   *See* Tuscany.

TOSTATURA *(ITALY)*   *See* Charring.

TOT *(GERMANY)*   *See* Old.

TOTAL ACIDITY (TA)   A measurement of the potential acidity in *must* or a wine, usually expressed in terms of tartaric acid (United States) or sulfuric acid (much of Europe). Also known as *acidità totale* and *titratable acidity*.

TOTAL COST   The sum of fixed and variable costs.

TOTAL REVENUE   Total receipts from the sale of a product. When there is a single price, total revenue is the price times the quantity sold.

TOTAL SOLIDS   The degrees Brix of unfermented juice or dealcoholized wine.

TOTMUR   A white grape variety. Formerly known as *Baco 2-16*.

TOURAINE *(FRANCE)*   One of the wine-producing communes of the Loire Valley, best noted for red and rosé wine made mostly from Gamay grapes, and white wines from Sauvignon Blanc grapes.

TOURIGA BRANCA *(PORTUGAL)*   A white grape variety grown in the Douro region.

TOURIGA BRASILEIRA *(PORTUGAL)*   A red grape variety grown in the Douro region.

TOURIGA FRANCESA *(PORTUGAL)*   A red grape variety used in the making of port wine.

TOURIGA NACIONAL (PORTUGAL) A red grape variety used in the making of port wine.

TRADE BUYER Any wholesaler or retailer of distilled spirits, wine, or malt beverages.

TRADEMARK Any word, name, symbol, or device or any combination thereof adopted and used by a manufacturer or merchant to identify and distinguish his goods... from those manufactured and sold by others and to indicate the source of the goods. Also known as *marchio, marchio depositato, marchio registrato, markenwein, marque,* and *marque déposée. See* Brand Name and Logo.

TRADE SHOWS Events held in major cities, often in conjunction with industry conventions, where business firms can display, demonstrate, and sell their products.

TRADITIONELLE FLASCHENGAERUNG (GERMANY) Traditional fermentation in the bottle; also the current term for sparkling wines made in the traditional champagne method.

TRAILING GROWTH The growth habit of certain grapevines in which shoots tend to hang or droop.

TRAINING The systematic arrangement of the necessary parts of the grapevine on a wire trellis so as to position the leaves for best exposure to light and the fruit for ease of harvest. The grapevine shape in turn will influence the extent that the grapevine will grow, fruit will develop, and harvesting will take place. Also known as *arjoado, bardo,* and *cruzeta. See* Cordon Training, Head Training, and Shoot Positioning.

TRAJADURA (PORTUGAL) A white grape variety used in the making of Vinho Verde wine.

TRAKHYS (GREECE) *See* Rough.

TRALCIO (ITALY) A grapevine shoot.

TRAMINER The former name of the Gewürztraminer grape variety, now seldom used. *See* Gewürztraminer.

TRAMINER AROMATICO (ITALY) *See* Gewürztraminer.

TRAMINER MUSQUÉ (FRANCE) *See* Gewürztraminer.

TRAMINI PIROS (HUNGARY) *See* Gewürztraminer.

TRANESE (ITALY) *See* Uva di Troia.

TRANQUILLO (ITALY) *See* Still.

TRANSFER METHOD A method of making sparkling wines, developed in Germany in the 1930s, that is a modification of the *méthode champenoise*. In fact, the two methods are identical except that the transfer method does not employ the riddling technique. Instead, when the wine is sufficiently aged, the bottles are moved to a large tank in which pressure is used to remove the corks, suck the wine out of the bottles, and then chill it to below 32 degrees Fahrenheit. After being filtered, the wine is transferred to clean bottles, and the final dosage is added. This does appear to be an easier and certainly cheaper way of making high-quality sparkling wines. However, during the filtering process it has been found that the filtration can strip the subtlety that the winemaker has worked so diligently to create. The reverse is also true—if the winemaker starts off with a mediocre wine, the filtering can improve the wine by clearing it of off flavors. Sparkling wines made in this manner are labeled *fermented in the bottle. See* Transvasage.

TRANSFER TO BAR   Foods requisitioned from the kitchen by the bar staff for use in the preparation and service of drinks. Examples are citrus fruits, dairy products, and eggs.

TRANSPIRATION   The water loss from the leaves on a grapevine; it is affected by light intensity, temperature, humidity, and wind. Warm days and cool nights increase pigmentation in grapes. The color and taste of grapes is also influenced by pH, the level of which is affected by temperature during ripening.

TRANSVASAGE *(FRANCE)*   The transfer under pressure of sparkling wine or champagne from standard-size bottles to larger or smaller bottles. Most sparkling wines are traditionally fermented in 375 or 750-milliliter, magnum, or double magnum bottles. Other sizes, both larger and smaller, are hand-filled from 750-milliliter bottles. The hand-filling does not violate the AOC regulations relative to *méthode champenoise* and, as a matter of fact, is commonly practiced in Champagne, where the regulations originate. *See* Transfer Method.

TRAPPIST   Strong beer brewed by Trappist monks in Belgium and the Netherlands. The name "Trappist" is authorized by law for those beers brewed exclusively by the monks. Most of the beers are deeply colored, with high levels of alcohol.

TRASFEGA *(PORTUGAL)*   *See* Racking.

TRASIEGO *(SPAIN)*   *See* Racking.

TRAUBE *(GERMANY)*   *See* Grape.

TRAUBEN *(GERMANY)*   To ferment.

TRAUBENSAFT *(GERMANY)*   *See* Grape Juice.

TREADING   A technique formerly used in many parts of Europe, especially Portugal and Spain, that consisted of teams of male workers interlocking arms and treading on the grapes for several hours at a time in shallow stone tanks. Also known as *foulage à pied* and *pisador*.

TREBBIANO *(ITALY)*   A white grape variety grown primarily in Italy, although it is also grown in lesser quantities in France and California. The grape is believed to have originated in Tuscany in the thirteenth century and exported to France around the time of the Pope's transfer to Avignon from Rome. There was once even a black Trebbiano grape, no longer in existence, around the mid-1300s. In the Cognac region of France the grape is known as *St-Emilion* and in California as *Ugni Blanc*.

Also known as *Albano, Procanico, Rossetto, Rossola, Spoletino, Trebbiano d'Abruzzo, Trebbiano di Lugana, Trebbiano di Romagna, Trebbiano di Soave, Trebbiano Giallo, Trebbiano Nostrano*, and *Trebbiano Toscano*.

TREBBIANO D'ABRUZZO *(ITALY)*   A white grape variety used to make a dry, white DOC wine of the same produced in the southern region of Abruzzo.

TREBBIANO DI LUGANA *(ITALY)*   *See* Trebbiano.

TREBBIANO DI ROMAGNA *(ITALY)*   *See* Trebbiano.

TREBBIANO DI SOAVE *(ITALY)*   *See* Trebbiano.

TREBBIANO GIALLO (ITALY)   *See* Trebbiano.

TREBBIANO NOSTRANO (ITALY)   *See* Trebbiano.

TREBBIANO TOSCANO (ITALY)   *See* Trebbiano.

TREGNUM   *See* Tappit-Hen.

TREIXADURA (SPAIN)   *See* Trajadura.

TREN (SPAIN)   A bottling line, used in preparation for shipping.

TRENTINO-ALTO ADIGE (ITALY)   The northernmost of the twenty wine-producing regions; it makes some of the finest red and white wines, many of which are of DOC quality. Such diverse grape varieties as Chardonnay, Gewürztraminer, Pinot Bianco, Pinot Grigio, and Sauvignon Blanc constitutes the whites, and Cabernet Sauvignon, Merlot, Pinot Noir, and Schiava make up the reds.

TRESALLIER (FRANCE)   *See* Sacy.

TRESTER (GERMANY)   *See* Grappa.

TREVISO (ITALY)   One of the seven provinces that make up the region of Veneto; also known as the *Marca Trevigiana*, it borders on the Dolomite Mountains to the north, the region of Friuli-Venezia Giulia to the east, the province of Venice, twenty-five miles to the south, and Padua to the west. The Piave River, one of Italy's most important waterways, flows south through the province to the Adriatic.

A wide range of both native and imported grape varieties are grown in the area. Of the total wine production, 60 percent is red and 40 percent white. Most of the wine produced in Treviso comes from six grape varieties. Three are white: Prosecco, Verduzzo, and Tocai Italico; and three are red: Merlot, Cabernet, and Raboso. Other varieties grown are Verdiso, Pinot Bianco, Pinot Grigio, Pinot Noir, Riesling Italico, and Sauvignon Blanc.

TRIAGE (FRANCE)   *See* Épluchage.

TRICHLOROANISOLE   *See* Corked.

TRIM   That part of a product removed to prepare the item for consumption.

TRINCADEIRA (PORTUGAL)   A white grape variety grown in the Douro and Alentejo regions.

TRIOSE   A monosaccharide, having three carbon atoms in its molecule; it is often used for sweetening alcoholic and nonalcoholic beverages.

TRIPLE SEC   A clear, sweet, orange-flavored liqueur. *See* Curaçao.

TROCKEN (GERMANY)   *See* Dry.

TROCKEN (GERMANY)   A wine designation that was put into effect by the wine authority of the Common Market in Brussels on August 1, 1977. The reason for this designation was that some people prefer wines drier than most of the German wines on the market.

Trocken wines contain a maximum of nine grams per liter of residual sugar (which can also be expressed as 0.9 grams per hundred milliliters, or 0.9 percent residual sugar). The sugar level cannot exceed the acidity level by more than two grams. For example, if a wine has five grams of acidity, its maximum sugar level can only be seven grams per liter.

TROCKENBEERENAUSLESE (GERMANY) Sometimes abbreviated TBA. A wine made entirely from late-picked, individually selected grapes (resembling raisins) that have been allowed to dry and shrivel on the grapevine after they've been attacked by *Botrytis cinerea*. These grapes, which are extremely high in sugar, produce one of the sweetest and rarest wines in the world, extremely rich and luscious-tasting. *See Botrytis Cinerea.*

TROIANO (ITALY) *See* Uva di Troia.

TROISIÈME TAILLE (FRANCE) The third pressing of the grapes in champagne-making, no longer permitted under AOC regulations (1992).

TROJA (ITALY) A red grape variety grown primarily in Apulia.

TROLLINGER (GERMANY) *See* Schiava Grossa.

TRONÇAIS OAK (FRANCE) A single, small, state-owned forest in the Allier region, just south of Nevers, noted for its production of extremely hard wood. Tronçais has a medium-tight grain and moderate flavor and tannin extraction. Its flavors are similar to Allier, though slightly richer, with an intense, undefined, spicy component. Tronçais is used with Nevers and Allier oak in Burgundy as well as in Bordeaux for Chardonnay and Cabernet Sauvignon.

TROUBLE (FRANCE) *See* Turbid.

TROUSSEAU *See* Bastardo.

TROUSSEAU GRIS *See* Chauché Gris.

TRUNK The relatively permanent, above-ground, main stem or body of the grapevine. There may be one or more trunks per grapevine.

TRYFERÓS (GREECE) Mild.

TSIGOUTHIA (GREECE) *See* Grappa.

TUFA (ITALY) Volcanic soil. Also spelled *tufo.*

TUFO (ITALY) *See* Tufa.

TUILÉ (FRANCE) The brick-red or tile-red color often displayed by red wines when they are becoming old and tired.

TULE REEDS Thin strips of a flexible grass that grows in marshes, especially in the southwest United States; they are utilized in barrel making. These thin strips are often placed between the wooden staves of a barrel, forming a tight joint that prevents leakage.

TULILLAH (AUSTRALIA) A white grape variety.

TULIP-SHAPED GLASS The proper glassware for champagne and sparkling wines; it is in the shape of a tulip and has a capacity of eight to ten ounces. *See* Flute-Shaped Glass and Saucer-Shaped Glass.

TUMBLER *See* Old-Fashioned Glass.

TUMULTUOSA (ITALY)   *See* Tumultuous.

TUMULTUOUS   Describes the noisy and sometimes violent bubbling observed during the primary fermentation of wine, beer, or distilled spirits. Also known as *fermentación tumultuosa* and *tumultuosa*.

TUN   *See* Barrel.

TUN TAVERN   The first recruiting of marines is reported to have been done at this Philadelphia tavern. The proprietor of the inn, one Robert Mullan, was commissioned a captain of the marines and served as one of the chief marine recruiters during the Revolutionary War. Lures for the recruits included offers of prize money, bounties, promises of pensions, and prospects of ample grog and other rations. Tun Tavern is traditionally regarded as the birthplace of the United States Marine Corps.

TURBID   Describes a cloudy or muddy beer or wine, the result of having its sediment stirred or shaken up. Also known as *torbido, turbio,* and *trouble.*

TURBIO (SPAIN)   *See* Turbid.

TURM (GERMANY)   Tower.

TURNOVER   The frequency and number of times a stock of beverages is sold and replenished in a given operating period of time; an activity ratio.

TURNSOLE   A purple vegetable dye obtained from the *Croton tinctoria* plant, sometimes used in the nineteenth century by the French to darken the wines of Bordeaux.

TUSCANY (ITALY)   One of twenty wine-producing regions, located in central Italy, north of Latium, famous for its production of Chianti, Carmignano, Brunello di Montalcino, and Vino Nobile di Montepulciano (red wines), and Vernaccia di San Gimignano, Galestro, and Vin Santo (white wines). Known as *Toscano* in Italy.

TWADELL   A seldom-used measuring system in the United States utilizing a hydrometer for determining degrees of sugar in the *must. See* Hydrometer.

TWIGGY   *See* Stemmy.

TWIST   A strip of citrus fruit peel used as a garnish in some cocktails.

TYLOSES   The internal grain patterns of wood (used in barrel making), with their maze of interwoven crossmembers.

TYPE   Further division of the classes of alcoholic beverages. Thus whiskey types, brandy types, and so on, used in the Universal Numeric Code (UNIMERC). *See* Class.

TYPHA LATIFOGLIA   A plant whose broad, flat leaves are occasionally dried and used to patch leaks in wooden barrels, almost like gasket material. In Italy, it is used as a wrapping for fiasco-shaped wine bottles. *See* Paraffin.

UARNACCIA *(ITALY)* *See* Guarnaccia.

ÜBERSCHWEFELT *(GERMANY)* Wines that are overly sulfured; the sulfer can be detected by its pungent odor.

UBHIYA The term for beer in the Zulu nation of Africa. *See* Beer.

UBRIACO *(ITALY)* Inebriate.

ÙE *(ITALY)* A distillate from a mixture of pomace and wine. *See* Grappa.

UGHETTA *(ITALY)* A red grape variety.

UGNI BLANC *See* Trebbiano.

UGNI NOIR *See* Aramon.

UISGEBEATHA Gaelic word meaning "water of life." *See* Aqua Vitae.

ULLAGE The air space in a bottle between the top of the wine and the bottom of the cork. Also known as *coulage*. *See* Headspace and Leakage.

ULL DE LLEBRE *(SPAIN)* The local name in Catalonia for the Tempranillo grape variety. *See* Tempranillo.

ULTRA BRUT *See* Extra Brut.

ULTRAFILTRATION A tangential-flow filtration system that utilizes a high pressure range (usually from 10 to 150 psi) membrane system in order to separate high molecular weight dissolved materials from aqueous solutions on the basis of size. Lower weight molecules (such as salts, sugars, color pigments, flavor constituents) can pass through membranes designed for wine filtrations, while solids, colloids, and larger molecules cannot pass through. *See* Filtering.

UMBRIA *(ITALY)* One of twenty wine-producing regions; it is surrounded by Tuscany, Latium, and the Marches. It is known as "the green heart of Italy" because it lies in the center of the peninsula and is rich in woods and pastures. The hillsides and gentle inclines of the Umbrian landscape are carpeted with olive trees and grapevines; the region's major freshwater lake—Trasimeno, which gives its name to one of the area's three DOC wines—is surrounded by vineyards. The Tiber River flows from north to south through the eastern part of the region, creating the Upper Tiber Valley, a major viticultural zone of Umbria. Perugia, the region's capital city, stands on a hilltop just east of Lake Trasimeno. The smaller towns of Orvieto and Torgiano have lent their names to the DOC and DOCG wines of the region.

Umbria's major wine-producing areas include the Colli Altotiberini to the north, the Colli del Trasimeno to the west, Torgiano (near Assisi), and the well-known Orvieto zone in the southwest.

UNBALANCED   Describes a wine whose various components have not cohesively come together (for instance, alcohol, tannin, fruit, and acidity). The opposite of balanced. Also known as *unharmonisch*.

UNCINULA NECATOR   *See* Powdery Mildew.

UNCTUOUS   Describes a wine that is rich, fat, and lush-tasting, with an almost oily texture to it; unctuousness is found in some full-bodied, very sweet wines. Also known as *onctueux* and *untuoso*. *See* Oily.

UNDERBACK   The receiving tank for the *wort*, necessary in the brewing process of beer.

UNDERBAR   That part of the bar that houses equipment (blenders, etc.), ice bins, bottle wells, speed racks, and other supplies necessary for the production of cocktails.

UNDERPROOF   Describes a distilled spirit containing less than 100 proof.

UNDER THE TABLE   *See* Intoxicated.

UNDEVELOPED   Describes wines that need further aging, either in wooden barrels or in glass bottles. Also known as *unenwickelt*.

UNENWICKELT (GERMANY)   *See* Undeveloped.

UNFILTERED   Describes a wine that has been bottled without being clarified or stabilized by filtration. However, the wine could have received other cellar treatments (e.g., fining). *See* Filtering.

UNFINED   Describes a wine that has been bottled without being fined by one of many fining agents. However, the wine could have received other cellar treatments (e.g., filtering). *See* Fining.

UNGEZUCKERT (GERMANY)   Unsugared; pure.

UNHARMONISCH (GERMANY)   *See* Unbalanced.

UNIMERC   *See* Class and Type.

UNION   Where the stock and scion of the grapevine are joined.

UNIT   A specified quantity, usually referring to the number or amount in a pack; may be expressed as weight in pounds or ounces; volume in quarts, liters, or gallons; or count in each dozen, case, gross, and so on.

UNIT COST   The price paid to acquire a specific unit.

UNITED STATES WINE   Wine produced on bonded wine premises in the United States.

UNIT PRICE   A supplementary system of pricing commodities, especially beverages, by showing the prices in terms of standard units (ounces or milliliters); it facilitates a comparison of prices of competing items.

UNIVERSITY OF BORDEAUX ENOLOGY INSTITUTE *(FRANCE)*   The name of Bordeaux's premier enological and viticultural school; it was founded in February 1948.

UNIVERSITY OF CALIFORNIA, DAVIS   The name of California's premier enological and viticultural school, located in Sacramento. The university purchased the Davis Farm in 1906.

UNMERCHANTABLE WINE   Wine that had been taxpaid, removed from bonded wine premises, and subsequently returned to a bonded wine premises for the purpose of reconditioning, reformulation, or destruction.

UNRIPE   Describes wines made from grapes that have not reached physiologic maturity. These wines lack aroma, taste, and other tactile impressions displayed in mature grapes. They also tend to be thin and watery, with relatively high levels of acidity. *See* Green and Young.

UNSOUND   The opposite of sound.

UNTER *(GERMANY)*   Below.

UNTERSCHWEFELT *(GERMANY)*   Lacking sulfur; those wines with insufficient levels of sulfur dioxide oxidize quickly and are subject to bacterial infestation.

UNTUOSO *(ITALY AND SPAIN)*   *See* Unctuous.

UP   Any drink that is served without ice or *straight up*, meaning "up off the ice." Also known as *straight up*.

UPCHARGE   Premium charged on a gift product to either fully or partially capture the additional cost of the gift wrap, carton, and so forth.

URALT *(GERMANY)*   Brandy that has been aged at least one year.

URBANA   A grape variety developed from a cross of Governor Ross and Mills at the New York State Experimental Station in 1912.

UR-BOCK *(GERMANY)*   A beer that has a darker color and is slightly fuller in body than traditional *bock beer*. *See* Bock Beer.

URSPRUNGSBEZEICHNUNG *(GERMANY)*   A statement of origin.

URZIGER *(GERMANY)*   A small village in the northern part of the Mosel region; it produces dry white wines with a spicy character that are slow-maturing.

USABLE PORTION   The portion of a product that has a value; the amount being used in a recipe that has a resale value.

USÉ *(FRANCE)*   *See* Tired.

USQUEBAUGH   *See* Aqua Vitae.

USSALARA *(ITALY)*   A white grape variety.

UVA *(ITALY* AND *SPAIN)*   *See* Grape.

UVA AMERICANA *(ITALY)*   *See* Isabella.

UVA ASPRINA *(ITALY)*   *See* Asprinio.

UVA CANE *(ITALY)*   *See* Negro Amaro.

UVA DELLA MARINA *(ITALY)*   *See* Uva di Troia.

UVA DE MESA *(SPAIN)*   A dessert grape.

UVA DI CANOSA *(ITALY)*   *See* Uva di Troia.

UVA DI CORATO *(ITALY)*   *See* Primitivo di Gioia.

UVA DI TROIA *(ITALY)*   A red grape variety grown primarily in Apulia. Also known as *Barlettana, Nero di Troia, Tranese, Troiano, Uva della Marina, Uva di Canosa*, and *Vitigno di Barletta*.

UVAGGIO *(ITALY)*   *See* Cuvée.

UVA NAVARRA *(ITALY)*   *See* Gaglioppo.

UVA PASAS *(SPAIN)*   *See* Raisins.

UVA RARA *(ITALY)*   A red grape variety grown in Lombardy.

v \'vē\ *n, often cap, often attrib*

VA   *See* Volatile Acidity.

VACCARÈSE *(FRANCE)*   A red grape variety grown in the Rhône Valley.

VALAIS *(SWITZERLAND)*   Valley.

VALAIS *(SWITZERLAND)*   One of the most famous wine districts in Switzerland. It is a deep, sheltered valley at the headwaters of the Rhône, where carefully grown and terraced vineyards step up the mountainsides, reaching very high altitudes (the Visperterminen vineyard, the highest in Europe, is at four thousand feet). The high Alps shield Valais from winds and storms, giving it one of Switzerland's most temperate climates in summer, although the winters are bitterly cold. Since Valais is the most arid section of Switzerland, the grapevines are irrigated with water taken from mountainside canals fed by the melting glaciers. The rich lowlands of Valais are famous for their lush fruits, especially the pears that are used to make Switzerland's celebrated pear brandy. Winemakers of the Valais district produce delicate white wines and Dôle, a full-bodied red wine.

VAL D'AOSTA *(ITALY)*   *See* Valle d'Aosta.

VALDEPEÑAS *(SPAIN)*   A red grape variety also grown in California.

VALDEPEÑAS *(SPAIN)*   A grape-growing district located in the La Mancha area, south of Madrid. Its name means "valley of stones." Valdepeñas produces a large quantity of light-bodied red wines referred to as *vino manchego*.

VALDIGUIÉ *(FRANCE)*   A red grape variety. Also known as *Napa Gamay*. *See* Gamay.

VALÉRIEN   A white grape variety. Formerly known as *Seyve-Villard 23410*.

VALGELLA *(ITALY)*   A full-bodied red wine produced primarily from the Nebbiolo grape variety in the Valtellina district of Lombardy, located in the north.

VALIANT   A red grape variety developed at the University of South Dakota.

VALLE D'AOSTA (ITALY) Smallest of Italy's twenty wine-producing regions, located in the northwest corner, producing some well-made white and red wines. Also spelled *Val d'Aosta*.

VALLÉE DE LA MARNE (FRANCE) A premium vineyard site in Champagne for the growing of Meunier grapes.

VALMUR (FRANCE) One of the seven *grand cru* vineyards of Chablis.

VALPOLICELLA (ITALY) A dry, light-bodied red wine from the region of Veneto, produced from a blend of Corvina, Rondinella, Molinara, and other grape varieties. The consorzio of Valpolicella features the Roman arena at Verona on its neck label.

VALTELLINA (ITALY) A grape-growing district in the region of Lombardy, situated in the Adda River Valley in the northern province of Sondrio, near Switzerland (about sixty miles northeast of Milan). It is one of the few places where the Nebbiolo grape, called *Chiavennasca*, has been growing since the fifth century A.D. Nebbiolo is the principal variety of the area and is grown in the terraced vineyards that scale the steep, rugged north bank of the valley. Here the grapes receive optimum exposure to the sun as well as all the other microclimatic conditions needed to flourish. Among the grape varieties grown are Rossola, Brugnola, Pignola Valtellinese, Merlot, and Pinot Noir.

The area's two DOC wines, Valtellina and Valtellina Superiore, are produced from the Nebbiolo grape. The bottle label of a Valtellina Superiore will usually carry the name of the designated area where the wine was produced. DOC law recognizes only four such geographic subdistricts for Valtellina Superiore: Sassella, Grumello, Valgella, and Inferno.

VAN BUREN A red grape variety developed in 1935 from a cross of Fredonia and Worden at the State Experimental Station in Geneva, New York.

VANILLA The smell of vanilla-bean extract that is evident in certain wines, especially Chardonnay and Cabernet Sauvignon that have been aged in certain types of new oak barrels.

VANESSA SEEDLESS A white grape variety developed in 1965 from a cross of Bath and Interlaken at the State Experimental Station in Geneva, New York.

VAPID *See* Insipid.

VAPPA (ITALY) *See* Acetic.

VARIABLE COSTS Costs that increase or decrease in direct relationship with the volume of business. A cost that is controlled by an individual (such as department head) in a company. In this case, the manager can exert some influence and act to lower the expense. Also referred to as *controllable costs*.

VARIETAL A wine made wholly or predominantly from a single grape variety identified on the label (for example, Cabernet Sauvignon, Chardonnay, Pinot Noir, Zinfandel).

VARIETAL CHARACTER The specific and unique combination of odor, taste, and sometimes tactile impression of a wine, directly attributable to the source grape variety. Also known as *sortenbukett*.

VARIETAL DESIGNATION The name of the dominant grape used in a wine. Cabernet Sauvignon, Merlot, Pinot Noir, Baco Noir, Chardonnay, Seyval, Johannisberg

Riesling, and Sauvignon Blanc are examples of grape varieties. A varietal designation on the label requires an *appellation of origin* and means that at least 75 percent of that grape variety is used in the wine. Wines made from *Vitis labrusca* grapes (a species of grapevine native to eastern North America) such as Concord are an exception because of the grape's intense flavor. *Labrusca* wines must contain a minimum of 51 percent of the specified grape variety; this is stated on the label. If the label carries no percentage statement, the wine must contain at least 75 percent of the *labrusca* variety. *Vitis vinifera* are European grapevine species, considered by many to be the world's premium wine grapes.

Wine labels are not required to bear a varietal designation. Other designations such as "red wine," "white wine," and "table wine" are used to identify the wine or the type of grape used or where it was grown. On California wine labels, designations such as "Chablis" or "Burgundy" indicate wines similar in name only to the wines originally made in geographic regions indicated by those names. Other notable examples of United States-produced generic wines are sauterne, rhine, chianti, champagne, tokay, madeira, sherry, and port. There are no federal regulations that stipulate the grape varieties that American-produced generic wines may contain.

Some wines, such as Pommard (*France*), Rüdesheimer (*Germany*), and Chianti (*Italy*) are designated with distinctive names that are permissible only on specific wines from a particular site or region within the country of origin.

VANN (*NORWAY*) *See* Water.

VARIETY *See* Grape Variety.

VARNISH *See* Lacquer.

VAROUSSET A red grape variety. Formerly known as *Seyve-Villard 23657*.

VARYS (*GREECE*) *See* Heavy.

VASO VINARIO (*ITALY*) Any type of vessel that contains wine, including the modern tanks of stainless steel.

VAT (*ENGLAND*) A tub or barrel; a large container used for the fermentation or storage of wine, beer, and distilled spirits. *See* Barrel.

VAT-ROOM A seldom-used name for the building where all the vinification processes are carried out and the barrels filled with wine or distilled spirits stored. *See* Wine Cellar.

VATTING Prior to being bottled, the flavoring whiskeys are mixed with a proportion of grain whiskey and left to marry for several weeks.

VATTING A process used during fermentation wherein the grape skins are left in contact with the *must* for a longer period of time than usual so to extract additional tannin, color, and flavonoids. *See* Extended Skin Contact.

VAUD (*SWITZERLAND*) A wine-producing canton that is made up of three grape-growing areas: Chablis, which is upstream from where the Rhône enters Lake Geneva; Lavaux, bordering the lakefront east of Lausanne; and La Côte, located between Lausanne and Geneva. Nearly all of Vaud's wines are white, called Dorins. Many also use on their labels the name of the commune or village from which the wines come. Charming, fragrant reds, labeled Salvagnins, are also produced throughout Vaud from a blend of Pinot Noir and Gamay grapes.

VAUDÉSIR (FRANCE) One of the seven *grand cru* vineyards of Chablis.

VDQS (FRANCE) *See* Vins Délimités de Qualité Supérieure.

VECCHIO (ITALY) Old.

VEEBLANC A white grape variety developed in 1953 from a cross of Cascade and Seyve-Villard 14287 at the Horticultural Research Institute, Vineland, Ontario, Canada.

VEEPORT A white grape variety developed in 1961 from a cross of Wilder and Winchell at the Horticultural Research Institute, Vineland, Ontario, Canada.

VEGETAL Describes an odor and/or taste of cooked vegetables—asparagus, bell pepper, broccoli, or cabbage—occasionally detected in some wines made from Cabernet Sauvignon and Sauvignon Blanc grapes. *See* Grassy and Herbaceous.

VEIN DE NUS (ITALY) A red grape variety grown in the region of Valle d'Aosta.

VEINS The ribs forming the interconnected framework on a grape leaf.

VELDT (FRANCE) A now obsolete unit of measurement that was used in the Cognac region. It measured approximately two gallons (twenty-seven veldts equaled a cognac barrel of 205 liters; thirty-five veldts equaled seventy-two gallons). Also spelled *veltes*.

VELHISSIMO (PORTUGAL) *See* Old.

VELHO (PORTUGAL) Old.

VELINCH *See* Wine Thief.

VELLUTATO (ITALY) *See* Velvety.

VELO (SPAIN) A surface film made primarily of *flor* which forms in certain barrels of sherry wine.

VELOCITY The turnover rate or sales volume of a particular item as compared to the rest of its competitive set.

VELOUTÉ (FRANCE) *See* Velvety.

VELTES (FRANCE) *See* Veldt.

VELVETY Describes a soft, silky, and smooth-tasting wine that is opulent and textured on the palate. This term could also be applied to some beers and distilled spirits. Also known as *samtig, vellutato*, and *velouté*. *See* Silky.

VENANGO A red grape variety first grown at Fort Venango on the Allegheny River in the United States. Also known as *Minor's Seedling*.

VENDANGE (FRANCE) *See* Année.

VENDANGE TARDIVE (FRANCE) *See* Late Harvest.

VENDANGEUR (FRANCE) A grape picker.

VENDANGE VERTE (FRANCE) *See* Crop Thinning.

VENDEMMIA (ITALY) Also known as *annata*. *See* Vintage.

VENDIMIA (SPAIN) Also known as *añada, año*, and *cosecha*. *See* Vintage.

VENDOR *See* Supplier.

VENENCIA *(SPAIN)* A special elongated silver receptacle that has a flexible whale-bone handle with a silver cup at one end and a decorative hook, also of solid silver, at the other end. This cup is plunged into a barrel and immediately filled with sherry wine. It is then removed and poured into several glasses from a height of perhaps twelve to eighteen inches.

VENENCIADOR The user of a *venencia*.

VENETO *(ITALY)* One of twenty wine-producing regions, located in the northeast. Veneto takes its name from its capital, Venice, once one of the most powerful sea nations in all history.

There are three distinct wine zones in Veneto: the Verona area, famous for Soave, Valpolicella, Amarone, and Bardolino; the Euganean hills between Vicenza and Padua, where table wines are made; and the areas of Treviso and Conegliano, which lie about forty miles due north of Venice. The latter are best known for excellent varietal wines, especially Tocai, Merlot, and Cabernet Sauvignon.

VENTILATING BUNG *See* Fermentation Lock.

VENTURA A red grape variety developed from a cross of Chelois and Elvira at the Horticultural Research Institute, Vineland, Ontario, Canada.

VENUS SEEDLESS A red grape variety developed in 1964 from a cross of Alden and New York 46000 by Dr. James N. Moore at the Arkansas Agricultural Experiment Station.

VÉRAISON *(FRANCE)* The commencement of maturation of grapes; it is distinguished by a change of color: the original green gives way to the true color (usually red) of the grape prior to it reaching its final maturity. Also known as *invaiatura*.

VERBAND DEUTSCHER SEKTKELLEREIEN *(GERMANY)* The Association of German Sekt Wineries.

VERBESSERN *(GERMANY)* A formerly used term to denote *chaptalization*. Replaced by *anreichern*. *See* Chaptalization.

VERBRAUCHER *(GERMANY)* A consumer.

VERDE *(ITALY)* *See* Green.

VERDECA *(ITALY)* A white grape variety grown primarily in Apulia and Latium.

VERDEJO *(SPAIN)* A white grape variety.

VERDELET A white grape variety developed in the late 1880s from a cross of Plantet and Seibel 4938 by Louis Seibel in France. Formerly known as *Seibel 9110* and called *Verdelet Blanc*.

VERDELET BLANC *See* Verdelet.

VERDELHO *(PORTUGAL)* A white grape variety grown primarily on the island of Madeira, where it used to produce a fortified wine called Verdelho. The Verdelho grape is believed to be a cross between the Spanish Pedro Ximénez and the Greek Verdea grape varieties. Also known as *Gouveio*.

VERDELHO FEIJÃO *(PORTUGAL)* A red grape variety, not related to the Verdelho grape, grown in the Minho area.

VERDELLO *(ITALY)*   A white grape variety used in the blend of Orvieto wine, from Umbria.

VERDICCHIO *(ITALY)*   A white grape variety grown primarily in the region of Marches, where it produces dry, white wines made from a blend of Verdicchio with the possible addition of Trebbiano Toscano and Malvasia Toscana.

Verdicchio is an indigenous grapevine that, according to legend, was used to make the wine consumed by the Visigoths in 410 A.D. as they sacked Rome. Verdicchio is occasionally bottled in the traditional amphora-shaped bottles that were used to bring wine from Greece to the Italian peninsula in ancient times. It is one of the oldest wine bottle shapes in the world, predating the Bordeaux bottle. The *consorzio's* neck label on bottles of Verdicchio depicts a heraldic lion.

VERDISO *(ITALY)*   A white grape variety.

VERDOGNOLO *(ITALY)*   Greenish reflections, as detected in some freshly made white wines.

VERDOLINO *(ITALY)*   Light green.

VERDOSO *(SPAIN)*   *See* Green.

VERDOT *(FRANCE)*   *See* Petit Verdot.

VERDUZZO *(ITALY)*   A white grape variety.

VERGENNES   A white grape variety originally found as a seedling in the garden of William E. Green at Vergennes, Vermont, in 1874.

VERGINE *(ITALY)*   *See* Marsala Vergine.

VERKAEUFER *(GERMANY)*   A vendor.

VERKEHRT *(AUSTRIA)*   A coffee containing one part coffee to four parts milk.

VERMENTINO   A white grape variety grown primarily on the islands of Corsica and Sardinia as well as in the Italian region of Valle d'Aosta.

VERMOUTH   According to the United States Bureau of Alcohol, Tobacco, and Firearms, vermouth is a type of apéritif wine that is made from grape juice and has the taste, aroma, and characteristics generally attributed to vermouth. The BATF regulations also state that apéritif wines fulfilling the characteristics of vermouth shall be so designated. Vermouth, although fortified (containing between 15 to 21 percent alcohol), is often referred to as an "aromatic" or "aromatized" wine, meaning a wine that has been altered by the infusion of *Artemisia absinthium* (any of a number of related aromatic plants) or bitter herbs. Some of the ingredients used (there are more than one hundred) are allspice, angelica, angostura, anise, benzoin, bitter almond, bitter orange, celery, chamomile, cinchona, cinnamon, clove, coca, coriander, elder, fennel, gentian, ginger, hop, marjoram, mace, myrtle, nutmeg, peach, quinine, rhubarb, rosemary, saffron, sage, sandalwood, savory (summer), thyme, vanilla, and woodruff, which is used to make May wine.

The red vermouths, most notably those from Italy and France, are always sweet and contain approximately 130 to 160 grams of sugar per liter (13 to 16 percent residual sugar per hundred milliliters). The white vermouths, also mainly from Italy and France, can be dry, semidry, or sweet, and contain less than forty grams of sugar per liter (4 percent or less residual sugar per hundred milliliters). Also known as *vermut*.

VERMUT (SPAIN) *See* Vermouth.

VERNACCIA DI ORISTANO (ITALY) A white grape variety grown primarily in Sardinia.

VERNACCIA DI SAN GIMIGNANO (ITALY) A white grape variety native to Tuscany, although small parcels are also grown on the island of Sardinia. It is also a DOCG white wine made from a blend of Vernaccia di San Gimignano and other white, non-aromatic grape varieties.

VERNATSCH (ITALY) *See* Schiava Grossa.

VERONA (ITALY) A picturesque wine-producing town located in the northeast region of Veneto; it rests on the river Adige near Lake Garda, just fifty miles west of the romantic and canal-latticed city of Venice. Verona is famous for the production of Soave, Valpolicella, Amarone, and Bardolino.

VERRE (FRANCE) Glass. The traditional Bordeaux tasting glass is tulip-shaped and preferably crystal to capture the brilliant reflections of the *robe*. It must be large enough to allow the swirling motion that releases all the subtleties of the bouquet.

VERRE ANGLAIS (FRANCE) English glass.

VERRE NOIR (FRANCE) Black glass.

VERSCHLOSSEN (GERMANY) *See* Closed In.

VERSCHNITT (AUSTRIA) *See* Blending.

VERSCHNEIDEN (GERMANY) The blending or mixing of various grape varieties or wines according to the German Wine Laws. *See* Blending.

VERT (FRANCE) *See* Green.

VERTICAL TASTING An organized tasting (generally of wines) that refers to the *depth* or extent to which particular regions and/or vintages of certain wines are represented. For example, a tasting of ten vintages of Cabernet Sauvignon from one California winery. *See* Horizontal Tasting.

VESOU (SPAIN) Sugarcane juice. In the making of rum, the sugarcane, minus its leaves, is cut and shredded by heavy rollers. The resultant *vesou* is collected, strained, decanted, and filtered.

VESPAIOLO (ITALY) A white grape variety grown in the Veneto region.

VESPARO (ITALY) A red grape variety.

VESPOLINA (ITALY) A red grape variety from Piedmont.

VEUVE (FRANCE) Widow.

VEVAY *See* Alexander.

VICTORIA (AUSTRALIA) A major grape-growing state located south of New South Wales. Its most popular grape growing areas are Bendigo, Great Western, Macedon, Murray River, and Yarra Valley.

VID (SPAIN) *See* Grapevine.

VIDAL 256 *See* Vidal Blanc.

VIDAL BLANC   A white grape variety developed in 1929 from a cross of Ugni Blanc and Rayon d'Or by J.L. Vidal, director of the Fougerat Research Station at Bois-Charente (in the Cognac region of France). Formerly known as *Vidal 256.*

VIDEIRA (*PORTUGAL*)   *See* Grapevine.

VIDUENO (*SPAIN*)   A white grape variety.

VIDURE (*FRANCE*)   *See* Cabernet Sauvignon.

VIEILLE RÉSERVE (*FRANCE*)   A label designation on armagnac, calvados, and cognac bottles that indicates that the youngest brandy used in the blend is at least six years old (armagnac), four years old (calvados), and 6-1/2 years old (cognac) (although they contain a very high percentage of brandy that has been aged for twenty, thirty, or forty years or more).

VIEILLES VIGNES (*FRANCE*)   Ungrafted grapevines.

VIEILLISSEMENT (*FRANCE*)   The maturing of wines by laying them down in a cellar with proper storage conditions (e.g., light, heat, humidity, and so on).

VIEJISIMO (*SPAIN*)   Very old.

VIEJO (*SPAIN*)   Old.

VIEN DE NUS (*ITALY*)   A red grape variety grown in the Valle d'Aosta region.

VIENNA BEER   Amber-colored beer, medium-bodied, with pronounced malty flavors. Although this was once a style of beer emanating from Vienna, it is now produced all over the world; the name now carries little meaning.

VIERTELSTÜCK (*GERMANY*)   A barrel used in the Rhine region with a capacity of approximately seventy-nine gallons. *See* Barrel.

VIEUX (*FRANCE*)   A label designation on calvados and cognac bottles that indicates that the youngest brandy used in the blend is at least three years old (calvados) or 6-1/2 years old (cognac), although they contain a very high percentage of brandy that has been aged for twenty, thirty, or forty years or more.

VIF (*FRANCE*)   *See* Lively.

VIGNA (*ITALY*)   *See* Single-Vineyard.

VIGNAIOLA (*ITALY*)   *See* Vigneron.

VIGNE (*FRANCE*)   *See* Grapevine.

VIGNERON (*FRANCE*)   A vineyardist; one who nurtures grapevines; a grape-grower; also a combination winemaker and grape-grower. Also known as *vignaiola. See* Vintner.

VIGNETI (*ITALY*)   *See* Single-Vineyard.

VIGNETO (*ITALY*)   *See* Single-Vineyard.

VIGNOBLE (*FRANCE*)   *See* Vineyard.

VIGNOLES   A white grape variety developed in 1929 from a cross of Pinot Noir and Seibel 6905 by J.F. Ravat. Formerly known as *Ravat 51.*

VIGOR   The rate of growth of a grapevine.

VIGOROUS   *See* Lively.

VIGOROUS GRAPEVINES   Grapevines with shoots that grow rapidly and produce considerable growth.

VIILE *(ROMANIA)* *See* Vineyard.

VIJIRIEGAS *(SPAIN)* A white grape variety grown in Málaga.

VILLA *(ITALY)* A country manor house.

VILLARD BLANC A white grape variety developed in 1924 from a cross of Seibel 6468 and Seibel 6905. Formerly known as *Seyve-Villard 12375*.

VILLARD NOIR A red grape variety developed from a cross of Chancellor and Seibel 6905; it was released in 1930. Formerly known as *Seyve-Villard 18315*.

VIN *(FRANCE* AND *NORWAY)* *See* Wine.

VIÑA *(SPAIN)* *See* Vineyard.

VINACCIA *(ITALY)* *See* Pomace.

VINAI *(ITALY)* Winemakers. *See* Winemaker.

VINAIGRE *(FRANCE)* *See* Vinegar.

VINAIGRIER *(FRANCE)* The small wooden barrels in which vinegar is made.

VIN AROMATIQUE *(FRANCE)* A wine that displays a very pronounced aroma or scent.

VIN BLANC *(FRANCE)* *See* White Wine.

VINCENT NOIR A red grape variety developed in 1967 at the Horticultural Research Institute, Vineland, Ontario, Canada.

VIN CHAUD *(FRANCE)* *See* Mulled Wine.

VIN CLAIR *(FRANCE)* A clear wine. *See* Clear.

VIN CUIT *(FRANCE)* Also known as *cuit*. *See* Cooked Wine.

VIN DE CARAFE *(FRANCE)* *See* House Wine.

VIN DE COULE *(FRANCE)* Wine made from the first pressing of the grapes.

VIN DE CUVÉE *(FRANCE)* Wine made from the pressing of the grapes in Champagne.

VIN DE GARDE *(FRANCE)* Wine for keeping or laying down. Due to the richness of its components (color, tannin, and bouquet), it develops slowly and preserves all its qualities while reaching a grand old age.

VIN DE GOUTTE *(FRANCE)* *See* Free-Run Juice.

VIN DE L'ANNÉE *(FRANCE)* *See* Nouveau.

VIN DE MESSE *(FRANCE)* *See* Sacramental Wines.

V

VIN DE PAILLE (SPAIN)   *See* Straw Mats.

VIN DE PAYS (FRANCE)   A classification of wines, established in 1973, which are one step above *vin ordinaire* in quality.

VIN DE PRESSE (FRANCE)   *See* Press Juice.

VIN DE PRIMEUR (FRANCE)   *See* Nouveau.

VIN DE SABLE (FRANCE)   Wines made from grapes grown predominantly in sandy soil.

VIN DE TABLE (FRANCE)   *See* Vino da Tavola.

VIN DE TAILLE (FRANCE)   Wine made from the harder and less desirable pressings of the grapes, used in making champagne. This is no longer permitted under AOC regulations (1994).

VIN DE TÊTE (FRANCE)   *See* Tête de Cuvée.

VINDIMA (PORTUGAL)   Also known as *ano de colheita*. *See* Vintage.

VIN DOUX NATUREL (FRANCE)   A category of sweet, fortified dessert wines, red or white, with an alcoholic content in excess of 14 percent by volume.

VIN DU PAYS (FRANCE)   Country wine; used to describe ordinary wines of each region that are consumed locally. This term carries no legal meaning.

VIN DU ROI (FRANCE)   The wine of kings.

VINE   Any plant with long, thin stems that grows above the ground or climbs a wall or other supports by means of tendrils.

VINE CAPACITY   The capability of the total growth of the grapevine in one season. It is measured by determining the weight of annual cane prunings. *See* Cane Weight.

VIÑEDO (SPAIN)   *See* Vineyard.

VINEGAR   Wine or wine product not for beverage use, which contains not less than 4.0 grams (4 percent) of volatile acidity (calculated as acetic acid and exclusive of sulfur dioxide) per hundred milliliters of wine. Also known as *aceto, vinaigre*, and *wine vinegar*. *See* Volatile Acidity.

VINER (FRANCE)   The practice of adding alcohol to a wine in order to fortify it.

VINERED   A white grape variety developed in 1964 from a cross of Brocton and Ontario at the State Experimental Station in Geneva, New York.

VINE SIZE   *See* Cane Weight.

VINE STOCK   The name given to the different varieties of grapevines from which wines are generally made.

VINEUX (FRANCE)   *See* Vinosity.

VINE VIGOR   The seasonal rate of growth of the shoots of a grapevine.

VINEYARD   Land devoted to the growing of grapevines. Also known as *einzellage, lozia, vignoble, viile, viña, viñedo, vinha, vinhedo*, and *weinberg*.

Vin Gris (FRANCE)   Describes the pale, almost rosé color of certain wines made either with limited skin contact or with grapes grown in those geographical areas of the world far from the equator, where the red grapes do not fully ripen and therefore the color is not deeper or darker. Occasionally referred to as *oeil de perdrix*—literally, eye of the partridge. Also known as *gris*.

Vinha (PORTUGAL)   *See* Vineyard.

Vinhão (PORTUGAL)   A red grape variety used in the making of Vinho Verde wine.

Vinhedo (PORTUGAL)   Small vineyard. *See* Vineyard.

Vinho (PORTUGAL)   *See* Wine.

Vinho Abafado (PORTUGAL)   Fortified wine. Also known as *abafado* and *vinho alcolisado*.

Vinho Alcolisado (PORTUGAL)   Also known as *alcolisado*. *See* Vinho Abafado.

Vinho Aperitive (PORTUGAL)   *See* Apéritif Wine.

Vinho Branco (PORTUGAL)   *See* White Wine.

Vinho Canteiro (PORTUGAL)   Wine that has been made and matured without being put through the process of *estufagem*.

Vinho Clarete (PORTUGAL AND SPAIN)   *See* Clarete.

Vinho Consumo (PORTUGAL)   *See* Ordinary.

Vinho de Mesa (PORTUGAL)   *See* Vino da Tavola.

Vinho do Rodo (PORTUGAL)   *See* Sparkling Wine.

Vinho Engarrafado (PORTUGAL)   Bottled wine.

Vinho Espumante (PORTUGAL)   Also known as *espumante* and *vinho do rodo*. *See* Sparkling Wine.

Vinho Estufado (PORTUGAL)   Wine that has already been through the process of *estufagem*. Also known as *estufado*.

Vinho Liquoroso (PORTUGAL)   *See* Dessert Wine.

Vinho Maduro (PORTUGAL)   *See* Maturity.

Vinho Rosado (PORTUGAL)   *See* Rosé Wine.

Vinho Seco (PORTUGAL)   Dry wine. *See* Dry.

Vinho Tinto (PORTUGAL)   *See* Red Wine.

Vinho Verde (PORTUGAL)   A term meaning "green wine." It is produced in the northwest corner of Portugal. These wines are often quite young, most of them bottled only four months after harvest, and are not meant to be stored away for prolonged aging. Their charm lies in their youthfulness, spritzy character, and absolutely clean, crisp, and refreshing taste.

Vini (ITALY)   Wines.

VINI BIANCHI *(ITALY)* White wines.

VINICULTURA *(SPAIN)* *See* Viniculture.

VINICULTURE The theory, art, and science of winemaking. Also known as *vinicultura*.

VINIFERA *See Vitis Vinifera.*

VINIFICATION The entire process of converting grapes or other ripe fruits into wine, which includes crushing/destemming, fermenting, pressing, aging, bottling, and so on. Also known as *vinificato, vinificazione, vinify,* and *weinbereitung.*

VINIFICATO *(ITALY)* Vinified. *See* Vinification.

VINIFICATO IN BIANCO *(ITALY)* *See* Blanc de Noirs.

VINIFICAZIONE *(ITALY)* *See* Vinification.

VINIFY *See* Vinification.

VINI PREGIATI *(ITALY)* Valued wines.

VINI ROSATI *(ITALY)* Rosé wines.

VINI ROSSI *(ITALY)* Red wines.

VINI TIPICI *(ITALY)* A category below DOC for wines typical of certain defined geographical areas. Also known as *vino tipico.*

VIN MOUSSEUX *(FRANCE)* Also known as *mousseux. See* Sparkling Wine.

VIN NATURE *(FRANCE)* A natural, still, or sparkling wine that has not been sweetened. The term carries no legal meaning.

VIN NATURE DE LA CHAMPAGNE *(FRANCE)* An obsolete term once used to describe the still wines of Champagne. *See* Coteaux Champenoise.

VINO *(ITALY* AND *SPAIN)* *See* Wine.

VINO ABOCADO *(SPAIN)* *See* Semidry Wine.

VINO BIANCO *(ITALY)* *See* White Wine.

VINO BLANCO *(SPAIN)* *See* White Wine.

VINO CLARETE *(PORTUGAL* AND *SPAIN)* *See* Clarete.

VINO COMÚN *(SPAIN)* *See* Ordinary.

VINO CORRIENTE *(SPAIN)* *See* Ordinary.

VINO COTTO *(ITALY)* *See* Cooked Wine.

VINO CRUDO *(SPAIN)* *See* Young.

VINO DA PASTO *(ITALY)* *See* Ordinary.

VINO DA TAGLIO *(ITALY)* *See* Blending.

VINO DA TAVOLA *(ITALY)* Table wine; a defined wine classification according to the laws of 1963, equivalent to *normalwein* (Austria); *stolno vino* (Yugoslavia); *vin de table* (France); *tafelwein* (Germany), *vinho de mesa* (Portugal), and *vino de mesa* (Spain). *See* Table Wine.

VINI BIANCHI (ITALY)

V

VINO DE AGUJA *(SPAIN)* *See* Spritz.

VINO DE CALIDAD *(SPAIN)* Quality wine. Must be a *denominación de origen* wine made from the free-run or lightly pressed juice of ripe, healthy grapes that has undergone a controlled fermentation.

VINO DE COSECHA *(SPAIN)* Wines of a particular vintage year. In special cases, if the purpose is to maximize the quality of the wine, a maximum of 15 percent of wine of a previous year may be added. Also known as *vino de vendimia*.

VINO DE COSECHA PROPIA *(SPAIN)* Estate bottled.

VINO DE CRIANZA *(SPAIN)* *See* Crianza.

VINO DE MESA *(SPAIN)* *See* Vino da Tavola.

VINO DE PASTO *(SPAIN)* *See* Ordinary.

VINO DE RANCIO *(SPAIN)* *See* Rancio.

VINO DE VENDIMIA *(SPAIN)* *See* Vino de Cosecha.

VINO DE XÉRÈS *(SPAIN)* Sherry wine.

VINO ESPUMOSA *(SPAIN)* Also known as *espumosa. See* Sparkling Wine.

VINO FRIZZANTE *(ITALY)* *See* Spritz.

VINO GASIFICADO *(SPAIN)* *See* Charmat Method.

VINO GENEROSO *(SPAIN)* *See* Generous.

VINO JOVEN *(SPAIN)* Also known as *joven. See* Young.

VINO LIQUOROSO *(ITALY)* *See* Dessert Wine.

VINOMETER An instrument utilized to measure the approximate alcohol content of dry wines. It consists of a capillary tube with a scale on one end and an opening at the other end where wine is poured for measuring. The device is not very accurate and is used mostly by home winemakers.

VINO NOBILE DI MONTEPULCIANO *(ITALY)* A dry, full-bodied red wine produced in a small area surrounding the town of Montepulciano in the province of Siena in Tuscany.

This wine was famous in the fourteenth and fifteenth centuries and was a favorite of Pope Paul III. Its name, which means "noble wine," derives from the fact that it was produced exclusively for the titled families who lived in the area.

Vino Nobile de Montepulciano was granted its DOCG status in 1982. It must be aged a minimum of two years and, if aged three years, it is entitled to be labeled *riserva*. It must have a minimum of 12.5 percent alcohol and be made from a blend of Prugnolo Gentile (Sangiovese Grosso), Canaiolo Nero, Malvasia del Chianti, and several other grape varieties. The Vino Nobile di Montepulciano *consorzio* features on its neck label a griffin rampant on a white background within a red circle.

VIN NOUVEAU *(FRANCE)* *See* Nouveau.

VINO NOVELLO *(ITALY)* A new or freshly fermented wine similar to the Beaujolais Nouveau of France. An Italian law of 1989 stipulates that the appellation *vino novello* can be applied only to table wines with a designated geographic origin or possessing characteristics typical of the growing zone of the grape. Vino novello must be made with grapes of the current vintage and bottled before December 31, but may not be released before November 6. The maximum limit on residual-reducing sugars cannot exceed 0.6 grams per hundred milliliters. The minimum alcohol level is set at 11 percent. At least 30 percent of the wine must be obtained through the *carbonic maceration* system in which the entire grape is used. The wine is also required to bear a vintage date. Also known as *novello*. *See* Nouveau.

VIN ORDINAIRE *(FRANCE)* Inexpensive, common, ordinary, everyday wines below the VDQS level of quality. The term includes almost 70 percent of all French wines; they are not controlled by the government. *See* Ordinary.

VINO PRETTO *(ITALY)* A wine that is pure or genuine. Also known as *pretto*. *See* Vin Santo.

VINO ROSADO *(SPAIN)* *See* Rosé Wine.

VINO ROSATO *(ITALY)* *See* Rosé Wine.

VINO ROSSO *(ITALY)* *See* Red Wine.

VINOTHEK *(AUSTRIA)* *See* Enoteca.

VIN SANTO *(ITALY)* This unfortified dessert wine is produced in several regions of Italy, each claiming that theirs is the true area of origin. Vin Santo Toscano is made from the ripest Malvasia del Chianti grapes (although Trebbiano Toscano, Grechetto, or even red grapes can be utilized), which are tied together and either hung from the beams of a well-ventilated room or dried on straw mats. This process results in the evaporation of a high percentage of the grapes' water content, at the same time increasing the percentage of sugar. The higher the sugar content of the grape, the higher the resulting alcoholic content and the richer the final product. For a sweet Vin Santo, the bunches are left to raisin for about two-and-one-half months; for a Vin Santo that is semidry to dry, they are left about two months.

The grapes are crushed during the winter and the *must* placed in oak barrels with a capacity of approximately fifty-nine gallons for a period of about two years, followed by three years in smaller chestnut or oak barrels called *caratelli,* which have a capacity of approximately thirteen gallons. The same barrels are used over and over again and a small amount of the previous Vin Santo (*madre*) is always left inside to blend with the new must (similar to sherry *solera* production). The barrels are filled to three-quarters capacity, closed with a cork or wooden bung, and placed in the winery's attic or a heated room called a *vinsanteria*, where the wine is left to slowly ferment. Each winter, fermentation is interrupted by the cold, but it starts again in the spring. During fermentation, carbon dioxide accumulates and creates high pressure that slows down the process. For this reason the barrels are stored directly under the roof of the winery, where the summer heat causes the wood of the top part of the barrel not in contact with the wine to contract, allowing air to enter and oxidation to occur. This gives Vin Santo its characteristic amber-brown color and contributes to the complexity of its aroma. Another characteristic of this special aging process is the development of a sort of cooked or *maderized* taste in the wine.

This famous Tuscan dessert wine was called *Vino Pretto* until 1349, when the name was changed to Vin Santo. The origin of this unusual name has not been firmly established. Some sources claim the wine is called "saintly" because it is used during Holy Mass or because the grapes are crushed during Holy Week. Others claim that during the

VIN ORDINAIRE (FRANCE)

V

Ecumenical Council in Florence called by Pope Eugenius VI in 1349, Cardinal Bessarione of Nicaea, patriarch of the Greek Orthodox church, upon being served a glass of Vin Pretto, exclaimed, "This is the Wine of Xantos," referring to a wine from his homeland. His colleagues understood him to be calling the wine "Santo" and the name stuck. Whichever story one believes, one thing is for sure: the name Vin Santo literally means "holy wine" or "wine of the Saints." Vin Santo is occasionally spelled *vino santo*. *See* Vino Pretto.

VINOS DE MISA (SPAIN)   *See* Sacramental Wines.

VINO SECCO (ITALY)   Dry wine. *See* Dry.

VINO SECO (SPAIN)   Dry wine. *See* Dry.

VINOSITY   The wine-like aroma or flavor of wine, which is due to its alcohol content. Also known as *vineux, vinoso, vinous flavor, weinig*, and *winy*.

VINOSO (ITALY)   *See* Vinosity.

VINO SPUMANTE (ITALY)   *See* Sparkling Wine.

VINO TIPICO (ITALY)   *See* Vini Tipici.

VINOUS   A term applied to a wine without a specific, distinguishable odor or flavor, however well it is made. Also known as *eklektós* and *franc de goût*.

VINOTHÉQUE (FRANCE)   *See* Enothéque.

VINO TINTO (SPAIN)   *See* Red Wine.

VIN ROSÉ (FRANCE)   *See* Rosé Wine.

VIN ROUGE (FRANCE)   *See* Red Wine.

VINS DÉLIMITÉS DE QUALITÉ SUPÉRIEURE (VDQS) (FRANCE)   A classification of wines that is just slightly below the AOC designation in quality. First authorized for use on December 18, 1949.

VIN SEC (FRANCE)   Dry wine. *See* Dry.

VINTAGE   The year that the grapes were picked or harvested for the making of wine, with the date shown on the label. A season of unusually favorable growing conditions is called a "vintage year" and is said to produce "vintage wines," connoting a very good year. Also known as *jahrgang, vendemmia, vendimia*, and *vindima*. *See* Harvest, Vintage Wine, and Year of the Harvest.

VINTAGE CHARACTER (PORTUGAL)   A port that is made from a blend of two or more vintages; it is similar in style and character to a late-bottled vintage port. Also known as *tipo vintage* and *vintage style*.

VINTAGE CHART   A report, chart, or guide developed to give retailers, restaurateurs, and consumers an indication of how a particular vintage or growing season progressed and what the final outcome was relative to the quantity and quality of the grapes harvested.

VINTAGE DATE   A vintage date on the label indicates that 95 percent or more of the wine is produced from grapes grown in that year. If a vintage date is shown on the label, an appellation of origin other than a country will also be shown.

VINTAGE PORT   Vintage port constitutes only about 2 percent of Portugal's port production and is produced only in years that are declared by the majority of shippers to be among the very best (usually only three or four vintages in a decade). A vintage port must be declared by the shipper between January 1 and September 30 of the second year after the harvest. It is aged for two years in wooden barrels, then bottled sometime between July 1 of the second year and June 30 of the third year after the harvest. Vintage port is very difficult to drink in its youth because it is fiery and peppery, with an almost black color. Its sweetness is masked by concentrated packed fruit, high extract, and dry, mouth-puckering tannins.

Surprisingly, it was not until 1775 that the first vintage port was produced. Beginning with vintages after 1970, all port must be bottled by the producer and since 1975, all vintage port must be bottled in Oporto, Portugal.

VINTAGE STYLE   *See* Vintage Character Port.

VINTAGE WINE   Wine from a single year stated on the label rather than a blend from several years. Also known as *millésimé*. *See* Harvest and Vintage.

VINTED AND BOTTLED BY   *See* Cellared and Bottled By.

VINTNER   One who sells wine. The term is used broadly to designate grape-growers, wine blenders, and wholesaler wine merchants. *See* Vigneron.

VINUM   Latin for wine. *See* Wine.

VIOGNIER *(FRANCE)*   A white grape variety grown primarily in the Rhône Valley, although it is believed to have been brought there by the Greeks more than two thousand years ago. Viognier produces wines that are full-bodied and rich-tasting, with fine floral fragrances often reminiscent of orange blossoms and honeysuckle as well as pear, peach, and melon. Some Viognier is grown in California.

VIOLACEO *(ITALY)*   Violet-colored. *See* Purple.

VIOLETS   An intriguing scent occasionally detected in some red wines, mostly from northern Italy as well as Bordeaux and the Rhône Valley of France.

VIOSINHO *(PORTUGAL)*   A white grape variety used in the making of white port wine.

VIRGIN BRANDY   *See* Alcools Blancs.

VIRGIN DRINKS   *See* Mocktails.

VIRGINIA   In Jamestown in 1608, the first wine bottles in the future United States were produced.

VIRGINIA SEEDLING   *See* Norton.

VIRGIN MARY   A Bloody Mary minus the vodka.

VIRIL *(FRANCE)*   Virile. *See* Powerful.

VIRUS-FREE GRAPEVINE STOCK   Grapevine stock developed at the University of California at Davis during the past forty years. This budwood is free of virus disease that weakens the grapevine and limits production.

VISCOSITY   *See* Viscous.

VISCOUS   Describes full-bodied red or white wines that taste concentrated and fat, almost thick and syrupy, with a high extract level and usually considerable alcohol. This term also can be applied to intensely sweet dessert wines that have that syrupy character. Also known as *viscosity* and *zähflüssig*.

VITAMIN C ASCORBIC ACID   *See* Antioxidant and Campden Tablet.

VITE (ITALY)   *See* Grapevine.

VITICOLE (FRANCE)   A viticultural region.

VITICOLTURA (ITALY)   *See* Viticulture.

VITICULTEUR (FRANCE)   *See* Viticulture.

VITICULTURA (SPAIN)   *See* Viticulture.

VITICULTURAL AREA   In the United States, a viticultural area is a well-defined grape-growing region with soil, climate, history, and geographic features that set it apart from the surrounding areas and make it ideal for grape-growing. A viticultural area appellation on the label indicates that 85 percent or more of the wine is produced from grapes grown in the particular area.

VITICULTURE   The growing of grapevines or the theory, science, or study of the production of grapes. Also called *viniculture* when applied to the growing of grapes for wine. Also known as *viticoltura, viticulteur, viticultura*, and *weinbau*.

VITIGNO (ITALY)   *See* Grape Variety.

VITIGNO DI BARLETTA (ITALY)   *See* Uva di Troia.

VITIS   Grapevine; derives from the Latin *vitaceae*, which refers to woody, climbing plants, and *vinifera*, which refers to the berries or grapes that the plant produces.

VITIS AESTIVALIS   A species of grapevines native to eastern North America.

VITIS LABRUSCA   A species of grapevines native to eastern North America that display a sort of foxy aroma and flavor. The grapevines were first identified in the early part of the seventeenth century. Also known as *fox grape* and *labrusca*. *See* Foxy and Native American Grape Varieties.

VITIS RIPARIA   A species of grapevines native to North America. Also known as *riparia*.

VITIS ROTUNDIFOLIA   A species of grapevines native to North America, grown primarily in the south Atlantic states where they are generally identified as *Muscadine* grapes. Also known as *rotundifolia*.

VITIS RUPESTRIS   A species of grapevines native to North America. Also known as *rupestris*.

VITIS SYLVESTRIS   The original group of wild grapevines native to western Europe; the name means "grape of the forests."

VITIS VINIFERA   European grapevine species considered by many to produce the premium grapes in winemaking (e.g., Chardonnay, Cabernet Sauvignon, Johannisberg Riesling, Pinot Noir).

VIURA *(SPAIN)* The local name in the Rioja region for the *Macabeo* grape variety.

VIVACE *(FRANCE* AND *ITALY)* *See* Vivacious.

VIVACIOUS Describes a wine or beer that is fresh, full of life, spirited, or lively. Also known as *briso* and *vivace*. *See* Lively.

VIVANT A white grape variety developed at the Horticultural Research Institute, Vineland, Ontario, Canada.

VO *(FRANCE)* (Very Old) A label designation used on armagnac, calvados, and cognac bottles to indicate that the youngest brandy used in the blend is at least five years old (armagnac and calvados) or 4-1/2 years old (cognac), although they contain a very high percentage of brandy that has been aged for twelve to twenty years or more.

VODKA An alcoholic distillate from a fermented mash of primarily grain; it is distilled at or above 190 proof, bottled with aging at not less than 80 proof, and processed further to extract all congeners with the use of activated charcoal. According to the United States federal standards of identity, the final product must be "without distinctive character, aroma, taste or color." However, no federal law requires vodka to be entirely without aroma or taste; therefore, some vodkas display distinctive characteristics in aroma and taste. Federal law governs the production of vodkas in the United States.

Vodka seems to have first appeared in either Russia or Poland around the twelfth century, when it was known as *zhizenennia voda* (water of life) in the Russian monastery-fort of Viatka. The word *vodka* is a diminutive of the Russian word for water, *voda* (although it has been proved that the Russians took this word from the Poles). By the fourteenth century, vodka began to be used as a beverage; formerly, it was mainly used in perfumes and cosmetics. However, it was primarily employed as the base ingredient of many wonder drugs or cure-all elixirs. During the fifteenth century, Poland produced many types of vodka as well as several grades that varied according to the number of times the vodka was distilled and refined.

Vodka was originally made from the most plentiful and least expensive ingredients available, which in most cases was the potato. Nowadays, grain rules as the main base ingredient for vodka throughout the world. The early vodkas, even if made from grains, were strongly flavored, and therefore it became a common practice to add certain spices to mask the sometimes harsh, raw taste of the grain. It was not discovered until the early 1800s that charcoal could be used to absorb most or all of the aromas and flavors of congeners in the vodka—thus, the relatively tasteless, colorless vodka that is produced today. Also known as *wódka*.

VOLATILE ACIDITY (VA) Refers to a high level of acetic acid, usually associated with the formation of vinegar. Volatile acidity covers most of the spoilage acids in wine, including acetic, butyric, formic, and propionic, formed during fermentation. These can be detected in the aroma and taste. Also known as *acetic, acetic acid, acidità volatile, flüchtige säure, piqué, pungent*, and *vinegar*. *See* Acescence, Acetaldehyde, Acetic, Acetobacter, and Vinegar.

VOLATILE FRUIT-FLAVOR CONCENTRATE Any concentrate produced by any process that includes evaporation from any fruit mash or juice.

VOLATILE OIL An oil that readily evaporates or vaporizes. Volatile oils give their distinctive odors and flavors to grapevines and other fruit-bearing plants.

VOLATILIZATION   The evaporation of substances (esters, aldehydes, and so forth) in an alcohol beverage from liquid to vapor.

VOLIDZA (GREECE)   A red grape variety.

VOLLMUNDIG (GERMANY)   *See* Mouthfilling.

VOLNAY (FRANCE)   A red-wine-producing village located in the Côte de Beaune between Pommard and Meursault; it produces outstanding, light-bodied red wines that are delicate and quite fruity. The vineyards were originally named after Volen or Velen, the Gaulish Goddess of spring. Volnay was the favorite wine of King Louis XI of France, who reigned from 1461 to 1483.

VOLPINO (ITALY)   *See* Foxy.

VOLSTEAD ACT   *See* Prohibition.

VOLUME   The measure of a three-dimensional object, expressed as "cubic"; it is the length multiplied by the width multiplied by the height.

VOLUME DISCOUNT   *See* Quantity Discount.

VONKELWYN (SOUTH AFRICA)   *See* Sparkling Wine.

VORNEHM (GERMANY)   *See* Noble.

VÖRÖS (HUNGARY)   *See* Red.

VÖRÖSBOR (HUNGARY)   *See* Red Wine.

VOSGES OAK (FRANCE)   Oak trees of an isolated forest located in the evergreen Vosges mountains behind Alsace. Vosges oak has a tight wood grain due to modest rainfall, with a relatively neutral oak flavor and medium tannin extraction that remains in the background. Vosges is traditionally used for large wine barrels.

VOSNE-ROMANÉE (FRANCE)   A red-wine-producing village in the Côte de Nuits district of Burgundy; it makes exceptional wines with good bouquet, balance, and flavor.

VOUGEOT (FRANCE)   A small wine-producing village located in the Côte de Nuits district of Burgundy, world-famous for its production of fine red and white wines. Its most famous vineyard is Clos de Vougeot.

VOUVRAY (FRANCE)   A white wine made from Chenin Blanc grapes, known locally in the district of Anjou in the Loire Valley as Pineau de la Loire or Blanc d'Anjou. The taste of Vouvray can range from bone dry to semidry and even sweet. There is also a sparkling version produced in limited quantities.

VRANAC (YUGOSLAVIA)   A red grape variety.

VS (FRANCE)   (Very Superior) A label designation used on armagnac and cognac bottles that indicates that the youngest brandy used in the blend is at least three years old, although they usually contain a blend of five to nine years old.

VSOP (FRANCE)   (Very Superior Old Pale) A label designation on armagnac, calvados, and cognac bottles that indicates that the youngest brandy used in the blend is at least five years old (armagnac), 4-1/2 years old (cognac), and five years old (calvados),

VSOP (FRANCE)

V

although they contain a very high percentage of brandy that has been aged for twelve to twenty years or more.

VUOTO *(ITALY)* Empty. *See* Shallow.

VVSOP *(FRANCE)* (Very, Very, Superior Old Pale) A label designation on cognac bottles that indicates that the youngest brandy used in the blend is at least 6-1/2 years old although they contain a very high percentage of brandy that has been aged for twenty, thirty, or forty years or more.

w \ ' d ə b - ə l - (ˌ) y ü , - y ə (- w) , *r a p i d* ' d ə b (- ə) - y ə (- w) , ' d ə b - y ē \ *n , o f t e n c a p , o f t e n a t t r i b*

WACHAU (AUSTRIA) A wine-producing district in the Kamp Valley; it is considered the wine paradise of Lower Austria. It is noted for making Rhine Rieslings and Schluck, a dry white wine made from the Sylvaner grape.

WACHENHEIM (GERMANY) A wine-producing town in the Pfalz, noted for its production of medium-bodied, dry white wines, made primarily from Sylvaner and Johannisberg Riesling grapes.

WACHSTRUM (GERMANY) Term used until 1971 to designate a "growth" or vineyard, usually followed by the name of the proprietor or producer. Also known as *crescenz, gewächs,* and *kreszenz.*

WAFFLED *See* Intoxicated.

WALDMEISTER (GERMANY) *See* Woodruff.

WALK-IN REFRIGERATOR *See* Cold Box.

WÄLSCHRIESLING (GERMANY) *See* Welschriesling.

WALTHAM CROSS (AUSTRALIA) A white grape variety used primarily as a table grape but also in the production of brandy.

WAPANUKA A white grape variety developed by Thomas Volney Munson (1843–1913) of Denison, Texas.

WARMTH The sensation felt when consuming brandy or similar types of distillates; a noticeable flavor characteristic of wines made from grapes from hot climates. Also known as *caldo, chaud,* and *quente.*

WASH The liquid obtained by fermenting *wort* with yeast. The wash forms the raw material of the first distillation in the *pot still* process and of the only distillation in the *continuous still* process. Also known as *beer.*

WASH STILL The still utilized for the primary distillation of alcoholic wash.

WASSAIL   The ancient name for toasting, derived from the Old English *waes* and *whal*, which meant "be whole" or "be well." Also a large bowl of spiced ale or wine, roasted sliced apples, sugar, and spices. The exact ingredients vary according to locality. *See* Mulled Wine.

WASSER (GERMANY)   *See* Water.

WASTE   That portion of a product that is not usable or edible.

WATER   Also known as *acqua, agua, água, eau, su, vann, wasser*, and *wode*. *See* Drinking Water and Natural Water.

WATER BUNG   *See* Fermentation Lock.

WATERED DOWN   Describes wine that results from the use of a seldom-employed technique whereby water is added to *must*, wine, beer, or distilled spirits to stretch it for increased volume. Also known as *mouillé*. *See* Elongated Wine, Jerk Wine, and Piquette.

WATERING HOLE   A slang expression for a bar. *See* Bar.

WATER JACKET   *See* Jacketed Tank.

WATER MANAGEMENT   Adding water to grapevines (or other plants utilized in making alcoholic beverages) at the appropriate time and place and in the correct amount.

WATER OF LIFE   *See* Aqua Ardens and Aqua Vitae.

WATER-SEAL   *See* Fermentation Lock.

WATER SPROUT   A shoot that originates along the trunk or arms on a grapevine from wood older than the previous season's wood. Water sprouts seldom bear fruit, but in the next season, shoots growing from them are fruitful.

WATER TABLE   The top of a permeable body of rock of a zone saturated with water.

WATER TREATMENT   The addition of various chemicals or other substances to water in order to adjust its hardness, pH, and acidity.

WATER VALVE   *See* Fermentation Lock.

WATERY   *See* Thin.

WATKINS   A red grape variety.

WAX LINED   *See* Paraffin.

WAXING   *See* Paraffin.

WEAK   *See* Thin.

WEDGE   *See* Scantling.

WEED CONTROL   A procedure necessary to prevent weeds from robbing vital nutrients from the soil, to maximize air circulation around the grapevines, and as a means of insect control, since weeds harbor certain insects that can carry grapevine diseases.

WEEDY   *See* Stemmy.

WEEPER *See* Leakage.

WEEPING The secretion of lymph from the incisions made in pruning of grapevines.

WEHLEN *(GERMANY)* A famous vineyard village in the Mittelmosel region whose wines are characterized by a flowery bouquet, excellent balance, and a little natural sparkle.

WEICH *(GERMANY)* *See* Thin.

WEIGHT The measure of mass; the heaviness of a substance expressed in ounces, pounds, tons, grams, or kilos.

WEIN *(GERMANY)* *See* Wine.

WEINBAU *(GERMANY)* *See* Viticulture.

WEINBAUGEBIET *(GERMANY)* A viticultural region.

WEINBAUGEBIETE *(AUSTRIA)* A viticultural region.

WEINBEERE *(GERMANY)* *See* Grape.

WEINBERG *(GERMANY)* *See* Vineyard.

WEINBEREITUNG *See* Vinification.

WEINGÄRTEN *(GERMANY)* Wine-gardens where beer festivals often take place.

WEINGESETZ *(GERMANY)* Wine law, with reference to the current laws adopted on July 14, 1971.

WEINGUT (GERMANY) Wine estate.

WEINGÜTESIEGEL ÖSTERREICH *(AUSTRIA)* The seal of quality that appears on labels of Austrian wines.

WEINGUTSBESITZER *(GERMANY)* The owner of a vineyard property.

WEINHÄNDLER *(GERMANY)* A wine merchant or shipper.

WEINIG *(GERMANY)* *See* Vinosity.

WEINKELLER *(GERMANY)* *See* Wine Cellar.

WEINKELLNER *(GERMANY)* *See* Sommelier.

WEINLESE *(GERMANY)* *See* Harvest.

WEINMOND *(AUSTRIA)* Wine month.

WEINPRESSE *(GERMANY)* *See* Wine Press.

WEINPROBE *(GERMANY)* Wine-tasting.

WEINREB *(GERMANY)* *See* Grapevine.

WEINSBERG SCHOOL *(GERMANY)* Germany's oldest experimental viticulture facility, founded in 1868 by King Karl of Württemberg. Among its many contributions to the industry was the development of the Kerner grape variety.

WEINSCHLAUCH *(GERMANY)* *See* Wine Skin.

WEINSTEINE (GERMANY)   *See* Crystalline Deposits.

WEINTRAUBE (GERMANY)   *See* Cluster.

WEISS (GERMANY)   *See* Wheat.

WEISSE (GERMANY)   *See* White.

WEISSBIER (GERMANY)   *See* Wheat Beer.

WEISSBURGUNDER (AUSTRIA AND GERMANY)   *See* Pinot Blanc.

WEISSHERBST (GERMANY)   A rosé wine of a minimum QbA quality, popular in Baden.

WEISSWEIN (GERMANY)   *See* White Wine.

WEIZEN (GERMANY)   The plural of wheat. *See* Wheat.

WEIZENBIER (GERMANY)   *See* Wheat Beer.

WELCH (GERMANY)   *See* Thin.

WELDRA (SOUTH AFRICA)   *See* Chenel.

WELL-BALANCED   A term used to describe wines or beers whose many odors, flavors, tastes, and other components are cohesive and in perfect harmony with each other. Also known as *ampleur* and *bien equilibré*. *See* Balance.

WELL BRANDS   House brands with little name recognition that are generally lower in quality and price. They are used when customers ask for generic drinks. Also known as *bar brands, bar whiskey, house brands, house whiskey*, and *well-stock*.

WELL-STOCK   *See* Well Brands.

WELSCHRIESLING   A white grape variety grown primarily in Austria, Germany, Hungary, Italy, Romania, and Yugoslavia. Also known as *Olaszriesling, Olasz Rizling, Riesling Italico*, and *Wälschriesling*.

WET BAR   A small drink preparation area with sewer and water lines permanently hooked up to the front bar; it is separate from other facilities.

WET COUNTY   Counties in the United States permitting the sale of alcoholic beverages by the drink (on-premise) and by package (off-premise), or by package only. Under this definition, counties can have private clubs or unlicensed outlets selling distilled spirits and still be considered legally dry for distilled spirits, or a wet county could be without a distilled spirit outlet. *See* Dry County.

WETTABLE POWDER (WP)   A chemical powder that can be added to water for spray applications on grapevines.

WHEAT   An annual cereal grain used in making some distilled spirits and, occasionally, beers. Also known as *weiss* and *weizen*. *See* Wheat Beer.

WHEAT BEER (GERMANY)   A beer made either entirely or predominantly of wheat. It is usually unfiltered and contains some yeast residue and therefore is often cloudy in appearance. It is acidic, crisp, and acrid-tasting, often being served with raspberry syrup or essence of woodruff. Also known as *weissbier* and *weizenbier*. *See* Berliner Weisse, Lambic, and White Beer.

WHEEL   A citrus fruit sliced in the shape of a wheel and used as a garnish on some beverages.

WHISKEY   An alcoholic distillate made from a fermented mash of grain, distilled at less than 190 proof in such a manner that the distillate possesses the taste, aroma, and characteristics generally associated with whiskey. Whiskeys are distinguished by the grain used, the proof at which the mash is distilled, and the age. The minimum proof that a whiskey can be bottled at is 80; there are no maximum proof standards.

Whiskey obtains its characteristic brown color from four sources: coloring matter from the barrel, oxidation, charred barrels, and the addition of caramel for color adjustment. *See* American-Made Whiskey.

WHISKEY SOUR   *See* Sour.

WHISKY   This spelling identifies the distilled spirits of Scotland and Canada.

WHISTLE-BELLY VENGEANCE   A drink made from sour beer, molasses, and crusts of brown bread. It was popular in the future United States during the late 1600s and early 1700s.

WHITE   A clear, colorless, or lightly tainted color, usually straw, gold, and yellow. Used to describe certain types of alcoholic and nonalcoholic beverages. Also known as *beloe, beyaz, bianco, bijelo, bjalo, blanc, blanco, branco*, and *weisse*.

WHITE BEER   A beer first produced in 1543 in Belgium from a combination of barley, wheat, and oats. Also known as *whitbier*. *See* Wheat Beer.

WHITE GOODS   A term often used to describe those distilled spirits that are clear in color and usually not aged in wood. These distilled spirits lack the distinctive flavor generally associated with whiskey and are perceived as being lighter by most consumers. Examples are gin, rum, tequila, and vodka. *See* Brown Goods.

WHITE LIGHTNING   *See* Moonshine.

WHITE PORT (PORTUGAL)   Port wines made exclusively from white grapes; they tend to run from dry and slightly tangy to a medium-sweet character. Generally, the *must* is allowed to ferment longer (or closer to dryness) than wines destined to become red port.

WHITE RIESLING   *See* Johannisberg Riesling.

WHITE RUM   *See* Light Rum.

WHITE VERMOUTH   *See* Vermouth.

WHITE WINE   A wine made without any trace of the red coloring matter that is usually derived from contact with the skin of the red grape. White wines may run in color from a pale, almost watery appearance to a deep gold and even amber, yet all are considered white wines. Also known as *fehér bór, vin blanc, vinho branco, vino bianco*, and *vino blanco, and weisswein*

WHITE ZINFANDEL   An extremely popular and quaffable *varietal* wine produced primarily in California from the red Zinfandel grape variety. White Zinfandel is a white wine made by limited skin contact (several hours) or no-skin contact with red Zinfandel grapes, extracting a hint of color. White Zinfandel is generally quite fruity smelling, with some residual sugar, which adds to the sensory impression of the wine.

The first successful white Zinfandel was made in 1869 by George West near Stockton, California.

WHOLE BERRY FERMENTATION   *See* Carbonic Maceration.

WHOLE MILK   Milk that contains not less than 3.25 percent milkfat and not less than 8.25 percent nonfat solids.

WHOLESALE   The sale of beverages (alcoholic and nonalcoholic) in quantity for resale to consumers.

WHOLESALERS   A merchant middleman who sells chiefly to retailers. *See* Distributors.

WHORTLEBERRY   A species of European blueberry occasionally used in making fruit-flavored liqueurs or brandies.

WICKER   *See* Straw Mats.

WICKER BASKET   *See* Wine Cradle.

WILD BEER   Draft beer that froths uncontrollably when dispensed due to excessively warm temperatures; it is a temporary condition.

WILDER   A red grape variety developed by Edward S. Rogers of Salem, Massachusetts. Formerly known as *Rogers 4*.

WILD GRAPEVINES   *See* Native American Grape Varieties and Vitis Labrusca.

WILD MUSTARD   The green *Brassica* plants (planted in the fall) whose blossoms paint the vineyard with a golden color, are rich in nitrogen, and are usually plowed into or disked into the ground for needed nutrients in the springtime. Also known as *mustard*. *See* Cover Crops.

WILD YEAST   Yeasts indigenous to certain vineyards. They collect on the grape's waxy outer layer during the growing season and are used to make the wine instead of inoculating it with pure cultured strains. It is estimated that there are more than ten million yeast cells, plus assorted molds and bacteria, on a grape skin. *See* Yeast.

WILMINGTON RED   *See* Wyoming.

WILTINGEN (GERMANY)   An important vineyard village of the Saar River near Trier famous for its production of dry white wines made from Johannisberg Riesling.

WINBRUDERSCHAFT (GERMANY)   Wine brotherhood.

WINCHELL   A white grape variety.

WINE   A living alcoholic beverage produced by fermenting grape juice. This includes alcoholic beverages made in the manner of wine, including sparkling and carbonated wine, wine made from condensed grape *must*, wine made from agricultural products other than the juice of sound, ripe grapes, imitation wine, compounds sold as wine, vermouth, cider, and perry. In each instance, it is considered wine only if containing not less than 7 percent and not more than 24 percent of alcohol by volume, and if for nonindustrial use. Also known as *bor, chiu, oinos, sarap, vin, vinho, vino, vinum, wein, wino,* and *yayin. See* Grape Wine and Wine Product.

WINE BAR   A bar that features a selection of wines and that provides customers with the opportunity of ordering wine by the taste, by the glass, and by the bottle.

WINE BASKET   *See* Wine Cradle.

WINE BROKER   *See* Broker.

WINE BROTHERHOODS OR FRATERNITIES (*FRANCE*)   Membership organizations within an appellation or region composed of grape growers, shippers, or brokers whose main concern is to maintain traditions of quality. Some of the Bordeaux wine fraternities are:

 la Jurade de Saint-Émilion

 la Commanderie du Bontemps de Médoc et des Graves

 la Commanderie du Bontemps de Sauternes et Barsac

 la Commanderie du Bontemps de Saint-Croix-du-Mont

 la Compagnons de Bordeaux

 la Confrérie des Hospitaliers de Pomerol

 la Gentilshommes du Duché de Fronsac

 la Compagnons de Loupiac

 la Vignerons de Montagne-Saint-Émilion

 les Baillis de Lalande-de-Pomerol

 les Echevins de Lussac-Saint-Émilion-Puisseguin Saint-Émilion

 la Connétablie des Premières Côtes de Bordeaux et des Graves

 la Connétablie des Côtes de Blaye

 la Connétablie des Côtes de Bourg

 la Connétablie de l'Entre-Deux-Mers

These fifteen wine fraternities are also members of the Grand Conseil du Vin de Bordeaux.

WINE BUCKET   *See* Ice Bucket.

WINE BUTLER   *See* Sommelier.

WINE BY THE GLASS   The merchandising of special wines by the individual glass rather than only by the bottle.

WINE CAPTAIN   *See* Sommelier.

WINE CELLAR   A storage or aging facility (generally subterranean) where wine is kept under optimum conditions of temperature, light, humidity, and security. Also known as *adega, bodega, cave, cellar, cocedero, kellergasse, maturing cellar, tinaia*, and *weinkeller*. *See* Cellar Temperature and Vat-Room.

WINE COOLERS   Also known as *coolers*. *See* Low-Alcohol Refreshers.

WINE CRADLE   A wicker or straw basket designed to hold a bottle of mature wine (usually red) containing sediment in nearly the same horizontal position it occupied in the cellar. The basket permits the removal of the bottle from storage without disturbing its sediment, for eventual opening and decanting. Also known as *basket, cradle, wicker basket, wine basket*, and *wire basket*.

WINE GALLON   *See* Gallon.

WINEGLASS   A stemmed glass with a capacity of eight to ten ounces, in which wine is served.

WINE GROWING   Because wine is a farm product, usually produced by the grower, who both cultivates the vineyard and ferments the grapes into wine on the farm, the entire production is referred to as *wine growing* and the producer is called a *wine grower*. It is preferred to *wine manufacturer*, as is the word *manufacture* in connection with wine. One of the highest recommendations for wine and one of the reasons for its purity, its dietary and health values, and the regard in which it is held by the medical profession, is the fact that it is a product of nature—a beverage grown, not manufactured.

WINE KEY   *See* Corkscrew.

WINE KING   A red grape variety developed by Thomas Volney Munson (1843–1913) of Denison, Texas.

WINEMAKER   A term used to describe the person in charge of producing wine in a winery. Also known as *bodeguero* and *vinai*. *See* Enologist.

WINE MERCHANT   *See* Vintner.

WINE PREMISES   Premises on which wine operations are authorized to be conducted.

WINE PRESS   A machine by which direct pressure extracts the juice from the skins of grapes. Older presses were hand-operated; then hydraulic presses were introduced. Modern electric presses utilize a system that resembles *bladders* to gently press the skins to liberate the juice. Also known as *grape press, kelter, pigiatrice, prensa, press, pressoir, torchio*, and *weinpresse*. *See* Basket Press and Cocquard.

WINE PRODUCT   A wine that contains in excess of 24 percent alcohol by volume is classified as a distilled spirit and taxed accordingly. *See* Dessert Wine and Wine.

WINE RACK   A fixed rack (generally made of wood or metal) with alternating stacked compartments and individual openings for the horizontal storage and display of wine bottles.

WINERY   The building in which the juice of grapes is fermented into wine. The term is not properly applied in the United States to any except bonded winery premises. It is preferred to *plant* or *wine factory*, which creates the incorrect impression of manufacturing. Also known as *casa vinicola* and *cuverie*.

WINE SKIN   A large bag, generally made from the skin of an animal (usually goat), for holding or transporting wine. Also known as *boracho, odre, otre, pellejo*, and *weinschlauch*. *See* Askos.

WINE SPIRITS   Brandy or wine spirits authorized for use in wine products.

WINE STEWARD   *See* Sommelier.

WINE TASTER   A person with a trained palate who specializes in the organoleptic evaluation of alcoholic beverages, especially wine.

WINE THIEF   Glass, stainless steel, or plastic tube or cylinder used to extract samples of wine, *must*, or distilled spirits from a barrel for analytical purposes. Also known as *baster, barrel thief, canuto, chantepleure, preuve, saggiavino, thief*, and *velinch*.

WINE VINEGAR   *See* Vinegar.

WINE WAITER   *See* Sommelier.

WINGED   Describes a grape cluster with two separate, distinct parts attached at the main stem.

WINKEL (*GERMANY*)   A famous vineyard town located in the Rheingau that produces fine quality, dry white wines.

WINNIE   *See* Alexander.

WINO (*POLAND*)   *See* Wine.

WINO   A slang term for a person who is addicted to cheap wine.

WINTER HARDINESS   The ability of a grapevine to survive the freezing cold of winter; refers to timing and dormancy, age, size, and vigor of the grapevine.

WINY   Also known as *inódis*. *See* Vinosity.

WINZERFEST (*GERMANY*)   Wine festival.

WINZER (*GERMANY*)   A grape-grower.

WINZERGENOSSENSCHAFT (*GERMANY*)   Grape-growers' cooperative association.

WINZERVEREIN (*GERMANY*)   Grape-growers' cooperative.

WINZERSEKT (*GERMANY*)   A sparkling wine created by an individual winery with its own special taste. It is produced by the traditional champagne method.

WIRE BALE   *See* Wire Hood.

WIRE BASKET   *See* Wine Cradle.

WIRE HOOD   A wire that holds sparkling wine and champagne corks in place and that must be twisted counterclockwise to remove from the bottle. Also known as *cage, ficelage, muselet, wire bale*, and *wire muzzle*.

WIRE MUZZLE   *See* Wire Hood.

WIŚNIÓWKA (*POLAND*)   A cherry-flavored liquer.

WITBIER (*BELGIUM*)   *See* White Beer.

WITHERED   A term applied to a wine that has lost its freshness, bouquet, fruit, and flavor due to prolonged storage in a barrel or a bottle, or after being opened too long.

WITHDRAWALS   In the United States, taxpaid withdrawals are the quantity of distilled spirits removed from government-supervised premises and on which federal excise taxes are determined. Tax-free withdrawals are withdrawals of distilled spirits free, or without payment, of the federal excise tax. Examples of such withdrawals are denatured alcohol (treated to make it unfit for consumption), shipments destined for export in bond, tax-free alcohol for use at hospitals, and so forth, and distilled spirits for use by the United States government. *See* Entering Trade Channels and Imports for Consumption.

WODE (*POLAND*)   *See* Water.

WÓDKA (*POLAND*)   *See* Vodka.

WÓDKA (POLAND)

W

WOOD   *See* Barrel.

WOOD AGING   *See* Aging and Barrel Aging.

WOOD ALCOHOL   *See* Methyl Alcohol.

WOOD PORT   A term formerly used to denote port wines that were aged in wooden barrels and consumed soon after bottling.

WOODY   Describes a characteristic odor and/or flavor of certain wines or distilled spirits aged in wooden barrels longer than necessary. *See* Oaky and Over-Aged.

WOODRUFF   Any of a genus (*Asperula odorata*) of wild plants of the madder family, a perennial, grown in moist rich soil in the woods, that also makes an excellent ground cover. Woodruff has small, white, pink, or blue lily-shaped flowers, and is used to flavor wine. Also known as *waldmeister*. *See* May Wine.

WORDEN   A red grape variety grown in 1863 by Mr. Schuyler Worden of Minetto, New York.

WORK STATION   That area behind the bar where fruit can be cut, drinks assembled, and glasses stacked as well as washed.

WORM   On a corkscrew, the piece that is inserted into the cork. Also known as *bore* and *screw*.

WORM   The worm and its surrounding bath of cold running water, or worm-tub, together form the condenser unit of the *pot still* process of manufacture. The worm itself is a coiled copper tube of decreasing diameter attached by the lyne arm to the head of the pot still and kept cold by continuously running water. In it the vapors from the still condense. Fed by the still, it in turn feeds the receiving vessel with the condensed distillate. The worm is being gradually replaced by the more modern tubular condenser. Also known as *worm box* and *flake stand*.

WORM BOX   *See* Worm.

WORM HOLES   Canals formed in a cork by burrowing worms.

WORMS (GERMANY)   A vineyard town located on the Rhine River near the southern edge of the Rheinhessen. Worms produces dry white wines that are mostly used in the production of Liebfraumilch.

WORT   The liquid drawn off the mash-tun in which the malted and unmalted cereals have been mashed with warm water. Wort contains all the sugars of the malt and certain secondary constituents. After cooling, it is passed to the fermenting vats. In *malt* distilleries, the cereals are all malted; in *grain* distilleries, only a proportion is malted.

WP   *See* Wettable Powder.

WROTHAM PINOT   A red grape variety grown in Great Britain.

WSWA   Wine and Spirits Wholesalers of America.

WUCHTIG (GERMANY)   *See* Fat.

WÜRTTEMBERG (GERMANY)   One of thirteen Qualitätswein (quality) grape-growing regions; it is noted for its production of red wines. This region is separated from Baden by the famed Black Forest. Thousands of Württemberg's small growers produce pleasant red and white wines mostly from Trollinger, Schwarzriesling, Spätburgunder, Portugieser, Johannisberg Riesling, and Müller-Thurgau grape varieties.

WÜRZBURG *(GERMANY)* A city in Franken noted for its production of dry and austere white wines with a fullness of body.

WÜRZER *(GERMANY)* A white grape variety developed in 1927 from a cross of Gewürztraminer and Müller-Thurgau in the Rheinhessen.

WÜRZIG *(GERMANY)* *See* Fruity.

WYOMING A red grape variety introduced in 1861 by S.J. Parker of Ithaca, New York. Also known as *Hopkins Early Red,Wilmington Red*, and *Wyoming Red*.

WYOMING RED *See* Wyoming.

W

XXX

x \\'eks\\ *n, often cap, often attrib*

XAMPAN *(SPAIN)*   The Catalonian term for a sparkling wine. *See* Sparkling Wine.

XAMPANERIA *(SPAIN)*   A Catalan term for a champagne bar.

XAREL-LO *(SPAIN)*   A white grape variety used primarily in making sparkling wines. Also known as *Pansa Blanca* and *Xarello.*

XARELLO *(SPAIN)*   *See* Xarel-Lo.

XÉRÈS *(FRANCE)*   Sherry.

XIRÓS *(GREECE)*   *See* Dry.

XITHUM   Egyptian beer made from barley.

XYNISTERI *(CYPRUS)*   A white grape variety.

XYNOMAVRO *(GREECE)*   A red grape variety.

XO *(FRANCE)*   (Extremely Old) A label designation on armagnac or cognac bottles that indicates that the youngest brandy used in the blend is at least six years old (armagnac) and 6-1/2 years old (cognac), although they contain a very high percentage of brandy that has been aged for twenty, thirty, or forty years or more.

XXX   An ancient Egyptian symbol denoting purity. Originally, distillers used the symbol "X" to indicate the number of times the product was distilled, "XXX" signifying a triple-distilled product. More than a century ago, brewmasters adopted the "XXX" designation for use on certain beer bottles. The "X" symbol, however, has no legal meaning.

y \\'wī\\ *n, often cap, often attrib*

YARD OF ALE An elongated drinking glass measuring approximately thirty-six inches and containing forty-two ounces of ale. It was used primarily in England during the seventeenth and eighteenth centuries in roadside taverns or pubs, where keepers kept them close to the door so that pint-sized waitresses could easily pass up a cold ale to stagecoach drivers who were required to stay aboard to contain the horses.

YARD OF FLANNEL A reputed remedy for colds. It is made by mixing ale with eggs, brown sugar, and nutmeg. It is then served at a rather warm temperature.

YATES A red grape variety developed in 1937 from a cross of Mills and Ontario at the State Experimental Station in Geneva, New York.

YAYIN The Hebrew term for wine. *See* Wine.

YEAR OF THE HARVEST *See* Harvest and Vintage.

YEAST Microorganisms of the family *Saccharomyces cerevisiae*, in which the unicellular form is conspicuous. They are fungi. The size and shape of yeast cells can vary in length and width and can be spheroidal, ellipsoidal, cylindrical, or even pear-shaped. Yeast multiplies by budding. When a cell has reached a certain size, it starts to form a bud, which grows until it is only a little smaller than the mother cell. Yeast brings about fermentation in the making of alcoholic beverages by converting sugar (a mixture of glucose and fructose) into roughly equal parts of ethyl alcohol and carbon dioxide under the generation of heat. Also known as *fermenti, hefe, levadura, lievito,* and *levure. See* Calcium Alginate Beads, Encapsulated Yeasts, and Wild Yeast.

YEAST ENERGIZERS *See* Nutrients.

YEAST NUTRIENTS *See* Nitrogen and Nutrients.

YEAST STARTER *See* Nutrients and Starter.

YEASTY Describes the fresh, unoxidized odor of freshly-made bread, often detected in newly made wines, or the odor of fermentation or its *lees*, which are comprised primarily of dead yeast cells. It is a positive odor when associated with some young white or sparkling wines. If detected in red or other wines, it is a negative sign. Also known as *hefig* and *kahmig*.

YEMA *(SPAIN)*   *See* Free-Run Juice.

YEÓDIS *(GREECE)*   *See* Earthy.

YESO *(SPAIN)*   *See* Plastering.

YIELD   The amount of usable or edible parts of a product.

YIELD OF EXTRACT   The number of pounds of extract obtained from one hundred pounds of brewing material, generally expressed as a percentage.

YIELD   The production of a given acre of vineyard land, expressed as tons per acre in the United States and as hectoliters per hectare in Europe. It also refers to the yield of juice extracted from each ton of grapes pressed.

YIELD PER ACRE   *See* Yield.

YIELD PER TON   *See* Yield.

YOUNG   Describes a fresh, undeveloped wine (often just past fermentation) that has not yet reached its peak and needs barrel and/or bottle aging to improve. Also known as *giovane, immature, jung, jungwein, vino crudo*, and *vino joven. See* Fresh, Green, and Unripe.

YONNE *(FRANCE)*   A small wine-producing town in the northern part of Burgundy that produces average wines.

YORK LISBON   *See* Alexander.

YVORNE *(SWITZERLAND)*   One of the better-known white wines produced in the Chablis district, southeast of Lake Geneva, from the Chasselas grape variety.

z \\'zē, *chiefly Brit* 'zed\\ *n, often cap, often attrib*

ZACINKA *(YUGOSLAVIA)*   A red grape variety.

ZAGARÉSE *(ITALY)*   *See* Primitivo di Gioia.

ZÄHFLÜSSIG *(GERMANY)*   *See* Viscous.

ZALEMA *(SPAIN)*   A white grape variety.

ZANTE CURRANT   *See* Black Corinth.

ZART *(GERMANY)*   *See* Delicate.

ZECHFENTHAL   *See* Zinfandel.

ZELL *(GERMANY)*   A vineyard town located in the lower Mosel, famous for its production of large quantities of QbA wines under the name of Zeller Schwarze Katz (*The Black Cat*).

ZELTINGEN *(GERMANY)*   The largest wine-producing town in the Mittelmosel; it produces a large quantity of dry white wine from the Johannisberg Riesling grape.

ZENFENTHAL   *See* Zinfandel.

ZERN   A measure of Scotch whisky taken during or immediately following an outdoor sporting event to repel the chill.

ZEST   The outer layer or peel of a citrus fruit; it contains the coloring and essence of oils. Used in cooking and certain alcoholic drink recipes.

ZESTER   A small, hand-held tool used to obtain zest from citrus fruit. *See* Zest.

ZESTY   *See* Lively.

ZHIZENNIA VODA   The twelfth-century name for vodka; it meant "water of life" in Russia and Poland. Also spelled *zhiznennia*.

ZHIZNENNIA VODA   *See* Zhizennia Voda.

ZIBIBBO (ITALY)   A white grape variety grown primarily in the south. Pliny the Elder called this grape *Scibellita*. *See* Muscat of Alexandria.

ZIERFANDLER (AUSTRIA)   A white grape variety usually blended with Rotgipfler to produce Gumpoldskirchner. Also known as *Spätrot*.

ZIN   *See* Zinfandel.

ZINFANDEL   A red grape variety grown throughout California for more than a century. Although now believed by some *ampelographers* to be the same grape as the Italian Primitivo, its European origin is still somewhat uncertain. The Primitivo grape was probably growing in Bari in the late 1860s, perhaps earlier.

In 1967 Dr. Austin C. Goheen, a United States Department of Agriculture research plant pathologist, first discovered the similarity of Primitivo and Zinfandel. The enzyme patterns of Primitivo were electronically compared with those of Zinfandel and found to be identical. In 1976 University of California, Davis, scientist Wade Wolfe tested both varieties by the isozyme fingerprinting technique and determined them to be the same.

In California, the Zinfandel grape produces pleasant, good, and often complex and excellent dry red wines, with a distinctly spicy, berry-like flavor reminiscent of blackberries or raspberries. Black pepper, raisin, and soy are also often detected. Considerable quantities of a semidry white Zinfandel or blush are also produced. In addititon, Zinfandel can be vinified into a rosé wine or a big, full-bodied, late-harvest style, often resembling port. With extended bottle age, Zinfandel takes on a surprisingly Cabernet-like character. California's first varietally labeled rosé Zinfandel was introduced in 1958 by Pedroncelli Winery.

Also known as *Black St. Peters, Black Zinfandel, Zinfenthal, Zechfenthal, Zenfenthal*, and *Zin*. *See* Primitivo di Gioia and Prince, William Robert.

ZINFANDEL CLUB   An informal wine club located in London, England, that was founded in October 1976.

ZINFENTHAL   *See* Zinfandel.

ZING   A property of an exciting, refreshing beer or wine that usually displays good acidity.

ZÖLDSILVÁNI (HUNGARY)   *See* Sylvaner.

ZOLFO (ITALY)   *See* Sulfur Dioxide.

ZOMBIE   A cocktail consisting of light rum, dark rum, gold rum, pineapple juice, papaya juice, lime juice, falernum or simple sugar, apricot-flavored brandy, orange curaçao or passion fruit syrup, and 151-proof Demeraran rum. A cocktail developed by Los Angeles restauranteur Don the Beachcomber that featured perhaps every type of rum he had on hand at his bar. This drink boasted a challenge that many simply could not pass up: "only one to a customer."

ZONA (ITALY)   Zone.

ZONKED   *See* Intoxicated.

ZUBRÓWKA   A flavored vodka produced in Slavic countries; it has a yellow-green tinge and a distinctive smell and taste derived from various added botanicals. Bottles of it at one time contained a single blade of grass, but these are no longer available in the

United States because scientists believed that the grass contained *coumarin*, a toxic compound found in some plants and said to cause liver cancer. The vodka, minus the grass, is currently available in the United States and is free from anything harmful. Also known as *Bison Vodka* or *Buffalo Vodka*.

ZUCCHERAGGIO *(ITALY)* *See* Chaptalization.

ZUCKERREST *(GERMANY)* *See* Residual Sugar.

ZUKUNFT *(GERMANY)* A wine that has a good aging potential or future.

ZUSAMMENSCHLUSS *(GERMANY)* An association, organization, or cooperative involved in the production or sale of wine or other alcoholic beverages.

ZUSETZEN *(GERMANY)* The addition of legal additives in making alcoholic beverages.

ZWEIGELT BLAU *(AUSTRIA)* A red grape variety developed from a cross of Blaufränkisch and St-Laurent by Dr. Zweigelt at the Klosterneuburg Institute.

ZWICKEL A device, similar to a spigot on a wine barrel (test petcock), that enables the brewmaster to sample the aging beer for evaluation purposes. *See* Spigot.

ZWICKER *(FRANCE)* A term formerly used to designate a blended wine; it was phased out on July 5, 1972. *See* Edelzwicker.

ZWICKLE A bung tap used to loosen or tighten bungs on a barrel. *See* Bungstarter.

ZYMASE An enzyme present in yeast that promotes fermentation by breaking down glucose and some other carbohydrates into alcohol and carbon dioxide. The term was coined by Edward Buchner (1860–1917), a microbiologist.

ZYMURGY That branch of applied chemistry that deals with the fermentation process, especially with respect to beer and wine.

ZYTHOS *(GREECE)* *See* Beer.

ZYTNIA *(POLAND)* A type of vodka.

ABOUT THE AUTHORS

BOB LIPINSKI

As a professional speaker and educator, Bob Lipinski has conducted seminars and workshops worldwide. He has given presentations to the White House executive waitstaff on how to pair wine with food, proper wine service, and sensory evaluation skills. He has conducted seminars for food and beverage trade shows, as well as hotels, cruise ship tours, colleges, wine and food societies, resorts, and conventions. Bob is a TV wine and food celebrity with extensive experience as a host, writer, producer, and guest. He has written more than 500 articles and is the coauthor of *Professional Beverage Management* and *Professional Guide to Alcoholic Beverages* published by Van Nostrand Reinhold. Bob was also the associate director and professor of the school of Hotel, Restaurant Administration and Culinary Arts at New York Institute of Technology.

KATHIE LIPINSKI

Kathie Lipinski, RN, MSN, CDE, is a holistic nurse in private practice in Louisville, Kentucky. She has more than twenty years experience as a healthcare professional. Her broad nursing background includes intensive-care, nursing administration, diabetes education, and writing for various healthcare publications as well as being coauthor of *Professional Beverage Management* and *Professional Guide to Alcoholic Beverages* published by Van Nostrand Reinhold. She is currently a nurse–massage therapist and a Reiki Master/Teacher. Her work focuses on stress reduction, pain relief, and relaxation, which aid the body in its own ability to heal.